HARNESSING FOREIGN INVESTMENT TO PROMOTE ENVIRONMENTAL PROTECTION

Harnessing Foreign Investment to Promote Environmental Protection investigates the main challenges facing the implementation of environmental protection and the synergies between foreign investment and environmental protection. Adopting legal, economic and political perspectives, the contributing authors analyse the various incentives which encourage foreign investment into pro-environment projects (such as funds, project-finance, market mechanisms, payments-for-ecosystem services and insurance) and the safeguards against its potentially harmful effects (investment regulation, corporate social responsibility and accountability mechanisms, contracts and codes of conduct).

PIERRE-MARIE DUPUY is Emeritus Professor at the University of Paris II (Panthéon-Assas) and at the Graduate Institute of International and Development Studies in Geneva. He also held the Chair of General International Law at the European University Institute in Florence (2000–8). Professor Dupuy has extensive experience in international law practice, in particular as counsel for governments in numerous cases before the International Court of Justice and as international arbitrator in the field of international investments law. He is a member of the Institut de Droit International (International Law Institute).

JORGE E. VIÑUALES is the Pictet Chair of International Environmental Law and an assistant professor of public international law at the Graduate Institute, Geneva, where he is also the Director of the Programme on Environmental Governance at the Centre for International Environmental Studies.

HARNESSING FOREIGN INVESTMENT TO PROMOTE ENVIRONMENTAL PROTECTION

Incentives and Safeguards

Edited by
PIERRE-MARIE DUPUY
and
JORGE E. VIÑUALES

CAMBRIDGE
UNIVERSITY PRESS

CAMBRIDGE UNIVERSITY PRESS
Cambridge, New York, Melbourne, Madrid, Cape Town,
Singapore, São Paulo, Delhi, Mexico City

Cambridge University Press
The Edinburgh Building, Cambridge CB2 8RU, UK

Published in the United States of America by Cambridge University Press, New York

www.cambridge.org
Information on this title: www.cambridge.org/9781107030770

First published 2013

Printed and bound in the United Kingdom by the MPG Books Group

A catalogue record for this publication is available from the British Library

Library of Congress Cataloguing-in-Publication Data

Harnessing foreign investment to promote environmental protection : incentives and
safeguards / edited by Pierre-Marie Dupuy, Jorge E. Viñuales.
pages cm
ISBN 978-1-107-03077-0
1. Environmental economics. 2. Environmental protection. 3. Environmental policy.
4. Environmental law. 5. Investments, Foreign. I. Dupuy, Pierre-Marie,
editor of compilation. II. Viñuales, Jorge, editor of compilation.
HC79.E5H3538 2013
333.72–dc23
2012035201

ISBN 978-1-107-03077-0 Hardback

CONTENTS

FIGURES

TABLES

CONTRIBUTORS

NATASHA AFFOLDER – **University of British Columbia**

Natasha Affolder is an associate professor at the University of British Columbia (UBC) Faculty of Law. She is a faculty associate at the Liu Institute for Global Issues and the Peter Wall Institute for Advanced Studies. Professor Affolder holds an LLB from the University of Alberta and a Bachelor of Civil Law (BCL) and doctorate in law from Oxford University where she was a Rhodes Scholar. Prior to joining UBC, Professor Affolder practised law in private practice in Boston, Massachusetts and held a research associate position in the area of large project negotiation at Harvard Business School. She has also worked in various capacities for international non-governmental and intergovernmental organisations including Oxfam and the United Nations Environment Programme (UNEP). Professor Affolder publishes and lectures widely on diverse aspects of transnational environmental law. Among her professional activities, Natasha is on the board of the Canadian Council of International Law, and she is an expert advisory board member of the journals *Transnational Environmental Law* and the *McGill Journal of International Sustainable Development Law*. Natasha is active in knowledge translation through research presentations to policymakers, industry, NGOs and judicial training on sustainable development law. She is the recipient of numerous awards, including, in 2011, UBC's Killam Faculty Research Fellowship.

KONSTANTINA K. ATHANASAKOU – **White & Case LLP**

Konstantina Athanasakou is a senior associate with White & Case LLP, Geneva Office. She practises primarily in the area of international trade law with an emphasis on energy and environment issues. Ms Athanasakou advises clients on WTO issues, including energy trade, market access, anti-dumping and subsidies, compliance, trade negotiations and dispute resolution, and on G20 matters, such as energy and commodities trade as well as environment and climate change issues. Ms Athanasakou has experience in US trade policy, including bilateral and regional trade agreements and trade remedy matters in relation to litigation in the US Court of International Trade and the WTO Appellate Body. Her experiences also includes advising multinational corporate clients on international business transactions and regulatory compliance matters, in corporate, intellectual property, antitrust, environmental, trade and customs, and labour law matters. Prior to joining White & Case, Ms Athanasakou worked for the European Commission Delegation in Washington, DC, for a law firm in New York, in-house for a large multinational company in New York and for a global trading and investment group in Boston.

PIERRE-MARIE DUPUY – **The Graduate Institute, Geneva/University of Paris II (Panthéon-Assas)**
Professor of International Law, the Graduate Institute of International and Development Studies, Agrégé des facultés de droit (France), PhD Sciences Po Paris. Professor Dupuy joined the Graduate Institute in 2008. He is also a professor at the University of Paris II (Panthéon-Assas) as well as visiting professor at the Universities of Michigan (Ann Arbor), Munich and Madrid (Complutense). From 2000 to 2008, he held the Chair of General International Law at the European University Institute in Florence. He gave the general course of public international law at The Hague Academy of International Law in 2000. He is the author, with Y. Kerbrat, of *Droit international public* (10th edn, 2010) as well as of numerous books and articles on the theory of international law, general international law, state responsibility, human rights, international environmental law and international economic law. He appears regularly as counsel before the International Court of Justice. He also regularly serves as arbitrator in investment cases.

ZACHARY DOUGLAS – **The Graduate Institute, Geneva**
Zachary Douglas is an associate professor of international law at the Graduate Institute of International and Development Studies, Geneva. He joined the Graduate Institute in 2011 from the University of Cambridge, where he lectured in public international law and international dispute settlement. His research focuses upon areas at the intersection of public and private international law such as investment arbitration, international law in domestic courts and financial crime. His published work includes, among others, *The International Law of Investment Claims* (Cambridge University Press, 2009) and 'The Hybrid Foundations of Investment Treaty Arbitration' (*British Yearbook of International Law*). He has also published more widely on topics of general international law. In addition to his academic activities, Professor Douglas maintains a practice as counsel,

expert witness and arbitrator before international courts and tribunals and is an academic member of Matrix Chambers in London.

DANIEL M. FIRGER – **Real Options International, Inc.**
Daniel M. Firger is Vice President of Real Options International, Inc., a carbon markets consultancy founded by the former head of carbon finance at the World Bank. He previously served as a US Associate in the environmental and climate change practice at Linklaters, LLP and as a postdoctoral research fellow and associate director of the Centre for Climate Change Law at Columbia University. He holds a JD from NYU School of Law and a Master's in Public Affairs from the Woodrow Wilson School at Princeton University.

FRANCESCO FRANCIONI – **European University Institute**
Professor of International Law and Human Rights, European University Institute, and Law Faculty of the University of Siena. Doctor of Laws (Florence), LLM (Harvard). Francesco Francioni is also General Editor of the *Italian Yearbook of International Law*, member of the Board of Editors of the *European Journal of International Law*, member of the American Law Institute and of the Executive Board of the European Society of International Law, and a member of the Italian delegation at many diplomatic conferences and international negotiations, especially in the field of environmental law and cultural heritage. He has taught courses at The Hague Academy of International Law (1995), Cornell Law School (1983–6), Texas Law School (1988–2007) and Oxford University (1999–2003).

MAGNUS JESKO LANGER – **The Graduate Institute, Geneva**
Magnus Jesko Langer is currently a teaching and research assistant and a PhD candidate at the Graduate Institute, Geneva. He worked in a number of cases as legal adviser before the International Court of Justice, including the Case concerning Pulp Mills on the River Uruguay (*Argentina* v. *Uruguay*). His research focuses on the fields of international environmental law and international investment law, as well as international dispute settlement. His thesis analyses the question of how international environmental law has impacted the entitlements that states enjoy over their natural resources. He holds degrees in international law (HEID) and international relations (HEI), and a Bachelor in Law (University of Geneva).

SHAUN LARCOM – **University of Cambridge**
Shaun Larcom is an affiliated lecturer at the Department of Land Economy at the University of Cambridge and a PhD candidate at the Centre for Law

and Economics, Faculty of Laws, University College London. He began his career as an economist at the Australian Treasury, primarily working on environmental policy. He has also worked at the Papua New Guinean Treasury, the Cape York Institute for Indigenous Policy and on European Union and Asian Development Bank projects. His current research is focused on the interaction of state and non-state legal orders.

URS LUTERBACHER – **The Graduate Institute, Geneva**
Urs Luterbacher is Emeritus Professor of Political Science at the Graduate Institute of International and Development Studies, where he taught from 1973 to 2010. He has done work on problems of international conflict and cooperation and international environmental problems using formal models and game theory. He is also a member of ProClim, the Forum for Climate and Global Change of the Swiss Academy of Sciences, and of the Consultative Body on Climate Change, a committee set up by the Swiss Academy of Sciences to advise the Swiss government on climate change.

SANDRINE MALJEAN-DUBOIS – **CNRS**
Director of Research at the French Centre National de la Recherche Scientifique (CNRS) and Director of the Centre d'études et de recherches internationales et communautaires (CERIC), Aix-en-Provence. Sandrine Maljean-Dubois has edited several books in international and European environmental law. She has published numerous articles in this field, especially relating to the protection of biodiversity and biosecurity, as well as on the articulation between international environmental law and WTO law.

ELISA MORGERA – **University of Edinburgh**
Lecturer in European Environmental Law, University of Edinburgh, School of Law. Elisa Morgera specialises in European, international and comparative environmental law. She has researched specifically in the area of environmental integration in the European Union external relations, biodiversity conservation and sustainable use, international environmental governance and corporate environmental accountability. Elisa joined the School of Law in 2009. She directs the LLM programme in Global Environment and Climate Change Law, and is a member of the Europa Institute and the Scottish Centre for International Law. She is currently participating in the EU-funded project 'Study of the legal framework on human rights and the environment applicable to European enterprises operating outside the European Union' and in the project 'Obtaining, protecting and using essential environmental technologies: a holistic analysis'. As a former legal officer of

the United Nations Food and Agriculture Organization, she advised over fifty countries in Africa, Asia, Latin America and the South Pacific on improving domestic legislation on natural resources. Previously, she also served as environmental management officer for the United Nations Development Programme in the Eastern Caribbean. Elisa holds law degrees from the University of Trieste (Italian law degree), the University of London (LLM) and the European University Institute (PhD), as well as certificates from the University of Liege and Boston University Law School. She is a regular contributor to the *Yearbook of International Environmental Law*, the *Review of European Community and International Environmental Law*, and the *Max Planck Encyclopedia of Public International Law.*

RICCARDO PAVONI – **University of Siena**
Associate Professor of International and European Union Law, University of Siena, Faculty of Law. Doctor of Laws (Siena), MJur (Oxford). Professor Pavoni is the associate editor of the *Italian Yearbook of International Law.* He is also a member of the editorial board of the *Oxford Reports on International Law in Domestic Courts.* He has been a visiting professor at various universities, including the University of Amsterdam (2006), Charles University in Prague (2008) and the University of Tulane School of Law (2010). Professor Pavoni is a member of the European Society of International Law and the Italian Society of International Law. He is co-director of the Tulane-Siena Institute for International Law, Cultural Heritage and the Arts. Currently, his main research areas cover the relationship between domestic, European and international law, international environmental law, international cultural heritage law and the law of international immunities.

VANESSA RICHARD – **CNRS**
Researcher at the French Centre National de la Recherche Scientifique (CNRS) and the Centre d'études et de recherches internationales et communautaires (CERIC), Aix-en-Provence. Vanessa Richard has published numerous articles in the field of international environmental law. Her research focuses on the international law applicable to freshwater and international non-compliance procedures and non-judicial remedies.

BENJAMIN J. RICHARDSON – **University of British Columbia**
Professor and Canada Research Chair in Environmental Law and Sustainability, University of British Columbia, Faculty of Law. Professor Richardson joined the UBC Faculty of Law in January 2011, and holds the Senior (tier 1) Canada Research Chair in Environmental Law and Sustainability.

Previously, he was a professor at Osgoode Hall Law School of York University (2003–10) and earlier was a senior lecturer at the law faculties of the University of Manchester and University of Auckland. Prior to working in academia, Professor Richardson was a policy adviser to the NSW National Parks and Wildlife Service in Australia, and a legal consultant to the International Union for Conservation of Nature (IUCN) in Nepal and Kenya. He completed his undergraduate studies in law and political science with honours at Macquarie University and his PhD at the Australian National University. Professor Richardson's principal research area is socially responsible investment and its regulation. His scholarship also includes Aboriginal peoples and the environment, and climate change law. His recent publications include *Local Climate Change Law* (2012), *Climate Law and Developing Countries* (2009), *Indigenous Peoples and the Law* (2009), *Socially Responsible Investment Law* (2008) and *Environmental Law for Sustainability* (2006). Among his professional responsibilities, Professor Richardson is an elected member of the Governing Board of the IUCN Academy of Environmental Law and co-chairs the SRI Research Cluster of the Canadian Business Ethics Research Network.

SWENJA SURMINSKI – **London School of Economics**
Senior Research Fellow, Centre for Climate Change Economics and Policy, London School of Economics. Swenja Surminski was a Fulbright Scholar in the United States, studying environmental economics and international relations at the University of New Hampshire. In 2002, Swenja received a PhD in political science/economics from Hamburg University for her work on 'Climate Change and the Insurance Industry'. She joined the London School of Economics in September 2010, after eight years working in the insurance industry. Swenja's current research interests include linking adaptation and disaster risk reduction, the role of insurance in climate adaptation and mitigation, and the economics of natural disasters. From April 2007 until September 2010, Swenja worked for the Association of British Insurers (ABI) as Climate Change Adviser. Her key areas of work were climate impacts, mitigation policies and the role of insurance in the climate change context. Swenja coordinated the ABI's response to the 2007 summer floods in the UK, led several industry research projects on climate change and sat on various research steering groups, guiding the knowledge exchange between climate scientists and the insurance industry. Swenja has been a member of the Management Committee of the industry's ClimateWise initiative, of the European Insurance Industry Climate Change Taskforce (CEA) and of the London Climate Change Partnership Steering Group. She has been advising

on climate change risks at UN, EU and UK level and is the author of several papers on these topics. Prior to taking up her role at the ABI, Swenja was working in the Risk Management division of insurance broker Marsh McLennan and in the Geoscience Team at Munich Reinsurance.

TIMOTHY SWANSON – **The Graduate Institute, Geneva**
André Hoffman Chair of Environmental Economics, Graduate Institute of International and Development Studies, Director, Centre for International Environmental Studies. Professor Swanson holds graduate degrees in law and economics, completing his PhD at the London School of Economics under the supervision of Nick Stern. Previously, he was the holder of the Chair of Law and Economics at University College London, a lecturer at Cambridge University and the Research Director for the UK's National Centre on Social and Economic Research on the Global Environment (CSERGE). Recently, he has led research teams on issues dealing with: environmental governance in China (for the China Council and the Asian Development Bank), biodiversity management domestically and globally (for various developing countries as well as the European Union's BioEcon programme), EU water management, as well as intellectual property rights and biotechnology regulation (EU and European Science Foundation). He has advised many international agencies (OECD, UNEP, World Bank) on issues dealing with burden sharing and institution-building under international environmental agreements such as the Montreal Protocol and the Convention on Biological Diversity. His publications appear in journals which focus on economics, international affairs and development, environmental studies, as well as law and economics.

JORGE E. VIÑUALES – **The Graduate Institute, Geneva**
Pictet Chair in International Environmental Law and an assistant professor of public international law at the Graduate Institute, Geneva. Jorge E. Viñuales is also the Director of the Programme on Environmental Governance at the Centre for International Environmental Studies (CIES). He is currently active both as an academic and a practitioner in the fields of international environmental law and foreign investment law. Professor Viñuales has substantial experience as a practising international lawyer in his specialty areas. He has worked on many cases under ICSID, UNCITRAL, PCA, ICC or LCIA rules, including several high-profile inter-state, investor-state and commercial disputes, and he also has experience advising companies, governments, international organisations or major NGOs on different matters of international law. He has published widely in major academic and practitioner

journals and he has recently completed *Foreign Investment and the Environment in International Law* (Cambridge University Press, 2012). Professor Viñuales was educated in France (Doctorat – Sciences Po, Paris), the United States (LLM – Harvard), Switzerland (*Licence* and *Diplôme d'études approfondies* in international relations – HEI; *liz jur* – Universität Freiburg; *Licence* and *Diplôme d'études approfondies* in political science – Université de Genève) and Argentina (*Abogado* – UNICEN). His native language is Spanish and he is fluent in English, French and Italian.

ABBREVIATIONS

AAU	assigned amount unit
ABS	access and benefit-sharing
ACHPR	African Commission on Human and Peoples' Rights
ACHR	American Convention on Human Rights
ADB	Asian Development Bank
AfDB	African Development Bank
AFL–CIO	American Federation of Labor and Congress of Industrial Organizations
AGF	Advisory Group on Climate Change Financing
ASRIA	Association for Sustainable & Responsible Investment in Asia
ATA	Air Transport Association
ATCA	Alien Torts Claim Act
BGB	Bürgerliches Gesetzbuch
BIT	bilateral investment treaty
BOAD	Banque ouest-africaine de développement (West African Development Bank)
BSA	benefit-sharing agreement
CABEI	Central American Bank for Economic Integration
CAC	command and control
CAF	Corporación Andina de Fomento
CAFTA-DR	Dominican Republic–Central America Free Trade Agreement
CalPERS	California Public Employees for a Responsible Retirement
CAO	compliance adviser/ombudsman
CARIFORUM	Caribbean Forum
CBD	Convention on Biological Diversity
CCS	carbon capture and storage
CCX	Chicago Climate Exchange
CDB	Caribbean Development Bank
CDM	clean development mechanism
CDP	Carbon Disclosure Project
CEE	Central and Eastern European
CER	certified emissions reduction

CERCLA	Comprehensive Environmental Response, Compensation and Liability Act
Ceres	Coalition for Environmentally Responsible Economies
CIAA	Common Investment Area Agreement
CIEL	Centre for International Environmental Law
CIFOR	Center for International Forestry Research
CIME	(OECD) Committee on International Investment and Multinational Enterprises
COMESA	Common Market for Eastern and Southern Africa
CoP	Communication on Progress
COP	conference of the parties
CRC	Convention on the Rights of the Child
CRISA	Code for Responsible Investing in South Africa
CSR	corporate social responsibility
CTE	Committee on Trade and Environment
CTESS	Committee on Trade and Environment Special Session
CTPs	cleaner technology and products
CTR	Claims Tribunal Report
CTS	Council for Trade in Services
CTSSS	Council for Trade in Services Special Session
DEFRA	Department for Environment, Food and Rural Affairs
DLDCs	developing and least-developed countries
E&S	environmental and social
EADB	East African Development Bank
EAN	enhanced analytics network
EBRD	European Bank for Reconstruction and Development
ECHR	European Convention on Human Rights
ECJ	European Court of Justice
ECOSOC	(United Nations) Economic and Social Council
ECT	Energy Charter Treaty
ECtHR	European Court of Human Rights
EGS	environmental goods and services
EHS	environmental, health and safety
EIB	European Investment Bank
EITI	Extractive Industries Transparency Initiative
EKC	environmental Kuznets curve
ELI	Environmental Law Institute
EMAS	Eco-Management and Audit Scheme
EMS	environmental management system
EPA	Economic Partnership Agreement
EPFIs	Equator Principles Financial Institutions
EPP	environmentally preferable product

ERU	emissions reduction unit
ESG	environmental, social and governance
ETF	exchange-traded fund
ETS	emissions trading scheme
EU EPA	European Union Economic Partnership Agreement
Eurosif	European Social Investment Forum
FAO	Food and Agriculture Organization
FCCC	Framework Convention on Climate Change (see also UNFCCC)
FDI	foreign direct investment
FET	fair and equitable treatment
FGD	flue-gas desulphurisation
FI	finance initiative
FIDH	Fédération internationale des ligues des droits de l'homme (International Federation for Human Rights)
FIELD	Foundation for International Environmental Law and Development
FRC	Financial Reporting Council
FSU	former Soviet Union
FTA	free trade agreement
GARP	growth at a reasonable price
GATS	General Agreement on Trade in Services
GATT	General Agreement on Tariffs and Trade
GC	Global Compact
GEF	global environment facility
GHG	greenhouse gas
GRI	Global Reporting Initiative
HRC	Human Rights Council
IADB	Inter-American Development Bank
IAIC	Inter-American Investment Corporation
IBRD	International Bank for Reconstruction and Development
ICCPR	International Covenant on Civil and Political Rights
ICESCR	International Covenant on Economic, Social and Cultural Rights
ICJ	International Court of Justice
ICommHR	Inter-American Commission on Human Rights
ICSID	International Centre for Settlement of Investment Disputes
IDB	Islamic Development Bank
IDLO	International Development Law Organization
IELMT	International Environmental Legal Materials and Treaties
IET	international emissions trading
IETA	International Emissions Trading Association
IFC	International Finance Corporation
IFI	international financial institution

IFPMA	International Federation of Pharmaceutical Manufacturers and Associations
IHRP	international habitat reserve programme
IIA	international investment agreement
ILC	International Law Commission
ILM	International Legal Materials
ILO	International Labour Organization
IMA	investment management agreement
INCR	Investor Network on Climate Risk
IPBES	Intergovernmental Platform on Biodiversity and Ecosystem Services
IPCC	Intergovernmental Panel on Climate Change
IPR	intellectual property rights
ISO	International Organization for Standardization
ITC	investment tax credit
ITLOS	International Tribunal for the Law of the Sea
ITPGR	International Treaty on Plant Genetic Resources (for Food and Agriculture)
IUCN	International Union for Conservation of Nature
JI	joint implementation
JISC	Joint Implementation Supervisory Committee
JVETS	Japanese Voluntary Emissions Trading Scheme
LDC	least-developed country
LRTAP	long-range transboundary air pollution
LULUCF	land use, land-use change and forestry
MCII	Munich Climate Insurance Initiative
MDB	multilateral development bank
MEA	multilateral environmental agreement
MFI	multilateral financial institution
MIGA	Multilateral Investment Guarantee Agency
MNC	multinational corporation
MOX	mixed oxide fuel
MRV	monitoring, reporting and verification
MTA	material transfer agreement
NAFTA	North American Free Trade Agreement
NAMA	non-agricultural market access
NAV	net asset value
NCP	national contact point
NETS	Norwegian Emissions Trading System
NGO	non-governmental organisation
NSW GGAS	New South Wales Greenhouse Gas Reduction Scheme

NTB	non-tariff barrier
OECD	Organisation for Economic Co-operation and Development
OPEC Fund	OPEC Fund for International Development
OPIC	Overseas Private Investment Corporation
OSPAR Convention	Oslo–Paris Convention for the Protection of the North-East Atlantic (i.e., Convention for the Protection of the North-East Atlantic)
PE	private equity
PES	payment for ecosystem services
POP	persistent organic pollutant
PPM	process and production method
PPP	public–private partnership
PRI	principles for responsible investment
PTC	production tax credit
QELR	quantified emission limitation reduction
QMM	QIT Madagascar Minerals
R&D	research and development
RAN	Rainforest Action Network
RCADI	*Recueil des Cours de l'Académie de Droit international*
RECIEL	*Review of European Community and International Environmental Law*
REDD	reducing emissions from deforestation and forest degradation
RFP	request for proposal
RMU	removal unit
S&D	special and differential
SAI	Social Accountability International
SBI	subsidiary body for implementation
SBSTA	Subsidiary Body for Scientific and Technological Advice
SFDI	Société française pour le droit international
SICAV	société d'investissement à capital variable
SMTA	standard material transfer agreement
SRI	sustainable and responsible investment/socially responsible investing
SSRN	Social Science Research Network
TBT	technical barriers to trade
TREM	trade-related environmental measure
UEBT	Union for Ethical BioTrade
UNCITRAL	United Nations Commission on International Trade Law
UNCLOS	United Nations Convention on the Law of the Sea
UNCTAD	United Nations Conference on Trade and Development
UNDRIP	UN Declaration on the Rights of Indigenous Peoples
UNEP	United Nations Environment Programme
UNEP-FI	United Nations Environment Programme Finance Initiative
UNFCCC	United Nations Framework Convention on Climate Change

UNISDR	United Nations International Strategy for Disaster Reduction
UNPRI	United Nations Principles of Responsible Investing
UNRISD	United Nations Research Institute for Social Development
UNTS	United Nations Treaty Series
VCLT	Vienna Convention on the Law of Treaties
WBCSD	World Business Council for Sustainable Development
WEC	World Energy Council
WFP	World Food Programme
WHO	World Health Organization
WIPO	World Intellectual Property Organization
WSSD	World Summit on Sustainable Development
WTO	World Trade Organization
WWF	World Wildlife Fund

Introductory observations

PIERRE-MARIE DUPUY AND JORGE E. VIÑUALES

It no longer seems controversial to state that the private sector has a very significant role to play in protecting the environment. Yet, as both the main producer (hence the main polluter) and the main holder of financial and technology resources, the role of the private sector is ambiguous. The purpose of this volume is to explore one central aspect of this role, namely the possibility of harnessing foreign direct investment to promote environmental protection. Foreign investment is a key vector of both financial and technology transfers to countries that are particularly exposed to environmental challenges. This is all the more so in an era of economic crisis where public budgets can hardly meet – whether for economic or political reasons – the increasing demand for development aid and environmental protection measures. In this context, the editors of this book considered that it would be useful to ask a selected number of academics and practitioners working on the legal, economic and political aspects of environmental protection to share their views on the question of how to channel foreign investment into pro-environment projects. With this purpose in mind, a conference was convened in May 2011 at the Graduate Institute, Geneva, where the role of the private sector in protecting the environment was analysed in detail. The present volume gathers most of the papers presented at that meeting as well as other chapters that were specifically commissioned afterwards to cover questions not addressed during the meeting. The book is structured in three parts.

The first part situates the specific question addressed in the book within the broader context of global environmental governance. In Chapter 1, Pierre-Marie Dupuy provides a macro-level view of the last four decades of global efforts to curb environmental degradation highlighting the three main trends that characterise the process, namely a gradual expansion of the geographical and substantive scope of international environmental law, the increasing complexity entailed by such expansion, and the persistence of the initial tensions, particularly between environmental protection and economic growth/development. One can gather from this initial chapter that the main challenge facing international environmental law today is one of implementation. In Chapter 2, Francesco Francioni dissects the different dimensions of this challenge and offers three distinct but interrelated perspectives for improving implementation. First, from a normative perspective, Francioni argues that the concept of sovereignty should be reconceptualised in functional terms, so as to redefine the powers of the state over its natural resources. Second, from a judicial perspective, he investigates the extent to which existing international courts and tribunals could be used to advance environmental protection. Third, from an institutional perspective, he explores ways to enhance global environmental governance and oversight mechanisms. Francioni highlights the need to engage with the private sector in order for these three transformations to be achieved. The remaining three chapters of the first part focus on questions of political, legal and economic 'infrastructure'. In Chapter 3, Urs Luterbacher analyses the fundamental political constraints within which global environmental negotiations take place. Luterbacher examines the cooperation, coordination and enforcement problems that must be overcome by international legal regimes dealing with environmental concerns. Using the example of climate change, he advocates for a system of 'transfers' from developed to developing countries that could make both groups better off under some specific conditions. In Chapter 4, Sandrine Maljean-Dubois and Vanessa Richard explore a fundamental legal question, namely the extent to which international environmental law can be directly applied to multinational corporations. They argue that although international environmental law may not apply 'directly' to corporations it does apply 'indirectly' through a variety of means, including internationally induced domestic law, human-rights-based approaches to environmental protection, soft law instruments stemming from both international and private institutions and the practice of a variety of oversight and compliance bodies. In Chapter 5, Shaun Larcom and Timothy Swanson explore the economic rationale that may incite governments to intervene into their economies to shift investment towards green industries. As shown by Larcom and Swanson by reference to the cases of Japan and Denmark, the main reason why it may pay to be a leader in technologies and industries that are more environmentally friendly is that technology leadership provides a first-mover advantage in terms of competitiveness. Overall, the five perspectives offered in this first part of the book are intended to provide a broad picture of how we got here (Dupuy), what to do next (Francioni) and what are the main political (Luterbacher), legal (Maljean-Dubois and Richard) and economic constraints (Larcom and Swanson) affecting efforts to move forward. It is in this context that a more detailed analysis of incentive mechanisms and safeguards can be conducted.

The second part of the book devotes five chapters to the analysis of the main avenues that can be explored to channel financial and technology resources into pro-environment projects. In Chapter 6, Magnus Jesko Langer provides a panoramic view of the complex field of environmental finance, focusing on the role of private funds, project-finance mechanisms and market mechanisms. Langer's chapter provides a general account of how these different financial tools can play a role in channelling much-needed resources towards pro-environment projects. The following four chapters discuss more specific sets of techniques to achieve this end. In Chapter 7, Daniel M. Firger analyses the operation and future potential of the market mechanisms developed within the context of the climate change regime, namely emissions trading, the joint-implementation mechanism, the clean development mechanism and the so-called REDD-plus mechanism, which focuses on financial incentives to avoid deforestation. Based on his analysis of the climate change policies, he advocates for the use of international law as a 'catalyst' for private investment in low-carbon growth. In Chapter 8, Riccardo Pavoni examines two main mechanisms used to promote the conservation of biodiversity, namely access-and-benefit-sharing agreements and payments-for-ecosystem-services schemes. He highlights that although both mechanisms may serve to channel investment into environmental protection initiatives their legal bases are profoundly different. Whereas ABS agreements are the expression of a fundamental principle of the Convention on Biological Diversity, now fully spelled out in the 2010 Nagoya Protocol, PES schemes have no clear legal or institutional basis. Pavoni calls for this lacuna to be filled, particularly because the potential of PES schemes to mobilise investment into conservation seems superior to that of ABS agreements. In Chapter 9, Swenja Surminski engages with a key financial instrument that has received little attention in environmental law and policy circles, namely insurance schemes. Taking climate change as an example, Surminski identifies three potential roles for insurance schemes: compensating victims and funding clean-up processes; incentivising risk-reduction efforts; and fostering environmental investments by transferring some of the investment risks. However, Surminski acknowledges that this is a relatively new area and that an overall assessment of the effectiveness of insurance schemes in this connection has yet to be conducted. The final chapter (Chapter 10) of the second part, by Konstantina Athanasakou, takes a different angle and explores the potential of the current negotiations on environmental goods and services as a trade-related incentive mechanism to diffuse, among others, environmental technologies. Athanasakou argues that a shift in the focus on these negotiations towards the question of technologies could create significant incentives for investing in pro-environment technology. Overall, the second part of the book provides both a panoramic view (Langer) and a specific analysis of four key sets of techniques (Firger, Pavoni, Surminski, Athanasakou) that could be used to channel investment into pro-environment projects.

The third part of the book looks at the other side of the 'investment/environment' coin by analysing the 'safeguards' available to ensure that the pro-environment nature of the investments thus channelled is not jeopardised. Indeed, foreign investment has sometimes been seen not only as a vector of technology and financial transfers but also as a source of social and environmental problems. The five chapters of the third part examine different techniques to subject the activities of foreign investors to adequate environmental protection standards. In Chapter 11, Jorge E. Viñuales analyses the impact of bilateral investment treaties on the ability of states to regulate the activities of foreign investors. He argues that international environmental law is playing a growing role in legitimising environmental regulation and that investment tribunals are gradually carving out some room for such regulation in their interpretation of investment disciplines. The subsequent chapters analyse four techniques to exercise some control over the activities of foreign investors. In Chapter 12, Elisa Morgera maps the evolution of the instruments used to define the corporate social responsibility of multinationals from voluntary codes to increasingly strong accountability mechanisms with a significant institutional component. She shows that the risks arising from the proliferation of different standards and accountability mechanisms are significantly mitigated by the substantive convergence of the standards used to guide and assess the conduct of private companies. In Chapter 13, Natasha Affolder advocates for a different level of analysis, namely the study of investment projects and their contractual arrangements. She provides a typology of the environmental contracts used to manage the social and environmental aspects of certain investment schemes, particularly in the extractive industries, as an illustration of a broader trend towards the contractualisation of environmental governance in foreign investment projects. In Chapter 14, Benjamin J. Richardson looks at another technique for subjecting the activities of companies to certain environmental standards, namely the role of voluntary codes applicable to financial intermediaries. As noted by Richardson, in recent years, the longstanding movement for 'sustainable and responsible investment' or 'socially responsible investing' (SRI) has become increasingly sensitive to environmental questions. Companies are now being encouraged to comply with certain social and environmental standards in order to attract financial resources from SRI sources. Finally, in Chapter 15, Zachary Douglas assesses the prospects for enforcing environmental norms in investment treaty arbitration both through the medium of a claim by the claimant investor and a counterclaim by the respondent host state. Drawing an analogy between investment proceedings and the Alien Torts Statute in the USA, he explores the possibility that investment tribunals might be able to operationalise international environmental norms as actionable standards for counterclaims against foreign investors. Overall, the 'safeguards' examined in these five chapters suggest that despite differences in their scope and effectiveness there are several avenues to keep the activities of foreign investors within reasonable bounds.

Taken together, the essays gathered in this volume are an attempt at providing a unified and coherent view of ways to harness foreign investment to promote environmental protection. It is intended for both practitioners and academics engaged in the formulation and/or the analysis of pro-environment policies. A detailed analysis of the most salient legal issues arising from the policies discussed in this volume is provided in a companion book published by the same publisher.[1] For those readers interested in exploring further the policy dimensions of the topics covered in the present volume, we have asked contributors to provide a list of bibliographic suggestions, which can be found at the end of each chapter. We hope that this collection of essays will help clarify the important synergies that could be achieved between foreign investment and the protection of the environment.

[1] See J. E. Viñuales, *Foreign Investment and the Environment in International Law* (Cambridge University Press, 2012).

I

Protecting the environment in the twenty-first century: the role of the private sector

1

International environmental law: looking at the past to shape the future

PIERRE-MARIE DUPUY

INTRODUCTION

Barely half a century ago, there were already discussions on the 'preservation of nature', but not yet on the 'protection of the environment'. Retrospectively, one may wonder if the substitution of the former by the latter in the UN 1972 Stockholm Declaration necessarily represents a step forward even if one must acknowledge that the Declaration recognises that 'Man is both creature and moulder of his environment'.[1] Not only has 'Nature' an existence of its own, but it also existed prior to the arrival of human beings and their culture. The environment, by contrast, cannot be conceived without reference to the human being, as it is the latter, with his needs and perceptions, which entirely defines the former. Hence, the paradox: in the 1970s, environmental law began to emerge, based on a rather ambiguous assertion found in the Stockholm Declaration, which had been adopted under the auspices of the United Nations: Nature was per se entirely dependent on humans.[2] Such a concept seems to have acknowledged one of the last avatars of the foundations of modern technocratic and consumerist western philosophy: the human being must establish itself as the 'master and owner' of the world, instead of accepting its dependence upon it.[3]

[1] A. Kiss, 'The International Protection of the Environment', in R. St J. Macdonald and D. Johnston (eds.), *The Structure and Process of International Law: Essays in Legal Philosophy, Doctrine and Theory* (The Hague: Martinus Nijhoff, 1983), 1069.

[2] Declaration of the United Nations Conference on the Human Environment, Stockholm, 16 June 1972, part I, para. 1: 'Both aspects of man's environment, the natural and the man-made, are essential to his well-being and to the enjoyment of basic human rights'. See also A. Kiss and J. Sicault, 'La Conférence des Nations Unies sur l'Environnement' (1972) 18 *Annuaire français de droit international* 603.

[3] Symbolically, the origins of this view are often associated with the Cartesian method. See R. Descartes, *Discours de la méthode* (Paris: Flammarion, 1966 [1637]), 84.

Such an assumption, which may appear to some extent realistic but which also potentially represents a great threat, is intensively challenged by many organisations of the international civil society. Nonetheless, it is still a prevailing concept in the mentality of the majority of the world's government officials, from both the North and the South, whose political culture clearly stands in the way of a fundamental truth: the survival of people must take precedence over state sovereignty. This is also the main reason why the environment still remains, first and foremost, subject to the territorial jurisdiction of the state.

However, the increasingly catastrophic consequences of such a concept show that, unlike Protagoras' famous saying, the human being is no longer 'the measure of all things'.[4] The accelerated melting of glaciers and poles, the increasing drying of the Sahelian area, the acidification of the oceans and perhaps in the near future the disruption of their currents, are numerous natural examples, which bring to mind another figure of Greek mythology: global Chaos, which the idea of national territory – and its derisory insignificance – is tragically incapable of resisting.

Moreover, what has become apparent in the last forty years is that environmental problems are by their very essence global. Ecology is by definition the science of interdependence.[5] Likewise, international environmental law is no longer defined by the approximate laying out, or interaction, of state sovereignties on a planet that has become too small and cramped. More than a right of joint ownership, international environmental law has become the responsibility of the whole. As the Belgian legal philosopher François Ost puts it: 'holism has replaced individualism'.[6]

If one tries to assess the evolution of international environmental law over the last four decades in order better to understand the topic of this book, three fundamental trends can be identified: first, a gradual expansion of its scope (1.1); second, a higher level of complexity due to this expansion (1.2); and third, the persistence of the initial tensions, which have shaped international environmental law from its inception (1.3).

[4] See the last edition of the Club of Rome's outlook on the potential scenarios for the next forty years: J. Randers, *2052: A Global Forecast for the Next Forty Years* (Rotterdam: The Club of Rome, 2012).

[5] See R. Carson, *Silent Spring* (Boston, Mass.: Mariner Books, 2002), 189. See also F. Ost, *La Nature hors la loi, l'écologie à l'épreuve du droit* (Paris: Editions La Découverte, 1995), 91–3.

[6] Ost, *La Nature hors la loi*, 13.

1.1 Gradual expansion

This expansion can be shown by reference to two main phenomena: the expansion of the spatial scope of application of international environmental law (1.1.1) and the expansion of its substantive scope (1.1.2).

1.1.1 An expanding spatial scope

International environmental law was originally concerned with and was intended to regulate spaces that lay precisely at the heart of the idea of joint ownership: transboundary rivers and lakes such as the Rhine,[7] the Danube[8] or the Mekong,[9] the Great Lakes on the border between Canada and the USA,[10] Lake Geneva[11] as well as enclosed or semi-enclosed seas such as the Baltic[12] or the Mediterranean Sea.[13] Therefore, it was initially

7 See e.g. Convention Establishing Uniform Regulations Concerning Fishing in the Rhine Between Constance and Basel, Berne, 9 December 1869, 9 IPE 4695; Convention between the Riverine States of the Rhine Respecting Regulations Governing the Transport of Corrosive and Poisonous Substances, Mannheim, 11 May 1900, 25 IPE 214; Agreement Concerning the International Commission for the Protection of the Rhine against Pollution, Berne, 29 April 1963, 994 UNTS 3; Convention for the Protection of the Rhine River against Chemical Pollution, Bonn, 3 December 1976, 1124 UNTS 375; Convention on the Protection of the Rhine River against Pollution by Chlorides, Bonn, 3 December 1976, 16 ILM 265 (1977).

8 See e.g. Convention concernant l'exploitation et la conservation des pêcheries dans la partie-frontière du Danube, Belgrade, 15 January 1902, 190 CTS 344; Convention Concerning Fishing in the Waters of the Danube, Bucharest, 29 January 1958, 339 UNTS 23.

9 Agreement on the Cooperation for the Sustainable Development of the Mekong River Basin, Chiang Rai, 5 April 1995, 2069 UNTS 3.

10 See e.g. Treaty Relating to the Boundary Waters and Questions Arising Along the Boundary between the United States and Canada, Washington, 11 January 1909, 10 IPE 5158; Agreement between the United States and Canada on the Water Quality of the Great Lakes, Ottawa, 22 November 1978, 30 UST 1383.

11 Convention Concerning the Protection of Waters of Lake Geneva against Pollution, Paris, 16 November 1962, 922 UNTS 49.

12 Convention on Fishing and Conservation of the Living Resources in the Baltic Sea and the Belts, Gdansk, 13 September 1973, 12 ILM 1291 (1973), as amended by the Warsaw Protocol, 11 November 1982, 22 ILM 704 (1982); Convention on the Protection of the Marine Environment of the Baltic Sea Area, Helsinki, 22 March 1974, 13 ILM 546 (1974).

13 Convention for the Protection of the Mediterranean Sea against Pollution, Barcelona, 16 February 1976, 15 ILM 290 (1976); Protocol for Co-operation in Combating Pollution of the Mediterranean Sea by Oil and other Harmful Substances in Cases of Emergency, Barcelona, 16 February 1976; Protocol for the Prevention of Pollution of the Mediterranean Sea by Dumping from Ships and Aircraft, Barcelona, 16 February 1976; Protocol for the Protection of the Mediterranean Sea against Pollution from Land-based Resources, Athens, 17 May 1980, 19 ILM 869 (1980); Protocol Concerning Mediterranean Specially Protected Areas, Geneva, 3 April 1982, IELMT 982:26.

conceived as being the law of good neighbourly relations. However, its global dimension rapidly emerged accompanied by the motto 'we have only one planet', which was popularised during the 1972 Stockholm Conference. Thereafter, this idea made its way through a variety of channels, reaching important dimensions in the 1980s. A major illustration is provided by the increasing global awareness of the damage to the ozone layer, which resulted in the adoption of the Vienna Convention on the Protection of Ozone Layer in 1985,[14] promptly followed by the quite revolutionary Montreal Protocol.[15] The latter paved the way for the adoption, at the Rio Conference, of the United Nations Framework Convention on Climate Change[16] and the Convention on Biological Diversity,[17] which were in turn followed by more specific protocols.[18] Such a progression clearly demonstrated the inextricable – and inexorable – global dimension of international environmental law.

As the idea of 'global commons', namely those goods jointly owned by all members of the human race, became progressively influential in the international debate, some states sought to mobilise it in order to justify a logic of 'trusteeship'.[19] Whether such logic is solely based on genuine altruism,[20] or hides behind some universalist alibi to increase the spatial

[14] Convention for the Protection of the Ozone Layer, Vienna, 22 March 1985, 26 ILM 1529 (1985).

[15] Protocol on Substances that Deplete the Ozone Layer, Montreal, 16 September 1987, 26 ILM 154 (1987).

[16] United Nations Framework Convention on Climate Change, New York, 9 May 1992, 31 ILM 849 (1992).

[17] Convention on Biological Diversity, Rio de Janeiro, 5 June 1992, 31 ILM 822 (1992).

[18] Kyoto Protocol to the United Nations Framework Convention on Climate Change, Kyoto, 11 December 1997, 2303 UNTS 148; Cartagena Protocol on Biosafety to the Convention on Biological Diversity, 29 January 2000, 39 ILM 1027 (2000); The Nagoya–Kuala Lumpur Supplementary Protocol on Liability and Redress to the Cartagena Protocol on Biosafety, 16 October 2010; Nagoya Protocol on Access to Genetic Resources and the Fair and Equitable Sharing of the Benefits Arising from their Utilization to the Convention on Biological Diversity, 29 October 2010 (these two instruments are available at www.cbd.int (accessed 11 May 2012).

[19] For instance, Canada sought to extend its jurisdiction in the Arctic waters to a 100 nautical mile ecological zone by adopting the Arctic Waters Pollution Prevention Act in 1970; See J.-Y. Morin, 'Le Progrès technique, la pollution et l'évolution récente du droit de la mer au Canada, particulièrement à l'égard de l'Arctique' (1970) 7 *Canadian Journal of International Law* 158. In 2003, France adopted legislation creating an ecological protection zone in the Mediterranean; loi no. 2003–346 of 15 April 2003 and décret no. 2004–33 of 8 January 2004. For general remarks on unilateralism, see P.-M. Dupuy, 'The Place and Role of Unilateralism in Contemporary International Law' (2000) 11 *European Journal of International Law* 19.

[20] See the chapter by F. Francioni in this book, discussing the idea of 'functional sovereignty'.

extension of national sovereignty, remains to be analysed on a case-by-case basis. Nowadays, as the different physical dimensions of the environment coexist, without being truly intertwined, one can safely state that most of these spaces are regulated, at least from a legal point of view, by international environmental law.

1.1.2 Framework of intervention

The aforementioned ideas and principles resulted in the development of the substance of international environmental law. International environmental law is no longer exclusively aimed at the protection of freshwater and maritime spaces, the prevention of deforestation, the protection of endangered species, the preservation of biological diversity, the fight against climate change or the regulation of fishing activities or transboundary pollution. It has now become a body of law acknowledging the ecological dimension of the human rights to water, health and life.[21] Thus, international environmental law will inevitably interact with other regulatory fields, such as trade law, investment law or intellectual property law.

This cross-cutting and global phenomenon, as reflected in the multiple fields of international law addressing ecological concerns, has now gained such magnitude that it must be acknowledged that international environmental law per se is no longer a mere 'branch' of international law; it is rather a 'dimension' inherent to each internationally regulated human activity.[22] It cannot therefore be limited in some sort of a normative ghetto, following the logic of the fragmentation of international law, as it is too often invoked by many scholars with admittedly parochial reflexes. To the contrary, international environmental law has now entered the

[21] See e.g. the General Comments of the Committee on Economic, Social and Cultural Rights: General Comment No. 15 (2002) on the right to water, E/C 12/2002/11, 20 January 2003; General Comment No. 14 (2000) on the right to the highest attainable standard of health, E/C 12/2000/4, 11 August 2000; and General Comment No. 12 on the right to adequate food, E/C 12/1999/5, 12 May 1999.

[22] Referring to international development law, the late Michel Virally spoke of a 'perspective' rather than of a mere 'branch' of international. Such a perspective had to be integrated in all areas of international. The same can be said of international environmental law. See P.-M. Dupuy, 'Où en-est le droit de l'environnement à la fin du siècle?' (1997) 101 *Revue générale de droit international public* 873. On Virally's understanding of international development law and its link to sustainable development law, see J. E. Viñuales, '"The Secret of Tomorrow": International Organisation through the Eyes of Michel Virally' (2012) 23 *European Journal of International Law* 1.

realm of those few 'federal' fields capable of consolidating international law via a few main axes whose ultimate beneficiary is the human being.

It is undeniable that such a holistic approach, the roots of which are overlapping or even conflicting with international obligations, raises and will continue to raise complex issues of interpretation and enforcement of international norms. These norms, and in particular those arising from treaties, reflect de facto the politically hard choices to be made by states, which are not really willing to define any pre-established hierarchy regarding social priorities. This situation is likely further to complicate the task of the judges, both national and international, who find themselves in the delicate position of having to replace the state in dealing with such matters. It is here that the second characteristic of the contemporaneous international environmental law emerges, namely its complexity.

1.2 Increasing complexity

The increasing complexity of international environmental law can be characterised in numerous ways. However, two main features deserve to be highlighted, namely the normative methods (1.2.1) and the institutional mechanisms (1.2.2), which in many ways lack sufficient coordination.

1.2.1 Normative methods

A first indication of a trend towards greater complexity in international environmental norms can be found in the multiplicity of the types of norms. By this, I do not refer to the broad substantive coverage of environmental norms. Rather, I would like to focus on their formal characteristics in order to shed light on the long-standing debate among legal commentators regarding hard law versus soft law.[23] More precisely, the heart of the debate lies in the compatibility and coordination between 'hard' norms – those which have been granted a formally binding character – and 'soft' norms, which at best call for the respect of guidelines, the multiplication and the convergence of which should inevitably characterise the 'regular' behaviour of a well-governed state.[24]

[23] See further P.-M. Dupuy, 'Soft Law and the International Law of the Environment' (1990–1) 12 *Michigan Journal of International Law* 420.

[24] See S. Toope, 'Formality and Informality', in D. Bodansky, J. Brunnée and E. Hey (eds.), *The Oxford Handbook of International Environmental Law* (Oxford University Press, 2007), 107.

The standard-based practice therefore takes on a special significance. Since the early days of international environmental law in the 1970s, various intergovernmental organisations, from the World Food Programme (WFP) to the World Health Organization (WHO), the United Nations Environment Programme (UNEP) or the International Labour Organization (ILO), adopted 'eco-standards' whose content was, if not always technical, at least quantified. The issuance of 'guidelines' to manage transboundary pollution or the equitable use of shared natural resources rapidly developed in contexts such as the Organisation for Economic Co-operation and Development (OECD), UNEP or various regional organisations.[25] Since then, some international institutions, such as the International Financial Corporation, a branch of the World Bank, have adopted environmental standards to guide their operations as well as – indirectly – those of the receivers of institutional funds.[26]

The complexity of the relationship between 'hard' and 'soft' law is further amplified by the fact that 'hard' instruments, such as legally binding treaties, often formulate obligations in vague terms, thereby limiting the effect of otherwise binding provision. By contrast, 'soft law' instruments may establish substantively rigorous objectives regarding, for instance, the quality of water destined to human consumption. This paradox can sometimes lead to rather ambiguous state obligations, and it may explain to some extent why there has been little resort to the rules of state responsibility in cases concerning compensation for transboundary damages or, more generally, for any type of environmental damage. Similarly, the leading cases dealing with environmental issues before the International Court of Justice, such as *Gabčíkovo–Nagymaros*[27] or *Pulp Mills on the River Uruguay*,[28] show the difficulty the judges face when it comes to applying – and adapting – traditional legal instruments to specific ecological matters. Here, one may point out inherent cultural

[25] See e.g. OECD, *Legal Aspects of Transfrontier Pollution* (Paris: OECD, 1977); Cairo Guidelines and Principles for the Environmentally Sound Management and Disposal of Hazardous Wastes, UNEP/GC/DEC 14/30, 17 June 1987.

[26] See the recently updated IFC Performance Standard on Environmental and Social Sustainability, 1 January 2012. See the chapters by E. Morgera and B. Richardson in this book. See more generally E. Morgera, *Corporate Accountability in International Environmental Law* (Oxford University Press, 2009); B. J. Richardson, *Socially Responsible Investment Law: Regulating the Unseen Polluters* (Oxford University Press, 2008).

[27] *Gabčíkovo–Nagymaros Project* (*Hungary/Slovakia*), Judgment, ICJ Reports 1997, 7.

[28] *Case Concerning Pulp Mills on the River Uruguay* (*Argentina* v. *Uruguay*), Judgment, 20 April 2010.

differences between the legal and scientific worlds. Indeed, international judges seem bewildered by the scientific statistical models used to estimate the long-term ecological impact of an industrial project. In such cases, they would rather rely on an approximate estimation of the actual damage instead of depending on an uncertain assessment of future potential risks resulting from a specific activity. This situation may seem sub-optimal. Yet, it would be unimaginable to replace judges by non-lawyer experts who, incidentally, often disagree with each other. Only a judge is capable of determining the judicial 'truth', and such a determination may not necessarily coincide with the results of scientific models, whose predictions – should I say 'prophecies' – are often divergent. The tension between a 'scientific' approach to the assessment of environmental damages, based on statistical and sometimes speculative forecasts, and a 'normative' one, stressing the actual occurrence of a quantified damage, is also a manifestation of the growing complexity of adjudicating environmental disputes, irrespective of the adjudicatory body, which may be international or domestic.

1.2.2 Institutional mechanisms

Another indication of the above-mentioned trend towards greater complexity is provided by the multiplication of supervisory mechanisms and competing procedures potentially dealing with environmental questions. This phenomenon is the direct consequence of the overlap of legal regimes and norms, which in many cases may apply simultaneously to the same activity. As highlighted by the International Tribunal for the Law of the Sea (ITLOS) in the *Southern Bluefin Tuna Case*: 'it is commonplace within international law and state practice for more than one treaty to bear upon a particular dispute'.[29] And yet, it is not uncommon for each of these treaties to establish their own dispute-settlement mechanism. Cases such as *Southern Bluefin Tuna*, *Mox Plant*,[30] the *Iron Rhine*[31] or

[29] *Southern Bluefin Tuna (New Zealand–Japan, Autralia–Japan)*, Reports of International Arbitral Awards, vol. 23 (2004), 40–1, para. 52.

[30] For a discussion of the Mox plant cases, see references, below, n. 34.

[31] *Award in the Arbitration Regarding the Iron Rhine ('Ijzeren Rijn') Railway between the Kingdom of Belgium and the Kingdom of the Netherlands*, decision of 24 May 2005, RIAA, vol. 27, 46–7, paras 13–15.

Pulp Mills[32] illustrate the array of competing dispute-settlement procedures that may be pursued to solve a given environmental dispute.[33]

In the *Mox Plant* case, which provides the most striking illustration of this point, the then European Court of Justice finally asserted its exclusive competence on the matter while condemning Ireland for failing to seek the Court's jurisdiction.[34] In fact, Ireland had successively asked for the establishment of an arbitration tribunal according to various overlapping legal regimes: first, the provisions of the Convention for the Protection of the North-East Atlantic (OSPAR Convention);[35] second, the United Nations Convention on the Law of the Sea (UNCLOS),[36] in order to be granted provisional measures against Great Britain; and finally an arbitral

32 Different aspects of this case that centred around the construction of, initially, two pulp mills, then one, on the border between Uruguay and Argentina were pleaded by different actors in different forums. Regarding the inter-state aspects of the dispute, Uruguay sought to obtain relief from a Mercosur ad hoc arbitral tribunal on the question of the blocking of international bridges by the Argentinean population that opposed the construction of the mills. See Laudo del Tribunal Arbitral 'ad hoc' del Mercosur constituido para entender de la controversia presentada por la República Oriental del Uruguay a la República Argentina sobre 'Omisión del Estado Argentino en adoptar medidas apropiadas para prevenir y/o hacer cesar los impedimentos a la libre circulación derivados de los cortes en territorio argentino de vías de acceso a los puentes internacionales Gral. San Martín y Gral. Artigas que unen la República Argentina con la República Oriental del Uruguay', 6 September 2006. The legal aspects concerning the authorisation and construction of the pulp mills were pleaded in front of the International Court of Justice. See *Pulp Mills on the River Uruguay* (*Argentina* v. *Uruguay*), ICJ, Judgment of 20 April 2010.

33 On this topic, see generally Y. Shany, *The Competing Jurisdictions of International Courts and Tribunals* (Oxford University Press, 2003); J.-C. Martin and Q. Liénard, 'La Concurrence des procédures de règlement des différends internationaux environnementaux', in Y. Kerbrat (ed.), *Forum Shopping et concurrence des procédures contentieuses internationales* (Brussels and Aix-en-Provence: Bruylant/CERIC, 2011), 183–251.

34 *Commission of the European Communities* v. *Ireland* (2006) 45 ILM 1051. See S. Majean-Dubois and J.-C. Martin, 'L'Affaire de l'usine Mox devant les tribunaux internationaux' (2007) 134 *Journal du droit international* 437; Y. Kebrat, 'Le Différend relative à l'usine MOX de Sellafield (*Irlande* v. *Royaume-Uni*): Connexité des procédures et droit d'accès à l'information en matière environnementale (2004) 50 *Annuaire français de droit international* 607; C. Romano, '*Commission of the European Communities* v. *Ireland*' (2007) 101 *American Journal of International Law* 171; S. Mardsen, '*Mox Plant* and the Espoo Convention: Can Member State Disputes Concerning Mixed Environmental Agreements be Resolved Outside EC Law?' (2009) 18 *RECIEL* 312; T. Stephens, *International Courts and Environmental Protection* (Cambridge University Press, 2009), 295–302.

35 Convention for the Protection of the Marine Environment of the North-East Atlantic, 22 September 1992, 2354 UNTS 67.

36 United Nations Convention on the Law of the Sea, 10 December 1982, 1833 UNTS 397.

tribunal established under Article 287 of UNCLOS. Furthermore, this case demonstrated the ineffectiveness of the *lis pendens* doctrine in these particular matters: both the ITLOS and the OSPAR tribunal applied the *lex specialis* interpretative rule to assert their jurisdiction. The same could be said of the application of the *res judicata* rule in the *Pulp Mills* case.[37]

Understandably, legal commentators have widely discussed the reasoning put forward by each jurisdiction, especially in the *Mox Plant* case, as well as on the futility of resorting to norms and general principles of private international law to resolve these issues.[38] Thus, international environmental law is likely to contribute, for the time being, to *forum shopping*, as there appears to be no existing rule of exclusivity or priority in favour of any relevant jurisdiction. As a consequence, in addition to the normative complexity, one can also add the organic complexity resulting from the numerous dispute-settlement mechanisms. Such a situation may generate lots of legal work for law firms but it is likely to undermine the real protection of the environment, especially considering that many of the tensions that were present in the early days of international environmental law still haunt international negotiations.

1.3 Persistence of initial tensions

Since its inception, international environmental law has faced several Gordian knots that make the attainment of its goals particularly challenging. Here I will mention only two of them, which have yet to be untied or cut: the confined mindset through which governments still approach environmental problems (1.3.1) and the delicate question of balancing environmental protection and other, mostly economic, interests (1.3.2).

1.3.1 A confined mindset

From Bali to Durban, via Copenhagen, the difficulties in the progress of the negotiations aiming to reach a new agreement on climate change demonstrate the slow evolution of governments' attitudes across the world.[39]

[37] *Pulp Mills on the River Uruguay (Argentina* v. *Uruguay), Provisional Measures, Order of 23 January 2007*, ICJ Reports 2007, 3.

[38] A. Gattini, 'Un Regard procédural sur la fragmentation du droit international' (2006) 110 *Revue générale de droit international public* 303.

[39] On this process, see J. E. Viñuales, 'Le Bon Dosage du droit international: les négociations climatiques en perspective' (2010) 56 *Annuaire français de droit international* 437.

Some scientists already believe that reaching a deal by 2015, as agreed during the Durban Conference in December 2011, may be insufficiently ambitious. Such an agreement would indeed come too late to curb global warming, whose links to human activities are no longer seriously challenged by anyone, save for a tiny community of experts who are often more concerned with raising doubts than with clarifying the problem.[40]

The climate change issue is but one particularly striking illustration of a broader problem, namely the persistent gap between the acceleration of the phenomena resulting from climate change and the political will to reach efficient outcomes. Government officials are still reluctant to acknowledge the dangers resulting from the destruction of certain fundamental ecosystems of global importance. This is mainly due to their short-term political horizons as defined by electoral deadlines, which, in turn, shows the extent to which the political mindset is still confined to an 'insular' national dimension fundamentally inadequate for the protection of the global environment.

1.3.2 Environmental protection and economic interests

Despite the spectacular progress in certain areas over the last forty years, international environmental law continues to face recurring enforcement problems. It is in this context that the current and future roles of private companies in the protection of the environment can be highlighted, especially in the field of foreign investment. This is a key concern of this book, which focuses on both 'incentives' to pro-environment foreign investment, particularly in developing countries, and 'safeguards' to ensure that investment schemes are properly regulated. Regarding 'incentives', a variety of instruments and approaches have been developed in the last several years in order to channel foreign investment towards sustainable development projects. Part II of this book explores the main instruments used for this purpose, including private finance,[41] climate-related market mechanisms,[42] payments-for-ecosystem-services

[40] See N. Oreskes and E. Conway, *Merchants of Doubt: How a Handful of Scientists Obscured the Truth on Issues from Tobacco Smoke to Global Warming* (New York: Bloomsbury Press, 2010).

[41] See the chapter by M.-J. Langer in this book. See more generally C. Krosinsky and N. Robins (eds.), *Sustainable Investing: The Art of Long-Term Performance* (London: Earthscan, 2008).

[42] See the chapter by. D. Firger in this book. See more generally D. Freestone and C. Streck (eds.), *Legal Aspects of Carbon Trading* (Oxford University Press, 2009).

schemes,[43] insurance schemes[44] and the ongoing discussion in the trade arena on the liberalisation of environmental goods and services.[45] Although international investment law could also be mentioned here, as the protection it offers to foreign investors is no doubt an incentive to undertake both pro-environment and other investment transactions abroad, this book approaches it as a potential obstacle to the regulatory changes entailed by a transition to a green economy. One cannot fail to note the rapidly increasing number of investment claims arising from environmental protection measures.[46] Foreign investors frequently consider that environmental measures adopted by the host state are discriminatory or arbitrary and, therefore, they stand in the way of their investments. Nonetheless, the activities of some sectors of the economy such as the extractive or the chemical industries can cause major catastrophes. There is unfortunately a plethora of examples, such as the Bhopal tragedy in India, the BP oil spill in the Gulf of Mexico or the Total gas leak in the North Sea.

On the one hand, although private companies have a direct right of action against states under most bilateral or multilateral investment treaties, they still presume that they are not subject to any of the international obligations incumbent upon states.[47] On the other hand, the lack of coordination between public authorities on a regional, national or local level may hamper the efficiency of private investments otherwise necessary for economic development. In this context, the protection of the environment suffers not from the fragmentation of international law but from the partitioning of legal orders. Private

[43] See the chapter by R. Pavoni in this book. See more generally P. ten Brink (ed.), *The Economics of Ecosystems and Biodiversity in National and International Policy Making* (London: Earthscan, 2011).

[44] See the chapter by S. Surminski in this book. See more generally K. Warner, N. Ranger, S. Surminski et al., 'Adaptation to Climate Change: Linking Disaster Risk Reduction and Insurance', paper prepared for the United Nations International Strategy for Disaster Reduction (UNISDR), 2009, available at www.preventionweb.net (accessed 14 March 2012).

[45] See the chapter by K. Athanasakou in this book. See more generally A. Vikhlyaev, 'Environmental Goods and Services: Defining Negotiations or Negotiating Definitions?' (2004) 38 *Journal of World Trade* 93.

[46] See the chapter by J. E. Viñuales in this book. See more generally J. E. Viñuales, *Foreign Investment and the Environment in International Law* (Cambridge University Press, 2012).

[47] Wolfgang Friedmann indicated already in 1964 that private corporations could be considered as 'participants in the evolution of international law'; W. Friedmann, *The Changing Structure of International Law* (London: Stevens & Sons, 1964), 230.

companies often play on the differences resulting from their respective legal capacity in both the national and the international legal orders, but simultaneously claim that they are entitled to access international arbitral justice when their interests are jeopardised. One can see the investors' preference for benefiting from international rights without having to assume the obligations deriving from them. However, it is essential to highlight the fact that private investors are often direct vectors of environmental protection – for example, when they are put in charge of managing water resources or waste disposal. As a consequence, the diversification of actors under international environmental law can be added to the spatial and substantive expansion of its scope; their standing as subjects of international law should no longer be challenged from a legal perspective.

While not yielding to the mirage of a monistic Utopia of international law, it is, however, essential to contemplate the idea of better interaction between – or even integration of – the international and national legal orders, in order to achieve two main objectives. First, a need clearly exists to consolidate standards, whose uniform application would contribute to the harmonisation of due diligence criteria incumbent not only upon states but also private companies that are likely to have an impact on the environment.[48] Most often, the effect of these companies' activities is international, even though they take place within national boundaries. Second, the academic and judicial communities must challenge the classical conception of inter-state obligations: some obligations contribute to promoting good governance of private companies, and thus should no longer be regarded as applying solely to contracting states.[49] As previously highlighted, civil society organisations have begun paving the way for the acceptance of a concept in which norms are considered international due to their substance and objective, rather than due to the subjects who have adopted them.

In these times, which witness the acceleration of history as well as the increasing disturbances of Mother Nature, no one, whether individuals, private companies or states, would dare endorse the famous as well as frightening words of the cynical and unfortunately prophetic French King Louis XV: 'Après moi, le déluge!'[50]

[48] See the chapters by E. Morgera and B. J. Richardson in this book.

[49] See the chapter by S. Maljean-Dubois in this book.

[50] 'After me, the deluge!'

Select bibliography

Dupuy, P.-M., 'Soft Law and the International Law of the Environment' (1990–1) 12 *Michigan Journal of International Law* 420.

'Où en-est le droit de l'environnement à la fin du siècle?' (1997) 101 *Revue générale de droit international public* 873.

'The Place and Role of Unilateralism in Contemporary International Law' (2000) 11 *European Journal of International Law* 19.

Freestone, F., and C. Streck (eds.), *Legal Aspects of Carbon Trading* (Oxford University Press, 2009).

Friedmann, W., *The Changing Structure of International Law* (London: Stevens & Sons, 1964).

Gattini, A., 'Un Regard procédural sur la fragmentation du droit international' (2006) *Revue générale de droit international public* 303.

Kebrat, Y., ' Le Différend relative à l'usine MOX de Sellafield (*Irlande* v. *Royaume-Uni*): connexité des procédures et droit d'accès à l'information en matière environnementale (2004) 50 *Annuaire français de droit international* 607.

Kiss, A., 'The International Protection of the Environment', in R. St. J. Macdonald and D. Johnston (eds.), *The Structure and Process of International Law: Essays in Legal Philosophy, Doctrine and Theory* (The Hague: Martinus Nijhoff, 1983), pp. 1069–93.

Kiss, A., and J. Sicault, ' La Conférence des Nations Unies sur l'Environnement' (1972) 18 *Annuaire français de droit international* 603.

Maljean-Dubois, S., and J.-C. Martin, ' L'Affaire de l'usine Mox devant les tribunaux internationaux' (2007) 134 *Journal du droit international* 437.

Martin, J.-C., and Q. Liénard, 'La Concurrence des procédures de règlement des différends internationaux environnementaux', in Y. Kerbrat (ed.), *Forum Shopping et concurrence des procédures contentieuses internationales* (Brussels and Aix-en-Provence: Bruylant/CERIC, 2011), pp. 183–251.

Morgera, E., *Corporate Accountability in International Environmental Law* (Oxford University Press, 2009).

Morin, J.-Y., 'Le Progrès technique, la pollution et l'évolution récente du droit de la mer au Canada, particulièrement à l'égard de l'Arctique' (1970) 7 *Canadian Journal of International Law* 158.

Oreskes, N., and E. Conway, *Merchants of Doubt: How a Handful of Scientists Obscured the Truth on Issues from Tobacco Smoke to Global Warming* (New York: Bloomsbury Press, 2010).

Ost, F., *La Nature hors la loi, l'écologie à l'épreuve du droit* (Paris: Editions La Découverte, 1995).

Randers, J., *2052: A Global Forecast for the Next Forty Years* (Rotterdam: The Club of Rome, 2012).

Richardson, B. J., *Socially Responsible Investment Law: Regulating the Unseen Polluters* (Oxford University Press, 2008).

Romano, C., 'Commission of the European Communities v. Ireland' (2007) 101 *American Journal of International Law* 171.

Shany, Y., *The Competing Jurisdictions of International Courts and Tribunals* (Oxford University Press, 2003).

Stephens, T., *International Courts and Environmental Protection* (Cambridge University Press, 2009).

ten Brink, P. (ed.), *The Economics of Ecosystems and Biodiversity in National and International Policy Making* (London: Earthscan, 2011).

Toope, S., 'Formality and Informality', in D. Bodansky, J. Brunnée and E. Hey (eds.), *The Oxford Handbook of International Environmental Law* (Oxford University Press, 2007), pp. 107–24.

Viñuales, J. E., 'Le Bon Dosage du droit international: les négociations climatiques en perspective' (2010) 56 *Annuaire français de droit international* 437.

Foreign Investment and the Environment in International Law (Cambridge University Press, 2012).

'"The Secret of Tomorrow": International Organisation through the Eyes of Michel Virally' (2012) 23 *European Journal of International Law* 1.

2

The private sector and the challenge of implementation

FRANCESCO FRANCIONI

INTRODUCTION

Forty years on,[1] and, residual uncertainties in scholarship notwithstanding,[2] environmental law has become an established branch of public international law. As such, it regulates relations between states by means, primarily, of bilateral and multilateral treaties and, to a lesser extent, by soft law, general principles and customary norms. The obligations arising from these sources of international law are addressed to states, but their primary goal is to reduce the adverse effects of human activities on the natural world. A logical implication of this is that environmental law is also concerned with the safeguarding of the living conditions of human beings and with the future sustainability of the ecosystems that contain our life on the planet.

This character of environmental law makes the role of the private sector *lato sensu* particularly relevant in the creation and implementation of international norms of environmental protection. At the substantive level, individuals and private entities, such as business companies, NGOs and civil society at large, are indispensable stakeholders in the prevention and reduction of environmental degradation. They participate in the process of standard-setting, both as actors in the transnational private regulation and as participants in traditional intergovernmental negotiations. They are an

[1] Forty years have passed since the adoption of the UN Declaration on the Human Environment, Stockholm, and 16 June 1972, generally recognised as the birth of international environmental law.

[2] See E. Fisher, B. Lang, E. Scotford and C. Carlane, 'Maturity and Methodology: Starting a Debate about Environmental Law Scholarship' (2009) 21 *Journal of Environmental Law* 213, with a response by R. Macrory. See also the critical observations on the lack of a customary law dimension in international environmental law by B. Conforti, *Diritto internazionale*, 8th edn (Naples: Editoriale scientifica, 2010), 219–25.

important factor in the enforcement of international norms in domestic courts and international forums, and, through the instrument of corporate social responsibility (CSR) they are active partners with public authorities and international institutions in the implementation of international environmental standards. In more advanced contemporary forms of private–public partnership, the private sector has also become a vehicle for the mobilisation of financial resources in support of environmental programmes, to channel investments in addressing global environmental problems and for the payment of 'ecosystem services', such as reforestation and biodiversity preservation.[3] Without the contribution of the private sector, many of these programmes would be beyond the economic capabilities of the territorial states.

Besides these substantive forms of public–private partnership, the role of the private sector can be appreciated also at the formal normative level as a factor connecting environmental law with other branches of international law that are concerned with human welfare and human development. It is easy to understand that these branches include international human rights norms, the law of international economic relations as well as the law promoting and protecting cultural diversity and the cultural rights of specific groups, such as indigenous peoples. Private actors promote interaction and mutual supportiveness with these different categories of international law by bringing claims before domestic courts and international forums in which the human-right and commercial aspects of a dispute are more and more frequently linked to environmental questions that need to be adjudicated incidentally or as an integral part of the subject-matter of the dispute.

In this context, it is evident that the enforcement of international environmental standards influences the implementation of a plurality of other systems of international law and it contributes to the idea of the 'unity' of the international legal order rather than to its fragmentation.[4]

2.1 Implementation of international environmental law in context

Given this premise, the question I have been asked to address in this chapter – the challenge of implementation – cannot be simply answered

[3] See chapters by M.-J. Langer, D. Firger, R. Pavoni, N. Affolder and B. Richardson in this book.

[4] P.-M. Dupuy, *L'Unité de l'ordre juridique international* (Leiden: Brill, 2003).

by a mechanical application of the traditional methods of international law implementation. These methods, as we know, are (i) the incorporation into domestic law of relevant international norms; (ii) their judicial enforcement by national courts; and (iii) the international enforcement by means of dispute-settlement mechanisms consented to by the parties in case of dispute. But this traditional paradigm of international law enforcement remains to a large extent refractory to the implementation of international environmental law.

First, with regard to domestic law enforcement, the object of international environmental law continues to remain indeterminate and elusive. It is not possible today to find general consensus on what constitutes a 'good', 'safe' or 'healthy' environment. Even more difficult is to give legal content to concepts such as 'sustainable development' and 'precautionary approach', with regard to which one must admit that international practice is still uncertain or openly divided.[5] The role of law becomes even more precarious when science itself shows variable interpretations of such concepts and thus variable conclusions as to what 'sustainability', 'critical environmental load' or 'sufficient evidence' of risk really mean.[6] This produces conflicting views on the response strategies required at the international level and the implementation schemes suitable to bring domestic law in conformity with international standards. This is made evident by the persistent divergence of legal and policy positions with regard to the planetary problem of what measures are necessary to mitigate and adjust to climate change.

[5] On sustainable development see the penetrating analysis by V. Lowe, 'Sustainable Development and Unsustainable Arguments', in A. Boyle and D. Freestone (eds.), *International Law and Sustainable Development* (Oxford University Press, 1999), 19–37 and, for a more positive evaluation of international practice, also F. Francioni, 'Sviluppo sostenibile e principi di diritto internazionale dell'ambiente', in P. Fois (ed.), *Il principio dello sviluppo sostenibile nel diritto internazionale ed europeo dell'ambiente* (Naples: Editoriale Scientifica, 2007), 41–62.

[6] For an early examination of the interaction between science and environmental degradation, see B. R. Doos, 'Environmental Issues Requiring International Action', in W. Lang, H. Neuhold and K. Zemanek (eds.), *Environmental Protection and International Law* (Dordrecht: Martinus Nijhoff, 1991), 1–54. On the role of scientific evidence in relation to the interpretation and implementation of the law, see the essays gathered in M. C. Malaguti, C. Dordi, S. Di Benedetto and A. Alemanno (eds.), *Scientific Evidence in International and European Law* (Lecce: Argo editore, 2010); F. Francioni and M. Montini, 'Integrating Scientific Evidence into Environmental Law: The International Dimension', in A. Biondi, M. Cecchetti, S. Grassi and M. Lee (eds.), *Scientific Evidence in European Law Making* (The Hague: Kluwer, 2003), 17–40.

Second, and most importantly, at the level of enforcement, international environmental law continues to lag behind in the process of development and consolidation of adjudicatory mechanisms that characterise other sectors of international law. In the field of human rights, we have witnessed the rise of regional courts in Europe, America and Africa and of quasi-judicial supervisory bodies with worldwide competence within the UN human rights treaties system.[7] The adjudication procedures in this field have been opened to applications by individuals and private entities, a development that has permitted a quasi-constitutional review of states' compliance with human rights obligations. This has proved to be not only a guarantee of the effectiveness of the law; it has provided the platform for the elucidation of the law, its jurisprudential development into a living body of norms and principles beyond the bare skeleton of the constitutive treaties. Thanks to this jurisprudential development, today we can speak of a true 'international legal order' of human rights protection. This legal order is constantly renewed and refined by the inter-judicial dialogue and comparative law analysis of different adjudicatory bodies.[8] This feature contributes in no small measure to the universality of human rights.

Similar considerations apply to other areas of international law relevant to the subject of this book, such as international trade and international investment law. In the domain of trade, the 'softness' of traditional norms, their reciprocal character and their subordination to diplomatic means of enforcement, has been overcome by the establishment of the compulsory and binding dispute settlement mechanism of the WTO,[9] now applicable to the overwhelming majority of the states

[7] Notably, the Human Rights Committee established pursuant to Article 28 of the International Covenant on Civil and Political Rights (ICCPR), 16 December 1966, 999 UNTS 171. Under the optional clause of Article 41, this Committee has also competence to receive and consider individual communications alleging violations of the ICCPR by a state party.

[8] Dialogue through judgments can take place in a vertical dimension between international and national courts (see e.g. *In Re P.* House of Lords, 2008 UK HL 38, opinion of Lord Hoffman, on the concept of discrimination) and also at a horizontal level between international courts. See the reference by the Inter-American Commission on Human Rights (ICommHR) to the ECtHR jurisprudence on the meaning of 'contracting parties' jurisdiction' for the purpose of extraterritorial application of the relevant convention norms. ICommHR Report No. 112/10, 21 October 2010.

[9] Understanding on Rules and Procedures Governing the Settlement of Disputes, Annex 2 to the Agreement Establishing the World Trade Organization, Marrakech, 15 April 1994, 1867 UNTS 154.

generating and controlling the world economy. Although the enforcement mechanism adopted in the WTO system is not as progressive as that of human rights (it is not open to claims from private parties; it follows the traditional model of inter-state claims; and the rulings are not self-executing but must be 'adopted' at the governmental level), it is nevertheless a system in which the enforcement of the obligations undertaken by the WTO members is legalised, foreseeable, subject to precise procedures and capable of resulting in effective sanctions in case of non-compliance. In short, it is an effective multilateral mechanism of law enforcement.

In the field of international investments, compulsory and binding arbitration is now a permanent feature of bilateral investment treaties (BITs) and international investment agreements (IIAs), of national laws, regional agreements (e.g., the NAFTA[10]), and of the ICSID established in 1965.[11] The strength of this law is guaranteed by the possibility for private actors, essentially the business corporations engaged in foreign investment ventures, to bring claims directly against the host state of the investment, thus bypassing the past hurdles of prior exhaustion of local remedies and of diplomatic protection by the national state. The effectiveness of the system is further guaranteed by the enforceability of arbitral awards in all state parties of the ICSID Convention.[12] This system has spurred a vast jurisprudence that today amounts to a new type of international administrative law under which the legality of state action – legislative, administrative and judicial – in the field of foreign investments is reviewed and adjudicated.

When compared with this general trend, international environmental law has remained impervious to the adoption of adjudicatory and enforcement mechanisms. The short-lived special environmental chamber of the ICJ[13] shows that even the characterisation of a dispute as 'environmental' may have discouraging effects on the willingness of states to submit that dispute to the ICJ. The International Tribunal for the Law of the Sea (ITLOS), in spite of having been seized of important

[10] North American Free Trade Agreement, 17 December 1992, 32 ILM 296.

[11] Convention on the Settlement of Investment Disputes between States and Nationals of Other States, 18 March 1965, 575 UNTS 159 (ICSID Convention).

[12] *Ibid.*, art. 54.

[13] The environmental chamber of the ICJ was established in July 1993 pursuant to article 26 (1) of the Statute of the International Court of Justice (press release 93/20, Constitution of a Chamber of the Court for the Environmental Matters, 19 July 1993). It was never utilised and, in 2006, the Court decided not to reconstitute it.

environmental disputes,[14] has been unable to adjudicate them for discontinuance of the cases, and is still far from realising its potential as a forum for marine environment disputes. The proposed international environmental court remains a 'pie in the sky', insofar as its creation is confined to academic speculations and conspicuously absent at the level of policy initiatives. This notwithstanding, some encouraging signs emerge from the more frequent resort to arbitration procedures applicable to the resolution of inter-state disputes involving an environmental dimension[15] and from an appreciable increase of environment-related disputes before the ICJ. The latter trend is shown by the *Pulp Mills*[16] dispute between Argentina and Uruguay decided in 2010, and the pending cases on *Aerial Herbicide Spraying,*[17] *Whaling in the Antarctic,*[18] and, most recently, *Construction of a Road in Costa Rica along the San Juan River.*[19]

It is not the purpose of this chapter to engage in a detailed analysis of the structural causes that have hindered the development of effective adjudication mechanisms in international environmental law. I have discussed such causes elsewhere.[20] My goal in the following sections of this chapter is to explore avenues through which we can meet the challenge of implementation of environmental standards taking into account existing international law and institutions and suggesting possible ways forward with the support of civil society and the private sector,

[14] I refer in particular to the *Case Concerning the Conservation and Sustainable Exploitation of Swordfish Stock in the South-Eastern Pacific Ocean* (*Chile–European Union*), ITLOS Case No. 7, Order 2009/1 (16 December 2009), and *Southern Bluefin Tuna* (*New Zealand and Australia* v. *Japan*), ITLOS Cases Nos. 3 and 4, Order (27 August 1999).

[15] See e.g. the important arbitral award in the *Iron Rhine* dispute between Belgium and the Netherlands: *Iron Rhine* ('*IJzeren Rijn*') *Railway Arbitration* (*Belgium/Netherlands*), RIAA, vol. 27 (2005), 25.

[16] *Pulp Mills in the River Uruguay* (*Argentina* v. *Uruguay*), *Judgment* (*20 April 2010*), General List No. 135.

[17] *Aerial Herbicide Spraying* (*Ecuador* v. *Colombia*). Proceedings were instituted by Ecuador before the International Court of Justice on 31 March 2008, alleging damage to human health, property and the environment by the deposit in its territory of toxic herbicide by Colombia.

[18] *Whaling in the Antarctic* (*Australia* v. *Japan*). This case was introduced by Australia against Japan in May 2012.

[19] This case was brought before the ICJ by Nicaragua against Costa Rica on 22 December 2011.

[20] F. Francioni, 'Dispute Avoidance in International Environmental Law', in A. Kiss, D. Shelton and K. Ishibashi (eds.), *Economic Globalisation and Compliance with International Environmental Agreements* (The Hague: Kluwer, 2003), 229 ff.

and through the strengthening of global environmental governance. With this in mind, I will discuss three distinct but interrelated perspectives for improving implementation: a *normative* perspective that presupposes a reconceptualisation of sovereignty in a way as to make it functional to environmental protection as an 'international public good' (2.2); an operational *judicial* perspective which can offer options for effective enforcement of international environmental law 'by other means', i.e., by existing dispute-settlement mechanisms (2.3); and an *institutional* perspective the entails rethinking the role of international institutions to improve environmental governance and oversight (2.4). As I will show, in all these three scenarios the role of the private sector is essential.

2.2 A normative perspective of 'functional' sovereignty

In modern international law, the most spectacular form of privatisation has taken place through the invention of the nation state and the consequent appropriation of portions of the physical space of the world and its resources under the mantle of 'territorial sovereignty'. In its classical formulation, as can be found in the *Island of Palmas* arbitration[21] or the *Lotus* case,[22] territorial sovereignty is understood as the unfettered dominion and power of government over the physical space subject to national jurisdiction, with the exception of recognised common spaces, such as the high seas, the seabed area and outer space. The rise of modern international environmental law requires a reconceptualisation of this idea of sovereignty. Like many other norms of international law – such as human rights, aliens rights and immigration – environmental law increasingly addresses private actors and regulates private activities[23] that in the past were sheltered from international regulation by the concept of 'domestic jurisdiction' or *domaine réservé*. Further, international environmental law is premised on the idea that the general environment must be protected as an international public good[24] to be

[21] *Island of Palmas Case* (*Netherlands–United States of America*), Award (4 April 1928), RIAA, vol. 2 (1928), 838.

[22] *SS Lotus, PCIJ, Series A, No. 10* (7 September 1927), 18–19.

[23] See the chapter by S. Maljean-Dubois and V. Richard in this book.

[24] I do not use the expression 'public goods' in the orthodox sense attributed to it by disciplines other than law, especially economic science – i.e., goods characterised by 'non rivalry and non excludability' (see P. A. Samuelson, 'The Pure Theory of Public Expenditure' (1954) 36 *Review of Economics and Statistics* 387) – but rather in a non-technical

administered and maintained in the general interest of humanity and of the generations to come. From a legal point of view, this idea underlies the development of the category of *erga omnes* obligations. More importantly for present purposes, this idea has generated the concept of 'common concern of humankind' applicable to the elements of the global environment, such as climate[25] and biodiversity,[26] whose safeguard is considered to be in the general interest of the international community as a whole. The novelty of the concept of 'common concern', as opposed to that of 'common heritage', is that it does not presuppose the exclusion of sovereignty and the establishment of an international regime of conservation and management of the relevant resource. On the contrary, it implies that such environmental goods, their protection and the activities related to or impacting on them remain subject to national sovereignty and to its exercise. Such exercise, however, must be in conformity with international law. The introduction of this simple concept is important for the implementation of international environmental law because it entails a normative perspective in which sovereignty is no longer seen as absolute power and control over the physical space subject to national jurisdiction but is analysed through the lens of its *functional* relationship to the general interest of the world community to respect and protect environmental values. This configuration of sovereignty is not dissimilar from the concept of private property in domestic law, which is the dominion of a person over a material or intangible good whose possession and disposal remain subject to the public interest and limited by the social function that the legal order attributes to it.[27]

legal sense of 'common goods' to which the law attaches a public interest and guarantees open access. An early statement of the concept can be traced to Principle 2 of the Stockholm Declaration on the Human Environment, which proclaims: 'The natural resources of the earth including the air, water, land, flora and fauna and especially representative samples of natural ecosystems must be safeguarded for the benefit of present and future generations through careful planning or management, as appropriate'. Declaration of the United Nations Conference on the Human Environment, A/CONF.48/14/Rev. 1 (1973).

25 See United Nations Framework Convention on Climate Change (UNFCCC), 29 May 1992, 31 ILM 849 (1992), preamble, first para.

26 See Convention on Biological Diversity (CBD), 5 June 1992, 31 ILM 818 (1992), preamble, 3rd para.

27 This is the social function recognised to property in modern constitutions (see e.g. Article 42, para. 2 of the 1947 Italian Constitution: 'La proprietà privata è riconosciuta e garantita dalla legge, che ne determina I modi di acquisto e, di godimento e I limiti allo scopo di assicurarne la funzione sociale'). This public function is reflected also in Article 1,

This functionalisation of sovereignty in view of fostering the implementation of international environmental standards has important implications at the theoretical and practical levels. At the theoretical level, it enables some of the ideological obstacles relating to the perceived deficit of 'legitimacy' and democratic decision-making that so far have hindered the effective implementation of international environmental norms to be overcome. These obstacles consist essentially in the difficulty of perceiving international environmental standards that restrict human freedom, and especially economic freedoms, as 'legitimate', in the sense of being the result of democratic-majoritarian decision-making of the people with regard to the use of natural resources. This perception is also induced by the persistence of people's loyalty to national institutions and interests, rather than loyalty to a remote international public interest to the preservation and protection of the environment. The perspective proposed here of a 'functional' sovereignty enables the perception of international environmental standards as the product of a remote and unaccountable authority that subtracts important environment-related matters from the democratic process within the state to be avoided. It brings under the scope of national sovereignty the task of interpreting environmental obligations and balances them against other legitimate aims relating to economic/social development. Thus, the implementation of international environmental law becomes part of a responsible exercise of sovereignty for the attainment of a common good, rather than the execution of an external prescription of an unaccountable authority.

The functionalisation of sovereignty for the respect and protection of the environment as an international public good also allows the limits of the economic theories that tend to reduce the natural world to a pure economic resource subject only to the logic of the market to be illuminated. This logic has gone very far in recent years. It has led to the very controversial reduction of water to a tradable commodity, thus obscuring its inherent value as a common good indispensable for human life.[28]

Protocol 1 additional to the Convention for the Protection of Human Rights and Fundamental Freedoms, 4 November 1950, 213 UNTS 221.

[28] Negative repercussions at international level of the trend towards propertisation of water are evident in the number of investment disputes arising from the privatisation of water supply systems. The most prominent example is that of the 'Cochabamba water war' triggered by the long-term concession by Bolivia to a subsidiary of the US company Bechtel of exclusive water sources previously held by public municipal institutions. The steep increase in water price that followed the concession sparked massive protests and a widespread rebellion which eventually forced the Government of Bolivia to terminate the

It has supported the claim to the appropriation of biogenetic resources, both as a medium of genetic information and as tangible material useful for the production of goods and services.[29] This race to the enclosure of the most intimate essence of life, the biogenetic heritage of plants and animals, has been accepted by the Convention on Biological Diversity insofar as it restates the 'sovereign right' of all states 'to exploit their resources pursuant to their own environmental policies'.[30] But, at the same time, the Convention proclaims the conservation of biodiversity as a 'common concern of humankind'[31] and sets as its fundamental objectives the 'sustainable use' of biodiversity[32] and the 'fair and equitable sharing of the benefits' arising out of the utilisation of genetic resources and from the exploitation of local knowledge and practices,[33] 'including appropriate access' to them and 'appropriate transfer of technology'.[34] This is a good example of how sovereignty can be recognised on the basis of the classical territorial link and at the same time be made functional to the achievement of international environmental goals. It also shows how market and private regulation can function effectively in the shadow of the overarching principle of the 'common concern of humankind'.

The role of the private sector can be an important component in the reinterpretation of sovereignty in the functional perspective of the achievement of environmental public goods. This is especially true in the field of foreign direct investment. A recent practice shows that an increasing number of *land deals* have been made in order to secure the acquisition of large tracts of fertile land in developing countries by foreign states and their agencies with a view to 'externalising' the production of agricultural commodities.[35] It is clear that these deals, also

concession contract and re-establish the public regime of water supply. For the history of this failed investment, see *Aguas del Tunari SA* v. *Republic of Bolivia*, ICSID Case No. ARB/02/3, Decision on Objections to Jurisdiction (21 October 2005). For a comment, see R. Glennon, 'Water Scarcity, Marketing and Privatization' (2005) 83 *Texas Law Review* 1873.

29 The tension arisen in this field between the commercial interests of investors (IPR) and the socio-economic and cultural interests of the local communities and the territorial state underlies the adoption of the 2010 Nagoya Protocol on Access to Genetic Resources and the Fair and Equitable Sharing of Benefits Arising from their Utilisations to the Convention on Biological Diversity, 29 October 2010, UNEP/CBD/COP/DEC/X/1. For further comments on the implications of this Protocol for the relations between the public and the private sectors, see the chapter by R. Pavoni in this book.

30 CBD, art. 3. 31 *Ibid.*, preamble, 3rd para. 32 *Ibid.*, art. 1.

33 *Ibid.*, art. 8(j). 34 *Ibid.*, art. 16.

35 See UNCTAD, *World Investment Report 2009*, available at www.unctad.org (accessed 15 April 2012).

named as *land grabs* by those who give them a negative connotation, may result in adverse effects on the local population and the sustainable use of their natural resources[36] and open the way to unsustainable uses of agricultural land to the extent that agricultural production is redirected from sustainable production of food for local needs to exported crops and to energy in the form of biofuels. To contrast this trend, it is necessary that investment law and especially the responsible exercise of sovereignty by host states in the regulation of related foreign activities takes into account the environmental and human rights implications of the investment and the need to make its performance compatible with objectives of general interest, such as the fight against hunger and the safeguarding of biodiversity.[37]

The use of the expression 'responsible sovereignty' should not be understood only in strict relation to the territorial sovereignty of the state. Also the exercise of 'sovereign' rights and competences transferred by states to international organisations with an autonomous standing and role in international relations can be made functional to the respect and fulfilment of environmental objectives of general interest under international law. This is certainly the case of the European Union, which maintains concurrent competence in environmental matters and has even exclusive competence in fields that are directly relevant to environmental protection, such as trade, fisheries and foreign investments. It is significant that the European Union has begun to exercise its 'sovereign' competence in these fields with a view not only to promote its own economic and political interests but to contribute to the implementation of environmental standards which are required for the protection of the common interest of the international community as a whole. An example of such an exercise of competence is the decision by the European Union to apply its emissions trading scheme to foreign airline companies whose planes are landing in or taking off from the territory of the European

[36] See e.g. *Attorney-General* v. *Lohay Akonaay and Another*, Court of Appeal of Tanzania, Civil Appeal No. 31 of 1994. Reported in [1995] 2 LRC 399; *Centre for Minority Rights Development (Kenya) and Minority Rights Group International on behalf of Endorois Welfare Council* v. *Kenya*, ACHPR Communication 276/2003, 27th Activity Report of the ACHPR (2009).

[37] See R. Künnemann, 'Foreign Investment and the Right to Food', in S. Murphy and A. Paasch (eds.), *The Global Food Challenge: Towards a Human Rights Approach to Trade and Investment Policies* (Cologne and Minneapolis: FIAN et al., 2009), 50–9, available at www.fian.org (accessed 15 April 2012). See further the chapter by J. E. Viñuales in this book.

Union.[38] This decision has been challenged by non-EU airlines on the basis of EU law and international law,[39] as well as by some states, including China, the USA, Japan, India and Russia. Yet it is difficult to deny that it represents an effective use of 'sovereign powers' at the service of the legitimate international aim of countering the catastrophic effects of global warming.[40] It is a responsible use of sovereign powers especially called for at a time when the clash of national economic interests block the reaching of consensus over a mechanism effectively to counteract a common threat such as climate change. It is also a rationally and morally justifiable choice, since it calls into play the private actors – the aviation companies – which contribute with their business to the increase in the emissions of greenhouse gases that are the cause of global warming.

It would be a mistake to consider that this approach based on the idea of 'responsible sovereignty' necessarily entails only negative burdens for the state. It may also entail benefits for states enforcing environmental standards. This is the case in relation to the implementation of the principle of 'common but differentiated responsibilities' (Principle 7 of the 1992 Rio Declaration), as well as in relation to the financial remuneration of states and private entities that make available environmental resources, such as forestry in the REDD programme, and in the context of the system of 'access and benefit-sharing' applicable to the prospecting and exploitation of biogenetic resources. In these cases the territorial

[38] The EU decided in 2008 to include aviation in its emissions trading scheme (ETS) and to extend such scheme to all emissions generated by flights arriving or departing from the EU territory. See Directive 2008/101/EC of the European Parliament and of the Council of 19 November 2008 amending Directive 2003/87/EC so as to include aviation activities in the scheme for greenhouse gas emissions allowance trading within the Community (OJ 2009 L 8, p. 3) and Articles 3a–3g and 25a of the Directive 2003/87/EC of the European Parliament and of the Council of 13 October 2003 establishing a scheme for greenhouse gas emissions allowance trading within the Community and amending Council Directive 96/61/E, OJ 2003 L 0087 – EN – 25.06.2009 – 004.001 (consolidated version) (ETS Directive).

[39] The Court of Justice of the European Union has decided in a preliminary ruling incidental to proceedings brought before a British court by the US Air Transport Association (ATA) that the ETS Directive did not violate international law. See *Air Transport Association of America and others* v. *Secretary of State for Energy and Climate Change*, CJEU Case C-366/10, Judgment of the Court (Grand Chamber) (21 December 2011). The ruling is consistent with the Opinion of Advocate General J. Kokott published in October 2011.

[40] On this initiative, see K. Kulovesi, '"Make Your Own Special Song, Even if Nobody Else Sings Along": International Aviation Emissions and the EU Emissions Trading Scheme' (2011) 2 *Climate Law* 535; J. Scott and L. Rajamani, 'EU Climate Change Unilateralism' (2012) 23 *European Journal of International Law* 469.

state accepts certain limitations to the principle of 'permanent sovereignty over natural resources' and participates with the private sector in a variety of partnerships and contractual arrangements whose common denominator is the positive remuneration of the territorial state for making its sovereignty over natural resources functional to the pursuit of an international public interest.[41]

2.3 Implementing environmental standards by 'other' means

In addition to the reconceptualisation of sovereignty as an agent of international environmental law implementation, another avenue to be considered is the use of existing international dispute-settlement mechanisms to develop an environmental dimension in the relative practice of international law enforcement.[42] The environmental dimension of many international litigation proceedings has become a structural feature in the case law of at least three sets of international forums: (1) the human rights courts and supervisory bodies; (2) investment arbitration; and (3) trade disputes.

In the field of human rights law, the spectacular development of an international jurisprudence in Europe, America and now in Africa has also had a positive impact on the enforcement of international environmental law. This has happened by way of an expansive interpretation of the applicable provisions of human rights treaties whenever a certain type of environmental degradation amounted to a breach of a human right. In Europe, the Strasbourg Court has made extensive use of articles 2 (the right to life) and 8 (the right to private and family life), to extend the protection of the European Convention to individuals exposed to hazardous industries, extractive activities and technological operations incompatible with the respect of such rights.[43] It has developed the

[41] On the role of the private sector in the implementation of the principle of access and benefit sharing (ABS), see the chapter by R. Pavoni in this book.

[42] Some authors have used the expression 'borrowed forums' (see e.g. J. E. Viñuales, 'Foreign Investment and the Environment in International Law: An Ambiguous Relationship' (2009) 80 *British Yearbook of International Law* 244; Viñuales, 'Managing Abidance by Standards for the Protection of the Environment', in A. Cassese, *Realizing Utopia* (Oxford University Press, 2012), 326–39), which I avoid because it gives the idea of a temporary and precarious lending of such institutions to environmental goals, while I envisage a systemic integration of environmental values in the jurisprudence of such forums.

[43] See e.g. *Lopez-Ostra* v. *Spain*, ECtHR Application No. 16798/90, Judgment (9 December 1994); *Guerra and others* v. *Italy*, ECtHR Application No. 14967/89, Judgment (19 February

concept of 'positive obligations' of state parties effectively to enforce legal, administrative and judicial measures designed to prevent or remedy harmful environmental interference by private parties, especially private actors engaged in economic activities, with the sphere of protected rights of other individuals or groups. Further, in the absence of specific treaty provisions, the Strasbourg Court has developed procedural requirements of information, consultation and participation of affected parties in the public decision-making process, in accordance with the standards laid down in the Aarhus Convention of 1998.[44] The practice of the Inter-American Court and of the African Commission warrants similar conclusions.[45]

In the field of investment law a phenomenon of gradual attraction of environment-related disputes within the sphere of compulsory investment arbitration has occurred in the past ten years. This has been facilitated by the direct access enjoyed by private investors to international arbitration and by their readiness to defend their investors' rights under relevant international treaties whenever such rights were felt diminished or nullified by environmentally motivated host states' regulatory measures. The jurisprudence developed in this field shows that investment arbitration can be an important forum for the enforcement of international environmental standards. After an early case law rather impervious to the introduction in the arbitral process of legitimate environmental considerations,[46] recent arbitral practice shows a more prudent opening to environmental values.[47] This is evident especially in two recent arbitral awards involving the USA, *Methanex*[48] *and Glamis*

1998); *Oneryldiz* v. *Turkey*, ECtHR Application No. 48939/99, Judgment (30 November 2004); *Fadeyeva* v. *Russia*, ECtHR Application No. 55723/00, Judgment (9 June 2005).

44 Convention on Access to Information, Public Participation in Decision-making and Access to Justice in Environmental Matters, 25 June 1998, 2161 UNTS 447.

45 For a detailed analysis of this case law, see F. Francioni 'Human Rights in an Environmental Horizon' (2010) 21 *European Journal of International Law* 48 ff.

46 See the first arbitral award under chapter 11 of the NAFTA: *Metalclad Corporation* v. *United Mexican States*, ICSID Case No. ARB(AF)/97/1, Award (25 August 2000). See also *Compañía del Desarrollo de Santa Elena SA* v. *Republic of Costa Rica*, ICSID Case No. ARB/96/1, Award (17 February 2000).

47 A detailed discussion of this point is provided in the chapter by J. E. Viñuales in this book and, more generally, in the companion volume to this book, J. E. Viñuales, *Foreign Investment and the Environment in International Law* (Cambridge University Press, 2012).

48 See *Methanex Corporation* v. *United States of America*, NAFTA (UNCITRAL), Award (3 August 2005).

Gold.[49] The first concerned a compensation claim brought by a foreign investor engaged in the production of a fuel additive that had been banned by the law of the State of California for its polluting effects on surface and ground water. The claim, based on alleged loss of property, loss of market share and discrimination, was rejected on the grounds that the environmental goal pursued by the State of California was legitimate, indistinctly applicable and adopted pursuant to democratic process open to advice by independent scientific bodies. In short, it was environmentally sound and justifiable. Similarly, in *Glamis Gold*, environmental regulations adopted at the state and federal levels to protect an environmentally and culturally sensitive area from the adverse effects of a mining project were deemed legitimate by the NAFTA arbitral panel despite their negative impact on the economic interests of a foreign investor.[50] The integration of environmental considerations in investment law and dispute settlement is not limited to the advancement of the natural environment. It can also include the preservation of the 'cultural' environment and in particular of the urban landscape in which a large portion of the human population lives today. A good example of this inclusion is provided by the *Parkerings-Compagniet* award where an ICSID tribunal ruled that the claim brought by a Norwegian investor against Lithuania for breach of the most-favoured-nation clause of the applicable bilateral investment treaty (BIT) was to be rejected because the claimant's project was not similar to that of the competing foreign bidder. Specifically, the claimant's project had a higher impact on the sensitive cultural environment of the Old City of Vilnius, a cultural site included in the UNESCO World Heritage List.[51]

In the field of trade disputes, the very existence of a strong system of international enforcement has attracted also environment-related disputes for which no alternative specialised environmental forum was available. After some early disappointing rulings,[52] the WTO

[49] See *Glamis Gold Ltd* v. *The United States of America*, NAFTA Arbitration (UNCITRAL), Award (16 May 2009).

[50] *Ibid.*, paras 824–30.

[51] See *Parkerings-Compagniet AS* v. *Republic of Lithuania*, ICSID Case No. ARB/05/8, Award (11 September 2007).

[52] I refer especially to the notorious 1991 *Tuna Dolphin* ruling under pre-WTO dispute settlement procedure in which the Panel rejected the USA's claim that its unilateral import ban on tuna from Mexico could be justified by the objective of discouraging the incidental killing of dolphins that was caused by the Mexican methods of tuna harvesting. The text of the ruling is reprinted in ILM (1991) 1594.

dispute-settlement panels, and especially the Appellate Body, have shown the willingness to move towards a certain opening for the accommodation of the trade obligations arising under the WTO and the covered agreements with the need to give proper consideration to the inherent sovereign rights of member states to set the appropriate level of protection of their local environment and also of the general environment in accordance with international law. This task has been accomplished by the interpretive tool offered by Article 31(3)(c) the Vienna Convention on the Law of Treaties,[53] by an expansive interpretation of the general exceptions under Article XX (g) of the GATT (concerning the exception related to the 'conservation of exhaustible natural resources'), through a more flexible interpretation of GATT Article III ('like products'), and by giving relevance to the Preamble of the WTO constitutive treaty, which refers to the need to conduct trade in accordance with 'the objective of sustainable development' and the protection of the environment.[54] Unfortunately, there have been instances in which the WTO adjudication process has proved to be impervious to considerations of environmental safety and sustainability. This can be seen in the *Biotech* case[55] involving the claim by the USA and other countries that the precautionary procedure adopted by the European Community (now the European Union) for the authorisation of the import and marketing of genetically modified products amounted to undue delay and thus to a violation of the European Union under WTO. Although the European Union position was motivated by legitimate environmental concerns and was prima facie consistent with international standards as reflected in the Cartagena Protocol on biosafety,[56] the Panel ruled that the precautionary approach followed by the European Union could not justify its departure from the

[53] Vienna Convention on the Law of Treaties, 23 May 1969, 1153 UNTS 331.

[54] This exception, originally conceived only in relation to mineral resources, was given an evolving interpretation so as to encompass living resources of the sea. See *United States – Import Prohibition of Certain Shrimp and Shrimp Products*, WT/DS58/AB/R (12 October 1998); *European Communities: Measures Affecting Asbestos and Asbestos-Containing Products*, WT/DS 135/AB/R (12 March 2001); *Brazil – Measures Affecting Imports of Retreaded Tyres*, Panel Report, WT/DS 332/R (12 June 2007) and Appellate Body Report, WT/DS 332/AB/R (17 December 2007) (finding that environmental and health considerations may justify the adoption of an import ban on retreaded tyres).

[55] *European Communities – Measures Affecting the Approval and Marketing of Biotech Products*, Report of the Panel, WT/DS 291/R, WT/DS 292/R, WT/DS 293/R, Final Report (29 September 2006).

[56] Cartagena Protocol on Biosafety to the Convention on Biological Diversity, 29 January 2000, 39 ILM 1027 (2000).

timely observance of the WTO obligations under the Sanitary and Phyto-Sanitary Agreement.[57] One of the arguments used by the Panel in reaching this controversial decision was that a multilateral environment agreement, such as the Cartagena Protocol, to which the European Union was a party, could not be invoked to legitimise regulation adopted for environmental purposes unless all members of the WTO were also parties to it. It is regrettable that this ruling was never challenged before the Appellate Body, because it is wrong, as a matter of both law and policy. From a legal point of view, WTO obligations are typically reciprocal obligations, so the Panel should have recognised that the Cartagena Protocol could have been 'applicable' in the relations between the EU and any other WTO Member which was also a party to the Protocol, in accordance with Article 30(3)–(4) of the Vienna Convention on the Law of Treaties. From a policy perspective the ruling runs against the fundamental goal of interpreting WTO norms as far as possible in a way that is compatible with legitimate aims of environmental protection. This is the approach mandated by the NAFTA system, with its side agreement on environmental protection,[58] and followed in the EU where the Court of Justice has always assessed the legality of measures restricting the free circulation of goods under the double criterion of (i) the necessity to pursue a legitimate environmental goal and (ii) the proportionality of the trade impact with the environmental goal pursued.[59]

The role of the private sector in the adjudicatory process before the above international forums can be important at two distinct levels. At the substantive level it may provide evidence that its contribution in terms of technical expertise and capacity-building is a factor in improving compliance with environmental law obligations of other states, especially developing states which are host states of international investments. The recent litigation between Argentina and Uruguay before the ICJ on *Pulp Mills*[60] indicates that an investor's technology, know-how and financial capacity can help ensure state compliance with international law obligations to prevent damage to the shared resources of a trans-boundary water system. At the procedural level, the private sector *lato*

57 Agreement on Sanitary and Phytosanitary Measures, 15 April 1994, 1867 UNTS 493.

58 North American Agreement on Environmental Cooperation, 17 December 1992, 32 ILM 1519.

59 See the seminal cases: *Danish Bottles*, Case 120/78, 1979, ECR 649; *Walloon Waste*, Case C-2/90, 1992, ECR I-4431; *Danish Bees*, Case C-67/97, 1998 ECR 4607; *Peruse Elektra*, Case C-379/98, 2001, ECR I-2099.

60 See *Pulp Mills*, above, n. 16.

sensu may contribute to the indirect enforcement of environmental standards by way of *amici curiae* participation in international litigations. The institution of *amici curiae* permits private actors, concerned individuals, associations and NGOs to intervene in dispute-settlement proceedings as non-disputing parties and to provide useful factual information and scientific evidence, as well as legal insights in addition to those provided by the parties to the dispute. As is well known, this type of participation is not contemplated in proceedings before the ICJ, and this has raised important issues in the just-mentioned *Pulp Mills* case, where some criticism was levelled against the lack of a proactive role of the Court in finding its own independent source of scientific evidence of a potential or actual environmental danger involved in the contested construction and operation of the pulp plant. The main concern was the assessment of scientific evidence by the Court and the fact that it did not use its power to appoint its own expert.[61] But the intervention of certain well-reputed organisations as *amici curiae* could also be helpful to provide the Court with a broader view as to the social and environmental implications of a dispute.

This situation can be contrasted with the practice of the WTO dispute-settlement body and that of investment arbitration, where *amicus* intervention is increasingly and quite widely accepted. In the WTO context, the absence of specific provisions in the Dispute Settlement Understanding and an initial opposition by certain developing countries has not deterred the dispute-settlement body from allowing *amicus* intervention on the basis of an expansive interpretation of the rules of procedure. Since the 2001 *Asbestos* ruling,[62] the Appellate Body has adopted specific rules and time limits to permit the orderly participation of *amici curiae* and to prevent abuses and undue delays in the procedure. The same pattern can be found in investment arbitration. High-profile litigations involving sensitive questions of environmental policy have been brought before ICSID and NAFTA tribunals. The relative proceedings have seen the active participation of *amici curiae* and representatives of the private sector who have contributed to highlight the environmental dimension of

[61] See in particular the joint dissenting opinion by judges Al-Khasawneth and Simma, who have criticised the methodological approach adopted by the court in relying on the parties' expert evidence to assess the possibility of environmental damage consequent to the realisation of the contested industrial project and have argued for the court independent fact finding or for an intensive cross-examination of the parties' experts.

[62] See *EC–Asbestos*, above, n. 54.

the dispute and the necessity of reviewing the conduct of the respondent state also in light of its responsibility to ensure the appropriate protection of the environment. This approach is particularly evident in the two already mentioned arbitrations in *Methanex* and *Glamis Gold*.[63] It is worth noting that this practice of *amici curiae* participation has been formally endorsed in a statement of the NAFTA Free Trade Commission[64] and by a formal amendment of the ICSID Rules of Arbitration.[65]

2.4 Improving the effectiveness of international environmental law through institutional reform

Besides the two *de lege lata* avenues described above, i.e., exercising sovereignty in a way that is functional to the protection of the environment as an international public good and integrating environmental considerations in existing international adjudicatory procedures, the question that remains to be examined is whether a more effective implementation of environmental law is possible by appropriate use of existing global institutions and whether a reform of these institutions is necessary or desirable *de lege ferenda*.

On the first point, it is not the purpose of this chapter to revisit the theme of the non-compliance procedures included in some multilateral environmental agreements, following the path-breaking model of Article 8 of the Montreal Protocol.[66] These procedures have been already the object of a vast literature which has exhaustively analysed their merits and shortcomings.[67] I would like to refer instead to two important instruments for bringing together the private sector and the public interest in the pursuit of more effective enforcement of environmental standards.

[63] See *Methanex* v. *United States of America*, above, n. 48; *Glamis Gold* v. *United States of America*, above, n. 49.

[64] See FTC Statement (7 October 2003), available at www.trade.gov (accessed 15 April 2012).

[65] See ICSID Rules of Procedure for Arbitration Proceedings (version in force since 10 April 2006), art. 37(2), available at http://icsid.worldbank.org (accessed 15 April 2012).

[66] Montreal Protocol on Substances that Deplete the Ozone Layer, 16 September 1987, 152 UNTS 3.

[67] See, among the many contributions, T. Treves, L. Pineschi, A. Tanzi et al. (eds.), *Non-Compliance Procedures and Mechanisms and the Effectiveness of International Environmental Agreements* (The Hague: TMC Asser Press, 2009); R. Wolfrum, 'Means of Compliance with and Enforcement of International Environmental Law', in *Recueil des cours de l'Académie de droit international* 272 (1998), 9–154.

The first instrument, the guidelines for policy and performance standards on social and environmental sustainability elaborated by the International Finance Corporation (IFC), was adopted in 2006. These guidelines are aimed at orienting foreign investments in developing countries in such a way as to prevent and minimise negative impacts on the host state's environment and local population. Private parties can raise violations of the policy and performance standards of the IFC before a Compliance Adviser Ombudsman who has the power to conduct a non-judicial review of the projects financed by the IFC.[68] These guidelines complement other UN initiatives aimed at establishing standards of responsible behaviour and accountability by corporations involved in transnational business, such as the Global Compact and the 2011 Principles elaborated by the UN Special Representative on human rights and business corporations.[69] Several cases are relevant for the discussion in this context, among them the *Bulyanhulu Gold Mine* case, involving a complaint against a MIGA-insured project by the Canadian company Barrick Gold in Tanzania,[70] and the *Kalahari Diamonds* case, which concerns IFC-supported mining operations in Botswana.[71]

The second instrument for securing a more proactive role of the private sector in environmental compliance is the OECD system of national contact points, which are competent to receive complaints relating to the conduct of multinational enterprises and, in the event of

[68] For a general overview of the Ombudsman functions, see CAO, *Review of IFC's Policy and Performance Standard on Social and Environmental Sustainability and Policy on Disclosure of Information* (Washington, DC, 2010).

[69] See Guiding Principles on Business and Human Rights: Implementing the United Nations 'Protect, Respect and Remedy' Framework, Report of the Special Representative of the Secretary-General on the Issue of Human Rights and Transnational Corporations and other Business Enterprises, J. Ruggie, Human Rights Council, A/HRC/17/31, 21 March 2011. See also the chapters by E. Morgera and B. Richardson in this book.

[70] See *Assessment Report Summary Complaint Regarding MIGA's Guarantee of the Bulyanhulu Gold Mine, Tanzania* (2002–5).

[71] See *Assessment Report – Complaint Regarding IFC's Investment in Kalahari Diamonds Ltd, Botswana* (June 2005). This case involves the forced relocation of the Kalahari peoples from their ancestral lands. It is a typical case in which the alleged justification adduced by the Government of Botswana, i.e., the safeguarding of a wildlife reserve, results in a conflict with the human rights of the indigenous and local population not to be removed from their land (Article 10, UN Declaration on the Rights of Indigenous Peoples, 13 September 2007, *Official Records of the General Assembly, Sixty-first Session, Supp.* No. 53 (A/61/53)).

an ascertained infraction of the OECD Guidelines, can act as mediators between the respondent company and the complainants.[72]

These are 'soft' mechanisms of environmental law implementation. Nevertheless, they are important because they can address *ex ante* problems of environmental impact posed by projects financed by the World Bank and by activities of transnational corporations. The 'internationalisation' of the local problem posed by such projects and activities can help correct environmental impacts that are incompatible with international standards and can facilitate appropriate monitoring of the activities conducted by the private actors. Despite their potential as the embodiment of an additional avenue, these mechanisms are, as such, limited in scope and the more fundamental question remains whether the implementation and institutional deficit of international environmental law makes necessary or desirable a reform of the global institutional framework of environmental governance.

In this respect, two approaches are theoretically possible within the perspective of a progressive development of the law. The first approach would consciously shun the need for institutional reform as too costly and ineffective, and would rely on market mechanisms of self-regulation and transnational private enforcement. The second approach would entail a reform of the institutional system of environmental governance by creating effective multilateral institutions that can mirror what has been done in the other areas of international law examined in this chapter, namely international economic law and human rights.

It is the opinion of this writer that the two approaches are not mutually exclusive. They can be complementary because the first one could not work properly without the second. The reason is simple. In order to be truly effective, international–transnational private regulation (such as trade in emissions allowances, the clean development mechanism, private investment in ecosystem services and forest conservation) must operate not only at a contractual level but also within the public sphere of state control and within the framework of relevant international environmental standards. A pure system of transnational private governance would pose in the long term an undesirable challenge to the very idea of sovereignty over the national territory and its resources

[72] For a detailed examination of the role of the OECD 'National Contact Points', see M. R. Cutillo, 'I National Contact Points dell'OCSE sulle imprese multinazionali: un meccanismo di accesso alla giustizia effettivo per la società civile', in F. Francioni, M. Gestri, N. Ronzitti and T. Scovazzi (eds.), *Acesso alla giustizia dell'individuo nel diritto internazionale e dell'Unione Europea* (Milan: Giuffrè, 2008), 233–54.

which, as we have seen, remains the cornerstone of the present system of international environmental law. Besides, a realistic approach in this field cannot ignore the bitter lesson of the contemporary economic crisis generated by the spectacular market failure of a financial system out of control, the decline of confidence in 'private' mechanisms of rating and self-control and the consequent shift of focus back to the role of the state in regulating, monitoring and supporting essential aspects of economic and social life. It would be foolish to think that this shift of focus should not include the way in which we ensure respect and protection for the vital components of the Earth's environment.

Thus, it is certainly desirable and necessary to re-examine *de lege ferenda* what kind of improvements are needed and are politically feasible in order to modernise and strengthen the institutional framework of environmental governance. In this respect, an opportunity for institutional reform and for improved global environmental governance was offered by the 2005 UN reform. Several critical issues were on the table at that time, and had been clearly articulated also with the support of academic studies and research in which the present writer directly participated.[73] In the end, however, the 2005 UN mini-reform did not produce any meaningful improvement to the UN architecture of global environmental governance, and the institutional deficit remains unresolved at a time when we are facing the most dangerous of environmental threat, climate change.

How can legal imagination contribute to the improvement of the institutions of global environmental governance? The simplest way would be to proceed with the strengthening of the existing institutions, in particular the United Nations Environmental Programme (UNEP). This was the route which was indicated by the UN Secretary-General in his 2005 Report on the reform of the UN system[74] and which UNEP itself

[73] See F. Francioni and P.-M. Dupuy, 'Preliminary Feasibility Study for the Establishment of a UN Environmental Organisation or Agency', study commissioned by the French Ministry of Foreign Affairs, European University Institute, Florence, 2005; F. Francioni, 'The Role of the EU in Promoting Reform of the UN in the Field of Human Rights and Environmental Protection', Chaillot Paper 78 (Paris: ISS/EU, 2005), 32 ff.; F. Biermann, 'The Emerging Debate on the Need for a World Environmental Organisation: A Commentary' (2001) 1 *Global Environmental Politics* 45; S. Charnowitz, 'A World Environmental Organization' (2002) 27 *Columbia Journal of Environmental Law* 321; R. G. Tarasofsky and A. L. Hoare, *Implications of a UNEO for the Global Architecture of the International Environmental Governance System* (London: Chatham House, 2004).

[74] Kofi Annan, 'In Larger Freedom – Towards Development, Security and Human Rights For All', 20 March 2005, UN Doc. A/59/2005.

is exploring at the time of writing.[75] This route is certainly still feasible, as suggested by options discussed as part of the 'institutional framework' component of the 2012 Rio Summit on Sustainable Development. However, to yield a reasonable expectation of effective improvement, certain functional conditions should be kept in mind. First, if UNEP were to remain a 'programme' as it is today, it would need to rely on adequate, predictable and stable funding. This is not the situation today. From the mid-1990s, funding has declined, both because of creeping dissatisfaction of some major contributing countries and because of increasing competition by other UN programmes, such as the United Nations Development Programme, which has an important role in promoting environmental sustainability. Secondly, an enhanced role of UNEP would be possible only to the extent that it is given real authority and operational capacity with regard to the mounting complexities of the threats to the global environment. Since the time of its creation, following the 1972 Stockholm Conference, the UNEP mandate has been quite limited. It was meant to provide monitoring of environmental developments, serve as a 'clearing house' for environmental information and provide impetus and coordination for the development and implementation of international environmental agreements. UNEP has performed these functions quite well. In some respects, it has outperformed its original mandate, notably in its normative role as a sponsor of a great variety of multilateral environmental agreements ranging from hazardous waste to trade in dangerous chemicals, air pollution, land degradation, regional seas and water resources management. Today, however, it seems that it is stretched to its limits, and it is doubtful that more authority and enhanced operational capacity can be achieved without institutional reform and substantial upgrading.

This brings us to the examination of the second option, namely the creation of a new environmental organisation. This project could be pursued in two alternative directions. One would be the creation of a UN environmental agency, which would be an organisation endowed with its own legal personality but placed within the UN system. The other alternative would be the creation of an independent world environmental organisation on the model of the WTO, with a distinct membership, secretariat and implementing mechanisms. In spite of the intrinsic

[75] See UNEP Governing Council Decision 25/4 on International Environmental Governance, 25th session, 16–20 February 2009, and Governing Council Decision SS XI/1, 11th special session, 24–6 February 2010.

differences between these two models, they have in common several advantages. First, they would place the current system of international environmental governance on a more stable institutional basis. Secondly, they would bring under the same institutional umbrella the vast and diversified array of multilateral environmental agreements which today are served by sector-specific and often competing secretariats. Thirdly, they could work as a catalyst for stronger environmental solidarity and for the development of a fiduciary spirit among participants in view of greater coherence in the efforts for environmental protection. Finally, they could provide a single forum for global environmental monitoring, an issue that is acutely felt in the current post-Kyoto negotiations on climate change, and for dispute settlement.

There is no hiding that the creation of any of these environmental organisations would entail the investment of enormous political capital, in terms of limitations of national sovereignty necessary to establish a system of effective multilateral cooperation. It would entail also technical obstacles linked to the intractable issue of the reform of the UN Charter, or to the adoption of a new multilateral treaty, for which complex negotiations would be required. But that would also be an opportunity for a fresh approach involving in the negotiation process not only states but also relevant UN agencies and programmes, the main secretariats of multilateral environmental agreements, the World Bank, the private sector and the leading environmental NGOs. This is not an easy task. But I see no easy solution to the daunting challenge posed to the international community by the global environmental crisis. This is time to rebuild consensus, not to drift in the hope that something good will come from continuing with the 'creative destruction' of the environment we have pursued so far.

Select bibliography

Biermann, F., 'The Emerging Debate on the Need for a World Environmental Organisation: A Commentary' (2001) 1 *Global Environmental Politics* 45.

Charnowitz, S., 'A World Environmental Organization' (2002) 27 *Columbia Journal of Environmental Law* 321.

Cutillo, M. R., ' I National Contact Points dell'OCSE sulle imprese multinazionali: un meccanismo di accesso alla giustizia effettivo per la società civile', in F. Francioni, M. Gestri, N. Ronzitti and T. Scovazzi (eds.), *Acesso alla giustizia dell'individuo nel diritto internazionale e dell'Unione Europea* (Milan: Giuffré, 2008), pp. 233–54.

Doos, B. R., 'Environmental Issues Requiring International Action', in W. Lang, H. Neuhold and K. Zemanek (eds.), *Environmental Protection and International Law* (Dordrecht: Martinus Nijhoff, 1991), pp. 1–54.

Dupuy, P.-M., *L'Unité de l'ordre juridique international* (Leiden: Brill, 2003).

Francioni, F., 'Dispute Avoidance in International Environmental Law', in A. Kiss, D. Shelton and K. Ishibashi (eds.), *Economic Globalisation and Compliance with International Environmental Agreements* (The Hague: Kluwer, 2003), pp. 231–43.

'Sviluppo sostenibile e principi di diritto internazionale dell'ambiente', in P. Fois (ed.), *Il principio dello sviluppo sostenibile nel diritto internazionale ed europeo dell'ambiente* (Naples: Editoriale Scientifica, 2007), pp. 41–62.

'Human Rights in an Environmental Horizon' (2010) 21 *European Journal of International Law* 41.

Francioni, F., and P.-M. Dupuy, 'Preliminary Feasibility Study for the Establishment of a UN Environmental Organisation or Agency', Study Commissioned by the French Ministry of Foreign Affairs, European University Institute, Florence, 2005.

Francioni, F., and M. Montini, 'Integrating Scientific Evidence into Environmental Law: The International Dimension', in A. Biondi, M. Cecchetti, S. Grassi and M. Lee (eds.), *Scientific Evidence in European Law Making* (The Hague: Kluwer, 2003), pp. 17–40.

Glennon, R., 'Water Scarcity, Marketing and Privatization' (2005) 83 *Texas Law Review* 1873.

Künnemann, R., 'Foreign Investment and the Right to Food', in S. Murphy and A. Paasch (eds.), *The Global Food Challenge: Towards a Human Rights Approach to Trade and Investment Policies* (Cologne and Minneapolis, Minn.: FIAN et al., 2009), pp. 50–9.

Lowe, V., 'Sustainable Development and Unsustainable Arguments', in A. Boyle and D. Freestone (eds.), *International Law and Sustainable Development* (Oxford University Press, 1999), pp. 19–37.

Malaguti, M. C., C. Dordi, S. Di Benedetto and A. Alemanno (eds.), *Scientific Evidence in International and European Law* (Lecce: Argo editore, 2010).

Tarasofsky, R. G., and A. L. Hoare, *Implications of a UNEO for the Global Architecture of the International Environmental Governance System* (London: Chatham House, 2004).

Treves, T., L. Pineschi, A. Tanzi, C. Pitea, C. Ragni and F. Romanin Jacur (eds.), *Non-Compliance Procedures and Mechanisms and the Effectiveness of International Environmental Agreements* (The Hague: TMC Asser Press, 2009).

Viñuales, J. E., 'Foreign Investment and the Environment in International Law: An Ambiguous Relationship' (2009) 80 *British Yearbook of International Law* 244.

Foreign Investment and the Environment in International Law (Cambridge University Press, 2012).

'Managing Abidance by Standards for the Protection of the Environment', in A. Cassese (ed.), *Realizing Utopia* (Oxford University Press, 2012), pp. 326–39.

Wolfrum, R., 'Means of Compliance with and Enforcement of International Environmental Law', in *Recueil des cours de l'Académie de droit international* 272 (1998), pp. 9–154.

3

The political environment of environmental law

URS LUTERBACHER

INTRODUCTION

As in other areas of law, the dynamics of domestic and international environmental law are constrained by political structures and activities. Indeed, the effectiveness of law depends ultimately on two factors: on the one hand, a sufficient prevalence of cooperative attitudes among agents subject to the laws and, on the other, the possibility to enforce them through institutionalised coercive mechanisms or through individual retaliatory measures. In both of these instances political processes are at work. In an open society the existence of law enforcement and coercive actions is not enough to explain the observance of norms, which depends on members' willingness to cooperate and coordinate among themselves or with established authorities. Coercion is thus only an ultimate deterrent, rarely used under normal conditions except to keep under control and punish fringe behaviour, which does not conform to prevailing rules. However, its existence is crucial to the continuation of an existing cooperation regime because it provides a trigger mechanism[1] that sanctions violations of norms. These statements are only generalities about the relations between politics and law. The narrower question to be faced is whether they also apply to environmental problems. Environmental problems present a certain level of difficulty for the law/politics nexus that is greater than in some other classical applications of normative arrangements such as international trade. These are worth examining in more detail.

Difficulties are embedded in the nature of environmental issues as these are often connected with the overuse of natural resources, broadly defined,[2] due to paradoxical human behaviour. The essence of the

[1] This trigger mechanism might be somewhat probabilistic in nature, in the sense that it is not necessarily used all the time but only with greater likelihood.

[2] This includes climate change as it is due in some sense to the overuse of the atmosphere as a repository of greenhouse gases.

paradox opposes here short-term individual advantages to long-term collective benefits. These are linked ultimately to the lack or insufficient adaptation of institutional settings that can lead to inadequate incentive structures. Institutional factors leading to resource scarcities and thus to environmental problems gained prominent attention through the 'tragedy of the commons' argument put forward by Garrett Hardin.[3] Hardin's piece highlighted how the nature of property regimes directly influences resource use and showed that some forms of collective management create incentives to dissipate resources. This is the case, for instance, when a field or a meadow is open to all herders of a community to use for grazing their cattle. Since, by assumption, the herders do not have to cover the maintenance costs of the meadow they will have an incentive to put more and more cattle into it leading to its complete degradation and uselessness. The grass is here a 'fugitive' good – in other words an item that belongs to somebody only if it is caught or consumed by him or her. The same can be said for fish in the ocean or game in the wild. In Hardin's construct the grass is open to all and is nobody's defined property.

3.1 Analysing the 'commons'[4] problem

Hardin thought that the absence of a unique feature, namely the lack of a private property system, is at the roots of the deterioration. However, shortly after the publication of Hardin's article, a vast empirical literature demonstrated that a balance between people and resources had been achieved in many parts of the world without recourse to private property structures.[5] Moreover, Hardin had presented a 'common sense' argument, based on the narrow context of cattle herding on a meadow whose access is open to anyone. This open access feature leads then to

[3] G. Hardin, 'The Tragedy of the Commons' (1968) 162 *Science* 1243.

[4] The term 'commons' is to some extent a misnomer since most historical commons are highly regulated environments and are very different from the open-access system described by Hardin.

[5] See generally B. J. McCay and J. Acheson (eds.), *The Question of the Commons* (Tucson: University of Arizona Press, 1987); E. Ostrom, *Governing the Commons: The Evolution of Institutions for Collective Action* (Cambridge University Press, 1990). It should be clear from the discussion that Hardin's story is but an extreme 'ideal type' representation of an environmental situation and not the norm. Nevertheless, it is worthy to use his approach as a baseline theoretical occurrence against which other empirical cases can then be evaluated.

overgrazing as stated above. A formalised version of Hardin's reasoning and a generalisation of his approach were presented later by Dasgupta and Heal[6] and then further developed by Chichilnisky.[7] Their work shows that Hardin's presentation is only a special case of a situation where individual incentives lead to socially inferior outcomes. They also insist upon the fact that many of these incentive structures do not permit the development of long-term retaliation strategies such as 'tit for tat' in a prisoners' dilemma game to help foster cooperation.[8] So cooperating for the organisation of environmental regulations often presents great difficulties.

In order to understand the problem raised by Hardin, one must therefore look at the general question of how regulatory structures such as property rights can be initiated. As suggested by Dasgupta and Heal's analysis, some regulatory structures might not bring about optimal results. Some might be too restrictive to permit innovation and development; others might be too loose and imprecise to protect natural resources. These could trigger desires to appropriate or overuse resources at the expense of other groups or individuals. Indeed, it can be stressed again[9] that no 'dominant strategy', i.e., a strategy that gives better outcomes in all circumstances than any other strategy, is available to actors operating in an open access type of situation. Thus, as already mentioned, the prisoners' dilemma is not an apt metaphor for such circumstances. However, one can clearly see that whereas no producer has a dominant strategy to keep on extracting more, no one can oppose a credible threat[10] to prevent others from doing so. Hence, the behaviour of actors in an open access type situation is closer to that of players in a 'chicken game', where there is a competition for the first move and where agents try to gain an advantage over the others before the latter make a move.[11] The corollary of the absence of credible threats is the existence of

[6] P. S. Dasgupta and G. M. Heal, *Economic Theory and Exhaustible Resources* (Cambridge University Press, 1979).

[7] See G. Chichilnisky, 'North–South Trade and the Global Environment' (1994) 84 *American Economic Review* 851.

[8] See R. Axelrod, *The Evolution of Cooperation* (New York: Basic Books, 1984).

[9] Dasgupta and Heal, *Economic Theory and Exhaustible Resources*, 59.

[10] See U. Luterbacher and D. Sprinz, 'Problems of Global Environmental Cooperation', in U. Luterbacher and D. Sprinz, *International Relations and Global Climate Change* (Cambridge, Mass.: MIT Press, 2001), 13.

[11] In a 'chicken game' the problem is catastrophe avoidance instead of conflict avoidance like in the prisoners' dilemma.

an intense competition for the first move: the first mover enjoys a durable advantage over his opponent; this in turn yields a subgame-perfect Nash equilibrium,[12] where gains (or losses) are disproportionately distributed in favour of the first. Given the asymmetry at the equilibrium, it is extremely difficult to reach another outcome, thus patterns of behaviour exhibiting strong inequalities can easily be maintained through long periods of time. Moreover, entitlements to the products in managed common-property systems across the globe have mostly been based on private holdings, such as land lots or cattle privately held.[13] These institutional arrangements tend therefore to replicate the inequalities in terms of wealth among participants at the level of resource use. Hence, even when access to a common pool resource is restricted, it is likely to provide the privileged with greater parts of the benefits. To be sure, the asymmetry in resources and capabilities provides the first mover with credible threats when it comes to devising collective agreements to control the exploitation of the environmental base.

Besides, one needs not assume asymmetric players (e.g., elite versus non-elite) to obtain a stable unequal distribution of benefits accruing from the exploitation of the resource. Such agreements are easily supported by specific types of retaliatory strategies, such as the threat not to participate in maintenance activities crucial to the production of the resources.[14] Moreover, as scarcities occur (e.g., as the availability of arable land decreases), the bargaining power of certain groups of population is altered by changes in relative prices: actors with few resources may put a premium on the short term. Indeed, in such instances, small parcels of land may be sold to powerful landowners to obtain liquidities rapidly. Furthermore, as competition intensifies, it becomes perfectly rational for individuals to over-exploit these open access resources in order not to be the last one without resources to tap.

[12] Recall that a 'Nash equilibrium' is an outcome of a game that nobody has an incentive to leave unilaterally. A unilateral move from the outcome makes the given agent worse off. A subgame-perfect equilibrium cannot be undermined except by a non-credible threat, i.e., a threat that is not rational to carry out.

[13] M. A. McKean, 'Management of Traditional Common Lands (Irialchi) in Japan', in D. W. Bromley, D. Feeny, M. A. McKean et al. (eds.), *Making the Commons Work: Theory, Practice, and Policy* (San Francisco, Calif.: Institute for Contemporary Studies Press, 1992), 63–98.

[14] P. S. Dasgupta, 'Common Property Resources: Economic Analytics' (2005) 40 *Economics & Political Weekly* 16.

This type of behaviour is duplicated at the international level and can best be illustrated by the failure so far of various efforts to control global environmental evolutions and especially climate change since the 1992 Rio Conference. The Kyoto Protocol elaborated in 1997 can best be described as a relative local success but a global failure. Indeed, as the goals of the protocol are reasonably fulfilled by the countries that ratified it (with a few prominent exceptions such as Japan or Canada, which are likely to exceed their ceilings), overall emissions have increased even at an accelerated pace throughout the 2000s. And even in those cases where the quantified targets seem to be fulfilled, this is largely due to the so-called Eastern hot air, i.e., the overhaul of the economies of the former Soviet Union and the Eastern European states. This phenomenon resulted in a significant decrease of greenhouse gas emissions with respect to 1990 especially in Russia and the Ukraine but also in most Eastern European countries which are now part of the European Union. Even the core group of the Kyoto Protocol, the fifteen members who were part of it when the protocol was elaborated, benefited from these circumstances in the sense that when West Germany absorbed the German Democratic Republic the total German emissions also went down significantly with respect to 1990. Despite this, significant additional efforts were made, albeit not uniformly, within the EU 15 so that the overall emissions have gone down over the period from 1997 to the present. However, the fact that the Kyoto Protocol is formally working does not mean that world emissions have diminished. As mentioned before, this is far from being the case. In fact, the 'good European example' has failed to convince the rest of the world, especially since the USA decided not to come on board for Kyoto and emerging countries such as China, Brazil or India did not undertake (and still have not undertaken) quantified emissions-reduction targets.

This evolution is mostly due to what is called 'carbon leakage', i.e., the transfer of production to parts of the world that are less constraining than the countries of origin. Even though environmental constraints are not the only reason for these developments they add to other production costs such as labour and manpower. A number of empirical studies demonstrate the significance of carbon leakages. In a simulation, Felder and Rutherford found marginal leakages, defined as the additional amount of leakage caused by an increase in environmental regulations, to be in the order of 25 per cent.[15]

[15] S. Felder and T. F. Rutherford, 'Unilateral CO_2 Reductions and Carbon Leakage: The Consequences of International Trade in Oil and Basic Materials' (1993) 25 *Journal of Environmental Economics and Management* 162.

Babiker empirically measured carbon leakages and found them to be as large as 50 per cent to 130 per cent.[16] According to Wiener, such large leakages can be attributed to the unexpectedly fast shift of emissions towards Asia.[17] That relocation to Asia has a very high cost in terms of greenhouse gas efficiency. By way of illustration, Chinese production is three to four times less efficient in terms of emissions compared with European production.[18]

To some extent, these outcomes could have been predicted since several economists and political scientists who study unilateral regulation had warned that local action to reduce greenhouse gas emissions would have negligible, or even perverse, effects on aggregate global emissions. This argument is formalised by Michael Hoel,[19] whose game theoretic model consists of two representative individuals who make decisions regarding a purely public good, anticipating the expected responses of each other. Hoel's game theoretic approach to public goods yields a grim view of unilateral and localised emissions regulation. Not only would the degree of localised regulation be below the globally optimal level, but, in addition, the effects of localised emissions reduction on global emissions would be both diluted and even reversed by international carbon leakage.[20]

3.2 The problem of cooperation

As shown in the previous section, efforts to regulate environmental resources at both the domestic and international levels require substantial cooperation in order to implement solutions that prevent the dysfunctional outcomes evoked above. An important question in this regard

[16] M. Babiker, 'Climate Change Policy, Market Structure, and Carbon Leakage' (2005) 65 *Journal of International Economics* 421.

[17] J. Wiener, 'Think Globally, Act Globally: The Limits of Local Climate Policies' (2007) 155 *University of Pennsylvania Law Review* 1972.

[18] This estimate concerns all industries in the aggregate and is based upon European Environmental Agency, World Resource Institute numbers and calculations by the author.

[19] M. Hoel, 'Global Environmental Problems: The Effects of Unilateral Actions Taken by One Country' (1991) 20 *Journal of Environmental Economics and Management* 55.

[20] See also R. Schmalensee, *Greenhouse Policy Architectures and Institutions* (Cambridge, Mass.: MIT Joint Program on the Science and Policy of Global Change – Report No. 13, 1996); J.-P. Amigues, U. Chakravorty and M. Moreaux, 'Think Globally, Act Locally? Stock vs Flow Regulation of a Fossil Fuel', University of Toulouse, School of Economics (2009) (manuscript on file with author).

is how such cooperation may be initiated? Traditionally, the international politics literature on the subject has relied on analogies to domestic conditions to explain cooperation and negotiations among states, especially in connection with environmental problems. These issues have often been theorised in terms of certain well-established paradigms that were originally meant to apply to domestic situations such as the Coase theorem.[21] The reason for this was the original objection to the realist assertion that the self-interest of countries leads to a world of 'anarchy' at the international level where cooperation can only be ephemeral. This counterclaim to realism contends that rational maximisations of national interests can actually result in long-term institutionalised cooperative structures at the international level in order to solve externality issues. The Coase theorem is popular in this regard because of two of its main features.

First, applying the theorem strictly under its standard assumptions would result in cooperation mostly at the bilateral level where, according to Coase, mutually beneficial solutions can be worked out between two entities through negotiations. Such arrangements can, however, only be worked out if core assumptions of the theorem are fulfilled, primarily the absence of significant transaction costs. Thus a negative or 'inverted' interpretation of the Coase theorem was developed in the literature on international cooperation, which justifies institutionalised multilateral collaboration as a necessity in a world where transaction costs are high, property rights are not well defined and generally uncertainty is great: all inverted statements of Coase's original premises.[22] This 'inversion' of the theorem's assumptions was relatively easy to formulate since Coase himself had used such arguments to justify a new theory of the firm. In this new theory, Coase claims that business firms, i.e., complex institutionalised forms of organisation of output generation, result precisely from high transaction costs, unclear property rights and uncertainties, which penalise direct contractual arrangements for production between individuals or household groups.[23]

Second, the Coase theorem applies most readily to relationships between firms for, as will be discussed in this chapter, only then will income effects become irrelevant to one of its main conclusions, namely

[21] R. H. Coase, 'The Problem of Social Cost' (1960) 3 *Journal of Law and Economics* 1.

[22] R. Keohane, *After Hegemony: Cooperation and Discord in the World Political Economy* (Princeton, NJ: Princeton University Press, 1984), 88.

[23] R. H. Coase, 'The Nature of the Firm' (1937) 4 *Economica* 386.

that the mutually beneficial bargaining outcomes between two agents are not affected by an initial assignment of property rights to one or the other. Therefore, a reliance on the Coase theorem even in an inverted interpretation keeps theorists from having to 'unpack' state structures to get to a reasonable explanation of institutionalised international cooperation. In other words, by using the inverted Coase theorem, it is possible to justify the existence of international collaboration by using basic assumptions similar to the realists and thus to keep the analogy introduced by Kenneth Waltz[24] between states and firms which are both, according to him, competing in market-like structures. However, if as I will show here, income effects are taken into account, then the 'unpacking' of state structures into their components becomes unavoidable. In fact, as pointed out by Hurwicz, firms belong to shareholders who will be affected by different attributions of property rights, and governments are subject to either voter or other validation groups who are again likely to react to wealth transfers.[25] I will elaborate more on this below.

Generally speaking, the proposition that the inverted Coase theorem might explain international cooperation is quite debatable. As mentioned above, if all its assumptions are fulfilled, the theorem leads to bilateral agreements but not necessarily to multilateral ones. As stressed by Varouj Aivazian and Jeffrey L. Callen,[26] multilateral cooperation cannot be explained by using the Coasean framework since, already when three agents are involved, bargaining between them can lead to an empty core or, in other words, to a situation where it is impossible to find an agreement that makes them all better off. Thus, if liabilities are not defined at the onset in a specific way (e.g., the polluters have to pay the victims of the pollution), bargaining between parties leads to endless discussions. If one follows this argument, Aivazian and Callen show that even if positive transaction costs are assumed to exist, bargaining still leads to an empty core.[27] Therefore, what seems to matter to explain multilateral cooperation in this sense are not transaction costs but precisely the kind of liabilities that are imposed upon parties. The issue arises of whether there is an incentive structure that ensures the

24 K. Waltz, *Theory of International Politics* (Reading, Mass.: Addison-Wesley, 1979).

25 L. Hurwicz, 'What is the Coase Theorem?' (1995) 7 *Japan and the World Economy* 69.

26 V. Aivazian and J. L. Callen, 'The Coase Theorem and the Empty Core' (1981) 24 *Journal of Law and Economics* 175.

27 *Ibid.*, 181.

emergence of a preset liability system where transfers should occur in a particular direction from wealthier to less wealthy.[28] At the domestic level, such transfers are embedded in the principle of progressive taxation, which is justified by the fact that the marginal utility of consumption is much greater for poorer as opposed to richer members of society. These kinds of taxation principles have been shown to be efficient.[29]

The above issues can be highlighted by the problems currently facing the international climate change negotiations. One is now confronting a very difficult situation in which developing and industrial countries are to some extent blaming each other for responsibility for climate change, a situation that explains in part the stalemate that we are in now. Quite clearly, the bone of contention lies with the following issue: while some industrial countries have accepted the need to achieve greenhouse gas reductions, what are developing and emerging countries going to do and under which conditions? The interpretation of the notion of common but differentiated responsibility has always meant for developing countries if not exemption from reduction efforts then at least some important compensations in exchange for lowering their emissions either soon or in some distant future. In other words, compensations and probably substantial ones seem to be essential to satisfy developing countries and to get them to negotiate emissions reduction now or in the future in exchange for abandoning their current status.

3.3 Negotiating environmental problems: the example of climate change

The question then boils down to the following: are we, as mentioned in a statement by Nouriel Roubini, in a world where 'the major powers now see these issues [climate change, among others] as zero-sum games rather than positive-sum games. Ours is, in essence, a G-Zero world'?[30] In such a universe negotiation outcomes can be quite random and essentially

[28] See G. Chichilnisky and G. Heal, 'Who Should Abate Carbon Emissions? An International Perspective' (1994) 44 *Economic Letters* 443; G. Chichilnisky, G. Heal and D. Starrett, 'Equity and Efficiency in Environmental Markets: Global Trade in Carbon Emission Reductions', in G. Chichilnisky and G. Heal (eds.), *Environmental Markets, Equity and Efficiency* (New York: Columbia University Press, 1998), 46–68.

[29] See J. A. Mirrlees, 'Optimal Tax Theory: A Synthesis' (1976) 6 *Journal of Public Economics* 327.

[30] N. Roubini, 'A World Adrift', *Slate Magazine*, 15 February 2011, available at www.slate.com (accessed 15 April 2012).

driven by short-term power and economic advantages.[31] Or is there an inherent advantage in cooperating about climate change especially through the process of some agreed compensation mechanism between developing and developed countries? If this were the case there would be, at least, a major additional incentive to cooperate at the international level to create a more effective climate change regime over a long time horizon. Cooperation would not be guaranteed as shown by the political economy literature on trade and domestic interests[32] but at least one could demonstrate that cooperative advantages exist.

3.3.1 Negotiations and the Coase theorem

The proposition that cooperation on climate change makes everybody better off whenever compensations are given from the richer to the poorer parties has been regularly challenged in the literature on the grounds that, under the Coase theorem, it does not matter in which direction compensations are given. In other words, whether they are given from poorer to richer or the other way round is not important, as both forms are Pareto optimal. If this is the case, then we are, in a way, back to the situation described by Roubini where random elements will determine the outcome of the negotiation. This principle of the 'independence' of compensations or initial allocations of rights (the two are equivalent if property rights over an externality are allocated in a given way) was recently reaffirmed by Hahn and Stavins.[33] The only factors that could invalidate the result according to them would be those at odds with the basic assumptions of the Coase theorem, namely significant transaction costs, market-power absence of competition, uncertainty and some other characteristics linked to the behaviour of firms dealing with the externalities, such as for instance non-profit maximising. These are usually, as already mentioned, the standard reasons given for the explanations of cooperative behaviour in the international political

31 Zero-sum situations are characterised by an empty core, which essentially is responsible for this conclusion. Aivazian and Callen, 'The Coase Theorem and the Empty Core', show that this is also the case for some non zero-sum structures as defined by the Coase theorem.

32 See e.g. G. M. Grossmann and E. Helpman, 'Protection for Sale' (1994) 84 *American Economic Review* 833.

33 R. W. Hahn and R. N. Stavins, 'The Effects of Allowance Allocations on Cap and Trade System Performance' (2010) National Bureau of Economic Research, Working Paper 15854.

economy literature, which refers also to the Coase theorem.[34] According to this body of literature, cooperative institutions at the international level have been created because the assumptions of the Coase theorem are not verified within the global world system.

3.3.2 Significance of the Coase theorem

But these approaches neglect one of the significant features of the Coase theorem, which has been recognised by Hurwicz,[35] namely that the independence principle is only valid if no income effects are present in the compensatory mechanisms envisaged or, in other words, if agents do not get richer or poorer as a result of the bargaining process. Indeed, this is unlikely to occur in a society where agents react differentially to increases or decreases in their wealth according to their position on the socio-economic ladder. For wealthy people an additional amount of wealth is of much smaller additional utility than for poor people. Wealth effects should not matter for firms but they certainly are of importance to households. Moreover, as emphasised by Hurwicz, firms are in the end owned by shareholders who will either benefit or suffer from the evolution of their shares. So, even if firms as such are not affected by a decision about who gets to be compensated, their effective owners are.

A more interesting question can be raised about states, which are the parties in the climate change negotiations: to what extent is the analysis of firms or households applicable to states? Clearly some theoreticians of international politics have defined states in close analogy to firms. For instance, Kenneth Waltz raises the analogy between international systems and market structures: 'International political systems, like economic markets, are formed by the co-action of self-regarding units' and 'International politics is structurally similar to a market economy'.[36] Therefore, like a market, the international system will select adequate behaviour for its units. These units, at least under present conditions, are primarily states, according to Waltz, which are closely assimilated to firms. Clearly, Hahn and Stavins claim implicitly that Waltz is right since

34 See J. Conybeare, 'International Organization and Property Rights' (1980) 34 *International Organization* 307; Keohane, *After Hegemony*.
35 See Hurwicz, 'What is the Coase Theorem?'.
36 Waltz, *Theory of International Politics*, 91. See also K. Waltz, 'Political Structures', in R. Keohane (ed.), *Neorealism and its Critics* (New York: Columbia University Press, 1986), 88.

they do not evoke the income effects pointed out by Hurwicz. There is, however, a strong argument to be made that states are indeed sensitive to income effects. Even if governments could be conceived to be intrinsically insensitive to them, it would be unrealistic to assume that voters' preferences are not driven in any significant way by their incomes or that this does not influence government behaviour. Moreover, even in authoritarian systems, side-payments to important political actors whose support is essential for maintaining the regime will be sensitive to shifts in revenues. In the international political economy literature deviations from Coase-type negotiations between states have always been explained, like in the Hahn and Stavins paper, by the existence of high transaction costs. Coase himself attributed the organisation of production around the firm structure, rather than by self-employed individuals or households, to that factor. However, a strong argument can be made that firms, like states, are also created to reap the benefits from temporarily increasing returns to scale. This can imply that profits can only be made after a certain size in terms of labour or other inputs is reached: small production units might not be able to cover fixed costs per unit of input. Similarly, states only constitute viable political units if they reach a certain size.[37] This conception, in combination with the transaction cost notion, strengthens the importance of income effects: initial allocation of resources or rights can play a decisive role in bringing together or in coordinating the necessary amount of inputs.

In addition to the income effects pointed out by Hurwicz, a related weakness of the theorem, also neglected by Hahn and Stavins, is suggested by the fact that the theorem is unable to explain negotiations between three rather than two agents even in the absence of transaction costs. For instance, this is the case when two firms emit a pollutant that is harmful to the production of a third one. Varouj Aivazian and Jeffrey L. Callen[38] have shown that in such a case the bargaining game between the three firms has an empty core, which means, basically, endless negotiations without a rational issue and thus a situation very close to the one evoked by Roubini, i.e., random and thus fragile outcomes driven

[37] A thorough discussion of the size effect and increasing returns to scale is provided in C. Norrlof, *America's Global Advantage* (Cambridge University Press, 2010), 38–44.

[38] See Aivazian and Callen, 'The Coase Theorem and the Empty Core'. R. Keohane mentions this difficulty with the Coase theorem but does not give an indication in which ways it could be related to an institutionalised solution at the international level. See Keohane, 'The Nature of the Firm', 87.

by short-term considerations. According to Aivazian and Callen, if liabilities are defined for the polluters then a bargaining solution arises because rights are attributed *ab initio* to the victim (here the third firm). Clearly, if compensations are attributed to some parties by others, because it is eventually advantageous for the polluters so to do, then the 'empty-core' problem posed by Aivazian and Callen disappears. A grand collation between all parties will be both individually and collectively rational and the core will no longer be empty.

3.3.3 *Efficiency of compensations*

One can now return to the main question and ask whether unidirectional transfers from richer to poorer agents (here states) would provide an efficient bargaining solution. In fact, a convincing case can be made that such compensations are actually Pareto optimal and that they make both the richer and poorer parties better off under some specific conditions. Assume that we are dealing with a uniformly spread collective problem like climate change measured in terms of carbon dioxide concentrations in the atmosphere. Its removal, a collective good, has the same properties of a uniform distribution. Lowering emissions in China has the same effect on the climate system as curtailing them in the USA. What might differ significantly, however, are the costs of reducing them, which are much cheaper in an emerging or developing country than in an industrialised one. This occurs in part because an emerging or developing country's infrastructure is not yet established and can therefore be constructed or reconstructed quite easily with huge savings in terms of emissions. There are, however, also theoretical reasons for this occurrence, stemming from the relatively high marginal value of consumption for a developing or an emerging country compared to a developed one.[39] One can show that higher marginal utilities for the consumption of private goods have to lead to lower prices of collective goods.[40]

So a developing or emerging country has a relatively inexpensive public good available but wants, on the other hand, more private goods,

[39] See K. A. Sheehan, 'Who Should Abate Carbon Emissions? A Note' (2006) 35 *Environmental and Resource Economics* 89.

[40] See Chichilnisky and Heal, 'Who Should Abate Carbon Emissions? An International Perspective'; Chichilinisky, Heal and Starrett, 'Equity and Efficiency in Environmental Markets'; G. Chichilnisky and U. Luterbacher, 'Climate Change, Security, and Redistribution: How Can the Political Dilemmas Linked to the Global Environment be Solved?' (2012) 19 *Brown Journal of World Affairs*, forthcoming.

which are abundant in industrialised countries. If a developed country purchases public goods in a developing one it provides thus the possibility for the poorer country to acquire more private goods. In some sense the developing or emerging country will at the end of the process be better off because it acquires more private goods and the industrialised country will be better off because it has acquired public goods more cheaply. This can be done, for instance, by providing a significant amount of emissions rights to the developing country which will then have to be purchased by the industrialised country. Clearly, in this case, the developing country can then purchase more private goods.[41] It has to be emphasised here that the traditional trade-off between equity and efficiency does not hold since transfers from richer to poorer are associated with higher efficiency.

3.4 Implementation problems

Even though it can actually be shown, as I discussed above, that compensations via a greater attribution of property rights to the poorer party can be efficient and thus can constitute an incentive for cooperation, it is not clear that such a scheme can actually be implemented. Hurwicz raised the general issues of implementation in much of his work but particularly in a paper of 1998.[42] The problem, as he describes it, is linked to the institutional setting used to solve an externality problem such as climate change. To reduce greenhouse gas emissions globally, it was suggested to attribute a large quantity of permits to developing and emerging countries. These permits would then be purchased by industrialised states (actually firms and households within them). In other words, what would be necessary here is the establishment of a market for the externalities generated by greenhouse gas emissions. To operate properly, such a market has to be organised in order not to be too thin, i.e., that it involves a sufficient number of agents. Moreover, several authors[43] have

[41] A formal proof of this is given in G. Chichilnisky, 'A Comment on Implementing a Global Abatement Policy: The Role of Tranfers' (1993), paper presented at the International Conference on the Economics of Climate Change OECD/IEA, Paris, June 1993. Also see a proof for a non-concave utility function (a non-convex set) in Chichilnisky and Luterbacher, 'Climate Change, Security, and Redistribution'.

[42] See L. Hurwicz, 'But Who Will Guard the Guardians?' (2008) 98 *American Economic Review* 577.

[43] See D. A. Starrett, 'Fundamental Non-convexities in the Theory of Externalities' (1972) 4 *Journal of Economic Theory* 180; Dasgupta and Heal, *Economic Theory and Exhaustible*

pointed out that such a market could not operate properly if non-convexities are present in the production of the externality (e.g., if the firm has no incentive – no marginal cost – to take action to abate emissions until it reaches a certain emissions level which is likely to be set by regulation). Finally, and perhaps most importantly, the rights or certificates associated with emissions have to point to a real occurrence (i.e., a reduction of emissions or an increase in absorption) and not to some imaginary scheme. These cannot be inflated by referring several times to the same production processes: for instance, if a firm from an industrial country replaces a piece of equipment, for example, a furnace, with a more efficient heater that emits much fewer greenhouse gases, the older, inefficient device cannot be reused somewhere else. In other words, the market has to be strongly monitored and cheaters have to be severely punished, as is the case, for instance, in the US Clean Air Act with respect to sulphur dioxide emissions. To set up an effective monitoring regime is difficult, as the controversies over the control of the financial system, national and international, have demonstrated.

Hurwicz[44] raises the problem of preventing cheating and purposeful misrepresentation of preferences surrounding public goods, especially if they are connected to the realisation of a so-called 'Lindahl equilibrium'.[45] How can this difficulty be overcome? One can refer here to the importance at the domestic level of the rule of law and of the principle of the separation of powers, which allows a mutual control of one instance by others, a solution which is also mentioned by Hurwicz. But can this solution be transposed to the international level?

It is important here to evoke the crucial nature of the interplay between domestic and international spheres. Major international agreements are not possible without some domestic acceptance and their enforcement or lack thereof is also to some extent a function of the advantages or disadvantages they provide to local constituencies. Economists and political scientists have long been interested in the motivations

Resources; P. S. Dasgupta and K. G. Mäler, 'The Economics of Non-Convex Ecosystems: Introduction' (2003) 26 *Environmental and Resource Economics* 499.

44 Hurwicz, 'But Who Will Guard the Guardians?', 579.

45 A 'Lindahl equilibrium' derives from an exchange of benefits resulting from collective goods (e.g., access to a highway) or externalities between individual agents. In a Lindahl equilibrium prices for a given externality are in general not unique. They can become so only if some special additional assumptions are made, such as for instance a similarity of preferences among participants. See Dasgupta and Heal, *Economic Theory and Exhaustible Resources*, 44–8.

and strategies of movements opposed to legislation and treaties that seek to maintain or improve international social welfare. Two main questions arise in this context. The first is why such movements want to influence the political process and the second is why they are often successful. Several studies show how protectionist barriers that benefit small groups but harm society as a whole are established.[46] The story that emerges is one of companies who are threatened by regulation/deregulation and who prefer to invest in the political process to extract protective measures from legislation rather than to improve their own competitiveness or conform to rules. While trade/investment agreements differ fundamentally from environmental agreements, because in the latter case first-mover advantage presents immediate benefits for individual states,[47] consequences are fairly similar. In both cases, some industries or some segments of the population are more affected by the obligations stemming from the treaty than others. Thus, similar incentives exist to fight the ratification of particular agreements. So even though the costs of implementing an environmental agreement might be low for the society at large, and even if the agreement offers tangible long-term advantages, the immediate impact upon some segments and industries might be extremely large. This will lead them to fight the agreement.

Conversely, such internal forces might also have positive effects regarding the ratification and subsequent implementation of an agreement. When domestic interests benefit either morally or materially from an international cooperative structure, they have an incentive not only to promote it but also to check that it is indeed implemented by state authorities. In other words, domestic constituencies can play a major role in both initiating and then implementing an international environmental agreement.[48] Looking back at the evolution of the climate change regime one can say that these positive forces dominate in Europe, hence the adoption and observance of the Kyoto Protocol, but that negative influences predominate in the USA and more recently in Canada, so that the Protocol there is either no longer on the political agenda (USA) or is simply ignored (Canada).

[46] See e.g. Grossman and Helpman, 'Protection for Sale'.

[47] In this way somebody else is either taking care of the problem or can be blamed for it: the Global Climate Change Coalition's main argument was that large polluters such as China and India would be exempt from obligations.

[48] See X. Dai, *International Institutions and National Policies* (Cambridge University Press, 2007), 1–32, 140–51.

CONCLUSION

In summary, what can political analysis contribute to the understanding of environmental law? For an international legal structure to become established and to be effective it has to overcome intricate cooperation, coordination and enforcement problems that are inherent in the sort of first-mover advantage incentives that are the essence of environmental dilemmas.

As argued in this chapter, part of the solution will involve transfers from rich to poor or from developed to developing countries that can correct the income effects that were shown to be associated with the workings of the Coase theorem. Such transfers could take different forms, some of which are explored in detail in the second part of this volume, focusing on incentives to foreign investment in pro-environment projects. I have discussed here the advantages associated with the establishment of a market of externalities encompassing the most important countries contributing to the problem. Fine-tuning such structures is of course challenging. The perception that economic losses would trump all the benefits accruing from fixing the climate became widespread because not only business interests but also significant segments of the lower middle classes would have been affected.[49] These elements of society can only be convinced to come on board if significant compensation schemes are put in place. At the same time, these schemes must have a concrete counterpart. The problems of implementation identified in this chapter require careful attention, particularly those relating to monitoring. In this regard, a number of innovative tools will have to be developed, some of which are discussed in the third part of this volume, devoted to safeguards. Cracking these regulatory equations is not easy, but, as suggested by this chapter, it is far from impossible.

[49] See U. Luterbacher and I. Ajala, 'Le Changement climatique, le protocole de Kyoto et les relations transatlantiques' (2009) *Politique étrangere* 103.

Select bibliography

Aivazian, V., and J. L. Callen, 'The Coase Theorem and the Empty Core' (1981) 24 *Journal of Law and Economics* 175.

Axelrod, R., *The Evolution of Cooperation* (New York: Basic Books, 1984).

Babiker, M., 'Climate Change Policy, Market Structure, and Carbon Leakage' (2005) 65 *Journal of International Economics* 421.

Chichilnisky, G., 'North–South Trade and the Global Environment' (1994) 84 *American Economic Review* 851.

Chichilnisky, G., and G. Heal, 'Who Should Abate Carbon Emissions? An International Perspective' (1994) 44 *Economic Letters* 443.

Chichilnisky, G., G. Heal and D. Starrett, 'Equity and Efficiency in Environmental Markets: Global Trade in Carbon Emission Reductions', in G. Chichilnisky and G. Heal (eds.), *Environmental Markets, Equity and Efficiency* (New York: Columbia University Press, 1998), pp. 46–68.

Chichilnisky, G., and U. Luterbacher, 'Climate Change, Security, and Redistribution: How Can the Political Dilemmas Linked to the Global Environment be Solved?' (2012) 19 *Brown Journal of World Affairs*, forthcoming.

Coase, R. H., 'The Nature of the Firm' (1937) 4 *Economica* 386.

'The Problem of Social Cost' (1960) 3 *Journal of Law and Economics* 1.

Conybeare, J., 'International Organization and Property Rights' (1980) 34 *International Organization* 307.

Dai, X., *International Institutions and National Policies* (Cambridge University Press, 2007).

Dasgupta, P. S., 'Common Property Resources: Economic Analytics' (2005) 40 *Economics & Political Weekly* 16.

Dasgupta, P. S., and G. M. Heal, *Economic Theory and Exhaustible Resources* (Cambridge University Press, 1979).

Dasgupta, P. S., and K. G. Mäler, 'The Economics of Non-Convex Ecosystems: Introduction' (2003) 26 *Environmental and Resource Economics* 499.

Felder, S., and T. F. Rutherford, 'Unilateral CO_2 Reductions and Carbon Leakage: The Consequences of International Trade in Oil and Basic Materials' (1993) 25 *Journal of Environmental Economics and Management* 162.

Hahn, R. W., and R. N. Stavins, 'The Effects of Allowance Allocations on Cap and Trade System Performance' (2010) National Bureau of Economic Research, Working Paper 15854.

Hardin, G., 'The Tragedy of the Commons' (1968) 162 *Science* 1243.

Hoel, M., 'Global Environmental Problems: The Effects of Unilateral Actions Taken by One Country' (1991) 20 *Journal of Environmental Economics and Management* 55.

Hurwicz, L., 'What is the Coase Theorem?' (1995) 7 *Japan and the World Economy* 49.

'But Who Will Guard the Guardians?' (2008) 98 *American Economic Review* 577.

Keohane, R., *After Hegemony: Cooperation and Discord in the World Political Economy* (Princeton, NJ: Princeton University Press, 1984).

Luterbacher, U., and I. Ajala, 'Le Changement climatique, le protocole de Kyoto et les relations transatlantiques' (2009) *Politique étrangere* 103.

Luterbacher, U., and D. Sprinz, 'Problems of Global Environmental Cooperation', in U. Luterbacher and D. Sprinz, *International Relations and Global Climate Change* (Cambridge, Mass.: MIT Press, 2001), pp. 3–22.

McCay, B. J., and J. Acheson (eds.), *The Question of the Commons* (Tucson: University of Arizona Press, 1987).

McKean, M. A., 'Management of Traditional Common Lands (Irialchi) in Japan', in D. W. Bromley, D. Feeny, M. A. McKean et al. (eds.), *Making the Commons Work: Theory, Practice, and Policy* (San Francisco, Calif.: Institute for Contemporary Studies Press, 1992), pp. 63–98.

Mirrlees, J. A., 'Optimal Tax Theory: A Synthesis' (1976) 6 *Journal of Public Economics* 327.

Norrlof, C., *America's Global Advantage* (Cambridge University Press, 2010).

Ostrom, E., *Governing the Commons: The Evolution of Institutions for Collective Action* (Cambridge University Press, 1990).

Sheehan, K. A., 'Who Should Abate Carbon Emissions? A Note' (2006) 35 *Environmental and Resource Economics* 89.

Starrett, D. A., 'Fundamental Non-convexities in the Theory of Externalities' (1972) 4 *Journal of Economic Theory* 180.

Waltz, K., *Theory of International Politics* (Reading, Mass.: Addison-Wesley, 1979).

'Political Structures', in R. Keohane (ed.), *Neorealism and its Critics* (New York: Columbia University Press, 1986), pp. 70–97.

Wiener, J., 'Think Globally, Act Globally: The Limits of Local Climate Policies' (2007) 155 *University of Pennsylvania Law Review* 1961.

4

The applicability of international environmental law to private enterprises

SANDRINE MALJEAN-DUBOIS AND VANESSA RICHARD

4.1 Conceptualising the problem

The perception of the role of corporations in environmental protection efforts has evolved greatly. This is clearly suggested by a comparative reading of three statements that have punctuated the short history of international environmental law.

In 1972, the private sector was almost absent from the Stockholm Declaration, which refers first to 'Man', 'governments', 'countries' and even to 'peoples'. The Preamble only mentions 'enterprises' when specifying that 'to achieve this environmental goal will demand the acceptance of responsibility by citizens and communities and by enterprises and institutions at every level, all sharing equitably in common efforts'.[1] The Declaration was deeply embedded into a state-centred, interventionist vision of economic policy. At Rio in 1992, corporations were given limited room. Agenda 21[2] mentioned the role of 'business and industry' but only after that of women, children and youth, indigenous peoples, workers etc. The private sector was still suspicious. It was perceived rather as a threat to environmental protection and even if some principles largely concerned corporations the relevant obligations were imposed on states. By way of example, Principle 15 of the Rio Declaration on Environment and Development states that

> In order to protect the environment, the precautionary approach shall be widely applied *by States* according to their capabilities. Where there are threats of serious or irreversible damage, lack of full scientific certainty

[1] Declaration of the United Nations Conference on the Human Environment, A/CONF.48/14/Rev. 1 (1973), Preamble.

[2] Report of the United Nations Conference on Environment and Development, A/CONF.151/26/Rev. 1 (vol. 1), Resolution 1, Annex 2: Agenda 21 (Agenda 21).

> shall not be used as a reason for postponing cost-effective measures to prevent environmental degradation.[3]

Similarly, Principle 17 underlines that 'Environmental impact assessment, as a national instrument, shall be undertaken for proposed activities that are likely to have a significant adverse impact on the environment and *are subject to a decision of a competent national authority*.'[4] At Johannesburg in 2002, the private sector came to the forefront of the international scene. The agreed Declaration and the Plan of Implementation reflected a true paradigm shift. The relative failure of the 'Rio promises' was acknowledged and the private sector was no longer seen as a threat but as part of a solution in achieving sustainable development or, in other words, as a relay or even a substitute for the action of states and/or international organisations. Kofi Annan, then UN Secretary-General, declared indeed that 'more and more we are realizing that it is only by mobilizing the corporate sector that we can make significant progress'.[5] In addition, the private sector was well represented at Johannesburg.[6] Taking into account the decline of official development aid, the goal became to encourage private initiative, to remove international trade barriers and to attract foreign direct investment by granting additional protection. Marxism and the New International Economic Order had by then definitively given way to the liberal dogma. The primary goal of the Johannesburg documents was to promote the role of businesses and to encourage good practices rather than to regulate their activities or subject them to increased control. The Rio +20 Summit in 2012, with the emphasis put on a *Green Economy*, will most likely follow a rather similar perspective.

Although brief, the foregoing survey suggests that, so far, two different approaches have been pursued, i.e., a 'regulatory' approach reflected by multilateral environmental agreements (command and control) and a more liberal one promoted by international trade and financial institutions (laissez-faire and protect). Whereas Rio mainly

[3] Rio Declaration on Environment and Development, UN Doc. A/CONF.151/26, vol. 1 (1992), Principle 15 (italics added). See also Principles 11, 13, 14, 16.

[4] *Ibid.*, Principle 17 (italics added).

[5] Speech, Lekgota: Business Day, 1 September 2002, Johannesburg, South Africa; 'Johannesburg Summit: Big Business Gets Green Light from Kofi Annan', *Earth Time*, 2 September 2002.

[6] S. Maljean-Dubois, 'Environnement, développement durable et droit international. De Rio à Johannesburg: et au-delà?' (2002) 48 *Annuaire français de droit international* 592.

reflects the first approach and Johannesburg the second, it cannot be said that either one has prevailed – even temporarily – over the other. Reality is more complex and the UN itself is often torn between these two logics. We reach here a first paradox. In order to be effective, international environmental law cannot afford not to influence the behaviour of multinational corporations. But its grip on enterprises is generally indirect, made possible through the intermediation of domestic law. In an international society consisting of states, corporations are only secondary, 'non-prescribing' actors, lacking the ability to produce legal standards. Although they do not, as such, participate in inter-state relations, they are, nevertheless, very present. They operate in the backstage of inter-state relations, a backstage characterised by an array of cross-border economic relations.[7] From this point of view, economic globalisation further strengthens their freedom and autonomy.[8]

If one characterises a subject of international law by reference to its rights and obligations as well as by the possibility of bringing an action against a state before an international court or tribunal (provided that this state has expressed its consent to jurisdiction),[9] it would be difficult to deny that multinational corporations have some measure of legal subjectivity in international law. There is no need to reopen here this long-standing theoretical debate. Suffice it to recall that the International Court of Justice itself has recognised that 'The subjects of law in any legal system are not necessarily identical in their nature or in the extent of their rights, and their nature depends upon the needs of the community.'[10] Whether one accepts or rejects the use of the term 'subject of international law' as applied to private parties, one cannot ignore the legal capabilities enjoyed by individuals (including corporations) in contemporary international law.[11] Indeed, although they lack an

[7] H. Ascensio, 'Rapport introductif', in H. Ghérari and Y. Kerbrat (eds.), *L'entreprise dans la société internationale* (Paris: Pedone, 2010), 24.

[8] P. Kahn, 'Les Investissements internationaux, nouvelles donnes: un droit transnational de l'investissement', in P. Kahn and T. W. Wälde (eds.), *Les Aspects nouveaux du droit des investissements internationaux/New Aspects of International Investment Law* (Leiden: Martinus Nijhoff Publishers, 2007), 7.

[9] C. Leben, 'La Théorie du contrat d'état et l'évolution du droit international des investissements' (2003) 302 *RCADI* 308.

[10] *Reparation for Injuries Suffered in the Service of the United Nations, Advisory opinion of 11 April 1949*, ICJ Reports 1949, 178.

[11] Leben, 'La Théorie du contrat d'état', 301.

international or internationalised status, corporations can nevertheless benefit from certain rights or be subject to certain obligations arising from international law.[12]

International law provides a good measure of protection to corporations. This is particularly the case in the field of international investment law, where corporations are the direct addressees of certain norms. Some treaties – obviously concluded by states – give corporations numerous rights both substantive and procedural. One can think of the 2,600 bilateral investment treaties (BITs) establishing the terms and conditions for private investment by nationals and companies of one state in another state, or of the 1965 Washington Convention on the Settlement of Investment Disputes between States and Nationals of Other States establishing the International Centre for Settlement of Investment Disputes (ICSID),[13] or, still, of chapter 11 of the North American Free Trade Agreement (NAFTA).[14] Foreign investors are accorded a certain level of treatment, generally including fair and equitable treatment, full protection and security, protection against expropriation, most-favoured-nation and national treatment and the possibility freely to transfer their assets. Most notably, they can bring a claim for breach of these standards before international arbitral tribunals.[15] Another example is given by state contracts, whereby corporations enter into contractual relations with states on an equal footing, their relationship being governed, at least partly, by public international law. International trade law also grants corporations numerous guarantees. For example, some scholars consider that in the field of intellectual property such guarantees have gone too far, at least in some areas (e.g., patents law), breaking the balance between the interests of large companies and the general interest.[16] In an entirely different area, one could also mention the decision of the Paris Court of Appeals of 30 March 2010 in the case concerning marine pollution from the *Erika*. In this case, the French multinational Total was able to escape civil liability for damage despite

[12] Ascensio, 'Rapport introductif', 24.

[13] Convention on the Settlement of Investment Disputes between States and Nationals of other States, 18 March 1965, 575 UNTS 159 (ICSID Convention).

[14] North American Free Trade Agreement, 17 December 1992, 32 ILM 296 (NAFTA).

[15] C. Leben, 'L'Évolution du droit international des investissements', in SFDI, *Un accord multilatéral sur l'investissement, d'un forum de négociation à l'autre* (Paris: Pedone, 1999), 11.

[16] B. Remiche, 'La Protection de la propriété intellectuelle et industrielle: la lutte contre la contrefaçon', in Ghérari and Kerbrat, *L'Entreprise dans la société internationale*, 137.

being found guilty of a *délit* of pollution.[17] The firm was considered to be the charter company of the vessel, or lessee, which allowed it to benefit from the principle of immunity stemming from the regime of the 1969 International Convention on Civil Liability for Oil Pollution Damage (as amended by the Protocol of 27 November 1992).[18] Hence, the plaintiffs could not assert their claims against the most solvent debtor.[19] The outcome is paradoxical: here international environmental law 'protected' the polluter.

But even if corporations can avail themselves of certain investment disciplines, a different question is whether they can be systematically subject to *obligations arising from international law*. There are two main possibilities in this regard. First, such obligations may be indirect, i.e., in order to apply to corporations international environmental obligations would have to be incorporated into domestic law. Second, these obligations may directly apply to corporations irrespective of their incorporation into domestic law. Historically, corporations have been subject to indirect obligations only and, even if the situation is evolving, most of the obligations nowadays governing the activities of corporations are still indirect in character. As Yann Kerbrat rightly notes:

> a closer examination of the development of international law shows, indeed, that private operators can today commit direct breaches of international law and therefore be held responsible for breaches of international law. Such development is nevertheless not a general trend. It is mainly perceptible in two fields: international criminal law and international human rights law.[20]

In this context, one may wonder about the situation of corporations in respect of international environmental standards.

[17] French criminal law distinguishes between *contravention*, *délit* and *crime*, categories that relate to the gradation in the seriousness of the punishment the defendant incurs. Those who commit a *délit* incur both a fine and a prison sentence.

[18] Protocol of 1992 to amend the International Convention on Civil Liability for Oil Pollution Damage, London, 27 November 1992, UNTS, vol. 2048 (2001), 36.

[19] Such qualifications have been sharply criticised to the extent that it does not relate to an effective legal situation but to a fiction resulting from the de facto power the company has on the ship's running. Total is seen as a de facto charter company although it is legally the owner of the cargo. See the commentary of L. Neyret, 'L'Affaire Erika: moteur d'évolution des responsabilités civile et pénale' (2010) 34 *Recueil Dalloz* 2241.

[20] Y. Kerbrat, 'La Responsabilité des entreprises peut-elle être engagée pour des violations du droit international?', in Ghérari and Kerbrat, *L'Entreprise dans la société internationale*, 93 (our translation).

Intersections between international environmental law and international criminal law are scarce with respect to corporations. In fact, international criminal responsibility only concerns individuals and not corporations.[21] Conversely, there are important intersections between international human rights law and international environmental law, in particular through the human right to a healthy environment. But, even in this case, the incidence of international environmental law would remain indirect, as human rights norms impose obligations on states. Thus, one can conclude that, as a general matter, the incidence of international environmental norms on enterprises is only indirect. International law grants enterprises a significant measure of protection without imposing on them correlative duties. This situation offers multinational companies a number of advantages to the extent that they can locate their activities in 'pollution havens' or 'tax havens' so as to benefit from lower regulatory standards. This explains also why they may oppose international efforts to develop a stronger governance framework adverse to their interests.[22] Yet, normative constraints weighing down on enterprises seem to be on the rise. The forms and terms of these constraints are quite diverse. Traditional sources of international law are but one of the many layers of the 'normative *millefeuille*' increasingly influencing the activities of enterprises. Newer sources – of a transnational rather than inter-state nature – also regulate such activities. Paradoxically, binding law (treaty and customary rules) has only a limited normative power because its incidence is indirect (4.2), whereas softer normative incentives have a very direct influence on the behaviour of enterprises (4.3).

4.2 The incidence of 'inter-state' international environmental law

4.2.1 A growing hold on enterprises

If international law has an increasing hold over enterprises it is because it has undergone deep transformations. International environmental law has played a significant role largely in the transition from an international law of coexistence to one of cooperation, to use Wolfgang Friedman's famous dichotomy. In other words, international

[21] Ascensio, 'Rapport introductif', 31.

[22] O. Godard and T. Hommel, 'Les Multinationales, un enjeu stratégique pour l'environnement et le développement durable?' (2005–6) 60 *Revue internationale et stratégique* 101.

environmental law has very little in common with the law defined from Vattel to Charles Rousseau as 'the law of the distribution of competences'.[23] It is, rather, part of the 'providence-international law' described by Emmanuelle Jouannet,[24] according to whom:

> like liberal internal States which have become in Europe providence-States, contemporary international law has evolved from a liberal law, restricted to its essential primary functions of regulation and coexistence, to a multifunctional providence-law which regulates the life of States and individuals and which is considered to be the ultimate guarantor of the collective well-being.[25]

One important consequence of this transformation is the 'blurring and progressive disappearance of a clear boundary between what is international and what is domestic'.[26] International law seeps into new fields and gives birth to new branches. International economic law, international labour law, international human rights law, international environmental law are some of these new branches which 'constitute unique and complex conglomerations of domestic and international law, thus reconstructing large sections of traditional law into a new material and spatial dimension', what Robert Kolb calls 'amphibious' matters.[27] This 'domestically consumed'[28] international law increases its hold over private individuals and corporations within national boundaries.

Many international (state) obligations, either customary or treaty-based, affect enterprises as their final addressees. As regards customary principles, one can, for example, think of what is entailed by the obligation to prevent environmental harm in other countries or in areas beyond the limits of national jurisdiction. The International Court of Justice (ICJ) stated in the 2010 *Pulp Mills* case that a 'State is thus obliged to use all the means at its disposal in order to avoid activities which take

[23] G. Abi-Saab, 'Cours général de droit international public' (1987) 207 *RCADI* 78 (our translation).

[24] E. Jouannet, 'Le Même et l'autre', in E. Jouannet, H. Ruiz Fabri and J.-M. Sorel (eds.), *Regards d'une génération de juristes sur le droit international* (Paris: Pedone, 2008), 222.

[25] E. Jouannet, 'À quoi sert le droit international? Le droit international providence du XXIème siècle' (2007) 1 *Revue belge de droit international* 11 (our translation).

[26] R. Kolb, 'Mondialisation et droit international' (2005) 3 *Relations internationales* 70 (our translation).

[27] *Ibid.*, 78.

[28] S. Laghmani, 'Droit international et droits internes: vers un renouveau du *jus gentium?*', in R. Ben Achour and S. Laghmani (eds.), *Droit international et droits internes: développements récents* (Paris: Pedone, 1999), 34 (our translation).

place in its territory, or in any area under its jurisdiction, causing significant damage to the environment of another State'.[29] Similarly, the ICJ clearly considers as customary the obligation 'to undertake an environmental impact assessment where there is a risk that the proposed industrial activity may have a significant adverse impact in a transboundary context, in particular, on a shared resource'.[30] Treaty obligations likely to affect enterprises are particularly detailed and specific, even if usually they do not have a direct impact. The spread of international law has taken it into questions as diverse as the international trade of wild fauna and flora species, hazardous waste, living modified organisms, production and trade of chemicals, the emission of greenhouse gases, oil transportation, nuclear safety, civil liability regimes, rights to environmental information, participation in decision-making, access to (national) justice and many others. Although enterprises are not formally associated to the definition of the norms adopted by states, they are in practice quite present in their negotiation. One good illustration is provided by the BINGOs (business-initiated NGOs) active in climate negotiations, a category of NGOs created by transnational enterprises in order to counterbalance the influence of NGOs coming from the civil society, and which are usually organised industrial federations or coalitions.

In addition to international environmental obligations, international human rights law contributes to the protection of the environment, inter alia, through the recognition of the human or peoples' right to a healthy environment. The case law of the European Court of Human Rights is quite remarkable in this respect. The Court has imposed on states positive obligations to ensure that the rights granted by the European Convention on Human Rights[31] are not jeopardised by the environmental degradation caused by third parties. The responsibility of the state in this connection may be engaged by both public and private interferences. It can thus result from the grant of an administrative authorisation or from the failure to adopt regulations or appropriate measures related to the activities of the private sector.[32] In the *Hatton* case, the Grand

[29] *Pulp Mills on the River Uruguay* (*Argentina* v. *Uruguay*), Judgment (20 April 2010), para. 101.

[30] *Ibid.*, para. 204.

[31] Convention for the Protection of Human Rights and Fundamental Freedoms, Council of Europe, European Treaty Series ETS No. 5.

[32] F. Haumont, 'Le Droit fondamental à la protection de l'environnement dans la Convention de sauvegarde des droits de l'homme et des libertés fondamentales' (2008) *Aménagement-Environnement* (special issue) 25.

Chamber stated indeed that 'the State's responsibility in environmental cases may also arise from a failure to regulate private industry in a manner securing proper respect for the rights enshrined in Article 8 of the Convention'.[33] The protection thus offered has therefore a rather extensive scope, to the extent that it can be invoked not only when the pollution, or nuisance, arises from the state or its instrumentalities, but also when it arises from private activities, according to the theory of the indirect horizontal effect of the Convention.[34] In line with this precedent, some national tribunals directly refer to international human rights law to settle disputes between private parties.[35] There is here a shock wave the impact of which is still ongoing. The European continent is not the only geographical area concerned. The African Commission on Human and Peoples' Rights emphasised in the 2001 *Social and Economic Rights Action Center and Center for Economic and Social Rights* v. *Nigeria* (Ogoniland) case that 'Governments have a duty to protect their citizens, not only through appropriate legislation and effective enforcement but also by protecting them from damaging acts that may be perpetrated by private companies'.[36] After having concluded that Nigeria had breached the right of the Ogoni population to a healthy environment, as guaranteed by Article 14 of the African Charter,[37] the Commission added that Nigeria had to 'ensur[e] adequate compensation to victims of the human rights violation ... [by] undertaking a comprehensive cleanup of lands and rivers damaged by oil operations'.[38]

4.2.2 But a fragile hold

The incidence of international environmental law on multinational enterprises is rather limited. The shortcomings of international environmental law are both known and relatively well understood, from

[33] *Hatton and others* v. *the United Kingdom*, ECtHR Application No. 36022/97, Judgment (8 July 2003), para. 119. See also para. 98.

[34] On this theory, see J.-P. Marguénaud, 'La Charte constitutionnelle de l'environnement face au droit de la Cour européenne des droits de l'homme' (2005) *Revue juridique de l'environnement* (special issue) 206.

[35] Kerbrat, 'La Responsabilité des entreprises', 102.

[36] Communication 155/96, para. 57, available at www.achpr.org (accessed 15 April 2012).

[37] African [Banjul] Charter on Human and Peoples' Rights, adopted 27 June 1981, OAU, CAB/LEG/67/3 rev. 5, 21 ILM 58 (1982).

[38] Decision Regarding Communication 155/96 (*Social and Economic Rights Action Center/Center for Economic and Social Rights* v. *Nigeria*), Case No. ACHPR/COMM/A044/1, §56.

upstream factors – the 'bad quality' of international rules (non-specific, conditioned, voluntarily ambiguous, non self-executing obligations) – to downstream reasons – for example, the cost of their implementation or the lack of appropriate local 'capacities', to use the UN terminology. The Ruggie Report echoes those explanations, noting that:

> The failure to enforce existing laws that directly or indirectly regulate business' respect for human rights is often a significant legal gap in State practice. Such laws might range from non-discrimination and labour laws to *environmental*, property, privacy and anti-bribery laws. Therefore, it is important for States to consider whether such laws are currently being enforced effectively, and if not, why this is the case and what measures may reasonably correct the situation.[39]

National tribunals rarely refer to international environmental law directly. By way of illustration, references to international environmental law by French domestic courts in connection with the behaviour of subjects of domestic law are scarce.[40] The federal courts of the USA seem somewhat more open. On this issue, one cannot avoid to mention the famous Unocal case before US courts. In the mid-90s, the American firm Unocal was accused of having benefited from the forced labour of Burmese villagers in the building of a pipeline in Burma. It was sued before US tribunals under the Alien Torts Claim Act (ATCA) for complicity in forced labour, rape, torture and murder. The Court of Appeals of the Ninth Circuit pondered on how the responsibility of Unocal could be determined in the event a breach of international law was found. Should it be determined under principles stemming from federal common law or from international law, including the case law of the Nuremberg and other international criminal tribunals? The Court considered that to find support on 'new' international law standards could lead to chaos and rather opted for the well-established federal common law standards.[41] Until now, US tribunals have

[39] Report of the Special Representative of the Secretary-General on the Issue of Human Rights and Transnational Corporations and Other Business Enterprises, John Ruggie, Guiding Principles on Business and Human Rights: Implementing the United Nations 'Protect, Respect and Remedy' Framework, A/HRC/17/31, 21 March 2011, p. 8 (italics added).

[40] M. Francheteau-Laronze, 'L'Application du droit international de l'environnement par le juge national: éléments d'analyse comparative', in S. Maljean-Dubois and L. Rajamani (eds.), *Implementation of International Environmental Law* (Leiden: Martinus Nijhoff, 2011), 607–52.

[41] J. Hoppin, '9th Circuit Wrestles with ATCA Standards', *Recorder*, 18 June 2003. Naomi Norberg, 'Entreprises multinationales et lois extraterritoriales: l'interaction entre le droit américain et le droit international' (2005) *Revue de science criminelle* 739; O. de Schutter,

never admitted the responsibility of enterprises in international law, but the case law is not stabilised yet.[42] Even when tribunals do acknowledge that the invoked international legal principles might well belong to customary international law, multiple obstacles remain: *forum non conveniens*, the non-invocability of rules made for inter-state relations against corporations, non-interference with other countries' environmental policies, the political question doctrine as a ground to dismiss the request etc.[43] But decisions that send negative signals on the possibility of using the ATCA to sue corporations for alleged violations of international law can also open new doors. The *Texaco* cases before US courts allowed the identification of the *forum conveniens* and finally resulted in Chevron – through the former operations of its subsidiary Texaco Petroleum Company – being sued before the Ecuadorian courts, triggering a renewed flurry of judicial attacks and counterattacks.[44] The Second Circuit's reasoning in the *Kiobel* case that rules out the possibility to use the ATCA against *corporations*[45] 'may in fact give a boost to cases against individuals who acted on behalf of foreign states or corporations'.[46]

'Les Affaires *Total* et *Unocal*: complicité et extraterritorialité dans l'imposition aux entreprises d'obligations en matière de droits de l'homme' (2006) 52 *Annuaire français de droit international* 55.

42 H. Ascensio, 'Le Pacte Mondial et l'apparition d'une responsabilité internationale des entreprises', in L. Boisson de Chazournes and E. Mazuyer (eds.), *The Global Compact of the United Nations 10 Years Later* (Brussels: Bruylant, 2011), 167.

43 See inter alia *Aguinda* v. *Texaco, Inc.*, 945 F. Supat 625, 627 (SDNY, 1996). *Bano* v. *Union Carbide Corat*, No. 99 Civ. 11329 (JFK) (SDNY, 2003). *Beanal* v. *Freeport-McMoRan, Inc.*, 969 F. Supat 362 (E.D. La. 1997) (No. 96 –1474). *Sarei* v. *Rio Tinto PLC*, 221 F. Supat 2d 1116 (CD Cal. 2001). For further details, see E. Morgera, *Corporate Accountability in International Environmental Law* (Oxford University Press, 2009), 123–33; N. L. Bridgeman, 'Human Rights Litigation Under the ATCA as a Proxy For Environmental Claims' (2003) 6 *Yale Human Rights and Development Law Journal* 1.

44 The latest episode of which is the resort by Chevron to an arbitration hosted by the Permanent Court of Arbitration under the UNCITRAL investment disputes rules, Chevron claiming Ecuador has breached its obligation under the Ecuador–US investment treaty to guarantee fair trial: B. Reddall and E. Garcia, 'Arbitrators Say They Can Hear Chevron-Ecuador Case', *Reuters*, 28 February 2012, www.reuters.com (accessed 15 April 2012).

45 On the basis that 'the fact that corporations are liable as juridical persons under domestic law does not mean that they are liable under international law (and, therefore, under the ATCA)', the Second Circuit deduces that only individuals (or states) can be sued under the ATCA: *Kiobel* v. *Royal Dutch Petroleum*, No. 06–4800-cv, 06–4876-cv, 2010 WL 3611392 (2nd Cir. 17 September 2010).

46 C. I. Keitner, 'Kiobel v. Royal Dutch Petroleum: Another Round in the Fight Over Corporate Liability Under the Alien Tort Statute' (2010) 30 *ASIL Insight*, online version available at www.asil.org/insights100930.cfm (accessed 15 April 2012).

More generally, to rely entirely on domestic tribunals to control multinational enterprises' compliance with internationally guaranteed rights would miss an important point, namely that in many countries remedies only exist on the surface, because of a lack of means, and/or of corruption and/or of the lack of independence of the judiciary.

International tribunals are also called on to make an increasing use of international environmental law, in order to articulate it with its normative environment. One important area is the interface between international environmental and investment law. There are a growing number of investment disputes involving environmental aspects, although only a few significant awards have been rendered so far. Practice is quite diverse but it is bound to develop with the quantitative and qualitative development of international environmental law. The *S.D. Myers* v. *Canada*[47] or the *Pyramids*[48] cases suggest that obligations stemming from international environmental conventions could prevail over investment disciplines, or at least that a conciliatory interpretation of those two normative fields must be performed.[49] Moreover, in a recent NAFTA Chapter XI arbitration, arbitrators clearly admitted that a measure taken in pursuance of an international environmental obligation – in this case obligations arising from the Aarhus Protocol on POPs to the Long-Range Transboundary Air Pollution (LRTAP) Convention[50] – was legitimate and valid under international law, and that it did not amount to a breach of the NAFTA, even though it did have an economic impact of the investment.[51] Another important interface, which has received much more attention in the literature, is that between international environmental law and international trade law. Despite significant efforts, the incidence of international environmental law on the interpretation of trade disciplines remains limited. In both areas, the main question is essentially the same, i.e., whether obligations arising from international

47 *S.D. Myers, Inc.* v. *Government of Canada*, NAFTA (UNCITRAL Rules), Partial award (13 November 2000).

48 *Southern Pacific Properties (Middle East) Limited* v. *Egypt*, ICSID Case No. ARB/84/3, Award (20 May 1992).

49 J. E. Viñuales, 'Conflits normatifs en droit international: normes environnementales vs. protection des investissements', in Société française pour le droit international, *Le droit international face aux enjeux environnementaux* (Paris: Pedone, 2010), 407.

50 Protocol on Persistent Organic Pollutants to the LRTAP Convention, 24 June 1998, 37 ILM 513.

51 See *Chemtura Corporation* v. *Government of Canada*, NAFTA (UNCITRAL Rules), Award (2 August 2010).

environmental law could counterbalance the advantages enjoyed by enterprises under current international investment or trade law.

4.3 Development and diversification of international environmental legal norms affecting enterprises

4.3.1 Features: soft law and soft regulation

According to Francis Snyder, the beginning of the twenty-first century witnesses a striking variety of forms and legal regimes which can substantially differ from traditional, state-centred 'governance' patterns by their nature, content, scale and operative terms. There are nowadays multiple 'governance sites' which supplement, complement or compete with the state, hence the use of the word 'governance' instead of 'government'.[52] This phenomenon influences the form taken by regulatory action, which has increasingly diversified to make room for incentives as well as for private actors to initiate new norms, participate in their elaboration and be involved in their implementation. One can speak in this regard of (public/private) co-regulation or else of self-regulation, where private actors regulate their own activities with almost no intervention from public authorities. In practice, however, such intellectual categories of regulation, co-regulation or self-regulation are inappropriate to describe a complex reality essentially characterised by hybridisation and overlaps between political decision makers (rule makers) and the addressees of such decisions (rule takers).

What some call the 'market for virtue',[53] better known as corporate social responsibility or CSR initiatives, shows an impressive flexibility. It consists of a 'legal mist' made from multiple soft law and soft regulation instruments and initiatives, even though international environmental law appears as a strong contextual element. This 'market for virtue' took off as a consequence of the Rio Summit in 1992, which largely contributed to the promotion of principles that have progressively become actual 'common frames of reference' at the international level: sustainable development, the polluter-pays principle, the right to a healthy

[52] F. Snyder, *The EU, the WTO and China: Legal Pluralism and International Trade Regulation* (Oxford: Hart Publishing, 2010), 11–41.

[53] D. Vogel, *The Market for Virtue: The Potential and Limits of Corporate Social Responsibility* (Washington, DC: Brookings Institution Press, 2005).

environment and so on.[54] These principles have often been taken up in international conventions but, aside from two of them (i.e., the prevention principle and the requirement to conduct an environmental impact assessment), their customary status remains controversial. This does not prevent them from being influential and from materialising into the 'managerial projects' of big companies.[55] As the Rio conference drew nearer, some multinational enterprises joined a club, named the World Business Council for Sustainable Development (WBCSD), which has set up a Charter for good environmental behaviour, standing for the leader in the business world for the promotion of sustainable development.[56]

One can of course wonder about the real incidence of international law in the development of 'corporate social and environmental responsibility'. For enterprises it is a question of corporate image and, more precisely, of the perception that investors, shareholders and consumers may have of the enterprise's activities. This is largely the result of denunciation campaigns by unions and associations, and perhaps much more attributable to the work of NGOs, such as Greenpeace or WWF, than to the incidence of international environmental law. This said, one must keep in mind that NGO campaigning is largely based on international environmental standards. The fact remains, however, that big companies have actively contributed to the development of *global* environmental and social norms through their lobbying activities, their partnerships and the highlighting of good practices.[57]

Despite the wide variety of conceptions and practices, CSR conveys the idea that the role of enterprises is not restricted to the maximisation of profit but that they must get involved at the social and environmental levels. The European Commission defines it as 'A concept whereby companies integrate social and environmental concerns in their business operations and in their interaction with their stakeholders on a voluntary basis.'[58] The efforts were initially aimed at shareholders and corporate officers (corporate governance aspects) but they have progressively

[54] B. Jobert and P. Muller, *L'État en action* (Paris: Presses universitaires de France, 1987); A. Faure, G. Pollet and P. Warin (eds.), *La Construction du sens dans les politiques publiques* (Paris: L'Harmattan, 1995).

[55] F. Aggeri and O. Godard, 'Les Entreprises et le développement durable' (2006) 45 *Entreprises et histoire* 6 (our translation). See also Chapter 12 of this volume.

[56] Aggeri and Godard, 'Les Entreprises et le développement durable', 6.

[57] *Ibid.*, 8.

[58] European Commission Green Paper, Promoting a European Framework for Corporate Social Responsibility, COM (2001) 366 final, 18 July 2001, para. 8.

encompassed other areas of corporate activity. Similarly, CSR initially focused on the largest firms, whereas today it also concerns small- and medium-sized enterprises, for example, in connection with their relations with suppliers or subcontractors. Although CSR is mainly a form of self-regulation, enterprises often seek to institutionalise their practice through the creation of 'labels' or the adoption of 'codes of conduct'.[59] In addition, significant efforts towards the development of standardised best practices have been carried out by a private regulatory body, i.e., the International Organization for Standardization (ISO). Major examples include the ISO 14000 'family' of standards on environmental management or the ISO 26000 'Guidance on Social Responsibility' adopted in November 2010. One could also refer to other standardisation attempts, such as the SA 8000 standard developed by Social Accountability International (SAI), an NGO which has been proposing since 1997 a standard based on compliance with the principles of the Universal Declaration on Human Rights,[60] the International Covenant on Economic, Social and Cultural Rights,[61] international workplace norms of International Labour Organization (ILO) conventions,[62] the New York Declaration on the Rights of the Child[63] and the Rio Declaration on Environment and Development.[64] Quite understandably, the development of technical standards stemming from private sources, and/or the enterprises associated with the setting up of such standards, has attracted some attention from legal scholars. As a normative phenomenon, it suggests that 'economic regulatory initiatives, whether collective or individual, multiply, tangle, and end up generating new methods for the public action of States and international institutions confronted with the evolution of market rules'.[65]

Intergovernmental institutions are also involved in these normative efforts. By way of illustration, one can mention UN/business initiatives to

[59] See Chapters 12 and 15 of this volume.

[60] Adopted by UN General Assembly, Resolution 217 A (III) of 10 December 1948.

[61] International Covenant on Economic, Social and Cultural Rights, 16 December 1966, 993 UNTS 3.

[62] For example, ILO Convention 138 and Recommendation 146 (Minimum Age) or ILO Convention 183 (Maternity Protection).

[63] Adopted by UN General Assembly, Resolution 1386 (XIV) of 10 December 1959.

[64] Rio Declaration on Environment and Development.

[65] I. Cadet, 'La Norme ISO 26000 relative à la responsabilité sociétale: une nouvelle source d'usages internationaux' (2010) 4 *Revue internationale de droit économique* 405 (our translation).

develop public–private partnerships (PPPs). PPPs show a great variety of scale, content and partners. Public partners can be intergovernmental organisations, states, but also territorial subdivisions or public enterprises. It is significant that PPPs were introduced in 2002 as one of the 'tangible results' of the Johannesburg Summit for Sustainable Development. Indeed, for the first time, a UN conference resulted in the elaboration of 'Type II commitments' (PPPs) in addition to the traditional 'Type I (non-binding) commitments'. These 'partnerships' are voluntary, rather informal, and subject to vague 'guidelines'.[66] The concrete terms of their implementation, monitoring and control remain to be defined.[67] According to some NGOs, PPPs acted as a smokescreen to hide the glaring lack of governmental commitments, and in particular the abandonment of the project to adopt an international convention governing the activities of multinational enterprises.[68] The interest of some projects, which seemed to meet the sole economic interests of the major groups concerned and were nevertheless formally 'endorsed' as Summit results, was also questioned.[69] There are to date more than 300 PPPs showing notable differences in terms of thematic interest, management structures,

[66] See www.un.org/esa/sustdev/partnerships/guiding_principles7june2002.pdf (accessed 15 April 2012).

[67] See Report of the Secretary-General, 'Follow-up to Johannesburg and the Future Role of the CSD – The Implementation Track', E/CN.17/2003 /2, 18 February 2003.

[68] S. Jacob Scherr and R. Juge Gregg, 'Johannesburg and Beyond: The 2002 World Summit on Sustainable Development and the Rise of Partnerships' (2006), 18 *Georgetown International Environmental Law Review* 440; C. Bruch and J. Pendergrass, 'Type II Partnerships, International Law, and the Commons' (2003) 15 *Georgetown International Environmental Law Review* 877–82; G. R. Pring, 'The 2002 World Summit on Sustainable Development: International Environmental Law Collides with Reality, Turning Jo'burg into "Joke'burg"' (2002) 30 *Denver Journal of International Law and Policy* 410.

[69] See e.g. the Italian project on 'Sustainable Biotechnology and Agriculture in Africa' introduced as a 'Strategic Plan for the Development of Biotechnology and their Use in Agriculture', or else the WASH project coordinated by the World Bank, the London School of Hygiene and Tropical Mediçine, UNICEF, the World Health Organization and major soap producers, aiming at improving hygiene and reducing diarrhoea and mortality. The involvement of Unilever, Procter & Gamble, and Colgate–Palmolive as the choice of the Indian State of Kerala to welcome the pilot project gave rise to wave of protests. Indian defenders of public health objected that the sanitary situation in Kerala was similar to that of some western countries and that advertising for multinational enterprises' soap had nothing to do with sustainable development. See Observatoire de l'Europe industrielle, 'Les Nations Unies colonisées par les lobbies industriels' (2005) 34 *Revue Agone* 135. Also, L. B. Andonova and M. A. Levy, 'Franchising Global Governance: Making Sense of the Johannesburg Type II Partnerships' (2003–4) 8 *Yearbook of International Co-operation on Environment and Development* 19.

size and geographical cover. According to a report of the UN Secretary-General, their effectiveness still has to be proved.[70]

Another illustration of UN efforts to engage with the private sector is the Global Compact (GC), which is a set of principles that enterprises are invited to adhere to and implement. Contents-wise, the GC draws on instruments such as the Universal Declaration of Human Rights,[71] the ILO's Declaration on Fundamental Principles and Rights at Work[72] and some others. It contains three principles focusing on the protection of the environment.[73] In March 2012, more that 8,000 adhering enterprises from 132 countries were registered. Moreover, about fifty of them have embarked on a 'Global Compact Lead' to go beyond the Global Compact. They are committed to applying fifty concrete criteria mentioned in the 'Blueprint for Corporate Sustainability Leadership'.[74] Despite the apparent success, the GC generated sharp criticism in particular from the International Federation for Human Rights (Fédération internationale des ligues des droits de l'homme or FIDH), which highlighted that the GC operates a worrying inversion:

> human rights are proposed to enterprises as facultative provisions when they should be imposed on enterprises, because they are by essence humanity's common values. By proposing the Global Compact, the UN agrees to, not to say encourages, the subjection of the general interest to individual interests. It signs here a serious resignation of the international community.[75]

Because of its flexibility, the GC can apply to a group as a whole – including subsidiaries or outlets – since the adhesion of a parent company entails consequences for its whole sphere of influence.[76] At the beginning, there was no application control mechanism. In January 2003,

[70] Partnerships for Sustainable Development, Report of the Secretary-General, E/CN.17/2008/10, 6 February 2008.

[71] Universal Declaration, above, n. 60.

[72] See ILO Declaration on Fundamental Principles and Rights at Work, June 1998, 37 ILM 1237 (1998).

[73] 'Businesses should support a precautionary approach to environmental challenges' (principle 7), undertake initiatives to promote greater environmental responsibility (principle 8), and 'encourage the development and diffusion of environmentally friendly technologies' (principle 9)

[74] The blueprint is available on the Global Compact website at www.unglobalcompact.org (accessed 15 April 2012).

[75] Text reproduced in W. Bourdon, *Face aux crimes du marché: quelles armes juridiques pour les citoyens?* (Paris: La Découverte, 2010), 200–1 (our translation).

[76] Ascensio, 'Le Pacte Mondial', 167.

the Global Compact adopted a basis for a 'Communication on Progress' (CoP). Being purely procedural and devoid of control on the substance of the implementation of the GC,[77] the CoP asks adhering enterprises to communicate annually with their stakeholders (consumers, employees, unions, shareholders, media, public authorities etc.) on the progress made in the integration of the GC's principles, through their annual activity report, sustainable development report or other public reports, their website or any other communication means. Since 2004, enterprises which do not report can be excluded from the GC and recently more than 2,000 enterprises (a quarter of them!) were indeed expelled.[78] In 2005, a loose grievance mechanism was created to examine allegations of 'systematic or egregious abuses with respect to the Global Compact's principles and related commitments'.[79] Despite its weaknesses, some scholars have wondered whether the Global Compact could constitute a step towards a form of legal responsibility detached from domestic laws.[80] Beyond the GC, other codes of conduct and guidelines have been proposed by international organisations as a tool to govern the activities of the private sector. One can mention the 1977 Tripartite Declaration of Principles Concerning Multinational Enterprises and Social Policy,[81] or the 1980 UNCTAD Set of Multilaterally Agreed Equitable Principles and Rules for the Control of Restrictive Business Practices[82] or the Policy and Performance Standards on Social and Environmental Sustainability of the IFC.[83]

International institutions and the UN in particular also include the need to respect human rights as part of corporate social responsibility. In 2003, the Sub-Commission on the Promotion and Protection of Human Rights thus adopted the 'Norms on the responsibilities of transnational

[77] H. Ghérari, 'Le profil juridique et politique du Pacte mondial', in Boisson de Chazournes and Mazuyer, *The Global Compact*, 7.

[78] Specifically, 2,393 'business participants' were 'delisted': see *UN Global Compact Monthly Bulletin*, June 2011, www.unglobalcompact.org/NewsAndEvents/UNGC_bulletin/2011_06_01.html (accessed 3 March 2012).

[79] Ghérari, 'Le profil juridique et politique', 7.

[80] Ascensio, 'Le Pacte mondial', 167.

[81] Available at http://actrav.itcilo.org/actrav-english/telearn/global/ilo/guide/triparti.htm (accessed 15 April 2012).

[82] Available at http://r0.unctad.org/en/subsites/cpolicy/docs/CPSet/cpset.htm (accessed 15 April 2012). The Set was approved by the UN General Assembly in its Resolution 35/63, 5 December 1980.

[83] Available at www1.ifc.org/wps/wcm/connect/115482804a0255db96fbffd1a5d13d27/PS_English_2012_Full-Document.pdf?MOD=AJPERES (accessed 15 April 2012).

corporations and other business enterprises with regard to human rights'. According to the Norms:

> even though States have the primary responsibility to promote, secure the fulfilment of, respect, ensure respect of and protect human rights, transnational corporations and other business enterprises, as organs of society, are also responsible for promoting and securing the human rights set forth in the Universal Declaration of Human Rights.

Moreover, 'transnational corporations and other business enterprises, their officers and persons working for them are also obligated to respect generally recognized responsibilities and norms'[84] contained in a list of international instruments expressly mentioned. As for environmental protection, the Norms provide that:

> Transnational corporations and other business enterprises shall carry out their activities in accordance with national laws, regulations, administrative practices and policies relating to the preservation of the environment of the countries in which they operate, as well as in accordance with relevant international agreements, principles, objectives, responsibilities and standards with regard to the environment as well as human rights, public health and safety, bioethics and the precautionary principle, and shall generally conduct their activities in a manner contributing to the wider goal of sustainable development.[85]

One can also refer to the work of John Ruggie, the UN Secretary-General's Special Representative for Business and Human Rights, who has defined a framework (Protect, Respect and Remedy) and proposed guidelines for its implementation by enterprises.[86] The Guiding Principles 'apply to all States and to all business enterprises, both transnational and others, regardless of their size, sector, location, ownership and structure' but they explicitly mention that 'Nothing in these Guiding Principles should be read as creating new international law obligations, or as limiting or undermining any legal obligations a State may have undertaken or be subject to under international law with regard to

[84] Preamble, Sub-Commission on the Promotion and Protection of Human Rights thus adopted in 2003 the Norms on the Responsibilities of Transnational Corporations and other Business Enterprises with Regard to Human Rights, E/CN. 4/Sub. 2/2003/12/Rev. 226, August 2003.

[85] *Ibid.*, para.14.

[86] See Report of the Special Representative of the Secretary-General on the Issue of Human Rights and Transnational Corporations and Other Business Enterprises, John Ruggie, Guiding Principles on Business and Human Rights: Implementing the United Nations 'Protect, Respect and Remedy' Framework, A/HRC/17/31, 21 March 2011.

human rights.'[87] Ruggie considered that the drafting of a binding text would be premature. As a result, he preferred to offer principles that would synthesise and make existing rules consistent, sticking to a soft framing which advances the idea of due diligence. As such, the framework gives a sense of responsibility without making it compulsory.

Another interesting initiative illustrating the dynamics of soft law/soft regulation combined with 'traditional' sources of international environmental law is the cross-fertilisation at work in the framework of the OECD Guidelines for Multinational Enterprises. These Guidelines are 'recommendations addressed by [adhering] governments to multinational enterprises' and, since 1976, they have progressively incorporated environmental, human rights and social concerns. The 2001 version had integrated principles stemming from the Rio Declaration, the Aarhus Convention on access to information, public participation and access to justice in environmental matters, and ISO 14000 'family' of standards.[88] The latest version (May 2011) of the Guidelines draws additional inspiration from a variety of more recent instruments, such as the Global Compact, the ISO 26000 guidance, the 2006 Policy and Performance Standards on Social and Environmental Sustainability of the IFC, the Equator Principles, Special Representative John Ruggie's works on Business and Human Rights, the UN Convention on Climate Change, the ADEME Bilan Carbone, the Greenhouse Gas Protocol Initiative etc.[89]

Still another illustration of hybridisation is provided by the climate change regime and, more precisely, by the efforts to achieve voluntary greenhouse gas (GHG) emissions compensation, which use standardisation techniques in order to ensure their credibility, whether one looks at the Bilan Carbone or at the certification of offsets.[90] One can indeed think of the voluntary tools enterprises can use, at least theoretically, to improve their image, make sustainable investments and earn money,

[87] *Ibid.*, 6.

[88] Commentary on the OECD Guidelines for Multinational Enterprises (2001 version), para. 30. The Commentary specifies that 'the fact that the Guidelines are addressed to enterprises means that no existing instrument is completely adequate for expressing this recommendation. The Guidelines therefore draw upon, but do not completely mirror, any existing instrument': para. 38.

[89] OECD Guidelines for Multinational Enterprises: Update 2011, Note by the Secretary-General, C(2011) 59, 3 May 2011, 8.

[90] B. Leguet, 'La Participation à des programmes de compensation volontaire', in S. Maljean-Dubois and A. Roger (eds.), *L'Implication des entreprises dans les politiques climatiques: entre corégulation et autorégulation* (Paris: La Documentation française, 2011), 51.

for example, in the framework of project-based mechanisms of the Kyoto Protocol[91] (joint implementation, clean development mechanism) and possibly in that of the REDD mechanism, by allowing enterprises to invest in projects leading to carbon offsets in several Eastern European or developing countries.[92] Here the international climate regime – hard law regime made from the UNFCCC[93] and its Kyoto Protocol – gives room for voluntary tools – offsets, or else sectoral voluntary approaches in the steel, aluminium or cement industries[94] – or promotes such tools – project-based mechanisms.

Hybridisation truly characterises such soft regulation. As the above examples show, traditional instruments promote or are complemented by more innovative instruments, public initiatives by private initiatives. The development of CSR instruments from private sources is clearly connected to the absence of a direct responsibility of enterprises under international law. It is both the pressure from civil society and international organisations to fill this gap and the enterprises' eagerness to do it themselves that may explain the strong development of self-regulation. But private initiatives are themselves mixed. An enterprise which develops its CSR policy may assess its GHG emissions, choose to carry out compensation projects, adopt a code of conduct and have recourse to the certification (labels) of some of its products/processes, and will as a rule prefer to do so under the umbrella of internationally recognised standards. These, in turn, often stem – ultimately – from international organisations.

4.3.2 Does 'soft regulation' mean 'soft implementation'?

The development of soft law and soft regulation, with its 'new' tools, suggests that enterprises are likely to implement the commitments they have voluntarily assumed. One may, however, wonder what are the mechanisms and processes that, in practice, induce an enterprise to abide by its voluntary undertakings. One such mechanism is, of course, transparency. In order to establish their credibility, enterprises are increasingly 'forced' to account for their activities. Social communication and the

[91] Kyoto Protocol to the United Nations Framework Convention on Climate Change, Kyoto, 11 December 1997, 2303 UNTS 148.

[92] See Chapter 7 of this volume.

[93] United Nations Framework Convention on Climate Change, 9 May 1992, 31 ILM 849.

[94] M. Colombier and R. Baron, 'Les Approches sectorielles, quelles perspectives?', in Maljean-Dubois and Roger, *L'Implication des entreprises dans les politiques climatiques*, 123.

rendering of accounts are standardised at the global level,[95] or framed by mechanisms such as the Global Reporting Initiative (GRI).[96] Enterprises adhere voluntarily, but once they have adhered the mechanism regulates their reporting practices, for example, the format of disclosure, its scope, the assurance that the data is reliable and that reports are freely accessible. Although sponsored by the OECD and UNEP, the GRI is a private initiative. The same pattern applies to the Principles for Sustainable Investment defined by institutional investors, which are sponsored by UNEP and the Global Compact,[97] or to the Equator Principles, a voluntary framework initiated by a group of financial intermediaries to guide their social and environmental policies, procedures and practices.[98] With respect to such initiatives, intergovernmental organisations are more often spectators than actual actors.

One must not equate the considerable amount of self-regulation with its actual effectiveness. Reality is far from being the bed of roses that a naive observer would be tempted to derive from such initiatives. Moreover, these 'soft tools' are not necessarily outside the legal radar. In this regard, the law has shown a remarkable ability to adapt to new situations.[99] Although self-regulation is often consciously used to escape formal regulatory schemes, some measure of normative constraint lurks in the shadows.

An example is the use of environmental certification. Voluntary certification initiatives may provide a competitive advantage. But such schemes may come under scrutiny of the WTO as non-tariff barriers inconsistent with the Technical Barriers to Trade (TBT) Agreement. This, in turn, encourages states to seek international harmonisation through mutual recognition or recourse to technical standards.[100] As a result, technical standards and environmental eco-label certification are, in practice, acquiring a quasi-binding character within the WTO.[101]

[95] The ISO 26000 guidance mentions a responsibility to account.

[96] See www.globalreporting.org (accessed 15 April 2012).

[97] See www.unpri.org (accessed 15 April 2012).

[98] See www.equator-principles.com (accessed 15 April 2012). Also Chapter 6 in this volume.

[99] P. Deumier, 'La Question de la sanction', in Boisson de Chazournes and Mazuyer, *The Global Compact*, 155–66.

[100] S. Lavallée and K. Barentsein, 'La Régulation et l'harmonisation internationale des programmes d'écolabels sur les produits et les services' (2004) 1 *Revue internationale de droit économique* 61.

[101] E. Truilhé-Marengo and E. Brosset (eds.), *Les Enjeux de la normalisation internationale: entre environnement, santé et commerce international* (Paris: La Documentation française, 2006).

Voluntary agreements between the car industry and the European Commission show a soft/hard dialectic: 'soft' when 'hard' is not available, 'hard' because of the failure of the 'soft'.[102] Carbon markets, where a similar dynamic could be observed, are in a wait-and-see position because of the slowness of international climate negotiations.[103]

The CSR policy of a multinational enterprise is supposed to bind its subcontractors by the contracts they signed, even if the US *Wal-Mart* case illustrates a restrictive approach to this issue.[104]

In the field of foreign investment, arbitral tribunals could take CSR into account in assessing an investor's good faith or the legitimacy of its expectations.[105] In a sort of 'boomerang effect', not always anticipated, enterprises could be held accountable for the achievement of their voluntary commitments. Indeed, under Article 1.8 of the Unidroit Principles of International Commercial Contracts, 'A party cannot act inconsistently with an understanding it has caused the other party to have and upon which that other party reasonably has acted in reliance to its detriment.'[106] One prominent illustration of such unanticipated effects is provided by the judgment of the California Supreme Court in the 2002 *Kasky* v. *Nike* case.[107] Mr Kasky claimed that Nike had undertaken numerous commitments (and issued several statements in this connection)[108] and subsequently failed to comply with them. According to the corporation, voluntary commitments arising from CSR could not trigger the corporation's liability. The Court decided that the veracity of Nike's statements, which were characterised as commercial speech, could be challenged before the courts and that, under some circumstances, the corporation could be sanctioned on false advertising and unfair

[102] A. Roger, 'Corégulation et politique climatique de l'Union européenne: le rôle des accords environnementaux', in Maljean-Dubois and Roger, *L'Implication des entreprises dans les politiques climatiques*, 51.

[103] S. Maljean-Dubois and M. Wemaëre, *La Diplomatie climatique: les enjeux d'un régime international du climat* (Paris: Pedone, 2010); O. Godard and P. Crifo, 'Des politiques publiques au service de l'économie verte' (2010) 355 *Cahiers français*.

[104] Ascensio, 'Le Pacte mondial', 168. See also the contribution of N. Affolder in this book.

[105] Ascensio, 'Le Pacte mondial', 168.

[106] Article 1.8 (Inconsistent Behaviour), Unidroit Principles of International Commercial Contracts, 2010, available at www.unidroit.org (accessed 15 April 2012).

[107] *Kasky* v. *Nike, Inc.*, 27 Cal. 4th 939, No. S087859, 2 May 2002. F.-G. Trébulle, 'Responsabilité sociale des entreprises et liberté d'expression. Considérations à partir de l'arrêt Nike v/ Kasky' (2004) *Revue des sociétés* 261.

[108] According to which Nike was making its subcontractors respect regulations related to minimal working age, working time, health and security of workers, environmental protection, etc.

competition grounds. In other words, the California Supreme Court laid down a 'demand for the truthfulness of voluntary declarations'.[109] This decision has been heavily criticised by enterprises on the grounds that it would create a discouraging, not to say chilling, effect on CSR commitments.

As a general matter then, good faith considerations would preclude enterprises from going back on the legitimate expectations they have themselves created on the basis of their previous behaviour. If they commit to observe guiding principles, codes of conduct or any other CSR instrument, they would not be allowed to abandon their commitments any more on the pretext that they are voluntary. Corporations' customers or rival firms can thus refer to such initial commitments to base their own behaviour. If the promise is broken, the affected party can bring legal action to gain compensation for the harm suffered and the argument stressing the voluntary nature of initial commitments would be ineffective.[110] A fine observer of these practices notes that although CSR commitments 'still appear as a relatively vague notion to many, not very likely to create legal implications, some recent cases support the analysis according to which it is actually a source of obligations for the enterprises who adopted them'.[111] In addition, the trend seems to favour the legal framing of CSR practices.[112]

One may also add that non-binding instruments may provide the basis for the establishment of accountability mechanisms. Apart from the example of the Global Compact mentioned above, this is also the case of the OECD Guidelines, the implementation of which can be the object of specific instances brought before national contact points (NCPs) established in each of the forty-two countries adhering to the Guidelines. The Guidelines are a set of voluntary principles aimed at ensuring that multinational enterprises operating in and from adhering countries[113]

[109] Trébulle, 'Responsabilité sociale', 261 (our translation).

[110] R. Geiger, 'Responsabilité sociale et développement durable: le rôle des entreprises', in Ghérari and Kerbrat, *L'Entreprise dans la société internationale*, 173.

[111] Trébulle, 'Responsabilité sociale', 261.

[112] For an example of the 'hardening' of CSR commitments by the French legislator, see V. Mercier, 'Responsabilité sociétale des entreprises et droit des sociétés: entre contrainte et démarche volontaire' (2011) 4 *Droit des societés* 4.

[113] Note that 'In addition to addressing adverse impacts in relation to matters covered by the Guidelines, [enterprises should] encourage, where practicable, business partners, including suppliers and sub-contractors, to apply principles of responsible business conduct compatible with the Guidelines': OECD Guidelines, General Policies, para. A(13).

adopt a socially and environmentally responsible behaviour. NCPs can examine grievances relating to the implementation of the Guidelines brought by the 'business community, worker organisations, other non-governmental organisations and other interested parties'[114] and issue recommendations. By examining 'compliance' with the Guidelines, NCPs could also assess compliance with some international law principles (precautionary approach, environmental impact assessments etc.). Between the 2000 update of the Guidelines and June 2010, some 100 complaints were brought by NGOs before an NCP (half of them partly or totally dealing with environmental concerns) and more than 100 by workers organisations.[115] In this context, the British NCP recently (March 2011) gave six NGOs satisfaction on their complaint against the building of the Baku–Tbilisi–Ceyhan (BTC) pipeline, recognising that the consortium led by British Petroleum and Total had breached the Guidelines, inter alia, in connection with the lack of consideration given to the rights of local communities. The project had indeed been presented as an exemplary application of the Equator Principles and as such had benefited from the financial support of many institutions including the World Bank and the European Bank for Reconstruction and Development.[116] The grievance mechanism of the OECD Guidelines nevertheless counts few environmental success stories. It remains hardly reliable due to the divergent practice of each NCP and its lack of transparency. Few complaints pass the eligibility examination and even when serious violations are established the reports issued by NCPs do not have as such any binding consequences.[117]

CONCLUSION

Does international environmental law apply to private enterprises? Not directly, which does not mean it does not apply at all. The hold of

[114] Decision of the Council on the OECD Guidelines for Multinational Enterprises, enclosed in the Declaration on International Investment and Multinational Enterprises, para. I(1).

[115] OECD Watch, *10 Years On: Assessing the Contribution of the OECD Guidelines for Multinational Enterprises to Responsible Business Conduct*, June 2010, available at http://oecdwatch.org/publications-en/Publication_3550 (accessed 15 April 2012).

[116] 'Violation des droits humains: Le Royaume-Uni donne raison aux ONG pour leur plainte OCDE sur la construction de l'oléoduc BTC', *Dépêche AEDD*, 15 March 2011.

[117] V. Richard, 'L'Accountability comme alternative à la responsabilité? Réflexions en droit international de l'environnement', in E. Vergès (ed.), *Droit, sciences et techniques, quelles responsabilités?* (Paris: LexisNexis, 2011), 523–41.

international environmental law takes subtle twists and turns. Indirect application results not only from situations when, in order to apply to corporations, international environmental obligations must be incorporated into domestic law, but also from the use of human rights-based approaches to bring forth environmental issues, from the hybridisation of the content of international legal norms with that of a wide array of soft law instruments and private standards, or else from the not-always-explicit use of international environmental law by non-judicial grievance mechanisms. Freedom, constraint and incentives seem to combine into complex configurations.[118] Under pressure from citizens–consumers–unions–shareholders (supported, in turn, by the existence of international standards) or from investors (through rating agencies), enterprises are increasingly subject to market-based regulatory constraints of different natures, including hard law and soft law, binding or voluntary, public and private, international and domestic instruments. The interactions between these normative and para-normative layers are complex and not fully coherent. To these systemic difficulties, one must also add the strong resistances from the regulated entities. Yet, the general trend is rather one of progressive standardisation and universalisation of the relevant standards, some 'homogenisation of the normative space at the global scale',[119] and the strength of international norms as a new *lex communis.*[120]

[118] Deumier, 'La Question de la sanction', 155.

[119] A. Supiot, *Homo Juridicus: essai sur la fonction anthropologique du droit* (Paris: Seuil, 2005), 168 (our translation).

[120] J.-L. Halperin, *Profils des mondialisations du droit* (Paris: Dalloz, 2009), 240–2.

Select bibliography

Aggeri F., and O. Godard, 'Les Entreprises et le développement durable' (2006) 45 *Entreprises et histoire* 6.

Andonova, L. B., and M. A. Levy, 'Franchising Global Governance: Making Sense of the Johannesburg Type II Partnerships' (2003–4) 8 *Yearbook of International Co-operation on Environment and Development* 19.

Blin-Franchomme, M.-P., I. Desbarats, G. Jazottes and V. Vidalens, *Entreprise et développement durable: approche juridique pour l'acteur économique du XXIe siècle* (Paris: Lamy, 2011).

Boisson de Chazournes, L., and E. Mazuyer (ed.), *The Global Compact of the United Nations, 10 Years Later* (Brussels: Bruylant, 2011).

Bourdon, W., *Face aux crimes du marché: quelles armes juridiques pour les citoyens?* (Paris: La Découverte, 2010).

Bridgeman, N. L., 'Human Rights Litigation Under the ATCA as a Proxy For Environmental Claims' (2003) 6 *Yale Human Rights and Development Law Journal* 1.

Bruch, C., and J. Pendergrass, 'Type II Partnerships, International Law, and the Commons' (2003) 15 *Georgetown International Environmental Law Review* 855.

Cadet, I., 'La Norme ISO 26000 relative à la responsabilité sociétale: une nouvelle source d'usages internationaux' (2010) 4 *Revue internationale de droit économique* 405.

Crane, A., A. McWilliams, D. Matten, J. Moon and D. S. Siegel (eds.), *The Oxford Handbook of Corporate Social Responsibility* (Oxford University Press, 2009).

De Schutter, O., 'Les Affaires *Total* et *Unocal*: complicité et extraterritorialité dans l'imposition aux entreprises d'obligations en matière de droits de l'homme' (2006) 52 *Annuaire français de droit international* 55.

Gherari, H., and Y. Kerbrat (eds.), *L'Entreprise dans la société internationale* (Paris: Pedone, 2010).

Godard, O., and T. Hommel, 'Les Multinationales, un enjeu stratégique pour l'environnement et le développement durable?' (2005–6) 60 *Revue internationale et stratégique* 101.

Kerbrat, Y., and S. Maljean-Dubois (eds.), *The Transformation of International Environmental Law* (Paris and Oxford: Pedone/Hart Publishing, 2011).

Lavallée, S., and K. Barentsein, 'La Régulation et l'harmonisation internationale des programmes d'écolabels sur les produits et les services' (2004) 1 *Revue internationale de droit économique* 61.

Maljean-Dubois, S., and L. Rajamani (eds.), *Implementation of International Environmental Law* (Leiden: Martinus Nijhoff, 2011).

Maljean-Dubois, S., and A. Roger (eds.), *L'Implication des entreprises dans les politiques climatiques: entre corégulation et autorégulation* (Paris: La Documentation française, 2011).

Mercier, V., 'Responsabilité sociétale des entreprises et droit des sociétés: entre contrainte et démarche volontaire' (2011) 4 *Droit des societés* 4.

Morgera, E., *Corporate Accountability in International Environmental Law* (Oxford University Press, 2009).

Richard, V., 'L'Accountability comme alternative à la responsabilité? Réflexions en droit international de l'environnement', in E. Vergès (ed.) *Droit, sciences et techniques, quelles responsabilités?* (Paris: LexisNexis, 2011), pp. 523–41.

Richardson, B. J., *Socially Responsible Investment Law: Regulating the Unseen Polluters* (Oxford University Press, 2008).

Sobczak, A., and N. Minvielle, *Responsabilité globale: manager le développement durable et la responsabilité sociale des entreprises* (Paris: Vuibert, 2011).

Truilhé-Marengo, E., and E. Brosset (eds.), *Les Enjeux de la normalisation internationale: entre environnement, santé et commerce international* (Paris: La Documentation française, 2006).

Viñuales, J. E., 'Conflits normatifs en droit international: normes environnementales vs. protection des investissements', in Société française pour le droit international, *Le droit international face aux enjeux environnementaux* (Paris: Pedone, 2010), pp. 407–27.

Vogel, D., *The Market for Virtue: The Potential and Limits of Corporate Social Responsibility* (Washington, DC: Brookings Institution Press, 2005).

5

Economics of green economies: investment in green growth and how it works

SHAUN LARCOM AND TIMOTHY SWANSON

INTRODUCTION

In early 2011, the United Nations Environment Programme issued its report on The Green Economy.[1] The report details the types of industries that underlie many nations' attempts at developing their economies around less environmentally intensive enterprises. Many advocates make the point that government spending should be geared towards such green industries.[2] It is clear that such a strategy, if adopted by any developing country, would be of great benefit to the environment. It is less clear why the fostering of such green industries is good for the countries themselves. Why is it the case that investment in less environmentally intensive industries might benefit countries pursuing growth and development? The purpose of this chapter is to explain some of the basic economics of why state intervention can be good for both the economy as well as the environment. This is the economic rationale for why countries should give some thought to intervening to make their economic growth more 'green'.[3]

We are grateful for the comments of the discussants at the workshop on the role of the private sector in protecting the environment, held at the Graduate Institute in May 2011, and to two anonymous reviewers. The chapter is also the result of work with the United Nations Environment Programme as well as of a Workshop on Designing Paths to Green Economies, held at the Graduate Institute in December 2011.

1 See UNEP, *The Green Economy Report – A Synthesis for Policy Makers* (Nairobi: UNEP, 2011)

2 See e.g. E. B. Barbier, 'The G20 Agenda Should Include Implementing a Global "Green" New Deal', Macroeconomics, a Global Crisis Debate, http://VoxEU.org (March 2009); E. B. Barbier, *A Global Green New Deal: Rethinking the Economic Recovery* (Cambridge University Press, 2010); E. B. Barbier, 'Green Stimulus, Green Recovery and Global Imbalances' (2010) 11 *World Economics* 1.

3 See T. Swanson and Z. Ziegelhofer, 'Economic Frameworks for Thinking about Growth, Sustainability and State Intervention: Paths to Green Economies', UNEP Working Paper (2011).

The basic idea is that good environmental outcomes are desirable not only for the country investing in them, but it can also be desirable for many other countries that might want to pursue such outcomes at some point in the future. In that case it can pay to be a leader in the search for technologies and industries that are more environmentally friendly. One of the primary reasons why states achieve competitiveness on the world stage is through such forms of technological innovation and leadership. There are much-reduced benefits from coming anything other than first in a new field. Adoption of other countries' technologies may be an avenue to other goals, such as employment or income equality, but it cannot generate the benefits that are derived from actual innovation. Developing countries may have a period of time during which imitation and transfer are the only real options regarding technological change, but (as the technological frontier is approached) there can be no substitute for actual innovation.[4]

Competitiveness in innovation is then determined by reference to the ability of the state to introduce new technologies, rather than simply adopt pre-existing ones. This can generate competitiveness in terms of market leadership in the innovative product but also in terms of the sales of the technology to others who wish to produce it. So, once leadership in a technology is established, competitiveness is measured in terms of both own production and other countries' production under licence.

Regulation is an important means by which a state might drive its industries to develop frontier-level technologies. Placing constraints upon an industry makes demands upon it to innovate, i.e., to develop new methods for doing things. These new techniques may then be marketed if it comes to pass that either (a) the implied constraint becomes a real one or (b) other states become convinced to adopt the same constraint. So, a regulatory policy can be translated into technological leadership if either the regulated resource becomes scarcer or if other countries become persuaded to adopt the regulation. If the state is able to see slightly further than others, or to be persuasive concerning its view, then the technologies it encourages become demanded worldwide.

In the remainder of this introduction we outline the very general argument for the use of environmental policy to drive green investment, industrial development and competitiveness. Then we turn from the abstract to the concrete by considering a couple of case studies

[4] See T. Swanson and T. Lin (eds.), *Economic Growth and Environmental Regulation: The People's Republic of China's Path to a Brighter Future* (London: Routledge, 2010).

(Japan and Denmark) that demonstrate this sort of approach to industrial and development policy. In general, the argument is that states should see policies regarding environment, investment and innovation as one seamless problem to be solved.

5.1 Environmental policy as development policy

The design of green economies considers the impact of environmental policies within the broader context of innovation and industrial policies more generally.[5] In this view, governments must intervene within economies in order to encourage innovation and growth (e.g., intellectual property rights policies).[6] Such intervention is important as a means for inducing innovation, and for choosing the direction of change within the economy.[7]

State intervention within an economy is critically important for these purposes. Governments must intervene in industries in order to provide incentives for investment in research and development (R&D).[8] This is because industries in competitive markets have few incentives to invest in technological change or even in product innovation, since any returns would be immediately competed away. This is one of the best-known examples of market failure in the context of competitive markets, and provides the rationale for various forms of interventions.[9]

Hence, environmental policies may be seen within this context as just one more instrument in society's toolkit of economy-directing interventions. They specify the problems that the society is targeting for solution, and place an emphasis on the accumulation of certain

5 This point has been debated since at least the time of the initial statement of the 'Porter hypothesis'. Porter argued that environmental regulation might have a positive impact on growth through the dynamic effects it engendered within an economy. See M. E. Porter and C. van der Linde, 'Toward a New Conception of the Environment-Competitiveness Relationship' (1995) 9 *Journal of Economic Perspectives* 97.

6 See P. Stoneman (ed.), *Handbook of the Economics of Innovation and Technological Change* (Oxford: Blackwell, 1995).

7 See D. Foray, *The New Economics of Technology Policy* (Cheltenham: Edward Elgar, 2010).

8 It has been known since at least the time of the seminal work of Kenneth Arrow: 'The Economic Implications of Learning by Doing' (1962) 29 *Review of Economic Studies* 155 and the structural work of Kamien and Schwarz (M. I. Kamien and N. L. Schwartz, *Market Structure and Innovation* (Cambridge University Press, 1982)) that competitive firms and competitive markets need not produce the optimal amount of innovation and growth within an economy.

9 See R. D. Blair and T. F. Cotter, *Intellectual Property: Economic and Legal Dimensions of Rights and Remedies* (Cambridge University Press, 2005).

forms of capital (natural, human, knowledge-based) for the accomplishment of those solutions.

This shift in priorities may be seen in the histories of many recently emerged economies. In the 1950s and 1960s, South Korean and Japanese governments chose the direction of technological change through importing the elections of other countries.[10] This changed in the 1970s when these economies shifted to aggressive policies for encouraging energy-efficient innovation. Shortly afterward, Japan was one of the leading economies in the world in terms of R&D investment in these industries.[11] A simple shift in environmental policies had changed the entire direction of these economies.

This example illustrates three points. First, environmental policies play an important and central role in determining the *direction of development* within an economy. It does so by providing incentives for particular pathways of technological change. Placing restrictions on the use of scarce resources (such as energy, water or air) encourages firms and industries to invest in ways that will conserve on these resources in order to minimise these costs. So, environmental regulation is just one manner in which firms and industries are provided direction on how and where to invest. It is a means for electing the direction in which the economy should move, by indicating the sets of problems on which the economy should work.

Secondly, environmental policies play a critical role in determining the *form of development* existing within an economy. Development that is based on underpriced resources and undervalued natural capital is skewed towards an exploitation and mining-based economy. When natural capital is free to the production sector, there is little reason for that sector to invest in or to accumulate other forms of productive capital (human, physical, knowledge). On the other hand, the creation of green policies encourages the development of a problem-solving sector within the economy, and this places an emphasis on the accumulation of other forms of capital and their employment in the creation of new types of activities. It is a clear shift in emphasis away from the extractive to the inventive economy.

[10] See D. J. Teece, 'The Market for Know-how and the Efficient International Transfer of Technology' (1981) 458 *Annals of the Academy of Political and Social Science* 81.

[11] By 1987, Japan was the world leader in R&D per unit GDP (at 2.8%) and the world leader in the proportion of that spent on energy-related R&D (at 23%). See D. Mowery, 'The Boundaries of the US Firm in R&D', in N. R. Lamoreaux and D. M. G. Raff (eds.), *Coordination and Information: Historical Perspectives on the Organization of Enterprise* (Chicago University Press, 1995), 147–72.

Thirdly, environmental policies play a fundamental role in defining the *governmental role* in choosing the development path. Economies that abdicate that leadership role to the private sector will not necessarily point the economy in the direction most beneficial to the society at large. This returns us to the initial point of this section – environmental policy as a part of innovation policy more generally. It is a core governmental function to determine which set of problems to prioritise, and the failure to do so simply leaves the economy without direction.[12]

In sum, the future path of an economy is a governmental choice. Environmental policies play a critical role in determining both the form of development and the direction for the development of an economy. Such policies help to prioritise the problems that society wishes to target, and to identify the means by which they are to be pursued. Green policies help to enable the shifting of the emphasis of an economy away from extractive and primitive industries and towards economies based on the development of human, natural and knowledge-based capital for the achievement of prioritised problem-solving.

5.2 Green development paths: the direction of development

The *direction of development* refers to the mix of goods and services that an economy targets. One of the key functions of environmental policy is simply to ensure that the economy is producing the precise mix of goods and services that citizens desire.[13]

This is an essential role for environmental policy in any economy. A purely market economy is only able to produce those goods and services that are able to be supplied through private markets and transactions. When this is the case the market must oversupply any and all private-market goods and services relative to public goods such as environmental goods and services.[14] Environmental regulation is then the means for supplying that mix of public and private goods that is demanded.

[12] Foray, *The New Economics of Technology Policy*.

[13] See A. B. Jaffe, S. R. Peterson, P. R. Portney and R. N. Stavins, 'Environmental Regulation and the Competitiveness of US Manufacturing: What Does the Evidence Tell Us?' (1995) 33 *Journal of Economic Literature* 132.

[14] This observation points to the 'demand-side' role for cost-benefit analysis and the 'supply-side' role for environmental regulation in the mixed economy. Cost-benefit analysis becomes the government's means for assessing the appropriate mix of goods and services actually demanded by consumers.

The implied relationship between economic growth and environmental regulation is also apparent from this description. As economic growth advances in an unregulated market, the mix of private and public goods becomes increasingly unbalanced. Since the market will respond to the demand for private goods but not to public, increasing growth must continue to contribute to this unbalance. The unmet demand for public goods then translates into a demand for environmental regulation to supply them.[15] Then environmental policies are put into place simply to choose a particular complex of goods and services.[16]

Environmental policy in this view is primarily the means for providing the link between societies' demands for goods and services and the mechanism for the supply of the goods demanded. In an exclusively market-based economy all production will be private goods production, until environmental policies are installed to make more complex forms of demand and supply feasible. Here the choice of a green development path is simply the choice of the mix of desired goods and services.

5.3 Green development paths: the form of development

Environmental regulation does more than shift production towards environmental goods and services. Environmental regulation also places a value on the environment, and disallows its unregulated use in production. For the first time the economy is provided with signals and prices that indicate that the public good is valued and that its production should be targeted. It is the creation of this signal that adds to the efficiency of the overall economy and provides the potential for dynamic impacts beyond the change in static production priorities.

Of course, the efficiency impact of any signal depends upon the quality of the signal provided, and this depends upon the form and substance of the environmental regulation. Nevertheless, movement away from an economy that signals that one set of goods is valued at or near zero costs

[15] See N. L. Stokey, 'Are There Limits to Growth?' (1998) 39 *International Economic Review* 1.

[16] This shift away from private-only provision and towards mixed goods and services, in combination with increased growth, can then be charted as the 'environmental Kuznets curve' (EKC) (G. Grossman and A. Krueger, 'Economic Growth and the Environment' (1995) 110 *Quarterly Journal of Economics* 353). In this respect the EKC charts nothing other than the simple observation that there are diminishing returns to continuing supplies of unrestricted private goods, and that a more complex mechanism – for registering social demand and generating supplies – is required after private good production has passed some 'tipping point'.

(when clearly there are opportunity costs) must be efficiency enhancing. It provides the initial signal to the effect that the economy must expend some efforts on *investing* in conserving these resources and *innovating* around the restrictions they impose.

How much impact does regulation generate? The dynamic effect of the introduced signal is to be found in the reports on the 'costs of environmental regulation', in countries such as the USA, where regulation has long existed.[17] In response to US environmental regulation, R&D expenditures have comprised about 5 per cent to 6 per cent of all expenditures by US businesses on abatement costs. This is indicative of the amount of 'new thinking' that was instilled into the US economy as a result of the introduced regulation. These R&D expenditures are evidence of investments into changing the direction of the economy.

An example of such induced innovation might be the use of tradable permit systems to induce innovation in the production of combined energy-generation plants in the USA and the EU. Both jurisdictions imposed aggregate constraints on sulphur oxide (SO_X) production, implying a reduction of about 50 per cent in emissions of SO_X over a period of about ten years commencing from the mid-1990s. Such an aggregate constraint on SO_X production places an implicit price on the SO_X generated in energy production and creates an incentive to invest in techniques capable of reducing SO_X emissions per unit of energy.

How well did this new regulation work to alter the approach of industry in these jurisdictions? Once the regulation was in place and enforced,[18] the industry threw substantial resources into the resolution of the problem. A wide range of potential solution concepts was considered.[19] Potential solution concepts included new abatement technologies (e.g., high efficiency burners and flue-gas desulphurisation or FGD), new inputs (e.g., low-sulphur coal) and new locations (e.g., away from urban areas). In the USA, the introduction of SO_X regulation induced large investments in FGD and costs of abatement that were a small fraction of those initially projected.[20]

[17] See Jaffe et al., 'Environmental Regulation', 137.

[18] The US invested substantial resources into 'real time' monitoring system that is credited with giving real effect to the investment incentives achieved.

[19] The form of regulation is critical to the response achieved. At the same time a tradable permit system was implemented in the USA that enabled many processes and innovations to be considered for these purposes.

[20] The actual costs of abatement (measured in terms of FGD costs) were a small fraction of those that the industry claimed would be imposed via environmental policy. This is

This is a broad-based phenomenon. In a recent cross-EU study by Oosterhuis et al., the authors charted the decline of abatement costs after regulation in several recently regulated industries. They compared the costs of abatement *ex ante* (prior to regulation) to those existing *ex post* (after regulation was imposed). In general, the finding was that the costs of abatement across sectors declined by a factor of two. The introduction of incentives to investigate and implement resource-conserving technologies was effective in cutting production costs in half, once the regulations were introduced.[21]

This is indicative of the manner in which environmental policy shifts incentives for investments and decision-making within an industry. When resources are initially underpriced and systems undervalued, there is no reason to invest in thinking about conservation. Investments in such economies are simple and extractive. The adoption of environmental policies has the impact of causing the industry to think, for the first time, about how to be more efficient in the use of these resources. The industry shifts from being simple, extractive and consumptive, to having a problem-solving sector existing within its core.

In sum, environmental policy has an important role in determining the form of development in the country concerned. Environmental policy shifts the emphasis in an economy away from pure extraction and towards invention and innovation. It incentivises the creation of a problem-solving sector, and so encourages investments in human, natural and knowledge-based capital stocks. This is a clear and critical role for environmental policies in determining the form of future development.

5.4 Competitiveness: the benefits from green development paths

Environmental policies are key to shifting the emphasis of an economy onto a new *green development path*. This new development path is distinguished both by its *direction* – incorporating problem-solving at

because the industry's initial cost projections assumed that the industry would remain extractive and uninteresting, rather than dynamic and problem-solving. See S. Sorrell, 'Why Sulphur Trading Failed in the UK', in S. Sorrell and J. Skea (eds.), *Pollution for Sale: Emissions Trading and Joint Implementation* (Cheltenham: Edward Elgar, 1999), 170–207.

[21] See F. Oosterhuis et al., 'Ex-post Estimates of Costs to Business of EU Environmental Legislation', EU-Projekt, vorläufiger interner Schlussbericht, IVM (Amsterdam: Institute for Environmental Studies, 2006).

its core – and by its *form* – investing in new forms of capital to achieve new types of solutions.

The movement onto a green development path is almost certainly a means for attaining welfare improvements across a society, but it is often a means for attaining future growth improvement as well. This is because a shift away from basic production modes of development based on extraction and consumption, and towards more complex modes of development, can be a good long-term strategy for growth. There are several reasons why this shift might be good for long-term *competitiveness*, as well as for social welfare.

First, employing resource pricing can drive inefficiencies out of the economy, by removing those firms and industries that only exist on account of these implicit subsidies. The uncharged use of air, water and ecosystems is not a free good for anyone in an economy, and it is simply subsidising negative net worth activities. The first role of environmental regulation is to drive the economy in a more efficient direction.

Second, this is important not just for the pricing of natural capital and services but also for pricing all of the other inputs within the economy. An economy allocates its efforts and expenditures according to relative prices, and underpriced resources result in unbalanced economies. Economies should be targeting the future that they wish to achieve, and this will usually require a higher relative price on resources. An economy that wishes to develop around knowledge, R&D, human capital and innovation should not be providing free natural resources.

Third, employing resource pricing drives investments in R&D. It does so because the avoidance of costly resource use can be accomplished by means of finding new methods of production. Creating these positive resource prices creates the incentives to invest in finding new methods of production. Investment in innovation is driven through environmental regulation. This will include investment in all of the factors (human capital, knowledge) and all of the activities (R&D, innovation) listed above. Resource pricing is shifting the economy towards an emphasis upon different foundations of development.

Fourth, these investments may then generate innovation rents. Resource pricing that reflects scarcities that are prevalent in the local economy can also reflect scarcities prevalent more widely. For this reason, a solution to a problem of resource scarcity identified locally (via R&D investments) may have applicability and hence marketability more globally. The first solution to a widely experienced problem can be patented, licensed and marketed widely.

Fifth, aggressive environmental regulation may anticipate future widely experienced scarcities – and hence provide a template for other jurisdictions to follow. Such 'policy leadership' can be the first step in the process of innovation, investment, regulation and resource pricing described above.

Finally, environmental regulation may be more about complementarities than about competitiveness. Economies that resemble or move together are more likely to fit together well. Environmental regulation that is consonant with that of other countries may aid the general functioning of the economy in trade and production relationships.

In sum, the benefits from environmental regulation flow down the environment pathway that comes from altering the direction of an economy. Regulation that enhances perceived resource prices creates incentives to shift the economy onto a completely different foundation: one based more on investments in innovation and its inputs – human capital, knowledge and R&D.

5.5 Choosing development pathways: the governmental role

Clearly, it is important to introduce environmental policies for the purpose of protecting environmental goods and services. This is the most basic role of environmental regulation – it provides some mechanism for creating the appropriate mix of both private and public goods (such as ambient air and water quality).

More importantly, environmental policies are a means for implementing a particular development path, not just a mix of goods and services. That is, it expressly provides the economic signals for the investments required to shift the economy in the desired direction. It is important that this forward-looking role of environmental regulation is recognised. It is not enough for regulation to be a simple engineering matter of cleaning up already existing messes from past production. The point of environmental policy is more directed to selecting the path forward than it is to clearing up the path behind.

It is the role of government to establish the priorities within an economy, and so the direction and form that development should take. Priority setting is a governmental role that cannot be abdicated to the market. The question of which problems to target is one that only society can answer – this is the core message of the economics of innovation policy. Governments must decide on the problems to target and the policies that will be used to engender investments in their resolution. It is this initial and fundamental governmental intervention that then generates the shift towards a problem-solving economy based on human, natural and knowledge-based capital.

It is important to recognise the role of environmental policy as one of a government's core instruments for the choice of the future of the economy. This is a role that cannot be abdicated. Governmental policies do elect the future path of development (direction and form), and it is simply a question of whether or not states employ this power to good use.

5.6 Green economies, green development paths and innovative investments

In the remainder of this chapter we set out the basic structure of analysis for understanding how environmental regulation can result in industrial prowess. We examine the arguments more specifically in the context of two case studies: one on Japan's industrial policy and another on Denmark's. In both cases we see how the prescient policies of these governments enabled their industries to take leadership in particular fields of important technologies. These were, basically, accurate forecasts of specific resource scarcities – which the governments got right.

5.6.1 Innovation and rents: the basic economics

The value of innovation lies in the conjunction of two distinct events: (a) the creation of an idea or innovation that makes it possible to achieve some consumer welfare at a reduced cost and (b) the ability to keep other firms from making use of this idea or innovation without permission (e.g., by taking out a patent).

Figure 5.1 assumes that the industry is an otherwise competitive one, with free entry and exit. This simply means that there are no barriers to markets and all factors of production (resources, labour and capital) are available to any potential entrant. These are reasonable assumptions with regard to most globalised industries. The initial level of production in such an industry is at Q, where the price of each unit is driven down to the minimum average cost of production (P = ACmin). This means that each plant in the industry is operating at an efficient scale, and selling at the same price.

The act of innovation may be represented by the shifting of the cost curves of a specific firm to the dashed lines set out in Figure 5.1. This means that this single firm has conceived of a way in which the same

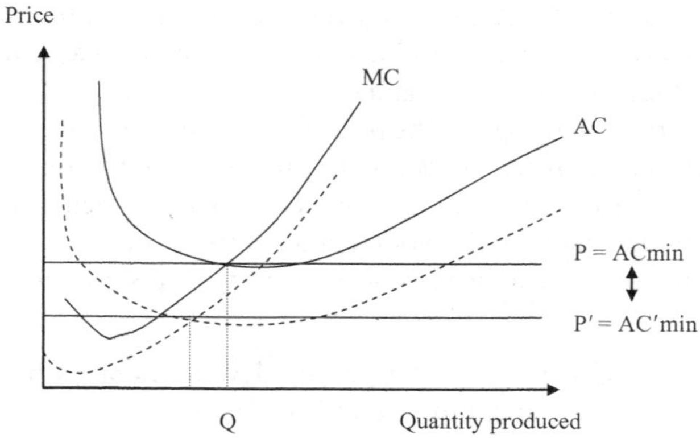

Figure 5.1 *The impact of an innovation – industry equilibrium and rent capture*

outcome (or output) may be achieved at a lower social cost – here represented by a shifting down of the cost of each unit of production (the dashed cost curves). If the innovating firm could not keep other firms from using the innovation, then the price of the good would fall to the new average cost (AC) and the consumers would capture all of the benefits (rents) of the innovation as the worldwide price fell to the new (lower) average cost (AC′min).

Rent-capture is available if the innovating firm is able to prevent other firms from freely using its innovation – for example, patents that make it possible for the innovating firm to prevent others from using its innovation without its permission. The innovating firm would then be able to charge every other firm a licensing fee (or 'innovation rent') equivalent to the difference between the average costs (ACmin – AC′min) on each unit of production, thereby capturing all of the benefits from its innovation in these licensing fees. Importantly, the global industry would be very likely to continue to operate precisely as before, with the same number of firms, the same amount of global output and very probably the same amount of output per firm; but now the innovator would be able to appropriate an 'innovation rent' on each unit of the good sold worldwide.

Then, in a sense, all of the firms in the industry would be working for the innovator. Their entry and continued operation in the industry continues only to the extent that they are able to generate this flow of licensing fees to the innovator. If the innovator feels that it is being cheated or disallowed its full rents by a firm, then it can simply withdraw its permission for the use of its technology and hence shut down the operation of that firm (since the firm cannot operate effectively in a global industry without the technology). Firms continuing in the industry may generate employment, production and even dividends – but the only real rents in the industry are being captured by the innovator. In that sense, technology leadership equates with ownership.

5.6.2 *Technology and policy leadership: the case of Japan*

Clearly, one way in which new ideas and innovative methods may be developed is by the industries themselves. Another way is for the government to take the lead. If a government foresees important scarcities or problems, and believes that it can take the lead in addressing them, then it may show policy leadership that may translate into technological leadership. In this case the government is choosing an industrial policy that will cause its industries to invest in particular cost-saving technologies. It is a gamble to do so – the government is betting that it is more accurate about future scarcities than is the general market view; however, there are many instances in which this has been the case.

Furthermore, all innovation requires some manner of government support, as discussed above. It is simply a matter of the government being proactive in its choice of development path, and hence its innovation pursuits. The following case study demonstrates how Japan made these choices in the 1970s, and thus developed world-leading technologies based upon its foresight regarding future energy prices.

5.6.2.1 Technology leadership

Japan is known for having done this in the case of energy efficiency. In the 1970s, the country took the decision to pursue policies supporting energy efficiency in its industries, cities and general way of life. At the time this was a reasonable policy to pursue in the face of high oil prices (on account of the OPEC crisis) and Japan's famous lack of indigenous oil resources. Japan undertook policy initiatives in industry (development of the hybrid car), in construction (development of solar heating and energy-efficient construction) and transportation (development of high-speed rail transit). For many years, these policies seemed poorly designed relative to current prices, as the oil price declined to reach historical lows by the end of the 1990s. Nevertheless, the continued pursuit of the policy gave Japan technology leadership in many of these fields. Its general lead in energy efficiency is indicated by its general level of economy-wide efficiency. As a result of these innovations, Japan now uses one-half the energy per unit of GDP as other developed countries and only one-fifth the energy per unit of GDP as China.[22]

More importantly, Japan now possesses the rights over specific technologies that other countries' firms will have to purchase if they wish to follow in Japan's path. An example of the sheer volume of innovations generated by this campaign is indicated by those cited in regard to car energy efficiency. Note that hybrid engine technologies are listed here as only one of twenty-eight different energy-saving technologies developed by the Japanese car industry (listed second from last in Figure 5.2).

Finally, these technological leads may then be converted back into policy leadership, when Japan asks other countries to adopt energy-efficiency policies similar to Japan's but twenty years later. Persuading other countries now to follow suit in policy means that the governments of other states then mandate (by parallel policies) that their industries adopt Japanese technologies (and pay Japanese firms the rents for their innovations). To illustrate how effective this policy leadership cycle can be, Prime Minister Fukuda has announced that Japan will support sector-based energy efficiency standards in the next phase of negotiations over a new climate change protocol. Adoption of this approach to climate change policy in a new climate change agreement would translate into an internationally adopted requirement that all firms purchase much of their technology from Japanese sector leaders (such as that listed in Figure 5.2).

5.6.2.2 Policy leadership in environmental regulation

Technology leadership comes when a country is successful at (a) creating unique innovations by making an investment in R&D related to future scarcities that are not yet widely perceived and (b) cementing leadership in those industries via the patenting of those innovations. When this is done successfully, and other countries' industries wish to pursue those technologies, then they have little choice other than to license them from the technology leader. In this way, and in accord with Figure 5.1, a technology leader is able to appropriate the rents of innovation from the need of others to follow that lead.

Why would other countries' industries wish to follow that lead? There are two fundamental reasons. First, it could be the case that the

[22] See International Energy Agency, *Energy Policies of IEA Countries* (Paris: OECD, 2008).

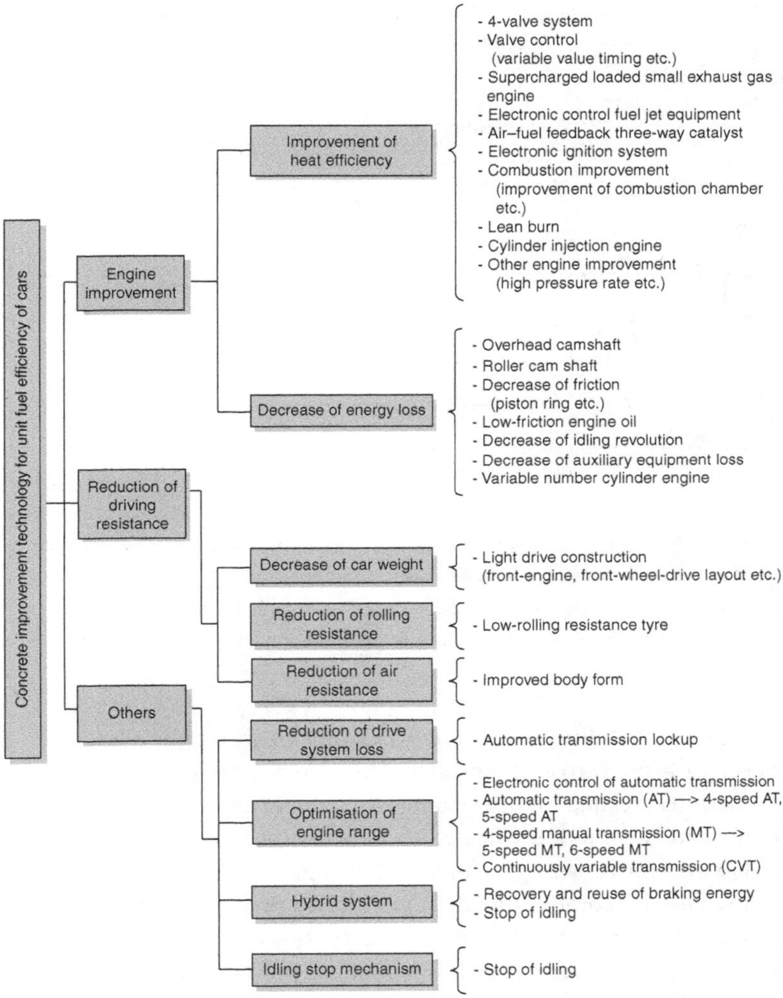

Figure 5.2 *Policy-driven innovations in the Japanese car industry*
Source: Energy Conservation Centre, *Japan Energy Conservation Handbook* (Tokyo: ECC, 2004–5), 243.

technology leader actually does bet on a particular form of resource scarcity in advance of its general recognition. Japan did this in the 1970s with regard to energy-conservation, and established a lead that is important now that the price of energy has increased significantly in real terms.

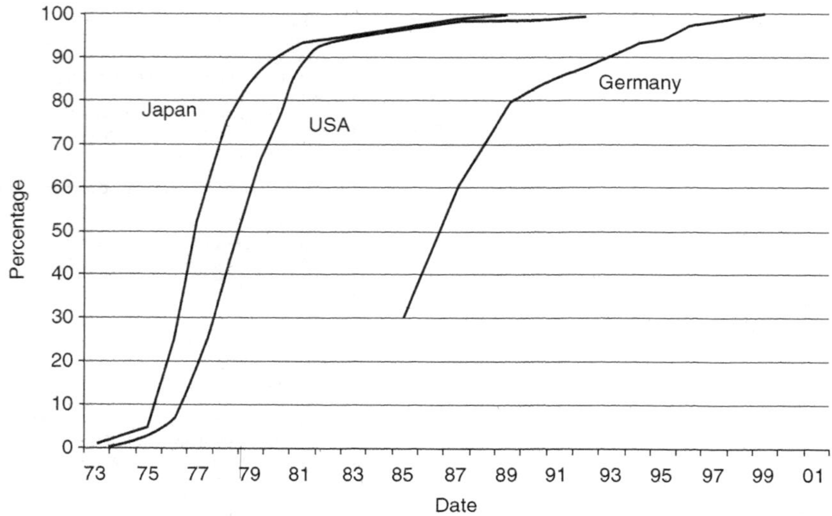

Figure 5.3 *The diffusion of catalytic converter technology – a function of policy leadership (share of passenger vehicles equipped with technology), 1973–2001*
Source: M. Beise, J. Blazejczak, D. Edler et al., *The Emergence of Lead Markets for Environmental Innovations* (Berlin: Forschungsstelle für Umweltpolitik, 2003), 20.

Another possibility is for a country to invest in a policy, and then see the policy diffuse across other states. This also happens in many cases, and is sometimes related to the change in real prices (e.g., in relation to energy) and is sometimes related to anticipating the directions in which societies will move with growth and development. For example, societies with increased incomes often demonstrate increased demand for particular sorts of goods, such as leisure, recreation, nature, health and other environmentally related goods. Establishing policy leadership in relation to the supply of these goods, and then having other states follow, can be sufficient to create technological and (consequently) industrial leadership.

There are numerous examples of the diffusion of technologies as a result of the diffusion of policies. One such example is the policy-related adoption of catalytic converters for the processing of emissions from car engines. This technology initially derived from the adoption of clean air emissions standards regarding mobile sources (cars) in 1970 in Japan and the USA, and then spread later throughout the developed world. Figure 5.3 illustrates the typical diffusion process of innovations, commencing with the states that were policy leaders and then diffusing later to those that were followers. Of course, the diffusion of the policies relating to car emissions was reflected in the adoption of the technology as well, and this resulted in the substantial transfer of policy-related rents to the early innovators.

More generally, the role of policy leadership is to anticipate the demands of the citizenry for changes in the sets of goods and services produced by the economy and to establish the policies that will meet these demands. As societies change, grow and develop, it is predictable that their citizens want and need different things, rather than simply more of the same. For this reason, the income-elasticities of different goods differ substantially over the course of development; some goods are demanded proportionally less as incomes rise (e.g., food), while others are demanded proportionally more as incomes rise (recreation, health and environment). One of the basic functions of environmental regulation is to anticipate these changes and to determine the relative proportions of different forms of goods and services produced by an economy.[23]

In any event, states that anticipate future change and establish desired policies first have the ability to become policy leaders in the field, and hence potentially establish technology leadership as well. Since the inception of environmental regulation, the policy leaders in this field have been the Scandinavian countries, the USA and Japan (see Table 5.1).

This policy leadership has often been translated into technology leadership, as industries respond to national policies with R&D and resultant patenting. The important consequence of such patenting concerns its adoption by others, and is represented by the proportion of patents won in other countries. This is demonstrated in Table 5.2, where it is shown that the majority of foreign patents in these fields have been won by the USA and Japan.

Note that Germany (not as much of a policy leader as the USA or Japan in these fields) needed to purchase the majority of its environmental technology from other states initially (71 per cent in air, 50 per cent in water and 52 per cent in car emissions), but then rapidly moved towards establishing technological leadership within its own borders. The USA on the other hand was a technological leader in all three fields, but lost its advantage particularly in the case of automotive emissions technologies. Japan started as a leader in these fields, and fortified its

23 See Stokey, 'Are There Limits to Growth?'.

Table 5.1 Policy leaders in environmental regulation

Country	1970–1985	1985–2000
Sweden (11)	7	4
USA (10)	8	2
Japan (9)	8	1
Denmark (9)	5	4
Finland (8)	4	4
France (7)	5	2
Germany (7)	5	2
The Netherlands (7)	3	4
UK (6)	4	2
Canada (6)	2	4
	51	29

Source: M. Janicke and K. Jacob, 'Lead Markets for Environmental Innovations: A New Role for the Nation State' (2004) 4 *Global Environmental Politics* 37.

positions across the board. In particular, Japan became the clear technological leader in the case of automotive emissions, after starting out as a joint policy leader together with the USA.

Despite these changing leads, it is important to recognise that the returns from initial policy leadership can be long-lasting, as important patents can have lifetimes of twenty years. It is possible to 'innovate around' existing patents, but many times it is necessary to pay the licensing fees to the initial innovator in order to stay in the industry. So, even if a state establishes leadership only briefly, it may be living off of the rents of that leadership for decades.

These patterns demonstrate how policy leaders benefit from anticipating emerging trends. The first state to establish an important policy, which then diffuses to others, is presenting its industry with the opportunity to establish technological leadership in an important global industry. A policy-induced patent that is filed first is sufficient not only to grant that industry domestic leadership but also the opportunity to capture global rents once the policy diffuses.

5.6.3 *Technology leadership: the Danish windmill industry*

It well known that Denmark has succeeded in acquiring a first-mover advantage on the world market for electricity production from wind

Table 5.2 Technology leadership resulting from policy leadership (sources of foreign patents by nationality of inventor)

Nationality of inventor	Industrial air				Water				Vehicle air			
	1972	1977	1982	1986/7	1972	1977	1982	1986/7	1972	1977	1982	1986/7
USA												
Japan	48%	28%	11%	38%	0%	21%	15%	23%	38%	82%	90%	35%
Germany	36	38	64	28	0	21	41	35	45	12	7	51
Other OECD	16	31	25	31	100	49	38	28	18	6	4	11
Other	0	0	0	3	0	9	6	3	0	0	0	2
Foreign/total in field	21%	32%	28%	32%	20%	33%	34%	26%	40%	66%	68%	65%
Japan												
USA	50%	46%	42%	64%	48%	44%	50%	83%	47%	33%	60%	100%
Germany	25	15	42	14	7	22	17	15	47	33	30	0
Other OECD	20	31	16	14	44	44	17	15	7	22	0	0
Other	0	0	0	0	0	0	17	0	0	0	0	0
Foreign/total in field	20%	13	19%	14%	27%	9%	6%	6%	15%	9%	10%	11%
Germany												
USA	37%	34%	45%	15%	40%	20%	22%	19%	35%	34%	70%	19%
Japan	48	34	16	27	10	14	11	3	50	48	11	27
Other OECD	13	32	37	58	50	61	57	71	15	8	20	46
Other	1	0	3	4	0	4	8	6	0	0	0	8
Foreign/total in field	71%	47%	38%	26%	50%	49%	37%	31%	52%	50%	56%	26%

Source: J. Lanjouw and A. Mody, 'Innovation and the International Diffusion of Environmentally Responsive Technology' (1995) 25 *Research Policy* 563.

Table 5.3 Wind resource availability in the European Union (relative onshore wind resources in the country case studies)

Country	TWh per year wind electricity production potential
Denmark	26
Spain	86
Germany	24
Scotland	54
The Netherlands	7
England and Wales	52

Source: D. Toke, S. Breukers and M. Wolsink, 'Wind-power Deployment Outcomes: How Can We Account for the Differences?' (2008) 12 *Renewable and Sustainable Energy Reviews* 1132.

power.[24] The industry began in the 1970s following active support from the government in response to the oil crisis, and was an outcome of that government's view that it was likely that there ultimately would be shortages of traditional energy sources such as oil and gas.[25]

Interestingly, Denmark is not one of the world's leaders in the availability of wind resources (Table 5.3). Many other states in Europe have greater wind resources. For example, Denmark's neighbour Norway has double the potential for wind generation but had less reason to look for policy leadership in this field (owing to Norway's energy resources). It was not the availability of the natural resource that determined Denmark's leadership, but rather the idea that some day this technology would be of importance in energy generation and the decision to take policy leadership in this field.

How did Denmark establish policy leadership? According to Hansen et al.,[26] the development of wind power technologies and the electricity produced has been encouraged through state subsidies prior to other states' intervention. Subsidies employed in Denmark included a price

[24] See J. Buen, 'Danish and Norwegian Wind Industry: The Relationship between Policy Instruments, Innovation and Diffusion' (2006) 34 *Energy Policy* 3887.

[25] See L. M. Kamp, R. E. H. Smits and C. D. Andriesse, 'Notions on Learning Applied to Wind Turbine Development in the Netherlands and Denmark' (2004) 32 *Energy Policy* 1625.

[26] See J. D. Hansen, C. Jensen and E. S. Madsen, 'The Establishment of the Danish Windmill Industry – Was it Worthwhile?' (2003) 139 *Review of World Economics* 335.

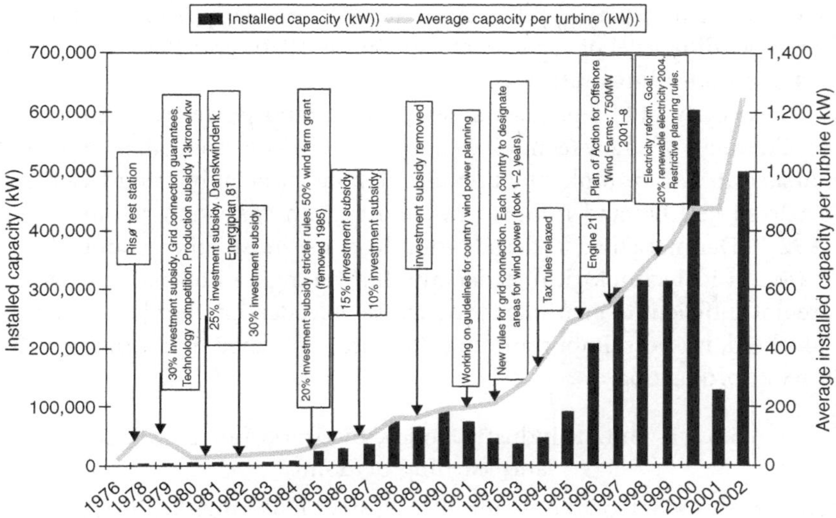

Figure 5.4 *Denmark's technology leadership and installed capacity*
Source: J. Buen, 'Danish and Norwegian Wind Industry: The Relationship between Policy Instruments, Innovation and Diffusion' (2006) 34 *Energy Policy* 3889.

guarantee per produced kilowatt hour to the owners of windmills, R&D subsidies, investment subsidies and an initially publicly funded wind energy research department.[27]

Hansen et al.[28] conclude that the price guarantee to owners of windmills was perhaps the most important of these as it made electricity produced from windmills profitable for private investors and hence competitive on the market for electricity produced by fossil fuels. Kamp et al.[29] highlight the importance having both producers and consumers of windmills close by at early stages of development so that the producers can gain continual feedback on their products from their customers in what they label as 'learning by interacting'.

In any event, it is clear that Denmark was the earliest proponent of the technology and one of the few states to invest in its development from a point as early as the 1970s (California also offered tax rebates on wind power generation in that decade).[30] Figure 5.4 illustrates the range of

[27] See Kamp, Smits and Andriesse, 'Notions on Learning', 1640.
[28] Hansen, Jensen and Madsen, 'The Establishment of the Danish Windmill Industry', 349.
[29] Kamp, Smits and Andriesse, 'Notions on Learning', 1642.
[30] Buen, 'Danish and Norwegian Wind Industry', 3892.

policies put into place by Denmark across these early decades and the corresponding level of capacity created in the 1970s and 1980s by reason of these leadership strategies.

These early public policies in support of wind power resulted in the development of a new technology a few years before most other countries pursued it. For example, the first installations in neighbouring Germany occurred in 1990 and in Spain (a country with vast wind resources) in 1992.[31] Denmark had a decade-long lead on most other countries by reason of its technological leadership. But timing and technology choice are not sufficient to guarantee the success of leadership. For leadership to take hold, it is also important that the state concerned invest in a certain level of production.

5.6.3.1 Infant industry policy, the importance of scale and learning by doing

The development of the windmill industry in Denmark illustrates the application of an 'infant industry' strategy as well as technological leadership. It is important to recognise that technological leadership consists of *early* backing for a novel technology and also of backing at a *scale* sufficient to encourage its development.

Scale of production is critical in the development of a new technology. The first units of production are always the most expensive in any production process with fixed costs, but especially so when large amounts of R&D are involved in the production process. This is simply by reason of the amount of fixed costs involved in developing ideas for new processes, prototypes for production processes and trials of the processes and products. All of these costs must be borne as R&D costs before a single unit of real production can occur. For this reason, subsequent units of product (for an accepted technology) will be produced at a much lower cost than the first units. The impact of scale is apparent in Danish wind turbine development after the initial developments in the 1970s. The average real cost of windmill production in Denmark more than halved over the period from 1983 to 1998.

Table 5.4 illustrates the yearly production of windmills in Denmark since 1983 measured by both number of windmills produced and 'total effect' or installation measured in megawatt hours. (It should be noted that in the early stages of development windmills were generally much

[31] See P. E. Morthorst, 'Capacity Development and Profitability of Wind Turbines' (1999) 27 *Energy Policy* 779.

Table 5.4 Production, effect and costs of Danish windmills, 1983–1998

Year	Number of mills	Effect in MW	Effect per mill in kW	Price per mill in DKK/kW (1980 prices)	Export ratio
1983	1,279	40	31	6,846	0.28
1984	1,694	117	69	6,287	0.93
1985	3,812	243	64	5,598	0.91
1986	2,246	212	94	5,176	0.84
1987	767	88	115	4,845	0.59
1988	597	102	171	3,978	0.23
1989	754	136	180	4,082	0.38
1990	723	162	224	4,323	0.54
1991	778	166	213	4,482	0.54
1992	712	165	232	4,343	0.71
1993	689	210	305	4,142	0.83
1994	1,144	368	322	3,882	0.88
1995	1,530	574	375	3,369	0.87
1996	1,360	726	534	3,433	0.69
1997	1,644	968	585	3,328	0.69
1998	1,742	1,216	698	3,191	0.74

Source: D. Hansen, C. Jensen and E. S. Madsen, 'The Establishment of the Danish Windmill Industry – Was it Worthwhile?' (2003) 139 *Review of World Economics* 327.

Note: Calculations in fixed prices are based on the deflator for gross factor income for the period 1983–93 and gross domestic product for 1993–8.

smaller and that larger windmills required considerably more technological expertise in developing but are far more efficient.) Column five lists the average real price of a windmill and column six lists the export ratio of windmills produced in Denmark. It can be seen that in five years the price per unit of capacity has fallen by more than half the price of 1983. As noted by Hansen et al.,[32] the substantial fall in price points to strong technological progress in the sector and that the data from statistical regressions they have run are consistent with the hypothesis of productivity growth by learning-by-doing (see below). Table 5.4 also

[32] Hansen, Jensen and Madsen, 'The Establishment of the Danish Windmill Industry', 338.

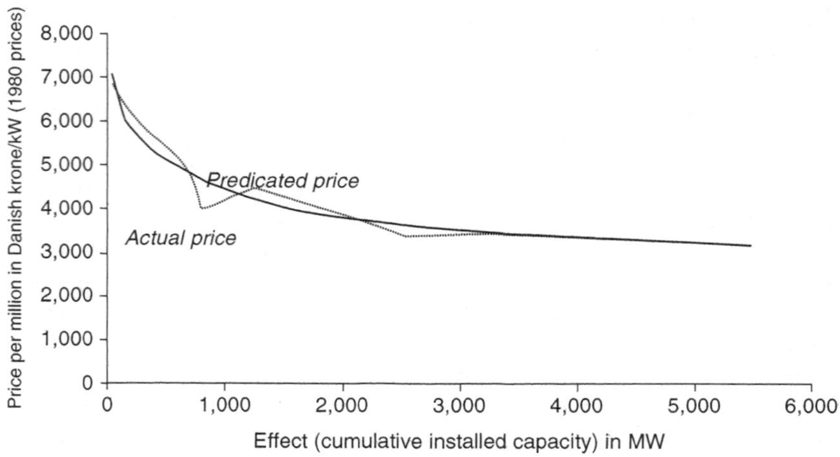

Figure 5.5 *Declining costs with scale of production (Danish experience)*
Source: D. Hansen, C. Jensen and E. S. Madsen, 'The Establishment of the Danish Windmill Industry – Was it Worthwhile?' (2003) 139 *Review of World Economics* 332.

shows that for most of the years the export share of total production has been above 70 per cent apart from a period in the late 1980s and early 1990s when the industry was in recession, most likely due to a slow response of the industry to demand for larger windmills.[33] Figure 5.5 graphs this decline in the costs of production as a function of scale.

This is a fairly general phenomenon. Lewis and Wiser[34] in their survey of wind power policies in twelve different countries concluded that policies that supported a sizeable and stable market for wind power were the most likely to result in the establishment of an internationally competitive industry. In short, any policy that assures a certain scale of production (after innovation) will both reduce average costs and encourage initial outlays on the R&D required to establish production.

5.6.3.2 The impact of technological leadership: enjoying success

As mentioned at the outset, a state pursuing technological leadership must have a vision of the future and must have that vision come to pass.

[33] *Ibid.*, 340.
[34] J. I. Lewis and R. H. Wiser, 'Fostering a Renewable Energy Technology Industry: An International Comparison of Wind Industry Policy Support Mechanisms' (2007) 35 *Energy Policy* 1844.

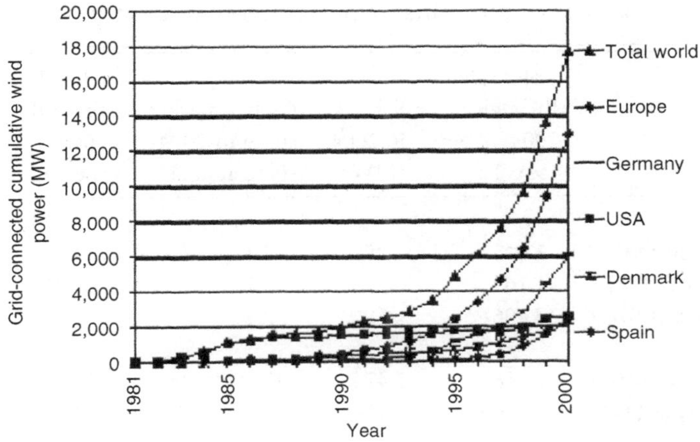

Figure 5.6 *Worldwide grid-connected cumulative installed megawatt of wind power*
Source: P. H. Kobos, J. D. Erickson and T. E. Drennan, 'Technological Learning and Renewable Energy Costs: Implications for US Renewable Energy Policy' (2006) 34 *Energy Policy* 1652.

In the case of Denmark's investment in wind generation, it has been very lucky in its leadership. The global investment in wind generation technologies has skyrocketed in the decades after Denmark's early policy adoptions.

Figure 5.6 demonstrates how the market for wind power has grown exponentially since the early 1980s, and given current fossil fuel prices and likely policies it seems that this growth is liable to continue. Although Denmark probably did not foresee the furore caused by concern over climate change, it did correctly project that excessive worldwide dependence upon fossil fuels would be viewed as increasingly problematic. Betting on this vision a mere ten years before the remainder of the world shared it has been a boon for its industry.

The vision exhibited by Denmark meant that it had the lead and experience in the technology when other states turned to it. This could be translated into either straightforward technology licensing or continued leadership in production and export. Denmark has continued to dominate in both. Denmark maintains a position of leadership in the global market for wind turbines, as can be seen from Table 5.5. In 2004, windmills produced in Denmark were estimated to account for 38.7 per cent of global market share. This compares with 20.5 per cent for

Table 5.5 Top ten wind turbine manufacturers by country

Country and companies	Total sales through 2004 (MW)	Sales in 2004 (MW)	Global market share in 2004 (percentage)	Global market share through 2004 (percentage)
Germany				
Enercon (#3)	7,045	1,288	15.1	13.9
REpower (#7)	1,169	276	3.2	2.3
Nordex (#10)	2,406	186	2.2	4.7
Spain				
Gamesa (#2)	6,438	1,474	17.3	12.7
Ecotecnia (#9)	744	214	2.5	1.5
USA				
GE Wind (#4)	5,346	918	10.8	10.5
Denmark				
Vestas (#1)	17,580	2,783	32.7	34.6
Siemens (#5)	3,874	507	6.0	7.6
India				
Suzlon (#6)	785	322	3.8	1.5
Japan				
Mitsubishi (#8)	1,019	214	2.5	2.0
Others	4,359	334	3.9	8.6
Total	50,765	8,513	100	100

Source: J. I. Lewis and R. H. Wiser, 'Fostering a Renewable Energy Technology Industry: An International Comparison of Wind Industry Policy Support Mechanisms' (2007) 35 *Energy Policy* 1849.

Germany and 10.8 per cent for the USA. This feat is even more remarkable given that Denmark is one of the world's smallest countries, with approximately 5 million people. In addition, a significant number of the prevailing patents in wind turbine technology will be held by Danish citizens, so that the use of Danish technology is probably universal. Since 1975, Danish companies have been granted thirty-three patents relating to wind power.[35] The importance of leadership is that it produces value for the state, irrespective of its own production. Other states must purchase the technology, either by licence or embedded in the end product.

35 See Buen, 'Danish and Norwegian Wind Industry', 3895.

Table 5.6 Comparison of Danish and Norwegian wind industries

	Denmark	Norway
Employment	21,000	200–300[i]
Turnover (million €)	2,500	25–40[i]
Share of world market 2004 (percentage)	38.5	≈ 0[i]
Export (percentage of produce)	85–98[a]	95[i]
Cumulative installed capacity (MW end 2003)	3076	101
Share of electricity consumption (percentage)	19.7[b]	0.25
Patents (1975–2004)	33	6

Source: J. Buen, 'Danish and Norwegian Wind Industry: The Relationship between Policy Instruments, Innovation and Diffusion' (2006) 34 *Energy Policy* 3898 and references therein to BTM consult (2004) and windpower.org (2003). Own estimates (marked[i]) and search on 'wind', matched with 'Denmark' and 'Norway', respectively, in EPIDOS-INPADOC Patent Family and Numerical List (PFS/INL) databases (Delphion; www.delphion.com).
[a] Differs between the three major manufacturers. Average is about 95 per cent
[b] In 2003, 15 per cent, but would have been 19.7 per cent in normal wind year.

An additional value to 'learning by doing' lies in the capacity for the country to undertake the production for others at a significant scale and hence at least cost. This ensures that other goals (such as employment) can also be served. Table 5.6 illustrates the importance and strength of the Danish wind industry compared with its Scandinavian neighbour Norway (which holds double the wind resources of Denmark). As noted by Buen,[36] the wind industry is Denmark's third largest exporter, a major employer (21,000 people) and possesses a market turnover of €2.5 billion.

Denmark established leadership in this field, enabling it both to claim patent rights in an important technology and to stake out production advantages in an important field. The former was sufficient to enable the state to claim a significant share of the value created in the new industry, but the latter enabled the achievement of other goals as well (production, employment and exports). The vision that Denmark displayed in foreseeing problems with existing energy generation technologies created technology leadership and a burgeoning industry.

[36] See *ibid.*, 3898.

5.6.3.3 Policy and technology leadership: Danish wind turbine technologies

In short, Denmark managed to foresee the adoption of wind turbine technologies as an important policy goal at least one decade before other states. This lead allowed Denmark to undertake early investments to create novel technologies and to establish claims to the patents for important developments in the field. The thirty-three patents on wind turbine technology were sufficient to enable Denmark to stake a significant claim to all value that subsequently developed when other states adopted the technology.

Equally as important, Denmark also invested in developing sufficient scale of production in the industry to lower the costs of production and make itself the obvious candidate for continuing production of anything relying upon the technology. Other states must still invest in 'learning by doing', even if they decide to purchase the technology, and so Denmark's early technological leadership in the field has translated into ongoing demand for its production. This enables the achievement of other equally important industrial goals (production, employment).

States that do not pursue technological leadership opportunities are destined to purchase their technologies from others. This means that those states perceiving the direction of technological progress will always have others paying them to undertake production in the fields in which they are leaders. Just as importantly, states perceiving the direction of progress may also invest to stake claims to the production in those fields, and only give up those territories when other preferred modes of production appear. Failure to pursue these opportunities translates into voluntary relegation to the bottom tier of global production.

CONCLUSION

The pursuit of the green economy is a topic of conversation in many ministries at present, environmental and economic. It is clear that green growth is a desirable environmental outcome, but many persons and papers are also making claims for it as an economic pathway to success.[37]

[37] See above nn. 1 and 2.

This chapter has shown that environmental policies can be sound economic policies if the state concerned 'guesses right'. That is, these sorts of policies are examples of innovation policies operated by a state for purposes of pursuing either policy or technology leadership. When a state is able to achieve leadership through intervention and investment, there are real competitiveness returns to be acquired. The case studies of such interventions made by the governments in Japan and Denmark indicate how this has been done successfully in the past.

There are two important caveats to be made concerning such interventions. First, as the woes of the financial crisis reveal, speculative investments can go wrong as often as they go right. States that choose to invest in a particular development path can be right about being leaders, or very wrong, and the results that they achieve will depend upon the accuracy of their guesswork. The speculativeness of green growth policies is important to recognise.

Secondly, and equally significantly, it is important to recognise that the decision to invest in environmentally constructive industries is not a bad bet these days. The resources and the systems of the earth are under heavy stress and the rapid growth of populations and economies indicates that these stresses are on a steep trajectory. It is not terribly speculative to invest now in industries and innovations that might be able to avoid the worst of these pressures. It is probably more risky to continue to invest in industries that represent 'more of the same'.

So, the economics of the green economy indicates that state intervention is important for fostering investments in innovation and growth. The best sorts of interventions and investments will be those that are truly environmentally innovative, leading to new forms of enterprise that place less pressure on environmental resources. It is a good guess that other countries will also need to move in this direction – now or in the near future. Investing in the green economy is about taking the lead in making these investments when they really matter – for purposes of both environmental and economic outcomes. The time to make those investments is now – in order to be a leader in the competition to find ways of reducing pressure on environmental resources.

Select bibliography

Arrow, K., 'The Economic Implications of Learning by Doing' (1962) 29 *Review of Economic Studies* 155.

'Economic Welfare and the Allocation of Resources for Invention', in K. Arrow (ed.), *The Rate and Direction of Inventive Activity: Economic and Social Factors* (Princeton, NJ: Princeton University Press, 1962), pp. 609–25.

Barbier, E. B., *A Global Green New Deal: Rethinking the Economic Recovery* (Cambridge University Press, 2010).

'Green Stimulus, Green Recovery and Global Imbalances' (2010) 11 *World Economics* 1.

Blair, R. D., and T. F. Cotter, *Intellectual Property: Economic and Legal Dimensions of Rights and Remedies* (Cambridge University Press, 2005).

Foray, D. (ed.), *The Economics of Technology Policy* (Cheltenham: Edward Elgar, 2010).

Grossman, G., and A. Krueger, 'Economic Growth and the Environment' (1995) 110 *Quarterly Journal of Economics* 353.

Jaffe, A. B., R. Newell and R. Stavins, 'Environmental Policy and Technological Change' (2002) 22 *Environmental and Resource Economics* 41.

Jaffe, A. B., S. R. Peterson, P. R. Portney and R. N. Stavins, 'Environmental Regulation and the Competitiveness of US Manufacturing: What Does the Evidence Tell Us?' (1995) 33 *Journal of Economic Literature* 132.

Jaffe, A. B., and R. Stavins, 'Dynamic Incentives of Environmental Regulations: The Effect of Alternative Policy Instruments on Technology Diffusion' (1995) 29 *Journal of Environmental Economics and Management* 43.

Janicke, M., and K. Jacob, 'Lead Markets for Environmental Innovations: A New Role for the Nation State' (2004) 4 *Global Environmental Politics* 29.

Jorgenson, W., and P. J. Wilcoxen, 'Environmental Regulation and US Economic Growth' (1990) 21 *Rand Journal of Economics* 314.

Kamien, M. I., and N. L. Schwartz, *Market Structure and Innovation* (Cambridge University Press, 1982).

Kobos, P. H., J. D. Erickson and T. E. Drennan, 'Technological Learning and Renewable Energy Costs: Implications for US Renewable Energy Policy' (2006) 34 *Energy Policy* 1645.

Lanjouw, J., and A. Mody, 'Innovation and the International Diffusion of Environmentally Responsive Technology' (1995) 25 *Research Policy* 563.

Lewis, J. I., and R. H. Wiser, 'Fostering a Renewable Energy Technology Industry: An International Comparison of Wind Industry Policy Support Mechanisms' (2007) 35 *Energy Policy* 1844.

Porter, M. E., and C. van der Linde, 'Toward a New Conception of the Environment-Competitiveness Relationship' (1995) 9 *Journal of Economic Perspectives* 97.

Stoneman, P. (ed.), *Handbook of the Economics of Innovation and Technological Change* (Oxford: Blackwell, 1995).

Swanson, T., and Z. Ziegelhofer, 'Economic Frameworks for Thinking about Growth, Sustainability and State Intervention: Paths to Green Economies', UNEP Working Paper (2011).

Teece, D. J., 'The Market for Know-how and the Efficient International Transfer of Technology' (1981) 458 *Annals of the Academy of Political and Social Science* 81.

United Nations Environment Programme, *The Green Economy Report* (Nairobi: UNEP, 2011).

Williams, E., K. Macdonald and V. Kind, 'Unravelling the Competitiveness Debate' (2002) 12 *Journal of European Environmental Policy* 284.

11

Foreign investment and environmental protection: incentives

6

Key instruments of private environmental finance: funds, project finance and market mechanisms

MAGNUS JESKO LANGER

INTRODUCTION

Environmental finance is increasingly becoming a central preoccupation of most private-sector actors around the globe. In the context of a global framework for sustainable development and the latest proposals to shift global production systems into the new era of 'green economy', a multitude of financial instruments have been developed to respond to these new challenges and to provide new incentives for private-sector actors to invest a larger portion of their assets in environment-friendly technologies. This chapter analyses the three main pillars of the emerging environmental finance field, i.e., private funds, project finance and market mechanisms, and it assesses their effectiveness in providing the investments necessary for a sustainable world economy. The main contention of this chapter is that although profit-making remains the principal incentive among private-sector investors one cannot assess the growing role played by the private sector in environmental protection without understanding a series of financial instruments specifically designed for this purpose.

6.1 Environmental finance: an overview

Environmental finance or 'green investing' can be defined for the purposes of this chapter as the investment activities of the private sector designed to enhance the efficiency of production systems so as to reduce the ecological footprint of companies or projects.[1] Generally speaking,

[1] For the evolution in terminology, see R. Urwin and C. Woods, 'Sustainable Investing Principles: Models for Institutional Investors', paper presented at the PRI Academic Conference 2009, 1–3 October 2009, Ottawa, Canada. Robins, Krosinsky and Viederman

the main challenge is to develop innovative mechanisms that channel financial assets into markets for environmental technologies by providing convincing incentives for the private sector to engage in eco-friendly investing. Arguably, the notion of private sector, as opposed to public sector, is an extremely large category, which could potentially include consumers and most not-for-profit organisations, in particular NGOs. In this chapter, private sector refers to three main categories of actors: first, asset holders, including also individuals and NGOs desiring to invest their assets in green projects; secondly, asset managers, for example, managers of funds that can provide funding for foreign investments; and thirdly, corporations in need of funds that they intend to invest in new ventures abroad.

Although the focus here is on the private sector, one cannot ignore the importance of the public sector and its role in catalysing new investments in the green economy. Not only do states strive to create safe investment environments, to provide incentives, to channel public funds and to promote new innovations through research and development (R&D) projects,[2] but they also pool their efforts to create international structures that address environmental problems and that seek to incite the private sector to participate in the global effort to tackle the most serious environmental threats such as climate change, biodiversity loss, pollution, desertification and water management issues.[3] The international

provide the following definition of sustainable investing: 'Sustainable investing is an investment philosophy that explicitly considers *future* environmental and social trends in financial decision making, in order to provide the best risk-adjusted and opportunity-directed results for investors. By anticipating these trends ahead of the market, sustainable investing seeks to identify "predictable surprises" that can help protect & enhance shareholder value over the long-term.' N. Robins, C. Krosinsky and S. Viederman, 'After the Credit Crisis – the Future of Sustainable Investing', 1 September 2009, available at www.unpri.org (accessed 25 April 2011).

2 See e.g. Norway's efforts to channel resources into the promotion of sustainability with instruments such as the National Fund for Research and Innovation or the Government Pension Fund. See more generally OECD, *Policy Framework for Investment* (Paris: OECD Publications, 2006); OECD, *Promoting Private Investment for Development: The Role of ODA* (Paris: OECD Publications, 2006); OECD, *Tax Incentives for Research and Development: Trends and Issues* (Paris: OECD Publications, 2002). See also the *OECD Principles and Guidelines for Access to Research Data from Public Funding* (Paris: OECD Publications, 2007). For an analysis of the effectiveness of fiscal policies to stimulate private sector R&D, see B. Hall and J. van Reenen, 'How Effective are Fiscal Incentives for R&D? A Review of the Evidence' (2000) 29 *Research Policy* 449.

3 See e.g. UNEP's call for a Global Green New Deal and UNEP's efforts to articulate the new enabling conditions necessary to foster an effective transition towards a 'Green Economy'. UNEP, *Towards a Green Economy: Pathways to Sustainable Development and Poverty*

community of states has repeatedly called on the private sector to help in the effort to reduce the destruction of the world's ecosystems and to take the lead in financing such efforts.[4] In 2009, the Secretary-General of the United Nations, Ban Ki-moon, stated to the business community that the 'United Nations and business need each other. We need your innovation, your initiative, your technological prowess. But business needs the United Nations. In a very real sense, the work of the United Nations can be viewed as seeking to create the ideal enabling environment within which business can thrive.'[5] Also, according to the OECD Guidelines for Multinational Enterprises, corporations

> should, within the framework of laws, regulations and administrative practices in the countries in which they operate, and in consideration of relevant international agreements, principles, objectives, and standards, take due account of the need to protect the environment, public health and safety, and generally to conduct their activities in a manner contributing to the wider goal of sustainable development.[6]

Eradication (2011). See also E. B. Barbier, *A Global Green New Deal: Rethinking the Economic Recovery* (Cambridge University Press and UNEP, 2010).

[4] For instance, the following was stated in the World Summit Outcome held by the United Nations General Assembly in 2005 to review the implementation of the Rio plan: 'We acknowledge the vital role the private sector can play in generating new investments, employment and financing for development', A/RES/60/1, para. 23(e).

[5] Reproduced in *Revised Guidelines on Cooperation between the United Nations and the Business Sector*, 20 November 2009.

[6] See the 2011 edition of the *OECD Guidelines for Multinational Enterprises* (Paris: OECD Publications, 2011), 42, point VI. See more generally S. F. Vendzules, 'The Struggle for Legitimacy in Environmental Standards Systems: The OECD Guidelines for Multinational Enterprises' (2010) 21 *Colorado Journal of International Environmental Law* 451; G. Schuler, 'Effective Governance through Decentralized Soft Implementation: The OECD Guidelines for Multinational Enterprises' (2008) 9 *German Law Journal* 1753; C. N. Franciose, 'A Critical Assessment of the United States' Implementation of the OECD Guidelines for Multinational Enterprises' (2007) 30 *Boston College International & Comparative Law Review* 223; E. Morgera, 'An Environmental Outlook on the OECD Guidelines for Multinational Enterprises: Comparative Advantage, Legitimacy, and Outstanding Questions in the Lead Up to the 2006 Review' (2006) 18 *Georgetown International Environmental Law Review* 751; B. Utz, 'Die OECD-Leitsätze für multinationale Unternehmen: Eine erste Bilanz der Wirkungsweise des Vermittlungs- und Schlichtungsverfahrens der Leitsätze anhand der abgeschlossenen Beschwerdefälle bei Nationalen Kontaktstellen 2000 bis 2005', Artec-Paper No. 134, Universität Bremen, July 2006; M. Klinkenberg, 'Die Leitsätze der OECD für multinationale Unternehmen' (2002) 101 *Zeitschrift für vergleichende Rechtswissenschaft* 421; S. Tully, 'The 2000 Review of the OECD Guidelines for Multinational Enterprises' (2001) 50 *International and Comparative Law Quarterly* 394.

There are many different techniques to provide environment-related economic incentives for the private sector. Economic incentives usually supplement the more traditional command-and-control (CAC) approaches adopted by most states.[7] One distinguishes generally between negative and positive incentives. Negative incentives or disincentives are regulatory measures prohibiting, restricting or taxing certain activities that are considered as having a negative impact on the environment. For instance, the 1987 Montreal Protocol[8] prohibits the production of certain ozone-depleting substances that are directly relevant for private-sector activities. Positive incentives on the other hand are designed to provide monetary or non-monetary advantages to those private-sector actors adopting certain behaviours that are presumed to be beneficial for the environment. Such incentives may be of a regulatory nature, such as certification schemes, investment tax credits,[9] export credit guarantees, subsidies or the recently developed feed-in tariff schemes for the production of electric energy using renewable resources in Germany, Spain or Italy, or the Renewables Obligation schemes in the United Kingdom. Yet, most positive incentives are increasingly based on market mechanisms developed by the private sector itself.[10] Indeed, these range from the creation of sustainability

[7] The US Environmental Protection Agency defines economic incentives as 'any instrument that provides continuous inducements, financial or otherwise, to encourage responsible parties to reduce their releases of pollutants or make their products less polluting. This definition includes fees, charges and taxes, charges on polluting inputs and outputs, tradable permits, subsidies, deposit-refund systems, as well as reporting requirements, and liability for harms. Some voluntary mechanisms also are included'; *International Experiences with Economic Incentives for Protecting the Environment*, November 2004, at p. i. As explained in this report, the main difference between economic incentives and CAC methods is that each unit of pollution has a continuous cost under the economic incentives approach, whereas pollution may have no cost or nearly no cost once CAC regulations have been satisfied. Economic incentives 'give those responsible for sources of pollution … an incentive to reduce pollution below permitted amounts when it is relatively inexpensive to do so', *ibid.*, 2.

[8] Montreal Protocol on Substances that Deplete the Ozone Layer, 16 September 1987, 1522 UNTS 3 (Montreal Protocol).

[9] The USA has used investment tax credits (ITCs) and production tax credits (PTCs) as a means to stimulate growth in the renewable energy sector. See e.g. R. Wiser, M. Bolinger and G. Barbose, 'Using the Federal Production Tax Credit to Build a Durable Market for Wind Power in the United States', *The Electricity Journal* (2007) 20.9 77–88; J. Logan and S. M. Kaplan, 'Wind Power in the United States: Technology, Economic, and Policy Issues', Congressional Research Service, June 2008 www.fas.org/sgp/crs/misc/RL34546.pdf.

[10] A 2009 HSBC study estimates that governments have globally allocated over US$445 bn in green stimulus packages to boost investment in the low carbon economy. N. Robins,

indexes which seek to outperform core industry indexes to the possibility to increase the investors' exposure to emerging markets through diversification schemes, the facilitated access to funds for projects that engage in sustainable development practices, the lowering of the costs of capital or enhanced reputation. All this would ideally lead over time to an increase in competition in sustainable practices amongst private-sector entrepreneurs seeking access to so-called green capital. These latest developments may stem from the fact that the triangular relationship between civil society, public sector and private sector is shifting from an alliance between civil society groups and governments to a *rapprochement* between civil society and the private sector in order to overcome the hesitant policy signals given by governments, particularly when it comes to the design of a post-Kyoto climate change regime. In the end, the emergence of the so-called green economy will depend more on the ability of the private sector to respond to the needs of civil society, rather than on the capacity of the public sector to harness the private sector. If investors increasingly perceive and anticipate higher returns on eco-friendly production patterns, this would in turn facilitate the police function of states because they would then have to focus only on the recalcitrant producers that do not wish to engage in sustainability efforts.

This chapter focuses on three broad categories of financial instruments or techniques currently available to private-sector actors as incentives to invest in eco-friendly technologies or to adopt eco-friendly production methods. The first section of this chapter delves into the complex world of funds and analogous techniques (collective investment schemes). These are amongst the privileged means used by the private sector to channel the necessary assets into the so-called sustainability market. The second section will discuss project finance and its role in infusing sustainable production practices through contractual agreements that render the disbursement of funds conditional on compliance with specific environmental standards.[11] The International Finance Corporation (IFC) has led the way over the past decade on this front and serves as a model for other multilateral development banks, as well as for commercial development banks and other financial

R. Padamadan and R. Clover, 'More Green Money on the Table', *HSBC Global Research*, 31 March 2009, available at www.endseurope.com (accessed 25 April 2011).

[11] On project finance, see generally J. Dewar (ed.), *International Project Finance: Law and Practice* (Oxford University Press, 2011).

intermediaries.[12] In the third section, we briefly discuss certain market mechanisms which not only provide additional incentives for corporations to reduce their ecological footprint because of the cost of compliance but also allow corporations to manage their compliance issues through tradable pollution rights. Besides the well-known clean development mechanism (CDM) and joint implementation (JI) under the Kyoto Protocol,[13] other market mechanisms include the emerging framework on land use, land-use change and forestry (LULUCF),[14] together with the United Nations Collaborative Programme on Reducing Emissions from Deforestation and Forest Degradation in Developing Countries (UN-REDD Programme).[15] Attention will also

[12] See e.g. S. Park, 'World Bank Group: Championing Sustainable Development Norms?' (2007) 13 *Global Governance* 535; D. B. Hunter, 'Civil Society Networks and the Development of Environmental Standards at International Financial Institutions' (2008) 8 *Chicago Journal of International Law* 437; A. Hardenbrook, 'The Equator Principles: The Private Financial Sector's Attempt at Environmental Responsibility' (2007) 40 *Vanderbilt Journal of Transnational Law* 197; K. Herbertson and D. Hunter, 'Emerging Standards for Sustainable Finance of the Energy Sector' (2007) 7 *Sustainable Development Law & Policy* 4; R. F. Lawrence and W. L. Thomas, 'The Equator Principles and Project Finance: Sustainability in Practice' (2004) 19 *Natural Resources & Environment* 20; R. Bailey, T. Ryan and N. Hodges, 'Building on Sustainability into Syndication' (2006) *Environmental Finance* 28; C. Wright and A. Rwabizumbuga, 'Institutional Pressures, Corporate Reputation, and Voluntary Codes of Conduct: An Examination of the Equator Principles' (2006) 111 *Business & Society Review* 89; S. Hadfield-Hill, 'The Greening of Project Finance' (2007) 1 *Geography Compass* 1058; T. Papadopoulos, 'The "Greening" of Project Finance: Is this a Viable "Project"?' (2009) 7 *The Icfai University Journal of Banking Law* 8; M. Marco, 'Accountability in International Project Finance: The Equator Principles and the Creation of Third-Party-Beneficiary Status for Project-Affected Communities' (2011) 34 *Fordham International Law Journal* 452.

[13] D. Freestone and C. Streck (eds.), *Legal Aspects of Carbon Trading* (Oxford University Press, 2009); M. Wara, 'Measuring the Clean Development Mechanism's Performance and Potential' (2008) 55 *UCLA Law Review* 1759; N. Fujiwara, 'Flexible Mechanisms in Support of a New Climate Change Regime: The Clean Development Mechanism and Beyond', Centre for European Policy Studies (Brussels, 2009); A. M. Halvorssen, 'Kyoto Protocol and Developing Countries – The Clean Development Mechanism' (2005) 16 *Colorado Journal of International Environmental Law & Policy* 353; M. Moliner-Dubost, 'Le Mécanisme pour un développement propre: une nouvelle voie de coopération et de transferts nord/sud' (2004) *Revue générale de droit international public* 963.

[14] I. Sagemüller, 'Forest Sinks under the United Nations Framework Convention on Climate Change and the Kyoto Protocol: Opportunity or Risk for Biodiversity?' (2006) 31 *Columbia Journal of Environmental Law* 189; IUCN, *Carbon, Forests and People: Towards the Integrated Management of Carbon Sequestration, the Environment and Sustainable Livelihoods* (2002).

[15] A. J. Plantinga and K. R. Richards, 'International Forest Carbon Sequestration in a Post-Kyoto Agreement', in J. E. Aldy and R. N. Stavins (eds.), *Post-Kyoto International Climate*

be given to the so-called green investment schemes and the payment for environmental or ecosystem services (PES) schemes.[16] These instruments will only be briefly mentioned, as they are analysed in detail in Chapters 7 and 8.

The main conclusion that can be derived from this analysis is the existence of a plethora of financial instruments available to those private-sector actors that wish to invest their assets in sustainable production practices. Emerging economies, unlike many other developing countries, are increasingly successful in taking advantage of these new instruments by attracting such resources into their countries. Also, the temporal element is particularly relevant in this context. The existing financial techniques not only allow asset holders and asset managers to address short- or long-term risks, but through them corporations have the opportunity to obtain funds at all stages of the production cycle, from the start-up to the decommissioning of a project. Financial institutions, especially international financial institutions, also increasingly offer an added value to their strictly financial activities by providing advisory services that help investors and producers to manage their activities over long periods. Finally, it is notable that international law is becoming increasingly relevant in such matters as states try to push the

Policy: Implementing Architecture for Agreement (Cambridge University Press, 2010), 682–711; J. E. Viñuales, 'Análisis prospectivo del mecanismo de reducción de emisiones derivadas de la deforestación y de sus variantes (RED, REDD, REDD+)' (2009) 09 *Perspectivas*; C. Stockwell, W. Hare and K. Macey, 'Designing a REDD Mechanism: The TDERM Triptych', in B. J. Richardson et al. (eds.), *Climate Law and Developing Countries: Legal and Policy Challenges for the World Economy* (Cheltenham: Edward Edgar, 2009), 151–77; L. V. Verchot and E. Petkova, 'The State of REDD Negotiations: Consensus Points, Options for Moving Forward and Research Needs to Support the Process', Centre for International Forestry Research (Bogor, 2010); E. Myers, 'Policies to Reduce Emissions from Deforestation and Degradation (REDD) in Tropical Forests', Discussion Paper 07–50, Resources for the Future, Washington, DC (2007).

16 UNEP, *Payments for Ecosystem Services. Getting Started: A Primer* (UNEP, Forest Trends, 2008); R. Jindal and J. Kerr, 'Valuing Environmental Services', in *USAID PES Sourcebook: Lessons and Best Practices for Pro-Poor Payment for Ecosystem Services* (2007) Brief 3.2; S. Wunder, 'Payments for Ecosystem Services: Some Nuts and Bolts', Occasional Paper No. 42, CIFOR (2005); S. Scherr, A. White and A. Khare, 'For Services Rendered: The Current Status and Future Potential of Markets for the Ecosystem Services Provided by Tropical Forests', International Tropical Timber Organization (2004) www.forest-trends.org; K. Georgieva, S. Pagiola and P. Deeks, 'Paying for the Environmental Services of Protected Areas: Involving the Private Sector', paper presented at Fifth World Park Congress, Sustainable Finance Streams, IUCN (2003); G. Daily, *Nature's Services: Societal Dependence on Natural Ecosystems* (Washington, DC: Island Press, 1997).

sustainability agenda by creating new financial mechanisms regulated by international norms and practices.

6.2 Private funds

Funds, or, generally speaking, collective investment schemes, are pooled assets managed under a specific legal structure, designed for investment in profitable economic activities. There is a large variety of different funds that perform distinct tasks and have different approaches to risk management. The main incentive for asset holders to invest their assets in funds is to reduce their exposure to risk by diversifying their portfolio. Although private for-profit funds manage the overwhelming amount of available assets, increasingly more not-for-profit funds,[17] public funds[18] and international funds[19] are created which actively pool assets for

[17] For instance, the Living Planet Fund, the Environmental Defense Fund or the CDKN Innovation Fund.

[18] Such as the Austrian Climate Fund, the Bulgarian National Trust EcoFund, the Czech Environmental Protection Fund, the French Global Environment Facility, the German Climate Fund, the Lithuanian Environmental Investment Fund, the Polish EcoFund or the Slovenian Environmental Development Fund. See generally OECD, *Handbook for Appraisal of Environmental Projects Financed from Public Funds* (Paris: OECD, 2007).

[19] For instance, the Global Environment Facility (GEF), which, besides providing grants to developing and emerging economies for projects related to climate change, biodiversity, land, water and air degradation, and serving as a financial mechanism for four major multilateral environmental agreements, seeks to provide incentives for the private sector in order to leverage more funds into sustainability projects that are consistent with GEF objectives. The GEF has also sought to promote public–private partnerships by deploying pilot projects, some of which ultimately materialising into financial mechanisms such as the GEF Earth Fund. To this effect, the GEF has adopted various policy frameworks, such as the 'GEF Strategy to Enhance Engagement with the Private Sector', GEF/C.28/14, March 2006, and the 'Additional Information to Support the GEF Strategy to Enhance Engagement with the Private Sector', GEF/C.28/Inf. 4, 10 May 2006. For the revised strategy, see 'Strategy to Engage with the Private Sector', G/C.40/13, 25 April 2011, and 'Revised Strategy for Enhancing Engagement with the Private Sector', GEF/C.41/09/Rev. 01, 10 November 2011. See generally L. Boisson de Chazournes, 'The Global Environment Facility (GEF): A Unique and Crucial Institution' (2005) 14 *RECIEL* 193. For regular updates on international climate funds, see the Climate Funds Update website www.climatefundsupdate.org (accessed 25 April 2011). With regard to the climate change negotiations under the UNFCCC, and in accordance with the initial provisions contained in the Copenhagen Accord of 18 December 2009, the parties to the UNFCCC accepted at the end of 2011 in Durban to establish the Green Climate Fund, endowed with a private sector facility destined to finance private sector mitigation and adaptation activities and promote private sector involvement and participation. UNFCCC, 'Green Climate Fund', Draft Decision -/CP.17, available at http://unfccc.int/2860.php (accessed 20 December 2011). See also 'Copenhagen Accord', FCCC/CP/2009/11/Add.1, Decision 2/CP.15, paras

specific purposes, most notably for social and environmental purposes. The environmental component is playing a growing role both in the diversification schemes adopted by fund managers, notably to attract more capital, and in the creation of environmental funds that devote large amounts or all of their assets to environment-related objectives – 'sustainable and responsible investment' or 'socially responsible investing' (SRI). After a short outline of the volume of this market, the main types of investment vehicles will be presented and the regulatory framework from an international law perspective will be analysed.

6.2.1 *The SRI market in the private fund industry*

The global amount of private assets under professional management was estimated in 2009 at a stunning US$105 trillion.[20] The largest part is covered by conventional funds, around US$71 trillion, which include pension funds (US$28 trillion), mutual funds (US$22.9 trillion) and insurance funds (US$20.4 trillion).[21] The rest is made up of alternative funds, such as exchange-traded funds (ETFs), private equity (PE) funds or hedge funds, and the private wealth funds of high-net-worth individuals. Faced with such numbers, it becomes clear that the biggest stake lies in the capacity to tap into these capital markets to channel greater amounts of available funds into sustainable investing.

According to various reports, no other financial industry has grown more over the past two years than SRI, i.e., the green investment industry.[22] SRI is used here as a generic term 'covering any type of

8 and 10; 'The Cancún Agreements', FCCC/CP/2010/7/Add.1, Decision 1/CP.16, paras 102–11 and Appendix III, 'Terms of Reference for the Design of the Green Climate Fund'.

20 Fund Management 2010, TheCityUK, October 2010, 2. 21 *Ibid.*

22 In Germany, for instance, the SRI market has grown by 16% overall since 2007, and mutual funds engaged in SRI practices have grown by 37% to reach €5.9 bn, or 0.9% of the total volume of German mutual funds. See Eurosif, *European SRI Study 2010*, 36. The Social Investment Forum Foundation explains that 'the pool of assets engaged in SRI strategies has grown more rapidly than the overall investment universe due to a number of factors, including net inflows into existing SRI products, the development of new SRI products and the adoption of SRI strategies by managers and institutions not previously involved in the field', Report on Socially Responsible Investing Trends in the United States, Social Investment Forum Foundation, 2010 (Report SIF), 8. For an analysis of factors that hinder the emergence of an effective SRI market in Germany, see F. J. Preu and B. J. Richardson, 'German Socially Responsible Investment: Barriers and Opportunities' (2011) 12 *German Law Journal* 865.

investment process that combines investors' financial objectives with their concerns about Environmental, Social and Governance (ESG) issues'.[23] The global volume of SRI assets under management is estimated by the European Social Investment Forum at nearly €7.6 trillion in 2010.[24] According to a 2010 Report of the US Social Investment Forum, professionally managed assets in the USA working with ESG criteria represented an estimated US$3.07 trillion, i.e., over 12 per cent of the totality of assets under professional management in the USA, estimated at US$25.2 trillion.[25] Between 2007 and 2010, the number of US funds involved in SRI (ESG funds)[26] rose from 260 to 493, with an estimated total of US$569 billion of assets under management.[27] In the European Union, the assets under management incorporating ESG issues have doubled between 2008 and 2009 reaching around €5 trillion.[28] With respect to emerging economies, the Institute of International Finance estimates that net private capital inflows have reached US$908 billion in 2010 and are estimated to reach US$960 billion in 2011 and over US$1 trillion in 2012.[29] According to the IFC, some US$300 billion are

[23] Definition taken from Eurosif, *European SRI Study 2010*, 7. See also B. J. Richardson, 'Financing Sustainability: The New Transnational Governance of Socially Responsible Investment' (2007) 17 *Yearbook of International Environmental Law* 73.

[24] Eurosif, *European SRI Study 2010*, 59. The estimation lay at €5 trillion in the 2008 Study; Eurosif, *European SRI Study 2008*, 52.

[25] Report SIF, 8. According to a 2010 UK study, total conventional assets under management in the USA amounted to a little more than US$35 trillion. Of these, US$18 trillion are managed by pension funds, US$11 trillion by mutual funds and US$6.5 trillion by insurance companies. See Fund Management 2010, TheCityUK, October 2010, 2.

[26] These include mutual funds, closed-end funds, exchange-traded funds, alternative investment funds and other pooled products. Two hundred and fifty mutual funds were identified within the USA that incorporate ESG criteria in their investment decisions, with total assets under management worth US$316.1 bn.

[27] Report SIF, 9. SIF tracks the ESG record of US mutual funds in its *Socially Responsible Mutual Fund Charts*, available at www.socialinvest.org (accessed 25 April 2011).

[28] Eurosif, *European SRI Study 2010*. See also C. Juravale and A. Lewis, 'Identifying Impediments to SRI in Europe: A Review of the Practitioner and Academic Literature' (2008) 17 *Business Ethics: A European Review* 285.

[29] Institute of International Finance, Capital Flows to Emerging Market Economies, IIF Research Note, 24 January 2011. Out of the US$908 bn of net private capital inflows in 2010, equity investment represented the bulk, with net inflows of US$550 bn, including US$350 bn in direct investment and US$199 in portfolio investment. According to a 2008 report by the McKinsey Global Institute, developing countries held only around 20% of global financial assets, and accounted for almost 50% of the growth in that sector, reaching US$38 trillion in 2007. Equity markets grew most, accounting for 72% of the increase in 2007. See McKinsey Global Institute, *Mapping Global Capital Markets: Fifth Annual Report*, October 2008, 14.

invested in projects that incorporate ESG criteria in the developing world.[30] Although international financial institutions, analysed further below, make a targeted effort to channel private-sector investments to developing countries of Africa, the largest share of funds invested outside of Europe and North America flows to the emerging economies. The case of clean energy investments is telling in this respect.

Several studies have revealed that global investments in clean technology reached new heights in 2010 with US$243 billion.[31] The main beneficiaries of these capital flows have been G-20 countries, with China attracting the largest share.[32] The Pew Charitable Trust has analysed three scenarios of possible growth of clean energy investments throughout the G-20, which underlines the importance of clear policy signals from governments.[33] Under the first scenario, based on current policies, the cumulative investments between 2010 and 2020 could reach an estimated US$1.75 trillion. Under the second scenario, i.e., if all states adhered to the commitments made following the Copenhagen Accord of December 2009, the clean energy industry could generate cumulative investments over the next ten years of up to US$1.86 trillion. Finally, under the third scenario, which requires states to adopt enhanced clean energy policies in line with the recommendations made by the IPCC in its fourth Assessment Report, the estimated investments over the next ten years would represent a US$2.3 trillion opportunity. With the exception of South Africa, a member of G-20, the rest of Africa is excluded from the analysis. Conscious of this problem, the African Development Bank (AfDB) has developed various strategies to create a clean energy investment framework for Africa.[34]

30 H. Birgden, D. Guyatt and X. Jia, *Gaining Ground: Integrating Environmental, Social and Governance (ESG) Factors into Investment Processes in Emerging Markets*, IFC and Mercer, March 2009, 4, 14.

31 Pew Environment Group, 'Who's Winning the Clean Energy Race? G20 Investment Powering Forward', *Pew Charitable Trusts*, 2010 Edition, 4. This industry has grown from US$51 bn in 2004 to US$76 bn in 2005, US$113 bn in 2006, US$150 bn in 2007, US$180 bn in 2008 and US$186 bn in 2009. See also Clean Energy Investment Storms to New Record in 2010, Bloomberg New Energy Finance, press release, 11 January 2011.

32 China received clean energy investments in the order of US$54.4 bn. Germany accounted for US$41.2 bn, the USA for US$34 bn, Italy for US$13.9 bn, the rest of the European Union for US$13.4 bn, Brazil for US$7.6 bn, Canada for US$5.6 bn, Spain for US$4.9 bn, France for US$4 bn and India for US$4 bn. See 'Who's Winning the Clean Energy Race?', 11.

33 Pew Environment Group, 'Global Clean Power: A $2.3 Trillion Opportunity', *Pew Charitable Trusts*, 2010, 17–24.

34 *Proposals for a Clean Energy Investment Framework for Africa: Role of the African Development Bank Group*, Tunis, 25 April 2008.

6.2.2 *Diversification of SRI investment vehicles*

Traditional and more recent investment vehicles have largely been put at the disposal of SRI. For instance, all collective investment schemes, both conventional and alternative funds, have in some way or the other been utilised for SRI. Conventional funds include pension funds, insurance funds and mutual funds, whereas alternative funds of the private sector include PE funds, venture capital funds, exchange-traded funds and hedge funds. Whereas hedge funds mostly serve as an example of funds from which not much should be expected in terms of channelling resources into sustainable production systems, at least for the time being,[35] all other types of funds present promising opportunities for SRI. Furthermore, all these funds invest increasingly in different types of asset classes, moving slowly from equity-dominated portfolios to more balanced portfolios with investments in bonds and the money market.[36] This has stimulated certain countries and some international financial institutions to issue green bonds whose proceeds are used for sustainable development projects. Another important development has been the multiplication of sustainability indexes in the main financial stock exchanges around the world. Companies selected in these indexes are gaining facilitated access to investments and thus stimulate at the same time a competitive drive amongst capital-seeking companies in terms of sustainable governance.

For various reasons mutual funds present greater challenges in terms of SRI than other types of funds, one of them being the sheer amount of capital at their disposal, estimated globally at US$23 trillion. This amount is, however, only second to pension funds and not so far ahead of insurance funds. What distinguishes mutual funds from pension funds is mainly that the latter seem more prone to include SRI criteria in their investment strategies because their outlook is oriented in the long term.

[35] For instance, the Virgin Climate Change Fund has been reported to invest a good part of its assets in sin stocks such as alcohol or the arms industry. See C. Gilchrist, 'The Virgin Climate Change Fund is Too Hot to Handle', 23 January 2008, available at www.every-investor.co.uk (accessed 25 April 2011); F. Pearce, 'Virgin Money's Climate Change ISA Gets Richard Branson in a Pickle', 15 October 2009, available at www.guardian.co.uk (accessed 25 April 2011).

[36] Eurosif, *European SRI Study 2010*, 17. According to the study, 'equities have lost their preferred SRI asset class status, dropping down to 33% of total AuM, compared to 50% in 2008. Bonds are now the favoured asset class, representing 53% of assets at the European level.'

They would primarily look to place their equity investments in companies having long-term, sustainable, chances of success, which most likely includes reducing environmental risks as far as possible. The other reason is that pension funds exert a special social function of holding and managing the future retirement incomes of the working population. This explains why they are more regulated than mutual funds in general, and sometimes also with respect to ESG issues in particular. Thus, for instance, German[37] and UK pension funds are required to submit information, which should explain, 'the extent, if at all, to which social, environmental or ethical considerations are taken into account in the selection, retention and realisation of investments'.[38] Mutual funds, on the other hand, are the primary vehicle with which asset owners can exert their commercial freedom and invest in whatever assets seem most profitable. Thus, the regulatory framework around mutual funds frequently lags behind those applicable to pension or insurance funds. Mutual fund managers therefore need to show particular skills in sustainable investing if they intend to make a convincing business case for the green economy. On the other hand, they are less risk averse and may therefore provide significant capital flows to emerging market economies with safe investment environments and reliable policy signals from policymakers.

[37] Pension funds in Germany are held to disclose whether, and to what extent, ESG criteria are taken into account in their strategic investment decisions. See Section 7, para. 1 of the Altersvorsorgeverträge-Zertifizierungsgesetz, AltZertG of 26 June 2001 (Act on the Certification of Retirement Arrangement Contracts), as amended on 23 July 2009, BGBl. (Federal Gazette) 2009 vol. I, p. 1959.

[38] This is the so-called Statement of Investment Principles. See the Pension Protection Fund (Statement of Investment Principles) Regulations 2005 No. 675, 6 April 2005, sect. 4(2)(g). The same statement must also indicate the kinds of investments that are included in the Board's investment strategy (lit. (b)) and the Board's policy (if any) in relation to the exercise of the rights (including voting rights) attaching to investments (lit. (h)). See also Article 12 of the Directive 2003/41/EC of the European Parliament and of the Council of 3 June 2003 on the activities and supervision of institutions for occupational retirement provision. The OECD also recommends the adoption of socially responsible investment policies by pension funds: 'An investment policy is a key mechanism for identifying and managing investment risk. Pension funds should have a written policy in place, covering at a minimum strategic asset allocation, performance objectives, any broad decisions regarding tactical asset allocation, and trade execution. The use of external managers and establishing mechanisms for monitoring the costs of their services. A socially responsible investment policy may also be added to the overall investment strategy, outlining how the pension fund intends to consider environmental, social and governance risks.' See OECD/IOPS, *Good Practices for Pension Funds' Risk Management Systems*, 2011, para. 4.2.

Mutual funds are the most basic investment vehicles utilised by retail and institutional investors.[39] They are open-ended funds that pool together assets of private investors in order to invest them in various types of securities, such as stock, bonds or money market funds.[40] Today, there are over 65,000 mutual funds worldwide,[41] and whereas only a handful of mutual funds specifically incorporated ESG criteria in their investment policy at the beginning of the 1990s, there are several hundred mutual funds around the world today that explicitly engage in SRI. Interestingly, the issue of sustainable investing in this industry has largely been asset holder driven. It all started at the end of the 1980s and the beginning of the 1990s, when some asset managers were increasingly questioned by asset owners on where their capital would be invested.[42] For instance, the stockbroker Amy Domini and her partners first created the Domini 400 Social Index in 1989, a basket of stocks of 400 large-cap US corporations identified as sustainable, and then the Domini Social Equity Fund. They increasingly came to understand that smart asset management could yield equal if not superior returns when environmental factors were included in the decision-making process.[43]

[39] Mutual funds find their origin in the USA. They find their equivalent in the unit trust in the United Kingdom and the SICAV (société d'investissement à capital variable) in France, Switzerland, Italy and Spain. For general information on mutual funds, see H. Scott, *International Finance: Law and Regulation* (London: Sweet & Maxwell, 2008), 599–640.

[40] These types of funds have to be registered in their state of incorporation and typically involve a triangular legal structure composed of the fund shareholders, the fund manager and a trustee or board of directors, whereby the fund's assets are kept separated from those of the fund manager who makes the decisive investment decisions. They present the advantage for investors that their shares can be directly redeemed with the fund at the daily net asset value (NAV).

[41] Investment Company Institute, *Investment Company Fact Book 2010: A Review of Trends and Activity in the Investment Company Industry*, 50th edn (Investment Company Institute, 2010), 182.

[42] Ethical investing, i.e., the negative screening of sin stocks, such as alcohol, tobacco or arms, dates back to the 1930s in the United Kingdom and the 1970s in the USA. However, screening with respect to environmental issues only came to the forefront during the 1980s.

[43] There have been numerous studies that have sought to assess whether green investing outperforms more traditional investment benchmarks, such as the S&P 500 Index. For further references, see L. Renneboog, J. Horst and C. Zhang, 'Socially Responsible Investments: Methodology, Risk Exposure and Performance', Finance Working Paper 175/2007, 2007. For its part, the IFC has stated that there is a positive correlation between the inclusion of ESG criteria in its portfolio and financial performance. According to Haydee Celaya, Director of IFC's Private Equity and Investment Funds Department, 'results from analysis of IFC's own portfolio shows that companies with higher ESG scores also

Fund managers may decide to increase their exposure to the green market for a number of reasons. Private capital flows are increased when public resources are devoted to stimulate growth in a certain sector. An investor coalition stated in its 2010 'Investor Statement on Catalyzing Investment in a Low-Carbon Economy' that

> investors will seek every sound investment opportunity, but until governments establish policies and rules that make low-carbon strategies the *clear strategic choice* for all businesses, we will not be able to deploy capital into low-carbon investments at the scale required. Until then, our billions of dollars in investments will remain a 'drop in the bucket' compared to the trillions of dollars needed.[44]

This statement goes on to add 'it is imperative that public money allocated to address climate change be spent in a way that leverages private capital to the maximum extent possible by altering the risk–reward balance of private-sector investments'.[45]

Existing funds may start to include green investments in their portfolio merely to reduce risk through diversification. More fundamentally, fund managers adopt a wide array of strategies to manage and select their portfolio. They may have either a short-term or long-term outlook, they may choose to be value or growth investors (or a hybrid, such as GARP),[46] they may adopt passively or actively managed portfolios or simply be index-tracking, and they have various ways to incorporate ESG

perform better on financial criteria', cited in *Sustainable Investing in Emerging Markets: Unscathed by the Financial Crisis* (IFC, 2009), 20.

44 2010 Investor Statement on Catalyzing Investment in a Low-Carbon Economy (2010 Investor Statement), 3 (emphasis added), available at www.incr.com (accessed 25 April 2011). With regard to the question of the need for clear, certain and reliable policy signals from the public sector, Kevin Parker, global head of Deutsche Asset Management, says that 'what investors need most from national and state legislatures are transparency, longevity and certainty'. He further explains the impact that a lack of clear policy signals could have with the example of the USA. 'Until the US Congress passes climate regulation, America will be at a competitive disadvantage in the development of renewable energy and other climate change industries.' Cited in 'Investors Representing US$13 Trillion Call on US and other Countries to Move Quickly to Adopt Strong Climate Change Policies', *UN-Business Focal Point Newsletter*, Issue 13 (May 2010), available at http://business.un.org (accessed 15 April 2011).

45 2010 Investor Statement, 6. Thomas Werner, CEO of SunPower, stated the same idea in the following way: 'The key is to have incentives that last more than a year or two. It's hard for investors to commit with that kind of long-term uncertainty'. Cited in 'Who's Winning the Clean Energy Race?', 15.

46 GARP stands for 'growth at a reasonable price' and refers to a strategy that combines growth and value investing.

criteria in their decision-making process. For instance, 'analysis of market evaluations' and 'targeted stock selection strategies' are increasingly based on screening criteria reflecting certain ESG standards.[47] The European Social Investment Forum (Eurosif) distinguishes between core and broad SRI. With core SRI, asset managers select their stocks by excluding certain categories based on specific norms or values (negative screening) and further operate positive screening such as best-in-class or the choice of thematic funds. If, for instance, an investment manager decides to screen its potential equity investments against the ten principles of the Global Compact,[48] his or her investments would be considered as forming part of core SRI. Broad SRI on the other hand may include a lighter screening process, the simple integration of ESG criteria in their investment decision or the engagement with the corporations on ESG issues.[49] It has been estimated that out of the €5 trillion of SRI assets under management in Europe, €1.2 trillion are core SRI and €3.8 trillion fall under broad SRI.[50] As new environmental funds are created every year, the amount of core SRI is bound to increase in the years to come.

Aside from open-ended mutual funds, there are a variety of other collective investment schemes that provide additional choices and incentives for asset holders. Exchange-traded funds (ETFs) may provide a convenient way for retail investors to channel their assets into SRI. ETFs are asset pools that trade at the stock exchanges and track a specific index. Asset holders can either redeem their shares directly with the fund or sell them on the secondary market. They are very recent investment schemes that emerged in the USA in 1993 and were introduced into the EU in 2000, but their market share rapidly increased in the last years,

[47] C. Krosinsky, 'Sustainable Equity Investing: The Market-Beating Strategy', in C. Krosinsky and N. Robins (eds.), *Sustainable Investing: The Art of Long-Term Performance* (London: Earthscan, 2008), 19–30.

[48] See www.unglobalcompact.org (accessed 25 April 2011). For further information, see below, n. 61.

[49] Engagement usually takes the form of continuous dialogue on ESG issues or of direct shareholder activism.

[50] Eurosif, *European SRI Study 2010*, 11. According to an IFC study, only 7% of all financial products available in the emerging market economies are branded as SRI. The study explains that 'to some extent, this underestimates the true number of SRI funds available to investors, as there are a significant number of funds available which are not branded as SRI, but which do follow socially responsible practices ... Whilst only a small number of products are marketed as SRI, almost half of the products take ESG issues into account within their investment process. This corresponds to the 46% of managers who have a policy on ESG.' *Gaining Ground*, 16.

suggesting their significant potential for SRI.[51] In the case of SRI funds, they present the advantage for retail investors that they provide them with a predetermined portfolio of public equity investments in corporations that have good environmental ratings. An example is the Power Shares Global Clean Energy Portfolio, an ETF tracking the WilderHill New Energy Global Innovation Index. It is also possible to track the performance of ETFs against the traditional benchmarks of the finance industry such as the S&P 500 index. The trouble with ETFs or with mutual funds that invest in public equity is that their resources are overwhelmingly invested in mid- or large-cap companies and that insufficient resources are channelled into nano-, micro- and small-cap companies. These last categories are the preferred domain for PE funds, including venture capital funds.[52] Start-up and young firms that seek to develop innovative technologies are often constrained to have recourse to PE funds that seek higher returns for their investments. However, PE funds typically have a medium- to long-term horizon that may increase their interest for SRI.[53] Whereas the 2008 economic crisis has hit the PE industry hardest, reducing its capital flows by a staggering 70 per cent, PE investments still have the potential to provide valuable resources to small corporations in developing countries. The total assets under management are estimated to be at US$2.5 trillion, with around 40 per cent (or US$1 trillion) representing funds available for investment.[54] The vast majority of PE funds raised come from the USA (66 per cent), and the rest from Europe (15 per cent), Asia (15 per cent) and other parts of the world (4 per cent). Some 37 per cent of the funds raised are thereafter invested in Europe, 36 per cent in North America, 21 per cent in Asia/Pacific and 6

[51] There was a 45% increase in 2009 of assets invested in ETFs, reaching a record US$1.032 trillion. There were 1,939 ETFs trading on forty exchanges around the world. See Fund Management 2010, TheCityUK, October 2010, 4. Some observers indicate that socially responsible ETFs tend to outperform non-SRI ETFs. See J. Burton, 'Exchange-Traded Funds. Investing with Principles. Socially Responsibly ETFs are Multiplying, with a Variety of Approaches', *Wall Street Journal*, 4 April 2011.

[52] TheCityUK classifies venture capital into four possible stages: (1) the seed stage, which encompasses financing for research and feasibility studies before the start-up stage, (2) the start-up stage which refers to product development and initial marketing, (3) the expansion stage where funds are provided for growth and expansion of companies in good health and (4) replacement capital stage which applies to debt refinancing. See Private Equity 2010, TheCityUK, August 2010, 4.

[53] R. Kumar, 'Private Equity: Unlocking the Sustainability Potential', in Krosinsky and Robins, *Sustainable Investing*, 129–36.

[54] Private Equity 2010, TheCityUK, August 2010, 2.

per cent in other parts of the world.[55] Regarding venture capital, the global assets managed by venture capital funds are estimated at US$160 billion.[56] However, venture capital financing in the clean energy sector has rebounded strongly after the financial crisis, reaching US$8.1 billion in 2010, an increase of 26 percent over the last couple of years.[57]

Finally, it is worth mentioning that an increasing number of sustainability indexes are launched every year either at stock exchanges or by financial institutions. The main stock exchanges have engaged in this practice, thus providing more insight into the SRI industry and fostering disclosure of information.[58] The last stock exchange to have launched a new family of sustainability indexes is the German stock exchange in April 2011 with the STOXX Global ESG Leaders Indexes (including STOXX Global ESG Environmental Leaders).[59] This evolution is very positive as it not only illustrates a persistent drive of the investment community to receive easier access to information on companies and their ESG practices, but, more importantly, because it creates a competitive environment amongst publicly traded companies that need to incorporate ESG issues if they want to have facilitated access to capital by being listed on such sustainability indexes. Asset managers also use a variety of other eco-indexes tracking a specific sector or type of industry. Examples include the Bloomberg World Energy – Alternate Sources Index, the Merrill Lynch Renewable Energy Index or the Living Planet Green Tech Europe Index.

[55] *Ibid.* [56] *Ibid.*

[57] 'Who's Winning the Clean Energy Race?', 26. The report explains that out of the US$8.1 bn of venture capital SRI, the largest share was invested in energy efficiency (with US$2.8 bn), then in solar energy (US$1.5 bn), and the rest in wind energy, biofuels and other renewables.

[58] The more prominent examples are the large index families created by Stanley & Poor (S&P's global thematic index series, including S&P Global Clean Energy Index, S&P Alternative Energy Index, S&P Global Eco Index, or the S&P Global Water Index), FTSE (FTSE4Good Index Series or the FTSE Environmental Markets Index Series, including sector indexes such as FTSE EO Waste & Pollution Control Technology Index, FTSE EO Water Technology Index, FTSE EO Energy Efficiency Index, or the FTSE EO Renewable & Alternative Energy Index), NASDAQ (NASDAQ OMX Green Economy Index Family, NASDAQ OMX CRD Global Sustainability 50 Index, or the NASDAQ Clean Edge Green Energy Index), the Dow Jones (Dow Jones Sustainability Indexes, including Dow Jones Sustainability World Index or Dow Jones Sustainability Asia Pacific Index), or MSCI (MSCI Global Alternative Energy Index, MSCI Global Clean Technology Index, MSCI Global Sustainable Water Index, MSCI Global Green Building Index, or MSCI Global Pollution Prevention Index).

[59] See www.boerse-frankfurt.de (accessed 25 April 2011).

With these considerations in mind, two main observations can be made. First, the potential to channel funds into the green economy is enormous. The SRI market is booming and already mobilising several trillion US dollars for the purposes of sustainable investing. Second, traditional and new investment vehicles have become accessible for SRI. Investors wishing to include environmental criteria in their investment portfolio have the possibility to spread their risks by choosing from a wide panoply of financial tools. In fact, it is even plausible that many future innovations in the financial market will be SRI driven. What remains to be analysed is the legal framework surrounding SRI, i.e., to determine whether there is an emerging obligation incumbent upon investment managers and advisers to include ESG criteria in their investment decisions.

6.2.3 *Legal framework governing the investment industry*

With the exception of the European Union,[60] there is currently no international regulation of collective investment schemes. Funds are instead regulated under the jurisdictions where they have been incorporated or have registered. International regulatory efforts in the area of environmental finance have for the most part been channelled through UNEP FI and the UN Global Compact.[61] The Global Compact's 2004 'Who Cares Wins' initiative,[62] which sought to introduce ESG issues into

[60] Since 1985, the member states of the European Communities have sought to create a single market for financial services by adopting Council Directive 85/611/EEC on the coordination of laws, regulations and administrative provisions relating to undertakings for collective investment in transferable securities (UCITS Directive), last amended in 2008 through Directive 2008/18/EC. These UCITS are the equivalent of the French SICAV, the British unit trust or the American mutual fund.

[61] The UN Global Compact is a voluntary corporate citizenship initiative under the auspices of the United Nations. It was launched in July 2000 by UN Secretary-General Kofi Annan and pursues two objectives: to mainstream its ten principles into business activities around the world and to catalyse actions in support of UN goals. The Global Compact's ten principles touch on human rights, labour, the environment and anti-corruption. The three principles relating to the environment are derived from the Rio Declaration on Environment and Development, and read as follows: 'Businesses should support a precautionary approach to environmental challenges' (principle 7); 'undertake initiatives to promote greater environmental responsibility' (principle 8); and 'encourage the development and diffusion of environmentally friendly technologies' (principle 9).

[62] The Global Compact, *Who Cares Wins: Connecting Financial Markets to a Changing World* (December 2004). For an assessment of the 'Who Cares Wins' initiative, see IFC/FDFA/Global Compact, *Future Proof? Embedding Environmental, Social*

the investor community, was supplemented in 2006 by the 'principles for responsible investment' (PRI) initiative, a set of six principles on sustainable investment practices.[63] The PRI were launched in April 2006 at the New York Stock Exchange and they are intended to encourage large institutional investors to incorporate ESG issues into their decision-making processes. According to the latest numbers, 889 investment institutions have become signatories to these non-binding principles,[64] with an estimated US$25 trillion of assets under management. These efforts have been supplemented by many other initiatives of the business community, such as the Global Reporting Initiative,[65] the Carbon Disclosure Project and the revised OECD Guidelines for Multinational Enterprises. Thus, it seems fair to say that the current international framework heavily depends on the goodwill of the business community to incorporate ESG criteria as an integral part of its fiduciary duty.[66] Incentives are therefore largely developed by forces within the business community itself, levelling the way towards facilitated compliance with potential international norms that may emerge in the future. A myriad of business associations, networks, working groups and service providers have emerged seeking to foster sustainable investment practices within the business community, such as the US Social Investment Forum, Eurosif, the Association for Sustainable & Responsible Investment in

and Governance Issues in Investment Markets. Outcomes of the Who Cares Wins Initiative 2004–2008 (January 2009).

63 The six 'principles for responsible investment' are: (1) we will incorporate ESG issues into investment analysis and decision-making processes; (2) we will be active owners and incorporate ESG issues into our ownership policies and practices; (3) we will seek appropriate disclosure on ESG issues by the entities in which we invest; (4) we will promote acceptance and implementation of the principles within the investment industry; (5) we will work together to enhance our effectiveness in implementing the principles; and (6) we will report on our activities and progress towards implementing the principles. See www.unpri.org (accessed 25 April 2011).

64 Technically speaking, the signatories are not legally bound by these principles. However, the signatories voluntarily committed themselves to adopt the 'comply or explain' approach under which they undertake to comply with the principles and report on their implementation, or else to provide an explanation in cases of non-compliance.

65 See e.g. the 2002 Sustainability Reporting Guidelines, Global Reporting Initiative, available at www.epeat.net, and last version of March 2011, the G3.1 Guidelines, available at www.globalreporting.org/resourcelibrary/G3.1-Guidelines-Incl-Technical-Protocol.pdf (both websites accessed 25 April 2011).

66 Some have argued, however, that institutional investors shunning ESG screening may face lawsuits for negligence from their asset holders. See the 2009 UNEP FI Report, Fiduciary Responsibility: Legal and Practical Aspects of Integrating Environmental, Social and Governance Issues into Institutional Investment, UNEP FI, July 2009.

Asia (ASRIA), the Canadian Social Investment Organisation, the Sustainable Investment and Finance Association (UKSIF), the Coalition for Environmentally Responsible Economies (Ceres), the Enhanced Analytics Network[67] or companies such as Sustainalytics or Trucost.[68]

Yet, there is so far no regulation directing mutual funds to channel their assets through SRI. The main driver for SRI seems to come from the side of asset owners who are increasingly exercising pressure on their fund managers to disclose their investment policies. According to various surveys, the number of asset owners that include responsible investment factors into contracts with their external managers is growing.[69] With respect to climate change issues, a 2009 study indicates that asset owners increasingly push their asset managers to include considerations of climate change in their decision-making process. According to this study,

> asset owners are gradually becoming more proactive in asking climate change-related questions when meeting with potential managers (almost 60% in 2009 compared to 30% in 2007) and integrating climate change into Requests for Proposals (50% in 2009 compared to 40% in 2007). However, they have been much slower in integrating these issues into Investment Manager Agreements (less than 20% in 2009).[70]

This same trend accounts for the increasing demands of information disclosure that institutional investors place on the companies in which they invest.

[67] Enhanced analytics network (EAN) was a collaborative effort between asset owners and asset managers seeking to promote extra-financial research among institutional investors and asset managers. For more information, see web.archive.org/web/20110710192933/http://www.enhanced-analytics.com/portal/ep/home.do (accessed 11 December 2012).

[68] Trucost provides an analysis of the environmental impact of corporations and the environmental risk tied to their operations. See www.trucost.com (accessed 25 April 2011).

[69] Some 63% of surveyed asset owners put responsible investment elements into contracts for the external managers of their investment in 2009, an increase of 38% with respect to 2008. See H. Reichelt, 'Green Bonds: A Model to Mobilise Private Capital to Fund Climate Change Mitigation and Adaptation Projects', in World Bank, *The Euromoney Environmental Finance Handbook 2010*, p. 6 n. 6.

[70] Investor Statement on Climate Change Report 2009, Institutional Investors Group on Climate Change, 6. This contrasts with the 2008 Report: 'While the number of asset owners integrating climate change into Requests for Proposal (RFPs) is unchanged and the inclusion of the issue in Investment Management Agreements (IMAs) is still unusual, some asset owners stated that they would consider this approach in future'; Investor Statement on Climate Change Report 2008, Institutional Investors Group on Climate Change, 5.

In an interesting study published by UNEP FI in 2009 (Fiduciary II), the authors come to the conclusion that asset managers have a duty proactively to include ESG criteria in their investment decisions, and that those who refuse to do so may be found liable by courts for negligence.[71] According to Quayle Watchman Consulting, cited in Fiduciary II,

> In tendering for investment mandates, it would be expected that the investment consultant or asset manager would raise ESG considerations as an issue to be taken into account and discussed with the client even if the pension fund has not specified ESG considerations as material to tender. If the investment consultant or asset manager fails to do so, there is a very real risk that they will be sued for negligence on the ground that they failed to discharge their professional duty of care to the client by failing to raise and take into account ESG considerations.[72]

A previous study published by UNEP FI in 2005 had also come to the conclusion that notwithstanding the general duty of institutional investors to create financial benefits for their clients, the inclusion of ESG criteria in their investment policy was 'not only legally permissible but also potentially required to the extent that ESG factors will have a material impact on the financial performance of potential investments'.[73] Thus, whereas investment managers are not explicitly required to include ESG criteria in their investment strategy, nothing prevents them from doing so in performing their fiduciary duties. In fact, they may even be implicitly required to do so, as part of their fiduciary duty to include ESG factors when these are likely to 'have a material impact on the financial performance of potential investments'. This would arguably be the case for industrial activities with a significant environmental impact, such as extractive industries. Finally, investment management agreements can always be used by asset owners, and should be used with increased frequency, to impose on asset managers the obligation to take into account ESG criteria when making their portfolio selection.

[71] Fiduciary Responsibility: Legal and Practical Aspects of Integrating Environmental, Social and Governance Issues into Institutional Investment, UNEP FI (July 2009).

[72] *Ibid.*, 44.

[73] *Ibid.*, 64. See also Freshfields Bruckhaus Deringer, *A Legal Framework for the Integration of Environmental, Social and Governance Issues into Institutional Investment* (UNEP-FI, 2005), 13: 'On that basis, integrating ESG considerations into an investment analysis so as to more reliably predict financial performance is clearly permissible and is arguably required in any jurisdictions.'

6.2.4 *Challenges for the future growth of SRI*

There are essentially four major challenges for the future growth of this industry that require some comment. The first concerns the relationship between asset holders and asset managers and the possibility to include ESG criteria in investment management agreements. As explained in the previous section, asset owners increasingly ask their asset managers to include considerations of environmental protection in their decision-making process. Nonetheless, the extent to which this observable trend will yield successful outcomes is also linked to the capacity to solve or address the following challenges.

The second challenge stems from the legal definition of the term fiduciary duty and the legal limits to the discretion of asset managers to determine their investment strategy.[74] As outlined above, the argument that ESG-based decision-making may be in conflict with the financial fiduciary duty of asset managers has often been used as an argument against the unqualified acceptance of SRI. Yet, the current trend seems to go in the direction of interpreting the term of fiduciary duty as including not only an obligation to act prudently, but also to act proactively and to include ESG criteria where there may be material impact on the financial performance of the assets under management.[75]

The third major difficulty concerns the relationship between asset managers and the companies in which they invest, particularly in connection with disclosure and accountability. The disclosure of company practices seems indeed essential for asset managers to make informed investment decisions. Several initiatives, such as the Global Reporting Initiative, seek to foster disclosure of ESG policies by private-sector corporations. Another question is whether investment managers effectively use their proxy voting powers and actively engage the companies they invest in with ESG issues through the filing of shareholder resolutions. Although many existing funds seek to publicise their new eco-friendly approach and many new funds are created with this creed, it is often very difficult for any investor to be sure that the resources he or she wishes to invest in sustainable projects are actually employed for these purposes.[76] If sustainable investing is the true objective of asset

[74] S. Viederman, 'Fiduciary Duty', in Krosinsky and Robins, *Sustainable Investing*, 189–99.

[75] See references above, nn. 71 and 73.

[76] P. Hawken, 'Social Responsible Investing: How the SRI Industry Has Failed to Respond to People Who Want to Invest with Conscience and What Can Be Done to Change It' (2004) www.naturalcapital.org.

managers, then they must persuade their investors, through serious management decisions, that their fund allocation not only yields superior returns but also achieves eco-friendly results in the longer run. For this reason, asset holders need to choose their asset managers diligently, as some funds advertise SRI but in fact dedicate only a minimal amount of their resources to it.

A fourth major challenge is the ongoing difficulty in determining what SRI covers and, more specifically, in defining what qualifies as environmentally sound investing. Intuitively, one may think that SRI encompasses mainly investments designed to protect the environment or to develop eco-friendly technologies. One may also think that most SRI funds typically shun investments in industry sectors that have significant environmental impacts, such as the mining sector. However, it may also be argued that investments reducing the ecological footprint of large polluters or enhancing efficiency could also be considered as SRI, even if they are channelled towards activities with potentially significant environmental impacts. The case of rare earths mining serves as a topical example to highlight this difficulty. Until recently, China produced over 95 per cent of the global demand for rare earths while possessing only around 37 per cent of the global reserves. Two years ago, the Chinese government announced that it would crack down on illegal mining of rare earths and that it would therefore curtail the exports of these minerals. The reason was largely motivated by environmental concerns and strategic considerations. This not only prompted trade negotiations between China, the USA, the European Union, Japan and other importers of rare earths, but may well develop into a fully fledged dispute before the WTO Dispute Settlement Body.[77] Unsurprisingly, global investors have reacted to this change of policy by reassessing the potential of old mines in Australia or the USA.[78] One American company, Molycorp, Inc., has made a public offer in July 2010 for the sale of stock at a price of

[77] In a similar matter, the USA, the European Union and Mexico already submitted in 2009 a dispute with China concerning the imposition of export duties and quotas on nine raw materials to the WTO Dispute Settlement Body. The Panel found China's export duties and quotas to be inconsistent with its obligations under the Protocol of Accession. *China – Measures Related to the Exportation of Various Raw Materials*, Reports of the Panel, WT/DS394/R, WT/DS395/R, WT/DS398/R, 5 July 2011. Although both sides have pledged to appeal the Panel's report, this decision may well influence the trade negotiations on rare earths.

[78] K. Bradsher, 'After China's Rare Earth Embargo, a New Calculus', *New York Times*, 29 October 2010.

US$14 in order to recommission one of its old mines, Mountain Pass, located in California. One of Molycorp Minerals' investors is Resource Capital Funds,[79] a set of PE funds investing exclusively in the mining sector. Despite reported environmental harms created through rare earths mining and refining,[80] Molycorp Minerals not only pledges to conduct operations based on sound environmental strategies but commercialises its rare earths mining activity as a critical component for the development of future clean energy technologies.[81] The question that arises in this connection is whether it would be appropriate for such an investment to qualify as SRI.

6.3 Project finance

While the private sector has developed and is constantly developing a wider range of financial instruments channelling funds into green economy projects, the share of this funding going into the developing world is still insufficient. While the emerging economies, mainly China, Brazil and India, receive large amounts of foreign capital to be used for sustainable projects, other developing countries have difficulties in attracting foreign private capital. It is mainly for this reason that international financial institutions (IFIs), such as multilateral development banks (MDBs), have been created by states to provide the private sector in developing countries with access to financial products on competitive or even preferential terms. Project finance is the most common technique used by such institutions to channel funds into the private sector of developing countries.[82]

[79] See www.resourcecapitalfunds.com (accessed 2 May 2011). The Molycorp stock price rose from US$14 in July 2010 to US$73.33 at the end of April 2011, with a sharp increase since mid-March. See www.marketwatch.com (accessed 2 May 2011).

[80] K. Bradsher, 'Mitsubishi Quietly Cleans Up its Former Refinery', *New York Times*, 8 March 2011.

[81] See www.molycorp.com (accessed 2 May 2011).

[82] Project finance is defined as a 'method of funding in which the lender looks primarily to the revenues generated by a single project, both as the source of repayment and as security for the exposure. This type of financing is usually for large, chemical processing plants, mines, transportation infrastructure, environment, and telecommunications infrastructure. Project finance may take the form of financing the construction of a new capital installation, or refinancing of an existing installation, with or without improvements. In such transactions, the lender is usually paid solely or almost exclusively out of the money generated by the contracts for the facility's output, such as the electricity sold by a power plant. The borrower is usually a special purpose entity that is not permitted to perform any function other than developing, owning, and operating the installation. The

MDBs have led the way by acknowledging their special nature and their obligation to make sure that their activities coincide with international environmental norms. This evolution can best be analysed using the International Finance Corporation as an example. Its innovative approach has influenced not only other multilateral financial institutions but also increasingly their financial intermediaries and other commercial development banks.

6.3.1 Multilateral development banks engaging the private sector

There is only one MDB with a global reach that engages directly the private sector, namely the IFC.[83] All four other MDBs have a regional mandate that limits their territorial scope.[84] The common denominator is that all these institutions provide funds either to emerging economies or to developing countries. Developed countries do not, in principle, benefit from the loan and advisory services of MDBs. The European

consequence is that repayment depends primarily on the project's cash flow and on the collateral value of the project's assets.' International Convergence of Capital Measurement and Capital Standards: A Revised Framework, Basel Committee on Banking Supervision, November 2005, 49, paras 221–2. For more information on project finance, see J. Dewar, *International Project Finance: Law and Practice* (Oxford University Press, 2011); P. Wood, *Law and Practice of International Finance: Project Finance, Securitisations, Subordinated Debt*, vol. 5 (London: Sweet & Maxwell, 2007). See also the activities of the International Project Finance Association (IPFA), available at www.ipfa.org (accessed 25 April 2011).

83 The International Finance Corporations is an autonomous institution within the World Bank Group. IFC was established in 1956 as an affiliate of IBRD with the purpose of promoting private-sector investments in member countries. Article I of the IFC Articles of Agreement states that 'the purpose of the Corporation is to further economic development by encouraging the growth of productive private enterprise in member countries, particularly in less developed areas, thus supplementing the activities of the International Bank for Reconstruction and Development'. See Article I of International Finance Corporation Articles of Agreement, 25 May 1955, 264 UNTS 117 (entered into force 20 July 1956).

84 These are the four regional MDBs: European Bank for Reconstruction and Development (EBRD), Asian Development Bank (ADB), African Development Bank (AfDB) and the Inter-American Development Bank Group (IADB). There are other multilateral financial institutions (MFIs) that provide funds to developing countries and their private sector, such as the European Investment Bank (EIB), the Islamic Development Bank (IDB) or the OPEC Fund for International Development (OPEC Fund). Finally, sub-regional multilateral development banks exist primarily in Latin America and Africa, namely the East African Development Bank (EADB), the West African Development Bank (BOAD), the Corporación Andina de Fomento (CAF), the Central American Bank for Economic Integration (CABEI) and the Caribbean Development Bank (CDB).

Bank for Reconstruction and Development is the first bank to have explicitly incorporated ESG issues into its mandate. In fact, it is the only one that contains an explicit reference to the environment or to sustainability in its constituent instrument.[85] All other MDBs have subsequently adopted new mission statements focusing on the reduction of poverty through sustainable investments. For instance, the IFC adopted its own mission statement in 1998: 'Promoting sustainable private sector investment in developing countries, helping to reduce poverty and improve people's lives'.[86] By doing so, these financial institutions have acknowledged that their fiduciary obligations not only contain financial elements but also extra-financial elements which have become an integral part of the decision-making process. Finally, in 2000, all MDBs committed themselves to contributing to the achievement of the Millennium Development Goals (MDGs), which includes the goal to ensure environmental sustainability.[87]

The main actor in the field of project finance is the IFC seeking to foster environmental stewardship in the projects it invests in.[88] The only other MDB to have created a specific body dealing with the private sector

[85] Agreement establishing the European Bank for Reconstruction and Development, signed in Paris, 29 May 1990, 1646 UNTS 100. Article 2 lit. (vii) of the Agreement states that the Bank should 'promote in the full range of its activities environmentally sound and sustainable development'. The explanatory note on this provision states that 'Delegates recognized the serious environmental problems in Central and Eastern Europe, and emphasized that principles of environmentally sound development must be integrated into the full range of the Bank's operations. Thus Delegates intended "in the full range of its activities" to include all of the Bank's activities, including technical assistance and all special operations, and not merely that the Bank should be able to provide support directly for specific environmental projects.' See EBRD, Basic Documents of the European Bank for Reconstruction and Development, Explanatory Notes, 49, available at www.ebrd.com (accessed 25 April 2011).

[86] 'About IFC: IFC Mission Statement', available at www.ifc.org. This contrasts with IFC's comments at the end of the 1980s and the beginning of the 1990s, when it stated that the 'most fundamental way in which the Corporation contributes to development is by investing only in projects that offer a satisfactory ex-ante economic rate of return'. See IFC Economics Department, 'The Development Contribution of IFC Operations', IFC Discussion Paper 5, Washington, DC, The World Bank, 1989, 5. ADB's mission statement, available at www.adb.org, is to 'promote quality, knowledge, and innovation for sustainable development'. AfDB's mission statement, available at www.afdb.org, is 'to spur sustainable economic development and social progress in its regional member countries, thus contributing to poverty reduction' (all websites accessed 25 April 2011).

[87] A/RES/55/2, United Nations General Assembly Resolution, 18 September 2000.

[88] During 2009, IFC's portfolio included loans and equity investments in 129 countries and 1,579 companies, totalling US$23.8 bn of disbursed investments. See Moody's Investors Service, International Finance Corporation. Credit Analysis, June 2010, 6.

is the Inter-American Development Bank (IADB), through the creation of the Inter-American Investment Corporation in 1986.[89] Created in 1956, the IFC only came to appreciate the importance of ESG screening during the 1990s, but has quickly responded to the new challenges by mainstreaming environmental standards across its entire business activities. It has sought to engage the private sector in the development of international standards and the adoption of best practices. Since 2006, the IFC applies its own performance standards to project sponsors seeking IFC support and has developed environmental guidelines applicable to its own activities.[90] The question is interesting as a matter of international law. For there was some uncertainty as to whether an organisation like the IFC is bound by the rules of international environmental law, including customary rules, and whether it should comply with the conventional obligations assumed by its member states under various multilateral environmental agreements (MEAs), such as the Montreal Protocol or the CITES Convention. To the extent that the IFC has developed *proprio motu* its internal guidelines and performance standards which seek to reflect or even integrate international norms relating to environmental protection and climate change, the question may well remain open were it not for the temporal element of the question. Not only would the IFC have to integrate existing international environmental norms into its daily activities, but it would also have to adapt its policies to new emerging international standards.

The IFC, as an intergovernmental organisation comprising solely member states, established by a constitutive act and with a special mandate, endowed with international personality, and as a special agency of the United Nations, is a legal entity under international law, subject to rights and obligations deriving from that legal order.[91] As stated by the

[89] Agreement Establishing the Inter-American Investment Corporation, signed in Washington, DC, 19 November 1984, available at www.iic.org (accessed 25 April 2011).

[90] IFC's regulatory framework on sustainability includes the following documents: Policy on Social and Environmental Sustainability, 30 April 2006; Environmental and Social Review Procedures, version 4.0, 14 August 2009; Performance Standard on Social and Environmental Sustainability, 30 April 2006; and environmental, health and safety (EHS) guidelines. This architecture is supplemented by IFC's disclosure policy: Policy on Disclosure of Information, 30 April 2006. For more information, see E. Morgera, *Corporate Accountability in International Environmental Law* (Oxford University Press, 2009); M. J. Langer, *The International Finance Corporation and International Environmental Law: Mainstreaming, Standardization, Compliance* (Geneva: Graduate Institute, 2009).

[91] The ICJ first stated this principle in its first advisory opinion. See *Reparation for Injuries Suffered in the Service of the United Nations, Advisory Opinion*, ICJ Reports 1949, 179.

International Court of Justice (ICJ), 'international organizations are subjects of international law and, as such, are bound by any obligations incumbent upon them under general rules of international law, under their constitutions or under international agreements to which they are parties'.[92] For general rules of international environmental law, such as the general principles of prevention, precaution or no-harm, are primarily obligations incumbent upon states, but also on other international subjects. They do not directly address private-sector actors, but impose certain due-diligence standards upon the manner with which states are to regulate private-sector activities. Interestingly, the IFC has not only chosen to integrate evolving standards developed in other intergovernmental forums, but decided to take the lead in developing environmental standards applicable to its private-sector clients. The IFC has innovated in the sense that it incorporates international standards relating to ESG issues, such as its own performance standards, into the contractual loan agreements that it concludes with its clients. Thus, private-sector entrepreneurs investing in the developing world and wishing to obtain the IFC's financial support must conform not only to the environmental laws of the host state but must equally comply with international standards set by the IFC.[93] All other major multilateral development banks have successfully employed the same method. Thus, for instance, the Model Loan Agreement prepared by the Inter-American Investment Corporation, the private-sector arm of the IADB, provides the following definition of environmental and labour legislation that its clients are contractually expected to fulfil:

> 'Environmental and Labor Legislation' means the international, [particularly __________ include international provisions applicable to this specific project] national, state or municipal provisions, statutes, laws, regulations, decrees, resolutions, codes, orders, plans, judicial sentences, judicial or administrative decisions or interpretations stemming therefrom, governing or referring to issues in the areas of pollution, environmental protection, public health and safety, air emissions, discharges to the water, hazardous or toxic substances, solid or hazardous wastes, or

92 *Interpretation of the Agreement of 25 March 1951 between the WHO and Egypt, Advisory Opinion*, ICJ Reports 1980, 89–90.

93 IFC's Policy on Social and Environmental Sustainability clearly states that 'IFC will only finance investment activities that are expected to meet the requirements of the Performance Standard within a reasonable period of time. Persistent delays in meeting these requirements can lead to loss of financial support from IFC', Policy on Social and Environmental Sustainability, IFC, 1 December 2010, para. 21.

> occupational health and safety, including, but not limited to, all environmental and occupational standards in force in [country], as well as any applicable state and municipal environmental protection regulations.[94]

The same document not only obliges the borrower to present different environmental impact studies and an environmental management plan, but also states that the borrower and guarantor must 'conduct their business with due diligence, in an efficient and environmentally correct manner, adhering fully to customary practices in their area of business and ensuring that all their operations are carried out on an arm's-length basis'.[95] It further mandates that they 'shall use the Loan proceeds exclusively for carrying out the Project and executing the Environmental Management Plan'.[96] The result of this evolution is that MDBs have become agents for normative integration where international standards are applied to projects in countries that even may not have ratified the relevant international agreements. To remain with the example of the Montreal Protocol, it matters little that a particular developing country might not have ratified that agreement, because any private-sector investor in that country wishing to obtain funds from the IFC will not obtain such funds if the project involves, for example, the production of hydrofluorocarbons (HFCs) or other banned ozone-depleting substances.

The main techniques utilised by MDBs to select the projects they will support are the creation of an exclusion list,[97] the preliminary screening of the project, the inclusion of due-diligence obligations and default clauses in the loan contract and project supervision until the moment of divestment. This marks a stark difference to the approaches used by private fund managers, who usually do not have a fixed exclusion list (however, the number is on the increase) and do not include specific environmental clauses in their investment agreements. The exclusion list approach already encompasses a good part of commercial activities prohibited under international law, such as trade in endangered species. They further allow MDBs to exclude *ab initio* very controversial activities such as arms production or the construction of nuclear facilities. This initial negative screening is followed by an in-depth positive screening that seeks actively to engage the borrower in sustainable production practices by submitting environmental impact assessments, and

[94] Model Loan Agreement to Companies, IAIC, June 2007, available at www.iic.org (accessed 25 April 2011). See also Article VI (viii).

[95] *Ibid.*, Article VI (i). [96] *Ibid.*

[97] See e.g. the IFC Exclusion List, available at www.ifc.org (accessed 25 April 2011).

developing environmental management plans, which include corrective action plans and emergency plans. Once the gaps have been identified and corrective actions are determined in the loan agreement, the project's compliance with relevant environmental standards is supervised by the MDB until all funds have been reimbursed. There obviously remains a risk that project sponsors will not pursue their efforts to comply with environmental good practices after an MDB has exited a project. This potential reputational risk can only be indirectly managed by MDBs as they have no more legal leverage once they exited a project. The only effective means at their disposal is to imbue their clients with good governance practices during the investment period, to develop environmental management plans with long-term outlooks and to refuse any new investments with rogue companies that may affect their reputation.

Apart from channelling international funds into sustainable private-sector projects and providing risk mitigation for development projects, MDBs present several other advantages for the private sector. Additionality and leverage are the focal points here. Leverage describes here the capacity of the IFC to mobilise supplementary capital from the private sector when it invests in a certain project. Because the IFC consistently obtains triple A ratings from the rating agency Moody's,[98] it attracts more funds from the private sector for the projects it invests in. Thus, a potential client of the IFC has the encouraging prospect of gaining facilitated access to capital markets simply because the IFC's due-diligence procedure reduces credit and capital risks. The IFC indicates that for a total disbursement of US$38.8 billion it has managed to mobilise close to another US$10 billion.[99] Additionality, on the other hand, refers to value added from working with the IFC. Its unique position within the finance industry, its professional and worldwide experience and its high-quality advisory services provide the IFC with a comparative advantage that incites private-sector investors to cooperate with the IFC. Because the IFC's advisory services span the entire project cycle where the IFC is involved, the initial cost to comply with environmental standards imposed by the IFC may very well turn out to be an opportunity for investors. This may be explained by the fact that the progressive adoption of good governance practices under the diligent supervision of an external expert body such as the IFC is a cost that has

98 Moody's Investors Service, International Finance Corporation. Credit Analysis, June 2010.

99 IFC Annual Report 2010, 'Where Innovation Meets Impacts'.

long-term benefits, such as efficiency, sustainability and enhanced reputation. According to the IFC, its additionality is the main reason why clients choose to do business with it.[100]

That being said, the IFC and other MDBs engaging the private sector must be kept in perspective. Their role is crucial for catalysing entrepreneurship and sustainable finance in sectors and economies where insufficient capital can be raised through the commercial channels. This is also explained by the reduced amount of capital at the disposal of MDBs, and the relatively small amounts of loans (anywhere from US$1 to US$200 million). It is encouraging that the Inter-American Investment Corporation (IAIC) has been created with a specific mandate to foster sustainable growth in small- and medium-sized corporations in Latin America. For its part, the IFC has acknowledged that a disproportionate amount of its investments were located in the emerging markets and that Africa received close to no serious attention. In the last couple of years, the IFC has sought to correct this trend by focusing much more actively on sustainable growth in Africa. And yet, the IFC's role can only be supplemental to the efforts of the finance sector. 'IFC can influence the markets. But only local and regional banks, institutional investors, and other financial institutions have the power to change them.'[101] However, the IFC's impact has been much greater than simply engaging entrepreneurs and imposing environmental standards on their clients. On the one hand, the IFC has pledged to ensure that the financial intermediaries, such as commercial development banks, which receive the IFC's financial support, adopt the IFC's sustainability policies and standards in their own activities. On the other hand, the IFC has been a centrepiece of a much

[100] IFC defines its additionality as follows: 'IFC participates in an investment only when it can make a special contribution not offered or brought to the deal by other investors.' IFC Annual Report 2010, 'Where Innovation Meets Impacts', vol. 2, IFC Financials, Projects, and Portfolio 2010, 16. 'IFC is uniquely positioned to make a difference for the many people at the base of the global economic pyramid. We are the largest multilateral financial institution investing in private enterprises in emerging markets, with activities in 130 countries. We combine financing that helps local businesses grow quickly and sustainably with advice that helps them innovate, raise standards, mitigate risk, and share knowledge across industries and regions. Our affiliation with the World Bank Group gives us additional leverage in terms of skills and experience. We call this unparalleled set of comparative advantages our "additionality." It is the main reason our clients choose to work with us.' See IFC's 'Role and Additionality: A Primer', May 2009, available at www.ifc.org (accessed 25 April 2011). IFC now provides its ESG services through the Sustainable Business Advisory Business Line.

[101] *Ibid.*, 35.

larger effort to engage the entire project finance industry by developing the so-called Equator Principles (see section 6.3.3, below) that are tightly linked to the IFC's own ESG standards.

6.3.2 *Financial intermediaries*

In order to increase its outreach, the IFC provides loans to financial intermediaries who in turn lend on these assets in project finance. Such financial intermediaries may include local commercial banks, leasing companies, micro-financiers, investment funds, index-funds, PE funds and venture capital funds. It is one of the chosen paths to reach more efficiently small- and medium-sized enterprises in developing countries of Africa. The IFC explains that 'In Sub-Saharan Africa, we used to reach about 50 enterprises through direct investments, at considerable cost to IFC; last year [i.e., 2007], by comparison, financial intermediaries IFC had invested in/provided over 220,000 loans to micro, small, and medium enterprises.'[102] However, the IFC's attention has been called to the fact that projects financed indirectly by the IFC have shown poorer environmental performance, and the IFC has been criticised for poorly monitoring the activities of financial intermediaries.[103] For this reason, the IFC has started to control its financial intermediaries by imposing a review procedure on their activities where the projects they finance with the IFC's support may have environmental or social risks.[104] For instance, the IFC expects its financial intermediaries to apply a slightly augmented version of the IFC's exclusion list. Thus, in addition to all activities prohibited for IFC activities, financial intermediaries are prohibited from engaging in commercial logging operations in primary tropical moist forests and in the production or trade in wood or other forestry products other than from sustainably managed forests.[105] In any event, financial intermediaries are expected to

[102] IFC Annual Report 2008, 44.

[103] See e.g. 'Out of Sight, Out of Mind? IFC Investment through Banks, Private Equity Firms and other Financial Intermediaries', Bretton Wood Project, 22 November 2010, available at www.brettonwoodsproject.org (accessed 25 April 2011).

[104] See e.g. 'IFC's Environmental and Social Review Procedures', version 4.0, 14 August 2009, sects 7–10. Paragraph 7.2.9 provides that 'for FI investments where the IFC supported FI is engaged in financing or investing in market instruments for activities with E&S risk and where the FI has little or no leverage or no capacity to carry out a reasonable review of the project's risk (such as with distressed asset pools), apply the FI Exclusion List and a reputation risk screen in addition to any other Applicable Performance Requirements as can be reasonably implemented in the scope of the transaction.'

[105] IFC Exclusion List, available at www.ifc.org (accessed 25 April 2011).

apply IFC performance standards to their activities, thus reinforcing considerably the scope of the IFC's standard-setting role.

6.3.3 *The Equator Principles*

While significantly improving its own handling of environmental factors in its financing activities, the IFC's leverage has been extended also to other actors in the field of project finance. In addition to aligning to its policies the financial intermediaries with which it is cooperating, in 2003, at the request of some commercial banks, the IFC developed a set of principles – the Equator Principles[106] – which are meant to allow commercial banks and other monetary institutions engaging in project finance to address environmental or social issues by applying recognised international standards. The mechanism works on a voluntary basis, and, to date, seventy-two financial institutions (the Equator Principles Financial Institutions or EPFIs) have publicly adopted the Equator Principles.[107] These ten principles basically incorporate the due-diligence procedure applied by the IFC to its own activities, such as the categorisation of projects based on the magnitude of their potential impact,[108] and contain various clauses that refer directly to the IFC's performance standards and EHS guidelines.[109] The Equator Principles distinguish between projects in high-income OECD countries, where there is a presumption that their regulatory requirements either meet or exceed the IFC's standards, and all other countries where EPFIs are expected to apply the IFC's standards.[110]

Because the Equator Principles are considered to be a globally recognised benchmark, this initiative has so far been crowned with success. It demonstrates not only that the Equator Principles – and thus, implicitly, the IFC's environmental standards – are considered to be the financial industry's 'gold standard',[111] but also that these principles exert moral suasion on other actors of the financial industry. It is not only a question of managing reputational risk, it is a question of finding a common language and of having access to capital at lower costs. Thus, a

[106] For the last version, see www.equator-principles.com (accessed 25 April 2011). For references, see above, n. 12.

[107] See www.equator-principles.com (accessed 25 April 2011). [108] Principle 1.

[109] See above, n. 90. [110] Principle 3.

[111] As publicised on the Equator Principles website, available at www.equator-principles.com (accessed 2 May 2011).

competitive drive amongst financial institutions has been created turning around the concept of sustainability.

To conclude on this point, the IFC's role has been largely underestimated. Over the last decade, this organisation has passed from being heavily criticised for its involvement in environmentally harmful projects to emerging as the leader in international ESG standard-setting with an outreach far beyond its initial sphere of influence. The IFC's tentacles have taken a hold not only on the environmental performance of its own clients but also of its financial intermediaries and their clients. It has successfully engaged the wider industry of financial institutions and continues to try to convince them to increase their efforts for achieving sustainable project finance. With regard to the private sector, the sustainability frameworks promoted by international financial institutions serve as an important incentive to engage in sustainable production practices for several reasons. First, if corporations or entrepreneurs demonstrate a willingness to adopt eco-friendly behaviours, they are more likely to obtain facilitated access to foreign capital on preferential terms. Secondly, the loans provided by IFIs come in a package including advisory services helping corporations to achieve more efficiency over the long run, thus increasing returns on capital. Thirdly, private-sector actors that receive financial support from IFIs are more likely to keep up with international standards. This comparative advantage allows them to encounter less cost over time as states tighten their environmental regulations. Finally, it is to be expected that these corporations are also more likely to manage their reputational risk more effectively.

6.4 Market mechanism

Above, we have seen through which channels corporations and entrepreneurs can obtain facilitated access to funds if they qualify as sustainable producers. Eco-finance provided by funds (conventional or alternative) plays the most important role as institutional investors manage a large chunk of the world's private assets and therefore have crucial leverage on the successful emergence of sustainable finance as a whole. International financial institutions, on the other hand, facilitate corporations to manage their environmental risk, besides providing additional financial resources during the various stages of project operations. Critically, these institutions operate in countries where the investment environment does not allow attracting privately owned capital on reasonable terms, thus channelling 'green capital' to these places. This section deals with a third technique employed for the allocation of resources into eco-friendly production patterns, i.e., market mechanisms destined to achieve efficiency at the lowest possible cost for the society at large.

In general, the concept of market mechanism can be defined as 'the system whereby using prices, the interaction of supply and demand allocates inputs and distributes outputs'.[112] Regarding environmental protection, there are basically two ways to conceptualise market mechanism. There are those markets that appear spontaneously in the private sector through the interaction of supply and demand. This is the case with payment for environmental or ecosystem services schemes, which are discussed further below. The second type of market mechanism exists because it is the deliberate result of a political choice. Thus, instead of adopting stringent and inflexible command-and-control methods, states choose to give the private sector sufficient flexibility to achieve pollution reduction targets by those emitters bearing the least cost. Carbon markets and emissions trading are a prominent example of this second type, together with the other flexibility mechanisms under the climate change regime.

6.4.1 Carbon markets

Carbon markets can be organised at national, regional or multilateral levels.[113] As regulatory authorities set a cap on the total amount of emissions allowed and distribute (or auction) emissions units, markets are created through which producers can trade their emissions rights. The basic idea underlying carbon markets is that those emitters of carbon dioxide that have a comparative advantage in lowering their emissions at low cost should have the incentive to do so by allowing them to sell their reduction units at a fluctuating price to other companies which encounter higher cost in achieving more efficient production practices. The carbon market created under the climate change regime of the Kyoto Protocol[114] is one such example that is destined to curb carbon emissions

[112] See www.finance-lib.com (accessed 25 April 2011).

[113] The largest emissions trading scheme (ETS) to date is the European Union Emissions Trading Scheme (EU ETS). Other carbon markets exist at the national level, such as the UK ETS, the Chicago Climate Exchange (CCX), the Japanese Voluntary Emissions Trading Scheme (JVETS), New South Wales Greenhouse Gas Reduction Scheme (NSW GGAS) or the Norwegian Emissions Trading System (NETS).

[114] Kyoto Protocol to the United Nations Framework Convention on Climate Change, signed 11 December 1997, 2303 UNTS 148.

through the allocation of assigned amount units (AAUs) to each country signatory of the Kyoto Protocol and that can thereafter be traded under the specific terms of the Protocol and its regulatory framework.[115] In order for these states to comply with their commitments within the indicated commitment period (2008–12), they are authorised to take advantage of various flexibility mechanisms.

Flexibility mechanisms under the Kyoto Protocol allow the efficient allocation of financial burdens upon all carbon-emitting producers involved. The four principal flexibility mechanisms are the bubble, joint implementation (JI), the Clean Development Mechanism (CDM) and emissions trading. Because JI and CDM are discussed in more detail in other chapters in this book, it is not necessary to delve more deeply into their functioning. It is, however, worth mentioning that JI under Article 6 of the Kyoto Protocol stimulates the flow of financial resources into the emerging economies of Eastern Europe that are part of Annex I UNFCCC,[116] whereas the CDM under Article 12 of the Kyoto Protocol helps to channel resources for eco-friendly projects in non-Annex I countries. Under the emissions trading schemes envisaged under Article 17 of the Kyoto Protocol, state parties to the Protocol, having at their disposal unused spare emissions units, may sell these units to other parties of the Protocol. This allows for carbon to become a commodity traded on the carbon market. Apart from AAUs that can be traded under the Kyoto Protocol emissions trading scheme, carbon reduction units obtained through other flexibility mechanisms under the Protocol can also be traded on the carbon market. For instance, emissions reduction units generated through a JI project, certified emissions reduction generated under the CDM, or removal units obtained under the land use, land-use change and forestry (LULUCF) mechanism can all be traded under the scheme.[117]

One particular market mechanism, the Green Investment Scheme, has recently emerged in the context related to 'hot air' coming from Central and Eastern European (CEE) countries. 'Hot air' refers to the AAUs that

[115] See e.g. J. Lin, 'Private Actors in International and Domestic Emissions Trading Schemes', in Freestone and Streck, *Legal Aspects of Carbon Trading*, 134–54; M. Passero, 'The Voluntary Carbon Market: Its Contributions and Potential Legal and Policy Issues', *ibid.*, 517–33.

[116] United Nations Framework Convention on Climate Change, signed 9 May 1992, 1771 UNTS 107.

[117] For the modalities for the accounting of assigned amounts of the Protocol, see Decision 13/CMP.1, FCCC/KP/CMP/2005/8/Add. 2.

these countries could sell on the carbon market because their emissions sank drastically after the economic downturn of the early 1990s.[118] Carbon emissions in these countries did not decrease due to the adoption of more efficient production methods or through other specific efforts by these countries to lower their emissions but because of the economic collapse of wide sectors of their polluting industries. This has raised the fear among observers that Annex I countries that will not meet their reduction targets will purchase the AAU credits from countries such as Russia or Ukraine, or from the new EU members. For example, this has prompted the International Emissions Trading Association (IETA) to send a letter to the Ministry of the Environment of the Czech Republic stating that the 'surplus of unused and unsold Assigned Amount Units (AAUs) built up in the first Kyoto commitment period and the recent increase in size and frequency of un-greened AAU trades are extremely serious issues for the global carbon market'.[119] Although these specific units could well be traded under Article 17 of the Kyoto Protocol (with the eventual consequence of pushing the carbon price downwards), all interested parties have in principle pledged not to do this.[120] In fact, countries that may not achieve their carbon reduction targets during the 2008–12 commitment period, such as Japan or Spain, have announced that they will not purchase any 'hot air', while CEE countries in possession of these units have pledged to invest any revenues raised into so-called 'greening' activities. This has spawned the emergence of the Green Investment Scheme, a new technique to secure that financial resources are channelled into green economy projects and contribute to the mitigation of climate change. In principle, the trade in AAUs is limited to the governments of Annex I countries; however, private-sector corporations in Japan may also engage directly in the purchase of AAUs to meet their voluntary domestic targets.[121]

[118] CEE countries have an estimated surplus of 8–12 billion AAUs, most of which is considered to be 'hot air'.

[119] Letter of 17 June 2009 from Henry Derwent, President and CEO of the International Emissions Trading Association to Mr Pavel Zamyslicky, Head of Delegation, Climate Change Department, Ministry of the Environment of the Czech Republic, available at www.ieta.org (accessed 25 April 2011).

[120] N. Gorina, 'Cooling Down Hot Air' (2006) *Environmental Finance. Supplement: Global Carbon*, 46–7; A. Tuerk et al., 'Green Investment Schemes: First Experiences and Lessons Learned', Working Paper, Joanneum Research/Central European University (April 2010), 3.

[121] Paragraph 5 of the Modalities, Rules and Guidelines for Emissions Trading provides that 'Transfers and acquisitions between national registries shall be made under the

Green Investment Schemes are destined to improve the environmental element in international emissions trading.[122] The general idea underlying Green Investment Schemes is that the revenues raised from AAU sales are invested in so-called 'greening activities' that further the greening of the economy.[123] Green Investment Schemes are divided into two types of greening: *hard greening* encompasses activities which 'directly deliver measurable and quantifiable' emissions reduction, whereas *soft greening* refers to activities without any quantifiable or measurable emissions reduction.[124] The *greening ratio* serves to measure the emissions reduction achieved through the sale of a specific amount of AAUs.[125] An example of a successful trade in AAUs was announced at the beginning of March 2011 between Estonia and two Japanese companies. On the one hand, Estonia traded 10 million AAUs in exchange for 507 electric cars produced by the company Mitsubishi (together with 250 points for charging electric cars). On the other hand, Estonia sold an additional 5.5 million AAUs to the Japanese bank Sumitomo Mitsui and pledged to invest the revenues into energy efficiency improvements of government buildings

responsibility of the Parties concerned in accordance with the provisions in decision 13/CMP.1. A Party that authorizes legal entities to transfer and/or acquire under Article 17 shall remain responsible for the fulfilment of its obligations under the Kyoto Protocol and shall ensure that such participation is consistent with the present annex. The Party shall maintain an up-to-date list of such entities and make it available to the secretariat and the public through its national registry. Legal entities may not transfer and/or acquire under Article 17 during any period of time in which the authorizing Party does not meet the eligibility requirements or has been suspended.' Annex to Decision 11/CMP.1, FCCC/KP/CMP/2005/8/Add. 2.

122 S. Simonetti and R. De Witt Wijnen, 'International Emissions Trading and Green Investment Schemes', in Freestone and Streck, *Legal Aspects of Carbon Trading*, 157–75.

123 According to the EBRD, 'Greening is the process that links the sold AAUs to activities that can deliver climate or other environmental benefits: the AAU proceeds are earmarked for Greening Activities in the seller country, which may consist of emission reduction projects, other projects beneficial to the environment, or a combination thereof'. EBRD, GIS Manual (version 1.0). Manual for the Sale and Purchase of Assigned Amount Units under a Green Investment Scheme (16 March 2009), 10.

124 A. Tuerk et al., 'Green Investment Schemes', 3. This report mentions various examples of *soft greening*, such as capacity-building related to climate change, demand-side management programmes, capitalisation of energy service companies, insurance funds for energy efficiency investors or dismantling of energy subsidies.

125 The *greening ratio* is employed if buyers of AAUs want to ensure that the proceeds are invested by the seller country not only in greening activities but more specifically to achieve a certain amount of GHG emissions for each corresponding AAU sold. See EBRD, GIS Manual, 11.

and public universities in order to reduce energy consumption and carbon dioxide emissions.[126]

Because Green Investment Schemes are a relatively new technique in international emissions trading, no regulatory framework has yet emerged to address these questions in a systematic manner, although some efforts are under way. For instance, in 2009, the European Bank for Reconstruction and Development published a GIS manual containing a GIS model agreement enabling private-sector actors to enter as buyers of AAUs into contractual agreements with seller countries.[127] Proposals concerning payment and delivery mechanisms include the conclusion of custody and escrow arrangements whereby the seller would transfer AAUs to a custody account and the buyer would transfer the purchase price to an escrow account. The respective credits can only be released upon the satisfactory implementation of the greening activities undertaken in accordance with the agreement binding both parties (the 'Greening Plan').[128] Such developments demonstrate the dynamic evolution of green financial techniques meant to include private-sector efforts in the creation of sustainable market mechanisms. Whereas Green Investment Schemes have emerged within a given regulatory framework, for example, the international emissions trading scheme under the Kyoto Protocol, other market mechanisms have emerged spontaneously without the necessary participation of governments. This is especially the case with biodiversity conservation and the related problematic of ecosystem services.

6.4.2 Payment for environmental or ecosystem services

As a particular application of the Coase theorem, some private-sector actors have sought to secure the conservation of biodiversity through the payment of financial resources to other private-sector actors (such as landlords, farmers, communities etc.) so that they manage and maintain the integrity of specific ecosystems and the services they provide. The 2005 Millennium Ecosystem Assessment report defines ecosystem services as the benefits that people obtain from ecosystems. 'These include provisioning services such as food and water; regulating services such as

[126] '"Electric Cars in Exchange for Carbon Credits" AAU Deal Done by Japan', Climate Connect, 10 March 2011, available at www.climate-connect.co.uk (accessed 25 April 2011).

[127] EBRD, GIS Manual. [128] *Ibid.*, 19.

regulation of floods, drought, land degradation, and disease; supporting services such as soil formation and nutrient cycling; and cultural services such as recreational, spiritual, religious and other nonmaterial benefits.'[129] Various stakeholders, most importantly the public sector, but also the private sector, have increasingly acknowledged the economic value of ecosystem services. For instance, large metropolises that used to have access to clean drinking water have come to understand that it is sounder to manage and maintain the natural water filtering capacity of surrounding habitats than to build, at high cost, water purification stations providing an analogous service. Hungary seems to have realised this problem in the context of the Gabčíkovo–Nagymaros dam project that was at the heart of the dispute between Hungary and the Slovak Republic fought out before the ICJ.[130] Hungary alleged that the series of dams northwards from its capital Budapest would alter the filtering capacity of the riverbed and put at peril the provision of clean drinking water for the city.

The idea that underlies payment for environmental or ecosystem services schemes is that private parties can achieve an efficient outcome by bargaining around the allocation of resources. 'By offering economic incentives for maintaining ecosystem services, PES operates on the basis that market forces can offer an efficient and effective means of supporting sustainable development objectives.'[131] As an example, where private landowners destroy virgin forests in order to produce cattle and obtain a quantifiable benefit, other private-sector actors (or society at large) may have to support the corresponding cost of losing vital ecosystem services, such as carbon storage, water filtering, biodiversity etc. According to Ronald Coase, the interested parties can always find an efficient outcome if they only bargain around the allocation of the resources.[132] Thus, where the cost to society is larger than the benefit accrued by the private landlord, society or parts thereof should offer a price to the landlord so that he or she disengages in his or her destructive practices and contributes to the restoration of the ecosystem services

129 Millennium Ecosystem Assessment, *Ecosystems and Human Well-Being: Current State and Trends*, vol. 1 (Washington, DC: Island Press, 2005), 27. For further references, see above, n. 16.

130 *Gabčíkovo-Nagymaros Project (Hungary/Slovakia)*, Judgment, ICJ Reports 1997, 7.

131 UNEP/IUCN, 'Developing International Payments for Ecosystem Services: Towards a Greener World Economy' (2006), 2, available at www.unep.ch (accessed 25 April 2011). See also UNEP, 'Payments for Ecosystem Services: Getting Started' (2008).

132 R. Coase, 'The Problem of Social Cost' (1960) 3 *Journal of Law and Economics* 1.

provided before. PES schemes have commonly been defined as a 'voluntary transaction whereby a well-defined ecosystem service, or a land-use likely to secure that service, is being "bought" by at least one buyer from at least one provider – if, and only if, the provider secures the provision of the service'.[133]

Although the public sector has also used this technique to secure landscape conservation, the private sector has increasingly come to understand the importance of PES schemes. Thus, what distinguishes PES schemes from other forms of conservation (such as land acquisitions in order to evacuate the former polluter) is that PES schemes seek to involve the different service providers over long periods of time in order to engage them in the process of conservation. Besides being interesting contractual arrangements in the form of voluntary contracts between an ecosystem service provider and an ecosystem service buyer, PES is a new financial mechanism providing additional sources of funding for the environment and works as an incentive for the private sector to engage in environmental protection, such as biodiversity conservation or climate change mitigation.

CONCLUSION

The potentially successful outcome of a greener economy critically depends on the capacity to mobilise the efforts of the private sector, and in particular to channel the necessary funds into green production practices. This chapter has sought to present some of the main techniques that have been developed as incentives for private-sector actors to get involved in this process. Collective investment schemes present the biggest interest for a variety of reasons, not least because of the sheer amount of assets under professional management. Their analysis is complex because they involve different types of relationships amongst various actors. Thus, asset owners are increasingly deciding to increase their exposure to the SRI market and also pressure asset managers to include SRI criteria in their investment decisions. Collective investment schemes engaging in SRI provide an incentive for corporations to adopt eco-friendly production practices because this facilitates access to capital and eventually may even reduce the cost of

[133] *Ibid.* This definition has been adapted from Wunder's definition. See S. Wunder, 'Payments for Environmental Services: Some Nuts and Bolts', CIFOR Occasional Paper No. 42, 2005, at 3.

capital and increase returns on investment. The same can basically be said of international financial institutions, with the exception that these institutions, most prominently the IFC, engage their clients in long-term relationships where advisory services and monitoring play crucial roles. Thus, corporations benefiting from their financial support equally obtain valuable advice on how to mitigate their environmental risks. Market mechanisms for their part provide valuable tools for corporations to manage their polluting activities. With techniques such as emissions trading and carbon pricing, corporations that have a hard time reducing their emissions can still achieve compliance with their obligations by financing environment-friendly activities under the clean development mechanism or green investment schemes, for instance. These techniques thus also allow the channelling of private resources from big polluters to activities that foster a sustainable world economy.

Whether the existing financial architecture will effectively lead to a fundamental shift in global production patterns remains open to question, as the challenges are daunting. While some parts of the private sector may have come to understand the opportunities that lie behind the concept of a green economy, more clear policy signals from the international community are still needed; the efforts of several countries to provoke a change have not found generalised support. And, yet, even though there are no international rules governing the financial duties of asset managers, for instance, it has mainly been the private sector itself that has developed the financial techniques for channelling resources into sustainable projects. The market share of SRI should, however, not only be made up of investments of responsible investors alone; SRI should ideally become an integral part of any investment decision made by all relevant investors. This ideal situation seems, however, still to belong to a distant future.

Select bibliography

Barbier, E. B., *A Global Green New Deal: Rethinking the Economic Recovery* (Cambridge University Press and UNEP, 2010).

Bailey, R., T. Ryan and N. Hodges, 'Building on Sustainability into Syndication' (2006) *Environmental Finance* 28.

Boisson de Chazournes, L., 'The Global Environment Facility (GEF): A Unique and Crucial Institution' (2005) 14 *Review of European Community and International Environmental Law* 193.

Dewar, J. (ed.), *International Project Finance: Law and Practice* (Oxford University Press, 2011).

Freestone, D., and C. Streck (eds.), *Legal Aspects of Carbon Trading* (Oxford University Press, 2009).

Georgieva, K., S. Pagiola and P. Deeks, 'Paying for the Environmental Services of Protected Areas: Involving the Private Sector', paper presented at *Fifth World Park Congress, Sustainable Finance Streams*, International Union for Conservation of Nature (2003).

Hadfield-Hill, S., 'The Greening of Project Finance' (2007) 1 *Geography Compass* 1058.

Hall, B., and J. van Reenen, 'How Effective are Fiscal Incentives for R&D? A Review of the Evidence' (2000) 29 *Research Policy* 449.

Hardenbrook, A., 'The Equator Principles: The Private Financial Sector's Attempt at Environmental Responsibility' (2007) 40 *Vanderbilt Journal of Transnational Law* 197.

Herbertson, K., and D. Hunter, 'Emerging Standards for Sustainable Finance of the Energy Sector' (2007) 7 *Sustainable Development Law & Policy* 4.

Hunter, D. B., 'Civil Society Networks and the Development of Environmental Standards at International Financial Institutions' (2008) 8 *Chicago Journal of International Law* 437.

Juravale, C., and A. Lewis, 'Identifying Impediments to SRI in Europe: A Review of the Practitioner and Academic Literature' (2008) 17 *Business Ethics: A European Review* 285.

Krosinsky, C., and N. Robins (eds.), *Sustainable Investing: The Art of Long-Term Performance* (London: Earthscan, 2008).

Langer, M.-J., *The International Finance Corporation and International Environmental Law: Mainstreaming, Standardization, Compliance* (Geneva: Graduate Institute, 2009).

Lawrence, R. F., and W. L. Thomas, 'The Equator Principles and Project Finance: Sustainability in Practice' (2004) 19 *Natural Resources & Environment* 20.

Morgera, E., *Corporate Accountability in International Environmental Law* (Oxford University Press, 2009).

Organisation of Economic Co-operation and Development, *Handbook for Appraisal of Environmental Projects Financed from Public Funds* (Paris: OECD, 2007).

Park, S., 'World Bank Group: Championing Sustainable Development Norms?' (2007) 13 *Global Governance* 535.

Preu, F. J., and B. J. Richardson, 'German Socially Responsible Investment: Barriers and Opportunities' (2011) 12 *German Law Journal* 865.

Renneboog, L., J. Horst and C. Zhang, 'Socially Responsible Investments: Methodology, Risk Exposure and Performance', Finance Working Paper 175/2007 (2007).

Richardson, B. J., 'Financing Sustainability: The New Transnational Governance of Socially Responsible Investment' (2007) 17 *Yearbook of International Environmental Law* 73.

Schuler, G., 'Effective Governance through Decentralized Soft Implementation: The OECD Guidelines for Multinational Enterprises' (2008) 9 *German Law Journal* 1753.

Tuerk, A., D. Frieden, M. Sharmina, H. Schreiber and D. Ürge-Vorsatz, 'Green Investment Schemes: First Experiences and Lessons Learned', Working Paper, Joanneum Research/Central European University (April 2010).

United Nations Environment Programme, *Payments for Ecosystem Services. Getting Started: A Primer* (UNEP/Forest Trends, 2008).

Urwin, R., and C. Woods, 'Sustainable Investing Principles: Models for Institutional Investors', paper presented at the PRI Academic Conference 2009, Ottawa.

Vendzules, S. F., 'The Struggle for Legitimacy in Environmental Standards Systems: The OECD Guidelines for Multinational Enterprises' (2010) 21 *Colorado Journal of International Environmental Law* 451.

Wara, M., 'Measuring the Clean Development Mechanism's Performance and Potential' (2008) 55 *UCLA Law Review* 1759.

Wood, P., *Law and Practice of International Finance: Project Finance, Securitisations, Subordinated Debt*, vol. 5 (London: Sweet & Maxwell, 2007).

Wunder, S., 'Payments for Environmental Services: Some Nuts and Bolts', Occasional Paper No. 42, CIFOR (2005).

7

The potential of international climate change law to mobilise low-carbon foreign direct investment

DANIEL M. FIRGER

INTRODUCTION

International climate change law begins, for all intents and purposes, with Article 2 of the 1992 United Nations Framework Convention on Climate Change (UNFCCC), which calls for 'stabilization of greenhouse gas concentrations in the atmosphere at a level that would prevent dangerous anthropogenic interference with the climate system'.[1] Endorsed by 195 state parties,[2] this simple phrase articulates perhaps the greatest global challenge of our time: cutting greenhouse gas (GHG) emissions quickly and deeply enough to keep global temperatures from rising too far.[3] Yet, while the imperative to act has grown more urgent as GHGs continue to accumulate in the atmosphere, mitigating emissions has proven to be extraordinarily difficult.

In part, this is because climate change, like other cross-boundary environmental harms, presents a 'transnational cooperation dilemma.'[4]

[1] United Nations Framework Convention on Climate Change (opened for signature 20 June 1992, entered into force 1994) (1992) 31 ILM 848 (UNFCCC), art. 2.

[2] UNFCCC, Status of Ratification of the Convention, available at http://unfccc.int (accessed 1 March 2012).

[3] The relationship between GHG emissions, atmospheric concentrations of GHGs, global average temperature and climate change impacts is scientifically complex. The Intergovernmental Panel on Climate Change, in its Fourth Assessment Report, concluded that emissions should be reduced so as to hold the increase in global temperature to less than 2 degrees Celsius above the pre-industrial average, which represents the consensus scientific view on a threshold beyond which 'dangerous anthropogenic interference' will be unstoppable. Notably, this view was expressly endorsed for the first time by the international community in the 2009 Copenhagen Accord. UNFCCC Decision 2/CP.15 (2009) (Copenhagen Accord), para. 2, available at http://unfccc.int (accessed 14 March 2012).

[4] S. Barrett, *Environment and Statecraft: The Strategy of Environmental Treaty-Making* (Oxford University Press, 2003), 49 (describing international climate change policy coordination in game theoretical terms).

Since carbon dioxide (CO_2), the most abundant GHG, mixes uniformly throughout the Earth's atmosphere once emitted, no state acting alone can stop the global warming process and individual states have little incentive to reduce their own GHG emissions when others do not.[5] Moreover, unlike many environmental pollutants, CO_2 is emitted as a consequence of nearly every modern human activity, meaning that rewiring the world's energy systems to run on renewable rather than fossil fuels will be a monumentally expensive undertaking.[6] Effective climate change mitigation thus requires not only unprecedented levels of international cooperation but also enormous capital expenditures.

Recognising the need to mobilise huge financial flows to fund both emissions reductions in the developed world and low-carbon development in emerging economies, the international community codified a set of three market-based 'flexible mechanisms' in the 1997 Kyoto Protocol to the UNFCCC that seek, among other things, to incentivise private-sector investments across a range of climate friendly projects and activities.[7] By setting up the basic architecture for an international carbon market, these mechanisms have helped generate a wave of new green investments, both within individual countries and across international borders, with a total capitalisation far greater than the relatively small amount of public financing made available thus far for climate mitigation.[8] Subsequent climate agreements such as the 2007 Bali

[5] D. Bodansky, 'The Framework Convention on Climate Change: A Commentary' (1993) 18 *Yale Journal of International Law* 451. Although CO_2 is but one of several GHGs that contribute to climate change, this chapter will refer to CO_2 interchangeably with other gases. This follows the scientific convention of representing all GHGs in terms of the global warming potential of CO_2, known as CO_2 equivalent. See below, n. 37.

[6] In 2007, the United Nations Framework Convention on Climate Change estimated the cost of reducing GHG emissions by 25% below 2000 levels in 2030 to be US$200 bn to US$210 bn. UNFCCC, *Investment and Financial Flows to Address Climate Change* (2007), available at http://unfccc.int (accessed 14 March 2012). A year later, the figure was 170% higher, largely due to higher projected capital costs in the energy sector. UNFCCC, *Investment and Financial Flows to Address Climate Change: An Update*, FCCC/TP/2008/7 (2008), para. 60.

[7] Kyoto Protocol to the United Nations Framework Convention on Climate Change (opened for signature 16 March 1998, entered into force 16 February 2005) (1998) 37 ILM 22 (Kyoto Protocol), arts 6, 12, 17.

[8] According to the World Bank, the total value of the world carbon market in 2010, the most recent year for which data is available, was US$142 bn. This figure includes the transaction of allowances, spot and secondary Kyoto offsets, and project-based credits such as those generated by the clean development mechanism (CDM) and joint implementation (JI) programmes. World Bank, *State and Trends of the Carbon Market 2011*, available at www.worldbank.org.

Action Plan,[9] the 2009 Copenhagen Accord,[10] the 2010 Cancún Agreements[11] and the 2011 Durban Platform[12] have, together, gone much further to create incentives for, and provide a framework to govern, low-carbon foreign direct investment (FDI),[13] the subject of this chapter.

Of course, policies *other* than those initiated under the auspices of the UNFCCC are playing an increasingly important role in the transnational response to climate change. And firms may choose to invest in low-carbon projects abroad for any number of reasons that have nothing to do with climate change per se, such as gaining access to new markets or increasing the efficiency of their production chains. Nevertheless, because international climate change law increases the cost of carbon emissions (through domestic cap-and-trade programmes or taxes implementing international legal obligations), decreases the cost of low-carbon alternatives (through the offsetting role of market-based flexibility mechanisms), or creates other incentives for private-sector investments in GHG emissions mitigation, the UNFCCC-centred legal framework has been – and remains – a significant factor in determining the size, rate and direction of global (low carbon) FDI flows.[14]

This chapter addresses three of the chief policy instruments for low-carbon FDI under international environmental law: joint implementation (JI), the clean development mechanism (CDM), and reducing emissions from deforestation and forest degradation (REDD).[15] Section 7.1

[9] UNFCCC Decision 1/CP.13 (2007) (Bali Action Plan), available at http://unfccc.int (accessed 14 March 2012).

[10] Copenhagen Accord, above, n. 3.

[11] The set of texts agreed to in December 2010 at COP-16 are known collectively as the Cancún Agreements. UNFCCC Draft Decision -/CP.16 (2010) (Cancún Agreements), available at http://cancun.unfccc.int.

[12] UNFCCC Draft Decision -/CP.17 (2011) (Durban Platform), available at http://unfccc.int (accessed 14 March 2012).

[13] Climate change adaptation, as opposed to mitigation, has become an increasingly prominent part of international climate policy as average global temperatures continue to climb. See http://unfccc.int/adaptation (accessed 14 March 2012). While clearly important, adaptation is outside the scope of this chapter.

[14] See generally United Nations Conference on Trade and Development (UNCTAD), *World Investment Report 2010*, Sales No. E.10.II.D.2 (New York: United Nations, 2010).

[15] Although increasingly important drivers of clean energy investment, this chapter will not address the wide range of private-sector initiatives and voluntary climate policy mechanisms that help incentivise international investments in low-carbon development. Likewise, this chapter will not explore bilateral agreements or initiatives led by multilateral institutions such as the World Bank, which are also helping to shape the future of

begins with a brief discussion of the nature of international carbon markets, explaining how various regulatory regimes interact to create a new commodity, carbon credits and new mechanisms to buy, sell, trade and otherwise profit from GHG emissions mitigation activities. Sections 7.2, 7.3 and 7.4 take up each policy instrument in turn, addressing its essential features, analysing its effectiveness in mobilising low-carbon FDI and identifying key opportunities for reform. Section 7.5 concludes by examining recent trends in international climate policy, including developments since the 2011 Durban, South Africa climate change summit, which are both calling into question the continued viability of the aforementioned instruments and creating new opportunities for international cooperation on clean energy, GHG emissions mitigation and climate adaptation.

7.1 Understanding the carbon market(s)

International environmental law, together with a range of 'soft law' instruments, standards and norms,[16] has created a new commodity: carbon. More specifically, the UNFCCC, Kyoto Protocol and other climate policy mechanisms have effectively assigned value to a hitherto valueless substance, CO_2, and established a variety of rules by which this substance, in the form of so-called 'carbon credits,' can be bought, sold and traded. With entities forced to internalise the costs associated with their GHG emissions, previously costless activities that emit significant quantities of carbon into the atmosphere are becoming less affordable, while renewable energy projects and mitigation activities like afforestation are becoming increasingly attractive investment opportunities. Together with subsidies and other forms of state support for climate-friendly projects, a high carbon price is the single most important driver of low-carbon FDI.

Unlike the mature, liquid and relatively transparent markets for oil or orange juice, however, today's carbon markets are characterised by enormous regulatory ambiguity and are supervised, if at all, by a variety

low-carbon FDI. For a more detailed discussion of these and other mechanisms, see D. M. Firger and M. B. Gerrard, 'Harmonizing Climate Change Policy and International Investment Law' (2011) 3 *Yearbook of International Investment Law and Policy* 517.

16 See K. Abbott and D. Snidal, 'Hard and Soft Law in International Governance' (2000) 54 *International Organization* 421 (establishing a comprehensive analytical framework for thinking through similarities and differences between 'hard' and 'soft' law in international affairs).

of standard-setting bodies operating across multiple international, regional, national and subnational jurisdictions. This uncertainty not only renders carbon markets relatively illiquid and subject to huge price swings as shifting policy mandates influence investor behaviour, but also has prevented the emergence, thus far, of a single international market for fungible carbon credits.

Low-carbon FDI inhabits this confusing policy space. Firms invest in climate mitigation measures because they are profitable. And profitability is determined by, among other things, the price per ton of CO_2.[17] Understanding the incentives that drive low-carbon FDI thus requires an examination of the regulatory mechanisms that set carbon prices and govern the operation of a range of loosely interlinked carbon markets.

7.1.1 The 'regime complex' for climate change

International climate change policy is fragmented, polycentric and decentralised in nature, consisting of multiple organisations, standards and operational activities that interact in complex ways.[18] Notwithstanding two decades of diplomacy aimed at crafting a comprehensive international treaty regime to set a global cap on GHG emissions and establish coherent rules for a global carbon market, climate policy today is characterised by a constellation of overlapping regulatory regimes rather than any single overarching framework for global action.

Taking stock of this messy reality, analysts have begun describing climate policy as a 'regime complex',[19] characterised less by consistent rules than by 'connections between [...] specific and relatively narrow regimes [and] the absence of an overall architecture or hierarchy that structures the whole set'.[20] The regime complex for climate change

[17] Throughout this chapter I use the word 'ton' to signify the most common unit of measurement applied to CO_2. Scientifically, however, this unit is in fact a metric ton, or 'tonne'. An American ton, also known as a 'short ton', is equal to 2,000 pounds, or 907 kilograms. By contrast, a metric ton equals 1,000 kilograms.

[18] K. Abbott, 'The Transnational Regime Complex for Climate Change', 1 (manuscript on file with author).

[19] The concept of a 'regime complex for climate change' was first proposed by political scientists Robert Keohane and David Victor in 2010. See R. Keohane and D. Victor, 'The Regime Complex for Climate Change' (2011) 9 *Perspectives on Politics* 7. Keohane and Victor build upon earlier work introducing the concept of a regime complex and applying it to the issue area of plant genetic resources. K. Raustiala and D. Victor, 'The Regime Complex for Plant Genetic Resources' (2004) 58 *International Organization* 277.

[20] Keohane and Victor, 'The Regime Complex for Climate Change', 8.

consists of a variety of policy instruments that create incentives for low-carbon FDI. Some instruments are defined formally under public international law, through the UNFCCC, Kyoto Protocol and their subsidiary agreements. Others are established by soft law institutions and standard-setting bodies.[21] One recent paper identifies sixty-seven distinct organisations engaged in some form of regulatory standard-setting in the climate change regime complex.[22] Of course, much of this standard-setting activity deals with governance issues beyond the scope of this chapter (and addressed elsewhere in this volume). It is the structure and form of the international carbon markets, and their capacity to incentivise low-carbon FDI, which concern us here.

7.1.2 Creating carbon credits

The international community concluded the UNFCCC at the 1992 Earth Summit in Rio de Janeiro.[23] The Convention, along with its 1997 Kyoto Protocol establishing country-specific emissions reduction commitments for the period from 2008 to 2012, has been the primary public international law mechanism for dealing with climate change ever since.[24] At its core, international climate change law consists of a set of binding emissions reduction targets for developed country parties listed in Annex I of the UNFCCC (known as Annex I countries).[25] It is this obligation under international law to cut emissions that heretofore has constituted the prime driver of international carbon markets and, thus, much low-carbon FDI activity.[26]

Taken together, Annex I countries' targets, known as quantified emission limitation reduction (QELR) commitments and inscribed in Annex B to the Kyoto Protocol as 'assigned amounts',[27] set a goal of reducing aggregate GHG emissions in Annex I countries by at least 5 per cent

[21] For an excellent survey of many of these institutions, see K. Michonski and M. Levi, 'Working Paper: Harnessing International Institutions to Address Climate Change', Council of Foreign Relations, 2010, available at http://i.cfr.org (accessed 14 March 2012).
[22] See Abbott, *The Transnational Regime Complex*, 6.
[23] UNFCCC. The 'Rio +20' United Nations Conference on Sustainable Development took place in June 2012. See www.uncsd2012.org (accessed 14 March 2012).
[24] Kyoto Protocol. [25] UNFCCC, Annex I.
[26] As in the case of most other aspects of international law, it is in fact states' domestic legislation implementing international legal obligations, such as those imposed by the Kyoto Protocol, that force GHG emitters to purchase carbon credits and otherwise engage in climate-related market activity.
[27] Kyoto Protocol, Annex B.

below 1990 levels by 2012.[28] To achieve their QELR commitments, Annex I countries agreed to implement a variety of policies and measures, in accordance with national circumstances. These include, inter alia, energy efficiency measures, protection of GHG 'sinks and reservoirs' such as forests, research and development on renewable energy and carbon sequestration technologies, and the phase out of preferential tax treatment and subsidies for carbon intensive industries.[29] The conference of the parties (COP) to the UNFCCC meets annually to review implementation and negotiate further commitments,[30] while two permanent subsidiary bodies meet separately and advise the COP on scientific and technical matters.[31]

Crucially, the Kyoto Protocol also established a set of three 'flexible mechanisms' to enable Annex I countries to achieve their QELRs in a cost-effective manner. These mechanisms are: (i) international emissions trading (IET) between Annex I countries;[32] (ii) joint implementation, which allows Annex I countries to transfer among themselves carbon credits generated by low-carbon projects undertaken within other Annex I countries;[33] and (iii) the clean development mechanism, which authorises private entities in Annex I countries to finance and obtain credits for emissions reduction projects undertaken in developing (non-Annex I) countries.[34] Policies aimed at reducing emissions from deforestation and forest degradation (REDD) were not included in the Kyoto Protocol when it was adopted in 1997, but have subsequently been adopted by the international community.[35] Each of these mechanisms anticipates a role for the private sector in the creation, transfer or sale of carbon credits.[36] Thus, each also creates incentives for certain types of low-carbon FDI associated with the generation of such credits.

[28] *Ibid.*, art. 3. Notably, the USA is not a party to the Kyoto Protocol, and therefore is not legally bound to reduce its emissions, as are most other developed countries.

[29] *Ibid.*, art. 2.

[30] UNFCCC, 'Essential Background: Convention Bodies,' available at http://unfccc.int (accessed 14 March 2012).

[31] The Subsidiary Body for Scientific and Technological Advice (SBSTA) was established by Article 9 of the Convention, with a mandate to 'provide the Conference of the Parties and, as appropriate, its other subsidiary bodies with timely information and advice on scientific and technological matters relating to the Convention'. UNFCCC, art. 9. Article 10 of the Convention established the Subsidiary Body for Implementation (SBI), which is meant to 'assist the Conference of the Parties in the assessment and review of the effective implementation of the Convention'. UNFCCC, art. 10.

[32] *Ibid.*, art. 17. [33] *Ibid.*, art. 6. [34] *Ibid.*, art. 12 [35] See section 7.4, below.

[36] See K. Kulovesi, 'The Private Sector and the Implementation of the Kyoto Protocol: Experiences, Challenges and Prospects' (2007) 16 *RECIEL* 145.

7.1.2.1 Allowances

The basic unit of carbon currency under the Kyoto Protocol is an allowance called the assigned amount unit (AAU). An Annex I country's total 'assigned amount' is equivalent to that country's Annex B QELR objective, expressed in tons of CO_2 equivalent (CO_2e).[37] In other words, the assigned amount is the total volume of CO_2e an Annex I country is allowed to emit during the Kyoto Protocol's first commitment period, which runs from 2008 to 2012. Each ton of CO_2 in a given country's assigned amount is equal to one AAU, which may be acquired and transferred under the IET rules established pursuant to Article 17 of the Kyoto Protocol. Notably, the COP formally adopted eligibility requirements for IET only in 2005.[38] These requirements are relatively straightforward, and work to ensure only that before a country trades any AAUs across borders or allows a private entity to do so, it must have certified that, inter alia, it has a programme in place for measuring and registering its GHG emissions.[39]

At the Durban summit in December 2011, the COP adopted a decision expressing agreement to extend the Kyoto Protocol beyond its original 2012 expiration date by creating a second commitment period, running from 2013 to at least 2017.[40] This decision, among other things, contains proposed amendments to Annex B of the Kyoto Protocol detailing new QELR objectives for Annex I countries, alongside certain country-specific pledges for additional reductions by the year 2020.

[37] Each of the six GHGs for which emissions cuts are mandated under the Kyoto Protocol has a different global warming potential, meaning that a ton of each gas will heat up the atmosphere more or less than the same amount of another gas. For ease of use, scientists and policymakers express volumes for five of the gases in terms of the sixth, CO_2. For example, one ton of HFC-23, a particularly potent GHG, has the global warming potential of 11,700 tons of CO_2. See Intergovernmental Panel on Climate Change (IPCC), 'Fourth Assessment Report: Synthesis Report' (Geneva, 2007), table 2.14 (p. 212), available at www.ipcc-wg1.unibe.ch (accessed 14 March 2012).

[38] Decision 11/CMP.1, *Modalities, Rules and Guidelines for Emissions Trading under Article 17 of the Kyoto Protocol*, Decision adopted by the Conference of the Parties Serving as the Meeting of the Parties to the Kyoto Protocol, FCCC/KP/CMP/2005/8/Add. 2, 30 March 2006.

[39] T. Szymanski, 'The Evolution of Emissions Trading in Europe: Legal and Commercial Risks Facing Phase II of the EU Emissions Trading Scheme' (2007) 1 *European Business Law Journal* 583.

[40] UNFCCC, Outcome of the Work of the Ad Hoc Working Group on Further Commitments for Annex I Parties under the Kyoto Protocol at its Sixteenth Session, Draft Decision -/CMP.7 (2011) available at http://unfccc.int (accessed 14 March 2012).

7.1.2.2 Offsets

Unlike AAUs, which are government-created allowances with certain unique features under the UNFCCC treaty regime, carbon offsets are generated privately, through project-based transactions. International climate law has detailed rules and standards governing how and where such offsets can be created and how emitters can use them to comply with their emissions reduction commitments, but international law delegates much of the 'nuts and bolts' of offsets to the market. Offset credits associated with Article 12 of the Kyoto Protocol are called certified emissions reduction (CER) credits, and are generated by projects approved under the CDM and issued by the CDM's Executive Board (CDM EB) on the basis of an independently audited report that verifies actual reductions in GHG emissions as a result of the project.[41] Like AAUs, each CER credit is equivalent to one ton of CO_2.[42] CER credits may only be generated by projects within non-Annex I countries. In contrast, JI projects implemented under Article 6 of the Kyoto Protocol yield emissions reduction units (ERUs), each of which is created through the one-to-one conversion of an AAU (or a removal unit or RMU)[43] in the account of a project's host country.[44] Since JI projects take place between Annex I countries only, ERUs can be exchanged directly for AAUs, as opposed to the supplementary nature of CER credits generated from projects in non-Annex I countries.

Beyond the basic eligibility requirements for carbon units created pursuant to the Kyoto Protocol, the 2001 Marrakech Accords require Annex I countries to hold a minimum level of AAUs, CER credits, ERUs and/or RMUs in a so-called 'commitment period reserve', which cannot be transferred. Designed to ensure that the bulk of Annex I countries' mitigation activities take place within their own borders in accordance with Article 3 of the Kyoto Protocol, this minimum level is set at 90 per cent of a country's assigned amount or the amount of emissions reported in the country's most recent emissions inventory, whichever is lower.[45]

[41] For a discussion of the legal nature of CERs generated via CDM projects, see J. Lin, 'Private Actors in International and Domestic Emissions Trading Systems', in D. Freestone and C. Streck (eds.), *Legal Aspects of Carbon Trading: Kyoto, Copenhagen, and Beyond* (Oxford University Press, 2009), 142.

[42] *Ibid.*

[43] Removal units, equivalent to AAUs, are created via eligible sink activities in Annex I countries, in accordance with Articles 3.3 and 3.4 of the Kyoto Protocol.

[44] See M. Wemaere, C. Streck and T. Chagas, 'Legal Ownership and Nature of Kyoto Units and EU Allowances', in Freestone and Streck, *Legal Aspects of Carbon Trading*, 35.

[45] Decision 11/CMP.1, Annex 6.

The commitment period reserve thus operates as one of the most significant limitations to the growth of low-carbon FDI via the Kyoto Protocol's flexible mechanisms, since only roughly 10 per cent of total AAUs can be transferred via the carbon markets. Notably, however, at the 2011 Durban summit the COP adopted a decision calling for a review of 'the design of the commitment period reserve for the subsequent [second] commitment period to support the effective operation of emissions trading'.[46] A change to the rules regarding how the reserve operates could clearly have major implications for the future of low-carbon FDI.

7.2 Joint implementation

7.2.1 Background

When the UNFCCC and Kyoto Protocol were negotiated in the 1990s, the world's developed economies not only had been responsible for almost all historic GHG emissions but were also still generating the bulk of current emissions. Adhering to the principle of 'common but differentiated responsibilities',[47] the treaties reflected a shared understanding that the vast majority of emissions mitigation activity would take place within Annex I countries while non-Annex I countries, still by and large developing economies, would be left to their own devices. Thus, JI, discussed here, was designed for the use of Annex I countries exclusively.

Article 6 of the Kyoto Protocol allows Annex I countries to fund projects in other Annex I countries that 'reduc[e] anthropogenic emissions by sources or enhanc[e] anthropogenic removals by sinks of greenhouse gases in any sector of the economy'.[48] These projects yield ERUs, with each ERU, like each AAU or CER credit, equivalent to one ton of CO_2. So long as each JI project generates emissions reductions that are 'additional to any that would otherwise occur',[49] and provided the acquisition of ERUs is 'supplemental to domestic actions for the purposes of meeting commitments under Article 3',[50] an Annex I country may

[46] UNFCCC, Emissions Trading and the Project-based Mechanisms, Draft Decision -/CMP.7 (2011) available at http://unfccc.int (accessed 14 March 2012).

[47] UNFCCC, art. 3(1): 'The Parties should protect the climate system for the benefit of present and future generations of humankind, on the basis of equity and in accordance with their common but differentiated responsibilities and respective capabilities. Accordingly, the developed country Parties should take the lead in combating climate change and the adverse effects thereof.'

[48] Kyoto Protocol, art. 6. [49] *Ibid.*, art. 6(1)(b). [50] *Ibid.*, art. 6(1)(d).

count ERUs towards its own emissions reduction target, set out in Annex B of the Kyoto Protocol.[51] Since a ton of CO_2 emitted anywhere in the world is globally fungible, and since opportunities to reduce GHG emissions may be cheaper in the former Soviet Union (FSU) than in, say, France, the JI mechanism was expected to help entities maximise their climate mitigation investments by creating incentives for low-carbon FDI flows into countries where relatively cheap mitigation opportunities are readily available.

JI projects can be initiated by governments directly, but they are much more likely to be run, for profit, by private entities. Article 6 expressly permits Annex I countries to 'authorize legal entities to participate, under its responsibility, in actions leading to the generation, transfer or acquisition' of ERUs.[52] In order to register and receive credit for its ERUs, a project sponsor, whether private or public, must comply with the JI guidelines established by the UNFCCC Secretariat.[53] Once it meets the criteria, a JI investor can 'repatriate' its ERUs under the rules of its home country, either using them to offset the cost of complying with its own domestic cap on GHG emissions or selling them to other entities in the market for carbon credits. By allowing private parties to seek out opportunities to generate ERUs, Article 6 prefigures significant private-sector FDI flows into low-carbon mitigation projects.

The JI registry went live in January 2008 and will run until 2012, coinciding with the first commitment period of the Kyoto Protocol.[54] JI projects will continue to generate ERUs during the second commitment period, although the COP adopted a decision at the Durban summit inviting changes to the JI guidelines that may or may not alter the operation of the registry and the rules for issuance and use of such credits.[55] Notably, CDM projects got a seven-year head start over JI projects, since Article 12 of the Kyoto Protocol allowed for the registration of such projects starting in 2001. This meant that CER credits generated between 2001 and 2008, as well as those generated in the period from 2008 to 2012, could be used to meet emissions reduction goals during the first commitment period (2008–12).

[51] *Ibid.*, Annex B. [52] *Ibid.*, art. 6(3).

[53] Decision 9/CMP.1, Annex, FCCC/KP/CMP/2005/8/Add. 2.

[54] UNFCCC, Kyoto Protocol Mechanisms: Joint Implementation, available at http://unfccc.int (accessed 14 March 2012).

[55] UNFCCC, Guidance on the Implementation of Article 6 of the Kyoto Protocol, Draft Decision -/CMP.7, available at http://unfccc.int (accessed 14 March 2012).

By comparison, JI projects were allowed to generate ERUs only during the first commitment period itself.[56]

Nevertheless, hundreds of JI projects have been registered since 2008, accounting for upwards of 500 million tons of CO_2.[57] These projects range from the installation of wind farms in New Zealand to the capture and utilisation of methane from Polish swine manure,[58] with the majority of ERUs generated by reducing methane losses from leaky natural gas pipelines in the FSU.[59] Russia, the 'country with the largest potential for JI', according to the chairman of the Joint Implementation Supervisory Committee (JISC),[60] had not registered a single JI project until relatively recently. It submitted its first fifteen projects for approval in the summer of 2010,[61] heralding what some hope will be a period of explosive growth for JI.

7.2.2 Track 1 versus 2 projects

Climate mitigation projects in Annex I countries can be registered pursuant to the JI guidelines under one of two distinct procedures. The first procedure, known as Track 1, allows a project's host country independently to determine how to verify the project, without oversight from any outside entities. Under Track 1, the host country defines the criteria that eligible projects must meet, as well as the rules for verification of the actual emissions reductions represented by the ERUs granted to the project sponsor.[62] Track 2 projects, by contrast, are meant to operate under the supervision of the JISC, a formal UNFCCC body tasked under the Kyoto Protocol with developing registration and verification procedures for JI projects.[63] Project sponsors registering their activities under Track 2 must hire independent third-party auditors to ensure that all

[56] See J. Hoogzaad and C. Streck, 'A Mechanism with a Bright Future: Joint Implementation', in Freestone and Streck, *Legal Aspects of Carbon Trading*, 184. Notably, the rules for issuance of ERUs during the second commitment period were still being revised as this chapter was submitted for publication.

[57] See http://ji.unfccc.int/JI_Projects/ProjectInfo.html (accessed 14 March 2012).

[58] *Ibid.*

[59] UNEP RISO Centre, Content of the CDM/JI Pipeline: Number of JI Projects in per cent (updated 1 May 2011), available at http://cdmpipeline.org/ji-projects.htm#2 (accessed 14 March 2012).

[60] See www.bloomberg.com/news/2010–08–30/russia-submits-breakthrough-carbon-emissions-reduction-project-un-says.html (accessed 14 March 2012).

[61] *Ibid.*

[62] See Hoogzaad and Streck, 'A Mechanism with a Bright Future', 178.

[63] *Ibid.*

JISC guidelines have been met, imposing additional costs on their projects vis-à-vis comparable Track 1 projects.

Track 1 procedures were first developed by a small set of host country governments who were early movers on JI. These governments, which included France, Germany, Hungary, New Zealand and Romania, helped attract early investors by helping project sponsors calculate emissions reductions, establish baselines to determine project additionality, and develop and implement monitoring plans.[64] Because the JI guidelines for Track 2 projects were only published by the JISC in 2006, early projects had to rely either on host country government procedures developed under Track 1 or nothing at all. Despite the advantages of the streamlined Track 1 procedure, most investors have until recently preferred the certainty of Track 2, in part due to concerns about the environmental integrity of JI projects. In countries with relatively poor governance or where corruption is prevalent, ERU buyers under Track 1 cannot guarantee that the credits they hold will comply with the compliance requirements imposed by the own home country governments.

7.2.3 Outlook

Indeed, the market for ERUs has been plagued by concerns about lax monitoring, reporting and verification (MRV) of JI projects undertaken without the direct supervision of the JISC. This concern about the environmental integrity of emissions mitigation projects has kept many potential buyers away from Track 1 projects altogether. For this reason, ERUs have tended to trade at a discount relative to equivalent credits, known as CER credits, issued under the more robust CDM programme.[65] Of the 257 JI projects registered as of May 2011,[66] 229 were registered under Track 1, where verification procedures and the issuance of ERUs are left up to the host country. The remaining twenty-eight projects were registered under Track 2, leaving verification and issuance up to the JISC. Notably, Track 2 projects accounted for nearly 60 per cent of projects in the JI pipeline in 2011, and for 80 per cent of total ERU volume expected by the end of 2012.[67] However, with over 200 Track 2 projects in the

[64] *Ibid.*, 180.

[65] World Bank, *State and Trends of the Carbon Market 2010*, 50. For a fuller discussion of the CDM, see section 7.3.2, below.

[66] World Bank, *State and Trends of the Carbon Market 2010*, 50. [67] *Ibid.*

pipeline but only thirty-seven of them actually registered as of February 2012, Track 1 represented a greater proportion of available ERUs.[68]

Moreover, buyers from the EU, many of which had previously preferred the certainty that came along with Track 2 projects under the JISC's supervision, seem to be increasingly willing to accept ERUs generated from Track 1 projects as current EU emissions trading system (ETS) eligibility restrictions require that ERUs used for ETS compliance must be issued prior to December 2012.[69]

JI has proven to be a particularly advantageous avenue for generating low-carbon FDI in Russia and other members of the FSU, since the Kyoto Protocol set Annex I countries' baseline emissions at 1990 levels, and much of the FSU experienced major declines in energy consumption during the past two decades. Indeed, with aging industrial infrastructure and AAUs to spare, Russia and the Ukraine alone account for nearly half of all JI projects in the pipeline, and *more* than half of all ERUs expected to be issued by the end of 2012.[70] Over and above sealing leaky pipelines, the FSU could reap tremendous benefits from clean energy technologies and simple efficiency improvements across a range of industrial sectors. Beyond the FSU, the usefulness of the JI instrument for low-carbon FDI in more developed Annex I countries remains to be seen.

7.3 The clean development mechanism

7.3.1 Background

The CDM enables both private parties and governments of developed (Annex I) or developing (non-Annex I) countries to receive certified emissions reduction credits for implementing projects that reduce GHG emissions or increase GHG sinks within non-Annex I countries.[71] Like ERUs generated by JI projects, these CER credits, each equivalent to one ton of CO_2, help incentivise low-carbon FDI because governments and/or private parties can use them to meet their QELR targets under Article 3 of the Kyoto Protocol.[72] Project developers using the CDM to

[68] There were 229 Track 1 projects in the pipeline, with 114 of them registered, as of May 2011. See UNEP RISO Centre, above, n. 59, JI Pipeline Spreadsheet (May 2011), available at http://cdmpipeline.org/publications/JiPipeline.xlsx (accessed 14 March 2012).

[69] World Bank, *State and Trends of the Carbon Market 2010*, 50.

[70] See JI Pipeline Spreadsheet (May 2011).

[71] Kyoto Protocol, art. 12.

[72] *Ibid.* See also C. Streck and J. Lin, 'Making Markets Work: A Review of CDM Performance and the Need for Reform' (2008) 19 *European Journal of International Law* 409–20

generate CER credits can opt to use the CER credits themselves, contract to sell them to other entities, or trade them on secondary markets.[73]

For firms such as the approximately 11,000 entities regulated under the EU ETS and assigned a limited number of tradable emissions allowances,[74] investing in CDM projects directly or purchasing CER credits on the secondary market can be a meaningful, and profitable, compliance strategy; the CER credits generated from such projects help firms achieve what would otherwise be costly compliance with emissions reduction targets. Motivated by wholly different considerations, firms capable of efficiently reducing their GHG emissions below their allocated targets, as well as firms from non-Annex I countries (where no caps on emissions exist), may also seek to invest in CDM projects of their own in order to generate CER credits for sale to Annex I entities.[75]

Since it allows for projects to be undertaken across the entire developing world, as opposed to just within Annex I countries, the CDM has far greater potential than joint implementation to stimulate low-carbon FDI flows.[76] The CDM has indeed attracted significant investment, with over 2,900 transnational projects – worth billions of dollars – registered as of March 2011.[77] One recent study estimated that CDM projects initiated since 2002 represent US$150 billion in investment, although not all of this constitutes FDI since some project sponsors from major emerging

(describing the CDM); A. Arquit Niederberger and R. Saneer, 'Exploring the Relationship between FDI Flows and CDM Potential' (2005) 14 *Transnational Corporations* 1 (same).

73 See Niederberger and Saneer, 'Exploring the Relationship', 4 (discussing the characteristics of CDM transactions).

74 See http://ec.europa.eu/clima/policies/ets/index_en.htm (accessed 14 March 2012).

75 See Niederberger and Saneer, 'Exploring the Relationship', 12.

76 *Ibid.*, 1.

77 UNFCCC, 'CDM Statistics'. http://cdm.unfccc.int (accessed 22 Feb. 2012). The CDM market was worth roughly US$7.4 bn in 2007, according to an analysis published by the World Bank. World Bank, *State and Trends of the Carbon Market 2008*, 19. In just two years, however, that value had fallen by over 50%, with the CDM market worth only US$3.3 bn in 2009. World Bank, *State and Trends of the Carbon Market 2010*, 37. Two points should be noted in this regard. First, this volatility in CDM investments reflects, in part, the global financial crisis of 2008. It also reflects fundamental uncertainty about the future of climate policy, and therefore of carbon markets. Second, the figures cited by the World Bank do not represent the combined value of CDM investments, but merely the value of the primary market for CERs *generated by* these investments. According to the International Institute for Sustainable Development, 'The underlying investments that gave rise to those credits would be many times as large.' Fiona Marshall, 'Climate Change and International Investment Agreements: Obstacles or Opportunities', *International Institute for Sustainable Development, Trade, Investment and Climate Change Series* (March 2010), 73.

economies have provided their own financing.[78] And, in 2008, the peak year for CER credits market activity, total trading volume was valued at over US$32 billion, including both primary and secondary markets.[79] Of course, this number has come down significantly as a result of the global financial crisis. The recent drop in economic activity, particularly in Europe, home to the vast majority of CER credits' buyers, has led to a drop in emissions and thus an oversupply of CER credits and a steep drop in prices (alongside an even steeper drop in the price of EUAs, EU-specific emissions allowances traded under the EU ETS). Together with significant uncertainty about the continuation of the CDM in advance of the Durban summit in late 2011, these macroeconomic factors have led to stalled CDM project registrations, weak trading activity on the secondary markets and limited incentives for new low-carbon investments in non-Annex I developing and least-developed countries.

In Durban, the COP adopted a relatively lengthy and detailed decision extending the CDM to the Kyoto Protocol's second commitment period and committing to a far-ranging governance reform process.[80] CDM reform had – and has – been a significant issue for stakeholders around the world, including most prominently the European Commission, which solicited a 'study on the integrity' of the CDM in response to longstanding concerns about issues such as additionality, technology transfer and sustainable development.[81] With these reforms well under way (see section 7.3.2, below), the prospects for the CDM are somewhat improved from the abysmal state of the market in 2011.

7.3.2 Governance and reform

Since the market for CER credits is entirely contingent upon the binding obligation on developed countries under the Kyoto Protocol to comply with their QELR commitments (including national emissions caps such as the EU ETS that are legally tied into the Kyoto framework and those, such as Australia, which may soon allow CER credits to satisfy domestic

[78] UNCTAD, *World Investment Report 2010*, 139 (citing UNEP Risoe, 'CDM/JI Pipeline Analysis and Database', 1 March 2010).

[79] World Bank, *State and Trends of the Carbon Market 2009*, 1.

[80] UNFCCC, Further Guidance Relating to the Clean Development Mechanism, Draft Decision -/CMP.7, available at http://unfccc.int (accessed 14 March 2012).

[81] See AEA Technology plc, Stockholm Environment Institute, Centre for European Policy Studies & CO_2 Logic, Study on the Integrity of the Clean Development Mechanism (December 2011), available at http://ec.europa.eu (accessed 14 March 2012).

compliance obligations),[82] the driving force behind the decision to invest is policy dependent; uncertainty about the future form of the CDM after the Kyoto Protocol's expiry in 2012 caused a significant dip in project activity in 2010–11.[83] At the Cancún summit in December 2010, the COP took steps to reform and strengthen governance of the CDM,[84] while falling short of some parties' proposals that the CDM be linked to new instruments designed to stimulate FDI and deliver emissions reduction on a much larger scale.[85] A year later, the COP in Durban took further steps to move towards a reformed and better-governed CDM.

Reforming the CDM has proven necessary not just because, under the terms of the Copenhagen Accord, low-carbon FDI must increase fivefold by 2020,[86] but also because real challenges remain in meeting the CDM's original twin goals of emissions mitigation and sustainable development. Many observers have criticised the CDM's relatively lax governance structure and questioned the additionality of the CER credits issued as a result of CDM projects, calling into question the effectiveness of the scheme to achieve real emissions reduction.[87] Furthermore, CDM projects have been implemented extremely unevenly across developing countries. Countries with relatively high levels of development have attracted the majority of CDM projects, while least developed countries (LDCs) have hosted only a few. Indeed, 70 per cent of CDM projects

[82] See Kyoto Protocol, art. 3.

[83] World Bank, *State and Trends of the Carbon Market 2010*, 37.

[84] See UNFCCC, Further Guidance Relating the Clean Development Mechanism, Draft Decision -/CMP.6, available at http://unfccc.int (accessed 14 March 2012).

[85] UNCTAD, *World Investment Report 2010*, 139.

[86] The Copenhagen Accord calls for US$100 bn in annual climate finance by 2020. By comparison, the value of all CDM projects between 2002 and 2010 has been estimated at just US$150 bn, or about US$18.7 bn per year. See *ibid.*

[87] For an overview of the issues related to CDM governance and the environmental integrity of CERs, see generally C. Streck, 'Expectations and Reality of the Clean Development Mechanism: A Climate Finance Instrument between Accusation and Aspirations', in R. B. Stewart, B. Kingsbury and B. Rudyk (eds.), *Climate Finance: Regulatory and Funding Strategies for Climate Change and Global Development* (New York: NYU Press, 2009), 67–75. See also M. Wara, 'Measuring the Clean Development Mechanism's Performance and Potential' (2008) 55 *UCLA Law Review* 1759; J. F. Green, 'Delegation and Accountability in the Clean Development Mechanism: The New Authority of Non-State Actors' (2008) 4 *Journal of International Law and International Relations* 21; C. Carr and F. Rosembuj, 'Flexible Mechanisms for Climate Change Compliance: Emission Offset Purchases under the Clean Development Mechanism' (2008) 16 *New York University Environmental Law Journal* 44; D. Hirsch, 'Trading in Ecosystem Services: Carbon Sinks and the Clean Development Mechanism' (2007) 22 *Journal of Land Use and Environmental Law* 623.

registered by 2011 have been located in just three countries: China (41.2 per cent), India (22.3 per cent) and Brazil (7.1 per cent). Only 1.9 per cent of registered projects are in Africa, with South Africa leading the continent at seventeen projects as of 2011.[88]

A recent World Bank study highlights the extent to which the CDM is being underutilised in spurring low-carbon FDI to LDCs. The authors examine the reasons for the relative absence of projects in Sub-Saharan Africa, where, as of May 2008, countries only hosted fifty-three projects out of the 3,902 then in the CDM project pipeline.[89] The study concluded that lack of CDM-related low-carbon FDI in the region was not due primarily to a lack of project opportunities. Rather, it found that there was potential for more than 3,200 clean energy projects that, if fully implemented, could provide more than double the amount of the region's current power generation capacity, while avoiding 'about 740 million tCO_2 [of future GHG emissions] per year, more than the region's current annual GHG emissions (680 million tCO_2)'.[90]

Clearly, CDM reform, undertaken in the near future pursuant to the serial mandates of the Cancún Agreements and Durban Platform and driven by increasing demand from governments in Europe and other jurisdictions that are home to the majority of CER credits' buyers, has the potential to unlock significant new clean energy and low-carbon investment opportunities in the developing world. Much, however, depends on how such reform is undertaken. With non-Annex I country parties committed, under the terms of the Durban Platform, to negotiate a new treaty-based mitigation regime by 2015 to be operationalised by 2020, the role of the CDM remains somewhat uncertain; will China, for instance, allow domestic emitters to purchase CER credits to comply with any future compliance obligation such as that imposed under a national or subnational cap-and-trade scheme? For now, notwithstanding this

[88] UNFCCC, 'Registration: Registered Project by Region and Registered Project by Host Party', http://cdm.unfccc.int/Statistics/index.html (accessed 22 February 2012).

[89] C. de Gouvello, F. B. Dayo and M. Thioye, *Low-Carbon Energy Projects for Development in Sub-Saharan Africa: Unveiling the Potential, Addressing the Barriers* (Washington, DC: World Bank, 2008), p. xxii (noting that the estimates may be low because the CDM's Executive Board is approving new methodologies for CDM projects, and that for various types of projects, including geothermal, concentrated solar power, wind farms, small hydropower plants, waste-to-energy projects, building energy efficiency, solar water heaters and improved household stoves, the study team could not collect sufficient information to draw conclusions regarding their potential).

[90] *Ibid.*, p. xx.

lack of clarity, the CDM remains the most promising mechanism under the UNFCCC to generate large and sustained low-carbon FDI flows to the developing world.

7.4 REDD

7.4.1 Background

Tropical deforestation accounts for roughly one-fifth of global anthropogenic carbon emitted each year,[91] yet until relatively recently policies aimed at reducing emissions from deforestation and degradation (REDD) were not formally included within the UNFCCC system.[92] Concerned with complicated questions of additionality and unable to agree on standards for MRV of avoided deforestation projects, negotiators chose to leave REDD outside of the original Kyoto Protocol framework. But, since the late 1990s, political and economic changes in forest-rich countries like Brazil and Indonesia, together with advances in remote sensing technology, have provided solutions to many of these problems.[93] At COP-16, in December 2010, REDD represented a rare area of relative consensus among developed and developing countries,[94] and parties to the Convention left Cancún with a formal, albeit vague, agreement in hand on forest conservation and climate change.[95] Further

[91] See IPCC, 'Fourth Assessment Report: Synthesis Report'.

[92] Parties to the UNFCCC have had extensive discussions on deforestation since the COP-11 summit in Montreal in 2005, but the REDD policy framework was formally introduced at COP-13 in 2007, as a component of the Bali Action Plan. See UNFCCC Decision 2/CP.13 (Reducing emissions from deforestation in developing countries: approaches to stimulate action), UN Doc. FCCC/CP/2007/6/Add. 1, 14 March 2008, available at http://unfccc.int (accessed 14 March 2012).

[93] For a comprehensive overview of these recent developments and key issues relating to implementation of REDD, see Meridian Institute, *Reducing Emissions from Deforestation and Forest Degradation (REDD): An Options Assessment Report Prepared for the Government of Norway*, March 2009, available at www.redd-oar.org (accessed 14 March 2012).

[94] See Foundation for International Environmental Law and Development (FIELD), 'REDD-Plus Briefing Paper: UN Climate Change Conference in Cancun,' 22 November 2010, available at www.field.org.uk (accessed 14 March 2012).

[95] For instance, the REDD agreement negotiated at COP-16 included no mention of carbon markets as a mechanism to generate investment in avoided deforestation projects, casting some doubt on the potential scope of the REDD programme. See J. Efstathiou Jr. and A. Morales, 'Climate Talks Back $100 Billion Aid Fund, Forest Protection; No Kyoto Deal', 11 December 2010, available at www.bloomberg.com (accessed 14 March 2012). Other aspects of the REDD text were purposefully left ambiguous so that future negotiators can work to improve the agreement. See N. Hultman, 'The Cancun

progress was made at COP-17 in Durban, with parties reaching broad agreement on baseline emissions levels and forestry-specific MRV protocols, while sketching out a broad brushstrokes approach to thorny issues such as social and environmental safeguards,[96] as well as how to secure sources of long-term funding for forest-related mitigation activities.[97]

Even before COP-16, where REDD finally became legally operative under the Kyoto Protocol, forest protection schemes have been fairly well integrated into the international climate policy toolbox through the creative use of the CDM to finance forestry projects,[98] through multilateral funds such as the World Bank's Forest Carbon Partnership Facility,[99] and through bilateral mechanisms like Norway's International Climate and Forest Initiative.[100] The 2009 Copenhagen negotiations yielded a REDD negotiating text that could stand alone, even in the absence of a deal on post-2012 emissions reduction commitments by developed countries.[101] The USA, among others, favoured this approach in Cancún.[102]

Agreements on Climate Change', 14 December 2010, available at www.brookings.edu (accessed 14 March 2012): 'The agreements merely provide the framework and do not obligate any country to specific reductions. The hope is that future multi- or bilateral agreements could arise as a result of the more formalized REDD process imitated [*sic*] under the Cancun Agreements, but as of now this potential remains an open question.'

96 UNFCCC, Guidance on Systems for Providing Information on How Safeguards are Addressed and Respected and Modalities Relating to Forest Reference Emission Levels and Forest Reference Levels as Referred to in Decision 1/CP.16, Draft Decision -/CP.17, available at http://unfccc.int (accessed 14 March 2012).

97 UNFCCC, Outcome of the Work of the Ad Hoc Working Group on Long-term Cooperative Action under the Convention, Draft Decision -/CP.17, available at http://unfccc.int (accessed 14 March 2012).

98 In March 2010, the World Bank announced the registration of Africa's first large-scale forest CDM project, which followed on the heels of other forestry-related CDM projects in other regions. See World Bank, press release, 'Africa's First Large-Scale Forestry Project Under the Kyoto Protocol', 3 March 2010, available at http://web.worldbank.org (accessed 14 March 2012).

99 See Pew Center on Global Climate Change, 'Post-2012 Policy Brief: Strengthening International Climate Finance', available at www.pewclimate.org (accessed 14 March 2012) (describing the World Bank-administered Forest Carbon Partnership Facility).

100 Ministry of the Environment (Norway), Norwegian Climate and Forest Initiative, 'What Does the Norwegian Climate and Forest Initiative Finance?,' available at www.regjeringen.no (accessed 14 March 2012).

101 UNFCCC Negotiating Text, UN Doc. FCCC/AWGLCA/2009/8 (19 May 2009), available at http://unfccc.int (accessed 14 March 2012).

102 A. Ogle, 'Obama Pointman Dismisses Climate Change Skeptics', *Agence France Presse*, 18 November 2010: 'With a dimmed prospect of a path-breaking deal there, efforts have shifted towards more modest and incremental steps. Stern backed such steps on

Bolivia, on the other hand, led a coalition of developing countries to demand that any REDD agreement reflect the outcome of a 'Peoples' Climate Conference' held in Cochabamba in 2010,[103] which called for enhanced social safeguards and limits on financing for REDD through offsets. A key challenge for Cancún negotiators was thus to incorporate some of these demands while maintaining support from developed countries, for which forest-based offsetting is essential. Although the REDD agreements reached in Cancún and Durban leave many details to be determined by future COPs, they have provided enough certainty to help unblock, along with bilateral aid initiatives, relatively large inflows of capital to forest-rich developing countries in the medium term.

7.4.2 Challenges

A large forest's worth of paper has been printed with reports outlining various proposals for integrating a REDD mechanism into international carbon markets. But poor technical and institutional capacity in many forest-rich countries – together with socio-economic pressures driving tropical land-use change – means that the possibilities for legitimate forest conservation schemes that yield high-quality carbon credits will most likely be, at best, limited.[104]

The creation of avoided deforestation credits may create problems that call into question the administrability of a REDD mechanism as it is currently structured under the Cancún Agreements and subsequent decisions concluded at COP-17 in Durban. Such problems include: (i) the establishment of country-specific baselines; (ii) setting up workable systems for MRV; (iii) protecting against intra- and inter-national leakage; (iv) accounting for human-induced and natural impermanence and reversals; and (v) ensuring sufficient regulations to prevent market flooding and manipulation.

Thursday, saying the summit would focus on smaller and more achievable initiatives to address deforestation, financing and technology transfer.'

103 The World Peoples' Conference on Climate Change and the Rights of Mother Earth was held in Cochabamba, Bolivia in April 2010. The Conference yielded a 'Peoples' Agreement', which articulated many of the most strident developing country critiques of the Copenhagen Accord. See http://pwccc.wordpress.com (accessed 22 February 2012).

104 For a fuller account of these and other challenges, see D. Brown and N. Bird, 'The REDD Road to Copenhagen: Readiness for What?', *Overseas Development Institute Opinion 118*, December 2008, available at www.odi.org.uk (accessed 14 March 2012).

Most early proposals for the creation of a REDD mechanism envisioned measurement against a national reference level, or baseline rate, of deforestation. This was the approach taken by the REDD provisions in the Cancún Agreements and by negotiators in Durban.[105] A review of the technical details is beyond the scope of this chapter,[106] but even the most optimistic assessments identify significant methodological shortcomings that must be overcome before any accurate reference level can be ascertained.[107] Some baseline problems can be analogised to the fierce disputes about reference dates for Kyoto Protocol Annex I countries' QELR commitments. But many other problems are unique to forests and may prove difficult, if not impossible, to resolve. Some of the most trenchant criticism, and the best analysis of these issues, comes from the European Union, which remains strongly opposed to accepting REDD credits in the EU ETS.[108]

MRV is an issue that cuts across a range of climate change policies, but is particularly problematic in the REDD context because most heavily forested countries have limited technical capacity to gather and communicate the kinds of information likely to be required by purchasers of avoided deforestation credits. Advocates argue that many problems associated with forest carbon flux and MRV have been effectively solved by the advent of sophisticated remote sensing technologies. Indeed, progress in recent years has made basic satellite surveillance a real possibility for

[105] Decision 1/CP.1, para. 71(b), FCCC/CP/2010/7/Add. 1, available at http://unfccc.int (accessed 14 March 2012). See also above, n. 96 and accompanying text.

[106] A lengthy discussion of the methodologies likely to be used in establishing REDD baselines is described at length in J. Eliasch, *Climate Change: Financing Global Forests* (The Eliasch Review), UK Office of Climate Change, 2008, 130–43, available at www.occ.gov.uk (accessed 14 March 2012); see also Meridian Institute, *Reducing Emissions for Deforestation and Forest Degradation (REDD)* 13–18; C. Parker, A. Mitchell, M. Trivedi et al., *The Little REDD Book: A Guide to Governmental and Non-Governmental Proposals for Reducing Emissions from Deforestation and Degradation* (2009), 19, available at www.unfccc.int (accessed 14 March 2012); K. Dooley et al., 'An Overview of Selected REDD Proposals', FERN/Forest Peoples Programme, 2008, 7, available at www.redd-monitor.org (accessed 14 March 2012).

[107] See ICF International, *Fostering Carbon Market Investments in REDD: Final Report*, 2009, 18–19, available at www.redd-oar.org (accessed 14 March 2012).

[108] For a discussion of the major EU reservations to baseline setting methodologies, see A. Bozmoski and C. Hepburn, 'The Interminable Politics of Forest Carbon: A EU Perspective', Smith School of Enterprise and the Environment, University of Oxford (2009), 4, available at www.law.harvard.edu (accessed 14 March 2012).

many states and the international community. However, no system of remote sensing can supplement on-the-ground verification of forest integrity, which requires either domestic capacity or acquiescence to a third-party monitoring regime likely to involve teams of experts operating within a state's sovereign territory. Since many forest states lack local expertise, and have corruption problems, domestic MRV will be unworkable. At the same time, many (not all) forest states may resist third-party MRV of forestry projects under REDD; in 2008, Brazil expelled foreign environmental groups operating in the Amazon region, including groups engaged in REDD-like activities.[109] This does not bode well for the future of MRV under REDD, notwithstanding an agreement in principle reached by negotiators at COP-17.[110]

Emissions displacement, also known as 'leakage', occurs when mitigation in one area results, directly or indirectly, in emissions increases somewhere else.[111] Though leakage is a problem across the entire range of GHG emissions, it is especially problematic in land use and forestry, as leakage within and between countries is especially hard to quantify and track. The global market for tropical timber provides an easy-to-understand illustration of how international leakage threatens the integrity of a REDD system. In 2003, just one country – China – imported approximately 42 million cubic metres of timber products and another fifty-two million cubic metres of pulp and paper; Russia, Malaysia and Indonesia were its three largest suppliers.[112] So long as Chinese demand is constant, any change in supply from these countries due to REDD programmess will easily be met by timber exporters further down on China's list of suppliers, including Gabon, Papua New Guinea and Thailand.[113] Notably, significant quantities of tropical timber products entering the market from these countries are sourced illegally, compounding not just the leakage problem but also MRV efforts, as

[109] 'Brazil Seeks to Rein in Foreign Influence in Amazon', Reuters, 16 July 2008, available at www.planetark.com (accessed 14 March 2012). See also www.alertnet.org/thenews/newsdesk/N10517350.htm (accessed 14 March 2012).

[110] See above, n. 96 and accompanying text.

[111] As described by the USA, Views on Issues Related to Further Steps under the Convention Related to Reducing Emissions from Deforestation in Developing Countries: Approaches to Stimulate Action (UNFCC/SBSTA/2007/MISC.14, 10 September 2007), 43.

[112] See I. Fry, 'Reducing Emissions from Deforestation and Forest Degradation: Opportunities and Pitfalls in Developing a New Legal Regime' (2008) 17 *RECIEL* 173.

[113] *Ibid.*

described above. Of course, leakage may also involve indirect land-use change resulting from spikes in crop prices on global commodity markets.

Unlike decommissioning a coal-fired power plant or increasing the fuel efficiency of a fleet of vehicles, protecting a forest from logging requires continuous, long-term affirmative action. Policing compliance at the local level will be costly. The unpredictable nature of human activities and the socio-economic forces that may drive future land-use change make it impossible to ensure that a given hectare of forest will still be standing in fifty or 100 years. Beyond human-induced land-use change, the natural variability of forest ecosystems make it likely that at least some forests serving as net carbon sinks in 2010 will become net carbon sources by 2020, and vice versa. Furthermore, climate change itself may dry out wide swathes of tropical forest, including the Amazon basin. A REDD crediting system that fails to take into account the impermanence risk associated with forest carbon in these regions is destined to cause headaches.

Poor governance in forest states is characterised by pervasive or persistent illegal logging, endemic corruption and uncertain or unstable land tenure. A 2006 report by the World Bank on forests and governance emphasised the importance of law enforcement to the social, economic and ecological security of forested regions.[114] In a review of selected World Bank governance indicators for the eight countries that represent 70 per cent of total GHG emissions from land use (Bolivia, Brazil, Cameroon, DR Congo, Ghana, Indonesia, Malaysia and Papua New Guinea), researchers found a striking lack of capacity for regulatory effectiveness and the rule of law.[115] Furthermore, in order for foreign investors to gain REDD credits generated in a host state, that state must have stable and intelligible land tenure laws and clearly enforceable property rights. Even in states where the rule of law is relatively advanced, such as Brazil, basic property rights may be lacking in remote forested areas. In other places, traditional forms of ownership such as communal property complicate the idea of creating a REDD credit based on a given quantity of avoided

[114] See http://siteresources.worldbank.org (accessed 14 March 2012).

[115] See World Bank, 'Worldwide Governance Indicators Country Snapshot', available at http://info.worldbank.org (accessed 14 March 2012). See also C. Streck, R. O'Sullivan, T. Janson-Smith and R. Tarasofsky (eds.), *Climate Change and Forests* (Washington, DC and London: Brookings/Chatham House, 2008), 241.

deforestation. Additionally, the question of who will own the forest carbon embodied in a REDD credit, and how ownership rights in this new form of property will be determined, will in large part determine the distributional impacts of REDD.[116] If national governments are given free rein to assign the rights as they wish, it is likely that past inequalities will be reinforced. However, ensuring that such rights end up in the hands of those who actually live in the forests could be quite difficult, and may involve sovereignty issues that make it functionally impossible for an international treaty to ensure equity in the distribution of REDD ownership rights.[117] Potential investors in REDD projects and buyers of future REDD credits are thinking carefully about these issues, which have the potential to disincentivise not just low-carbon FDI but all forms of foreign investment in a developing country or LDC.

The majority of current REDD projects rely upon public rather than private capital, with most private-sector investments in REDD to date constituting mere pilot projects. To the extent today's projects, including those with government support, generate significant attention from investors, REDD represents a key policy area where climate change policy and low-carbon FDI will interact, both positively and negatively, for the foreseeable future.

[116] For example, on 5 May 2009, the Malaysian Federal Court ruled that indigenous people in Sarawak, the Malaysian part of Borneo, have rights to land they use for hunting and gathering as well as land they use for growing food. Previously, the Sarawak government did not recognise tribal peoples' rights over their traditional land unless they could show that they had grown crops there. This ruling clears the way for more formal land tenure, and casts plans for large-scale palm oil plantations in the region into significant doubt. See Survival International, press release, 'Landmark Court Ruling Could Help Tribes Stop Deforestation and Oil Palm Plantations', 8 May 2009, available at www.survival-international.org (accessed 14 March 2012).

[117] Tropical deforestation threatens the livelihoods and cultures of 1.2 billion forest-dependent people. C. Streck, 'Creating Incentives for Avoiding Further Deforestation: The Nested Approach', in C. Streck et al., *Climate Change and Forests*, 237. In many cases, these people represent the poorest, most marginalised communities in their countries. The issue of human rights and deforestation are already well documented. Creating new forest management schemes opens the door for progress on these intractable issues, but also increases the likelihood that some communities will be further taken advantage of. For instance, the international community recently complained that Indonesia has not adequately addressed indigenous rights in developing forest management policies. See www.thejakartaglobe.com/news/national/%20article/14191.html (accessed 14 March 2012).

7.5 Comparative assessment of future potential

The Kyoto flexibility mechanisms were, for a time, the primary international law tools available to policymakers seeking to engage the private sector, and markets, in transnational GHG emissions mitigation activities. This is no longer the case. New multilateral institutions such as the Green Climate Fund, proliferating bilateral arrangements on 'green' technology transfer and related topics, expanded private-sector investments in clean energy ventures in developing countries and the changing nature of global FDI flows – with increasing volumes originating in the Global South – are all calling into question the ongoing viability of the CDM, JI and even REDD as significant drivers of low-carbon FDI. These mechanisms made sense under the Kyoto regime, which envisioned a large group of industrialised countries cutting domestic emissions and bringing down the marginal cost of emissions abatement by allowing private parties to use the carbon markets to access a supply of relatively cheap credits from countries external to the system, whether those were CER credits created by mitigation projects in China, ERUs sourced in Russia or the Ukraine or REDD credits from forest-rich nations such as Brazil or Indonesia.

But faced with the deep US–EU recession starting with the financial crisis of 2008, the growth of emissions from non-Annex I countries such as China, India and Brazil, and the resulting diplomatic stalemate at COP-15 in Copenhagen, international climate change policy began quietly to diversify away from its UN roots. Instead of insisting upon the unattainable vision of a unitary global architecture to govern climate mitigation activities and the carbon market, the international community has in recent years turned to a range of other policies, instruments and forums that allow for progress to be made while circumventing a UNFCCC negotiating process that has come to be characterised as 'broken'.[118]

While the trend away from a centralised, top-down international climate policy had been apparent to many observers for some time, the first real fissures only became obvious at Copenhagen, when it was clear

[118] D. Freestone, 'The Copenhagen Accord: Train Wreck or Paradigm Shift?', in World Bank, *Law, Justice and Development*, available at http://go.worldbank.org/DAG-KAHU770 (accessed 14 March 2012): 'It is already clear that the UNFCCC process might be broken. The idea of 194 UNFCCC State Parties negotiating a huge number of important issues is becoming impossibly unwieldy.'

that a new, global treaty to extend and expand upon the Kyoto Protocol was not realistically achievable. Two years later, the Durban summit marked a turning point of sorts for the relationship between international climate change law and low-carbon FDI. At Durban, the international community took steps to operationalise many of the themes and commitments first articulated in Copenhagen and further elaborated in Cancún, including climate finance, adaptation and the breaking down of the outdated and troublesome distinction between Annex I and non-Annex I countries within the context of the still-important concept of 'common but differentiated responsibilities'.[119] Above all, COP-17 formally established the Green Climate Fund,[120] a new international financial institution first sketched out by negotiators in Copenhagen whose terms of reference include ample provisions for the mobilisation of private-sector investments in climate mitigation activities and the use of public funds to leverage larger pools of private capital, per the suggestion of the UN Secretary-General's High-Level Advisory Group on Climate Change Financing (AGF).[121]

As international climate diplomacy moves into a new phase dominated less by the Kyoto framework, including a carbon market structure built upon the distinction between Annex I and non-Annex I countries' emissions, future climate mitigation activities will necessarily come to be influenced by new policies and new models for cooperation, whether market-oriented or otherwise. The 'regime complex' for climate change

[119] Perhaps the single most important outcome of the Durban summit was the agreement, albeit vaguely worded, for developing countries that had thus far sat on the sidelines of international climate treaty-making as non-Annex I countries to participate in the process of negotiating a new 'protocol, another legal instrument or an agreed outcome with legal force under the Convention applicable to all Parties' through a new ad hoc working group on the Durban Platform. See UNFCCC, Establishment of an Ad Hoc Working Group on the Durban Platform for Enhanced Action, Draft Decision -/CP.17, para. 2, available at http://unfccc.int (accessed 14 March 2012).

[120] UNFCCC, Green Climate Fund – Report of the Transitional Committee, Draft Decision -/CP.17, available at http://unfccc.int (accessed 14 March 2012).

[121] AGF, 'Report of the Secretary-General's High-Level Advisory Group on Climate Change Financing,' 5 November 2010, available at www.un.org (accessed 14 March 2012). Following the recommendations laid out in the AGF report, the Green Climate Fund's terms of reference establish a specific 'private sector facility that enables [the Fund] to directly and indirectly finance private sector mitigation and adaptation activities at the national, regional and international levels' and to 'promote the participation of private sector actors in developing countries, in particular local actors, including small and medium-sized enterprises and local financial intermediaries'. See UNFCCC, Green Climate Fund – Report of the Transitional Committee, Draft Decision -/CP.17, paras 41–4.

now includes not just the rules for carbon markets dominated by UNFCCC-authorised offset credits, but bilateral treaties and other, less formal, arrangements, regional initiatives, and public–private partnerships in countries like China that may come to dominate the economics of climate change policy through sheer scale.[122] While, after Durban, no one is realistically arguing that the CDM will simply cease to exist, its future relevance, along with JI and REDD, remain uncertain.

CONCLUSION

Policies undertaken to combat climate change are increasingly oriented towards the mobilisation of low-carbon FDI such as renewable energy projects, efficiency improvements and tropical forest conservation schemes. Firms will continue to pursue low-carbon FDI whenever and wherever it makes economic sense to do so, but international climate policy instruments such as JI, the CDM and REDD have changed the economics of low-carbon investments by creating a new commodity, the carbon credit, and establishing the basic regulatory framework and price signals that, together, have allowed for the establishment and ongoing operation of international carbon markets. By imposing new costs on GHG emissions and creating a new form of quasi-currency that investors and states can buy and sell, these policy instruments have changed the rules of the game for low-carbon FDI.

Still, much more has to be done. The Kyoto Protocol will expire at the end of 2012 and, even with the Durban Platform's new mandate for a future treaty negotiation process, uncertainty about the precise form and content of such an agreement is casting a long shadow over the carbon markets, keeping prices quite low. Moreover, the EU ETS remains the primary engine for the generation of carbon offsets via the Kyoto mechanisms, yet the future of European climate policy remains highly uncertain, particularly in light of ongoing political and economic challenges associated with the Euro crisis, to say nothing of Europe's shrinking share of aggregate global emissions. While Australia recently adopted national climate change legislation, other developed countries, most notably the USA (with the exception of the state of California), have thus far failed to implement comparable legislation that can spur new overseas investments in GHG mitigation. Meanwhile, China and other fast-growing

[122] For further discussion, see Firger and Gerrard, 'Harmonizing Climate Change Policy'.

developing economies are generating significant new FDI flows that sideline the JI and, to some extent, the CDM as well. In light of this uncertain and rapidly changing landscape, innovative policies to incentivise low-carbon FDI are needed now more than ever. Policymakers would do well to expand upon the platform launched in Durban and seek out new ways to use international law as a catalyst, not a hurdle, for private investment in low-carbon growth.

Select bibliography

Abbott, K., and D. Gartner, 'The Green Climate Fund and the Future of Environmental Governance,' EARTH System Governance Working Paper 16 (2011).

Arquit Niederberger, A., and R. Saneer, 'Exploring the Relationship between FDI Flows and CDM Potential' (2005) 14 *Transnational Corporations* 1.

Barrett, S., *Environment and Statecraft: The Strategy of Environmental Treaty-Making* (Oxford University Press, 2003).

Bodansky, D., 'The Framework Convention on Climate Change: A Commentary' (1993) 18 *Yale Journal of International Law* 451.

'W[h]ither the Kyoto Protocol? Durban and Beyond', Working Paper – Harvard Project on Climate Agreements (2011).

Bozmoski, A., and C. Hepburn, 'The Interminable Politics of Forest Carbon: A EU Perspective', Smith School of Enterprise and the Environment, University of Oxford (2009).

Carr, C., and F. Rosembuj, 'Flexible Mechanisms for Climate Change Compliance: Emission Offset Purchases under the Clean Development Mechanism' (2008) 16 *New York University Environmental Law Journal* 44.

De Gouvello, C., F. B. Dayo and M. Thioye, *Low-Carbon Energy Projects for Development in Sub-Saharan Africa: Unveiling the Potential, Addressing the Barriers* (Washington, DC: World Bank, 2008).

Eliasch, J., *Climate Change: Financing Global Forests*, UK Office of Climate Change (2008).

Firger, D. M., and M. B. Gerrard 'Harmonizing Climate Change Policy and International Investment Law' (2010/11) 3 *Yearbook of International Investment Law and Policy* 517.

Freestone, D., and C. Streck (eds.), *Legal Aspects of Carbon Trading: Kyoto, Copenhagen, and Beyond* (Oxford University Press, 2009).

Fry, I., 'Reducing Emissions from Deforestation and Forest Degradation: Opportunities and Pitfalls in Developing a New Legal Regime' (2008) 17 *Review of European Community and International Environmental Law* 173.

Green, J. F., 'Delegation and Accountability in the Clean Development Mechanism: The New Authority of Non-State Actors' (2008) 4 *Journal of International Law and International Relations* 21.

Hirsch, D., 'Trading in Ecosystem Services: Carbon Sinks and the Clean Development Mechanism' (2007) 22 *Journal of Land Use and Environmental Law* 623.

Keohane, R., and D. Victor, 'The Regime Complex for Climate Change' (2011) 9 *Perspectives on Politics* 7.

Kulovesi, K., 'The Private Sector and Implementation of the Kyoto Protocol: Experiences, Challenges and Prospects' (2007) 16 *Review of European Community and International Environmental Law* 145.

Marshall, F., 'Climate Change and International Investment Agreements: Obstacles or Opportunities', *International Institute for Sustainable Development, Trade, Investment and Climate Change Series* (March 2010).

Parker, C., A. Mitchell, M. Trivedi, N. Mardas and K. Sosis, *The Little REDD Book: A Guide to Governmental and Non-Governmental Proposals for Reducing Emissions from Deforestation and Degradation* (2009).

Stewart, R., B. Kingsbury and B. Rudyk (eds.), *Climate Finance: Regulatory and Funding Strategies for Climate Change and Global Development* (New York: NYU Press, 2009).

Streck, C., R. O'Sullivan, T. Janson-Smith and R. Tarasofsky (eds.), *Climate Change and Forests* (Washington, DC and London: Brookings/Chatham House, 2008).

Szymanski, T., 'The Evolution of Emissions Trading in Europe: Legal and Commercial Risks Facing Phase II of the EU Emissions Trading Scheme' (2007) 1 *European Business Law Journal* 578.

United Nations Commission on Trade and Development, *World Investment Report 2010: Investing in a Low-Carbon Economy* (2010).

Wara, M., 'Measuring the Clean Development Mechanism's Performance and Potential' (2008) 55 *UCLA Law Review* 1759.

World Bank, *State and Trends of the Carbon Market 2010* (Washington, DC: World Bank).

8

Channelling investment into biodiversity conservation: ABS and PES schemes

RICCARDO PAVONI

INTRODUCTION: THE BUSINESS CASE FOR BIODIVERSITY AFTER THE FAILURE OF THE 2010 TARGET

The conference of the parties (COP) to the Convention on Biological Diversity (CBD)[1] has repeatedly expressed its resolve to promote and enhance the 'business case for biodiversity'.[2] Similarly, a recent report by the CBD Secretariat has concluded that 'There is a business case for private sector participation in financing the protection of ecosystem services'.[3] The COP has also exemplified the reasons in favour of a wide and sustained engagement of business in the realisation of the CBD's objectives, namely the conservation of biodiversity, the sustainable use of its components, and the fair and equitable sharing of the benefits arising from genetic resources.[4] It has thus noted that 'The private sector is arguably the least engaged of all stakeholders in the implementation of the Convention, yet the daily activities of business and industry have major impacts on biodiversity';[5] moreover, 'Individual companies and industry associations can be highly influential on Governments and public opinion';[6] and, finally, 'The private sector possesses biodiversity-relevant knowledge and technological resources, as well as more general management, research and communication skills, which, if mobilised, could facilitate the implementation of the Convention'.[7]

[1] Convention on Biological Diversity, 5 June 1992, 1760 UNTS 79 (CBD).
[2] COP-8, Decision VIII/17, paras 3 and 5; COP-9, Decision IX/26, para. 2, and Annex, para. 2.
[3] *Incentive Measures for the Conservation and Sustainable Use of Biological Diversity: Case Studies and Lessons Learned* (CBD Technical Series No. 56, 2011), 51.
[4] CBD, art. 1. [5] COP-8, Decision VIII/17, fifth preambular para.
[6] *Ibid.* [7] *Ibid.*

The above COP statements do not mention that, pragmatically, the main reason for the private sector's involvement in the CBD regime is the availability of financial resources that companies may increasingly be willing to channel into the international efforts to safeguard biological diversity *insofar as* market mechanisms for biodiversity-related products and services are fully institutionalised and developed. As a matter of fact, the idea of a 'business case for biodiversity' primarily speaks of markets, profitable transactions and economic incentives capable of attracting private investments in the global struggle over the protection of species, habitats and ecosystems.

It is indeed foreseeable that the role of the private sector will be a crucial factor in the operation of the CBD in its third decade of existence and beyond, because it opens up new scenarios, dynamics and hopes for the biodiversity challenge. All policies and mechanisms devised so far have proven unable to halt the loss and degradation of biodiversity in any significant way. As set by the global community in 2002,[8] the so-called '2010 Biodiversity Target', that is the achievement by 2010 of a significant reduction of the current rate of biodiversity loss at the global, regional and national levels, has dramatically been missed.[9] The contemporary pace and volume of biodiversity erosion are unprecedented, with some estimates referring to no fewer than 140,000 species becoming extinct each year and 30 per cent of all known species that might disappear by 2050. At the 2010 COP-10 in Nagoya, Japan, the Parties to the CBD renewed their commitments and adopted a 'Strategic Plan for Biodiversity' comprising twenty ambitious targets to be achieved in the period 2011–20. For instance, the overall mission target is to 'take effective and urgent action to halt the loss of biodiversity in order to ensure that by 2020 ecosystems are resilient and continue to provide essential services, thereby securing the planet's variety of life, and contributing to human well-being, and poverty eradication'.[10] As a result, the full involvement of businesses and their financial resources may now appear all the more inescapable and the COP has indeed urged governments to foster the effective contribution of the private sector in the implementation of the

[8] COP-6, Decision VI/26, point 11 of the Annex (Strategic Plan for the Convention on Biological Diversity); World Summit on Sustainable Development, Plan of Implementation (4 September 2002), para. 44.

[9] See COP-10, Decision X/2, points 5 and 7 of the Annex; A. Trouwborst, 'International Nature Conservation Law and the Adaptation of Biodiversity to Climate Change: A Mismatch?' (2009) 21 *Journal of Environmental Law* 419, 422–3.

[10] COP-10, Decision X/2, point 12 of the Annex.

Convention and its Strategic Plan[11] as well as 'to make the case for investment for biodiversity and ecosystem services'.[12]

A precondition for meaningful business engagement in the biodiversity challenge is the creation of market-based incentives and mechanisms that companies may welcome as opportunities for making profits or, at least, for internalising and offsetting the adverse environmental impacts of their activities. This emerging market paradigm for biodiversity protection is noteworthy and brings about an evident shift from the traditional perception of the CBD as an instrument running against the interests of the business community. Such a perception has historically arisen from concerns over alleged CBD inroads into the protection of intellectual property rights (IPR) associated with genetic resources coming from the southern hemisphere and into the free market for biodiversity-related products and services (e.g., the controversies about trade in genetically modified organisms). To be sure, an economic rationale has underlain the CBD since its inception. The prominent place attributed to the objectives of sustainable use and benefit-sharing in the CBD was indeed driven by economic considerations: developing and least-developed countries (DLDCs), endowed with most of the global biodiversity, would be more willing to strike deals with corporations based in industrialised countries and grant them access to their valuable bioresources if the profits resulting from any subsequent commercialisation were to be equitably shared between providers and users of such resources. This would create a virtuous circle by incentivising the protection of biodiversity on the part of DLDCs and their communities. It is, however, clear that these benefit-sharing agreements (BSAs) were primarily meant to offer incentives to DLDCs, and not so much to private undertakings which would rather retain the pre-CBD status quo, namely the absence of any explicit international legal obligation to reach an agreement with biodiversity-rich states. In evaluating the trends and developments that have emerged in the area of BSAs, section 8.2 of this chapter will seek to appraise to what extent the above considerations remain accurate and especially whether such agreements have also turned into an incentive for business engagement in the safeguarding of biodiversity.

Much more innovative is instead the other contractual mechanism examined in this chapter, i.e., schemes for payments for ecosystem

[11] *Ibid.*, para. 3(a). [12] *Ibid.*, para. 7.

services (PES), whereby certain users/beneficiaries of an ecosystem service (such as the availability of drinking water) derived from environmentally sound activities accept to reward economically the individuals/providers who carry out such activities. The current dimension of this market for ecosystem services as it specifically relates to biodiversity, together with its prospects and challenges, will be discussed in section 8.3.

A background assumption of the chapter is that it is unwarranted flatly to dismiss the emergence of biodiversity-related market mechanisms on the grounds that they constitute a distortion of the essential tenets underlying biodiversity law and policy, such as the intrinsic value of biodiversity and its status as a global public good (or a 'common concern of humankind')[13] with the consequent purported necessity to resist any commoditisation of biogenetic resources. Indeed, this chapter essentially supports the creation of market incentives as promising tools potentially capable of significantly *contributing* to the biodiversity challenge. On the contrary, such tools are not regarded as stand-alone policies supplanting traditional regulatory measures, nor should their steady emergence make us lose sight of the fundamental objective of biodiversity *conservation* through the enforcement of prohibitions and liabilities against environmentally destructive industrial processes and associated activities (section 8.1).

8.1 Market-based mechanisms and the regulatory 'command-and-control' approach: mutually exclusive or complementary?

What is the appropriate role for market-based mechanisms and private parties' autonomy within the global regimes aimed at the protection of biodiversity? On a general level, while it is frequently posited that economic mechanisms 'might be more flexible, cost-efficient and effective than a command and control approach',[14] it is, however, clear that the two approaches are to be complementary and mutually reinforcing. Indeed, biodiversity protection cannot be achieved by simply unleashing market forces. Biodiversity-related market and investment incentive mechanisms must be pursued according to clear standards and safeguards regulating such issues as bioprospecting and the use of genetic

[13] CBD, third preambular paragraph.

[14] T. Greiber (ed.), *Payments for Ecosystems Services: Legal and Institutional Frameworks* (Gland: IUCN, 2009), 2.

resources, the types of permitted transactions, the destination of profits and public participation. Most recently, the CBD COP has indeed recalled 'the *essential* role of regulation and the *complementary* role of market-based instruments'.[15] Commentators typically share this view,[16] notwithstanding the various potential advantages of such instruments as compared to orthodox regulatory measures.[17]

Yet, what is the *optimal* level and extent of regulation in the area of biodiversity, i.e., a form of regulation capable of preserving the basic values and legal tenets linked to biodiversity without discouraging businesses and private capital from investing in the emerging biodiversity markets? Regarding the level of regulation, the formulation of *international* legal instruments on biodiversity-related market mechanisms seems appropriate. Given the status of biodiversity as a global public good, it would be odd if in this area the international community were completely to abdicate its standard-setting function in favour of domestic laws and practices. On the contrary, policy and institutional guidance at the international level must be considered as a precondition for the successful implementation of economic instruments. The expected uniformity and predictability of national approaches would be an asset also for businesses engaging in biodiversity-related investments. Moreover, states should not simply leave the implementation of international environmental rules and standards to the private parties' goodwill, with the sole limitation arising from the need to respect the disparate contract and business laws and practices prevailing in each domestic system. Such a

[15] COP-10, Decision X/44, para. 10, emphasis added. This also seems the main lesson to be drawn from the forceful critique of market mechanisms under the Kyoto Protocol on Climate Change which has recently been offered by G. Winter, 'The Climate is No Commodity: Taking Stock of the Emissions Trading System' (2010) 22 *Journal of Environmental Law*, esp. 21–5.

[16] For instance, see, recently, C. T. Reid, 'The Privatisation of Biodiversity? Possible New Approaches to Nature Conservation Law in the UK' (2011) 23 *Journal of Environmental Law* 203, 224–5 (referring to market mechanisms as 'additions to rather than replacements for the current approach', as well as to the necessity of retaining 'at least a significant regulatory role for public authorities, rather than moving to complete reliance on a free-market approach').

[17] For a detailed overview, see R. B. Stewart, 'Economic Incentives for Environmental Protection: Opportunities and Obstacles', in R. L. Revesz, P. Sands and R. B. Stewart (eds.), *Environmental Law, the Economy, and Sustainable Development* (Cambridge University Press, 2000), 171–244. For a comparative illustration of pros and cons of certain innovative incentive mechanisms in the field of biodiversity, see L. Fromond, J. Similä and L. Suvantola, 'Regulatory Innovations for Biodiversity Protection in Private Forests – Towards Flexibility' (2009) 21 *Journal of Environmental Law* 1.

purely contractual approach would not be consistent with the states' due diligence obligation to oversee and control private parties' transactions and activities impacting upon global environmental resources.[18]

If deregulation does not therefore constitute a viable option, the breadth and depth of international regimes for biodiversity-related market mechanisms may be a matter of debate. The two key mechanisms analysed below, i.e., PES schemes and BSAs, lend themselves to different considerations. In respect of PES schemes, an international legal framework has not yet been devised, especially for payments specifically rewarding biodiversity conservation *in its own right*. A crucial development in this connection may result from the ongoing negotiations under the UN Framework Convention on Climate Change (UNFCCC) on an instrument outlining basic principles and rules for reducing emissions from deforestation, conservation of forest carbon stocks, sustainable management of forests and enhancement of forest carbon stocks in developing countries (REDD-plus).[19] However, it remains unclear to what extent this envisaged instrument will be suitable to provide *direct* benefits in terms of biodiversity protection. Moreover, its implementation through privately financed PES schemes is only one of the proposed options. At any rate, it seems that in the area of PES schemes a 'soft' approach to international regulation, in the form of broad principles, objectives and standards, would be consistent with the need to preserve the flexibility and variability evidenced by the host of disparate contractual arrangements that have already come to light.[20]

In the context of BSAs, the regulatory models emerging from the CBD and its 2010 Nagoya Protocol on Access and Benefit-Sharing[21] (Nagoya

[18] As recently confirmed in a comparable context (prospecting activities by private companies in the Area, i.e., the seabed and ocean floor beyond the limits of national jurisdiction) by the International Tribunal for the Law of the Sea (ITLOS), see ITLOS Seabed Disputes Chamber, *Responsibilities and Obligations of States Sponsoring Persons and Entities with Respect to Activities in the Area*, Advisory Opinion (1 February 2011), paras 223–6.

[19] COP-16, Decision 1/CP.16; cf. *REDD-plus and Biodiversity* (CBD Technical Series No. 59, 2011); A. Savaresi, 'Reducing Emissions from Deforestation in Developing Countries under the UNFCCC: Caveats and Opportunities for Biodiversity' (2010) 21 *Yearbook of International Environmental Law* 81; E. Morgera, 'Far Away So Close: A Legal Analysis of the Increasing Interactions between the Convention on Biological Diversity and Climate Change Law' (2011) 2 *Climate Law* 85.

[20] See section 8.3, below.

[21] Nagoya Protocol on Access to Genetic Resources and the Fair and Equitable Sharing of Benefits Arising from Their Utilization to the Convention on Biological Diversity

ABS Protocol), on the one hand, and from the International Treaty on Plant Genetic Resources for Food and Agriculture[22] (ITPGR), on the other, are paradigmatic of different options available for accessing, using and marketing biogenetic resources. The CBD and its Nagoya ABS Protocol promote an essentially *bilateral* (investor-state) approach to economic transactions about genetic resources, which are to be fundamentally governed by 'mutually agreed terms'[23] between providers and users. In principle, such treaties therefore imply a low degree of regulatory interference with private parties' autonomy. By contrast, the ITPGR establishes a Multilateral System of Access and Benefit-Sharing covering sixty-four food crops and forages that are essential to the world's food needs and agricultural biodiversity.[24] The System is closely tied to a Trust Account[25] administered by the ITPGR's Governing Body, where a share of the profits arising from ABS transactions must be transferred.[26] This *multilateral* model greatly reduces the scope for manoeuvre by parties engaging in ABS transactions pursuant to so-called material transfer agreements (MTAs). In 2006, the ITPGR's Governing Body has indeed approved a standard material transfer agreement (SMTA)[27] setting out the basic conditions and clauses that *must* be present in each specific contract between providers and recipients of plant genetic resources. Notably, under the SMTA, the Food and Agriculture Organization (FAO) must be the third-party beneficiary of any ABS contract and, as such, it is empowered to initiate dispute-settlement proceedings for non-fulfilment of the respective obligations of providers and recipients.[28]

The ITPGR's multilateral approach is arguably the appropriate solution in the area of BSAs. It is more in line with the status of biodiversity as a global common and, while not altogether depriving private parties of freedom of contract, it sets mandatory benchmarks for their negotiations and arrangements aimed at securing that the latter effectively contribute to the conservation and sustainable use of plant genetic resources. The

(Nagoya ABS Protocol), adopted at the CBD COP-10 on 29 October 2010 (see Annex I to Decision X/1), not yet in force.

22 International Treaty on Plant Genetic Resources for Food and Agriculture (ITPGR), 3 November 2001, 2400 UNTS 379.

23 See CBD, art. 15(4)(7), 16(3), 19(2) and Nagoya ABS Protocol, arts 5(1)(2)(5), 6(3)(e)(g), 7, 15(1), 16(1), 17(1)(b) and (3), 18(1)(2), 19.

24 ITPGR, arts 10–13 and Annex I.

25 *Ibid.*, art. 19(3)(f).

26 *Ibid.*, art. 13(2)(d)(ii).

27 See Resolution 1/2006 of 16 June 2006. See also ITPGR, art. 12(4).

28 SMTA, arts 4(3) and 8(1)(2)(3).

private sector's involvement is stimulated by a clear and predictable framework under which a provider country's refusal to grant access to resources included in the Multilateral System should be exceptional.[29]

The Nagoya ABS Protocol has done little to multilateralise the CBD regime for benefit-sharing. It contemplates the establishment of a global multilateral benefit-sharing mechanism, but this is *only* intended for situations involving transboundary genetic resources or the impossibility to grant prior informed consent for access to the resources (e.g., when the latter are located in areas beyond national jurisdiction).[30] Moreover, the Protocol does not expressly envisage the drafting of an internationally mandated standardised ABS contract along the lines of the ITPGR's SMTA.[31] Instead, a bottom-up approach is adopted by attributing a supervisory role for that task to the Parties, which are merely to encourage 'the development, update and use of sectoral and cross-sectoral model contractual clauses for mutually agreed terms',[32] while the Protocol's COP will just 'periodically take stock of the use'[33] of such clauses.

8.2 Positive incentive mechanisms to foster the conservation and sustainable use of biodiversity: benefit-sharing agreements

At the time of the adoption of the CBD, the need to devise market-based instruments for the protection of biodiversity was played down. This was reflected in the final text of the CBD, which did not explicitly refer to investments from the *private* sector as a means of contributing to the achievement of the Convention's objectives. Yet, investment opportunities associated with the biodiversity challenge were acknowledged. According to the preamble to the CBD, 'substantial investments are required to conserve biological diversity and […] there is the expectation of a broad range of environmental, economic and social benefits from these investments'.[34] More to the point, a provision on economic

[29] The ITPGR refers to 'facilitated access' to the materials covered by the Multilateral System (art. 12(1)(2)), a term which is intended to preserve the principle of sovereign rights over plant genetic resources and the correlative power of provider countries to ultimately deny access to their biodiversity. It is, however, clear that, when a state ratifies the ITPGR, that power is no longer absolute or unconditional. See ITPGR, art. 10.

[30] Nagoya ABS Protocol, art. 10.

[31] To be sure, nothing prevents the Protocol's COP from engaging with this issue as part of its implied powers. See *ibid.*, art. 26(4)(f).

[32] *Ibid.*, arts 19(1) and 12(3).

[33] *Ibid.*, art. 19(2).

[34] CBD, eighteenth preambular paragraph.

incentives made its way into the CBD. Under Article 11, Parties 'shall, as far as possible and as appropriate, adopt economically and socially sound measures that act as incentives for the conservation and sustainable use of components of biological diversity'. What at the time was a pioneering provision has now come to the fore as the key legal basis legitimising the design and formulation of economic mechanisms capable of contributing to the protection of biodiversity. The contemporary focus is clearly on *positive* incentive mechanisms (as opposed to perverse incentives such as environmentally harmful subsidies), namely those that are potentially beneficial to biodiversity conservation and sustainable use.

In economic terms, the sharing of profits flowing from access to genetic resources and resulting commercialisation of gene-based products through BSAs between provider countries and user companies can be regarded as one such mechanism.[35] ABS transactions may in fact operate as a positive incentive tool to channel investment into biodiversity protection, or as a framework ancillary to broader incentive schemes.[36] However, in legal terms, the fair and equitable sharing of the benefits arising from the utilisation of genetic resources is certainly more than just another market mechanism. It is a fundamental objective of the CBD and the ITPGR, the subject of the 2010 Nagoya ABS Protocol, and, arguably, a general principle of international (biodiversity) law.[37] Moreover, the rationale of this principle makes it suitable for application beyond the biodiversity regime to a wide range of activities involving environmental, developmental and health issues, as is demonstrated by the pertinent debates undertaken in a plethora of international organisations, such as the World Intellectual Property Organization (WIPO), the United Nations Conference on Trade and Development (UNCTAD) and the World Health Organization (WHO).

[35] According to *The Economics of Ecosystems and Biodiversity for National and International Policy Makers* (2009): 'ABS-related activities straddle payment schemes and market-based rewards', draft chap. 5, p. 3. Document available at www.teebweb.org (accessed 15 April 2012).

[36] See *Incentive Measures for the Conservation and Sustainable Use of Biological Diversity*, 17 (discussing the sharing of benefits from genetic resources and traditional knowledge as a measure to support community-based natural resource management programmes).

[37] See R. Pavoni, 'Biodiversity and Biotechnology: Consolidation and Strains in the Emerging International Legal Regimes', in F. Francioni and T. Scovazzi (eds.), *Biotechnology and International Law* (Oxford: Hart Publishing, 2006), 29, 39–42. For a different perspective, see F. Francioni, 'International Law for Biotechnology: Basic Principles', *ibid.*, 3, 22–3 (who subsumes benefit-sharing regarding genetic resources within the traditional principle of equitable remuneration of foreign investment).

Being an international legal standard, equitable benefit-sharing cannot be reduced to a purely economic issue governed by market forces, private contracts and private disputes. In particular, equity as the cornerstone of benefit-sharing under the biodiversity regime has to be considered the overarching principle which should guide and inform the interpretation and implementation of BSAs. It is especially a powerful tool that adjudicators of disputes arising from BSAs, mindful of the international obligations at stake, may legitimately use in order to accommodate the conflicting interests of the parties, fill in apparent gaps in the contractual scheme and formulate fair solutions.[38] At the same time, this special legal status of benefit-sharing in the field of biodiversity should not overshadow that BSAs are contractual transactions significantly shaped by market trends and perceptions. Building an ABS regime that appears legitimate, fair and predictable to the private sector is therefore key to its success.

Thus, BSAs have the potential of operating as a positive incentive tool whereby a provider country authorises foreign actors, either public or private, to access the genetic resources located in its jurisdiction for purposes of research and development, and on condition of receipt of an equitable amount of monetary or non-monetary benefits, including royalties resulting from the commercial exploitation of the resources. It should be noted that such contracts mostly work out as an *indirect* incentive, because biodiversity conservation may be achieved as a sort of by-product of transactions focusing on the exchange of value for economic benefits. Yet, it is here that the previously discussed distinction between the CBD and ITPGR models should once again be underscored.

The indirect nature of the contribution to biodiversity-friendly outcomes is undeniable in CBD-type BSAs, as there is no legal obligation in the CBD that the economic benefits flowing therefrom be channelled towards conservation or sustainable use purposes by recipients and providers of genetic resources. The Nagoya ABS Protocol is emblematic in this respect, as it *merely* requires the Parties to 'encourage users and providers to direct benefits arising from the utilisation of genetic resources towards the conservation of biological diversity and the sustainable use of its components'.[39] The same does not apply to

[38] See the compelling arguments by Francioni, 'International Law for Biotechnology', 24. See also F. Francioni, 'Equity in International Law', in R. Wolfrum (ed.), *The Max Planck Encyclopedia of Public International Law* (Oxford University Press, 2008–), online edition.

[39] Nagoya ABS Protocol, art. 9.

ITPGR-type BSAs pursuant to the SMTA. In this case, the ITPGR's Multilateral System as administered by the Governing Body performs an essential supervisory and intermediary function aimed at securing that the funds resulting from contractual transactions are effectively used for the protection of agricultural biodiversity. Thus, the ITPGR provides that the benefits shared under its Multilateral System 'should flow primarily […] to farmers in all countries, especially in developing countries, who conserve and sustainably utilise plant genetic resources'.[40] This soft provision is reinforced by making *agreed* plans and programmes for those farmers a priority of the Treaty's funding strategy.[41] The early practice under the ITPGR shows the determination of the Parties and treaty bodies effectively to pursue that approach. In 2009, eleven pilot projects to help developing countries protect crop diversity were financed through the ITPGR's Trust Account.[42]

However, considering the ITPGR's narrow scope and limited coverage,[43] it is clear that the CBD remains the cornerstone of the international biodiversity regime. Therefore, the divergent conception of benefit-sharing by the CBD and the ITPGR epitomises a key challenge for the future of BSAs. Indeed, the bilateral model endorsed by the CBD has frequently come under attack. For instance, the UN Special Rapporteur on the Right to Food has boldly stated that the CBD scheme has been unsuccessful, at least in the area of agrobiodiversity, and has highlighted the absence of concrete examples of successful benefit-sharing arrangements.[44] According to the Special Rapporteur, the CBD 'has failed to generate sufficient benefits to fund the conservation of biodiversity. It sometimes has created insuperable obstacles to the access of both researchers and the bioindustry to genetic resources.'[45] He has therefore urged states to endorse a shift from bilateral to multilateral benefit-sharing along the lines of the ITPGR.[46]

The above remarks of the Special Rapporteur are perhaps overstated, insofar as instances of successful, or at least promising and balanced,

[40] ITPGR, art. 13(3). [41] *Ibid.*, arts 18(5) and 15(1)(b)(iii).

[42] See E. Morgera and E. Tsioumani, 'The Evolution of Benefit Sharing: Linking Biodiversity and Community Livelihoods' (2010) 19 *RECIEL* 150, 158–9.

[43] The ITPGR covers agricultural seed and crop diversity regarding sixty-four food crops and forages. But it excludes major crops such as tomatoes, tea, coffee and soybeans.

[44] Interim Report, *Seed Policies and the Right to Food: Enhancing Agrobiodiversity and Encouraging Innovation*, UN Doc. A/64/170, 23 July 2009, para. 47.

[45] *Ibid.*, para. 20. [46] *Ibid.*, para. 57(a).

BSAs have been identified.[47] It is true that the available data is still partial and inconclusive, for instance, in respect of the total amount of monetary transfers to provider countries performed by user companies and institutions.[48] Moreover, the industries and businesses most concerned have frequently expressed scepticism over and unwillingness to act upon the ABS obligations set out in the CBD.[49] Yet, recent studies suggest that this negative attitude might be changing and that private companies, especially in the pharmaceutical and biotechnology sectors, are in fact increasingly involved in BSAs,[50] at both the policy[51] and operational levels. This said, widespread misgivings and reluctance towards the CBD are still a reality. Unlike the ITPGR's multilateral and standardised ABS model, the CBD is often seen as an unreliable, unpredictable and overbureaucratic framework.[52] Last, but not least, the CBD continues to be perceived as an instrument adverse to the enforcement of IPR relating to products and technologies developed from genetic resources. Obviously, IPR are a strategic corporate asset and IPR regulation is therefore crucial to the private sector's acknowledgement of the CBD as a fair regime providing veritable investment opportunities.

The protection of intellectual property in respect of gene-based inventions is indeed an enduring challenge for the global biodiversity and trade regimes. Here too, the ITPGR stands out as a more reliable framework for companies undertaking research and development on resources covered by its Multilateral System. The most controversial intellectual property-related provision in the ITPGR outlaws claims of IPR 'that limit the facilitated access to the plant genetic resources for food and agriculture, or their genetic parts or components, *in the form received* from the Multilateral System'.[53] This only seems to bar intellectual property claims over the *very same* seeds, and their genetic material, that have been

[47] See e.g. the case studies illustrated in *Access and Benefit-Sharing in Practice: Trends in Partnerships Across Sectors* (CBD Technical Series No. 38, 2008), 40–98.

[48] P. ten Brink et al., 'Rewarding Benefits through Payments and Markets', in P. ten Brink (ed.), *The Economics of Ecosystems and Biodiversity in National and International Policy Making* (London: Earthscan, 2011), chap. 5, p. 224.

[49] *Access and Benefit-Sharing in Practice*, 22–37, 121–30.

[50] *Ibid.*, 22.

[51] Also by means of self-regulation and private standard-setting, see especially the Guidelines for IFPMA Members on Access to Genetic Resources and Equitable Sharing of Benefits Arising out of their Utilization, first adopted in 2006 by the International Federation of Pharmaceutical Manufacturers and Associations (IFPMA), available at www.ifpma.org (accessed 15 April 2012).

[52] *Access and Benefit-Sharing in Practice*, 11–37.

[53] ITPGR, art. 12(3)(d), emphasis added.

accessed in accordance with the Treaty. It does not prevent the granting of IPR over products and DNA that have been modified and developed from the resources acquired through the System (for instance, genetically modified plant varieties and foodstuff). Tellingly, the European Union (EU) and most of the EU member states that have ratified the ITPGR have formulated declarations stating 'that plant genetic resources for food and agriculture or their genetic parts or components *which have undergone innovation* may be the subject of intellectual property rights'.[54] In sum, the ITPGR provides a fair solution in this area, one that significantly reduces the scope for encroachment upon intellectual property-related strategies and revenue expectations by businesses. Therefore, the disagreement by the USA and Japan over the treatment of IPR in the Treaty, and their resulting abstention at the time of its adoption and ongoing refusal to ratify, seem unwarranted. It is true that the ITPGR also imposes on companies that commercialise products incorporating material accessed from the System an obligation to transfer a fixed percentage of the revenue (including royalties from licences) arising from the sales of those products to the Treaty's Trust Account.[55] But this payment obligation (i) does not normally apply when the products are available without restriction to others for further research and breeding,[56] nor when the products are sold as commodities;[57] (ii) it is carried out under a predictable framework; and (iii) it does not seem to have deterred companies from widely engaging with the System. Although a precise estimate of the respective engagement of public and private entities is unavailable, it is known that between 600 and 800 samples of plant germplasm are exchanged *each day* under the Treaty's SMTA.[58]

In respect of the CBD regime, it must be acknowledged that the provisions impinging on the protection of IPR have been diluted in the final text of the Nagoya ABS Protocol. Unlike previous negotiating drafts, the Protocol does not explicitly envisage what was mostly opposed by the

[54] Emphasis added. The text of these declarations is available at www.fao.org (accessed 15 April 2012).

[55] ITPGR, art. 13(2)(d)(ii). This percentage is 1.1% less 30% of the sales of the products derived from the accessed material, or, alternatively, 0.5% of the sales of any products derived from the accessed material and of the sales of any other products that are plant genetic resources belonging to the same crop. See SMTA, Annexes 2 and 3.

[56] ITPGR, art. 13(2)(d)(ii).

[57] See *ibid.*, introductory para. to art. 2; and SMTA, Annex 2(1)(c).

[58] See www.planttreaty.org (accessed 15 April 2012).

business community, namely mandatory disclosure requirements (i.e., the duty to disclose the country of origin of genetic resources as a requirement for patentability) and IP offices as checkpoints for supporting compliance with BSAs.[59] It does, however, endorse various options for sharing intellectual property-related benefits that can be acted upon by provider countries when negotiating BSAs, such as the payment of royalties or licence fees, joint ownership of IPR and transfer of proprietary knowledge and technologies.[60] In sum, the usual problem underlying the CBD ABS regime, i.e., its essentially non-multilateral nature, also affects the issue of IPR in the Nagoya ABS Protocol. IPR negotiations are thus entirely a matter of private deals, and equity is left in the hands of the private parties, at least until an agreement is reached and subsequently becomes the object of a dispute. This may translate into a fragmented and cumbersome framework made up of disparate national regulatory requirements and unpredictable party-to-party affairs. The risk is not only that the ultimate aim of biodiversity protection may be undermined, but also that private actors refrain from actively participating in the BSA's process and rather shift their priorities towards other market sectors and opportunities.[61]

8.3 Payments for ecosystem services

The most generic definition of a PES scheme is that of 'a contractual transaction between a buyer and a seller for an ecosystem service or a land use/management practice likely to secure that service'.[62] Ecosystem

[59] Nagoya ABS Protocol, art. 17.

[60] *Ibid.*, Annex. On technology transfer, see also the rather weak provision set forth in art. 23: 'Parties undertake to promote and encourage'.

[61] From the perspective of IPR, another crucial determinant for future business engagement with BSAs will be the outcome of the relevant processes initiated at the WIPO Intergovernmental Committee on Intellectual Property and Genetic Resources, Traditional Knowledge and Folklore, and especially at the World Trade Organization (WTO) in the context of the Doha Round. On the proposed patent disclosure-of-origin amendment to the WTO Agreement on Trade-Related Aspects of Intellectual Property Rights, see R. Pavoni, 'Mutual Supportiveness as a Principle of Interpretation and Law-Making: A Watershed for the "WTO-and-Competing Regimes" Debate?' (2010) 21 *European Journal of International Law* 649, 669–72.

[62] Recommendations on Payments for Ecosystem Services in Integrated Water Resources Management, adopted by the Parties to the UNECE Convention on the Protection and Use of Transboundary Watercourses and International Lakes at their fourth meeting (Bonn, 20–22 November 2006) (Water Convention PES Recommendations), chap. 2. Available at www.unece.org (accessed 15 April 2012).

services, in turn, are the 'benefits people obtain from ecosystems'[63] and can be categorised into *provisioning services* (e.g., food, water, timber), *regulating services* (e.g., purification of air and water, stabilisation of climate), *supporting services* (e.g., nutrient cycling, soil formation) and *cultural services* (e.g., aesthetic beauty).[64] The economic case for the creation of PES schemes is well documented. They can indeed work out as a dynamic tool whereby an efficient and equitable allocation of environmental costs and benefits is achieved: sellers would be incentivised to pursue sound environmental management practices over and above existing regulatory requirements, and beneficiaries would be 'willing to pay to secure the services that underpin their businesses',[65] while at the same time internalising part of the costs associated with those business activities. In this connection, the CBD Principles of the Ecosystem Approach refer to a need for the 'alignment of incentives'[66] to promote biodiversity conservation and sustainable use.

Unlike BSAs, PES schemes can be considered as a *direct* positive incentive mechanism to foster biodiversity protection. The immediate object of PES contracts is indeed to grant monetary benefits on condition that one or more (biodiversity-related) ecosystem services are constantly provided by the seller.[67] Despite their recent pedigree, PES arrangements have been identified as 'one of the most frequently used economic instruments in biodiversity management', especially in the agriculture and forestry sectors.[68] The available overall figures are impressive: about 300 PES programmes are in operation in various parts of the world and their scale is growing by 10 per cent to 20 per cent annually; US$6.53 billion are mobilised as payments for the schemes that are in force in China, Costa Rica, Mexico, the United Kingdom and the USA alone.[69]

At any rate, it must be pointed out that PES schemes have so far mainly prevailed (i) at the national level without clear guidance from international institutions, whereas international PES (IPES) programmes

[63] *Ibid.*

[64] *Ibid.* See also, with further references, G. Heal, 'Markets and Sustainability', in Revesz, Sands and Stewart, *Environmental Law* 410, 411–12; P. ten Brink et al., 'The Global Biodiversity Crisis and Related Policy Challenge', in ten Brink, *The Economics of Ecosystems*, 7, 11.

[65] ten Brink et al., 'Rewarding Benefits through Payments and Markets', 182.

[66] COP-5, Decision V/6, Annex, Principle 4.

[67] This is why PES are also frequently termed 'performance payments'.

[68] *Incentive Measures for the Conservation and Sustainable Use of Biological Diversity*, 14.

[69] See the references in ten Brink et al., 'Rewarding Benefits through Payments and Markets', 194.

as measures to contribute to the achievement of the objectives of multilateral environmental agreements have not yet been officially launched;[70] (ii) in the water and carbon sectors; and (iii) in the form of *public* PES schemes, where public authorities' engagement and funding are fundamental. Mixed public–private schemes have also principally relied on public financing. It therefore seems necessary to promote wider investments from the private sector into *private* and *trading* PES schemes that are particularly designed to reward and incentivise the provision of services linked to the protection of biodiversity in its own right and, preferably, *at the ecosystem level.* A key question is whether and to what extent the private sector is willing to pay for the provision of such biodiversity-specific ecosystem services.

Existing practice suggests that, although there are exceptional instances in which PES schemes may be *exclusively* directed at the protection of species' and ecosystems' diversity and related services, the funding of such schemes comes from government authorities or non-governmental organisations (NGOs). For example, the payments for agri-environmental measures taken by farmers in various European regions under the auspices of the EU Common Agricultural Policy – which may directly target biodiversity benefits such as genetic diversity and preservation of landscapes – have traditionally been secured through public funds, which, in turn, heavily rely on tax revenues.[71] Alternatively, NGOs may be willing to finance PES programmes aimed at the conservation of endangered species, as in the interesting example of the performance payments made available by Sea Sense, a Tanzanian NGO, to reward individuals on Mafia Island (Tanzania) who report and agree not to poach sea turtle nests.[72]

Many other PES schemes ambitiously bundle the provision of biodiversity-related services with other ecosystem services, with a view to include biodiversity-friendly outcomes among those that are to be compensated. But even here the private sector seems reluctant to offer

[70] Negotiations for REDD-plus under the FCCC are ongoing and it is not yet clear to what extent privately financed PES schemes will be part of its funding strategy. A quite exceptional international (soft law) instrument on PES is represented by the Water Convention PES Recommendations, above, n. 62.

[71] *Ibid.*, Annex IV, 40–1.

[72] See ten Brink et al., 'Rewarding Benefits through Payments and Markets', 198; P. J. Ferraro, 'Performance Payments for Sea Turtle Nest Protection in Low-income Nations: A Case Study from Tanzania', available at www2.gsu.edu (accessed 15 April 2012).

payments for biodiversity-specific benefits. The much-imitated and celebrated *Pagos por Servicios Ambientales* (PSA) programme implemented in Costa Rica since 1997 is paradigmatic in this respect. This programme envisages monetary rewards to forest landholders who agree to carry out sustainable management practices for three distinct services, namely water-related services, carbon storage and biodiversity services. However, while private companies (i.e., power producers) have either substantially (for water-related services) or partially (for carbon storage) contributed to financing the PSA scheme, they have not supported biodiversity payments. Any efforts undertaken by the Costa Rican authorities in this regard, including with the eco-tourism industry, have proven unsuccessful. Certain funds for biodiversity-specific payments have only been provided by international institutions, such as the Global Environment Facility.[73]

The Costa Rican example shows that the actual positive contribution of current PES schemes to the protection of biodiversity is usually indirect. Frequently, such schemes may *in fact* be beneficial to species' and ecosystems' diversity. Nonetheless, this only occurs as a sort of *by-product* of PES arrangements that are primarily aimed at securing the provision of other ecosystem services, such as carbon sequestration or water quality. For instance, forest preservation and sustainable farming practices produce tangible benefits in terms of reduced greenhouse gas emissions and improved water quality and quantity. At the same time, they may also significantly contribute to the conservation of forest and agricultural crop diversity. Hence, the insistence in the pertinent literature and practice on the notion of *biodiversity co-benefits*[74] flowing from PES arrangements. This state of affairs is hardly satisfactory from the perspective of long-term and sustainable financing of biodiversity protection. As a matter of fact, private investment is typically channelled in the biodiversity regime only incidentally and haphazardly, that is, insofar as *complementary* measures to safeguard biodiversity are deemed necessary to avoid undermining investment projects and related businesses and PES schemes.

[73] See *Incentive Measures for the Conservation and Sustainable Use of Biological Diversity*, 42–3; ten Brink et al., 'Rewarding Benefits through Payments and Markets', 187.

[74] For a clear illustration of this notion and possible alternative paths in the context of REDD-plus initiatives, see ten Brink et al., 'Rewarding Benefits through Payments and Markets', 200–9.

This also seems true for certain major private business initiatives that have been considered a prototype of successful PES schemes. The Nestlé payments for improved watershed practices in Vittel's spring catchment area located in the Vosges Mountains in north-eastern France deserve special mention in this connection.[75] Since 1993, faced with increased levels of nitrates and pesticides in the area and the resulting threat for the viability of Vittel's business and brand name, Nestlé Waters approved a substantial investment in a complex scheme foreseeing a range of benefits for farmers entering into long-term contracts (eighteen to thirty years) to carry out sustainable farming practices (e.g., replacement of maize cultivation with feed cultivation and extensive dairy cattle ranching). The benefits included payments of approximately €200 per hectare per year over a seven-year transition period, reimbursements of new technological equipment for up to €150,000 per farm, and ongoing technical assistance and supervision. All the concerned farmers have been enrolled in the programme which has greatly contributed to preserve both water and environmental quality. Nestlé has therefore been encouraged to replicate the scheme in other spring catchment areas in France, as well as in other countries, such as Argentina.[76] At least in respect of Vittel's spring catchment area, measures specifically targeting biodiversity protection were also supported by Nestlé, insofar as these were functional to the realisation of the core objective of sustainable farming practices to maintain high-quality mineral drinking water. Thus, plant and animal species, such as natural predators of crop pests, were either the object of enhanced protection or were appositely released into the environment, and non-farm land was acquired and turned into green areas or sustainable tourism facilities in order to counter increased urbanisation pressure.[77] The Nestlé case may therefore be taken as a successful example of a focused local investment project, involving a narrow geographical area and farming community, which in the process has additionally financed certain biodiversity co-benefits. It is instead inherently unable to set a precedent suitable for replication at the global level and it does *not* suggest that the private sector is, under any circumstances, inclined to finance the provision of biodiversity services in and of themselves.

[75] See Water Convention PES Recommendations, Annex IV, 41–2; ten Brink et al., 'Rewarding Benefits through Payments and Markets', 191; *Incentive Measures for the Conservation and Sustainable Use of Biological Diversity*, 49–51.

[76] *Incentive Measures for the Conservation and Sustainable Use of Biological Diversity*, 50.

[77] *Ibid.*, 49–50.

To the contrary, the present situation is still one where private companies do not appear willing to pay for the provision of biodiversity services at the *components* level, at least where the preservation of species is not clearly functional to the profitability of a business, and especially at the *ecosystem* level. Unlike BSAs, where genetic samples are seen as valuable and tangible resources for research and development activities, no concrete benefits that would justify monetary disbursements are usually acknowledged in respect of ecosystems' diversity as a global public good.[78] In terms of economics, this is explained by highlighting that the burden of securing and rewarding the provision of public goods falls to public authorities, as such goods are by definition non-excludable and non-rival goods: 'this makes it hard for business or individuals to profit from producing them'.[79] That is also a well-known issue reflected in the international biodiversity legal regime, and traceable to the overall design of the CBD and the asymmetric implementation of its objectives. In the CBD, there is indeed a certain tension between the means for pursuing the conservation of biodiversity, on the one hand, and the sustainable use of (and equitable sharing of benefits arising from) its *components*, including biological resources, on the other.[80] In short, the CBD attaches economic value to, thereby triggering markets for, biological resources, and not for services produced by ecosystems themselves.[81] Ecosystems are thus an integral whole and cannot be itemised in terms of specific resources, nor easily monetised, valued or marketed according to economic rationalities.

Therefore, a key issue for the future of the private sector's investments in biodiversity-related PES schemes remains that of devising universally shared principles and economic methodologies for the valuation of ecosystem services and for measuring impacts on biodiversity at the

[78] This also explains why, usually, private PES schemes are aimed at rewarding carbon sequestration or water-related services. In the latter cases, the income generated by investing in carbon-friendly projects or in enhanced water quality and quantity is more easily quantifiable and measurable, as are the specific contributions to such income by service-suppliers' activities.

[79] *The Economics of Ecosystems and Biodiversity for National and International Policy Makers*, draft chap. 5, p. 30. See also Heal, 'Markets and Sustainability', 426–7.

[80] See CBD, art. 1. 'Biological resources' are in turn defined in art. 2 as including 'genetic resources, organisms or parts thereof, populations, or any other biotic *component* of ecosystems with actual or potential use or value for humanity' (emphasis added).

[81] For thoughtful insights into these themes, see e.g. D. Farrier and L. Tucker, 'Access to Marine Bioresources: Hitching the Conservation Cart to the Bioprospecting Horse' (2001) 32 *Ocean Development & International Law* 213, 220–2.

ecosystem level. Undoubtedly, scientific and economic disciplines have made substantial progress towards that objective, and relevant studies and projects have proliferated in the past few years.[82] However, fundamental challenges remain, such as whether and how one should account for the cultural services and the global and intrinsic values associated with biodiversity.[83] This task necessarily needs to be performed at the international level through an inclusive process allowing the participation of all stakeholders. The current debate on the establishment of biodiversity-related IPES schemes, as well as the ongoing negotiations on the REDD-plus mechanism under the UNFCCC, are likely to provide significant insights in this respect.

CONCLUSION

The present discussions over the need to create and expand market mechanisms to stimulate private investments in the protection of biodiversity have first of all clarified that the original economic rationale underlying the CBD is viable only if both providers *and users* of genetic resources and ecosystem services acknowledge and act upon biodiversity-related business opportunities.

This chapter has examined BSAs and PES as two distinct mechanisms which may provide incentives to the participation of business and its financial resources in the global effort to safeguard biodiversity. Although both are contractual transactions shaped by market forces and trends, their status is profoundly different. While BSAs constitute the output of a fundamental principle and objective of the CBD as now spelled out in the Nagoya ABS Protocol, PES are an innovative emerging instrument with only a tenuous link to CBD obligations. It is therefore necessary to institutionalise biodiversity-related PES at the international level, in order to provide standards and benchmarks for private parties' transactions.

It is indeed unthinkable that innovative market mechanisms be developed outside any clear guidance from the relevant international institutions. In this regard, the regulation of BSAs in the CBD regime

[82] For instance, see most recently, *Developing Ecosystem Service Indicators: Experiences and Lessons Learned from Sub-Global Assessments and other Initiatives* (CBD Technical Series No. 58, 2011). A key institutional role in respect of these issues is bound to be played by the Intergovernmental Platform on Biodiversity and Ecosystem Services (IPBES). See www.ipbes.net (accessed 15 April 2012).

[83] For a concise overview of the divergencies and limits of economic theories in this area, see Water Convention PES Recommendations, Annex II, pp. 25–31.

may provide useful insights, at least in terms of non-derogable overarching principles that must be followed by individual contracts, such as especially the principle of equity and fairness in the sharing of burdens and benefits flowing from biodiversity-relevant activities.

This chapter has shown that the engagement of business in BSAs has so far not been satisfactory. There exists ongoing business's resistance to regard the CBD and Nagoya Protocol's ABS frameworks as a real investment opportunity, rather than an obstacle to market freedoms and product development. To a certain extent, the bilateralisation of transactions involving genetic resources seems to have exacerbated the respective positions of providers and users, while the multilateral model supported under the ITPGR has instead resulted in a reliable regulatory environment and paved the way for a steady flow of genetic *and* financial resources.

On their part, PES schemes will undeniably play a role in future strategies to protect biodiversity. However, most of the funds necessary to reward providers of ecosystem services are still originating from governmental public sources, and thus ultimately from taxpayers. A wider participation of the private sector therefore appears essential. This is especially the situation prevailing in respect of biodiversity-related PES programmes. One of the main findings of this chapter is that in the few instances where such programmes have envisaged payments for the provision of biodiversity-dependent ecosystem services, private actors have refused to contribute or have only supplied a minor financial contribution. The main reason for this, which is also reflected in the elusive notion of ecosystems' biodiversity, is the need further to develop universally shared methodologies for measuring and allocating costs and benefits of the preservation of ecosystems. This seems an indispensable condition in order to persuade the private sector to devote an equitable share of its resources to the financing of biodiversity conservation.

Select bibliography

Bowman, M., P. Davies and C. Redgwell, *Lyster's International Wildlife Law*, 2nd edn (Cambridge University Press, 2010).

Farrier, D., and L. Tucker, 'Access to Marine Bioresources: Hitching the Conservation Cart to the Bioprospecting Horse' (2001) 32 *Ocean Development & International Law* 213.

Francioni, F., 'Equity in International Law', in R. Wolfrum (ed.), *The Max Planck Encyclopedia of Public International Law* (Oxford University Press, 2008–); online edition.

Fromond, L., J. Similä and L. Suvantola, 'Regulatory Innovations for Biodiversity Protection in Private Forests – Towards Flexibility' (2009) 21 *Journal of Environmental Law* 1.

Greiber, T. (ed.), *Payments for Ecosystems Services: Legal and Institutional Frameworks* (Gland: IUCN, 2009).

Heal, G., 'Markets and Sustainability', in R. L. Revesz, P. Sands and R. B. Stewart (eds.), *Environmental Law, the Economy, and Sustainable Development* (Cambridge University Press, 2000), pp. 410–27.

Morgera, E., 'Far Away So Close: A Legal Analysis of the Increasing Interactions between the Convention on Biological Diversity and Climate Change Law' (2011) 2 *Climate Law* 85.

Morgera, E., and E. Tsioumani, 'The Evolution of Benefit Sharing: Linking Biodiversity and Community Livelihoods' (2010) 19 *Review of European Community and International Environmental Law* 150.

Pavoni, R., 'Biodiversity and Biotechnology: Consolidation and Strains in the Emerging International Legal Regimes', in F. Francioni and T. Scovazzi (eds.), *Biotechnology and International Law* (Oxford: Hart Publishing, 2006), pp. 29–58.

Pavoni, R., 'Mutual Supportiveness as a Principle of Interpretation and Law-Making: A Watershed for the "WTO-and-Competing Regimes" Debate?' (2010) 21 *European Journal of International Law* 649.

Reid, C. T., 'The Privatisation of Biodiversity? Possible New Approaches to Nature Conservation Law in the UK' (2011) 23 *Journal of Environmental Law* 203.

ten Brink, P. (ed.), *The Economics of Ecosystems and Biodiversity in National and International Policy Making* (London: Earthscan, 2011).

Trouwborst, T., 'International Nature Conservation Law and the Adaptation of Biodiversity to Climate Change: A Mismatch?' (2009) 21 *Journal of Environmental Law* 419.

Winter, G., 'The Climate is No Commodity: Taking Stock of the Emissions Trading System' (2010) 22 *Journal of Environmental Law* 1.

9

The role of insurance risk transfer in encouraging climate investment in developing countries

SWENJA SURMINSKI

INTRODUCTION

Environmental change has profound effects on economies, wider society, individuals and ecosystems. Responding to threats such as pollution, loss of biodiversity or climatic changes requires public policy intervention, as well as private action and significant new capital investments. Under the caption of 'sustainable development' more and more private companies and national governments pledge to balance the economic, social and environmental effects of growth. Innovative solutions are being developed and tested, especially in the context of financing the required action. One particular area that receives increasing attention is how best to foster public and private investments in environmental protection. This is especially relevant for low-income countries: often those most exposed to environmental changes are least capable to respond to the threats, and require financial and technical support from developed countries and donors. Most commentators have focused on the role of public policy in facilitating the required environmental investments.[1] Conversely, the application of financial instruments such as insurance is still under-researched.

The author wishes to thank Andrew Williamson and Delioma Oramas-Dorta for their input and helpful comments.

[1] See D. Fiorino, *The New Environmental Regulation* (London: MIT Press, 2006); E. Somanathan and T. Sterner, 'Environmental Policy Instruments and Institutions in Developing Countries', in R. López and M. Toman (eds.), *Economic Development and Environmental Sustainability: New Policy Option* (Oxford University Press, 2006), chap. 7; F. Foxon and P. Pearson, 'Overcoming Barriers to Innovation and Diffusion of Cleaner Technologies: Some Features of a Sustainable Innovation Policy Regime' (2008) 16 *Journal of Cleaner Production* 148; S. Fankhauser, 'A Practitioner's Guide to a Low-Carbon Economy: Lessons from the UK', Policy paper, Centre for Climate Change Economics and Policy, 2012, available at www.cccep.ac.uk (accessed 24 January 2012).

Insurance risk transfer has been used for centuries as a tool to manage the risk of uncertain losses. In its most basic form insurance is a mechanism where risks or part of a risk are transferred from one party (the insured) to another party (the insurer) in return for a payment (the premium). The insurer pays out a previously agreed amount if the insured experiences a loss, or if a predefined event occurs.[2] In other words, the insured pays a certain premium to reduce the risk of an uncertain loss. This reduction in uncertainty is widely seen as an important mechanism driving our economic systems: without insurance many activities and processes would be deemed too risky and would not be undertaken. Moreover, in the event of a loss, those affected might struggle to recover. In economic terms the justification for any insurance is derived from the welfare function, which means that the provision of insurance can increase the expected utility of individuals, companies or society.

At first sight insurance seems an unusual choice for supporting environmental protection: the inherent problem of moral hazard can mean, in an environmental context, that the provision of an insurance policy triggers risky and unwanted polluting activities on the side of the insured. But safeguards can be designed in order to avoid moral hazard and incentivise risk reduction by the policyholder. An example is environmental-liability insurance, where the insured is often required to assess and improve standards and procedures that could lead to pollution. This creates an incentive for those companies seeking insurance to comply or exceed environmental standards as the policy will only pay out if the insured is compliant. In addition to this indirect risk-reduction role derived from the compensation function of insurance, there is another dimension of the environmental role of risk transfer: insurance can make investments less risky and therefore foster innovation and the development of cleaner technologies.

Most of the existing analytical work exploring the environmental role of risk transfer has focused on two risk areas: pollution liability and natural disaster insurance, which can both have catastrophic consequences. A 2003 OECD study finds that, with pollution insurance, the insurer may act as a private surrogate regulator aligning its interests with

[2] N. Ranger, S. Surminski and N. Silver, 'Open Questions about How to Address "Loss and Damage" from Climate Change in the Most Vulnerable Countries: A Response to the Cancún Adaptation Framework', Policy paper, Centre for Climate Change Economics and Policy, 2011, p. 9, available at www.cccep.ac.uk (accessed 15 March 2012).

those of high environmental standards.[3] The internalisation of environmental costs through the payment of premiums is compatible with the deterrence goal of any liability regime and with the polluter-pays principle. Conversely, Minoli and Bell[4] find in an evaluation of two leading UK insurance companies' pollution claims that the insurers' initial underwriting assessments and post-loss investigations are insufficiently developed. Similarly, the management practices of insured parties in connection with the prevention of pollution are also underdeveloped. Consequently, insurers' terms and conditions on policies are insufficient to work as an incentive to dissuade pollution losses. The effectiveness of environmental insurance has been extensively researched for the USA. Some studies show indeed that despite a range of practical barriers environmental insurance can achieve efficiency where government fines do not.[5] In the context of natural disaster, the main analytical focus has been on the potential for insurance risk transfer to be coupled with incentives (such as building standards and codes) and other regulatory instruments to reduce potential losses from natural disasters. Surminski[6] finds that there is evidence of insurers engaging in disaster risk reduction by raising awareness, promoting and supporting the risk-reduction activities of their clients, but measuring the effectiveness of these efforts remains a challenge.

While most of the literature has explored pollution liability and natural disaster insurance in the context of developed markets, there is now a growing focus on emerging markets and developing countries. Here the situation is characterised by low insurance penetration and growing risks. Freeman and Kunreuther[7] describe the challenges faced by developing countries when utilising insurance products for risk management.

[3] OECD, *Environmental Risks and Insurance: A Comparative Analysis of the Role of Insurance in the Management of Environment-Related Risks*, Policy Issues in Insurance, No. 6 (Paris: OECD Publishing, 2003), available at www.oecd-ilibrary.org (accessed 15 January 2012).

[4] See D. M. Minoli and J. N. B. Bell, 'Insurance as an Alternative Environmental Regulator: Findings from a Retrospective Pollution Claims Survey' (2003) 12 *Business Strategy and the Environment* 107.

[5] See H. Yin, A. Pfaff and H. Kunreuther, 'Can Environmental Insurance Succeed Where Other Strategies Fail? The Case of Underground Storage Tanks' (2011) 31 *Risk Analysis* 12.

[6] S. Surminski, 'Adapting to the Extreme Weather Impacts of Climate Change – How Can the Insurance Industry Help?', *ClimateWise*, November 2010, available at www.climatewise.org.uk (accessed 12 March 2012).

[7] P. K. Freeman and H. Kunreuther, *Managing Environmental Risk Through Insurance* (Boston, Mass.: Kluwer Academic Publishers, 1997), 159–89.

Pollution insurance or natural catastrophe risk insurance requires a sophisticated set of laws, regulations and administrative agencies. A 2012 report by Swiss Re, a large reinsurer, on the evolution of pollution insurance in China, notes that, while the potential for pollution insurance remains sizeable in China, several challenges remain.[8] These include the need for a developed legal framework, the current small market base for pollution insurance, firms' lack of in-house knowledge and client awareness and an absence of historical loss data. The existence of an appropriate legal framework seems particularly important. Warner and others[9] find that community risk awareness, dissemination of risk information and financial literacy are particularly important for disaster insurance schemes in developing countries.

In this context, the present chapter explores the potential of insurance instruments to tackle one major environmental challenge, namely climate change. It is well documented that the greatest threats from climate change are expected in those parts of the world that are most vulnerable. Assisting those countries in their efforts to become more resilient to climate risks is now a key part of the international climate negotiations under the UNFCCC.[10] Agreeing a suitable Adaptation Framework will require significant funds – and there are growing expectations amongst policymakers that this will be met to a large extent by the private sector. At the same time it is evident that any significant reduction in global emissions over the next decades will have to involve those countries with the highest current growth rate. Fostering low-carbon growth in developing countries is therefore a key goal of global climate policy. Financing this transition to 'greener' economies will require large investments, both publicly and privately.

Generally speaking, any investment carries risks and opportunities. Investments will only be made if the rate of return is high enough to justify the risks involved. In the context of climate mitigation and adaptation in developing countries the risks are often perceived to be particularly high (in some cases too high) to encourage private investment, with projects not meeting the required 'investment grade' status

[8] Swiss Re, 'Environmental Pollution Liability Insurance in China: A Bumpy Road Leading to a Bright Prospect' (2012). Available at www.swissre.com (accessed 11 March 2012).

[9] K. Warner, N. Ranger, S. Surminski et al., 'Adaptation to Climate Change: Linking Disaster Risk Reduction and Insurance', paper prepared for the United Nations International Strategy on Disaster Reduction (Geneva: UNISDR, 2009), available at www.preventionweb.net (accessed 14 March 2012).

[10] United Nations Framework Convention on Climate Change, 9 May 1992, 31 ILM 849.

required by many investors. This chapter explores if and how insurance risk-transfer schemes could encourage investment in climate-related projects in developing countries. The analysis focuses on the compensation, risk-reduction and supporting environmental investment functions of insurance schemes.[11]

After a brief discussion of the potential role of insurance in environmental protection in developing countries (9.1.), the chapter analyses the particular case of insurance of climate-change-related investment in developing countries, in the context of both mitigation and adaptation (9.2.). The chapter concludes with a summary and an outlook on future perspectives (9.3).

9.1 Financial instruments and environmental protection in developing countries: the role of insurance

Insurance is a widely used financial product in most developed countries, although availability, demand and scope vary significantly from country to country owing to local customs and traditions, different risk attitudes and regulation. Insurance can come in different forms and shapes: (i) it can be provided by public or private entities;[12] (ii) the insured might seek cover on a voluntary basis or it can be compulsory; (iii) it can cover individuals, businesses, insurers/reinsurers (via reinsurance), organisations or governments; (iv) it can cover different types of hazards (e.g., flood or illness) and exposures (homes, motor cars or business

[11] Insurance encompasses two kinds of activities: providing insurance risk transfer (liability side) and investing insurance funds (asset side). The liability side of insurance can be classified into different categories: life insurance, non-life insurance, reinsurance (insurance of insurers) and alternative risk transfers. The asset side of insurance is concerned with investing the funds accumulated and managing the capital base of an insurer. As institutional investors, insurers can influence capital flows across asset classes and markets. But this chapter only considers the liability side of insurance. Obviously there is an environmental role to play for insurers as institutional investors, just like for any other investors. But an assessment of this investment role is beyond the scope of the chapter.

[12] In general terms, insurance can be provided by the private sector or 'publicly' through governments and governmental agencies. Within this spectrum, variation exists and some large-scale risks, such as terrorism or natural catastrophe, are covered through public–private partnerships, where the private insurance industry and government share risks. Private companies can be domestic or foreign, and the cover can be provided directly or via reinsurers, who mainly operate at a global scale. Insurance companies can also take the form of mutuals, which are owned by the insured, and function like cooperatives.

interruption) and have different coverage designs (varying levels of cover, features such as deductibles, exclusions, conditions); (v) and the cover provided can be loss-based (a loss must be evident) or parametric (triggered by a certain event).

The provision of risk transfer is still in its infancy in most developing countries, as shown by the distribution of insurance premiums. In 2010, Europe (37 per cent) and North America (30 per cent) were the largest insurance markets in terms of premium volume. Asia accounted for 27 per cent of the global premium volume. In contrast, Latin America and Africa/Oceania only made up a 6 per cent share of the global insurance premiums (3 per cent each).[13] Most developing countries experience very low insurance penetration rates.[14] Insurance penetration shows the relationship between economic growth (GDP or GDP per capita) and insurance premiums, and it is an indicator of how active and developed the insurance sector is within a country.[15] Plotting penetration levels against per capita income for different countries produces the so-called Global Trend Line (Munich Re) or 'S-curve' (Swiss Re). This relationship suggests an income elasticity of insurance premiums, which typically varies with the stage of economic development: with growing income insurance penetration increases, after a certain level of GDP per capita is reached it tends to plateau.[16]

Mainly due to the growth of emerging economies, insurance activities are now spreading more widely across the globe (Figure 9.1). A range of studies have underlined the importance of stable and effective institutions for a functioning insurance market, such as law enforcement, but also the availability of risk data.[17] Education and financial literacy levels are also perceived to be driving factors for the development of

[13] See CEA, *European Insurance – Key Facts* (Brussels, 2011), 4, available at www.insuranceeurope.eu (accessed 21 January 2012).

[14] See H. Ibarra and J. Skees, 'Innovation in Risk Transfer for Natural Hazards Impacting Agriculture' (2007) 7 *Environmental Hazards* 62.

[15] See S. Hussels, D. Ward and R. Zurbruegg, 'Stimulating the Demand for Insurance' (2005) 8 *Risk Management and Insurance Review* 257.

[16] Data provided by Munich Re. See also N. Ranger and S. Surminski, 'A Preliminary Assessment of the Impact of Climate Change on Non-Life Insurance Demand in the BRICS Economies', Working Paper 72, Centre for Climate Change Economics and Policy (2011), available at www.cccep.ac.uk (accessed 17 January 2012).

[17] See L. Brainard, 'What is the Role of Insurance in Economic Development?', Zurich Government and Industry Thought Leadership Series (2008), No. 2; Hussels, Ward and Zurbruegg, 'Stimulating the Demand for Insurance'.

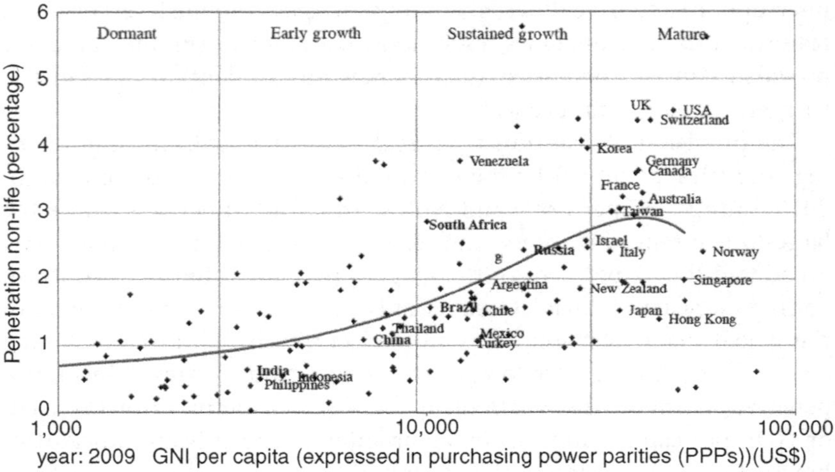

Figure 9.1 *Relationship between gross national income (GNI) per capita (expressed in purchasing power parities (PPPs)) and the penetration of non-life insurance (percentage of GDP) in 2009 for 200 countries*

Notes: The grey line is the 'global trend line'. The vertical lines indicate approximate phases of market development.

Source: Data provided by Munich Re. N. Ranger and S. Surminski, 'A Preliminary Assessment of the Impact of Climate Change on Non-Life Insurance Demand in the BRICS Economies', Working Paper 72, Centre for Climate Change Economics and Policy (2011), 9. Available at www.cccep.ac.uk (accessed 17 January 2012).

insurance.[18] In addition, the specific characteristics of a market, such as distribution channels and appetite for innovation in terms of products and services can drive or hold back the development of insurance.[19] The last decade has seen several efforts to liberalise the insurance industry. Despite some local differences, there is indeed a trend towards the opening up of national markets (such as in China and India) to foreign companies, international trade liberalisation and harmonisation of the EU insurance market.

The insurance products available in developing countries reflect the scope of coverage available in more established insurance markets,

[18] See P. Masci, L. Tejerina and I. Webb, 'Insurance Market Development in Latin America and the Caribbean', Inter-American Development Bank Sustainable Development Department Technical Papers Series, IFM-146, 2007.

[19] See UNCTAD, *Trade and Development Aspects of Insurance Services and Regulatory Frameworks, 2007*, available at www.unctad.org (accessed 11 March 2012).

including life and non-life (such as health, motor, property, crop, funeral, commercial) risks. Government schemes are also in operation, mainly in the social insurance context and for certain catastrophe types, backed by global reinsurance and/or international donors. Specifically designed for developing countries are micro-insurance and some new forms of parametric insurance, mainly used in the agricultural sector. Despite recent growth trends, both private and public insurance schemes still face a lot of challenges in developing countries, such as lack of capital by domestic players or governments due to weak finance sectors and limited access to global markets.

The main role of insurance is the transfer of risks and the provision of compensation in the event of a loss. Well-designed[20] insurance initiatives and markets can play a wider economic and social role by:

1. promoting financial stability and security at both the national and personal levels;
2. encouraging productive investments and innovation through the mitigation of the consequences of financial misfortune;
3. mobilising savings;
4. contributing to an efficient use of capital based on insurers' role as significant institutional investors;
5. facilitating firms' access to capital (as institutional investors);
6. reducing the capital firms' need to operate;
7. promoting sensible risk management through the price mechanism; and,
8. fostering stable consumption throughout the customer's life.[21]

Insurance can also play a social welfare role, taking over some public relief functions and being used as a tool for public policy, for example, in the context of social security.

Some of the factors from the list above hint at a potential role for insurance in environmental protection. Item (1) can be seen in the context of providing compensation for victims, for example, in the case of accidental pollution. Item (2) is about reducing the financial risk of a

[20] By contrast, badly designed insurance products and badly structured insurance markets can lead to moral hazard, maladaptation to future risks and to inefficiency.

[21] See Geneva Association, *Global Insurance Industry Factsheet* (2010), 4, available at www.genevaassociation.org (accessed 15 February 2011).

Table 9.1 Links among types of insurance, function and applications

Type of insurance	Risks covered	Environmental applications
Liability	Accidental pollution, directors and officers	Compensation of victims, funding of clean-up, fostering risk reduction = no. 1 + no. 7 of the insurance functions
Project insurance	Construction risks delivery failure, property damage, political risk, business interruption	Facilitating 'environmental' investment and supporting technological innovation by transferring risks = no. 2 of the insurance functions
Natural disaster	Property damage, business interruption	Compensation for damages, funding of recovery efforts, fostering risk-reduction = no. 1 + no. 7 of the insurance functions
Policy risks	Change in subsidies	Facilitating 'environmental' investment and supporting technological innovation by transferring risks = no. 2 of the insurance functions

particular activity, for example, for investors in new 'green' technologies. Item (7) touches on incentivising risk management, for example, by charging higher insurance premiums for those activities that might harm the environment. Table 9.1 provides an overview of different types of insurance and links them to the broad functions of insurance listed above, as well as with their more specific environmental applications.[22]

[22] In addition to these four categories there is a much broader range of environmental applications which are not considered in this analysis. They are often captured by the heading 'green products'. These are often adaptations of existing products, such as motor insurance, which are designed with a link to environmental aspects, such as pay-as-you-drive motor insurance policies that have been promoted as 'policies to reduce private usage of cars', and policies that achieve greater energy efficiency, such as 'eco homes' policies. A good overview is provided in E. Mills, *From Risk to Opportunity: Insurer Responses to Climate Change* (Boston, Mass.: Ceres, 2009).

Particularly the risk-reduction element (7) in the above framework is linked to the issue of moral hazard: pollution insurance and also natural disaster cover could be seen as a licence to pollute or a licence to build and operate in a way that is unnecessarily harmful to the environment, unless a direct link between the environmental efforts of the insured and the level of the premium is established. Here, insurance, if designed properly, can offer an incentive for prevention and risk reduction, for example, by imposing certain operational standards, which reduce pollution risks.

The application of these insurance instruments has been predominantly focused on developed countries and established insurance markets. Estimating the market size remains difficult. For natural catastrophe (or 'nat cat') insurance there is evidence of an insurance gap. Estimates indicate that in developing countries only 3 per cent of natural disaster losses are insured compared to 40 per cent in developed markets.[23] For pollution insurance anecdotal evidence suggests a global market size of around US$3 billion, which is heavily dominated by the US market.[24] For the size and spread of nat cat insurance the most commonly used indicator is insured loss, with a global figure of US$38 billion stated for 2010,[25] again heavily dominated by the US market and other developed countries. Only recently have there been increased efforts to provide risk transfer in a low-income country context. Guoqiang and Jinyan[26] analyse the progress of environmental insurance in China. In the municipalities Dalian, Changchuan, Shenyang and Jilin, pollution insurance was initially developed in the 1990s as a collaborative effort between the local environmental protection departments and insurance companies. The authors state that the initial development of pollution insurance was unsuccessful and that, in 2007, the State Environmental Protection

[23] K. Warner and A. Spiegel, 'Climate Change and Emerging Markets: The Role of the Insurance Industry in Climate Risk Management', in Geneva Association, *The Insurance Industry and Climate Change – Contribution to the Global Debate* (Geneva: Geneva Association, 2009), 83–96.

[24] Based on interviews with market players by the author in February 2012.

[25] Munich Re NatCat Service, 2011: Natural Catastrophes Worldwide 2010, available at www.munichre.com (accessed 13 Februrary 2011).

[26] R. Guoqiang and S. Jinyan, 'The Conditions of China's Environmental Liability Insurance System: Bioinformatics and Biomedical Engineering (iCBBE)', paper presented at the 2010 4th International Conference, available at http://ieeexplore.ieee.org (accessed 15 February 2011).

Department provided a framework to establish an environmental pollution liability insurance system that would serve gradually to expand pollution insurance coverage nationwide. Despite this road map, the industry still faces several challenges, including better scoping of coverage; a more scientific process for formulating premium prices; a much improved legal framework, including a clearer understanding of liabilities and compensation; strengthened government support; and improved general awareness for companies and households of environmental risk.

9.2 The case of insurance risk-transfer and climate-related investments in developing countries

9.2.1 Introductory observations

Triggered by a wide scientific consensus about the seriousness of the problem, there is growing international agreement on the need to take action now to avoid future catastrophic climatic changes. But decision-making on climate change activities is complicated by a prevailing level of uncertainty about the exact nature of climatic changes and the costs and benefits of the action required now and in the future. The risks and uncertainties arise directly from the physical impacts of climatic changes such as extreme weather events, natural disasters or slow-onset developments such as sea-level rise, but also indirectly from the political responses to these challenges. Mitigation targets, climate policies and promotion of low-carbon technologies are all subject to political negotiations and their implementation could be adjusted, cancelled or delayed depending on political decisions. For those who provide insurance-risk transfer this creates new risks, but also opportunities. Often triggered by large-scale losses from extreme weather events, some private insurance companies have explored the issue of climate change by collaborating with scientists, publicly engaging in policy debates and also assessing the climate impacts on and opportunities for their own products.[27]

[27] Individual companies and sector initiatives such as ClimateWise and UNEPFI's Insurance Working Group, as well as industry organisations such as the Chartered Insurance Institute, the Geneva Association and national trade bodies have started publicly to address this issue through statements, research and events.

As insurance is still in its infancy in the developing world, not much attention has been given to the role of risk transfer in supporting climate activities in those countries. But in the wake of international climate negotiations the issue of climate change in developing countries is now receiving more attention amongst those who provide insurance. For example, signatories to the ClimateWise industry initiative have pledged to 'consider how we can use our expertise to assist the developing world to understand and respond to climate change',[28] while other groups such as the Munich Climate Insurance Initiative (MCII)[29] work with the UN on proposals for climate insurance schemes in developing countries. The discussion about insurance as a tool to foster investment in climate activities in developing countries can be applied to both the adaptation and mitigation sides of climate change policies.

Adaptation to climate change is defined by the Intergovernmental Panel on Climate Change (IPCC) as 'adjustment in natural or human systems in response to actual or expected climatic stimuli or their effects, which moderates harm or exploits beneficial opportunities'.[30] It captures a range of efforts to manage the effects of climate change, such as building flood defences, developing water irrigation systems or educating people about coping with heat. In the past often regarded as the poor relative of climate mitigation, adaptation is now an accepted part of climate policy. Even if all proposed mitigation measures were to be successful and global emissions levels could be reduced, there would still be a need to adapt to those climatic changes induced by historic emissions. Adaptation comes in different forms and includes both soft (e.g., education) and hard measures (e.g., strengthening of buildings to withstand wind storms). Adaptation is of great importance to developing countries, which are often highly vulnerable to climate change. The international community has recognised this challenge. Following the 2010 Cancún climate negotiations, the UNFCCC is now exploring insurance solutions for most vulnerable countries as part of a 'loss and damage' work plan.[31] For insurers, the

[28] See ClimateWise – Principle No. 3 – Support Climate Awareness Amongst our Customers, available at www.climatewise.org.uk (accessed 11 March 2012).

[29] See www.climate-insurance.org (accessed 11 March 2012).

[30] Intergovernmental Panel on Climate Change (IPCC), *Climate Change 2007: Impacts, Assessment and Vulnerability. Contribution of Working Group II to the Fourth Assessment Report* (2007), technical summary.

[31] The plan appears in Decision -/CP.16, Outcome of the Work of the Ad Hoc Working Group on Long-Term Cooperative Action under the Convention, UNFCCC/AWGLCA/2010/L.7, paras 25–9, available at http://unfccc.int (accessed 11 March 2012).

concept of adaptation shows many similarities to the general principle of risk management: taking action to increase resilience and to reduce current and future risks. One could consider insurance itself as a form of adaptation, as it increases the financial resilience of policyholders, for example, through flood insurance. While some risks arising from climate change can be reduced through better preparedness, there will always be residual risks that can leave those exposed with significant financial gaps and increase poverty. One could also argue that adaptation is a way of maintaining the insurability of these risks, especially in the context of extreme weather events, and that effective adaptation may actually become a condition for granting insurance cover in the future, with insurance picking up the residual risks and extremes. A key question in this context is if and how insurance products could be designed in such a way that they trigger adaptive behaviour.

The IPCC defines climate mitigation as: 'implementing policies to reduce greenhouse gas emissions and enhance sinks'.[32] In the discussion about mitigation policies there is a growing focus on how financial instruments can help fostering low-carbon growth in developing countries through channelling investment flows into low-carbon technologies. The Copenhagen Accord[33] signified that deep cuts in global greenhouse gas emissions were required in order to hold the increase in global temperatures to below 2 degrees Celsius. This target was subsequently confirmed by the Cancún Agreements[34] and is expected to play a guiding role in the negotiations triggered by the Durban Platform.[35] Achieving these emissions reductions requires a shift to a low-carbon economy or, as noted by Nicholas Stern, 'a new industrial low-carbon revolution'.[36] The World Bank estimates that an amount of

[32] IPCC, *Climate Change 2007: Mitigation of Climate Change. Contribution of Working Group III to the Fourth Assessment Report* (2007), technical summary.

[33] Decision 2/CP.15, Annex (Copenhagen Accord), FCCC/CP/2009/11/Add. 1, para. 2.

[34] Decision 1/CP.16, The Cancun Agreements: Outcome of the Work of the Ad Hoc Working Group on Long-Term Cooperative Action under the Convention, 15 March 2011, FCCC/CP/2010/7/Add. 1, para. 138–40.

[35] Draft Decision -/CP.17, Establishment of an Ad Hoc Working Group on the Durban Platform for Enhanced Action, preamble.

[36] See 'Lord Stern: Avoid Dangerous Warming with "Industrial Low-Carbon Revolution"', 21 March 2011, available at www.climateactionprogramme.org (accessed 11 March 2012).

US$240–600 billion a year is required by developing countries for building low-carbon infrastructures.[37] Due to the magnitude of the funds needed it is clear that, alongside traditional public development funding, private investment will have to provide a large part of the funds required, mainly in the form of foreign investments in areas such as renewable energy, reforestation or low-carbon technology transfer. Therefore a lot of emphasis is currently placed on creating the right environment and conditions to facilitate private and public investment flows.[38]

At a 2010 roundtable discussion hosted by rating agency Standard & Poor's and specialist firm Parhelion, representatives from the capital markets concluded that climate change-related investments 'are fraught with risks'.[39] Participants listed twenty-eight specific risks they face when providing climate change finance, ranging from technology risk ('technology is not efficient and/or too complex and/or not publically accepted')[40] to human/operational risks ('lack of well-trained workforce to implement projects').[41] Against this backdrop the chapter now explores evidence of insurance risk transfer related to climate activities in developing countries, based on four risk-transfer categories: liability; project insurance; natural disaster cover; and policy risks.

9.2.2 Liability insurance

Environmental-liability or pollution insurance is available in most developed insurance markets.[42] Historically, environmental damage was usually covered under general-liability policies. In the 1990s, in the

[37] K. Neuhoff, S. Fankhauser, E. Guerin et al., 'Structuring International Financial Support to Support Domestic Climate Change Mitigation in Developing Countries', *Climate Strategies 2009*, 5, available at www.climatestrategies.org (accessed 1 March 2011).

[38] See *ibid.*, 14–22; UNEP, *Catalysing Low-Carbon Growth in Developing Economies: Public Finance Mechanisms to Scale Up Private Sector Investment in Climate Solutions.* Case Study Analysis (2009), available at www.unepfi.org (accessed 15 February 2012).

[39] Standard & Poor's/Parhelion, *Can Capital Markets Bridge the Climate Change Financing Gap?*, Report 2010, 2, available at www.parhelion.co.uk (accessed 16 February 2012).

[40] *Ibid.*, 4. [41] *Ibid.*, 3.

[42] For an overview of the insurance market, see European Commission, *Financial Security in Environmental Liability Directive*, Final Report (August 2008), available at http://ec.europa.eu (accessed 20 February 2012).

wake of growing environmental damage awards through the courts, the insurance industry started to move to the development of specific environmental-liability risk cover. As far as compensation is concerned, environmental-liability insurance cover offers *ex ante* protection rather than relying on *ex post* penalties and fines, which can be uncertain if a polluter faces insolvency after an event. Compliance with current environmental laws and regulations is a standard condition for this type of insurance. But expecting insurers to play a quasi regulatory role in environmental protection through their risk selection process may be overstretching the capacity of private insurers. The provision of cover can provide an additional incentive for a company taking out insurance to comply with regulatory requirements and improve its own environmental standards. But monitoring compliance requires additional tools and expertise and the private sector usually relies on public regulators to take this role rather than doing it themselves. Some commentators identify insurance as a 'surrogate regulatory tool', arguing that through their own risk assessment and the underwriting decisions insurers can drive the behaviour of the insured.[43] There is some empirical evidence suggesting that insurers may effectively exercise a quasi-regulatory capacity for potentially hazardous or polluting operations.[44] According to this literature, the main driver for deterrence is the risk of not gaining insurance cover if certain standards are not met. In general terms, insurance can trigger risk-reduction activities if it is beneficial for both the insured and the insurer. In the context of environmental-liability insurance, the link between risk reduction and provision of cover is evident: the adherence to high standards, such as a company's environmental management system, can be a condition for the provision of insurance, or it may justify a lower premium compared to those risks where lower (or no) pollution standards are implemented. For insurers this is a direct way to reduce and control insured losses during the lifespan of an insurance policy (usually a year).

To what extent is the provision of compensation to victims and reducing pollution by incentivising risk reduction relevant for climate change activities in developing countries? The consideration of

[43] OECD, *Environmental Risks and Insurance*, 53.

[44] See Yin, Pfaff and Kunreuther, 'Can Environmental Insurance Succeed'; B. J. Richardson, 'Enlisting Institutional Investors in Environmental Regulation: Some Comparative and Theoretical Perspectives' (2002) 8 *North Carolina Journal of International Law and Commercial Regulation* 247.

greenhouse gas emissions as pollution and the consequential award of damages from losses linked to the emissions is subject to legal discussions. Especially in the USA, several cases are currently being tested in the courts to see if a carbon liability exists.[45] The key difficulty is the establishment of a causal link between emitting activities and damages. This is referred to in climate change circles under the heading 'attribution': is it possible to determine how much of severe weather losses can actually be linked to climate change? If the courts were to conclude that carbon liability exists then one could envisage that liability insurers would incentivise policyholders to reduce their emissions activities and/or to incentivise adaptation activities. Yet, in practice, in such a scenario it is likely that most insurers would apply a cover exclusion for carbon liability.

9.2.3 Project insurance

9.2.3.1 Common project risks

There is evidence that risk transfer can facilitate climate investment and support the development of 'clean' technologies by removing some of the 'project risks' faced by investors. Common project risks such as construction risks, property damage, political risk and liability can usually be covered by traditional insurance in the same way as other large-scale international investment projects. A wide range of private insurers offer risk transfer of these mainly operational risks from project phase to completion. Challenges, such as lack of loss data for new technologies or unclear legal frameworks for liability, exist, but they can be overcome. This point can be illustrated by reference to three examples, as follows.

In April 2012, Aviva, a major UK insurance company, unveiled a range of new policies and services that cover operational risks for onshore wind, solar, waste-to-energy, biomass power, environmental consultancy and building technology firms. The firm offers public liability cover worth up to £1m and will also cover the failure to supply power to the electricity grid from a renewable energy project.

[45] For example, on 17 January 2012, the Supreme Court of Virginia set aside its groundbreaking judgment in *AES Corporation* v. *Steadfast Insurance Company*, 282 Va. 252 (2011), which held that the emission of carbon dioxide was not an 'occurrence' within the meaning of a general liability policy. See 'Virginia Court Grants Rehearing of Global Warming Claims Case', *Insurance Journal* (3 February 2012), available at www.insurancejournal.com (accessed 18 March 2011).

AIG provided one of the first ever insurance coverage for a carbon credit transaction back in 2007. The firm provided a letter of assurance to Chinese factories covering the commitment from a Japanese firm to honour the purchase of carbon credits generated under the Clean Development Mechanism.

The Overseas Private Investment Corporation (OPIC) recently provided one of the first political insurance contracts for a reducing emissions from deforestation and forest degradation (REDD) project. OPIC provided US$900,000 in political insurance to Terra Global Capital, an investor in the project. The specific REDD scheme aims to protect 64,318 hectares of forest in Cambodia and sequester approximately 8.7 million metric tons of CO_2.

Creating adaptation infrastructure and wider adaptive capacity in developing countries also requires significant funds and expertise. The private sector will have to play a role in providing these funds in the same way as in the mitigation projects outlined above. The adaptation investment projects, such as flood protection infrastructure or drought management solutions, require similar risk transfer during the project phase. This area has received scant attention and will require further elaboration, specifically in discussions on how to secure private-sector adaptation funding and where to spend the capital required for adaptation.[46]

9.2.3.2 Carbon-finance-specific risks

In addition to the above risks, low-carbon investments also face carbon-finance-specific risks. Since the establishment of international carbon-finance markets as part of the Kyoto Protocol,[47] insurance has been available to assist investors and transfer some of the risks, mainly in the context of the joint implementation (JI) and the clean development mechanisms (CDM), by combining traditional project insurance with cover for emissions credits, such as credit delivery guarantees. The cover is against lack of or under-performance of climate investment in terms of the underlying emissions reduction. An example would be an industrial facility funded through a CDM investment, which then fails to deliver the expected emissions reduction.

[46] For more information, see A. Persson et al., 'Adaptation Finance Under a Copenhagen Agreed Outcome' (2009), Research Report, SEI, Stockholm, available at www.sei-international.org (accessed 14 March 2012).

[47] Kyoto Protocol to the United Nations Framework Convention on Climate Change, Kyoto, 11 December 1997, 2303 UNTS 148.

These risk-transfer solutions are offered by the private insurance market, but often in close cooperation with international organisations. They are in direct response to the specific needs of climate investments. An example is Swiss Re's cover for CDM projects, developed in 2006,[48] or Munich Re's 'Kyoto Multi Risk Policy', developed for international carbon markets.[49] The growth in carbon markets has also led to the establishment of specialty insurance service providers such as Carbon Re and Parhelion, who offer assistance with risk solutions in carbon finance. Carbon Re, supported by the global environment facility (GEF) and the United Nations Environment Programme (UNEP) has developed an insurance product for renewable energy projects in developing countries. Besides the traditional insurance products for construction, operation and transit for renewable energy projects, the service offers bespoke covers such as carbon-counterparty credit risk insurance, carbon all-risk insurance and carbon delivery guarantee insurance/Kyoto multi-risk policy. But despite these developments it is difficult to assess the size of the transactions and the volume of supply and demand for these specific products, particularly with regards to projects based in developing countries.

9.2.3.3 Political risk

Investments in foreign countries face political risks. In the insurance industry, the term 'political risk' covers areas such as currency convertibility and transfer, expropriation, political violence, breach of contract by a host government and the non-honouring of sovereign financial obligations.[50] In the wake of globalisation and the growth of international trade, governments in the developed world have concluded that one way

[48] A brief characterisation of this instrument appears on the website of Swiss Re: 'The insurance product, which was developed by Swiss Re and RNK, covers Kyoto-related risk to carbon credit purchases by RNK. The policy, issued by Swiss Re subsidiary European International Reinsurance Ltd, provides coverage for the risks related to Clean Development Mechanism (CDM) project registration and the issuance of certified emissions reduction credits (CERs) under the Kyoto Protocol's CDM. These risks include the failure or delay in the approval, certification and/or issuance of CERs from CDM projects by United Nation Framework Convention on Climate Change (UNFCCC)', RNK Capital and Swiss Re Structure First Insurance Product for CDM Carbon Credit Transactions, available at www.swissre.com (accessed 11 March 2012).

[49] Munich Re, *Topics Geo: Natural Catastrophes 2006: Analyses, Assessments, Positions*, 2007, available at http://extremeweatherheroes.org (accessed 14 March 2012).

[50] Multilateral Investment Guarantee Agency (MIGA), *World Investment and Political Risk, 2009*, 28.

of encouraging further trade and investment by companies is the provision of political risk insurance, believing that this would provide positive externalities for the wider economy. Political risk cover is now available through (inter-)governmental agencies, for example, the World Bank Multilateral Investment Guarantee Agency (MIGA), and also some private insurers, such as Lloyd's of London, Atradius or Hiscox. The products offered by these public and private institutions can also be applied to climate-related investments in developing countries, as the political risks facing these investments are not different from those experienced in other sectors and in international trade.

An illustration of the importance of political risk for low-carbon investments is provided by the Desertec Industrial Initiative, launched in 2009 by a large group of leading companies from different sectors, including Munich Re. The project seeks to foster investment in the utilisation of renewable energy in North Africa. In light of current political changes in the North Africa and Middle East region the political risk of this project has received increased attention. Political risk insurance is a specialist area and some limitations on the type of risk and locations apply. Significantly, political risk insurance not always covers (or covers inadequately) regulatory risks, although these latter are increasingly viewed by investors as a major source of risk.[51]

But one can expect that extensions of existing political risk-transfer products will seek to provide coverage to climate-related projects. Such extensions could be operated either publicly – through government or governmental agencies – or privately. Similarly, they could be pursued either on a bilateral or on a multilateral basis. This could provide support to investors and reduce some of the investment risks in the transition to a low-carbon economy. Mills[52] outlines a range of insurance products pertaining to political and regulatory stability risk that could be relevant in this connection: companies providing political risk insurance include ACE and Zurich for carbon-emissions trading and carbon-credit projects. Munich Re includes political risk in its Kyoto policy and Carbon Re additionally offers political risk products as well as products covering other risks associated with carbon-reduction projects.

[51] MIGA, *World Investment and Political Risk, 2011*, 46.
[52] See Mills, *From Risk to Opportunity*, 40.

9.2.4 Natural disaster cover

Developing countries are at risk from changes in extreme events, owing to a combination of factors such as geography (with many being located in already hot tropical and sub-tropical regions), sensitivity of the economies to weather (because of the relative dominance of agriculture) and lack of resources to prepare for disasters or increase resilience levels.[53] The application of risk transfer to manage the impacts of natural disasters is relatively well researched, but unevenly applied across the world, with the extent and scope of risk transfer varying from country to country.[54] Over the last decade, more risk-transfer schemes have been developed in poor countries, often run as pilot projects between the private sector and public authorities. The recently published *Compendium of Disaster Risk Transfer Initiatives in the Developing World*[55] offers a snapshot of current risk-transfer activities in low- and middle-income countries.

The *Compendium* documents 123 existing initiatives in middle-income and lower-income countries that involve the transfer of financial risk associated with the occurrence of natural hazards. There appears to be potential in many places and a growing recognition of the possible roles for risk transfer in fostering risk-reduction activities. Closer examination shows that the schemes are truly diverse, often created to meet very specific needs in a particular community, with a wide range of stakeholders being involved, and differing levels of risk transfer being provided. The cover is provided via private insurers, governments or public–private partnerships. While agricultural insurance is the most common form in all countries, a particular geographical preference for other types of insurance is noticeable, such as micro-insurance against natural disasters in Asia. This may reflect local tradition and possibly also cultural differences, while other factors, such as links to micro-finance schemes, may also have an influence.[56]

53 A. Millner and S. Dietz, 'Adaptation to Climate Change and Economic Growth in Developing Countries', Grantham Research Institute on Climate Change and the Environment Working Paper 60 (2011), 2, available at www2.lse.ac.uk (accessed 24 February 2012).

54 CEA, *European Insurance – Key Facts*, 4.

55 ClimateWise, *Compendium of Disaster Risk Transfer Initiatives in the Developing World*, available at www.climatewise.org.uk (accessed 20 February 2012).

56 S. Surminski and D. Oramas-Dorta, 'Building Effective and Sustainable Risk Transfer Initiatives in Low- and Middle-Income Economies: What Can We Learn from Existing Insurance Schemes?', Policy paper, Centre for Climate Change Economics and Policy/

The main aim of these schemes is compensation after a loss. But depending on design and operation of the risk transfer this can also lead to risk reduction and greater resilience. As experience with flood and windstorm insurance in developed countries shows, there are some key principles that should be met when designing and regulating insurance schemes to make full use of their risk-reduction role: (i) risk levels should drive the pricing of insurance cover (risk-based pricing rather than cross-subsidisation); (ii) granting of cover must require certain measures of risk reduction to be in place (such as business continuity plans or strengthened roofs in exposed coastal areas); (iii) insurance payouts after a loss must increase resilience (for example, through resilient repair after a flood). Surminski and Oramas-Dorta show that the full potential for utilising risk transfer for adaptation is far from exhausted.[57] Only very few schemes have a direct operational link between risk transfer and risk reduction. Not surprisingly, the large majority of risk-transfer schemes focus on today's weather risks and do not capture climate change in vulnerable low-income countries. The Cancún Adaptation Framework, an outcome of the 16th Session of the Conference of Parties to the UNFCCC, highlights the need to strengthen international cooperation and expertise to understand and reduce loss and damage associated with the adverse effects of climate change. In this context, a new work programme on 'Loss and Damage' has been initiated in order to assess the potential of a wide range of adaptation and risk-management measures. One particular focus of this work stream is the proposal to create a climate insurance facility to provide cover against extreme weather events.[58]

9.2.5 *Policy risks*

Another challenge for investors in climate projects is the risk that underlying policy frameworks and subsidy schemes may change during the lifetime of their investment. Changing political landscapes can make an investment unprofitable, which is often highlighted by investors as a

Grantham Research Institute on Climate Change and the Environment (2011), 23, available at www.cccep.ac.uk (accessed 27 February 2012).

[57] *Ibid.*, 24.

[58] See http://unfccc.int/adaptation/cancun_adaptation_framework/loss_and_damage/items/6056.php (accessed 14 March 2012).

key barrier for climate investment flows into developing countries.[59] This policy risk is relevant not just in a developing country context, but also in established markets, where changes to climate policy may affect the validity of investments.

If we look first at mitigation efforts, low-carbon sectors such as renewable energy have been and continue to be hugely dependent on public policy, not just in terms of the usual subsidies and technology push measures, but also in terms of political decisions on emissions reduction and the structure of international carbon finance. This creates a degree of political dependence and uncertainty in terms of sudden policy changes, which may make investments unprofitable. This is often quoted as one of the key barriers to climate-related investment. The potential for transferring these risks has not been investigated in great detail, but an initial assessment by stakeholders such as the Climate Bonds initiative suggests that these type of risks might only be insurable through public schemes. Yet, there appears to be a possibility for some private insurance cover related to some retrospective changes to law and regulation, as illustrated by a recent insurance transaction developed by Lloyds Syndicate Kiln and specialists firm Parhelion. This collaborative offering provides an insurance product designed to compensate policyholders against changes in legislation in the European Union that could impact suddenly on the value of carbon credits or certified emissions reduction (CER) credits. The product is designed to create more certainty and stability for financial institutions trading carbon credits in Europe.

This is a very new area for insurers and it is too early to say if there will be a broader private market for these types of products or whether this will be a task for public institutions, possibly as an extension of the existing political risk schemes. This issue is also very relevant in the developed world context, where some recent policy changes have had significant implications for investors. Judicial proceedings triggered by these changes, which might possibly lead to compensation payments by governments, are still ongoing with an unclear outcome, as evidenced in the UK's legal dispute about the government's revision of renewable feed-in tariffs.[60]

59 Standard & Poor's/Parhelion, *Can Capital Markets Bridge the Climate Change Financing Gap?*, Report 2010, 3.

60 See Department for Energy and Climate Change, Application to the Supreme Court, 21 February 2012, available at www.decc.gov.uk/en/content/cms/news/fits_supcourt/fits_supcourt.aspx (accessed 15 March 2012).

With respect to adaptation, creating the necessary infrastructure and wider adaptive capacity in developing countries requires significant funds and also expertise. These adaptation investments, such as flood protection infrastructure or draught management solutions, face also policy risks. Yet, this area has been explored even less than mitigation investments, although it is likely to gain more prominence in the context of discussions about adaptation finance. When it comes to policy risks, in particular, the application of traditional risk transfer may prove difficult or impossible for private insurers owing to the nature of the risk and the high legal and political uncertainty attached to it. Thus, any solutions may have to involve the state. State involvement would be justified by a market failure (if no private cover can be offered) and/or by the overall political and economic rationale for supporting climate investments in developing countries.

While there are significant limits to insurability, a pragmatic view would suggest that market demand will eventually trigger supply. Strong regulatory systems and institutions will be key enabling factors for this type of policy.[61] But further research and market assessments are still needed to investigate the potential for this risk transfer.

CONCLUSION

Insurance risk transfer has for centuries been part of economic activity and provided financial resilience for individuals, companies and governments in the face of uncertain losses. This article has explored if and how this mechanism can be applied to harness investment in environmental protection in developing countries by investigating the case of climate change. Any investment faces risks. Underwriting some of these in exchange for a premium payment can reduce investors' uncertainty and make some investments more attractive.

The above analysis identified three potential roles for insurance risk transfer in the context of environmental protection: compensation for victims and funding of clean-up processes; incentivising risk-reduction efforts; and fostering environmental investments by transferring some of the investment risks. The compensation element is still of limited relevance in the climate change context, because the legal interpretation of liability for damages arising from greenhouse gas emissions is not clear

[61] J. Brown and M. Jacobs, 'Leveraging Private Investment: The Role of Public Sector Climate Finance', *ODI Background Notes* (April 2011), 3, available at www.odi.org.uk (accessed 5 March 2012).

yet. As seen in pilot projects in a range of developing countries, there is scope for insurance schemes to incentivise risk reduction and adaptation as well as regulatory compliance. But the effectiveness of this process depends on the design of the insurance products, an area which is currently investigated both by the insurance industry and by policy-makers. In the context of climate change investments there is evidence that the transfer of investment risks could provide a boost for private climate funding. While insurance solutions already exist for most of the common project risks and political risks attached to mitigation and adaptation investments, there are a range of specific risks for which no cover has been developed and where only public insurance schemes or public–private partnerships may be able to offer risk transfer. The existing political commitment to increased investment in climate change action could justify public support for risk-transfer solutions that reduce the investment risks as a way to reduce the barriers to private investment in climate action.

In addition to these three roles, there may be other reasons for insurers to promote mitigation through their products: they may see it as good citizenship under their wider corporate sustainability agenda; they may use climate-mitigation activities to create a positive image amongst stakeholders; or they may use certain green policies to target 'responsible' customers who are perceived to be less likely to experience losses than less environmentally conscious individuals or companies. Some insurers have developed specific policies, which seem to reward environmentally friendly behaviour. Some motor insurance policies charge less premium if a car is driven less, on the basis that this also reflects on the risk of accidents. The fact that this will also reduce the car emissions is a side effect, but not the main driving force for the insurer.

The application of insurance risk transfer in the context of climate-change investments is a relatively new area and an overall assessment of the effectiveness and efficiency of the solutions offered has not been conducted yet. There is growing knowledge about barriers and constraints and both industry and decision makers are exploring ways to improve and enhance the environmental role of risk transfer. This provides an opportunity for developing countries to avoid repeating past mistakes in the developed world and for the industry to become more innovative in linking the environmental role to other insurance functions. This could lead to sustainable insurance solutions that support environmental protection, but it will not replace the need for environmental regulation.

Select bibliography

Brainard, L., 'What is the Role of Insurance in Economic Development?', Zurich Government and Industry Thought Leadership Series (2008).

Brown, J., and M. Jacobs, 'Leveraging Private Investment: The Role of Public Sector Climate Finance', *ODI Background Notes* (April 2011).

Dlugolecki, A., 'Coping with Climate Change: Risks and Opportunities for Insurers', Chartered Insurance Institute, London, CII 3112 (2009).

Feyen, E., R. Lester and R. Rocha, 'What Drives the Development of the Insurance Sector? An Empirical Analysis Based on a Panel of Developed and Developing Countries', World Bank Working Paper S5572 (2011).

Freeman, P. K., 'Environmental Insurance as a Policy Enforcement Tool in Developing Countries' (1997) 18 *University of Pennsylvania Journal of International Economic Law* 477.

Freeman, P. K., and H. Kunreuther, *Managing Environmental Risk Through Insurance* (Boston, Mass.: Kluwer Academic Publishers, 1997).

Hussels, S., D. Ward and R. Zurbruegg, 'Stimulating the Demand for Insurance' (2005) 8 *Risk Management and Insurance Review* 257.

Ibarra, H., and J. Skees, 'Innovation in Risk Transfer for Natural Hazards Impacting Agriculture' (2007) 7 *Environmental Hazards* 62.

Linnerooth-Bayer, J., R. Mehler and S. Hochrainer, 'Insurance against Losses from Natural Disasters in Developing Countries: Evidence, Gaps, and the Way Forward' (2011) 1 *Journal of Integrated Disaster Risk Management* 1.

Masci, P., L. Tejerina and I. Webb, 'Insurance Market Development in Latin America and the Caribbean', Inter-American Development Bank Sustainable Development Department Technical Papers Series, IFM-146 (2007).

Millner, A. and S. Dietz, 'Adaptation to Climate Change and Economic Growth in Developing Countries', Grantham Research Institute on Climate Change and the Environment Working Paper 60 (2011).

Mills, E., *From Risk to Opportunity: Insurer Responses to Climate Change* (Boston, Mass.: Ceres, 2009).

Minoli, D. M., and J. N. B. Bell, 'Insurance as an Alternative Environmental Regulator: Findings from a Retrospective Pollution Claims Survey' (2003) 12 *Business Strategy and the Environment* 107.

Neuhoff, K., S. Fankhauser, E. Guerin, J.-C. Hourcade, H. Jackson, R. Rajan and J. Ward, 'Structuring International Financial Support to Support Domestic Climate Change Mitigation in Developing Countries', *Climate Strategies* (2009).

Organisation for Economic Co-operation and Development, *Environmental Risks and Insurance: A Comparative Analysis of the Role of Insurance in the Management of Environment-Related Risks,* Policy Issues in Insurance, No. 6 (Paris: OECD Publishing, 2003).

Ranger, N., and S. Surminski, 'A Preliminary Assessment of the Impact of Climate Change on Non-Life Insurance Demand in the BRICS Economies', Working Paper 72, Centre for Climate Change Economics and Policy (2011).

Ranger, N., S. Surminski and N. Silver, 'Open Questions about How to Address "Loss and Damage" from Climate Change in the Most Vulnerable Countries: A Response to the Cancún Adaptation Framework', Policy paper, Centre for Climate Change Economics and Policy (2011).

Richardson, B. J., 'Enlisting Institutional Investors in Environmental Regulation: Some Comparative and Theoretical Perspectives' (2002) 8 *North Carolina Journal of International Law and Commercial Regulation* 247.

Surminski, S., 'Adapting to the Extreme Weather Impacts of Climate Change – How Can the Insurance Industry Help?', *ClimateWise* (November 2010).

Surminski, S., and D. Oramas-Dorta, 'Building Effective and Sustainable Risk Transfer Initiatives in Low- and Middle-income Economies: What Can We Learn from Existing Insurance Schemes?', Policy paper, Centre for Climate Change Economics and Policy/Grantham Research Institute on Climate Change and the Environment (2011).

United Nations Commission on Trade and Development, *Trade and Development Aspects of Insurance Services and Regulatory Frameworks* (2007).

United Nations Environment Programme, *Catalysing Low-carbon Growth in Developing Economies: Public Finance Mechanisms to Scale Up Private Sector Investment in Climate Solutions*. Case Study Analysis (2009).

USAID, *Assessment of How Strengthening the Insurance Industry in Developing Countries Contributes to Economic Growth* (2006).

Warner, K., N. Ranger, S. Surminski, M. Arnold, J. Linnerooth-Bayer, E. Michel-Kerjan, P. Kovacs and C. Herweijer, 'Adaptation to Climate Change: Linking Disaster Risk Reduction and Insurance', paper prepared for the United Nations International Strategy on Disaster Reduction (Geneva: UNISDR, 2009).

Warner, K., and A. Spiegel, 'Climate Change and Emerging Markets: The Role of the Insurance Industry in Climate Risk Management', in Geneva Association, *The Insurance Industry and Climate Change – Contribution to the Global Debate* (Geneva: Geneva Association, 2009), pp. 83–96.

Yin, H., A. Pfaff and H. Kunreuther, 'Can Environmental Insurance Succeed Where Other Strategies Fail? The Case of Underground Storage Tanks' (2011) 31 *Risk Analysis* 12.

Zheng, W., L. Yongdong, L. and Y. Deng, 'A Comparative Study of International Insurance Markets' (2009) 34 *Geneva Papers* 85.

10

Trade-related incentives: the international negotiations over environmental goods and services

KONSTANTINA K. ATHANASAKOU

INTRODUCTION

This chapter will address another instrument that could be used to harness foreign investment to promote environmental protection, namely the removal or elimination of tariff and non-tariff barriers for environmental goods and services (EGS). The negotiations on EGS are currently taking place in the World Trade Organization (WTO) pursuant to the mandate provided in the Doha Ministerial Declaration. Trade liberalisation for EGS could provide a significant incentive for the dissemination of important technologies for the environment by lowering the costs of such technologies. Lower or no tariffs on EGS components of such technologies and lower transactions costs due to the elimination of non-tariff barriers would lower the costs of such technologies, thus making them more attractive for investors.

The technology dimension of the environmental goods and services negotiations has been often overlooked; however, new proposals and technological developments would mandate a closer look into these technologies and the ways to allow their wider deployment, especially through providing and encouraging investment incentives. This chapter will provide an overview of the WTO negotiations on environmental goods and services, highlighting key proposals and issues raised, particularly regarding technologies for the environment and their dissemination. It will show that the WTO EGS negotiations could create the necessary incentives for investment in key technologies for the environment.

10.1 WTO negotiations on environmental goods and services

10.1.1 The framework of the negotiations

The mandate for the WTO negotiations on environmental goods and services is provided in the Declaration resulting from the November 2001 WTO Ministerial Conference in Doha, Qatar (the Doha Declaration). Paragraph 31(iii) of the Doha Declaration reads as follows:

> 31. With a view to enhancing the mutual supportiveness of trade and environment, we agree to negotiations, without prejudging their outcome, on:
>
> ...
>
> (iii) the reduction or, as appropriate, elimination of tariff and non-tariff barriers to environmental goods and services.[1]

Also, paragraph 32 of the Doha Declaration[2] highlights that members 'should give particular attention' to:

> the effect of environmental measures on market access, especially in relation to developing countries, in particular the least-developed among them, and those situations in which the elimination or reduction of trade restrictions and distortions would benefit trade, the environment and development.

Therefore, the Doha Declaration emphasises that these negotiations should aim at achieving sustainable development by creating a 'triple win' situation for trade, the environment and development.

1 WTO Ministerial Conference Fourth Session, Ministerial Declaration, para. 31 WT/MIN (01)/DEC/1 (20 November 2001) (Doha Declaration).

2 Paragraph 32 of the Doha Declaration specifically states: 'We instruct the Committee on Trade and Environment, in pursuing work on all items on its agenda within its current terms of reference, to give particular attention to: (i) the effect of environmental measures on market access, especially in relation to developing countries, in particular the least-developed among them, and those situations in which the elimination or reduction of trade restrictions and distortions would benefit trade, the environment and development; (ii) the relevant provisions of the Agreement on Trade-Related Aspects of Intellectual Property Rights; and (iii) labelling requirements for environmental purposes.

Work on these issues should include the identification of any need to clarify relevant WTO rules. The Committee shall report to the Fifth Session of the Ministerial Conference, and make recommendations, where appropriate, with respect to future action, including the desirability of negotiations. The outcome of this work as well as the negotiations carried out under paragraph 31(i) and (ii) shall be compatible with the open and non-discriminatory nature of the multilateral trading system, shall not add to or diminish the rights and obligations of Members under existing WTO agreements, in particular the Agreement on the Application of Sanitary and Phytosanitary Measures, nor alter the balance of these rights and obligations, and will take into account the needs of developing and least-developed countries.'

In the WTO, the environmental goods negotiations are taking place in a Committee on Trade and Environment Special Session (CTESS). The environmental services negotiations are conducted in Council for Trade in Services Special Sessions (CTSSSs). The environmental goods and services negotiations are separate and distinct processes from the regular work of the WTO Committee on Trade and Environment (CTE) and the Council for Trade in Services (CTS).

As part of the overall Doha Round single undertaking,[3] the WTO environmental negotiations have suffered delays as members have focused on other aspects of the Doha mandate, such as agriculture and the non-agricultural market access (NAMA) negotiations, among others. In addition, it is not entirely clear how the results of any tariff reductions under NAMA, or one of the sectoral initiatives,[4] could impact other elements of the mandate, including tariff reductions on environmental goods. Members have also noted that agreement on one area would not necessarily mean agreement on the whole package, so the Doha negotiations have reached a stalemate and produced no outcome in the ten years since the Doha Ministerial Declaration.

10.1.2 Negotiations over environmental goods

A number of WTO members have submitted proposals on environmental goods for which tariff and non-tariff barriers should be eliminated under Paragraph 31(iii).[5] These proposals vary significantly as to their focus, as there is no agreement on the definition of environmental goods or the modalities (or approach) for these negotiations. In its report of

[3] The Doha single undertaking principle is defined as follows: 'Virtually every item of the negotiation is part of a whole and indivisible package and cannot be agreed separately. "Nothing is agreed until everything is agreed"'. See www.wto.org (accessed 12 February 2012).

[4] WTO Negotiating Group on Market Access, Sectoral Negotiations in Non-Agricultural Market Access (NAMA), JOB/MA/85 (10 March 2011) (listing the current WTO sectoral initiatives in the following sectors: automotives; bicycles and related parts; chemicals; electronics and electricals; fish and fish products; forest products; gems and jewellery; hand tools; enhanced healthcare; industrial machinery; raw materials; sports equipment; and toys).

[5] WTO Committee on Trade and Environment Special Session (CTESS), Report by the Chairman, Ambassador Manuel A. J. Teehankee, to the Trade Negotiations Committee, TN/TE/20 (21 April 2011) (Teehankee Report); WTO Committee on Trade and Environment Special Session, Compilation of Submissions under Paragraph 31(iii) of the Doha Declaration Pursuant to the CTESS Work Programme, JOB/TE/3/Rev. 1 (5 January 2011).

21 April 2011, the CTESS Chairman stated that 'The format of an outcome under Paragraph 31(iii) is still open although stated opinions and components have become clearer'.[6] On the identification of environmental goods, 'a number of technical difficulties remain'.[7]

The environmental goods definition has been a contentious issue and the inability of WTO members to reach an agreement on it has significantly delayed progress in the negotiations. Various definitions are generally available and some proposals have been submitted in the context of the CTESS negotiations. Members focused particularly on the distinction between 'single-use' and 'multiple-use' goods, because a number of the proposed goods could be used for non-environmental purposes.[8] Some members argued that only single-use goods should be included in the definition of environmental goods and be eligible for tariff liberalisation. Other members stressed the limitations of such an approach, as the number of single-use goods would be rather limited and would not be adequate to address the environmental needs of all WTO members.

A number of members made proposals seeking to overcome the definitional question. Some members proposed for liberalisation goods included in the environmental goods lists of international organisations, such as the OECD and APEC.[9] Other members proposed that the determination of whether a good is environmental hinges on its environmental performance, specifically on whether the good has 'high environmental performance or low environmental impacts'.[10] Members also considered whether 'cleaner technologies and products' (CTPs) and 'environmentally preferable products' (EPPs) could be considered as environmental goods.[11]

[6] Teehankee Report, para. 2. [7] *Ibid.*, para. 10.

[8] See the debates reported in Summary Report on the Nineteenth Meeting of the Committee in Trade and Environment Special Session, TN/TE/R/19 (8 August 2007). See also the following Summary reports: TN/TE/R/18 (8 June 2007); TN/TE/R/16 (22 December 2006); TN/TE/R/15 (5 April 2006); TN/TE/R/14 (9 February 2006); TN/TE/R/13 (11 October 2005); TN/TE/R/12 (14 September 2005).

[9] See CTESS, Submission by the USA, US Contribution on an Environmental Goods Modality, TN/TE/W/38, TN/MA/W/18/Add. 5 (7 July 2003) (Submission US – 7 July 2003); CTESS, Submission by the United States, Liberalizing Environmental Goods in the WTO: Approaching the Definition Issue, TN/TE/W/34, TN/MA/W/18/Add. 4 (19 June 2003) (Submission US – 19 June 2003).

[10] See Non-Paper by the European Communities, Technical Discussions under Paragraph 31(iii) of the Doha Declaration – Products with High Environmental Performance/Low Environmental Impacts, JOB(06)/177 (9 June 2006), para. 1.

[11] Non-Paper by Switzerland, Technical Discussions under Paragraph 31(iii) of the Doha Declaration – Market Access for Environmental Goods: Environmentally Preferable

Members have also considered environmental goods that are components of new key technologies for the environment, such as carbon capture and storage (CCS), gas flaring reductions and efficient consumption technologies.[12] The World Energy Council (WEC) has also provided a list of environmental goods for consideration by the WTO, which also has a technology focus and to a large extent mirrors the WTO-proposed environmental goods as components of these technologies.[13] The focus of these proposals on technologies brings a new dimension to the environmental goods negotiations, which is much broader than previously considered approaches and makes the linkage to technology dissemination and investment more apparent.

These various proposals for the definition of environmental goods have generated intense debate but produced no agreement on a definition or the criteria for selecting such goods. Members have proposed a number of different approaches in an effort to address the definitional question and to provide a way for the identification of environmental goods and a format for a final agreement on this issue. The proposed approaches are as follows:

(i) *List approach.* Members would propose and agree on a list of environmental goods.[14]
(ii) *Integrated/Project approach.* Designated national authorities would notify environmental projects of interest to them, potentially under the clean development mechanism (CDM), and goods and services included in these projects would be thus designated as environmental and therefore enjoy lower or zero tariffs for the duration of the project.[15]
(iii) *Request/Offer approach.* A member would 'propose, among the agricultural and non-agricultural goods it produces those that it

Products (EPPs), JOB(06)/179 (9 June 2006), paras 2–10; Non-Paper by Switzerland, Technical Discussions under Paragraph 31(iii) of the Doha Declaration – Market Access for Environmental Goods: Cleaner Technology and Products (CTPs), JOB(06)/178 (9 June 2006), paras 1–10.

12 Submission of Saudi Arabia JOB(09)/169 (6 November 2009), JOB(09)/169/Add. 1 (15 December 2009), JOB(09)/169/Add. 2 (21 July 2010) (Submission of Saudi Arabia).

13 The WEC list of environmental goods is available at www.worldenergy.org (accessed 14 March 2012).

14 See Submission US – 7 July 2003, paras 3–5; Submission US – 19 June 2003, paras 2, 9.

15 Submission by Argentina and India, Integrated Approach to Paragraph 31(iii), JOB(07)/77 (6 June 2007) (Argentina/India – Integrated Approach); Submission by India, An Alternative Approach for Negotiations under Paragraph 31(iii), TN/TE/W/51 (3 June 2005); Submission by India, Procedural and Technical Aspects of the Environmental Project Approach, TN/TE/W/60 (19 September 2005).

considers can contribute to the environment, while allowing others to examine which of them would not compromise their effort to develop environmental goods industries or other industries'.[16]

(iv) *Hybrid approach.* Under this approach, there would be a core list agreed by all WTO members and additional goods could be selected based on self-selection, request/offer or a particular project.[17]

(v) *Combined approach.* This includes a core list of agreed environmental goods, and a complementary list, which would be the multilateralised outcome of a request offer process.[18]

Until recently, the CTESS has focused most of its work on compiling a list of environmental goods of interest to members that will be subject to tariff elimination or reduction, pursuant to the list approach. Despite the lack of agreement on a specific list of environmental goods, the list approach appeared to be working quite well, as it generated a significant number of members' proposals for environmental goods of interest to them.[19]

On 21 April 2011, the CTESS produced a text with elements for an agreement on environmental goods and services under paragraph 31(iii) pursuant to the WTO Director-General's request to the Chairpersons of the negotiating groups to prepare new texts by this date in an effort to jumpstart the Doha Round.[20] This text is a mere assembly by the Chair of different proposed elements for a final agreement and does not reflect any agreement by members. Rather, to the extent that all positions have been accurately reflected in it, this text demonstrates the significant gap among the positions of members and the need for further extensive work in the CTESS.

According to the April 2011 Chair's text, members have submitted environmental goods under 'six broad categories': (i) air pollution

[16] Submission by Brazil, Environmental Goods for Development, JOB(07)/146 (1 October 2007), para. 7. See also Non-Paper by Brazil, Scheme for Request and Offer Procedure in Environmental Goods, JOB(09)/184 (15 December 2009).

[17] Submission by Australia, Colombia, Hong Kong, China, Norway and Singapore, A Hybrid Approach to the Liberalization of Environmental Goods under Paragraph 31 (iii), JOB/TE/15 (7 March 2011).

[18] Submission by Mexico and Chile, Combined Approach for Environmental Goods, JOB/TE/16 (11 March 2011) and JOB/TE/16/Corr.1 (21 March 2011).

[19] Teehankee Report, Annex II.A., Annex II.B.

[20] See CTESS, Textual Elements Derived from Members' Submissions under Paragraph 31 (iii), JOB/TE/20 (21 April 2011) (CTESS – Textual Elements); Teehankee Report, para. 11.

control, (ii) renewable energy, (iii) waste management and water treatment, (iv) environmental technologies, (v) carbon capture and storage and (vi) others.[21] In this categorisation by the WTO Secretariat, the term 'environmental technologies' appears to be used quite narrowly as renewable energy and carbon capture and storage could also be characterised as 'environmental technologies'. Again, this demonstrates the difficulties of identifying environmental goods and the challenge of capturing all members' interests in addressing environmental concerns. Needless to say, there is no agreement on any of the listed environmental goods.

In an effort to find a compromise, in March 2011, members submitted two new proposals for a combined or hybrid approach.[22] Both the combined and hybrid approaches would require an agreement by all members on a core list of environmental goods. This is essentially the same requirement as under the list approach and it is thus not clear whether the envisaged core lists would be any different, and how, from the list of environmental goods compiled thus far under the list approach. In particular, it is not clear whether the core lists under these newer proposals would be shorter than the list of environmental goods already existing under the list approach. Under the hybrid approach, a group of members have proposed 'on an illustrative and starting point basis, 26 tariff lines'.[23] However, there is no explanation on how these goods were selected and, certainly, this narrow list does not represent any consensus among WTO members on a core list. It appears to be uncertain that the hybrid and combined approaches could offer a meaningful alternative to identifying and agreeing on a common list of environmental goods under the list approach, and thus a way out of the impasse in the CTESS negotiations.

Again, it is important to note that these proposals were submitted in March 2011 and have not been extensively discussed and assessed by the WTO members. To the extent that these encompass elements of older proposals, such as lists of environmental goods (core, complementary or otherwise), members will need to assess whether they may suffer from the same shortcomings as the prior original proposals.

[21] Teehankee Report, Annex II.A. See also CTESS – Textual Elements.

[22] Teehankee Report, Annex II (providing an overview of the key elements of the combined and hybrid approaches, as well as of the project and request/offer approaches and stating that '[t]he coverage approaches necessarily focus on how Members can agree on an environmentally credible universe of products to which the treatment modalities could apply').

[23] *Ibid.*, Annex II, n. 10.

In addition to the modalities and definitional issues, there is no agreement on the other elements of a final agreement on environmental goods, such as non-tariff barriers (NTBs), special and differential (S&D) treatment and technology transfer and dissemination.[24] Thus far, it appears that these issues have attracted less attention, given members' inability to agree on the specific environmental goods.

In particular, the NTB issues have not been addressed at any extensive length despite proposals by members regarding specific NTBs that should be eliminated in order for members to achieve the full benefit of the tariffs' reductions on environmental goods.[25] This may be in part due to the fact that certain NTB issues are addressed in the NAMA negotiations where a number of members have submitted proposals for a framework agreement on NTBs and agreements on industry-specific proposals. These proposals are still under discussion, without any agreement on any particular issue.

Likewise, while it is widely recognised that a final agreement on environmental goods must also include special and differential treatment provisions for developing countries, the CTESS discussion on this issue has been limited to countries' submissions highlighting the need further to discuss such provisions in the context of these negotiations.[26]

The CTESS discussion of technology transfer and dissemination has been even more limited, even though developing members have repeatedly highlighted its importance and the need for members to discuss this issue more extensively.[27] Technology dissemination, which encompasses technology transfer and capacity-building, is an important element of the environmental goods negotiations for all members, especially developing and least-developed countries.[28] In its 2011 Report, the CTESS Chair

[24] *Ibid.*, paras 14, 18–19.

[25] See Submission of Saudi Arabia. See also Submission of the Philippines, Continued Work under Paragraph 31(iii) of the Doha Ministerial Declaration, JOB/TE/2 (16 February 2010).

[26] See Communication from Argentina and Brazil, Environmental Goods and Services – Paragraph 31(iii) – Special and Differential Treatment, TN/TE/W/76 (30 June 2010).

[27] See *ibid.*

[28] See Submission of Saudi Arabia. See *also* Communication by the Kingdom of Saudi Arabia, Technology Dissemination, WT/CTE/W/247 (29 October 2010) (Saudi Arabia – Technology Dissemination) (highlighting, at para. 2, that 'technology will play an increasingly important role in addressing environmental concerns for the foreseeable future' and that '[t]o provide the necessary enabling structure, Members need to identify and eliminate barriers to the dissemination of environmental technologies. Members should examine what trade measures impose costs and risks to the private

notes that 'Concerning environmental technologies, discussions have clearly highlighted the importance of these elements as being an integral part of an outcome'.[29] At this stage, it remains unclear how technologies will be further considered in the CTESS negotiations.

10.1.3 Environmental services negotiations

The negotiations on environmental services in the WTO CTSSS are not as well advanced as the negotiations on environmental goods in the CTESS.

According to a 2010 Background Note on Environmental Services,[30] prepared by the WTO Secretariat:

> The first challenge with environmental services is to define them. As many services can have an environmental end-use, it is difficult to draw the line between 'environmental services' *per se* and other services coming into play for the protection of the environment in a broad sense.[31]

In addition, national and international definitions and classification systems 'do not coincide' with either the WTO Sectoral Classification List, also known as 'W/120',[32] or with the United Nations Central Product Classification, version provisional 1991, also referred to as 'CPC', which are widely used for scheduling purposes under the WTO General Agreement on Trade in Services (GATS).[33]

Environmental services listed in W/120 include four subsectors: (i) sewage services, (ii) refuse disposal services, (iii) sanitation services and (iv) other.[34] The 'other' category 'is generally assumed to include the remaining elements of the CPC's environmental services category', which include 'cleaning of exhaust gases', 'noise abatement services', 'nature and landscape protection services' and 'other environmental protection services'.[35]

sector and thus preventing the industry from capturing the rewards of deploying these highly effective methods').

29 Teehankee Report, para. 21.

30 WTO Council for Trade in Services, Note by the Secretariat, Background Note on Environmental Services, S/C/W/320 (20 August 2010) (Background Note on Environmental Services).

31 *Ibid.*, para. 4.

32 WTO Sectoral Classification List of MTN.GNS/W/120 (10 July 1991).

33 Background Note on Environmental Services, para. 4.

34 *Ibid.*, para. 47.

35 *Ibid.*, para. 48.

The Secretariat Note also mentions that other services may have 'an environmental end-use' but 'as they are not exclusively environmental in nature and may have various other end-uses, they are classified under other generic items, in particular business and construction services'.[36] Relevant 'business services' may include engineering services, engineering design and advisory engineering services, among others.[37] 'Construction services' that may be also relevant include, among others, construction of waterworks, water plumbing, and thermal insulation.[38] Other relevant services may relate to transport services and storage services, as well as to management consulting services and banking services.[39]

The WTO list of environmental services is very narrow and does not appear to reflect recent developments and technologies for the environment. The Secretariat recognises in its Note that:

> Classification of environmental services contained in W/120 has been repeatedly criticized for being obsolete. Its focus on infrastructure services and end-of-pipe technologies is considered too narrow and many consider that it does not account for developments which have occurred in the environmental industry over the last 20 years.[40]

While the shortcomings of the current classification of environmental services appear to be generally known, the WTO Secretariat notes the challenge of changing or revising such classification. The issue concerns not only the identification of the environmental services but also the necessary related modifications of the services schedules in terms of headings and CPC definitions.[41] While technical issues concerning the scheduling of services are beyond the scope of this discussion, it is necessary to recognise that such technical concerns are important and have an impact on the environmental services negotiations.

The identification of environmental services deal with some of the same challenges encountered in the environmental goods negotiations. As noted, W/120 includes services that have a purely environmental end-use. However, other important services for the environment have uses beyond those for environmental purposes and would therefore need to be included as environmental services. In the environmental goods negotiations, the single/multiple-use question has been the subject of extensive debate and the issue remains unresolved.

[36] *Ibid.*, para. 50. [37] *Ibid.*, para. 50(a). [38] *Ibid.*, para. 50(b).
[39] *Ibid.*, para. 51. [40] *Ibid.*, paras 49 and 65. [41] *Ibid.*, paras 65 ff.

In addition, with regards to the other services that should be included, the unresolved issue relates to the selection and treatment of services already classified under different categories. For example, in a proposal by the USA and the EU,[42] that the environmental services negotiations under paragraph 31(iii) 'should cover "a broad set of environmental and climate-related services" ' and the proposed environmental services would include 'environmental, energy, construction, architectural, engineering and integrated engineering services'.[43] It is not clear how the related services would be selected, as this would require moving beyond the existing services classification.

The current classification of services does not allow for a broader consideration of environmental services pursuant to paragraph 31(iii) that are relevant to the environmental concerns of all members. For example, carbon capture and storage and renewables have been included as 'energy services' in a recent Secretariat Background Note on Energy Services.[44] This disparity between the different services classification and the reality of environmental technologies to address members' concerns should be addressed in order to ensure consistency of the environmental services negotiations with those for environmental goods, where CCS and renewable energy have been expressly recognised as environmental categories.

An idea that should also be considered in the environmental services context concerns technologies for the environment and the extent to which they can provide the basis on which services could be identified as environmental. Technologies encompass a number of different goods and services from their development to their deployment and commercialisation as well as their maintenance and upgrade. Also, since technologies are already considered in the environmental goods negotiations, they should also be addressed in the environmental services context. This would reinforce the complementarily of the environmental goods and services negotiations as thus far the two have moved in separate paths. It would also lead to a coherent outcome under paragraph 31(iii).

[42] See Non-Paper by the European Union and the USA, Proposal for a Result under Paragraph 31(iii) of the Doha Ministerial Declaration, JOB(07)/193/Rev. 1 (6 December 2007) (Non-Paper US/EU – 6 December 2007); CTSSS, Report of the Meeting Held on 15 November and 6 December 2007, TN/S/M/28 (5 May 2008) (CTSSS – TN/S/M/28).

[43] Background Note on Environmental Services, para. 72 (quoting the Non-Paper US/EU – 6 December 2007).

[44] CTS, Energy Services: Background Note by the Secretariat, S/C/W/311 (12 January 2010), paras 18–24, 36–9.

The inability of members to reach an agreement on a list of environmental services, as well as to overcome the technical difficulties regarding scheduling, have impeded progress in the CTSSS environmental service negotiations under paragraph 31(iii). The impasse experienced in the CTSSS is so severe that this Committee has basically abandoned the discussion under paragraph 31(iii) and the CTESS Chair has recently entertained the idea of discussing both environmental goods and services in the CTESS.[45] However, no consensus has been reached by the WTO membership on this issue due to the risk that any problems in the environmental services negotiations may impede further progress in the environmental goods negotiations.[46]

10.2 Technology dissemination in the context of the EGS negotiations

10.2.1 Environmental technologies as a criterion

As discussed above, an important dimension of the environmental goods and services negotiations that remains largely unexplored in the WTO negotiations is that of technologies. Important technologies for the environment could provide guidance in designating environmental goods and related environmental services for a final agreement under paragraph 31(iii). In other words, one of the main purposes of the EGS negotiations, i.e., identifying and fostering the dissemination of certain environmental technologies, could provide guidance for the identification of 'environmental' goods and services.

The 2009 proposal of Saudi Arabia to the CTESS provides some guidance as to how a technology element could assist in the negotiations.[47] Saudi Arabia's proposal to the CTESS introduced 'technologies' as a core element of countries' efforts to address their environmental concerns.[48] While the term 'technology' per se is not new in the CTESS discussions, the proposal to include technologies themselves as sets of components (goods and services) is new. Treating technologies as value chains with various inextricably linked components in the form of goods and services could serve as a useful framework within which environmental goods and services could be identified.

[45] Teehankee Report, para. 20.
[46] Informal communications with delegates attending the CTESS meeting.
[47] See Submission of Saudi Arabia. [48] *Ibid.*, para. 5.

This of course would entail a better understanding of the technologies and their environmental benefits. Technologies go beyond mere designation as environmental technologies and include consideration of the market, supply chains and infrastructure, and technology commercialisation and wide dissemination.[49] This is particularly the case for large-scale environmental technologies. For example, CCS is a technology with significant environmental benefits, especially because it is applied to the heavy industry sector. However, due to its infrastructure requirements, this technology is inextricably linked to the energy production process and may thus be misunderstood. It is therefore essential that such large-scale technologies are explained and considered in the CTESS negotiations as they can deliver substantial and proven environmental benefits.

A technology focus would assist WTO members in identifying key environmental goods for tariff liberalisation. This could be easily done under the list approach, especially since members and the WEC have already submitted relevant lists to the CTESS.[50] It would also help update the current environmental services list, bringing into light relevant services in the technology value chain. Moreover, a technology focus would provide much broader and longer lasting results than a project approach. Under the integrated/project approach, goods used in particular projects could enjoy tariff free treatment for the duration of the project.[51] However, a technology that relates to environmental protection would include a number of goods that would enjoy tariff treatment indefinitely, as well as a number of related services. Such an approach would shift the focus from a narrow list of environmental goods and services to a broader, evolving list, which would capture updates to the technologies as well as the introduction of new ones.

Importantly, a technology focus would conceptually expand the discussion of environment issues on the ways to address environmental concerns as key technologies for the environment would necessarily include those used by heavy industries. It would also enhance awareness of the benefits of these new and complex technologies, thus encouraging investment in the development, dissemination and commercialisation of these important technologies for the environment. Technologies are relevant for all sectors of the economy, particularly for the heavy industry

[49] See Saudi Arabia – Technology Dissemination.
[50] WEC list of environmental goods, available at www.worldenergy.org (accessed 14 March 2012).
[51] See Argentina/India – Integrated Approach.

sector where environmental concerns may be more prominent.[52] Technologies for the environment, among others, include CCS, gas flaring reduction technologies, efficient consumption and efficiency technologies, renewables, biofuels, solar panels etc. They encompass the different components (environmental goods), processes and related services.

10.2.2 EGS technologies and investment

Technologies have an important economic or market dimension and they entail substantial investment requirements, among others, for research and development (R&D), infrastructure, establishment of supply chains and consumer/market awareness.[53] In order to achieve environmental benefits, it is thus necessary to determine whether a technology is commercial, in that it can be meaningfully deployed in the necessary scale to bring the desired result.[54] Technology commercialisation requires large investment by private entities that wish to use these technologies in order to operate, manage, maintain and update them. Industry and private stakeholders will need to examine the economic factors in the technology value chain in order to determine whether the economic and environmental benefits of the particular technology will justify as a business matter the large investment required.[55]

A very useful example of how the technology value chains work is an illustration of the CCS process. CCS technologies capture CO_2 from fixed sources, such as power plants, gas plants and desalination plants prior to its release into the atmosphere, and then transfer and store the captured CO_2 in geological sinks such as deep saline aquifers and oil and gas reservoirs. The captured CO_2 is compressed and transported to the storage area primarily via high-pressure pipelines, but ships, trucks and trains may also be used for transport in areas where no storage is available. Storage involves the injection of CO_2 into the geological

[52] International Energy Agency, Energy Technology Transitions for Industry, www.iea.org (accessed 24 April 2012).

[53] Carbon Sequestration Leadership Forum, 2011 Technology Roadmap, www.cslforum.org (accessed 24 April 2012).

[54] International Energy Agency, Technology Roadmap: CCS (2009) (among others, highlighting at page 4 that 'CO_2 capture technology is commercially available today, but the associated costs need to be lowered and the technology still needs to be demonstrated at commercial scale'). Available at www.iea.org (accessed 24 April 2012).

[55] *Ibid.*

formation, which in turn enhances carbon recovery. CCS is a very complex set of separate and distinct processes, done at different stages. These stages are highly interconnected and constitute the CCS value chain.[56]

Like CCS, other environmental technologies, including efficiency technologies, also require a particulate setting to operate, including a number of components some of which are imported and some produced locally. Again, such technologies encompass complex value chains spanning across different countries and different continents. For these technologies to operate, it is necessary to ensure availability of the required components, related services and know-how.

CCS, efficiency technologies and other technologies for the environment encompass value chains, the economics of which determine whether investment in the particular technology is commercially meaningful for the industry. Among others, the ability for technologies to be commercialised by being widely deployed would increase the return on investment for the industry and enhance the benefits for the environment.[57] In this context, incentives to encourage investment in the development and dissemination of these technologies become essential. The reduction of tariff and non-tariff barriers for environmental goods and services pursuant to the mandate of paragraph 31(iii) provides such an incentive as it lowers the costs of these technologies. The reduction of tariff and non-tariff barriers to essential components for CCS or efficiency technologies will lower their costs, thus lowering the cost of using these technologies. Lower costs will make these technologies more attractive for investors thus leading into their greater deployment and commercialisation.

Moreover, technology dissemination and transfer provisions in a final agreement under paragraph 31(iii) would facilitate wider deployment of these technologies to developing countries by decreasing transaction and real costs, thus providing additional incentives for their utilisation and commercialisation, which in turn would make investment worthwhile and profitable. However, as noted above, the CTESS discussion on technology dissemination, including technology transfer and capacity-building, is lagging behind and at this point it is not clear how WTO members would wish to address these concerns in order to achieve greater benefits.

[56] See www.ipcc.ch/pdf/special-reports/srccs/srccs_summaryforpolicymakers.pdf (accessed 14 March 2012).

[57] See Saudi Arabia – Technology Dissemination, paras 4–8.

CONCLUSION

The WTO environmental goods and services negotiations are far from nearing completion. Despite the efforts to find a compromise solution, important differences in members' positions remain and would require a fresh look into these negotiations. One important element of the EGS negotiations that has the potential to facilitate the negotiations concerns the role of technologies.

As discussed above, a technology focus in the negotiations could provide a framework within which EGS would be identified and agreed as technology encompasses a very broad set of components in the form of goods and services. A technology focus would also facilitate the identification of related non-tariff barriers thus encouraging investment and technology dissemination. Such an approach would help address the environmental concerns of both developed and developing countries and would thus provide a balanced outcome.

Of course, there are challenges in deploying such an approach. A technology focus would essentially require that the CTESS shift its attention from end-uses of products to processes and related value chains. This market-related approach would require members carefully to assess national needs and strategies on environmental issues and also to consider the private sector when assessing incentives for investment and commercialisation of these technologies.

Technologies are instrumental in addressing global environmental concerns. Technology deployment is, however, linked to economic and market considerations. Consequently, investment to allow the commercialisation of these key technologies is essential to achieve significant environmental benefits. WTO members need to take this fact into account in the EGS negotiations and consider ways to address it more openly and more efficiently.

Select bibiliography

Carbon Sequestration Leadership Forum, *2011 Technology Roadmap* (2011).

Fliess, B., and J. A. Kim, 'Non-Tariff Barriers Facing Trade in Selected Environmental Goods and Associated Services' (2008) 42 *Journal of World Trade* 535.

Global CCS Institute, *CCS Ready Policy: Considerations and Recommended Practices for Policymakers* (2010).

International Energy Agency, *Solutions for the 21st Century. Zero Emissions Technologies for Fossil Fuels: Energy Security, Environmental Protection, and Economic Development* (2002).

Energy Technology Transitions for Industry (2009).

Technology Roadmap: CCS (2009).

Matthew, A. J., and S. Fernandez de Córdoba, 'Green Dilemma about Liberalization of Trade in Environmental Goods' (2009) 43 *Journal of World Trade* 379.

Organisation for Economic Co-operation and Development/Eurostat, *The Environmental Goods and Services Industry: A Manual for Data Collection and Analysis* (OECD and the European Communities, 1999).

Organisation for Economic Co-operation and Development, *Policy Brief: Opening Markets for Environmental Goods and Services* (2005).

Steenblink, R., and J. A. Kim, 'Facilitating Trade in Selected Climate Change Mitigation Technologies in the Energy Supply, Buildings, and Industry Sectors', OECD Trade and Environment Working Paper 2009–02 (4 May 2009).

Vikhlyaev, A., 'Environmental Goods and Services: Defining Negotiations or Negotiating Definitions?' (2004) 38 *Journal of World Trade* 93.

WTO Committee on Trade and Environment Special Session, Compilation of Submissions under Paragraph 31(iii) of the Doha Declaration Pursuant to the CTESS Work Programme, JOB/TE/3/Rev.1.

Report by the Chairman, Ambassador Manuel A. J. Teehankee, to the Trade Negotiations Committee, TN/TE/20 (21 April 2011).

WTO Council for Trade in Services, Note by the Secretariat, Background Note on Environmental Services, S/C/W/320 (20 August 2010).

III

Foreign investment and environmental protection: safeguards

11

The environmental regulation of foreign investment schemes under international law

JORGE E. VIÑUALES

INTRODUCTION

The protection of foreign investment is normally envisaged as an 'incentive' to investment in pro-environment projects rather than as a 'safeguard' against the potential problems arising from it. This is only natural. According to a recent report from the Multilateral Investment Guarantee Agency (MIGA), regulatory change is perceived by foreign investors as the riskier contingency they face when investing in developing countries.[1] Yet, investment law may also be seen as an obstacle to the transition towards a 'green economy' model. This model requires a shift of investment towards sustainable uses of natural resources and pro-environment projects.[2] In turn, this shift involves significant changes in the regulatory framework, such as the introduction of cost-internalising schemes in the energy sector or other policies tackling negative externalities.[3] These are the typical measures that could trigger investment claims from those investors adversely affected by the regulatory shift.

It is important to keep in mind that the 'transitional challenges' mentioned in the Green Economy Report prepared by the United Nations Environment Programme (UNEP) would have to include the considerable litigation risks resulting from the application of investment

[1] MIGA, *World Investment and Political Risk* (Washington, DC: World Bank, 2011), 20.

[2] UNEP, *Towards a Green Economy: Pathways to Sustainable Development and Poverty Eradication* (2011), 16.

[3] *Ibid.*, 214 ff. and 546 ff.; Intergovernmental Panel on Climate Change (IPCC), *Climate Change 2007: Mitigation of Climate Change. Contribution of Working Group III to the Fourth Assessment Report* (2007), sects 13.1.2 (Criteria for Policy Choice) and 13.2 (National Policy Instruments, their Implementation and Interaction), 750–68; International Development Law Organization (IDLO), *Green Economy for Sustainable Development: Compendium of Legal Best Practices* (June 2012).

disciplines. States should take such risks very seriously when deciding their own path to a green economy.[4] The current focus on trade disciplines[5] fails to capture this issue. Even a fully WTO-consistent set of green growth policies could potentially clash with investment disciplines and, quite significantly, the very same policy could be challenged by several independent investment claims, each leading, if successful, to the award of substantial amounts in damages (potentially amounting to billions of US dollars), including past and future losses and compound interest.[6]

In this context, this chapter seeks to explore this important risk through an assessment of the scope for the environmental regulation of foreign investment. Legal commentators have traditionally framed this issue from the perspective of investment or trade law. The question is the extent to which a given environmental measure is consistent with investment or trade disciplines. This is of course not the only way to frame the issue. Instead of assuming that the framework of reference is either investment or trade law and the 'object' to be evaluated is the 'environmental measure', one could change the terms of the equation and assess the consistency of an 'investment scheme' with environmental disciplines. This change in perspective would have significant legal consequences. If 'environmental measures' are only permissible within the bounds set by investment (or trade) disciplines, then they are in practice subordinated to investment (or trade) protection. The main argument underlying this approach is the legal priority of international law over domestic law. A domestic (environmental) measure must be consistent with international (investment or trade) standards. But this approach does not take into account the possibility that at least some domestic environmental measures may be required or authorised (I will use the term 'induced') by international environmental law.[7]

[4] See the chapter by S. Larcom and T. Swanson in this book.

[5] See e.g. UNEP, *Towards a Green Economy*, 24 or 64 ff.

[6] On the computation of damages in international investment law, see I. Marboe, *Calculation and Compensation of Damages in International Investment Law* (Oxford University Press, 2009).

[7] See e.g. *Southern Pacific Properties (Middle East) Limited (SPP)* v. *Arab Republic of Egypt*, ICSID Case No. ARB/84/3, Award (20 May 1992) (*SPP* v. *Egypt*) (link to World Heritage Convention); *Compañía del Desarrollo de Santa Elena SA* v. *Republic of Costa Rica*, ICSID Case No. ARB/96/1, Award (17 February 2000) (*CDSE* v. *Costa Rica*) (link to several biodiversity instruments, including the Convention on Biological Diversity); *S.D. Myers Inc.* v. *Canada, NAFTA Arbitration* (UNCITRAL Rules), Partial Award (13 November 2000) (*S.D. Myers* v. *Canada*) (link to Basel Convention on Hazardous Waste); *Parkerings-Compagniet AS* v. *Republic of Lithuania*, ICSID Case No. ARB/05/8, Award (11 September

In this case, the rule giving priority to international law over domestic law would not apply and there would be no legal reason, as a matter of principle, to consider that an internationally induced environmental measure inconsistent with an investment (or trade) discipline is illegal under international law. To the extent that the requirements of the applicable international environmental and investment (or trade) standards conflict with each other, their priority would have to be determined on the basis of a different set of conflict rules, which would not include the rule giving priority to international law over domestic law. As the chapter shows, this alternative model faces some important practical obstacles. But this is not to say that the scope for the environmental regulation of foreign investment schemes is not expanding through other avenues. Investment disciplines are increasingly being interpreted so as to leave considerable room for the accommodation of environmental considerations through a variety of legal concepts, such as environmental differentiation, the level of reasonableness expected from investors, the police powers doctrine or the scope of the necessity/emergency clauses.

In the following pages, after some preliminary considerations (11.1), I discuss *tour à tour* what I call the 'traditional' (11.2) and 'progressive' approaches (11.3) to the relationship between environmental and investment protection and then analyse the main avenues through which environmental considerations are being increasingly taken into account in investment disputes (11.4). I conclude with some prospective views on the evolution of the environmental regulation of foreign investment schemes (11.5).

11.1 'Legitimacy conflicts' versus 'normative conflicts'

In the last decade, a growing number of investment claims have been brought against states in connection with the adoption of environmental

2007) (*Parkerings* v. *Lithuania*) (link to World Heritage Convention); *Suez, Sociedad General de Aguas de Barcelona SA and InterAguas Servicios Integrales del Agua SA* v. *The Argentine Republic*, ICSID Case No. ARB/03/17 (*Suez* v. *Argentina – 03/17*) (link to the right to water as it arises from several treaties); *Suez, Sociedad General de Aguas de Barcelona, SA and Vivendi Universal, SA* v. *The Argentine Republic*, ICSID Case No. ARB/03/19 (*Suez* v. *Argentina – 03/19*) (link to the right to water as it arises from several treaties); *Chemtura Corporation (formerly Crompton Corporation)* v. *Government of Canada*, UNCITRAL, Award (2 August 2010) (*Chemtura* v. *Canada*) (link to POP Protocol to the LRTAP Convention and to POP Convention).

measures.[8] These measures have often a purely domestic legal basis[9] but in some cases they are 'induced' (required or authorised) by international environmental standards.[10] Yet, in practice, the treatment of purely domestic and internationally induced measures has been amalgamated by investment tribunals. Conflicts between two norms of international law ('normative conflicts') have thus been conflated with conflicts between a domestic (environmental) measure and an international (investment) norm ('legitimacy conflicts'). As a result, the impact of international environmental law on the regulation of foreign investment schemes remains unclear.

Traditionally, investment tribunals and legal commentators have taken environmental measures as the 'object' the legality of which must be assessed and investment disciplines as the governing 'legal standard'. Perhaps as a result of the facts of some early cases, 'environmental measures' have often been evaluated with a suspicious eye (as covert protectionism) and assumed to be subordinated to international (investment) law. This approach is understandable. Investment claims are as a rule brought by foreign investors who challenge the legality of a given measure with an adverse impact on their activities. Thus, the measure challenged is quite naturally the 'object' that must be assessed in the light of the 'legal standards' invoked in support of the claim, typically an investment treaty.

[8] See J. E. Viñuales, *Foreign Investment and the Environment in International Law* (Cambridge University Press, 2012), chap. 1.

[9] See e.g. *Robert Azinian, Kenneth Davitian and Ellen Baca* v. *United Mexican States*, ICSID Case No. ARB(AF)/97/02, Award (1 November 1999) (*Azinian* v. *Mexico*) (measure concerned: regulation banning trade in a gasoline additive); *Metalclad Corporation* v. *United Mexican States*, ICSID Case No. ARB(AF)/97/1, Award (25 August 2000) (*Metalclad* v. *Mexico*) (measures concerned: refusal of a permit to build a landfill and decree declaring the area a natural preserve); *Methanex Corporation* v. *United States of America*, NAFTA (UNCITRAL), Award (3 August 2005) (*Methanex* v. *United States of America*) (measure concerned: regulation indirectly banning the commercialisation of a fuel additive); *Técnicas Medioambientales Tecmed SA* v. *United Mexican States*, ICSID Case No. ARB(AF)/00/2, Award (29 May 2003) (*Tecmed* v. *Mexico*) (measure concerned: non-renewal of the operation permit of a waste treatment facility); *MTD Equity Sdn Bhd and MTD Chile SA* v. *Republic of Chile*, ICSID Case No. ARB/01/7, Award (25 May 2004) (measure concerned: refusal of a permit based on a zoning requirement); *Plama Consortium Ltd* v. *Republic of Bulgaria*, ICSID Case No. ARB/03/24, Award (27 August 2008) (measure concerned: change in domestic environmental laws); *Glamis Gold Ltd* v. *The United States of America*, NAFTA Arbitration (UNCITRAL), Award (16 May 2009) (*Glamis v. United States of America*) (measures concerned: delays and legislative/regulatory action based on environmental and cultural protection).

[10] See above, n. 7.

However, one important question that has sometimes been inadequately handled by investment tribunals is that of the legal effects attached to the justification of the measure. In an environmental context, this justification should be allowed to play a role at two levels. First, the legal basis of the measure is important. A measure adopted to comply with an international environmental obligation cannot be treated on the same footing as a purely domestic measure. The legal framework applicable to the assessment of the legality of a 'multilateral' measure is indeed different from that applicable to a 'unilateral' measure, at least as far as the applicable 'conflict rules' (the rules used to determine the priority of one norm over another) are concerned. Second, even for purely domestic measures, the interpretation of investment disciplines must leave sufficient room to accommodate environmental considerations. This is not always the case. By way of illustration, the use of the 'sole effects doctrine' in assessing claims for expropriation has led investment tribunals to pay little attention to the purpose of the measure when deciding questions of both liability[11] and damages.[12]

For the environmental justification of a measure to be properly taken into account, the 'traditional approach' described earlier would have to

[11] See e.g. *Tippetts, Abbett, McCarthy, Stratton* v. *TAMS-AFFA Consulting Engineers of Iran, the Government of the Islamic Republic of Iran*, Award (22 June 1984), Iran–US CTR, vol. 6, p. 225: 'The intent of the government is less important than the effects of the measures on the owner'; *Tecmed* v. *Mexico*, above, n. 9, para. 116: 'The government's intention is less important than the effects of the measures on the owner of the assets or on the benefits arising from such assets.'

[12] See e.g. *CDSE* v. *Costa Rica*, above, n. 7, para. 62: 'Expropriatory environmental measures – no matter how laudable and beneficial to society as a whole – are, in this respect, similar to any other expropriatory measures that a state may take in order to implement its policies: where property is expropriated, even for environmental purposes, whether domestic or international, the state's obligation to pay compensation remains.' See also *Marion Unglaube* v. *Republic of Costa Rica*, ICSID Case No. ARB/08/1, Award (16 May 2012); *Reinhard Unglaube* v. *Republic of Costa Rica*, ICSID Case No. ARB/09/20, Award (16 May 2012). See, by contrast, the decision of the European Court of Human Rights in *Case of Scordino* v. *Italy (No. 1)*, ECtHR Application No. 36813/97, Judgment (29 March 2006), paras 95, 97–8: 'Legitimate objectives in the "public interest", such as those pursued in measures of economic reform or measures designed to achieve greater social justice, may call for less than reimbursement of the full market value.' See also *Turgut* v. *Turkey*, ECtHR Application No. 1411/03, Judgment – Just Satisfaction (13 October 2009), para. 14. This case has influenced the outcome of other related cases: *Sarisoy* v. *Turkey*, Application No. 19641/05, Judgment (13 September 2011); *Ali Kilic and others* v. *Turkey*, Application No. 13178/05 Judgment (13 September 2011); *Erkmen and others* v. *Turkey*, Application No. 6950/05, Judgment – Merits (16 March 2010), Just Satisfaction (13 September 2011).

be revised. Two alternative models could be envisaged in this regard. A more 'progressive approach' distinguishing between internationally induced and purely domestic environmental measures could be developed in order to recalibrate the relationship between investment and environmental protection. An internationally induced measure would indeed be less 'suspicious' than a unilateral one and the relations between such a measure (required or authorised by international environmental law) and investment disciplines could not be approached as a conflict between a purely domestic measure and international law. This said, such an approach would be difficult in practice, because international environmental norms are often formulated in vague terms and, more generally, because investment tribunals seem rather reluctant to give international environmental law a larger room in their decisions.

Thus, a rather modest upgrade of the traditional approach may be a more realistic option. This 'upgraded approach' would carve out additional space in investment disciplines to make them more sensitive to environmental considerations. As will be discussed later in this chapter, this is currently being done through the use of certain legal concepts (e.g., environmental differentiation, the level of 'reasonableness' expected from investors, the police powers doctrine, or the scope of emergency/necessity clauses) that are important to interpret investment disciplines. In this upgraded approach, the question remains the assessment of the consistency of an environmental measure with investment disciplines, but the likelihood of such consistency is significantly increased. In other words, more room is left for the environmental regulation of foreign investment schemes.

11.2 The 'traditional approach'

The traditional approach to the relationship between environmental and investment protection can be seen, to some extent, as a generalisation of the holdings of certain tribunals in cases where a domestic environmental measure adversely affected the operations of a foreign investor in a manner inconsistent with international investment protection standards. It is important to keep in mind this initial context because it has influenced both the approach followed by investment tribunals and the way in which early commentators framed the question.

In the following paragraphs, I analyse how some features of this initial context – despite being dispute-specific – made their way into the general approach distilled from these disputes and still influences the way in which policy instruments frame the relationship between environmental measures and investment disciplines. Under this traditional approach, environmental measures are seen as 'suspicious', because they could hide a protectionist intent (11.2.1). Moreover, their legality is subject to their conformity with international (investment) law (11.2.2).

11.2.1 'Suspicious' environmental measures

The disputes that provided the initial context for the analysis of this question[13] – cases such as *Ethyl Corporation* v. *Canada*,[14] *Metalclad* v. *Mexico*, *S.D. Myers* v. *Canada*, or *Tecmed* v. *Mexico* – all shared the fact that the main purpose underlying the adoption of the relevant environmental measure had most likely not been genuinely environmental. This point is difficult to establish because tribunals tend to avoid taking bold stances on such issues. However, aside from *Ethyl Corporation* v. *Canada*, which was settled shortly after the decision of the tribunal asserting jurisdiction, a fine-grained analysis of the awards in the three other cases mentioned clearly suggests that the tribunals gave a considerable – and perhaps decisive – weight to the fact that the measures did not pursue a genuine environmental purpose.

In *Metalclad* v. *Mexico*, the tribunal seemed sceptical as to the grounds for declaring the land of the investor part of a natural preserve for the protection of cacti and simply disregarded the purpose of the measure.[15] In *S.D. Myers* v. *Canada*, the tribunal went a step further, explicitly noting that 'The evidence establishe[d] that Canada's policy was shaped to a very great extent by the desire and intent to protect and promote the market share of [Canadian] enterprises'[16] and that 'there was no legitimate environmental reason for introducing the ban'.[17] Similarly, in *Tecmed* v. *Mexico*, the tribunal considered that the measure challenged had been adopted on the basis of political (and not environmental) reasons.[18] This common feature of the initial context is significant because

[13] See e.g. T. Wälde and A. Kolo, 'Environmental Regulation, Investment Protection and "Regulatory Taking" in International Law' (2001) 50 *International and Comparative Law Quarterly* 837–9 (discussing *Ethyl Corporation* v. *Canada*, *Metalclad* v. *Mexico*, and *S.D. Myers* v. *Canada*); J. Abouchar, 'Environmental Laws as Expropriation under NAFTA' (1999) 8 *RECIEL* 209 (discussing the same three cases).

[14] *Ethyl Corporation* v. *Government of Canada*, NAFTA (UNCITRAL), Preliminary Award on Jurisdiction (24 June 1998).

[15] *Metalclad* v. *Mexico*, paras 109–11.

[16] *S.D. Myers* v. *Canada*, para. 162.

[17] *Ibid.*, para. 195.

[18] *Tecmed* v. *Mexico*, para. 128.

environmental measures appeared in a negative light, as a sort of disguise for the pursuit of protectionist or political purposes.

The 'suspicious' character of environmental measures can still be read between the lines in some policy instruments. By way of illustration, the Organisation for Economic Co-operation and Development (OECD) has recently referred to the risks of 'green protectionism' as a justification for the need to 'harness freedom of investment for green growth'. One of the draft papers circulated by the OECD staff as part of the consultation process defines 'green protectionism' as follows:

> Investment protectionism occurs when government policies and practices restrict the free flow of capital across the global economy and when such restrictions do not have a solid justification in safeguarding essential security interests and public order. Green investment protectionism occurs when environmental policies have this same effect and when the restrictions cannot be justified as advancing well-founded public-policy goals.[19]

It is therefore unsurprising that the 'OECD Statement on Harnessing Freedom of Investment for Green Growth', adopted in April 2011, impliedly subordinates environmental measures to investment protection standards when it states, in its fourth paragraph, that 'governments should review their new proposed environmental measures for compliance with investment law obligations'.[20] The latter point raises another question, namely the hierarchy between environmental and investment protection.

11.2.2 'Subordinated' environmental measures

Even in those cases where it is undisputed that the measure pursues a genuine environmental purpose, environmental law remains, as a matter of practice, subject to investment disciplines. From a legal perspective, this is mostly the result of the hierarchy of international law, which prevails over domestic law. In practice, the application of this rule depends on the tribunal addressing the conflict as well as of the characterisation of the conflict. The traditional approach is for investment

[19] K. Gordon, 'Green-Investment Protectionism: What is it and How Prevalent is it?' (2011) (OECD Paper), para. 16, available at www.oecd.org/dataoecd/8/3/46905672.pdf (accessed 12 March 2012).

[20] OECD, 'Harnessing Freedom of Investment for Green Growth', Freedom of Investment Roundtable, 14 April 2011.

tribunals to frame conflicts between environmental and investment protection as 'legitimacy conflicts' between a domestic (environmental) measure and an international (investment) norm, even when international environmental norms would be relevant to decide the case.

Perhaps the clearest illustration of the operation of the traditional approach in this regard is provided by *CDSE* v. *Costa Rica*. The dispute concerned the amount of compensation due by Costa Rica for the direct expropriation of a biodiversity-rich land that the investor, Compañía del Desarrollo de Santa Elena (CDSA), had acquired to develop a resort. We know from an article written by counsel for Costa Rica that, in its pleadings, the respondent had referred to the impact of certain environmental treaties on the assessment of compensation.[21] Yet, the tribunal disposed of Costa Rica's argument without even analysing the content of these treaties, stating that:

> the purpose of protecting the environment for which the Property was taken does not alter the legal character of the taking for which adequate compensation must be paid. The international source of the obligation to protect the environment makes no difference.[22]

It then added, in a footnote, that:

> For this reason, the Tribunal does not analyze the detailed evidence submitted regarding what Respondent refers to as its international legal obligation to preserve the unique ecological site that is the Santa Elena Property.[23]

In other words, according to this tribunal, international environmental law and, more generally, the environmental purpose of the measure would be completely irrelevant for the determination of quantum.

This conclusion is controversial. In the context of human rights, the environmental justification of a measure is recognised as a ground for reducing compensation. For instance, in *Turgut* v. *Turkey*, a case concerning the reclassification of certain lands as state forests, the European Court of Human Rights (ECtHR) reasoned that 'economic imperatives and even some fundamental rights, such as the right to property, should not be accorded primacy against considerations of environmental protection'.[24]

[21] See C. Brower and J. Wong, 'General Valuation Principles: The Case of Santa Elena', in T. Weiler (ed.) *International Investment Law and Arbitration: Leading Cases from the ICSID, NAFTA, Bilateral Treaties and Customary International Law* (London: Cameron May, 2005), 764.

[22] *CDSE* v. *Costa Rica*, above, n. 7, para. 71. [23] *Ibid.*

[24] See *Turgut* v. *Turkey*, ECtHR Application No. 1411/03, Judgment – Merits (8 July 2008) (*Turgut – Merits*), para. 90 (unofficial translation of the French text).

Fair compensation must be paid but, in practice, this means less than the full value of the property. As noted by the ECtHR, '[t]aking into account the foregoing considerations, the Court considers that, in the present case, the nature of the violation found does not allow the Court to use as a starting point the principle of *restitutio in integrum*'.[25] Another example is provided by *Theodoraki* v. *Greece*.[26] In this case, two hotel developers claimed that their right to property (article 1 of Protocol 1 to the ECHR) had been breached by reason of the measures adopted by Greece to protect endangered loggerhead turtles, pursuant to the Bern Convention. The European Court of Human Rights concluded that the measures amounted indeed to a deprivation of the right to property of the plaintiffs but it only accorded €3.7 million as fair compensation (instead of the €47 million requested). In the context of investment arbitration, a similar conclusion was reached by a tribunal chaired by the former president of the International Court of Justice. Indeed, in *SPP* v. *Egypt*, the tribunal excluded from the amount of compensation the damage corresponding to the period after the emergence of Egypt's obligations under the World Heritage Convention, noting that:

> From that date forward, the Claimant's activities on the Pyramids Plateau would have been in conflict with the Convention and therefore in violation of international law, and any profits that might have resulted from such activities are consequently noncompensable.[27]

For present purposes, however, suffice it to note that, in playing down the role of environmental law, the tribunal in *CDSE* v. *Costa Rica* framed the issue as a 'legitimacy conflict' and not as a 'normative conflict'. This is particularly significant in the context of this dispute. The main point of contention was whether the valuation of the property at stake should be governed by the laws of Costa Rica (as argued by Costa Rica) or by international investment law (as argued by the investor). The tribunal sided with the investor on the grounds that international (investment) law prevailed over domestic (environmental) law. It reasoned as follows:

> This leaves the Tribunal in a position in which it must rest on the second sentence of Article 42(1) ('In the absence of such agreement …') and thus

[25] *Ibid.*, Judgment – Just Satisfaction (13 October 2009), para. 14 (unofficial translation of the French text). The ECtHR then refers to paragraph 90 of its judgment on the merits, already quoted.

[26] *Theodoraki* v. *Greece*, ECtHR Application No. 9368/06, Judgment (2 December 2010).

[27] *SPP* v. *Egypt*, above, n. 7, para. 191.

> apply the law of Costa Rica and such rules of international law as may be applicable. No difficulty arises in this connection. The Tribunal is satisfied that the rules and principles of Costa Rican law which it must take into account, relating to the appraisal and valuation of expropriated property, are generally consistent with the accepted principles of public international law on the same subject. *To the extent that there may be any inconsistency between the two bodies of law, the rules of public international law must prevail. Were this not so in relation to takings of property, the protection of international law would be denied to the foreign investor and the purpose of the ICSID Convention would, in this respect, be frustrated ... [t]he parties' divergent positions lead, in substance, to the same conclusion, namely, that, in the end, international law is controlling.* The Tribunal is satisfied that, under the second sentence of Article 42(1), the arbitration is governed by international law.[28]

Yet, had the situation been characterised as a conflict between two norms of international law (one of international investment law and another of international environmental law), the priority of international law over domestic law would not have been applicable. Confining environmental considerations to the domestic level is therefore not an innocuous step. The use of the 'traditional approach' adds an important constraint on environmental regulation, namely the need to evolve within the bounds set by international investment law.

As 'suspicion', 'subordination' is still apparent in the manner in which some investment treaties are drafted. Despite the fact that the space devoted to environmental considerations in investment treaties and free-trade agreements (international investment agreements or IIAs) has been significantly expanded in recent years,[29] most of these 'environmental clauses' focus on legitimacy conflicts and seek to carve out some space for environmental regulation within investment disciplines. The seven main categories of environmental provisions in IIAs identified by the OECD Report are the following:

> [1] General language in preambles that mentions environmental concerns and establishes protection of the environment as a concern of the parties to the treaty [...]
> [2] Reserving policy space for environmental regulation [...]

[28] *CDSE* v. *Costa Rica*, above, n. 7, paras 64–5 (italics added).

[29] K. Gordon and J. Pohl, 'Environmental Concerns in International Investment Agreements: A Survey', OECD Working Papers on International Investment No. 2011/1 (2011) (OECD Report), 8.

[3] Reserving policy space for environmental regulation for more specific, limited subject matters (performance requirements and national treatment) [...]
[4] [P]rovisions that clarify the understanding of the parties that non-discriminatory environmental regulation does not constitute 'indirect expropriation' [...]
[5] [P]rovisions that discourage the loosening of environmental regulation for the purpose of attracting investment [...]
[6] [P]rovisions related to the recourse to environmental experts by arbitration tribunals [...]
[7] [P]rovisions that encourage strengthening of environmental regulation and cooperation.[30]

One may consider that such provisions could also accommodate normative conflicts between IIAs and environmental treaties. While this may be accurate to some extent, the formulation of these clauses is premised on the assumption that conflicts between environmental measures and investment disciplines are 'legitimacy conflicts'.

This is clear when one compares these clauses to another – much rarer – type of clause that specifically envisions the possibility of 'normative conflicts'. The clearest illustration is Article 104 of the NAFTA, which provides

1. In the event of any inconsistency between this Agreement and the specific trade obligations set out in:
   (a) the Convention on International Trade in Endangered Species of Wild Fauna and Flora, done at Washington, March 3, 1973, as amended June 22, 1979,
   (b) the Montreal Protocol on Substances that Deplete the Ozone Layer, done at Montreal, September 16, 1987, as amended June 29, 1990,
   (c) the Basel Convention on the Control of Transboundary Movements of Hazardous Wastes and Their Disposal, done at Basel, March 22, 1989, on its entry into force for Canada, Mexico and the USA, or
   (d) the agreements set out in Annex 104.1

such obligations will prevail to the extent of the inconsistency, provided that where a party has a choice among equally effective and reasonably available means of complying with such obligations, the party chooses the alternative that is the least inconsistent with the other provisions of this Agreement.[31]

[30] *Ibid.*, 11 (numbering added).

[31] North American Free Trade Agreement, 17 December 1992, 32 ILM 296 (NAFTA), art. 104.

Other comparable provisions have been included in the Caribbean Forum (CARIFORUM)–European Union Economic Partnership Agreement (EU EPA),[32] the EU–Russia Agreement on Partnership and Cooperation,[33] the Belgium–Luxembourg Model Bilateral Investment Treaty,[34] the Dominican Republic–Central America–United States Free Trade Agreement (CAFTA-DR)[35] or the USA–Singapore Free Trade Agreement.[36] The fact that this type of clause is much rarer than the previous type suggests that the prevailing understanding in investment treaty practice is still based on the traditional approach, but also that some attention is increasingly being paid to the impact of environmental treaties.

11.3 A more 'progressive approach'

As discussed in the previous section, the traditional approach to solving conflicts between environmental and investment protection has been influenced by the factual context of some early disputes. Environmental measures are often suspected of covert protectionism and even when their purpose is not in doubt they are deemed to be subordinated to investment disciplines.

Yet, this approach is controversial. In some of the early disputes, e.g., *S.D. Myers* v. *Canada* or *CDSE* v. *Costa Rica*, as well as in a number of subsequent disputes that will be discussed in the following paragraphs, there was a link between the measure challenged and an international environmental norm that, if spelled out, could have influenced the reasoning of investment tribunals. This influence can be summarised as follows: international environmental law may help reduce or eliminate suspicions of covert protectionism (11.3.1); and the recognition of the link between a domestic measure and an environmental treaty

[32] Economic Partnership Agreement between the CARIFORUM States and the European Community and its Member States, 15 October 2008, OJ 30/10/2008 – L 289/I/3, art. 72(c).

[33] Agreement on partnership and cooperation establishing a partnership between the European Communities and their member states, of one part, and the Russian Federation, of the other part, 26 June 1994, art. 69, reproduced in OECD, *International Investment Law: Understanding Concepts and Tracking Innovation* (2008) (OECD 2008 Study), 223–4.

[34] Belgian/Luxembourg Model BIT, art. 5(3), reproduced *ibid.*, 177.

[35] Dominican Republic–Central America–United States Free Trade Agreement, 5 August 2004, 43 ILM 514 (CAFTA-DR), art. 17.12.1.

[36] USA–Singapore FTA, art. 18.8, reproduced in OECD 2008 Study, 212.

would place the measure challenged at the same level as investment disciplines, thus excluding the application of the rule giving priority to international (investment) law over domestic (environmental) law (11.3.2).

11.3.1 Internationally induced measures are less suspicious

Regarding the first effect, the underlying rationale is that, as a rule, an internationally induced measure commands higher legitimacy.

This issue has been widely discussed in connection with so-called trade-related environmental measures or TREMs.[37] The dispute-settlement bodies in the trade context (as investment tribunals) frame conflicts between trade disciplines and environmental measures as legitimacy conflicts, i.e., environmental measures must evolve within the bounds set by trade disciplines. These bounds include some environmental exceptions, most notably Article XX, letters (b) and (g) of the GATT.[38] However, when a restriction to trade is required by an environmental treaty, a conflict arises between two norms of international law, one stemming from an environmental treaty and the other from a trade treaty. In the absence of a specific conflict norm, such as Article 104 of the NAFTA, trade tribunals address this situation by reference to general exceptions in trade treaties, such as Article XX of the GATT.

Irrespective of whether such exceptions may provide an adequate means to manage a normative conflict, this *modus operandi* has some difficulties. Aside from the allocation of the burden of proof, which would lie with the party invoking the exception (thus already implying a sort of priority of trade disciplines over environmental measures), the fact that – technically – these exceptions do not differentiate between unilateral and internationally induced environmental measures is problematic. This explains why the Doha Ministerial Declaration contemplated the need to conduct negotiations on 'the relationship between existing WTO rules and specific trade obligations set out in multilateral

[37] See WTO/CTE, Matrix on Trade Measures Pursuant to Selected Multilateral Environmental Agreements, 14 March 2007, WT/CTE/W/160/Rev. 4, TN/TE/S/5/Rev. 2 (CTE MEA Matrix), sect. II.

[38] General Agreement on Tariffs and Trade, 1947, incorporated into the General Agreement on Tariffs and Trade, of 15 April 1994 (GATT), Article XX(b) and (g). See S. Zleptnig, *Non-Economic Objectives in WTO Law* (The Hague: Kluwer, 2010).

environmental agreements (MEAs)'.[39] One of the proposals – put forward by the European Union – to address this problem introduced a presumption that TREMs are consistent with Article XX unless the contrary is established.[40] A pragmatic alternative to this approach would be to consider, in practice, that environmental measures adopted pursuant to an MEA are consistent with the chapeau of Article XX of the GATT, which excludes from the scope of the exception measures 'applied in a manner that would constitute arbitrary or unjustifiable discrimination [...] or a disguised restriction on international trade'.[41] Whether one follows the first or the second alternative, the key consideration for present purposes is that international environmental law would help reduce the suspicion of protectionism for most practical effects.

A similar effect of international environmental law can be detected in the investment context. An apposite illustration is provided by a NAFTA case, *Chemtura* v. *Canada*. The dispute concerned certain measures adopted by the Canadian environmental agency that resulted in the suspension and subsequent cancellation of the lindane-based pesticides produced and commercialised by the investor. The investor argued that the measures challenged (specifically the conduct of a scientific re-examination of the risks posed by lindane) had been triggered by a trade irritant and not as a result of a genuine environmental concern. The tribunal rejected this argument noting that:

> the evidence on the record [...] show[ed] that the Special Review was undertaken by the PMRA [Canada's environmental agency] in pursuance of its mandate and as a result of Canada's international obligations [under the POP Protocol to the LRTAP Convention].[42]

Thus, the link between international environmental law and the domestic measure challenged strengthened the legitimacy of the latter in a decisive manner.

[39] WTO Ministerial Conference Fourth Session, Ministerial Declaration, para. 31 WT/MIN (01)/DEC/1 (20 November 2001) (Doha Declaration), para. 31(i).

[40] Committee on Trade and Environment, Resolving the Relationship between the WTO Rules and Multilateral Environmental Agreements, communication by the European Communities of 19 October 2000, WT/CTE/W/170, para. 10, 15.

[41] GATT, art. XX, chapeau. See e.g. *United States – Import Prohibition of Certain Shrimp and Shrimp Products*, Report of the Appellate Body, WT/DS58/AB/R (12 October 1998), paras 166 ff. (suggesting that measures adopted pursuant to MEAs would a priori be justified under the chapeau of art. XX).

[42] *Ibid.*, para. 138.

11.3.2 Internationally induced measures are not subordinated

The second effect of international environmental law could be to change the characterisation of the conflict and, thereby, the set of rules applicable to solve it. When the challenged domestic measure is required or clearly authorised by an environmental treaty, a potential conflict with an investment discipline should be framed as a 'normative conflict' between two norms of international law. The view that environmental measures can only evolve within the bounds set by investment disciplines would no longer apply because the rule according to which international (investment) law prevails over domestic (environmental) law would not be applicable. The set of rules for solving normative conflicts would include principles such as *lex superior*,[43] *lex specialis*,[44] *lex posterior*,[45] some interpretation techniques[46] or a limited number of specific conflict norms already referred to.[47] However, there are some difficulties in establishing a link between international environmental law and a domestic environmental measure.

[43] On the hierarchical effects that could be attached to certain international environmental norms, see E. Kornicker, 'State Community Interests, Jus Cogens and Protection of the Global Environment: Developing Criteria for Peremptory Norms' (1998–1999) 11 *Georgetown International Environmental Law Review* 101.

[44] Conclusions of the work of the Study Group on the Fragmentation of International Law: Difficulties Arising from the Diversification and Expansion of International Law (2006), Doc. A/61/10/ (Conclusions-Fragmentation), paras 5–16. See also the Report of the Study Group on the Fragmentation of International Law: Difficulties Arising from the Diversification and Expansion of International Law, Finalized by Martti Koskenniemi, 13 April 2006, Doc. A/CN.4/L.682 (Report-Fragmentation), paras 46–222.

[45] See Vienna Convention on the Law of Treaties, 23 May 1969, 1155 UNTS 331 (VCLT), art. 30; Conclusions-Fragmentation, paras 24–30; Report-Fragmentation, paras 223–323.

[46] See R. Pavoni, 'Mutual Supportiveness as a Principle of Interpretation and Law-Making: A Watershed for the "WTO-and-Competing-Regimes" Debate?' (2010) 21 *European Journal of International Law* 649 (discussing 'mutual supportiveness' between trade and environment); C. McLachlan, 'The Principle of Systemic Integration and Article 31(3)(c) of the Vienna Convention' (2005) 54 *International and Comparative Law Quarterly* 279 (discussing the principle of systemic integration); *Gabčíkovo-Nagymaros Project* (Hungary/Slovakia), ICJ Reports 1997, 7, Weeramanty – Separate Opinion, 114 (discussing the principle of contemporaneity in the application of environmental law). On this latter principle, see also Iron Rhine ('IJzeren Rijn') Railway (Belgium/Netherlands), PCA Case, Award (24 May 2005), paras 59–60; *Dispute Regarding Navigational and Related Rights* (*Costa Rica* v. *Nicaragua*), Judgment of 13 July 2009, General List No. 133, para. 64; *Case Concerning Pulp Mills in the River Uruguay* (*Argentina* v. *Uruguay*), Judgment of 20 April 2010, General List No. 135, para. 204.

[47] See above, 11.2.2.

Perhaps the main difficulty arises from the broad formulation of environmental obligations. To develop this point it seems useful to provide some illustrations. Some provisions in environmental treaties are formulated in rather specific terms. For instance, Article 4(5) of the Basel Convention provides that 'A Party shall not permit hazardous wastes or other wastes to be exported to a non-Party or to be imported from a non-Party'.[48] This obligation would clearly require a source state to adopt and implement measures prohibiting exports to a developing country which is not a party to the Basel Convention. This provision can be contrasted to the much broader provisions contained in environmental treaties concerning the protection of biological resources, climate change or water resources. For example, Article 6 of the Convention on Biological Diversity provides that

> Each Contracting Party shall, in accordance with its particular conditions and capabilities:
>
> (a) Develop national strategies, plans or programmes for the conservation and sustainable use of biological diversity or adapt for this purpose existing strategies, plans or programmes which shall reflect, inter alia, the measures set out in this Convention relevant to the Contracting Party concerned; and
> (b) Integrate, as far as possible and as appropriate, the conservation and sustainable use of biological diversity into relevant sectoral or cross-sectoral plans, programmes and policies.[49]

It would be unclear whether a measure aimed at integrating 'the conservation and sustainable use of biological diversity' is required or, even simply authorised, by this provision. Similarly, Article 3(1) of the Kyoto Protocol provides that

> The Parties included in Annex I shall, individually or jointly, ensure that their aggregate anthropogenic carbon dioxide equivalent emissions of the greenhouse gases listed in Annex A do not exceed their assigned amounts, calculated pursuant to their quantified emission limitation and reduction commitments inscribed in Annex B and in accordance with the provisions of this Article, with a view to reducing their overall emissions of such gases by at least 5 per cent below 1990 levels in the commitment period 2008 to 2012.[50]

48 Basel Convention on the Control of Transboundary Movements of Hazardous Wastes and Their Disposal, of 22 March 1989, 1673 UNTS 57 (Basel Convention), art. 4(5).
49 Convention on Biological Diversity, 5 June 1992, 1760 UNTS 79 (CBD), art. 6.
50 Kyoto Protocol to the United Nations Framework Convention on Climate Change, Kyoto, 11 December 1997, 2303 UNTS 148 (Kyoto Protocol), art. 3(1).

It would again be unclear whether a measure such as the requirement imposed on airlines operating flights from or to Europe to present a certain amount of carbon offsets[51] is required or fully authorised by this provision. Still another example, this time in the area of water regulation, is provided by the right to water derived from Articles 11 (1) and 12(2)(b) of the Covenant on Economic, Social and Cultural Rights.[52] General Comment 15 of the Committee on Economic, Social and Cultural Rights defines this right as follows: 'The human right to water entitles everyone to sufficient, safe, acceptable, physically accessible and affordable water for personal and domestic uses'.[53] These and other provisions[54] are of particular relevance from a practical perspective, and they have been invoked in a number of investment proceedings.[55] For present purposes, it will be sufficient to make two observations concerning the *existence* and the *recognition* of the link between international environmental law and environmental measures.

Regarding the existence of the link, if one focuses on the environmental obligations that have been discussed in the practice of investment tribunals, they share a number of features: (i) they were adopted between the 1970s and the 1990s; (ii) most often they are broadly

[51] See Directive 2003/87/EC of the European Parliament and of the Council of 13 October 2003 establishing a scheme for greenhouse gas emissions allowance trading within the Community and amending Council Directive 96/61/E, OJ 2003 L 0087 – EN – 25.06.2009 – 004.001 (consolidated version) (ETS Directive). *Air Transport Association of America and others* v. *Secretary of State for Energy and Climate Change*, CJEU Case C-366/10, Judgment (21 December 2011).

[52] International Covenant on Economic, Social and Cultural Rights, 16 December 1966, 993 UNTS 3 (ICESCR).

[53] Committee on Economic, Social and Cultural Rights, General Comment No. 15 (2002), The Right to Water (Articles 11 and 12 of the International Covenant on Economic, Social and Cultural Rights), 26 November 2002, UN ESCOR Doc. E/C 12/2002/11 (GC 15), para. 2.

[54] See e.g. Protocol on Persistent Organic Pollutants to the LRTAP Convention, 24 June 1998, 37 ILM 513 (POP Protocol), Annex II; Convention on Wetlands of International Importance especially as Waterfowl Habitat, 2 February 1971, 996 UNTS 245, arts 2(1) and (4); Treaty between the United States of America and Mexico Relating to the Utilisation of the Waters of the Colorado and Tijuana Rivers and of the Rio Grande, 3 February 1944, 3 UNTS 314 (1944 Water Utilisation Treaty), art. 4; Convention on Nature Protection and Wild Life Preservation in the Western Hemisphere, of 12 October 1940, 56 Stat. 1354, TS 981 (Western Hemisphere Convention), arts II(1) and V(1); Convention for the Protection of the World Cultural and Natural Heritage, 16 November 1972, 1037 UNTS 151 (WHC), 4, 5(d) and 11.

[55] See above, n. 7.

stated; and (iii) their implementation is progressive and, to some extent, unclear. Perhaps to the exception of chemicals and waste regulation, which tends to be more precise, it seems difficult to assess in advance the impact of broad environmental obligations on the situation of foreign investors. This impact becomes clearer when some specific implementation measures have been adopted at the domestic level but, at this point, it is often too late to conduct a useful assessment of the regulatory risk. Yet, at the same time, the very existence of such clauses provides a signal that the host state will take regulatory action in the future, and foreign investors cannot safely disregard such a possibility. Thus, the main question posed by these environmental obligations is one of allocation of the regulatory risk between the investor and the state.

The second observation follows from the latter point. In practice, this risk allocation is carried out by investment tribunals, which, through the lens of the traditional approach, tend to see environmental measures as subordinated to investment disciplines. This perception prevents broad environmental norms from deploying the basic effects of other international obligations. This can be contrasted to the manner in which broad investment disciplines, such as the fair and equitable treatment clause, are interpreted by investment tribunals. It is also noteworthy that some domestic courts have recognised a direct effect to broad environmental obligations, such as Article 3 of the Ramsar Convention.[56] Thus, recognition of the link is a matter of perception as much (and perhaps even more) as it is one of law.

11.4 The 'upgraded approach'

Although investment tribunals are still reluctant to recognise the relevance of international environmental law for solving investment disputes, in the last few years they have increasingly carved out some space within investment disciplines for environmental considerations

[56] In the *Bonaire* case, the Dutch Council of State judged that Article 3 was directly enforceable at the domestic level and upheld on this basis an administrative decision cancelling a permit to build a holiday resort in a buffer zone surrounding a Ramsar protected site. See M. Bowman, P. Davies and C. Redgwell, *Lyster's International Wildlife Law*, 2nd edn (Cambridge University Press, 2010), 419.

to be taken into account. In doing so, they have placed themselves somewhere between the traditional and the progressive approaches. Indeed, while conflicts are still framed as 'legitimacy conflicts' (i.e., the link between international environmental law and domestic measures is not *formally* recognised), an additional measure of legitimacy is given to the environmental measure challenged (i.e., the link between international environmental law and domestic law is *informally* recognised or, at least, the environmental justification of the measure is given more weight). This practice is important for the environmental regulation of foreign investment schemes because it provides a clearer picture of the litigation risks entailed by host state regulatory action.

In the following paragraphs I analyse four 'upgrades' to the traditional approach: environmental differentiation (11.4.1); the level of 'reasonableness' expected from investors in the fair and equitable treatment standard (11.4.2); the police powers doctrine (11.4.3); and the scope of emergency/necessity clauses (11.4.4).

11.4.1 Environmental differentiation

The starting point of the discussion of environmental differentiation is the debate on 'green protectionism'. However, as noted in one of the papers prepared by the OECD as background for its 2011 Statement on Harnessing Freedom of Investment for Green Growth, so far green investment protectionism is not a problem in practice.[57] The fear of green protectionism comes rather from the early investment decisions discussed above as well as from the tendency to extrapolate trade reasoning[58] into the investment context. Yet, it is important not to conflate these two contexts. Trade disciplines are directly concerned with cross-border movements of goods/services and only indirectly concerned with production processes (e.g., through actionable subsidies etc.). The prevailing – albeit slowly eroding – understanding in the trade context is that similar products should be treated similarly at the border,

[57] OECD Paper, para. 19.

[58] On the debate of green protectionism in the trade context, see P. Sands, *Principles of International Environmental Law* (Cambridge University Press, 2003), 946–7; D. Bodansky, 'What's So Bad about Unilateral Action to Protect the Environment?' (2000) 11 *European Journal of International Law* 339.

irrespective of their (environmentally friendly or unfriendly) processes and production methods (PPMs).[59] Conversely, investment disciplines are directly concerned with the treatment of foreign producers based in the host state's territory and only indirectly with cross-border movements (e.g., through export restraints etc.). Differentiation based on PPMs is not only possible but central to investment regulation.

In the investment context, one important consideration in assessing whether two investors are in similar circumstances for purposes of non-discrimination standards is whether they face similar regulatory frameworks or, in other words, whether they have to evolve under the same overall constraints. This provides an important entry point for environmental differentiation. As noted by the tribunal in an early case, *S.D. Myers* v. *Canada*:

> the interpretation of the phrase 'like circumstances' in Article 1102 must take into account the general principles that emerge from the legal context of the NAFTA, including both its concern with the environment and the need to avoid trade distortions that are not justified by environmental concerns. The assessment of 'like circumstances' must also take into account circumstances that would justify governmental regulations that treat them differently in order to protect the public interest.[60]

From a legal standpoint, this statement can be seen as an application of the systemic integration interpretive technique for the determination of the meaning of 'like circumstances' in Article 1102 of the NAFTA. It thus opens the door to related and even separate environmental instruments

[59] On the issue of 'non-product-related PPMs' (i.e., differentiation on the basis of different PPMs that result in similar end-products), see R. Howse and D. Regan, 'The Product/Process Distinction – An Illusory Basis for Disciplining "Unilateralism" in Trade Policy' (2000) 11 *European Journal of International Law* 249; S. Charnovitz, 'The Law of Environmental "PPMs" in the WTO: Debunking the Myth of Illegality' (2002) 27 *Yale Journal of International Law* 59; J. Potts, *The Legality of PPMs under the GATT: Challenges and Opportunities for Sustainable Trade Policy* (Winnipeg: International Institute for Sustainable Development, 2008), 9–27; D. H. Regan, 'How to Think about PPMs (and Climate Change)', in T. Cottier, O. Nartova and S. Z. Bigdelli (eds.), *International Trade Regulation and the Mitigation of Climate Change* (Cambridge University Press, 2009), 97–123. Recently, the WTO Appellate Body considered that an environmental regulation differentiating among tuna exporters on the basis of their PPMs (the impact on dolphins of different ways of catching tuna) was consistent with Article 2.2. of the TBT Agreement. See *United States – Measures Concerning the Importation, Marketing and Sale of Tuna and Tuna Products*, WT/DS381/AB/R (16 May 2012) (US – Tuna/dolphin 2012), paras 311–33.

[60] *S.D. Myers* v. *Canada*, above, n. 7, para. 250.

in the assessment of likeness.[61] Another reference to the assessment of constraints was made in a subsequent case, *Methanex v. United States of America*, where the tribunal reasoned that local methanol producers (and not ethanol producers, as argued by the investor) were the proper comparator precisely because they evolved under the same regulatory constraints as the claimant.[62] These two early cases provide the background for the assessment of the contribution of the recent investment case law. I refer here to three cases: the first illustrates the impact of international environmental law on the assessment of likeness; the second shows that, even when two situations are deemed to be similar, international environmental law may play a role in justifying differential treatment; the third offers a more nuanced picture, highlighting the limits to the possibility of importing external legal elements into an investment treaty.

In the first case, *Parkerings* v. *Lithuania*, the investor claimed that it had been discriminated against because its project for the construction of a car park in the area of the old town of Vilnius had been treated less favourably than the one of another foreign investor. Lithuania argued that the two projects were not alike because the claimant's project had a higher impact on Vilnius' old town, a site included in the World Heritage List established by the World Heritage Convention.[63] The tribunal sided with Lithuania and reasoned that: 'The historical and archaeological preservation and environmental protection could be and in this case were a justification for the refusal of the project' and that, as a result, the claimant's project 'was not similar with the MSCP [multi-story car park] constructed by Pinus Propius [the comparator]'.[64] In this case, international environmental law was therefore important to assess 'likeness', despite the fact that the tribunal seemed to conflate this issue with the issue of justification (of differential treatment of two investors or investments recognised as being in a similar situation). This is consistent with the approach followed by some investment treaties, which explicitly refer, as part of the assessment of 'like circumstances' or 'similarity' to the

[61] See *ibid.*, paras 247–8 (referring inter alia to the North American Agreement on Environmental Cooperation, 17 December 1992, 32 ILM 1519, or the Rio Declaration on Environment and Development, 13 June 1992, UN Doc. A/CONF.151/26).

[62] *Methanex* v. *United States of America*, part IV, chap. B, paras 18–19.

[63] Convention for the Protection of the World Cultural and Natural Heritage, 16 November 1972, 1037 UNTS 151 (WHC).

[64] *Parkerings* v. *Lithuania*, above, n. 7, para. 392.

'effects on third persons and the local community' or to the 'effects on the local, regional or national environment, including the cumulative effects of all investments within a jurisdiction on the environment'.[65]

Even when two situations are explicitly considered as similar, international environmental law may play a role in 'justifying' differential treatment. This hypothesis can be illustrated by the *Arcelor* case decided by the European Court of Justice (ECJ).[66] Arcelor, a large steel producer, claimed that the Emissions Trading Directive[67] and the French implementing measures discriminated among similar sectors (the cap on emissions applied to steel production but not to chemical and aluminium production) in violation of the equal treatment standard.[68] Whether the ETS Directive can be considered as international law (community law is, technically, international law) or as a measure implementing the UNFCCC[69] and the Kyoto Protocol[70] is less important here than the reasoning of the ECJ (now the Court of Justice of the European Union). The ECJ considered indeed that the steel, chemical and aluminium sectors were 'in a comparable position',[71] and that they had been treated differently, but it concluded that the differentiation was justified[72] as an exercise of the ECJ's 'broad discretion'[73] on the basis of 'objective criteria appropriate to the aim pursued by the legislation [...] taking into account all the facts and the technical and scientific data available at the time of adoption of the act in question'[74] and 'all the interests involved'.[75] To support its conclusion, the ECJ referred, inter alia, to the administrative difficulties involved in including the chemical sector, made of some

[65] See COMESA Common Investment Area Agreement (COMESA CIAA) (23 May 2007), art. 17(2), referred to in S. A. Spears, 'The Quest for Policy Space in a New Generation of International Investment Agreements' (13) 4 *Journal of International Dispute Settlement* 1058.

[66] *Société Arcelor Atlantique et Lorraine et al.* v. *Premier Ministre, Ministre de l'Économie, des Finances et de l'Industrie, Ministre de l'Écologie et du Développement Durable*, ECJ Case C-127/07, Judgment (16 December 2008) (*Arcelor reference*). See also *US – Tuna/dolphin 2012*, paras 311–33. Technically, the discussion in the latter case was not about justification but about the scope of a primary norm (art. 2.2. of the TBT Agreement), which expressly allows for the protection of 'legitimate objectives', including environmental protection.

[67] The EU ETS Directive. [68] *Arcelor reference*, para. 23.

[69] United Nations Framework Convention on Climate Change, 9 May 1992, 31 ILM 849 (UNFCCC).

[70] *Arcelor reference*, paras 3–19. [71] *Ibid.*, para. 38. [72] *Ibid.*, paras 69 and 72.

[73] *Ibid*, para. 57. [74] *Ibid.*, para. 58. [75] *Ibid.*, para. 59.

34,000 companies, in the initial phase of the scheme,[76] as well as to the substantial 'difference in the levels of direct emissions between the two sectors concerned'.[77] For present purposes, this case suggests that international environmental law may be relevant – *informally* – to justify differential treatment of two similar situations.

The third case, *Grand River* v. *United States of America*, takes a different angle. In this case, a group of people belonging to first nations claimed that as a result of some human rights/environmental treaties and customary norms the investment disciplines of the NAFTA granted them a higher level of protection than that accorded to regular investors.[78] Thus, unlike the two previous cases, the environmental differentiation sought here by reference to international environmental law was not aimed to limit the scope of investment disciplines but rather to expand it. The tribunal rejected this claim. The case is relevant, however, for two main reasons. First, the tribunal considered

> the identity of the legal regime(s) applicable to a claimant and its purported comparators to be a compelling factor in assessing whether like is indeed being compared to like for purposes of Articles 1102 and 1103 [of the NAFTA].[79]

Second, the tribunal noted, in connection with the investors' claim for breach of the international minimum standard of treatment, that '[w]hile other legal rules may shape the context in which Article 1105 is applied, they do not alter the content of the customary international law minimum standard of treatment'.[80] The room left to international environmental law under this approach is unclear. The statement seems to draw a distinction between the application of the treaty provision (Article 1105) and the content of the customary norm. International environmental law would not have an effect on the latter, but it could influence the meaning of the former. The tribunal seems to confirm this understanding when it notes that

[76] *Ibid.*, para. 68. [77] *Ibid.*, para. 72.

[78] The claimants referred inter alia to the American Convention on Human Rights, 22 November 1969, 1144 UNTS 123 (art. 21), the International Labour Organizations' Convention (No. 169) concerning Indigenous and Tribal Peoples in Independent Countries, 27 June 1989, 28 ILM 1382 (1989) (art. 6(1)(a)), and the United Nations Declaration on the Rights of Indigenous Peoples (art. 17). *Ibid.*, para. 182(3).

[79] *Ibid.*, para. 167.

[80] *Ibid.*, para. 181. This statement is located in the section presenting the position of the claimant but it expresses the view of the tribunal.

> Even if one were to indulge a supposition that a customary rule required consultations directly with an individual First Nations investor under the circumstances of this case, it would be difficult to construe such a rule as part of the customary minimum standard of protection that must be accorded to every foreign investment pursuant to Article 1105. The notion of specialized procedural rights protecting some investors, but not others, cannot readily be reconciled with the idea of a minimum customary standard of treatment due to all investments.[81]

Thus, it is because this specific customary norm is a 'minimum' standard (and not because of its customary nature) that its 'content' cannot be redefined to offer special protection to certain minorities. In all events, the reasoning of the tribunal concerns an expansion of an investment discipline to accommodate special interests and not a restriction to accommodate environmental regulation.

11.4.2 Adjusting the level of 'reasonableness' expected from investors

International investment law provides some measure of protection to the 'legitimate' or 'reasonable' expectations of foreign investors, most notably under the fair and equitable treatment (FET) standard. To be protected, expectations must meet a number of conditions that have been identified by investment tribunals. According to one tribunal, such expectations have to be

> based on the conditions offered by the host state at the time of the investment; they may not be established unilaterally by one of the parties; they must exist and be enforceable by law; in the event of infringement by the host state, a duty to compensate the investor for damages arises except for those caused in the event of state of necessity; however, the investor's fair expectations cannot fail to consider parameters such as business risk or industry's regular patterns.[82]

Other tribunals have referred to largely similar conditions.[83] Irrespective of the potential differences that may exist among tribunals with respect

81 *Ibid.*, para. 213.

82 *LG&E* v. *Argentina*, ICSID Case No. ARB/02/1, Decision on Liability (13 October 2006) (*LG&E* v. *Argentina*), para. 130.

83 In *Parkerings* v. *Lithuania*, the tribunal reasoned that 'The expectation is legitimate if the investor received an explicit promise or guaranty from the host-State, or if implicitly, the host-State made assurances or representations that the investor took into account in making the investment. Finally, in the situation where the host-State made no assurance or representation, the circumstances surrounding the conclusion of the agreement are

to these conditions, there is wide agreement that in order to be protected the investor's expectations must be 'reasonable'.[84] Reasonableness is a broad concept that must be assessed in the light of a variety of circumstances, including 'business risk or industry's regular patterns'[85] or 'the political, socioeconomic, cultural and historical conditions prevailing in the host State'.[86] The definition of reasonableness thus offers another significant entry point for environmental considerations.

Two investment cases concerning purely domestic environmental measures provide the backdrop against which the impact of international environmental law must be assessed. In *MTD* v. *Chile*, a foreign investor claimed that the refusal of a zoning permit by the Chilean urban planning authorities was inconsistent with the previous authorisation to invest granted by another Chilean authority. Importantly, the investor had not conducted a due diligence assessment of the need for a zoning permit. The tribunal took into account both the inconsistent behaviour of the state and the lack of diligence of the investor. It concluded that Chile had breached the applicable bilateral investment treaty (BIT)[87] but that the compensation due to

decisive to determine if the expectation of the investor was legitimate. In order to determine the legitimate expectation of an investor, it is also necessary to analyse the conduct of the State at the time of the investment.' *Parkerings* v. *Lithuania*, above, n. 7, para. 331. Similarly, in *Duke* v. *Ecuador*, the tribunal considered that 'To be protected, the investor's expectations must be legitimate and reasonable at the time when the investor makes the investment. The assessment of the reasonableness or legitimacy must take into account all circumstances, including not only the facts surrounding the investment, but also the political, socioeconomic, cultural and historical conditions prevailing in the host State. In addition, such expectations must arise from the conditions that the State offered the investor and the latter must have relied upon them when deciding to invest.' *Duke Energy Electroquil Partners and Electroquil SA* v. *Republic of Ecuador*, ICSID Case No. ARB/04/19, Award (18 August 2008) (*Duke* v. *Ecuador*), para. 340.

84 *Waste Management Inc.* v. *Mexico*, ICSID Case No. ARB(AF)/00/3, Award (30 April 2004), para. 98.

85 *LG&E* v. *Argentina*, above, n. 82, para. 130; *Glamis* v. *United States of America*, above, n. 9, para. 767.

86 *Duke* v. *Ecuador*, para. 340.

87 It noted that 'the Tribunal agrees that it is the responsibility of the investor to assure itself that it is properly advised, particularly when investing abroad in an unfamiliar environment. However, in the case before us, Chile is not a passive party and the coherent action of the various officials through which Chile acts is the responsibility of Chile, not of the investor. Whether the Claimants acted responsibly or diligently in reaching a decision to invest in Chile is another question … Chile claims that it had no obligation to inform the Claimants and that the Claimants should have found out by themselves what the regulations and policies of the country were. The Tribunal agrees with this statement as a matter of principle, but Chile also has an obligation to act coherently and apply its policies consistently, independently of how diligent an investor is. Under international

the investor had to be reduced to account for latter's negligence.[88] In *Plama* v. *Bulgaria* the dispute concerned a change in the domestic environmental law as a result of which the investment vehicle had been made liable for past environmental damages. The investor argued that this change contradicted its reasonable expectations and was therefore in breach of the FET clause of the Energy Charter Treaty (ECT).[89] The tribunal rejected this claim. It noted that

> the ECT does not protect investors against any and all changes in the host country's laws. Under the fair and equitable treatment standard the investor is only protected if (at least) reasonable and justifiable expectations were created in that regard.[90]

Significantly, the tribunal considered, in connection with the claimant's argument that the regulatory change was still being discussed by the Bulgarian parliament at the time the investment had been made, that the 'parliamentary debates were in the public record and should have been known by [the investor's] Bulgaria advisors'.[91]

The latter point is important because, as already noted, the impact of broad environmental obligations arising from treaties ratified by the host state is difficult to assess in advance. Thus, the question is rather how the regulatory risk should be allocated. Whereas the decision in *MTD* v. *Chile* suggests that the risk should be split between the state and the investor, the *Plama* award places the burden entirely on the investor, perhaps because in this case no 'lack of due diligence in Respondent's treatment of Claimant and its investment with regard to the environmental amendments' could be identified.[92] In this context, the role played by international environmental law can be illustrated by reference to the *Chemtura* v. *Canada* case. As already noted, the dispute concerned a re-examination of lindane that eventually led to the cancellation of the investor's authorisation to produce certain pesticides. One important line of argument pursued by the investor was that Canada had acted disingenuously in launching *and* conducting the review of lindane. International environmental law was relevant for both issues. Regarding the launching of the review, the tribunal considered that Canada had acted

law (the law that this Tribunal has to apply to a dispute under the BIT), the State of Chile needs to be considered by the Tribunal as a unit.' *Ibid.*, paras 164–5.

88 *Ibid.*, paras 242–3.

89 Energy Charter Treaty, 17 December 1994, 2080 UNTS 95 (ECT).

90 *Plama* v. *Bulgaria*, above, n. 9, para. 219.

91 *Ibid.*, para. 221.

92 *Ibid.*, paras 220, 222.

pursuant to its international obligations under the POP Protocol, which required a re-examination of lindane.[93] As to the conduct of the review, the tribunal recalled that its task was not to settle the scientific debate over the consequences of lindane[94] but added that:

> irrespective of the state of the science [...] the Tribunal [could] not ignore the fact that lindane ha[d] raised increasingly serious concerns both in other countries and at the international level since the 1970s.[95]

One significant element in this regard was that in May 2009 lindane had been introduced in the list of substances banned under the POP Convention.[96] Moreover, the tribunal set a demanding standard of 'reasonableness' applicable to sophisticated investors. It noted indeed that:

> as a sophisticated registrant experienced in a highly-regulated industry, the Claimant could not reasonably ignore the PMRA's practices and the importance of the evaluation of exposure risks within such practices.[97]

This test is consistent with the previous case law, which referred, inter alia, to the need to anticipate changes[98] as well as to the industry's regular patterns.[99] Taken together, this body of case law suggests that regulatory changes induced by international environmental obligations would normally be part of an investor's business risk.

There are, of course, several techniques to manage regulatory risk, such as stabilisation or adjustment clauses[100] or, more generally, other types of specific assurances.[101] Yet, these techniques have limits. First, it

[93] *Ibid.*, para. 138. [94] *Ibid.*, para. 134. [95] *Ibid.*, para. 135.

[96] Stockholm Convention on Persistent Organic Pollutants, 22 May 2001, 40 ILM 532 (2001) (POP Convention).

[97] *Chemtura* v. *Canada*, above, n. 7, para. 149.

[98] *Plama* v. *Bulgaria*, above, n. 9, para. 221.

[99] *LG&E* v. *Argentina*, above, n. 82, para. 130; *Glamis* v. *United States of America*, above, n. 9, para. 767.

[100] On stabilisation and adjustment clauses, see generally E. Paasivirta, 'Internationalisation and Stabilisation of Contracts versus State Sovereignty' (1989) 60 *British Yearbook of International Law* 315; P. Bernardini, 'The Renegotiation of the Investment Contract' (1998) 13 *ICSID Review* 411; A. Shemberg, *Stabilization Clauses and Human Rights: A Research Project Conducted for IFC and the United Nations Special Representative to the Secretary General on Business and Human Rights*, 11 March 2008, available at www.ifc.org (accessed 31 December 2011); T. Wälde and G. N'Di, 'Stabilising International Investment Commitments' (1996) 31 *Texas International Law Journal* 215; P. Cameron, *International Energy Investment Law* (Oxford University Press, 2010), 68–83.

[101] The characterisation of specific assurances varies somewhat from one tribunal to the other. See *Methanex* v. *United States of America*, above, n. 9, part IV, chap. D, para. 7 (identifying five stringent conditions for the protection of specific assurances in the

is only natural that investors (as other businesses) operating in highly regulated markets bear part of the risk entailed by regulatory change. Even in cases where a specific clause in an investment contract provides for some sort of allocation of regulatory risk the validity of such clauses is not unlimited.[102] An often disregarded limitation stems from international environmental soft law. The OECD Guidelines for Multinational Enterprises specifically preclude covered companies, including foreign investors, from 'seeking or accepting exemptions not contemplated in the statutory or regulatory framework related to human rights, environmental, health, safety, labour, taxation, financial incentives, or other issues'.[103] Although the observance of these standards is 'voluntary and not legally enforceable',[104] they may become so if 'regulated by national law or international commitments'.[105] In all events, and perhaps most importantly, irrespective of their legally binding nature, nothing prevents an investment tribunal from taking such standards into account when assessing the level of reasonableness of an investor's expectations.

11.4.3 The use of the police powers doctrine

The police powers doctrine is a well established limitation to the constraints imposed by international investment law on environmental

context of an expropriation claim); *CMS Gas Transmission Company* v. *Argentina*, ICSID Case No. ARB/01/08, Decision on Annulment (25 September 2007), para. 95 (referring to similarly restrictive conditions in the context of the review of a claim for breach of an umbrella clause); *LG&E* v. *Argentina*, above, n. 82, para. 133 (providing a broader characterisation – including the domestic regulatory framework – in the context of a claim for breach of the FET standard); *Continental Casualty* v. *Argentina*, ICSID Case No. ARB/03/9, Award (5 September 2008), para. 261 (adopting a restrictive characterisation of specific assurances in the context of a claim for breach of the FET standard).

102 See L. Cotula, 'Reconciling Regulatory Stability and Evolution of Environmental Standards in Investment Contracts: Towards a Rethink of Stabilization Clauses' (2008) 1 *Journal of World Energy Law and Business* 158 (arguing by analogy with human rights law that states cannot legally undertake not to adopt environmental regulation); K. Tienhaara, 'Unilateral Commitments to Investment Protection: Does the Promise of Stability Restrict Environmental Policy Development' (2006) 17 *Yearbook of International Environmental Law* 139 (discussing from a pro-environment perspective the issue of regulatory chill arising from investment disciplines).

103 OECD, Guidelines for Multinational Enterprises, Annex I to the Declaration on International Investment and Multinational Enterprises, 25 May 2011 (OECD Guidelines), chap. 2, para. 5. This standard was at stake in a 'specific instance' brought before the UK National Contact Point. See 'Letter from Friends of the Earth to Wesley Scholz, Director, Office of Investment Affairs and National Contact Point for the OECD Guidelines for Multinational Enterprises, Department of State 3–8', 29 April 2003.

104 OECD Guidelines, chap. 1, para. 1. 105 *Ibid.*

regulation.[106] To understand the impact of international environmental law on the use of this instrument, it is, however, necessary to introduce a distinction between environmental regulation and targeted environmental measures. This distinction is rather intuitive. Whereas regulations are generally applicable, targeted measures concern one specific company. By way of illustration, the introduction of a tax or the prohibition to produce or commercialise certain substances is a regulation, whereas the refusal or the non-renewal of a permit is a targeted measure. Although both regulations and targeted measures can have expropriatory effects,[107] the overwhelming majority of the cases of indirect expropriation concern targeted measures.[108] In this context, an important question is whether the police powers doctrine could shield a targeted environmental measure.

Until recently, investment tribunals had only admitted the applicability of the police powers doctrine to shield environmental

[106] On the police powers doctrine, see American Law Institute (ALI), *Restatement (Third) of the Law of Foreign Relations of the United States*, 1986, sect. 712, commentary, letter (g). On the sources of the this doctrine, see, more generally, S. Friedman, *Expropriation in International Law* (London: Stevens, 1953), 51; L. B. Sohn and R. R. Baxter, 'Draft Convention on the International Legal Responsibility of States for Injuries to Aliens' (1961) 55 *American Journal of International Law* 545 (Harvard Draft 1961), art. 10(5); G. C. Christie, 'What Constitutes a Taking of Property under International Law' (1962) 38 *British Yearbook of International Law* 307; ALI, *Restatement (Second) of the Law of Foreign Relations of the United States*, 1965, sect. 197(1)(a); G. H. Aldrich, 'What Constitutes a Compensable Taking of Property? The Decisions of the Iran–United States Claims Tribunal' (1994) 88 *American Journal of International Law* 585; M. Kinnear, A. K. Bjorklund and J. F. G. Hannaford, *Investment Disputes under NAFTA: An Annotated Guide to NAFTA Chapter 11* (The Hague: Kluwer Law International, 2006), commentary to art. 1110, 49–55; I. Brownlie, *Principles of Public International Law* (Oxford University Press, 2008), 535–6.

[107] See *S.D. Myers* v. *Canada*, above, n. 7, para. 281 *in fine*.

[108] Out of the ten hypotheses of indirect expropriation mentioned by a leading textbook, only one (taxation) concerns general regulations: M. Sornarajah, *The International Law of Foreign Investment* (Cambridge University Press, 2010), 375. A similar pattern can be detected in the case law of the Iran–US Claims Tribunal. Aldrich distinguishes cases that amounted to an expropriation (aside from formal nationalisations, these are all targeted measures) from cases where no taking was found (including 'lawful regulations'). See G. H. Aldrich, *The Jurisprudence of the Iran–United States Claims Tribunal* (Oxford University Press, 1996), chap. 5. See also *SPP* v. *Egypt*, above, n. 7; *Metalclad* v. *Mexico*, above, n. 9; *Tecmed* v. *Mexico*, above, n. 9; *Compañía de Aguas del Aconquija SA and Vivendi Universal SA* v. *Argentine Republic*, ICSID Case No. ARB/97/3, Award (20 August 2007) (*Vivendi II*); *Biwater Gauff (Tanz.) Ltd* v. *United Republic of Tanzania*, ICSID Case No. ARB/05/22, Award (24 July 2008) (*Biwater* v. *Tanzania*); *Middle East Cement Shipping and Handling Co SA* v. *Egypt*, ICSID Case No. ARB/99/6, Award (12 April 2002).

regulations. In *S.D. Myers* v. *Canada*, the tribunal noted indeed that 'The general body of precedent does not treat *regulatory action* as amounting to expropriation'.[109] Similarly, in *Methanex* v. *United States of America*, the tribunal noted that 'a non-discriminatory *regulation* for a public purpose, which is enacted in accordance with due process and, which affects, inter alios, a foreign investor or investment is not deemed expropriatory and compensable'.[110] Still another illustration (although not concerning environmental regulation) is the case *Saluka* v. *Czech Republic*, where the tribunal noted, by reference to the *Methanex* award, that

> the principle that a State does not commit an expropriation and is thus not liable to pay compensation to a dispossessed alien investor *when it adopts general regulations* that are 'commonly accepted as within the police powers of States' forms part of customary law today.[111]

It is against this background that one must assess the contribution of *Chemtura* v. *Canada*. In this case, for the first time, an investment tribunal applied the police powers doctrine to shield a targeted environmental measure (i.e., the suspension and subsequent cancellation of the investor's registered pesticides):

> The Tribunal considers in any event that the measures challenged by the Claimant constituted a valid exercise of the Respondent's police powers. As discussed in detail in connection with Article 1105 of NAFTA, the PMRA took measures within its mandate, in a non-discriminatory manner, motivated by the increasing awareness of the dangers presented by lindane for human health and the environment. A measure adopted under such circumstances is a valid exercise of the State's police powers and, as a result, does not constitute an expropriation.[112]

[109] *S.D. Myers* v. *Canada*, above, n. 7, para. 281 (italics added). However, the term regulatory action here is somewhat unclear. The case concerned a targeted measure and, *in casu*, the tribunal did not apply the police powers doctrine. In *Tecmed* v. *Mexico*, the formulation of the police powers doctrine was also somewhat broader: 'The principle that the State's *exercise of its sovereign powers* within the framework of its police power may cause economic damage to those subject to its powers as administrator without entitling them to any compensation whatsoever is undisputable.' *Tecmed* v. *Mexico*, above, n. 9, para. 119 (italics added). The case also concerned a targeted measure and, again, *in casu* the tribunal did not actually apply the doctrine.

[110] *Methanex* v. *United States of America*, above, n. 9, part IV, chap. D, para. 7.

[111] See *Saluka Investments B.V.* v. *The Czech Republic*, UNCITRAL, Partial Award (17 March 2006) (*Saluka* v. *Czech Republic*), para. 262 (italics added).

[112] *Chemtura* v. *Canada*, above, n. 7, para. 266.

The reference in this paragraph to the discussion of the investor's claim for breach of Article 1105 of the NAFTA is important because, as noted in section 11.4.2., the tribunal considered that both the launching and the conduct of the review of lindane leading to the cancellation of the investor's registrations were justified, inter alia, by reference to Canada's international environmental obligations.[113]

The application of the police powers doctrine to targeted environmental measures is confirmed by the practice of other jurisdictions. In *Pine Valley* v. *Ireland*, the European Court of Human Rights considered indeed that a judicial decision enforcing a zoning plan (and thereby depriving the applicant of certain uses of its land 'so as to preserve a green belt') was not a 'disproportionate measure' and therefore did not amount to a violation of the right to property accorded by Article 1 of Protocol I to the European Convention on Human Rights.[114] Similarly, in another early case, *Fredin* v. *Sweden*, the revocation of a permit to exploit gravel was considered as a legitimate measure to control the use of property consistent with Article 1 of Protocol I.[115] Although these two cases do not refer to international environmental law to legitimise the measure (they apply the exception contained in Article 1 of Protocol I), they are relevant for present purposes because they suggest that in applying the police powers doctrine to shield a targeted environmental measure the *Chemtura* tribunal was simply coming closer to a well established principle in the field of human rights, i.e., that rights (or, by analogy, investment disciplines) can be limited through general and targeted measures without necessarily being breached.

11.4.4 A broader scope for emergency/necessity clauses

The impact of international environmental law on the operation of emergency/necessity clauses arising from either treaties or international customary law can be detected at two levels. First, the scope of certain clauses included in IIAs is explicitly or implicitly defined, inter alia, by reference to international environmental law. Second, the type of

113 *Ibid.*, paras 138, 135.

114 *Pine Valley Developments Ltd and others* v. *Ireland*, ECtHR Application No. 12742/87, Judgment (29 November 1991) (*Pine Valley* v. *Ireland*), paras 9, 55–60.

115 *Fredin* v. *Sweden*, ECtHR Application No. 12033/86, Judgment (18 February 1991) (*Fredin* v. *Sweden*), paras 41–56.

interests protected by the customary necessity defence may include the protection of the environment. In both cases, international environmental law plays a catalysing role: the emergence of international environmental norms protecting certain interests adds legitimacy to the claim that such interests must be protected under emergency/necessity clauses.

The trend to include environmental provisions in IIAs has been briefly discussed in section 11.2.2. Although such provisions are technically not emergency clauses, they carve out some space for environmental regulation, sometimes by reference to international environmental law. For example, Article 72(c) of the CARIFORUM-EPA provides that:

> Investors do not manage or operate their investments in a manner that circumvents international environmental or labour obligations arising from agreements to which the EC Party and the Signatory CARIFORUM States are parties.[116]

Similarly, under Article 5(3) of the Belgian/Luxembourg model BIT:

> The Contracting Parties reaffirm their commitments under the international environmental agreements, which they have accepted. They shall strive to ensure that such commitments are fully recognized and implemented by their domestic legislation.[117]

Still another illustration is provided by Article 17.12.1 of CAFTA-DR, according to which:

> The Parties recognize that multilateral environmental agreements to which they are all party play an important role in protecting the environment globally and domestically and that their respective implementation of these agreements is critical to achieving the environmental objectives of these agreements. The Parties further recognize that this Chapter and the ECA [side environmental agreement] can contribute to realizing the goals of those agreements. Accordingly, the Parties shall continue to seek means to enhance the mutual supportiveness of multilateral environmental agreements to which they are all party.[118]

Some other provisions do not explicitly refer to international environmental law but are nevertheless interesting because they would most likely have to be interpreted in the light of international environmental

[116] CARIFORUM-EPA, above, n. 32, art. 72(c).
[117] Belgian/Luxembourg Model BIT, above, n. 34, art. 5(3).
[118] CAFTA-DR, above, n. 34, art. 17.12.1.

law. For example, certain IIAs concluded by Canada contain a general exception clause similar to Article XX of the GATT:

> 1. Subject to the requirement that such measures are not applied in a manner that would constitute arbitrary or unjustifiable discrimination between investments or between investors, or a disguised restriction on international trade or investment, nothing in this Agreement shall be construed to prevent a Party from adopting or enforcing measures necessary:
> (a) to protect human, animal or plant life or health;
> (b) to ensure compliance with laws and regulations that are not inconsistent with the provisions of this Agreement; or
> (c) for the conservation of living or non-living exhaustible natural resources.[119]

The interpretation of this provision would in all likelihood be guided by the way WTO panels and the Appellate Body have interpreted Article XX of the GATT, i.e., by reference to international environmental law.[120] Another example, of significant practical importance,[121] is Article XI of the Argentina–USA BIT, according to which the treaty

> shall not preclude the application by either Party of measures necessary for the maintenance of public order, the fulfillment of its obligations with

[119] Reproduced in A. Newcombe, 'General Exceptions in International Investment Agreements', in M.-C. Cordonnier Segger, M. W. Gehring and A. Newcombe (eds.), *Sustainable Development in World Investment Law* (The Hague: Kluwer, 2011), 359.

[120] On the interpretation of art. XX of GATT, see S. Charnovitz, 'Exploring the Environmental Exceptions in GATT Article XX' (1991) 25 *Journal of World Trade* 37; A. Mattoo and P. Mavroidis, 'Trade, Environment and the WTO: The Dispute Settlement Practice Relating to Article XX of GATT', in E.-U. Petersmann (ed.), *International Trade Law and the GATT/WTO Dispute Settlement System* (The Hague: Kluwer, 1997), 327–43; D. M. McRae, 'GATT Article XX and the WTO Appellate Body', in M. Bronckers and R. Quick (eds.), *New Directions in International Economic Law: Essays in Honour of John H. Jackson* (The Hague: Kluwer Law International, 2000) 228–36; Zleptnig, *Non-Economic Objectives*, chap. 6.

[121] This provision has played a major role in a number of investment disputes against Argentina: *CMS Gas Transmission Company* v. *Argentine Republic*, ICSID Case No. ARB/01/08, Award (12 May 2005), Decision on Annulment (25 September 2007); *LG&E* v. *Argentina*, above, n. 82; *Enron and Ponderosa Assets* v. *Argentine Republic*, ICSID Case No. ARB/01/3, Award (22 May 2007), Decision on Annulment (30 July 2010) (*Enron* v. *Argentina – Annulment*); *Sempra Energy* v. *Argentine Republic*, ICSID Case No. ARB/02/16, Award (28 September 2007) (*Sempra* v. *Argentina – Award*), Decision on Annulment (29 June 2010) (*Sempra* v. *Argentina – Annulment*); *Continental Casualty* v. *Argentina*, above, n. 101.

> respect to the maintenance or restoration of international peace or security or the protection of its own essential security interests.[122]

The terms 'essential security interests' were interpreted by the tribunal in *Continental Casualty* v. *Argentina* by reference to the work of the International Law Commission (ILC) on the necessity defence. Quoting the commentary to the ILC Articles on State Responsibility,[123] the tribunal noted that 'States have invoked necessity "to protect a wide variety of interests, including safeguarding the environment" '.[124] Better to understand the link between necessity and international environmental law, it is useful to take a step back and look at the case law of the International Court of Justice (ICJ).

The ICJ recognised for the first time that the protection of the environment could be an 'essential interest' of the state under the customary necessity defence in the *Gabčíkovo-Nagymaros* case.[125] This step must be appraised in the light of its normative context. The year before, the ICJ had taken a fundamental step for the development of international environmental law. In paragraph 29 of its *Advisory Opinion on the Legality of Nuclear Weapons*, the Court had stated that

> The existence of the general obligation of States to ensure that activities within their jurisdiction and control respect the environment of other States or of areas beyond national control is now part of the corpus of international law relating to the environment.[126]

There is a link between this statement and the recognition of environmental protection as an essential interest. While an interest is conceptually different from a norm aimed at protecting it, the very existence of a

122 Treaty between the United States of America and the Argentine Republic concerning the Reciprocal Encouragement and Protection of Investment, 14 November 1991, 31 ILM 124 (Argentina–US BIT).

123 Responsibility of States for Internationally Wrongful Acts, GA Res. 56/83, UN Doc. A/RES/56/83, 12 December 2001 (ILC Articles).

124 *Continental Casualty* v. *Argentina*, above, n. 101, para. 175.

125 *Gabčíkovo–Nagymaros*, above, n. 46. The ICJ considered that 'the concerns expressed by Hungary for its natural environment in the region affected by the Gabčíkovo-Nagymaros Project related to an "essential interest" of that State, within the meaning given to that expression in Article 33 of the Draft of the International Law Commission' (para. 53), but it rejected the necessity defence because other conditions were not met. On the so-called 'ecological necessity', see A. Bjorklund, 'The Necessity of Sustainable Development', in Cordonnier Segger, Gehring and Newcombe, *Sustainable Development in World Investment Law*, 373.

126 *Legality of the Threat or Use of Nuclear Weapons*, ICJ Reports 1996, 226, at para. 29.

customary norm may suggest that international law attaches sufficient importance to the protection of that interest so as to justify its characterisation as an 'essential' interest.[127] In the *Gabčíkovo–Nagymaros* case, the Court explicitly justified this characterisation by reference to paragraph 29 of its *Advisory Opinion* of the previous year.[128] Thus, there is a link between the development of international environmental law and the operation of emergency/necessity clauses.

This link can also be discerned in the specific context of investment disputes. In two cases against Argentina,[129] the respondent argued that the measures challenged could be justified under the customary necessity defence. To buttress its argument, it specifically referred to the human right to water recognised in several international instruments.[130] Although the defence was rejected, the tribunals had no difficulty in acknowledging that 'The provision of water and sewage services ... certainly was vital to the health and well-being of [the population] and was therefore an essential interest of the Argentine State'.[131] Despite the rather cursory character of the tribunal's analysis, the references to the human right to water in the sections presenting the arguments of both the respondent and the *amici curiae*[132] as well as the assertiveness of the tribunal (conveyed by the word 'certainly' in the text quoted above) provide two indications that the existence of a right to water in international law had an impact on this conclusion. Of course, this is not to say that any interest protected by an international environmental norm could be characterised as 'essential' or be protected by an emergency clause. The conclusion suggested by the analysis of these cases is simply that international environmental law could provide – and, in practice, has provided – greater legitimacy to the protection of the environment through emergency/necessity clauses.

[127] J. E. Viñuales, 'The Contribution of the International Court of Justice to the Development of International Environmental Law: A Contemporary Assessment' (2008) 32 *Fordham International Law Journal* 249.

[128] *Gabčíkovo–Nagymaros*, above, n. 46, para. 53, *in fine*.

[129] See *Suez* v. *Argentina – 03/17 and Suez* v. *Argentina – 03/19*, both above, n. 7.

[130] *Suez* v. *Argentina – 03/17 – Liability*, para. 232; *Suez* v. *Argentina – 03/19 – Liability*, para. 252.

[131] *Suez* v. *Argentina – 03/17 – Liability*, para. 238; *Suez* v. *Argentina – 03/19 – Liability*, para. 260.

[132] *Suez* v. *Argentina – 03/19 – Liability*, para. 256.

11.5 Some prospective observations

The foregoing analysis suggests that international environmental law does have an impact on investment disputes, but only indirectly through 'upgrades' to the traditional approach. There seems to be considerable resistance to frame conflicts between environmental and investment protection as 'normative conflicts' and treat them accordingly. In this section, I discuss what I see as the main reasons explaining such resistance (11.5.1), as well as some avenues that could be pursued to help overcome it (11.5.2)–(11.5.3).

11.5.1 Obstacles to a 'progressive approach'

One of the main difficulties involved in the recognition of 'normative conflicts' is the prevailing formulation of international environmental norms as broad, often merely exhortative or even vague clauses in environmental treaties. I have discussed this issue in section 11.3.2 by reference to several illustrations. As noted then, due to their broad formulation, it may be very difficult to establish that a domestic environmental measure is required or authorised by an environmental treaty.

One may add here that even when this link exists and is invoked in an investment dispute it remains 'vulnerable' to challenges on grounds of proportionality and/or due process. Several illustrations of such vulnerability can be provided. In *S.D. Myers* v. *Canada*, the investor successfully challenged the measure adopted by Canada (a trade ban) on grounds of proportionality. The tribunal considered indeed that irrespective of whether the ban was required by the Basel Convention, or not, the measure had been disproportional:

> Even if the Basel Convention were to have been ratified by the NAFTA Parties, it should not be presumed that CANADA would have been able to use it to justify the breach of a specific NAFTA provision because ... *where a party has a choice among equally effective and reasonably available alternatives for complying ... with a Basel Convention obligation, it is obliged to choose the alternative that is ... least inconsistent ... with the NAFTA*. If one such alternative were to involve no inconsistency with the Basel Convention, clearly this should be followed.[133]

[133] *S.D. Myers* v. *Canada*, above, n. 7, para. 215 (italics original, referring to article 104 of the NAFTA).

In *Chemtura* v. *Canada*, the investor also challenged the measures adopted by Canada on grounds of due process, but the tribunal rejected the argument.[134] In the context of freshwater regulation, in *Suez* v. *Argentina* the investors argued that the measures adopted by Argentina to tackle the 2001–2 economic and social crises could not be justified under the customary necessity defence because they were disproportionally adverse to the investors' interests. The tribunal sided with the claimants on this point[135] noting that:

> Argentina could have attempted to apply more flexible means to assure the continuation of the water and sewage services to the people of Buenos Aires and at the same time respected its obligations of fair and equitable treatment. The two were by no means mutually exclusive.[136]

Regarding the protection of cultural sites, an interesting illustration of the vulnerability of the link between international environmental law and domestic environmental measures is provided by *SPP* v. *Egypt*. In this case, the tribunal interpreted the obligation arising from Articles 4, 5(d) and 11 of the World Heritage Convention in a manner that effectively neutralised the relevance of this treaty for the assessment of Egypt's liability. According to the tribunal, the obligation to protect a site had only arisen when the World Heritage Committee accepted the nomination of the site by Egypt.[137] As the measures challenged by the investor (the classification of the land as not suitable for tourism purposes and the revocation of the concession) had taken place between the date of nomination and the date of acceptance, the tribunal considered that they were not 'required' by the World Heritage Convention.

These examples suggest that the rather broad formulation of environmental norms makes the link between such norms and domestic environmental measures vulnerable. This, in turn, prevents the characterisation of conflicts as 'normative conflicts' between two norms of international law and favours the use of the traditional approach based on the concept of 'legitimacy conflicts'. However, formulation alone cannot account for the persistence of the traditional approach. As already

[134] *Chemtura* v. *Canada*, above, n. 7, paras 153–62 (concerning the review of lindane), 184–93 (concerning the phase-out conditions applied to the investor) and 200–25 (concerning the alleged excessive delays in the registration of the claimant's replacement product).

[135] *Suez* v. *Argentina – 03/19 – Liability*, above, n. 7, paras 239–43.

[136] *Ibid.*, para. 260.

[137] *SPP* v. *Egypt*, above, n. 7, para. 154.

noted, other broadly stated clauses – for example, Article 3 of the Ramsar Convention or the FET standard – have been successfully linked to more specific measures adopted at a lower legislative/regulatory level. What else is then preventing this link from being recognised?

This question leads me to the second reason, namely the system for the implementation of international environmental law. Unlike international investment law (or other branches of international law such as international trade law, international human rights law, international criminal law etc.), international environmental law has no system of compulsory adjudication capable of developing and refining the specific contents of broad environmental obligations.[138] It thus has to rely either on a variety of soft mechanisms (e.g., monitoring and reporting,[139] 'non-compliance procedures',[140] authoritative interpretations,[141] amicus intervention[142] etc.) or on judicial forums often specialised in other branches of international law. As I discuss next, both avenues could be useful if their potential for strengthening the link between domestic measures and international environmental law is more fully explored and understood by investment practitioners and tribunals.

138 However, there are a number of non-compulsory adjudication systems focusing on environmental matters. A 'Chamber for Environmental Matters' was created in 1993 under article 26(1) of the Statute of the International Court of Justice (press release 93/20, Constitution of a Chamber of the Court for the Environmental Matters, 19 July 1993). This Chamber was never used and in 2006 the Court decided not to reconstitute it. Another example is the 'Chamber for Marine Environmental Disputes' established by the International Tribunal for the Law of the Sea in 1997 pursuant to article 15(1) of its Statute (press release ITLOS/Press 5, 3 March 1997).

139 On these mechanisms, see K. Sachariew, 'Promoting Compliance with International Environmental Legal Standards: Reflections on Monitoring and Reporting Mechanisms' (1992) 2 *Yearbook of International Environmental Law* 31.

140 T. Treves, A. Tanzi, C. Pitea et al. (eds.), *Non-Compliance Procedures and Mechanisms and the Effectiveness of International Environmental Agreements* (The Hague: TMC Asser Press, 2009).

141 See e.g. Committee on Economic, Social and Cultural Rights, General Comment No. 15 (2002), The Right to Water (Articles 11 and 12 of the International Covenant on Economic, Social and Cultural Rights), 26 November 2002, UN ESCOR Doc. E/C 12/2002/11.

142 See B. Stern, 'Civil Society's Voice in the Settlement of International Economic Disputes' (2007) 22 *ICSID Review* 280; F. Grisel and J. E. Viñuales, 'L'*amicus curiae* dans l'arbitrage d'investissement' (2007) 22 *ICSID Review* 380. On *amicus* intervention before other international tribunals, see D. Shelton, 'The Participation of Nongovernmental Organizations in International Judicial Proceedings' (1994) 88 *American Journal of International Law* 611.

11.5.2 The contribution of soft mechanisms

Regarding the first avenue, its relevance for present purposes lies in the potential contribution of some soft mechanisms to encourage investment tribunals to treat conflicts as 'normative conflicts' or, in other words, to treat international environmental law on an equal footing with international investment law. This point can be illustrated by reference to three cases.

The first is *Chevron* v. *Ecuador*,[143] a dispute arising from the oil extraction activities of Texaco (subsequently acquired by Chevron) in Ecuador. Texaco's operations led to severe pollution of the Ecuadorian jungle with serious health consequences for the local population. After a failed attempt to hold Chevron liable before the courts of the USA, in February 2011 an Ecuadorian court ordered Chevron to pay some US$18 billion in environmental and punitive damages.[144] Chevron has replied among others by initiating arbitration proceedings against Ecuador under the Ecuador–US BIT.[145] According to Chevron:

> Ecuador's judicial branch has conducted the [domestic environmental litigation against the investor] in total disregard of Ecuadorian law, international standards of fairness, and Chevron's basic due process and natural justice rights, and in apparent coordination with the executive branch and the [...] plaintiffs.[146]

Interestingly, this claim could potentially oppose international investment law (customary law and a BIT) to the obligations of Ecuador under the American Convention on Human Rights.[147] The link between this treaty and the decision of the Ecuadorian court could be strengthened through the action of the Inter-American Commission on Human Rights

[143] *Chevron Corporation and Texaco Petroleum Company* v. *Republic of Ecuador*, PCA Case No. 2009-23 (UNCITRAL Rules), Jurisdictional Decision (27 February 2012) (*Chevron* v. *Ecuador II*).

[144] See Summary of Judgment and Order of Superior Court of Nueva Loja, *Aguindav. Chevron Texaco*, No. 2003-0002, 14 February 2011 and Excerpts from Judgment and Order of Superior Court of Nueva Loja (*Lago Agrio – first instance*), available at www.chevrontoxico.com (accessed 13 January 2012).

[145] *Chevron Corporation and Texaco Petroleum Corporation* v. *The Republic of Ecuador*, PCA Case No. 2009-23, Notice of Arbitration (23 September 2009) (*Chevron* v. *Ecuador – NoA*), paras 1–2.

[146] *Ibid.*, para. 4.

[147] American Convention on Human Rights, 22 November 1969, 1144 UNTS 123.

(ICommHR).[148] Already in 1997, the ICommHR had recommended that Ecuador ensure access to justice for the people affected by oil contamination to seek redress.[149] In early February 2012, the plaintiffs requested the ICommHR to issue an order barring Ecuador from interfering with the enforcement of the judgment against Chevron.[150] They were afraid that Ecuador may bow when faced with the increasing pressure put by the investor, particularly as a result of an interim order (subsequently converted into an interim award) issued by the investment tribunal seized of the matter ordering Ecuador:

> to take all measures at its disposal to suspend or cause to be suspended the enforcement or recognition within and without Ecuador of any judgment against the First Claimant in the Lago Agrio Case [Chevron].[151]

The plaintiffs withdrew their request in early March 2012, but the case illustrates how a 'normative conflict' could arise if the link between the domestic measure challenged and an international environmental obligation is spelled out by a quasi-adjudicatory body.

The second illustration is provided by the considerable development of *amicus* intervention in investment proceedings in the last decade. Investment disputes with environmental components are particularly prone to such intervention[152] and *amici curiae* often discuss in detail the link

[148] ICommHR, 'Report on the Situation of Human Rights in Ecuador', OEA/Ser.L/V/II.96, Doc. 10 rev. 1 (24 April 1997) (Ecuador Report), available at www.cidh.oas.org/countryrep/ecuador-eng/chaper-9.htm (accessed 21 December 2011).

[149] *Ibid.*, chap. 8, fourth recommendation: 'Given that the American Convention requires that all individuals of the Oriente have access to effective judicial recourse to lodge claims alleging the violation of their rights under the Constitution and the American Convention, including claims concerning the right to life and to live in an environment free from contamination, the Commission recommends that the State take measures to ensure that access to justice is more fully afforded to the people of the interior.'

[150] See J. Hepburn, 'Ecuadorian plaintiffs withdraw requests for protective measures, after sparring with Chevron over need for human rights authorities to intervene', available at www.iareporter.com (accessed 14 March 2012).

[151] *Chevron Corporation and Texaco Petroleum Corporation* v. *The Republic of Ecuador*, PCA Case No. 2009–23, First Interim Award on Interim Measures (25 January 2012).

[152] See *Methanex* v. *United States of America*, above, n. 9, Decision of the Tribunal on Petitions from Third Persons to Intervene as Amici Curaie (15 January 2001); *Aguas del Tunari SA* v. *Republic of Bolivia*, ICSID Case No. ARB/02/3, Letter by Tribunal President (29 January 2003); *Suez* v. *Argentina – 03/19*, above, n. 7, Order in Response to a Petition for Transparency and Participation as Amicus Curiae (19 May 2005), Order in Response to Amicus Petition (12 February 2007); *Suez* v. *Argentina – 03/17*, above, n. 7, Order in Response to a Petition for Participation as *Amicus Curiae* (17 March 2006); *Biwater* v. *Tanzania*, above, n. 108, Petition for Amicus Curiae Status (27 November 2006);

between international environmental law and the measures challenged by the investor. A good example is the *amicus* brief submitted in *Suez* v. *Argentina*,[153] which elaborates on the link between the measures adopted by Argentina and a number of human rights treaties:

> This dispute involves measures taken by the government of Argentina, during a period of severe economic and social crisis, to protect human rights. Inter alia, Argentina's measures have been adopted in furtherance of its obligation to progressively realize its citizens' right to water, as well as to protect and promote its citizens' right to health. Those rights are protected by several human rights treaties that were in force in Argentina before the investment was established.[154]

This argument had also been made by the respondent. In the award, the tribunal acknowledged that both international investment law and the right to water were applicable but considered that these two bodies of law did not conflict with each other.[155]

The third illustration is given by a case brought against Slovakia before the Compliance Committee of the Aarhus Convention[156] in connection

Glamis v. *United States of America*, above, n. 9, Decision on Application and Submission by Quechan Indian Nation (16 September 2005), Letters to the National Mining Association, the Quechan Indian Nation, Sierra Club and Earthworks, and Friends of the Earth (15 February 2007); *Piero Foresti, Laura de Carli and others* v. *Republic of South Africa*, ICSID Case No. ARB(AF)/07/1, Letter from the Secretary of the Tribunal to the Non-Disputing Parties (5 October 2009).

[153] *Suez* v. *Argentina – 03/19*, above, n. 7, Amicus Curiae Submission, 4 April 2007 (Suez – Amicus Submission), available at www.ciel.org/Publications/SUEZ_Amicus_English_4Apr07.pdf (accessed 13 January 2012).

[154] *Ibid.*, 14. In the footnote to this paragraph, the amicus brief refers to the following instruments: 'the International Covenant on Economic, Social and Cultural Rights (ICESCR), the Additional Protocol to the American Convention on Human Rights in the Area of Economic, Social and Cultural Rights (Protocol of San Salvador or San Salvador Protocol), the Convention on the Elimination of All Forms of Discrimination against Women (Women's Convention), the Convention on the Rights of the Child (CRC), the International Covenant on Civil and Political Rights (ICCPR), and the American Convention on Human Rights (American Convention). These treaties require Argentina to protect the right to water.'

[155] The tribunal stated the following: 'Argentina [was] subject to both international obligations, i.e. human rights *and* treaty obligations, and [had to] respect both of them equally. Under the circumstances of these cases, Argentina's human rights obligations and its investment treaty obligations [were] not inconsistent, contradictory, or mutually exclusive.' See *Suez* v. *Argentina – 03/19*, above, n. 7, para. 262 (italics original). See also *Suez* v. *Argentina – 03/17*, above, n. 7, para. 240.

[156] Convention on Access to Information, Public Participation in Decision-Making and Access to Justice in Environmental Matters, 25 June 1998, 2161 UNTS 447 (Aarhus Convention)

with the insufficient participation granted to civil society in the procedure leading to the authorisation of a foreign investment scheme in the nuclear energy sector.[157] The Compliance Committee found that the legal framework of Slovakia was not consistent with the participation standards of the Convention because it was 'not sufficient to provide for public participation only at the stage of the EIA [environmental impact assessment] procedure, unless it [was] also part of the permitting procedure'.[158] On this basis, it recommended that Slovakia 'review its legal framework so as to ensure that early and effective public participation is provided'.[159] According to some environmental groups, the fact that the European Union is a party to the Aarhus Convention would have the consequence that the European Commission is required to monitor that Slovakia suspends the scheme and conducts a new environmental impact assessment.[160] Should this situation (or another similar situation) give rise to an investment dispute, it would be difficult for the arbitral tribunal to ignore the link between the domestic measure and international environmental law.

11.5.3 The contribution of adjudication mechanisms

The latter point is also important in connection with the role of adjudication mechanisms. Judicial proceedings conducted in some international forums, such as human rights courts, could help strengthen the link between international environmental law and a domestic environmental measure.

For example, in the *Yakye Axa* case,[161] the Inter-American Court of Human Rights (ICtHR) stated that the 'restriction of the right of private individuals to private property might be necessary to attain the collective objective of preserving cultural identities in a democratic and pluralist society' and added that such a restriction would be 'proportional, if fair compensation is paid to those affected pursuant

[157] *Findings and Recommendations of the Compliance Committee with regard to Communication ACCC/C/2009/41 concerning compliance by Slovakia*, 17 December 2010 (Committee Findings (Slovakia), available at www.unece.org/env/pp/pubcom.htm (accessed 13 January 2012).

[158] *Ibid.*, para. 64. [159] *Ibid.*, para. 70.

[160] See 'Mochovce Public Participation Insufficient', in *Nuclear Monitor*, n. 722, 21 January 2011, available at www.nirs.org/mononline/nm722.pdf (accessed 13 January 2012).

[161] *Indigenous Community Yakye Axa* v. *Paraguay*, ICtHR Series C No. 125 (17 June 2005).

to Article 21(2) of the Convention'.[162] Similarly, in the *Sawhoyamaxa* case,[163] the ICtHR further stated that 'The restitution of traditional lands [...] is the reparation measure that best complies with the *restitutio in integrum* principle' and directed the state to ensure that the ownership rights of indigenous communities over their ancestral lands are respected.[164] These conclusions are consistent with those of the ECtHR in *Turgut* v. *Turkey*, where the courts noted that 'economic imperatives and even some fundamental rights, such as the right to property, should not be accorded primacy against considerations of environmental protection'.[165] Were a dispossessed investor to bring an investment claim as a result of a measure taken by the host state to comply with a judgment of the ICtHR or the ECtHR, it would, again, be very difficult for the investment tribunal seized of the matter to simply ignore the link between the measure and either the ACHR or the ECHR.[166]

Assuming that an investment tribunal is willing fully to recognise the link between international environmental law and a domestic environmental measure, an important question would be whether, from a legal standpoint, the tribunal has sufficient room for manoeuvre. This question concerns both the scope of jurisdiction of investment tribunals and the law applicable to investment disputes. I have analysed these issues elsewhere.[167] The basic conclusion of that research is that there is significant room for investment tribunals to assert jurisdiction over claims with environmental components or to apply international environmental law. The direct application of international environmental law to assess the legality of the host state's conduct was considered as self-evident by the tribunal in *SPP* v. *Egypt*. The tribunal noted indeed that there was no doubt that:

[162] *Ibid.*, para. 148.

[163] *Case of Sawhoyamaxa Indigenous Community* v. *Paraguay*, ICtHR Series C No. 146 (29 March 2006).

[164] *Ibid.*, para. 210.

[165] See *Turgut – Merits*, above, n. 24, para. 90 (unofficial translation of the French text).

[166] One may object that the ICtHR and the ECtHR require the payment of fair compensation and that, therefore, this case law has no real relevance. However, this 'practical' objection would itself be too 'theoretical' if one takes into account that the amounts of compensation granted by investment tribunals are – in practice – much higher than what an investor could expect from a human rights court. See the cases referred to above, n. 12, in fine.

[167] See J. E. Viñuales, 'Foreign Investment and the Environment in International Law: An Ambiguous Relationship' (2009) 80 *British Yearbook of International Law* 244.

> the UNESCO Convention [was] relevant: the Claimants themselves acknowledged during the proceedings before the French *Cour d'Appel* that the Convention obligated the Respondent to abstain from acts or contracts contrary to the Convention.[168]

Similarly, in *S.D. Myers* v. *Canada*, the tribunal had no difficulty in envisaging the application of the Basel Convention to review the conduct of Canada, although it concluded that this treaty could not justify the measure challenged.[169] Still another example is provided by *Chemtura* v. *Canada*. Here, the question was not whether the Aarhus Protocol to the LRTAP Convention was applicable to the dispute, which the tribunal considered as self-evident, but only whether the conduct of Canada was adopted pursuant to such treaty.[170] Thus, the application of international environmental law in investment disputes is not controversial. Of course, this is not to say that an investor may use an investment treaty as the jurisdictional basis to bring a claim for breach of an environmental treaty or that a state may do so to bring an environmental counter-claim. The possibility of bringing environmental claims or counter-claims through arbitration clauses will depend on a variety of factors, including the wording of the consent base (usually an arbitration clause in a contract or a treaty), the nature of the claim (contract or treaty-based) and the clause governing the applicable substantive law (domestic and/or international).[171] But those are different questions. The main point to be stressed is that an investment tribunal may apply international environmental law to all the extent relevant for the resolution of an investment dispute.

It is therefore a change of mindset rather than a change of law that is required for the progressive approach to gain increasing acceptance. The formulation of international environmental obligations may seem excessively broad, but it would be a mistake to conclude from this that they have no impact on investment disputes. This impact is becoming increasingly significant in the use of what I have called the 'upgraded approach'. This approach can be seen as an intermediate stage between the traditional approach and a more progressive one. Whether the integration of international environmental law in investment disputes pursues one or the other approach, both avenues suggest that environmental regulation

[168] *SPP* v. *Egypt*, above, n. 7, para. 78.
[169] *S.D. Myers* v. *Canada*, above, n. 7, paras 209–15.
[170] *Chemtura* v. *Canada*, above, n. 7, paras 139–41.
[171] See Viñuales, *Foreign Investment and the Environment in International Law*, chap. 5.

is here to stay, not as an anomaly belonging to the category of political risk but as a fact of life or, in other terms, as a normal commercial risk to be taken into account by foreign investors when planning their activities.

Select bibliography

Abouchar, J., 'Environmental Laws as Expropriation under NAFTA' (1999) 8 *Review of European Community and International Environmental Law* 209.

Bodansky, D., 'What's so Bad about Unilateral Action to Protect the Environment?' (2000) 11 *European Journal of International Law* 339.

Charnovitz, S., 'The Law of Environmental "PPMs" in the WTO: Debunking the Myth of Illegality' (2002) 27 *Yale Journal of International Law* 59.

Cordonnier Segger, M.-C., M. W. Gehring and A. Newcombe (eds.), *Sustainable Development in World Investment Law* (The Hague: Kluwer, 2011).

Cotula, L., 'Reconciling Regulatory Stability and Evolution of Environmental Standards in Investment Contracts: Towards a Rethink of Stabilization Clauses' (2008) 1 *Journal of World Energy Law and Business* 158.

Dupuy, P.-M., F. Francioni and E.-U. Petersmann (eds.), *Human Rights in International Investment Law and Arbitration* (Oxford University Press, 2009).

Fauchald, O. K., 'International Investment Law and Environmental Protection' (2006) 17 *Yearbook of International Environmental Law* 3.

Firger, D. M., and M. B. Gerrard, 'Harmonizing Climate Change Policy and International Investment Law' (2010–11) 3 *Yearbook of International Investment Law and Policy* 517.

Footer, M. E., 'BITs and Pieces: Social and Environmental Protection in the Regulation of Foreign Investment' (2009) 18 *Michigan State Journal of International Law* 33.

Gaines, S., 'The Masked Ball of NAFTA Chapter 11: Foreign Investors, Local Environmentalists, Government Officials, and Disguised Motives', in J. Kirton and V. MacLaren (eds.), *Linking Trade, Environment, and Social Cohesion: NAFTA Experiences, Global Challenges* (Aldershot: Ashgate, 2002), pp. 103–29.

Gordon, K., and J. Pohl, 'Environmental Concerns in International Investment Agreements: A Survey', *OECD Working Papers on International Investment* 2011/1 (2011).

Gowlland Gualtieri, A., 'The Environmental Accountability of the World Bank to Non-State Actors: Insights from the Inspection Panel' (2001) 72 *British Yearbook of International Law* 213.

Grisel, F., and J. E. Viñuales, 'L'*amicus curiae* dans l'arbitrage d'investissement' (2007) 22 *ICSID Review – Foreign Investment Law Journal* 380.

Howse, R., and D. Regan, 'The Product/Process Distinction – An Illusory Basis for Disciplining "Unilateralism" in Trade Policy' (2000) 11 *European Journal of International Law* 249.

Intergovernmental Panel on Climate Change (IPCC), *Climate Change 2007: Mitigation of Climate Change. Contribution of Working Group III to the Fourth Assessment Report* (2007).

McLachlan, C., 'The Principle of Systemic Integration and Article 31 3(c) of the Vienna Convention' (2005) 54 *International and Comparative Law Quarterly* 279.

Miles, K., 'Arbitrating Climate Change: Regulatory Regimes and Investor-State Disputes' (2010) 1 *Climate Law* 63.

Multilateral Investment Guarantee Agency, *World Investment and Political Risk* (Washington, DC: World Bank, 2011).

Nikken, P., 'Balancing of Human Rights and Investment Law in the Inter-American System of Human Rights', in P.-M. Dupuy, F. Francioni and E.-U. Petersmann (eds.), *Human Rights in International Investment Law and Arbitration* (Oxford University Press, 2009), pp. 246–71.

Pavoni, R., 'Mutual Supportiveness as a Principle of Interpretation and Law-Making: A Watershed for the "WTO-and-Competing-Regimes" Debate?' (2010) 21 *European Journal of International Law* 649.

Potts, J., *The Legality of PPMs under the GATT: Challenges and Opportunities for Sustainable Trade Policy* (Winnipeg: International Institute for Sustainable Development, 2008), pp. 9–27.

Richardson, B. J., 'Financing Sustainability: The New Transnational Governance of Socially Responsible Investment' (2006) 17 *Yearbook of International Environmental Law* 73.

Socially Responsible Investment Law: Regulating the Unseen Polluters (Oxford University Press, 2008).

Robert-Cuendet, S., *Droits de l'investisseur étranger et protection de l'environnement: contribution à l'analyse de l'expropriation indirecte* (Leiden: Martinus Nijhoff, 2010).

Schrijver, N., 'The Evolution of Sustainable Development in International Law: Inception, Meaning and Status', in *Recueil des cours de l'Académie de droit international*, vol. 329 (2008), pp. 217–412.

Shemberg, A., *Stabilization Clauses and Human Rights: A Research Project Conducted for IFC and the United Nations Special Representative to the Secretary General on Business and Human Rights* (11 March 2008).

Shihata, I., 'Implementation, Enforcement and Compliance with International Environmental Agreements – Practical Suggestions in Light of the World Bank's Experience (1996–97)' 9 *Georgetown International Environmental Law Review* 37.

Spears, S. A., 'The Quest for Policy Space in a New Generation of International Investment Agreements' (13)4 *Journal of International Dispute Settlement* 1037.

Tienhaara, K., 'Unilateral Commitments to Investment Protection: Does the Promise of Stability Restrict Environmental Policy Development?' (2006) 17 *Yearbook of International Environmental Law* 139.

United Nations Environment Programme, *Towards a Green Economy: Pathways to Sustainable Development and Poverty Eradication* (2011); www.unep.org/greeneconomy.

Viñuales, J. E., 'The Contribution of the International Court of Justice to the Development of International Environmental Law: A Contemporary Assessment' (2008) 32 *Fordham International Law Journal* 232.

'Foreign Investment and the Environment in International Law: An Ambiguous Relationship' (2009) 80 *British Yearbook of International Law* 244.

Foreign Investment and the Environment in International Law (Cambridge University Press, 2012).

Wälde, T., and A. Kolo, 'Environmental Regulation, Investment Protection and "Regulatory Taking" in International Law' (2001) 50 *International and Comparative Law Quarterly* 811.

Wälde, T., and G. N'Di, 'Stabilising International Investment Commitments' (1996) 31 *Texas International Law Journal* 215.

Zleptnig, S., *Non-Economic Objectives in WTO Law* (The Hague: Kluwer, 2010).

12

From corporate social responsibility to accountability mechanisms

ELISA MORGERA

INTRODUCTION

The international community has debated the need for international regulation and oversight of multinational companies for almost forty years.[1] While states have hitherto resisted the creation of an international legally binding instrument on the matter, voluntary[2] and soft law[3] international instruments and initiatives of intergovernmental and multi-stakeholder origin have proliferated to support and encourage an environmentally sound conduct of multinational and other companies. This chapter seeks to trace the evolution of such international practice with a view to highlighting a progressive shift from purely voluntary approaches (corporate social responsibility or CSR[4]) towards accountability mechanisms. To this end, the chapter will first briefly discuss the

[1] Early attempts were undertaken in the context of the UN Economic and Social Council that adopted a resolution in 1972 acknowledging the lack of an international regulatory framework for multinational corporations and the need to institutionalise international debate on that issue: ECOSOC Res. 1721 (LIII) 28 July 1972.

[2] This is notably the case of international public–private partnerships, which were endorsed as an official outcome of the World Summit on Sustainable Development in 2002. See C. Streck, 'The World Summit on Sustainable Development: Partnerships as the New Tool in Environmental Governance' (2003) 13 *Yearbook of International Environmental Law* 21; E. Morgera, *Corporate Accountability in International Environmental Law* (Oxford University Press, 2009), chap. 12; B. Richardson's contribution in this volume.

[3] This is the case of international standards on corporate environmental accountability elaborated in the context of international organisations, which will be discussed in detail in section 12.2, below.

[4] CSR is the label used to group efforts and initiatives that are purposely voluntary in their approach to sustainable corporate conduct. Even voluntary initiatives may have, however, legal implications or relevance. See D. McBarnet, A. Voiculescu and T. Campbell (eds.), *The New Corporate Accountability: Corporate Social Responsibility and the Law* (Cambridge University Press, 2007).

increasing convergence in the definition of international environmental standards for corporate accountability within a variety of international organisations and processes (12.1).[5] It will then focus on the most recent discussion on human rights and corporate accountability, with a view to determining whether environmental protection concerns are adequately taken into account (12.2). Attention will then concentrate on the growing number of international oversight and dispute avoidance mechanisms that provide a readily available and impartial avenue for addressing individuals', communities' and civil society groups' complaints against private companies and the possibility for international entities to operate on the ground for fact-finding and/or mediation purposes (12.3).

In concluding, this contribution aims to bring to light an understudied aspect of the proliferation of relevant international initiatives. An argument will be put forward that the risk of fragmentation of international guidance on corporate accountability due to the multiplicity of different international accountability processes now in existence is significantly mitigated by the convergence of the standards used to guide and assess private companies' conduct. Previous research of mine had indicated that international standard-setting initiatives were increasingly characterised by a significant degree of convergence.[6] In the early 2010s, this trend – as discussed in this contribution – has nothing but accelerated. The complementary finding of the present study is that the outcomes of international monitoring activities, which are equally carried out by a plethora of different international actors, also show increasing signs of convergence. Notably, the environmental standards elaborated within the framework of the Convention on Biological Diversity, in particular environmental–cultural impact assessments and benefit-sharing, are referred to in the decisions of different international corporate accountability mechanisms. This is a significant contribution to ensuring substantive unity[7] across different areas of international law, notably on the environment and on human rights, which may be negatively affected by the conduct of private operators (12.4).

[5] A more extensive treatment of this subject can be found in Morgera, *Corporate Accountability in International Environmental Law*, above, n. 2, chaps 4–8.

[6] *Ibid.*

[7] P.-M. Dupuy, *L'Unité de l'ordre juridique international* (The Hague: Martinus Nijhoff, 2003).

12.1 From corporate social responsibility to corporate accountability through converging environmental standards

The term 'corporate accountability' was endorsed by the international community at the 2002 World Summit on Sustainable Development (WSSD),[8] and can be understood as the legitimate expectation that reasonable efforts will be put in place, according to international standards, by private companies and foreign investors for the protection of a certain global interest or the attainment of a certain internationally agreed environmental objective.[9] The expectations and relevant international standards that make up corporate accountability in international environmental law have been gradually spelt out through various international processes, some of which pre-dated or ran in parallel with the WSSD. These processes are characterised by different approaches (regulation versus collaboration), nature (intergovernmental versus multi-stakeholder) and legal status (hard versus soft law). Nonetheless, upon closer inspection, they all build upon the same international standards for corporate environmental accountability.

These instruments include the ill-fated UN draft Code of Conduct for Transnational Corporations,[10] whose negotiations collapsed in the early 1990s,[11] and the UN Norms on the Responsibilities of Transnational Corporations and Other Business Enterprises with regards to Human Rights,[12] which were adopted by the UN Sub-Commission on the Promotion and Protection of Human Rights[13] (a body comprising independent human rights experts acting in their personal capacity) but not by the former UN Commission on Human Rights.[14] The UN Norms thus

[8] Paragraph 49 of the WSSD Plan of Implementation, UN Doc. A/CONF.199/20, Resolution 2, Annex, 4 September 2002.

[9] Morgera, *Corporate Accountability in International Environmental Law*, chap. 2.

[10] The Draft Code of Conduct on Transnational Corporations, UN Doc. E/1990/94, 12 June 1990 (UN Draft Code).

[11] W. Sprote, 'Negotiations on a United Nations Code of Conduct on Transnational Corporations' (1990) 33 *German Yearbook of International Law* 339.

[12] Commentary to the Norms on the Responsibilities of Transnational Corporations and other Business Enterprises with Regards to Human Rights, UN Doc. E/CN.4/Sub.2/2003/12/Rev. 2, 26 August 2003 (Commentary UN Norms).

[13] See 'Norms on the Responsibilities of Transnational Corporations and other Business Enterprises with Regard to Human Rights' (UN Doc. E/CN.4/Sub.2/2003/12/Rev.2, 26 August 2003).

[14] The Commission did not adopt, but only 'took note' of the 'Norms', stating that they had 'not been requested by the Commission and, as a draft proposal, had no legal standing, and that the Sub-Commission should not perform any monitoring function in this

reached a level of expert legitimacy, but no political legitimisation.[15] Relevant instruments also include the intergovernmentally approved OECD Guidelines for Multinational Corporations,[16] the partnership-focused principles of the UN Global Compact[17] (an initiative of the UN Secretary General with support from various UN bodies)[18] and the Policy and Performance Standards on Social and Environmental Sustainability of the IFC.[19] The last in particular includes environmental standards clearly identifying the responsibility of the private sector on the basis of international environmental agreements,[20] and has been widely followed by regional development banks as well as major commercial banks.[21]

regard'. Commission's decision 2004/116: The Responsibilities of Transnational Corporations and Related Business Enterprises with Regard to Human Rights (UN Doc. E/CN.4/DEC/2004/116, 20 April 2004), para. C.

15 See Simon Walker's contribution in United Nations Research Institute for Social Development, 'Corporate Social Responsibility and Development: Towards a New Agenda'. Summaries of Presentations Made at the UNRISD Conference (Geneva, 17–18 November 2003), 85.

16 OECD, *The OECD Guidelines for Multinational Enterprises* (OECD, 2011) (*OECD Guidelines*).

17 The website of the Global Compact can be found at www.unglobalcompact.org (accessed 14 March 2012). See also United Nations Guide to the Global Compact: A Practical Understanding of the Vision and the Nine Principles, 58, available at www.unglobalcompact.org.

18 In time, the Global Compact received an intergovernmental endorsement through General Assembly resolutions 62/211 'Towards Global Partnership' (2007), para. 9 and 64/223 'Towards Global Partnership' (2009), para. 13. The question of the intergovernmentally agreed mandate of the Global Compact remains open, however. See the Joint Inspection Unit, United Nations Corporate Partnerships: The Role and Functioning of the Global Compact, UN Doc. JIU/REP/2010/9 (2010), paras 13–18 and recommendation 1; and 'A Response from the Global Compact Office', 24 March 2011, 2.

19 IFC, Performance Standard on Social and Environmental Sustainability, adopted by the IFC Board on 21 February 2006 (2006 IFC Performance Standard). A revised version was adopted in 2011 and is discussed below: 2012 IFC Performance Standard, available at www.ifc.org (accessed 14 March 2012). See IFC press release, 'IFC Updates Environmental and Social Standards, Strengthening Commitment to Sustainability and Transparency', 12 May 2011.

20 For a more in-depth discussion, see Morgera, *Corporate Accountability in International Environmental Law*, chap. 7. Note that the IFC provides both direct and indirect investments: in the latter case, the performance standards apply to financial intermediaries rather than to private companies carrying out projects in developing countries. See B. J. Richardson, 'Financing Sustainability: The New Transnational Governance of Socially Responsible Investment' (2008) 17 *Yearbook of International Environmental Law* 73.

21 D. Ong, 'From "International" to "Transnational" Environmental Law? A Legal Assessment of the Contribution of the "Equator Principles" to International Environmental Law' (2010) 79 *Nordic Journal of International Law* 35; C. Wright, 'Setting Standards for

A series of common standards have emerged from these initiatives that appear to have reached a significant level of detail and acceptance at the international level as directly applicable to private companies. They include the environmental impact self-assessment, namely the ongoing assessment, beyond legal requirements at the national level, of the possible environmental impacts of private companies' activities before and during their operations, on the basis of scientific evidence, as well as communication with likely-to-be-affected communities.[22] On the basis of such continuous assessment, private companies are further to elaborate environmental management systems (EMSs) to assist in controlling direct and indirect impacts on the environment and possibly continually to improve their environmental performance.[23] In accordance with their environmental impact assessments and management systems, private companies are further expected to take reasonably active steps, including the suspension of certain activities, to prevent or minimise an environmental damage, particularly in case of likely transboundary environmental harm or environmental harm with serious human rights consequences.[24] In addition, in the face of scientific uncertainty, private companies are further expected to undertake precautionary action by taking the most cost-effective early action to prevent the occurrence of environmental harm, or by avoiding delays in minimising such harm.[25] Disclosure of public information,[26] direct consultations with

Responsible Banking: Examining the Role of the International Finance Corporation in the Emergence of the Equator Principles', in F. Biermann, B. Siebenhüner and A. Schreyrögg (eds.), *International Organisations in Global Environmental Governance* (Abingdon: Routledge, 2009), 51–70.

[22] Commentary UN Norms, above, n. 12 (b) and (c); *OECD Guidelines*, above, n. 16, chap. 6, para. 3; 2006 IFC Performance Standard, above, n. 19, paras 4–6 (cf. 2012 IFC Performance Standard 1, above, n. 19, paras 5–7).

[23] *OECD Guidelines*, above, n. 16, chap. 6, para. 1 and Commentary, para. 60; Commentary UN Norms, above, n. 12, sect. (g); 2006 IFC Performance Standard, above, n. 19, paras 16 and 23 (cf. 2012 IFC Performance Standard 1, above, n. 19, paras 17 and 24).

[24] *OECD Guidelines*, above, n. 16, chap. 6, para. 5; 2006 IFC Performance Standard 3, above, n. 19 (cf. 2012 IFC Performance Standard 3); implicitly, Principle 10 of the Global Compact (Guide to the Global Compact, above, n. 17, p. 64); Commentary UN Norms, above, n. 12 (e)–(g).

[25] The Global Compact, Principle 7 and Guide to the Global Compact, above, n. 17, p. 54; *OECD Guidelines*, above, n. 16, chap. 6, para. 4; UN Norms, above, n. 13, sect. G.

[26] UN Draft Code, above, n. 10, para. 42; Guide to the Global Compact, above, n. 17, p. 58; UN Norms, above, n. 13 (b) and (c); 2006 IFC Performance Standard 3, above, n. 19, para. 19 (cf. 2012 IFC Performance Standard 1, above, n. 19, para. 29); *OECD Guidelines*, above, n. 16, chap. 6, para. 2.

the public[27] and the creation of a review or appeal process for communities to express their complaints[28] are complementary and mutually reinforcing procedural standards. What has been more difficult to determine is a substantive standard for corporate environmental accountability: only the IFC Standards attempted to identify such a standard as the sustainable natural resource management[29] and respect for internationally protected sites.[30]

12.2 Increased convergence in 2011 reviews

Such convergence on international standard-setting became even more visible in 2011, when both the OECD Guidelines and the IFC Standards were revised in order, inter alia, to take into account the development of the UN Framework on Business and Human Rights (discussed below). The review brought about further convergence in the procedural standards for corporate environmental accountability and new developments in terms of substantive standards, in particular linked to biodiversity and climate change.

On the procedural side, the 2011 review of the OECD Guidelines stressed stakeholder engagement as an interactive and two-way process based on good faith for the planning and decision-making concerning projects or activities 'that may significantly impact local communities', such as those involving the intensive use of land and water, as well as disclosure of climate change and biodiversity-specific information.[31] In addition, it included references to due diligence, reflecting the key

27 Guide to the Global Compact, above, n. 17, p. 58; *OECD Guidelines*, above, n. 16, chap. 6, para. 2; 2006 IFC Performance Standard 3, above, n. 19, paras 19 and 23 (cf. 2012 IFC Performance Standard 1, paras 30–3); 6, paras 12; 7, objectives and para. 9; and 8, para. 6, all above, n. 19.

28 2006 IFC Performance Standard 3, above, n. 19, paras 16 and 23 (cf. 2012 IFC Performance Standard 1, above, n. 19, para. 35).

29 2006 IFC Performance Standard 1, above, n. 19, n. 7 made reference to 'sustainable resource management' as 'the use, development and protection of resources in a way or at a rate that enables people and communities to provide for their present social, economic and cultural well-being while also sustaining the potential of those resources to meet the reasonably foreseeable needs of future generations' (cf. 2012 IFC Performance Standard 6, above, n. 19).

30 2006 IFC Performance Standard 6, above, n. 19. For a more detailed discussion on these substantive standards, see Morgera, *Corporate Accountability in International Environmental Law*, chap. 8.

31 OECD Council, 'OECD Guidelines for Multinational Enterprises: Update 2011 – Note by the Secretary-General', OECD Doc. C (2011) 59 (3 May 2011), Appendix II, para. II. A.14;

concept underpinning the UN Framework on Business and Human Rights. These recent revisions, however, have been criticised by civil society for their lack of explicit reference to prior informed consent in the consultations with indigenous peoples, lack of indications on what constitutes an adequate impact assessment process, the lack of a requirement for environmental disclosure and lack of consideration for cumulative environmental impacts.[32]

The concomitant 2011 review of the policy and performance standards of the IFC went along similar lines, being equally influenced by the UN Framework on Business and Human Rights.[33] As opposed to the OECD Guidelines review, however, the IFC significantly strengthened its approach to community consultations, linking the need for companies to conduct 'informed consultation' with a specific and express (albeit qualified) requirement for prior informed consent. IFC clients are thus to 'consider' involving representatives of affected communities in monitoring the effectiveness of their environmental management programmes only 'where appropriate',[34] thus leaving a considerable margin of discretion to individual business entities. This is coupled with the creation of an 'external communications system' that will allow IFC clients to screen, assess and reply to communications from stakeholders with a view to continually improving their management system. The system is in turn subject to the requirement for a 'stakeholder engagement framework' in the case that the exact location of the project is unknown but the project is nonetheless reasonably expected to have significant impacts on local communities. More detailed indications regarding dissemination of information are provided when communities may be affected by risks

OECD Council, 'OECD Guidelines for Multinational Enterprises: Update 2011 - Commentaries', OECD Doc. C (2011) 59/ADD1, 3 May 2011, paras 25 and 33.

32 OECDWatch statement on the update of the OECD Guidelines for Multinational Enterprises: Improved Content and Scope, but Procedural Shortcomings Remain (25 May 2011); and Amnesty International, 'The 2010–11 Update of the OECD Guidelines for Multinational Enterprises has come to an end: the OECD must now turn into effective implementation' (23 May 2011).

33 Note that the UN Special Representative on Business and Human Rights that elaborated the UN Framework participated in both reviews: Report of the Special Representative of the Secretary-General on the Issue of Human Rights and Transnational Corporations and other Business Enterprises: Further Steps Toward the Operationalization of the 'Protect, Respect and Remedy' Framework (2010) UN Doc. A/HRC/14/27 (Report Operationalisation), para. 13.

34 2012 IFC Performance Standard 1, 'Assessment and Management of Social and Environmental Risks and Impacts', above, n. 19, para. 21.

of adverse impacts of the project. This is coupled with the significant specification that when stakeholder consultations are the responsibility of the host government the client is expected to conduct a complementary process if the government-led engagement does not meet the policy and performance standards of the IFC.[35]

Prior informed consent specifically needs to be obtained from IFC clients in three cases: potential relocation of indigenous peoples, impacts on lands and natural resources subject to traditional ownership or under customary use and projects proposing to use cultural resources for commercial purposes.[36] The IFC has also engaged in 'translating' the concept of prior informed consent for private companies: according to the performance standard on indigenous peoples, prior informed consent entails a good-faith negotiation with culturally appropriate institutions representing indigenous peoples' communities, with a view to reaching an agreement that is seen as legitimate by the majority within the community.[37] In addition, private companies are called upon to put in place mitigation measures, such as compensation and benefit-sharing, taking into account indigenous peoples' laws, institutions and customs, and to ensure that distribution of benefits be individually or collectively based or a combination of both. Benefits may include, according to the preferences of indigenous peoples, culturally appropriate improvement of their standard of living and livelihoods and the long-term sustainability of the natural resources on which they depend.[38] Benefit-sharing is further

[35] *Ibid.*, paras 26 and 30–1 and 38. Information to be disseminated to affected communities include: purpose, nature and scale of the project; duration of proposed project activities; risks and potential impacts on communities and relevant elements of the management programme; envisaged stakeholder engagement process; and grievance and redress mechanism.

[36] *Ibid.*, para. 35, where it is explicitly mentioned that 'consent does not necessarily require unanimity and may be achieved even when individuals and sub-groups explicitly disagree'. Compare with the understanding of prior informed consent proposed by the UN Special Rapporteur on indigenous peoples' rights (discussed below), who clarified that prior informed consent does not provide indigenous people with a veto power when the state acts legitimately and faithfully in the public interest, but rather 'establishes the need to frame consultation procedures in order to make every effort to build consensus on the part of all concerned' and that consensus-driven consultation processes should not only address measures to mitigate or compensate for adverse impacts of projects, but also explore and arrive at means of equitable benefit-sharing in a spirit of true partnership (Report of the Special Rapporteur on the Situation of Human Rights and Fundamental Freedoms of Indigenous People, UN Doc. A/HRC/12/34 (2009), paras 48 and 53).

[37] 2012 IFC Performance Standard 7: Indigenous Peoples, above, n. 19, para. 15.

[38] *Ibid.*, paras 12–13.

envisaged where the business entity 'intends to utilise natural resources that are central to the identity and livelihoods of indigenous peoples and their use exacerbates livelihood risk'.[39] With specific regard to involuntary resettlement, IFC clients are expected, according to one of the 2011 amendments, to implement measures to ensure, for communities with natural-resource-based livelihoods, the continued access to affected resources or alternative resources with equivalent livelihood-earning potential and accessibility. In return, IFC clients are to provide compensation and benefits associated with the natural resource use that 'may be collective in nature rather than directly oriented towards individuals and households', taking into account the ecological context.[40] Significantly, the 2011 IFC review relied on the legal concept of benefit-sharing, as a key link between prior informed consent and due diligence.[41]

Notably, the 2011 reviews also expanded on substantive standards of corporate environmental accountability. The 2011 review of the OECD Guidelines addressed a new recommendation on 'exploring and assessing ways to improve environmental performance' with reference to emissions reduction, efficient resource use, the management of toxic substances and the conservation of biodiversity.[42] Regrettably, this significant addition is not addressed in the commentary to the Guidelines. The concomitant 2011 review of the IFC Performance Standards focused more extensively on climate change, resource efficiency and biodiversity. The IFC Policy on Social and Environmental Sustainability, which targets the IFC itself, acknowledged the need to support the private sector's contribution to climate change mitigation and adaptation, building the capacity of the private sector in relation to climate change, biodiversity and resource efficiency, as well as to limit its impacts on ecosystem services,[43] and to reflect a human rights due

[39] *Ibid.*, para. 18.

[40] 2012 IFC Performance Standard 5: Land Acquisition and Involuntary Resettlement, above, n. 19, para. 26.

[41] In the previous version of the IFC Performance Standard the concept of benefit-sharing was only relied upon in the context of cultural heritage: 2006 IFC Performance Standard 8, above, n. 19.

[42] OECD Council, 'OECD Guidelines Update 2011 – Note by the Secretary-General', Appendix II, para. II.A.10 and *OECD Guidelines*, above, n. 16, chap. 6, para. 6(d).

[43] Which are defined at para. 2 of 2012 IFC Performance Standard 6, above, n. 19, 'Biodiversity Conservation and Sustainable Management of Living Natural Resources', as the 'benefits that people, including businesses, derive from ecosystem services' (emphasis added). The definition is clearly based on the Millennium Ecosystem Assessment, a global scientific process that facilitated intergovernmental endorsement of the

diligence approach across its sustainability principles.[44] In the Performance Standards addressed to private companies, the IFC then introduced very detailed standards on climate change, including that the client implements 'technical and financially feasible and cost-effective options to reduce project-related greenhouse gas emissions during the design and operation of the project', as well as more specific obligations in case of projects expected or actually producing more than 25,000 tonnes of CO_2 equivalent annually.[45] Resource efficiency also includes specific standards to reduce potentially significant water consumption and waste reduction, including checking whether contractors for the disposal of hazardous waste are reputable and legitimately licensed and their sites are operated in a manner consistent with acceptable standards. IFC clients are also to consider whether they should develop their own recovery or disposal facilities at the project site. They are further subject to the prohibition to purchase, store, manufacture, use or trade in products classified as extremely hazardous or highly hazardous by the World Health Organization.[46]

On biodiversity, the IFC Standards concerning natural habitats have been strengthened by making reference to establishing stakeholders' views on the extent of conversion or degradation and the identification and protection of 'set-aside areas'. The latter are excluded from development and targeted for conservation enhancement measures, which should be identified by their 'high conservation value' based on internationally recognised guidelines.[47] A new section on the management of ecosystem services has also been added, which calls upon the business entity to determine likely adverse impacts on ecosystem services, and systematically identify priority ecosystem services (either those having adverse impacts on affected communities or those on which the project will be directly dependent for its operations) with stakeholder participation. These are aimed to avoid negative impacts, or minimise

term 'ecosystem services': The Millennium Ecosystem Assessment, Ecosystems and Human Well-Being: Synthesis (2005), available at www.maweb.org (accessed 14 March 2012). For a discussion of legal implications, see E. Morgera, 'The 2005 UN World Summit and the Environment: The Proverbial Half-Full Glass' (2006) 15 *Italian Yearbook of International Law* 53.

44 2012 IFC Policy on Social and Environmental Sustainability, paras 10–11 and 15. Available at www.ifc.org (accessed 14 March 2012).

45 2012 IFC Performance Standard 3: Resource Efficiency and Pollution Prevention, above, n. 19, paras 7–8.

46 *Ibid.*, paras 9, 12 and 17.

47 2012 IFC Standard 6, above, n. 19, para. 14 and n. 10.

them and implement measures to increase the operations' resource efficiency.[48] Furthermore, additional requirements have been put in place for clients engaged in primary production of living natural resources (including forestry, agriculture, animal husbandry, fisheries and aquaculture), particularly in the absence of appropriate and applicable global, regional or national standards. These additional requirements include: committing to applying international industry operating principles and good management practices and available technology; actively engaging and supporting the development of national standards, for the definition and demonstration of sustainable practices; and (as was the case in the previous version of the Standards) committing to achieving certification.[49] Finally, private companies are also expected to prefer suppliers that can demonstrate that they are not significantly impacting on natural or critical habitats.[50]

The 2011 review of two of the most influential international sets of corporate environmental accountability standards has therefore led to a sophistication of the pre-existing procedural standards, bringing them into line with parallel developments related to business and human rights, and provided unprecedented guidance on substantive standards related to climate change, biodiversity and resource efficiency.

12.3 Business and human rights: what role for corporate environmental accountability standards?

Interestingly, little of the impressive normative convergence achieved by the mid-2000s on corporate *environmental* accountability had been used explicitly in the UN Framework on Business and Human Rights – the framework elaborated by the UN Special Representative on Business and Human Rights, John Ruggie, appointed by the UN Secretary-General to continue discussions on corporate accountability in the absence of state endorsement of the UN Norms.[51] It could rather be argued that the 2011 reviews of the OECD Guidelines and the Policy and Performance Standards of the IFC filled a gap concerning environmental accountability in the UN Framework.

[48] *Ibid.*, paras 24–5. [49] *Ibid.*, paras 26 and 29–30. [50] *Ibid.*, para. 31.

[51] UNCHR Res 2005/69 (20 April 2005), which proposed that the Special Representative: (i) identify and clarify standards of corporate responsibility and accountability for MNCs and other business; (ii) elaborate on the role of states in effectively regulating and adjudicating on the role of MNCs, including through international cooperation; (iii) develop methodologies for human rights impact assessment of activities of MNCs and other business; and (iv) compile a compendium of best practices of states, MNCs and other businesses.

The UN Framework emerged from the rejection of the idea that there are direct legal obligations arising of international law for companies, and from the support for international standards that are in 'the process of being socially constructed'[52] in the face of the 'fluid' applicability of international legal principles to companies' acts.[53] The Special Representative thus pointed to 'standards' governing corporate 'responsibility' – understood as the legal, social or moral obligations imposed on companies – and on corporate 'accountability' – understood as the mechanisms to hold companies to their obligations.[54] Ruggie did so on the understanding that corporations are under growing scrutiny by international human rights mechanisms and have been the object of the standard-setting, and accountability mechanisms created by international organisations, in light of 'social expectations by States and other actors'.[55] Such practice was considered by the Special Representative as 'blurring the lines between [what is] strictly voluntary, and mandatory' and recognising the need to 'exercise shared responsibility'.[56] As a result, the Representative put forward a Framework built on three pillars ('Protect, Respect and Remedy'), namely: the state duty to protect against human rights abuses by business; the corporate responsibility to respect human rights; and the need for greater access to effective remedies. Notably, the second pillar consists of the prevailing societal expectation that companies 'do no harm' and exercise 'due diligence'[57] – the same language that could already be found in the 2006 Policy and Performance standards of the IFC.[58]

[52] UNCHR, 'Interim Report of the Special Representative of the Secretary-General on the Issue of Human Rights and Transnational Corporations and other Business Enterprises', UN Doc. E/CN.4/2006/97 (2006), para. 55.

[53] *Ibid.*, para. 64.

[54] 'Report of the Special Representative of the Secretary-General on the Issue of Human Rights and Transnational Corporations and other Business Enterprises: Mapping International Standards of Responsibility and Accountability for Corporate Acts', UN Doc. A/HRC/4/35 (2007), para. 6.

[55] *Ibid.*, paras 44–6. [56] *Ibid.*, paras 61–2.

[57] HRC, 'Report of the Special Representative of the Secretary-General on the Issue of Human Rights and Transnational Corporations and other Business Enterprises: Protect, Respect and Remedy. A Framework for Business and Human Rights', UN Doc. A/HRC/8/5 (2008) (Report – Protect, Respect and Remedy), paras 25 and 58. Due diligence in the context of business and human rights is indeed defined as the 'process whereby companies not only ensure compliance with national laws but also manage the risk of human rights harm with a view to avoiding it', based on reasonable expectations (para. 25).

[58] For an earlier, more detailed assessment, see Morgera, *Corporate Accountability in International Environmental Law*, above, n. 2, 98–101.

The Special Representative stressed the importance for the Framework of international policy coherence,[59] with specific regard to 'prevailing social norms ... that have acquired near-universal recognition by all stakeholders.'[60] There was, however, no attempt to seek or acknowledge synergies between the UN Framework and relevant widely ratified international environmental agreements in the specific case of natural resource exploitation[61] – an area in which serious corporate abuses of human rights have been documented. Nonetheless, the Special Representative developed the procedural aspect of the human rights due diligence process on concepts and approaches[62] that have been developed and experimented in the environmental sphere, notably: (i) impact assessment; (ii) stakeholder involvement in decision-making; and (iii) life-cycle management.[63]

The 2011 Guiding Principles to implement the UN Framework clarify that there is a 'global standard of expected conduct for all business enterprises wherever they operate', that exists independently of states' abilities and willingness to fulfil their human rights obligations. Such global standard operates 'over and above compliance with national laws and regulations protecting human rights', basically requiring business entities to take adequate measures to prevent, mitigate and remediate adverse human rights impacts.[64] The Guidelines further clarify that the

[59] Report Operationalisation, above, n. 33, para. 52. [60] *Ibid.*, para. 13.

[61] The UN Representative indicated that the scope of corporate responsibility to respect human rights is defined by the actual and potential human rights impacts generated by business, which can be identified on the basis of an authoritative list of international recognised rights, including the 'International Bill of Rights', conventions of the International Labour Organization (ILO) and, depending on circumstances, also human rights instruments concerning specifically indigenous peoples and other vulnerable groups: Report of the Special Representative of the Secretary-General on the Issue of Human Rights and Transnational Corporations and other Business Enterprises, 'Business and Human Rights: Towards Operationalising the "Protect, Respect and Remedy" Framework', UN Doc. A/HRC/11/13 (2009), 15.

[62] *Ibid.*, 14.

[63] E. Morgera, Expert Report on Corporate Responsibility to Respect Human Rights in the Environmental Sphere, European Commission-funded Project, 'Study of the Legal Framework on Human Rights and the Environment Applicable to European Enterprises Operating Outside the European Union', May 2010, 12. The report is available at www.law.ed.ac.uk (accessed 14 March 2012).

[64] UN Special Representative on Human Rights and Business Enterprises, 'Guiding Principles on Business and Human Rights to Implement the UN Protect, Respect and Remedy Framework', UN Doc. A/HRC/17/31 (2011), para. 11 (the Guiding Principles were endorsed by the Human Rights Council by Resolution A/HRC/17/4 (2011)). See also Office of the UN High Commissioner on Human Rights press release, 'New Guiding

human rights due diligence process entails: (i) assessing actual and potential impacts with 'meaningful consultations' with potentially affected groups and other stakeholders at regular intervals; (ii) integrating the assessment findings in internal decision-making budget allocation and oversight processes; (iii) acting upon those findings; (iv) tracking responses (including by drawing on feedback from affected stakeholders); and (v) communicating how impacts are addressed to rights-holders in a manner that is sufficient for stakeholders to evaluate the adequacy of the company's response.[65] Companies are expected to prioritise the prevention and mitigation of most severe impacts or those that a delayed response would make irremediable.[66] Finally, enterprises 'should establish or participate in' legitimate, transparent, predictable, equitable and right-compatible grievance mechanisms that are directly accessible to individuals and communities that may directly be affected by their business operations, with a view both to supporting the identification of adverse impacts and systematic problems and remedying adverse impacts.[67] The Guiding Principles, therefore, continue the self-referential trend of the UN Framework, with no specific reference to the relevance of multilateral environmental agreements. No reference was made to specific rights of indigenous peoples either, which could have provided a bridge between human rights and environmental protection discourses.

This mismatch between the work of the UN Special Representative and international initiatives contributing to defining corporate environmental accountability standards has been recently picked up by the UN Rapporteur on indigenous peoples' rights, James Anaya, who started addressing corporate environmental accountability issues in 2009.[68] Anaya noted that private companies engaging in or promoting extractive or other development activities affecting indigenous peoples should themselves 'as a matter of company policy' endeavour to conform their behaviour at all times to relevant international norms concerning the rights of indigenous peoples, including those norms related to consultation. To this end, he recommended that companies identify, fully incorporate and make operative the norms concerning the rights of indigenous peoples within every aspect of their work carried out within

Principles on Business and Human Rights Endorsed by the UN Human Rights Council', 16 June 2011.

65 Guiding Principles, above, n. 64, paras 17–21. 66 *Ibid.*, para. 24.

67 *Ibid.*, paras 29 and 31. 68 A/HRC/12/34, above, n. 36, sect. E.

or in close proximity to indigenous lands. In addition, as part of their due diligence, companies should avoid endorsing or contributing to any act or omission on the part of the state amounting to a failure to consult adequately with the affected indigenous community before proceeding with a project. The Special Rapporteur furthermore recommended that states develop specific mechanisms to monitor closely company behaviour in order to ensure full respect for indigenous peoples' rights and that required consultations are fully and adequately employed.[69]

In 2010, Anaya expanded upon this preliminary guidance by devoting the substantive section of his annual report to corporate accountability. He thus fleshed out standards for corporate accountability emerging from the UN Declaration on the Rights of Indigenous Peoples (UNDRIP)[70] and other human rights instruments and processes, to be incorporated in the understanding of the due diligence framework developed by the UN Special Representative on Human Rights and Business.[71] Anaya proposed that companies identify prior to commencing their activities all matters related to the basic human rights of indigenous peoples with a view to taking them into account when their activities are carried out. He emphasised that social and environmental impact studies should be conducted on behalf of companies by independent experts under the supervision of the state, specifically referring in this respect to guidance on cultural, social and environmental assessments adopted under the Convention on Biological Diversity (CBD) – the Akwé: Kon Guidelines.[72] As a result of these assessments, companies are expected to take all possible technically feasible solutions to mitigate likely negative impacts on the environment and social, economic, cultural and spiritual life of indigenous peoples. Where adverse impacts cannot be avoided, Anaya indicated that indigenous peoples are entitled to just and fair redress.[73]

[69] *Ibid.*

[70] UN Declaration on the Rights of Indigenous Peoples, UN Doc. A/RES/61/295 (13 September 2007).

[71] Report of the Special Rapporteur on the Situation of Human Rights and Fundamental Freedoms of Indigenous People, James Anaya, UN Doc. A/HRC/15/37 (2010), sect. III.

[72] Akwé: Kon Voluntary Guidelines for the Conduct of Cultural, Environmental and Social Impact Assessment Regarding Developments Proposed to Take Place on, or which are Likely to Impact on, Sacred Sites and on Lands and Waters Traditionally Occupied or Used by Indigenous and Local Communities, in Article 8(j) and related provisions (CBD COP 7 Decision VII/16F, 13 April 2004).

[73] *Report of the Special Rapporteur*, above, n. 71, paras 73–4.

Anaya also devoted significant attention to the question of benefit-sharing – a concept that figured prominently in the 2011 revision of the IFC performance standards discussed above. He emphasised that in addition to entitlement to compensation, indigenous peoples have a right to share in the benefits arising from business activities taking place on their traditional lands or in relation to their traditionally used natural resources. Accordingly, he argued that due diligence would imply that companies set up specific benefit-sharing mechanisms, based on international standards, genuinely strengthening the capacity of indigenous peoples to establish and follow up on their development priorities and supporting communities' own decision-making mechanisms.[74]

Overall, Anaya clearly indicated that concepts such as benefit-sharing[75] and socio-cultural and environmental impact assessments, as elaborated upon under the CBD through the Akwé: Kon Guidelines, can significantly contribute to fleshing out standards for corporate accountability with respect to indigenous rights in the context of the due diligence framework developed by the UN Special Representative on Human Rights and Business. The same understanding seems to emerge from other indigenous rights processes. The Expert Mechanism on the Rights of Indigenous Peoples, in 2010, stressed the link between prior informed consent, benefit-sharing and mitigation measures in the context of large-scale natural resource extraction on indigenous peoples' territories or the creation of national parks, forest and game reserves. In that connection, the Expert Mechanism also underscored the importance of the CBD work programme on protected areas[76] and the Akwé: Kon Guidelines.[77] These references – which are reflected to a great extent in the IFC Performance Standards – are significant in providing evidence of a coherent approach to corporate environmental accountability across

74 *Ibid.*, paras 76–80.

75 The legal concept of benefit-sharing has been developed under the CBD not only in the context of access to genetic resources but also with regard to the conservation and sustainable use of biological resources (such as protected areas, tourism and forest management). See E. Morgera and E. Tsioumani, 'The Evolution of Benefit-sharing: Linking Biodiversity and Community Livelihoods' (2010) 19 *RECIEL* 150–73.

76 Programme of Work on Protected Areas, adopted by CBD COP Decision VII/28, Protected Areas (2004), Annex.

77 Expert Mechanism on the Rights of Indigenous Peoples, Progress Report on the Study on Indigenous Peoples and the Right to Participate in Decision-making, UN Doc. A/HRC/15/35 (2010); and Report of the Expert Mechanism on the Rights of Indigenous Peoples on its Third Session, Geneva (12–16 July 2010), UN Doc. A/HRC/15/36 (2010).

different international bodies, and ultimately to contribute to substantive unity across different areas of international law.

12.4 From corporate social responsibility to corporate accountability through multiple monitoring mechanisms

Several international initiatives have not limited themselves to standard-setting for corporate environmental accountability, but have also put in place mechanisms to monitor corporate conduct and/or to consider complaints from members of the public. These are key steps in bringing to light instances of unsustainable corporate conduct or proactively manage possible conflicts through an independent mechanism for assessing facts and facilitating the identification of constructive solutions.[78] These mechanisms may provide a readily available and impartial avenue for individuals, communities and civil society groups to have their complaints against private companies heard, going beyond the hurdles and bias that may be experienced in accessing justice at the national level. These mechanisms may also serve the legitimate interests of private companies to have allegations against them assessed by an independent entity through their fact-finding activities on the ground, and through the good offices of an independent mediator in helping prevent conflicts from emerging or escalating. From a broader perspective, these mechanisms also offer concrete opportunities to test the suitability of corporate environmental accountability standards, further clarifying the conditions for their applicability to private companies in different contexts. Furthermore, they may contribute to ensure a coherent approach to corporate accountability, by making systematic reference to those international standards that emerge as common from different international standard-setting initiatives.

Four illustrations of such international mechanisms will be offered in the following subsections, focusing first, briefly, on the more recent system for handling allegations of severe environmental damage under the UN Global Compact and the consideration of communications on alleged violations of indigenous rights by the UN Rapporteur on Indigenous Peoples' Rights. Then, two more in-depth case-studies will focus on the well-established practice of two other accountability systems: the

[78] On the limited role of national courts and the shortcomings of other traditional legal approaches, see Morgera, *Corporate Accountability in International Environmental Law*, above, n. 2, chap. 3.

international compliance body established by the IFC to resolve complaints related to its Performance Standards and the implementation procedure established under the OECD Guidelines for Multinational Enterprises.

12.4.1 The Global Compact's integrity measures

The UN Global Compact, even if it was 'not designed, nor does it have the mandate or resources, to monitor or measure participants' performance',[79] has developed a procedure to handle 'credible allegations of systematic or egregious abuse of the Global Compact's overall aims and principles'.[80] The procedure aims to safeguard the reputation, integrity and good efforts of the initiative, as well as to promote continuous quality improvement and assist participants in aligning their actions with their commitments. Abuse includes 'severe environmental damage',[81] which is particularly significant as the vast majority of companies participating in the Compact tend to emphasise their adherence to the environment-related principles of the initiative.[82]

According to the procedure, any written complaint can be submitted by any individual, organisation or state to the Global Compact Office, which will require the relevant company to provide written comments and keep it informed of action undertaken to address the situation. While the Office will not make any assessment of its own as to the matter at hand, it will provide guidance and assistance to the company in taking action to remedy the situation. More interestingly, the Office can also, including on its own initiative, refer the matter to the relevant UN entity (in the case of environmental principles, the UN Environment Programme) for advice, assistance or action. It can refer the matter to the Global Compact Board, to draw on its business members' expertise.

[79] UN Global Compact, 'Note on Integrity Measures', 12 April 2010 (Integrity Measures), 1, available at www.unglobalcompact.org (accessed 14 March 2012).

[80] *Ibid.* On the origins of the procedure, see K. Nowrot, 'The New Governance Structure of the Global Compact: Transforming a "Learning Network" into a Federalized and Parliamentarized Transnational Regulatory Regime', *Essays in Transnational Economic Law* 47 (2005), 24–30.

[81] UN Global Compact Office, 'Frequently Asked Questions on the Integrity Measures' (2009), available at www.unglobalcompact.org (accessed 14 March 2012).

[82] R. Barkemeyer, *Beyond Compliance – Below Expectations? Cross-border CSR, Development and the UN Global Compact* (2009), 15, available at www.ssrn.com (accessed 14 March 2012).

The Office may further share with parties information about the compliance procedure under the OECD Guidelines (discussed below), which could provide for some cooperation, or at least some linkages between two distinct international accountability processes. If a company refuses to engage in dialogue within two months or if the review of the complaint reveals something detrimental to the reputation and integrity of the Global Compact, the Office will remove the company from its list of participants.[83] Overall, the procedure has been described, in low-key terms, as a 'dialogue facilitation mechanism'.[84] It has already been suggested that the mechanism could be strengthened by empowering the Global Compact Office to 'mediate the process and seek to define conditions to be met by companies in order to remain a Compact participant'.[85]

While this mechanism has some potential to monitor private companies' compliance with the environmental principles of the Global Compact, information available on the complaints dealt with is at the time of writing very limited and would not allow a more detailed discussion in this chapter. This lack of transparency concerning the complaint procedure has already been highlighted within the UN system.[86] Information on integrity cases is being included in the Global Compact Annual Review starting from the 2009 edition, but to date these reports have limited themselves to note the number of cases received and handled by the Global Compact Office,[87] without providing any further information – not even with reference to the specific principles that were alleged to be seriously violated by the company. This practice can be contrasted with that of the implementation procedure of the OECD Guidelines, discussed below: although until the mid-2000s the OECD did

[83] Integrity Measures, above, n. 79, 2–4.

[84] U. Wynhoven and M. Stausberg, 'The United Nations Global Compact's Governance Framework and Integrity Measures', in A. Rasche and G. Kell (eds.), *The United Nations Global Compact: Achievements, Trends and Challenges* (Cambridge University Press, 2010), 262–3.

[85] E. Brugger and P. Maurer, 'Concluding Remarks', *ibid.*, 395.

[86] Joint Inspection Unit, above, n. 18, paras 70–3 and recommendation 6(d). See also 'A Response from the Global Compact Office' above, n. 18, p. 5.

[87] The 2010 edition of the Annual Report states that '21 separate matters alleging abuses of the Ten Principles by business entities were raised with the Global Compact Office in 2010 [of which] 3 matters were handled under the Integrity Measures dialogue facilitation mechanism' (UN Global Compact Office, *2010 Annual Report of the Global Compact* (UN, 2011), 42). Similar information is provided in the 2009 edition (UN Global Compact Office, *2009 Annual Report of the Global Compact* (UN, 2010), 20).

not publish the names of companies involved in instances under consideration by its implementation procedure, it provided an annual update of the status of each instance, with specific reference to the alleged non-complied-with guideline. This was, however, largely considered insufficient, and NGO 'OECDWatch' started independently to produce quarterly updates on the filing, conclusion or rejections of instances.[88]

12.4.2 Communications to the UN Special Rapporteur on indigenous peoples' rights

Attention can now turn to the incipient practice of the UN Rapporteur on Indigenous Peoples' Rights in addressing communications on alleged violations of indigenous rights.[89] In his first report to the General Assembly, James Anaya prioritised among four areas of work the task of responding on an ongoing basis to specific cases of alleged human rights violations. He noted that cases hitherto brought to his attention included infringements of the right to free, prior informed consent, especially in relation to natural resource extraction and displacement or removal of indigenous communities, and denial of rights of indigenous peoples to lands and resources.[90] Accordingly, the Special Rapporteur established a practice of gathering, requesting, receiving and exchanging information from all relevant sources, notably from indigenous peoples and governments, and carrying out on-site visits to examine the issues raised with a view to providing observations and recommendations on the underlying human rights issues.

While it is too early to draw definitive conclusions on this practice, it can be highlighted that it may provide a new avenue for indigenous communities' complaints against environmentally unsustainable corporate conduct. In a case concerning the Marlin mine project in Guatemala

[88] E. Morgera, 'An Environmental Outlook on the OECD Guidelines for Multinational Enterprises: Comparative Advantage, Legitimacy, and Outstanding Questions in the Lead-up to the 2006 Review' (2006) 18 *Georgetown International Environmental Law Review* 774. The OECDWatch database is still functioning at the time of writing and can be freely consulted at http://oecdwatch.org/cases.

[89] Report of the Special Rapporteur on the Situation of Human Rights and Fundamental Freedoms of Indigenous Peoples: Communications to and from Governments, UN Doc. A/HRC/15/37/Add.1 (2010).

[90] Report of the Special Rapporteur on the Situation of Human Rights and Fundamental Freedoms of Indigenous Peoples, UN Doc. A/64/338 (2009), Section D.

and Maya indigenous communities, for instance, Anaya focused mostly on the regulatory and administrative shortcomings of the state, but did not shy away from noting that private companies had an influence on the conflicts with indigenous peoples in that context. He therefore concluded that companies have a 'certain degree of responsibility with regard to the disrespect of indigenous rights, independently from the international obligations of the host state'.[91] Anaya further noted that the consultations undertaken by the company did not lead to an adequate understanding of the project impacts on the communities, did not take into account sufficiently the community concerns and in all events should have involved more fully the government. He thus called for a new consultation process focusing on mitigation measures, reparation of damage, establishment of a formal mechanism for benefit-sharing with full participation of the relevant communities and the establishment of a complaint and conciliation mechanism.[92] In his final recommendation on this case, Anaya confirmed that the private enterprises' faults in due diligence could not be justified only by the limitations of the host state legal framework.[93] He thus recommended that private enterprises adopt internal policies on indigenous peoples' rights and independent follow-up mechanisms, as well as permanent mechanisms for dialogue and grievance with the participation of state authorities.[94]

Anaya's monitoring and normative work appear to converge in his recognition that 'in its prevailing form, the model for advancing natural resource extraction within the territories of indigenous peoples appears to run counter to the self-determination of indigenous peoples in the political, social and economic spheres'.[95] This conclusion led the Special

[91] Report of the Special Rapporteur on the Situation of Human Rights and Fundamental Freedoms of Indigenous Peoples: Observaciones sobre la situación de los derechos de los pueblos indígenas de Guatemala en relación con los proyectos extractivos, y otro tipo de proyectos, en sus territorios tradicionales, advance unedited version of 4 March 2011, para. 69.

[92] *Ibid.*, paras 69–70.

[93] Report of the Special Rapporteur on the Situation of Human Rights and Fundamental Freedoms of Indigenous Peoples: Observaciones sobre la situación de los derechos de los pueblos indígenas de Guatemala en relación con los proyectos extractivos, y otro tipo de proyectos, en sus territorios tradicionales, UN Doc. A/HRC/18/35/Add.3 (2011), para. 69–72.

[94] *Ibid.*, paras 89–93.

[95] Report of the Special Rapporteur on the Situation of Human Rights and Fundamental Freedoms of Indigenous Peoples, Extractive Industries Operating Within or Near Indigenous Territories, UN Doc. A/HRC/18/35 (2011), para. 82.

Rapporteur to request in 2011 a mandate to elaborate a set of guidelines providing specific orientation to governments, indigenous peoples and corporations regarding the protection of indigenous peoples' rights in the context of resource extraction or development projects.[96]

12.4.3 *IFC ombudsman*

A more established practice can be studied in the context of the IFC performance standards. Complaints from those affected by IFC-financed projects can be filed before a compliance adviser/ombudsman (CAO), an independent oversight authority that reports directly to the President of the World Bank Group and that thus ascertains application of the IFC Standards to companies.[97] The CAO 'attempts to resolve complaints through a flexible problem-solving approach and to enhance the environmental outcomes of the project' (ombudsman function).[98] Any person, group or community affected, or likely to be affected, by a project is eligible, at any time in the project, to file complaints that may relate to any aspect of the planning, implementation or impact of the project, without the need to allege necessarily violations of specific IFC procedures and standards.[99] When the complaint is accepted, the CAO decides the best course of action. Besides seeking to resolve issues for individuals who are directly or likely to be directly affected by IFC projects, the CAO is also mandated to provide the IFC with policy and process advice on environmental and social performance, and conduct environmental and social audits and reviews as an aid to institution learning (compliance function). The CAO can thus decide to resolve a complaint by undertaking a compliance audit or exercising advisory functions instead of its ombudsman functions. In such cases, the complainant no longer controls the process.[100]

The ombudsman's modus operandi includes field visits to the site of contested projects and interviews with all parties involved: staff of the private company, local authorities, affected communities representatives,

[96] *Ibid.*, paras 74–5.
[97] 2012 IFC Policy on Social and Environmental Sustainability, above, n. 44, paras 54–7.
[98] *Ibid.*
[99] Centre for International Environmental Law (CIEL), *A Handbook on the Office of the Compliance Advisor/Ombudsman of the International Finance Corporation and Multilateral Investment Guarantee Agency*, September 2000 (CIEL Handbook), 5–6, 16, available at www.ciel.org (accessed 14 March 2012).
[100] *Ibid.*, 8.

other relevant local organisations and IFC staff. Complaints, reports of field missions and recommendations are all published on the CAO website, together with updates on ongoing investigations.[101] Among these, the most important document is the assessment report, which is intended both as a finding of facts by the CAO in relation to allegations contained in the complaint and as an assessment of the 'ripeness' of any conflict or tension for resolution or management.[102] Interestingly, after considering complaints, the CAO formulates recommendations not only to the IFC itself, but also directly to the private company involved, albeit such recommendations will then need to be endorsed by the IFC President. The latter would then transmit them to the private company and/or request the IFC to take the appropriate action.[103]

In a complaint regarding a hydropower project in India,[104] for instance, the CAO recommended the company provide for an independent study of environmental concerns, make it public, ensure the public monitoring of resulting commitments, and generally engage more constructively local communities also through the intermediation of independent facilitators or observers. The CAO further called for developing a schedule for implementation of commitments resulting from the environmental impact assessment on the basis of each of the IFC performance standards.[105] In addition, the CAO provided for both the IFC and the private company to engage in quality monitoring. The IFC, in turn, was requested to appoint an independent engineer to oversee the project and report on social and environmental matters, while the company was requested to report to the IFC on quarterly and annual bases on social, environmental and health issues.[106]

In several instances, the Ombudsman considered whether the private company had undertaken an appropriate environmental impact assessment and whether the IFC had appropriately reviewed such assessment.[107] In other instances, the Ombudsman even concluded that in the absence of formal non-compliance with IFC Standards, companies should still build a climate of trust and understanding with local

[101] See www.cao-ombudsman.org/html-english/ombudsman.htm, where all the CAO documents cited below can be found.

[102] CAO, Assessment Report on the Complaint Concerning COMSUR/Don Mario Mine, Bolivia, November 2003.

[103] *Ibid.*, 4. [104] *Ibid.*, 7. [105] *Ibid.*, 8–9. [106] *Ibid.*, 14.

[107] CAO, Assessment Report on the Complaint Regarding the Zambia Konkola Copper Mine Project, November 2003, particularly p. 16; CAO, Assessment Report of the Complaint Regarding Allain Duhangan Hydropower Project, India, March 2005.

communities with regards to the environmental impacts of the project.[108] One of the most striking features of the CAO's recommendations is thus the paramount attention devoted to the perception of the environmental and social performance of IFC-funded projects by local communities.

The CAO also undertook follow-up monitoring and site visits.[109] Where possible, it also engaged directly in the resolution of complaints, facilitating an agreement between the private sector and the complainants.[110] Based on its activities until 2006, it could be concluded that CAO provided individuals and communities an avenue for expressing their complaints and receive prompt consideration. In more recent cases, however, the CAO appears to have gradually abandoned its practice of establishing its own findings and making its own recommendations. The CAO rather focuses on creating the conditions for more collaborative interactions between the company and stakeholders, setting out steps for establishing or strengthening dialogue,[111] or where dialogue is not favoured by the complainants, it proposes to refer the case to the compliance facility.[112] This is confirmed by the fact that in recent reports the CAO explicitly cautions that it merely 'summarizes the views expressed by the various stakeholders without the intention to validate or deny any issues'.[113]

It is regrettable that the practice of the CAO has experienced a significant change, providing for visibly more limited discussion of the practical application of relevant international environmental law standards for corporate accountability. This is particularly so because the IFC Performance Standards remain the most explicit and elaborated substantive standards on corporate environmental accountability

[108] CAO, Assessment Report on the Complaint Regarding IFC's Investment in Kalahari Diamonds Ltd, Botswana, June 2005; CAO, Assessment Report of a Complaint in Relation to the Marlin Mining Project in Guatemala, September 2005.

[109] CAO, Follow-up Assessment Report on Complaint Regarding the Marlin Mining Project, May 2006.

[110] CAO, Assessment Report in Relation to a Complaint Regarding the Baku-Tbilisi-Ceyhan (BTC) Pipeline Project, Georgia, February 2006. See also 'Trouble in the Pipeline', *Guardian*, 3 September 2002.

[111] See e.g. CAO, Assessment Report of the Complaint Regarding the Electron Investment SA Pando-Monte Lirio Hydroelectric Project, Ciriqui Province, Panama, July 2010, 20–1.

[112] CAO, Assessment Report to Stakeholders Regarding Concerns of Local Stakeholders about the PRONACA Farms in Santo Domingo, Ecuador, June 2011.

[113] CAO, Pando Assessment Report, above, n. 111, p. 18.

that are explicitly based on multilateral environmental agreements, and particularly the CBD.[114]

12.4.4 OECD Guidelines implementation procedure

Although the OECD Guidelines are not as explicit or detailed with regard to corporate environmental accountability standards as the IFC Standards, their implementation procedure has contributed on occasions to flesh out the links between corporate accountability and multilateral environmental agreements. The procedure[115] is based on the creation of national contact points (NCPs) in adhering countries, to handle enquiries ('specific instances') at the national level.[116] The procedure is subject to the oversight by the OECD Committee on International Investment and Multinational Enterprises (CIME), which issues clarifications (providing additional information about whether and how the Guidelines apply to a particular business situation, without assessing the appropriateness of that enterprise's conduct), reviews the Guidelines and is ultimately responsible for their interpretation.[117] Specific instances are basically a means for any 'interested party' to draw the NCP's attention to a company's alleged non-observance of the Guidelines.[118] NCPs make an initial assessment of the issue and then offer their services as mediators. If the conflict is not resolved, it can be referred to the CIME, where non-binding decisions are taken by consensus. In the vast majority of cases, however, the onus of attempting to resolve specific instances and ensuring the effectiveness of the Guidelines is largely upon NCPs.[119]

114 In addition to 2012 IFC Performance Standard 6 (discussed under sect. 1, above), also 2012 IFC, Performance Standard 8: Cultural Heritage, above, n. 19, para. 1, is 'based in part on standards set by the Convention on Biological Diversity'.

115 The Implementation Procedure of the OECD Guidelines for Multinational Enterprises is included in Part II of the *OECD Guidelines*, above, n. 16, sect. I.

116 *Ibid.*, sect. II.

117 P. Acconci, 'The Promotion of Responsible Business Conduct and the New Text of the OECD Guidelines for Multinational Enterprises' (2001) 2 *Journal of World Investment* 140–1.

118 P. van der Gaag, 'OECD Guidelines for Multinational Enterprises: Corporate Accountability in a Liberalised Economy?' (November 2004), 3, available at www.oecdwatch.org (accessed 14 March 2012).

119 J. Karl, 'The OECD Guidelines for Multinational Enterprises', in M. K. Addo (ed.), *Human Rights Standards and the Responsibility of Transnational Corporations* (The Hague: Kluwer, 1999), 92–5.

Disappointment, however, has been expressed for quite some time about the weak implementation mechanism of the Guidelines,[120] including by the UN Special Representative on Business and Human Rights.[121] The lack of predictable timelines for NCPs to acknowledge receipt of, or respond to, instances in an efficient and timely manner also raised concerns.[122] To some extent these shortcomings were addressed in the 2011 review, which resulted in spelling out principles for NCP 'functional equivalence' (accessibility, transparency, predictability, impartiality, accountability, efficiency and timeliness). The review left adhering governments flexibility in setting up NCPs that are enabled to operate in an impartial manner while maintaining an adequate level of accountability to the adhering government.[123] The review also called for the systematic publication of the outcomes of the NCP procedure and detailed their minimum content: NCP statements should at a minimum describe the issue raised and the reasons for the NCP decision, and emit recommendations on the implementation of the Guidelines 'as appropriate'.[124] The review also provided indicative timelines: three months for the initial assessment of instances and three months for issuing a statement of report following the conclusion of the procedure, with a view to concluding the whole procedure in twelve months.[125]

120 Friends of the Earth, 'OECD Guidelines for Multinational Enterprises' (undated), 6, available at www.foe.org (accessed 14 March 2012); OECD, Roundtable on Corporate Responsibility: Encouraging the Positive Contribution of Business to Environment through the OECD Guidelines for Multinational Enterprises. Background Report, June 2004 (OECD 2004 Roundtable Background Report), 12, available at www.oecd.org (accessed 14 March 2012); UNCTAD, 'Disclosure of the Impact of Corporations on Society: Current Trends and Issues' (15 August 2003) UN Doc. TD/B/COM.2/ISAR/20, 6. Other critiques concerned the lack of independent verification of whether companies follow the Guidelines, the confidentiality rule applied in the 'best interests' of the implementation of the Guidelines and the failure by NCPs to issue statements and make recommendations when no agreement can be achieved between the parties concerned. V. Nilsson, 'The OECD Guidelines for Multinational Corporations in Practice', paper presented at the OECD Global Forum on International Investment – Investment for Development: Forging New Partnerships, 19–21 October 2004, available at www.oecd.org (accessed 14 March 2012).

121 Report – Protect, Respect and Remedy, above, n. 57, para. 98.

122 *Ibid.*

123 OECD Guidelines Update 2011 – Commentaries, above, n. 31, para. 9; and OECD Guidelines Update 2011 – Note by the Secretary-General, above, n. 31, Appendix III, sect. I, A and C. The 'Procedural Guidance' and its Commentary are included in Part II of the *OECD Guidelines*, above, n. 16.

124 OECD Guidelines Note by the Secretary-General, above, n. 31, Appendix III, sect. I.C, para. 3.

125 OECD Guidelines Update 2011 – Commentaries, above, n. 31, para. 40.

The 2011 review has, however, been criticised by civil society organisations for the lack of specification as to NCPs' role in identifying breaches of the Guidelines and providing recommendations, including consequences for companies' failure to engage in the implementation procedure, as well as in monitoring and following up on their recommendations.[126]

Instances considered before the 2011 review have concerned different parts of the environmental recommendations of the Guidelines, often focusing on the recommendation regarding assessment and communication to the communities affected by the environmental impacts of projects in developing countries. Many questions, however, remain unanswered as to the direct application to multinational enterprises of standards based on general environmental principles, such as precaution and sustainable development as reflected in the Guidelines. In some cases, the NCP recommended that in a weak legal and regulatory system multinational enterprises should do their utmost to implement the internationally acknowledged best practices that they follow in their own country on the construction site and for the people affected by their activity, making reference to environmental impact assessment and consultations.[127] In other instances, instead, the NCP recommended respecting the legal standards of the company's home country to its activities abroad.[128] In yet other instances, the NCP statement focused on institutionalising channels for communication and information exchange between the company and affected constituencies.[129]

Although NCPs have made uneven references to international standards for corporate accountability, the UK NCP set a significant precedent in 2009. It addressed a complaint brought to its attention by Survival International, a UK-based NGO, against Vedanta, a UK-registered

[126] See sources cited above, n. 33.

[127] French NCP, 'Recommendations Intended for EDF and its Partners with Regard to the Implementation of the "Nam Theun 2" Project in Laos' (1 April 2005), available at www.reports-and-materials.org (accessed 14 March 2012).

[128] Van der Gaag, above, n. 118, according to whom an NCP report in October 2003 recommended that environmental standards of Nutreco in Chile should progressively be brought into line with those found in the Netherlands.

[129] Government of Canada, 'Annual Report 2002: Canada's National Contact Point for the OECD Guidelines for Multinational Enterprises' (2002), available at www.ncp-pcn.gc.ca (accessed 14 March 2012). The NCP suggested establishing a Land Task Force Committee by the company, the local government and local NGOs, with the mandate to, inter alia, protect the environment, provide information to the public on land and environmental issues and resolve any land disputes at the local level.

mining company operating in India, concerning the use of forest land for bauxite mining near Lanjigarh and the failure to consult with an indigenous group affected by its operations, the Dongria Kondh. The NCP found, mostly on the basis of evidence from the complainant (as Vedanta did not engage fully in the procedure and its own investigations), that Vedanta had failed to put in place an adequate and timely consultation mechanism to engage fully the Dongria Kondh. Accordingly, the NCP declared non-compliance with, inter alia, the Guidelines sections on engaging in adequate and timely communication and consultation with the communities directly affected by the environmental policies of the enterprise and by their implementation. It further found that Vedanta did not respect the rights and freedoms of the Dongria Kondh in a manner consistent with India's commitments under various international instruments, including the CBD and the UNDRIP. Specifically, the NCP used the CBD Akwé: Kon Guidelines to interpret the OECD Guidelines provisions on consultations on environmental impacts[130] and determined that Vedanta did not employ the local language or means of communication other than written form for consultations with communities with very high rate of illiteracy. It also found that the environmental impact assessment that had been carried out, although including an analysis of the 'socio-economic environment' of the study area, did not address the impact of the mine on the community.[131] The NCP concluded that the company did not carry out adequate or timely consultations about the potential environmental impact of the construction of the mine.[132] The NCP thus recommended that Vedanta engage in consultations with the indigenous group on access to the project-affected area, ways to secure its traditional livelihood and alternative arrangements (other than resettlement) for the affected families according to the process outlined in the CBD Akwé: Kon Guidelines. At a minimum, the NCP expected Vedanta to advertise the consultation in a language and form that could be easily understood by the Dongria Kondh, thereby ensuring the participation of the maximum number of their representatives in the consultation.[133] Interestingly, the NCP also underlined that in carrying out a human rights impact assessment, as suggested by the UN Framework on Business and Human Rights, the

[130] UK NCP, Final Statement on the Complaint from Survival International against Vedanta Resources plc, 25 September 2009, paras 44–6, available at www.berr.gov.uk (accessed 14 March 2012).

[131] *Ibid.*, para. 57. [132] *Ibid.*, paras 65 and 67. [133] *Ibid.*, paras 73–4.

Akwé: Kon Guidelines could be used as a point of reference, particularly for carrying out indigenous groups' impact assessments.[134]

The follow-up statement by the NCP, however, provided a mixed picture, with the NGO claiming that no change in the company's conduct could be detected while Vedanta reported on specific action being undertaken following consultations with affected communities, and no comment provided by the NCP.[135] Nevertheless, the case remains groundbreaking in showing how the OECD Guidelines implementation procedure can significantly point to companies' shortcomings vis-à-vis international environmental standards, as well as lead to coherent interpretation and application of different international sources of corporate environmental accountability standards. To the latter end, the NCP proposed filling a gap in the UN Framework on Business and Human Rights through CBD guidelines.

12.5 Institutional fragmentation and substantive unity: the role of the CBD

Although the multiplicity of international standard-setting and monitoring mechanisms related to corporate accountability inevitably creates the risk of fragmentation of international guidance on corporate accountability, the above discussion has clarified that such risk is significantly mitigated by the convergence of the standards used to assess private companies' conduct. In particular, environmental standards for corporate accountability have explicitly or implicitly facilitated progress in standard-setting and influenced the international debate on corporate accountability tout court, by providing key elements of the due diligence framework on business and human rights such as impact assessment, stakeholder consultations and more recently benefit-sharing.

Specific guidance elaborated in the context of the CBD has clearly influenced the practice of corporate accountability mechanisms, providing detailed procedures that have received the endorsement of the CBD's virtually universal membership. Notably, the CBD Akwé: Kon Guidelines[136] have been used more and more often in different contexts to

[134] *Ibid.*, 79.

[135] Follow-up to Final Statement by the UK National Contact Point for the OECD Guidelines for Multinational Enterprises: Complaint from Survival International against Vedanta Resources plc (12 March 2010).

[136] Although they are directed to parties and governments, the Akwé: Kon Voluntary Guidelines, above, n. 72, are expected to provide a 'collaborative framework for

assess whether private companies' conduct is acceptable in light of international human rights standards, thus showing that it is possible to ensure substantive unity across different areas of international law that may be negatively affected by the conduct of private operators. Other CBD guidelines can also serve as a benchmark for the conduct of the private sector: this is the case of the Addis Ababa Principles and Guidelines on Sustainable Use,[137] the Guidelines on Biodiversity and Tourism Development[138] and the Tkariwaié:ri Code of Ethical Conduct on respect for the cultural and intellectual heritage of indigenous and local communities relevant for the conservation and sustainable use of biodiversity.[139] Other guidelines may also be relevant for corporate environmental accountability purposes, such as those included in the CBD work programmes on protected areas, mountain and forest biodiversity.[140] All these instruments include specific procedures underpinning private companies' interactions with indigenous and local communities.[141]

The CBD has thus provided a virtually universal forum for reaching intergovernmental consensus on standards for corporate environmental accountability with significant human rights dimensions.[142] This has occurred even before the Convention parties and Secretariat started

Governments, indigenous and local communities, decision makers and *managers of developments*' (para. 3) (emphasis added).

137 Addis Ababa Principles and Guidelines for the Sustainable Use of Biodiversity, CBD Decision VII/12, Sustainable Use (Article 10) (2004), Annex II, para. 1 clarifies that 'The principles provide a framework for advising Governments, resource managers, indigenous and local communities, the *private sector* and other stakeholders about how they can ensure that their use of the components of biodiversity will not lead to the long-term decline of biological diversity' (emphasis added).

138 International guidelines for activities related to sustainable tourism development in vulnerable terrestrial, marine and coastal ecosystems and habitats of major importance for biological diversity and protected areas, including fragile riparian and mountain ecosystems, CBD Decision VII/14, Biological Diversity and Tourism (2004), Annex, para. 2 clarifies that the Guidelines provide 'technical guidance to policy makers, decision makers and managers with responsibilities covering tourism and/or biodiversity, whether in national or local Government, *the private sector*, indigenous and local communities' (emphasis added).

139 CBD Decision X/42, The Tkarihwaié:ri Code of Ethical Conduct to Ensure Respect for the Cultural and Intellectual Heritage of Indigenous and Local Communities (2010).

140 Expanded Programme of Work on Forest Biological Diversity, CBD Decision VI/22, Forest Biological Diversity (2002), Annex.

141 Morgera and Tsioumani, 'The Evolution of Benefit-sharing', above, n. 75, 165 and 167.

142 E. Morgera and E. Tsioumani, 'Yesterday, Today and Tomorrow: Looking Afresh at the Convention on Biological Diversity' (2011) 21 *Yearbook of International Environmental Law* 3–40.

activities specifically targeting the involvement of the business community into the CBD implementation in 2005.[143] Notably, according to the most recent decision of the CBD Conference of the Parties on the subject of private-sector involvement, business entities are encouraged to monitor and assess impacts on biodiversity and ecosystem services, to develop and apply processes and production methods that minimise or avoid negative impacts on biodiversity and 'take into account, as appropriate, the Akwé: Kon Guidelines'.[144] The CBD normative activity is particularly significant in supporting a coherent approach to corporate environmental accountability bridging human rights and environmental perspectives with its focus on indigenous and local communities, and covering several environmental issues in light of the ecosystem approach,[145] particularly with regard to consultation, impact assessment and benefit-sharing.

On the other hand, the CBD Secretariat has participated in various activities that directly engaged private companies,[146] such as collaboration with the UN Permanent Forum on Indigenous Issues, and an association of private enterprises to elaborate guidance to the aromatic, perfume and cosmetics industry interacting with indigenous peoples.[147] Another example concerns the BioTrade Initiative that was initiated under the aegis of the UN Commission on Trade and Development[148] to engage private companies to develop a verification framework that will formally recognise their efforts towards conservation, sustainability and benefit-sharing.[149] The Union for Ethical BioTrade (UEBT), a non-profit

143 For an early assessment, see Morgera, *Corporate Accountability in International Environmental Law*, above, n. 2, chap. 8, based on CBD Decision VIII/11 'Private Sector Engagement' (2006) and CBD COP Decision IX/26 'Promoting Business Engagement' (2008).

144 CBD Decision X/21, 'Business Engagement' (2010), para. 2(b)–(c).

145 Principles of the Ecosystem Approach, in Ecosystem Approach (CBD Decision V/6, 22 June 2000), Annex B and Refinement and Elaboration of the Ecosystem Approach, Based on Assessment of Experience of Parties in Implementation, in Ecosystem Approach (CBD Decision VII/11, 13 April 2004), Annex I.

146 See discussion in Morgera and Tsioumani, 'The Evolution of Benefit-sharing', above, n. 75, 165–7.

147 See the report of the meeting 'Indigenous and Local Communities, Business and Biodiversity Consultation', held in New York on 12–13 May 2009 (13 May 2009), available at www.equatorinitiative.org (accessed 14 March 2012).

148 The term 'biotrade' refers to the 'collection, production, transformation, and commercialisation of goods and services derived from native biodiversity under the criteria of environmental, social and economic sustainability'. See the BioTrade Initiative (Biotrade, undated), available at www.biotrade.org (accessed 14 March 2012), which was referred to in Decision X/21, above, n. 144.

149 See BioTrade Principles and Criteria (Biotrade, undated), Principles 3–4 and 7, available at www.biotrade.org (accessed 14 March 2012).

entity emerged from the initiative and whose members[150] commit gradually to ensuring that their sourcing practices promote the conservation of biodiversity, respect traditional knowledge and assure the equitable sharing of benefits along the supply chain, signed a Memorandum of Understanding with the CBD Secretariat, with a view to raising the awareness of cosmetic and food companies on access and benefit-sharing principles.[151]

These and other initiatives[152] confirm that the CBD is not only contributing to the international debate on corporate accountability through standard-setting but also through direct engagement with the private sector.[153]

CONCLUSION

The trend towards setting and monitoring standards of corporate environmental accountability at the international level has intensified, as demonstrated by the 2011 review of the OECD Guidelines and the IFC Performance Standards, the recent practice of the Global Compact's integrity measures and the communications procedure initiated by the UN Special Rapporteur on Indigenous Peoples' Rights. Convergent international standards for corporate environmental accountability have also significantly impacted upon the international debate on corporate accountability and human rights – although the

[150] UEBT has two categories of members: trading and affiliate. Trading members are companies or other types of organisations that are actually involved in natural ingredient supply chains. Affiliate members may be NGOs or government-related agencies that support the principles of ethical biotrade in their work. No governments are currently members as such. See UEBT website at www.ethicalbiotrade.org (accessed 14 March 2012).

[151] Memorandum of Understanding between the CBD and UEBT, 18 August 2011, available at www.cbd.int (accessed 14 March 2012). For a discussion of the direct and indirect relevance of international rules and principles on access and benefit-sharing for business, see M. J. Oliva, 'The Implications of the Nagoya Protocol on Access and Benefit-sharing for the Ethical Sourcing of Biodiversity', in E. Morgera, M. Buck and E. Tsioumani (eds.), *The Nagoya Protocol on Access and Benefit-Sharing in Perspective: Implications for International Law and Implementation Challenges* (The Hague: Brill, 2012).

[152] Other initiatives can be found at www.cbd.int/business/tools/ (accessed 14 March 2012).

[153] Similarly to the case of the World Heritage Convention Secretariat discussed by N. Affolder, 'The Private Life of Environmental Treaties' (2009) 103 *American Journal of International Law* 510.

UN Framework on Business and Human Rights did not acknowledge it – by providing key tools such as impact assessment, stakeholder involvement and life-cycle management.

Overall, the resulting plurality of international avenues for addressing complaints against private companies not only supports those affected by corporate environmental damage, but may also protect the reputation of companies from unfounded allegations and contribute to the credibility of international standard-setting efforts. The risk of fragmented and possibly conflicting guidance to companies emerging from these international monitoring efforts appears for the great part averted by the significant convergence and increasing cross-fertilisation of international standards on corporate environmental accountability.[154] Specifically, concepts and guidelines elaborated under the CBD and adopted by consensus by its 193 state parties increasingly provide useful benchmarks to assess and guide corporate conduct towards environmental sustainability and the respect of relevant human rights. Accordingly, the 2011 review of the IFC Performance Standards, the UN Special Rapporteur on Indigenous Peoples' Rights and the OECD Guidelines implementation procedure[155] relied on the Akwé: Kon Guidelines and the concept of benefit-sharing developed under the CBD to complement and operationalise the UN Framework on Business and Human Rights.

[154] More systematic documentation of the operations and findings of international accountability mechanisms, however, would help in coherently developing international quasi-case law on corporate environmental accountability. In part, this was reflected in the 2011 review of the *OECD Guidelines*, where emphasis was placed on collecting and making publicly available information on recent trends among NCPs, findings and the establishment of a database on specific instances: OECD Guidelines Update 2011 – Note by the Secretary-General, above, n. 31, p. 29.

[155] Note that the CBD is the only multilateral environmental agreement cited in the list of international instruments of reference on which implementation of the *OECD Guidelines* should rely, together with an unclear reference to 'international treaties [*sic*] on persistent organic pollutants'. The Secretary-General's note stresses that 'the number of instruments and initiatives that are relevant to the Guidelines far surpasses the possibility for introducing explicit references to them in the text of the Guidelines. For this reason, there is general agreement that, as part of follow-up on the updated Guidelines, a resource document [will] be compiled' (OECD Guidelines Update 2011 – Note by the Secretary-General, above, n. 31, pp. 6 and 9).

Select bibliography

Addo, M. K. (ed.), *Human Rights Standards and the Responsibility of Transnational Corporations* (The Hague: Kluwer, 1999).

Affolder, N., 'The Private Life of Environmental Treaties' (2009) 103 *American Journal of International Law* 510.

Biermann, F., B. Siebenhüner and A. Schreyrögg (eds.), *International Organisations in Global Environmental Governance* (Abingdon: Routledge, 2009).

Calder, F., and M. Culverwell, *Following Up the WSSD Commitments on Corporate Responsibility and Accountability* (London: Royal Institute of International Affairs, 2004).

Hansen, M., 'Environmental Regulation of Transnational Corporations', in P. Utting (ed.), *The Greening of Business in Developing Countries* (London: Zed Books in association with UNRISD, 2002), pp. 159–86.

McBarnet, D., A. Voiculescu and T. Campbell (eds.), *The New Corporate Accountability: Corporate Social Responsibility and the Law* (Cambridge University Press, 2007).

Morgera, E., *Corporate Accountability in International Environmental Law* (Oxford University Press, 2009).

'*Human Rights Dimensions of Corporate Environmental Accountability*', in P.-M. Dupuy, E.-U. Petersmann and F. Francioni (eds.), *Human Rights, Investment Law and Investor-State Arbitration* (Oxford University Press, 2009), pp. 511–24.

'Multinational Corporations and International Environmental Law', in S. Alam, J. H. Bhuiyan, T. M. R. Chowdhury and E. J. Techera (eds.), *Routledge Handbook of International Environmental Law* (London: Routledge, 2012), pp. 189–206.

Nollkaemper, A., 'Responsibility of Transnational Corporations in International Environmental Law: Three Perspectives', in G. Winter (ed.), *Multilevel Governance of Global Environmental Change: Perspectives from Science, Sociology and the Law* (Cambridge University Press, 2006), pp. 179–99.

Ong, D., 'From "International" to "Transnational" Environmental Law? A Legal Assessment of the Contribution of the "Equator Principles" to International Environmental Law' (2010) 79 *Nordic Journal of International Law* 35.

Rasche, A., and G. Kell (eds.), *The United Nations Global Compact: Achievements, Trends and Challenges* (Cambridge University Press, 2010).

Shelton, D., 'The Utility and Limits of Codes of Conduct for the Protection of the Environment', in A. Kiss, D. Shelton and K. Ishibashi (eds.), *Economic Globalization and Compliance with International Environmental Agreements* (The Hague: Kluwer, 2003), pp. 211–27.

Sprote, W., 'Negotiations on a United Nations Code of Conduct on Transnational Corporations' (1990) 33 *German Yearbook of International Law* 331.

Zerk, J., *Multinationals and Corporate Social Responsibility* (Cambridge University Press, 2006).

13

Beyond law as tools: foreign investment projects and the contractualisation of environmental protection

NATASHA AFFOLDER

INTRODUCTION

Significant global attention is now being paid to land deals.[1] Particular concerns emanate from their secrecy, as well as from mounting evidence that these contracts are being concluded 'at the social, environmental and economic expense of local communities'.[2] One aspect of land deals that has yet to receive notice is the fact that they are symptomatic or representative of a legal phenomenon of wider significance: the contractualisation of environmental governance in foreign investment projects.

In individual investment projects, environmental protection initiatives are introduced through diverse forms of contractual arrangements. But our accounts of foreign investment and environmental law largely fail to account for these legal developments. These agreements, whether environmental agreements signed between communities and companies, biodiversity protection agreements emanating out of environmental assessment processes, commitments in loan agreements or insurance documents, or partnership agreements between conservation organisations and companies, largely operate below the radar of legal scholars. In projects where conservation is the foreign investment (conservation performance payment agreements, conservation concessions or access

[1] In 2011, land deals made the agenda of the World Economic Forum. In April 2011, an international conference on 'Global Land Grabbing – Land Deals Politics Initiative' was held in London. Land deals are the subject of ongoing debates in international journals and news media. See e.g. J. Vidal, 'How Food and Water are Driving a Twenty-first Century African Land Grab', *Observer*, 20 March 2010; L. Cotula, 'Deals Can Be Good News When Not Made Behind Closed Doors', *ibid.*, 7 March 2010, p. 29.

[2] 'When Others are Grabbing Your Land' *The Economist*, 7 May 2011, p. 65.

and benefit agreements, for example) the 'innovative' nature of these 'economic instruments' again obscures their legal content and function. The chapter is not a celebration of the innovative potential of contracts. Nor is it a detailed investigation into the effectiveness of contracts in diverse settings. Rather, emphasis is placed on the governance function of contracts as a neglected element of transnational law.

The objective of this chapter is to elucidate the contracts through which biodiversity conservation is channelled in project-specific settings – both in extractive projects and where conservation is the primary source of the foreign investment. I refer to these agreements as 'contracts' in this chapter because that word has a particular resonance for lawyers. This is not intended to obscure or gloss over the legal form and consequences of these agreements – rather it is intended to spark closer attention to issues of legality and to invite scrutiny of these agreements on planes other than their policy utility. On one level, then, this chapter's ambition is to account for the neglected role of contracts as an aspect of the environmental regulation of investment projects. On another, this chapter represents a deeper challenge to prevalent conceptualisations of environmental law within the literature on foreign investment. Rejecting a framing of environmental contracts and quasi-contractual agreements as 'safeguards' or 'tools', this chapter argues for a deeper reflection on the culture of contracting that pervades foreign investment projects, but which has received sparse attention from legal scholars. The importance of individual contracts, of deal-making, of agreements and partnerships in foreign investment projects becomes apparent by focusing attention at the individual project level.

Conservation biologists and conservation organisations have been debating the utility and effectiveness of project-specific conservation agreements for some time. Political scientists and policy scholars have drawn attention to the importance of private authority generally,[3] and partnerships specifically,[4] as aspects of environmental governance. Yet these agreements continue to be framed as policy and economic instruments. The consequence is that they largely remain invisible to our

[3] See e.g. A. C. Cutler, V. Haufleur and T. Porter (eds.), *Private Authority and International Affairs* (Albany, NY: SUNY Press, 1999); O. R. Young, *International Governance: Protecting the Environment in a Stateless Society* (Ithaca, NY: Cornell University Press, 1994).

[4] P. Glasbergen, F. Biermann and A. P. J. Mol (eds.), *Partnerships, Governance and Sustainable Development: Reflections on Theory and Practice* (Cheltenham: Edward Elgar, 2007).

accounts of environmental law, just as law remains for the most part invisible in debates on project-specific agreements. Where law is invoked, it is in a cut-and-paste way, analysing contractual clauses as autonomous, free-standing entities.

The failure to engage with contracts as *legal* instruments and as part of a wider architecture of environmental law represents a missed opportunity to articulate the complexity of environmental law. By drawing attention to the contractual and quasi-contractual basis of project-specific environmental governance, and to law's invisibility in the literature on contractual approaches, this chapter highlights areas for productive new research. This chapter also stresses the diversity of private-sector actors involved in environmental protection initiatives, with a focus on both companies and conservation organisations as foreign investors and environmental regulators. For scholars of international investment law, the chapter redirects attention towards avenues other than dispute resolution for assessing legal approaches to environmental protection. For scholars of international environmental law, contracts provide fertile ground for studying the dynamic processes of implementation of international environmental norms.

In focusing attention directly on agreements – rather than the legislative, regulatory and administrative structures that make individual agreements possible – this chapter at once invites us to consider 'new tools' of environmental law, but at the same time urges us to resist the temptation to conceptualise agreements as mere tools. The chapter proceeds in three parts. Following this introduction, the first part reflects on prevailing approaches to assessing foreign investment and environmental protection (13.1). Responding to the blind spots indentified in that review, the second part explores the contractual basis of environmental protection in foreign investment projects (13.2). It focuses on two blind spots in existing legal scholarship on foreign investment and environmental protection: the multilayered contractual agreements that address environmental protection in extractive industry investment projects (13.2.1) and conservation agreements governing investment projects where conservation is the foreign investment (13.2.2).

A close examination of environmentally relevant contractual agreements emerging in foreign investment contexts reveals the function of contracts both in setting limits on the operations undertaken by, or funded by, foreign investors and in providing the legal form through which investors can advance environmental protection initiatives. The environmental governance role of contracts (13.2.3) represents both a pushing to restrain economic activity with unacceptable environmental impacts and a pulling to encourage investment leading to beneficial environmental outcomes. Contracts as a governance mechanism do not operate in isolation from domestic and international law.

The objective in illuminating this range of contractual mechanisms is also to urge us to think more expansively about what counts as environmental law and the processes by which we find and study it. The third part thus offers methodological reflections on the challenges inherent in turning to new directions for future research (13.3). The conclusion returns us to more traditional ways of approaching international investment law. I close by suggesting that the sort of dynamic and iterative accounts of environmental law that will result from taking contracts seriously present a significant tension for international investment law and the demands of stability and predictability. Attempting to tame or restrain our accounts of environmental law is not the way to deal with this tension.

13.1 Environmental law as tools: prevailing approaches

Why do we know so little about the contractual elements of project-specific governance? This section provides an opportunity to situate a discussion of the contractual elements of environmental regulation in foreign investment projects within a wider reflection of the privileging of certain areas of scholarly enquiry in foreign investment law. A number of forces are at work. More specifically, I attribute the dearth of legal scholarship on contractual elements of environmental governance to three factors: the preference of legal scholars writing on environmental protection and foreign investment to neglect project-specific instruments in favour of studying treaties and investment dispute resolution (13.1.1), the (perhaps resulting) fact that information on project-specific contracts is produced by either business or non-governmental organisations (NGOs) (13.1.2) and the fact that conservation partnerships and contractual commitments seem to operate entirely beneath the legal radar (13.1.3). All of these factors contribute to a view of project-specific contracts as 'tools' or safeguards and a divorcing of these agreements from the wider legal and social settings in which they emerge. It thus makes sense to explore each of these factors in more detail.

13.1.1 The preferences of legal scholars

International investment law's view of environmental protection reflects a scholarly obsession with dispute resolution.[5] Topics that animate recent scholarship include the role of non-disputing parties,[6] interpretation of investment protection clauses,[7] the operation of necessity clauses[8] and the scope of regulatory expropriation.[9] The unit of analysis is the decision of an international court or arbitral tribunal.[10] For example, a valuable recent survey of the international legal interactions between foreign investment and environmental protection maps these interactions through the lens of 'the most significant questions posed by such interactions in the light of the relevant investment-related decisions from international courts and tribunals'.[11]

Analysis of dispute resolution is complemented in the legal scholarship on investment law by careful assessment of treaty requirements and at times national legislative requirements. But there is a tendency to stop our analysis of 'law' at the level of legislation or an international treaty. International lawyers are very good at collecting and collating treaty provisions. We well document relevant international resolutions but we are too often hesitant to roll up our sleeves and engage in the time-consuming and inherently messy work of seeing how these legal requirements are implemented in individual project settings.

5 See e.g. M. E. Footer, 'BITs and Pieces: Social and Environmental Protection in the Regulation of Foreign Investment' (2009) 18 *Michigan State Journal of International Law* 33.

6 See B. Stern, 'Civil Society's Voice in the Settlement of International Economic Disputes' (2007) 22 *ICSID Review* 280; E. Triantafilou, 'Amicus Submissions in *Investor-State Arbitration after Suez* v. *Argentina*' (2008) 24 *Arbitration International* 571.

7 See O. K. Fauchald, 'International Investment Law and Environmental Protection' (2006) 17 *Yearbook of International Environmental Law* 3; F. Ortino, 'Non-Discriminatory Treatment in Investment Disputes', in P.-M. Dupuy, F. Francioni and E.-U. Petersmann (eds.), *Human Rights in International Investment Law and Arbitration* (Oxford University Press, 2009) 344.

8 See D. Dobos, 'The Necessity of Precaution: The Future of Ecological Necessity and the Precautionary Principle' (2002) 13 *Fordham Environmental Law Journal* 375.

9 A. Newcombe, 'The Boundaries of Regulatory Expropriation in International Law' (2005) 20(1) *ICSID Review* 1.

10 See e.g. R. Pavoni, 'Environmental Rights, Sustainable Development, and Investor-State Case Law: A Critical Appraisal', in Dupuy, Francioni and Petersmann, *Human Rights*, 525.

11 J. E. Viñuales, 'Foreign Investment and the Environment in International Law: An Ambiguous Relationship' (2010) 80 *British Yearbook of International Law* 244.

Outside the world of legal scholarship, literature on foreign investment and environmental regulation also tends to cluster. It bunches around two questions: (1) the impact of host country environmental regulations on attracting or deterring foreign investment and (2) assessing whether foreign investment leads to higher or lower environmental standards.[12] Topics of perennial interest include debating 'race to the bottom' hypotheses and documenting how cases of liberalisation result in improved national policies. More recently the literature has taken a turn to document how foreign direct investment can serve as an important vector for the transfer of environmentally sound technologies.[13]

What this means in practice is that careful attention to the micro-level of project-specific regulation may only happen as part of a forensic examination of an environmental disaster, such as the Bhopal tragedy, or where the spotlight of attention is focused through transnational litigation, inquiries and campaigns, such as the Chad–Cameroon pipeline. Attention to specific contractual aspects of project governance is perhaps often viewed as the terrain of legal practitioners rather than scholars.[14] The result being that we have yet to gain a clear picture of the ways in which environmental protection is negotiated at the project level.

Another consequence of the privileging of dispute resolution in international investment law scholarship is that suggested avenues for reform tend to overemphasise dispute resolution remedies. Where issues of sustainability are given short shrift in decisions, the suggested remedy is the amicus curiae brief.[15] Where the exclusion of non-parties from adjudication is identified as problematic, the prescription is the use of more participatory and open procedures for arbitral tribunals. Less

[12] See e.g. K. Tienhaara, 'Mineral Investment and the Regulation of the Environment in Developing Countries: Lessons from Ghana' (2006) 6 *International Environmental Agreement: Politics, Law and Economics* 371; P. Stalley, 'A Double-edged Sword: Foreign Firms and Environmental Governance in China', PhD dissertation, George Washington University, 2006.

[13] G. Verhoosel, 'Foreign Direct Investment and Legal Constraints on Domestic Environmental Policies: Striking a "Reasonable" Balance between Stability and Change' (1998) 29 *Law and Policy of International Business* 451.

[14] See e.g. L. B. Ahearn, 'Environmental Aspects of International Transactions', in M. R. Sandstrom and D. N. Goldsweig, *Negotiating and Structuring International Commercial Transactions*, 2nd edn (Chicago, Ill.: American Bar Association, 2003), 451.

[15] See Footer, 'BITs and Pieces', 33–4 (exploring the incorporation of social and environmental issues in arbitral proceedings through the acceptance of amicus curiae briefs as evidence that 'foreign investment is developing a social conscience'); E. Savarese, 'Amicus Curiae Participation in Investor–State Arbitral Proceedings' (2007) 17 *Italian Yearbook of International Law* 99.

attention is given to reform of contract negotiation processes, where important participatory improvements could equally be advocated.

13.1.2 The sources of information on project-specific contracts

A concrete result of the fact that project-specific information and analysis is not being provided by scholars is that the available information on environmental aspects of specific projects comes from two sources: either companies or NGOs. In other words, it falls to the private sector to produce commentary on contractual agreements. This affects the questions asked. It affects the way the information is packaged. It leads to a view of individual contracts as autonomous entities rather than the product of wider social and legal processes. And it contributes to a tendency to view law as tools.

An instrumentalist view of law emerges from a context in which contracts are being assessed as tools or instruments for change. Existing work on contracts tends to be situated within a larger project of improving contractual negotiations and agreements. The Revenue Watch Institute has published a detailed analysis of concession agreement negotiations in Liberia: *Getting a Better Deal from the Extractive Sector.*[16] The International Institute for Sustainable Development has produced a *Model International Agreement on Investment for Sustainable Development.*[17] The International Institute for Environment and Development published in 2010 *Investment Contracts and Sustainable Development: How to Make Contracts for Fairer and More Sustainable Natural Resource Investments.*[18] These all represent exceptionally valuable contributions to the literature. They affirm the importance of investment contracts as instruments of governance. They all approach contracts with a reformist agenda – prescribing ways in which contracts can be improved to achieve more sustainable development.

[16] R. Kaul, A. Heuty and A. Norman, *Getting a Better Deal from the Extractive Sector: Concession Negotiation in Liberia, 2006–2008* (New York: Revenue Watch Institute, 2009).

[17] H. Mann, K. von Moltke, L.-E. Peterson and A. Cosbey, *IISD Model International Agreement on Investment for Sustainable Development: Negotiators Handbook*, 2nd edn (Winnipeg: IISD, 2006).

[18] L. Cotula, *Investment Contracts and Sustainable Development: How to Make Contracts for Fairer and More Sustainable Natural Resource Investments* (London: IIED, 2010).

13.1.3 *The limited scope of the legal radar*

A literature examining various conservation contracts is emerging. But it is largely emerging in the work of conservation biologists, economists and conservation organisations. Agreements are thus variously framed as 'economic instruments' or 'conservation tools'. Recent contributions to the literature from legal scholars echo this focus on the question: do these agreements work? Yet even when these developments take on an explicitly legally binding, contractual form, they seem to operate beneath the legal radar, invisible to law.[19] This again contributes to a view of contracts as tools; capable of seamless removal from their legal and social settings. The set of papers produced for this volume thus marks a particularly valuable contribution to the literature as they represent an effort to engage with economic and financial instruments on many levels and to situate these agreements within the wider challenge of implementing international environmental norms.

Conservation contracts provide an opportunity for important *intra*-disciplinary legal work. The insights of private law will be particularly valuable in understanding how contracts work and how they are embedded in legal frameworks of public and private law, national, transnational and international law.[20]

13.1.4 *Beyond an instrumentalist view of contracts*

There are thus various factors that explain why contracts, to the extent that they are analysed at all, are conceptualised as tools or instruments of environmental protection. I now turn to show why this view of contracts is unduly restrictive, and indeed problematic. This involves a critique of environmental law that is easy for me to identify, because it emerges from and applies to my own work.

Conceptualising agreements as tools emerges from a 'scholarly compulsion to point the way toward reform'.[21] The risk is that a focus on the

[19] Joanne Scott and Jane Holder make a similar observation with respect to partnerships that have emerged around the European Union's Water Framework Directive. See J. Scott and J. Holder, 'Law and New Environmental Governance in the European Union', in J. Scott and G. De Búrca (eds.), *Law and New Governance in the EU and the US* (Oxford: Hart Publishing, 2006), 211.

[20] See e.g. Hugh Collins' thought-provoking treatise exploring both how contracts regulate and are regulated: H. Collins, *Regulating Contracts* (Oxford University Press, 1999).

[21] P. W. Kahn, *The Cultural Study of Law: Reconstructing Legal Scholarship* (University of Chicago Press, 1999), 6.

innovative potential of a particular policy prescription produces a partial account of law. Particularly in the environmental context, there is a huge policy appetite for new, innovative approaches to governance. Much environmental law commentary, coming from both scholars and campaigners, is written from an activist perspective, with legal reform as the goal.[22] The consequence of this approach is that a certain conceptualisation of environmental law pervades scholarship. It privileges litigation and dispute resolution – cases in domestic law, arbitral tribunal rulings in foreign investment contexts. It also approaches individual projects with an eagerness to extract lessons, best practices and precedents to apply elsewhere. This can create a misleading picture of environmental law as populated by distinct, autonomous and transferable instruments. It can obscure the embeddedness of an agreement in its own cultural and legal context. And it can lead one to overplay 'success stories' and to giving insufficient attention to failures. Viewing contracts as tools can be problematic as it exaggerates their transferability.

A further consequence of conceptualising environmental law as 'tools' or 'safeguards' is that it contributes to a proceduralisation of environmental law. Environmental requirements can become categorised in a check-the-box way. We can be lured in by the simplicity of counting references to the precautionary principle in documents, counting references to environmental impact assessment in legislation. We can create a checklist of whether a project meets IFC performance standards or contains an appropriate environmental management plan. But we also need to map and look carefully at the documents that are generated by these checklists. This is the task I turn to in the next section.

13.2 Foreign investment projects and environmental protection: contracts as blind spots

This part of the chapter involves a preliminary mapping exercise; an opportunity to identify some of the contractual mechanisms for biodiversity protection in project-specific settings. This is far from a comprehensive picture of transnational contracts for biodiversity protection. Rather, I focus on two settings. First, I look to extractive industry projects with

[22] See e.g. J. Kimerling, 'International Standards in Ecuador's Amazon Oil Fields: The Privatization of Environmental Law' (2001) 26 *Columbia Journal of Environmental Law* 289; I. A. Bowles and G. T. Prickett, *Footprints in the Jungle: Natural Resource Industries, Infrastructure and Biodiversity Conservation* (Oxford University Press, 2001).

the aim of identifying the multiplicity of partnerships and agreements that pertain to biodiversity protection that might otherwise operate under the legal radar (13.2.1). Second, I examine transnational conservation contracts, i.e., agreements which address the protection of discrete areas of land or water to achieve conservation objectives involving actors in more than one country (13.2.2).

These two categories of agreements are chosen as they illuminate the topic of this volume – harnessing foreign investment to promote environmental protection. They exemplify the range of agreements being concluded by and between various private sectors, including corporations and conservation groups. That said, the identity of the actors involved as non-state actors is not a subject I dwell on here. That observation is well reflected already in the literature on private authority in international affairs, in debates on the retreat of the state, and in existing work on civil society networks and transnational social movements.[23] Instead of directing attention to the actors, my task is to illuminate the instruments involved.

13.2.1 *Extractive industry projects and contractual webs*

A neglected aspect of biodiversity governance is the project-specific agreement making that occurs as part of the approval process for large development projects. Large mining and oil and gas projects, for example, are routinely subject to a range of biodiversity protection demands from state and non-state communities of interest and must answer these demands to secure both legal and social licences to operate, particularly in ecologically sensitive sites. Contracts with governments, local communities and conservation organisations emerge as one mechanism for responding to demands for biodiversity protection. Natural-resource companies have also developed autonomous foundations that channel community development and environmental protection initiatives to project-affected communities. But little is known about these webs of agreements and institutions and how they are situated within the complex, multicentred and multilayered worlds of public and private law.

[23] See e.g. P. Wapner, *Environmental Activism and World Civic Politics* (Albany, NY: State University of New York, 1996); P. Glasbergen, 'Setting the Scene: The Partnership Paradigm in the Making', in Glasbergen, Biermann and Mol, *Partnerships, Governance and Sustainable Development*, 7.

Contracts are central to large project regulation. They provide a key mechanism for environmental regulation of project operations. Loan agreements,[24] insurance agreements,[25] investment agreements,[26] construction contracts,[27] environmental agreements[28] and community benefit agreements[29] are just a few examples of contracts that adopt environmental regulatory functions. The environmental significance of contracts can be obscured for a number of reasons. First, these contracts may not be public and thus their terms may be unknown. Second, as a form of private law, the wider public and political significance of contracts can easily be missed. Contracts are highly contextualised instruments that can fine tune regulatory responses to the challenges of specific situations and unknown contingencies. They can provide for environmental performance bonds, or security deposits, which provide a 'stick' should negotiated attempts to secure environmental outcomes fail. But contractual provisions can equally entrench environmental disregard and fail to provide for responsive approaches to environmentally destructive behaviour.

In the setting of large extractive projects, contracts are critical because so many aspects of regulation are one-off and negotiated. At the most general level, foreign investment contracts themselves raise significant environmental issues. Common forms of foreign investment contracts include concession agreements, production sharing agreements and

[24] See J. W. Head, 'Environmental Conditionality in the Operations of International Development Finance Institutions' (1991) 1 *Kansas Journal of Law and Public Policy* 15; I. F. I. Shihata, 'The World Bank and the Environment: A Legal Perspective' (1992) 16 *Maryland Journal of International Law and Trade* 1.

[25] See P. K. Freeman, 'Environmental Insurance as a Policy Enforcement Tool in Developing Countries' (1997) 18 *University of Pennsylvania Journal of International Economic Law* 477.

[26] For analysis of conservation issues in concession agreements, see D. N. Smith and C. F. Kormos, 'Conservation and Concession Contracts: Environmental Issues in Mineral Extraction Agreements', in Bowles and Prickett, *Footprints in the Jungle*, 233.

[27] See O. Perez, 'Using Private–Public Linkages to Regulate Environmental Conflicts: The Case of International Construction Contracts' (2002) 29 *Journal of Law and Society* 77 (arguing that standard form construction contracts can institutionalise ecological indifference).

[28] On the practice of environmental contracting in mining projects, see N. A. Affolder, 'Rethinking Environmental Contracting' (2010) 21 *Journal of Environmental Law and Policy* 155.

[29] Community benefit agreements were concluded, for example, in the West African Gas Pipeline Project in the form of Memorandums of Understanding signed by the company and fourteen affected communities. See Cotula, *Investment Contracts and Sustainable Development*, 12.

build–operate–transfer agreements. Individual aspects of these agreements, such as stabilisation clauses, have been identified as posing significant obstacles for environmental protection.[30] In earlier decades, government negotiators had considerable discretion in prescribing the terms of these agreements. This broad discretion has to some degree been curtailed by legislation and the use of model or standard contractual forms.[31]

Environmental regulation of large projects through contracts does not only happen through investment agreements. Contracts with governments, local communities and conservation organisations have emerged as one mechanism for responding to community demands for environmental safeguards in individual projects. Negotiated agreements with companies may take the form of environmental agreements, impact and benefit agreements or good neighbour agreements.[32] These negotiated agreements may respond to gaps in regulatory regimes and add an additional layer of project-specific environmental regulation. It is instructive to look at the example of a specific project to appreciate the multilayered contractual environmental commitments.

The QIT Madagascar Minerals (QMM) ilmenite mine well illustrates the tensions surrounding extractive activity in an environmentally sensitive site, and the emergence of project-specific contractual arrangements to respond to these tensions. The mine is situated in an area of Madagascar noted for its unique biodiversity. Madagascar is the home of many endemic species. The QMM project is a US$1.1 billion joint venture between Rio Tinto, which owns 80 per cent of QMM, and the Government of Madagascar, which holds the remaining 20 per cent. While prospecting, exploration and mining take place in Madagascar, once mined, the minerals are shipped to Quebec, Canada for processing.

A number of agreements that impact on the environmental regulation of this project are negotiated agreements. First, the company has agreed to certain biodiversity offset agreements. Offset agreements address conservation activities designed to compensate for the loss of or harm to

[30] *Ibid.*; P. Rosenblum and S. Maples, *Contracts Confidential: Ending Secret Deals in the Extractive Industries* (New York: Revenue Watch, 2009).

[31] D. N. Smith and L. T. Wells, *Negotiating Third-World Mineral Agreements, Promises as Prologues* (Cambridge, Mass.: Ballinger, 1975).

[32] See e.g. C. O'Faircheallaigh and T. Corbett, 'Indigenous Participation in Environmental Management of Mining Projects: The Role of Negotiated Agreements' (2005) 14 *Environmental Politics* 629.

biodiversity by development projects.[33] QMM agreed to forgo mining on 12 per cent of the deposit areas in a highly endangered littoral forest. Consequently, three conservation zones totalling 625 hectares have been created. The zones are legally protected under Madagascar's protected area system. Agreements to establish a community reforestation programme have also been concluded with the company.

As part of these commitments, the company established 37,500 hectares of legally protected biodiversity offsets. The company co-manages the conservation zones with local communities and the Malagasy forest department under a *dina* (a traditional Malagasy social contract).[34] The *dina* also incorporates the company's environmental and social programmes as set out in its integrated development plan. It is overseen by a committee consisting of communal authorities, community representatives and the company.[35] The *dina* thus creates a joint management construct for the Mandena area. It emerges from an approach of decentralising management of certain natural resources, introduced by the Malagasy Government through formal procedures known as the *Gestion locale sécurisée* and *Gestion contractuelle des forêts*. This joint management approach involved negotiations between the communities, the government and the company on land use plans, agreements and the *dina* itself. The process of negotiating contracts and finding workable frameworks for joint management has proven challenging, particularly given the lack of successful prior experiences upon which the stakeholders could build.[36]

A number of the commitments made by the company and described above are the result of the company's partnership agreements with various international non-profit organisations (including Kew Gardens, Birdlife International, Conservation International and Fauna & Flora International). These commitments focus on the development of

[33] See generally K. ten Kate, J. Bishop and R. Bayon, *Biodiversity Offsets: Views, Experience and the Business Case* (Gland: IUCN/Insight Investment, 2004).

[34] Rio Tinto Madagascar, 'Positive Impacts of the Project', online: Rio Tinto Madagascar, www.riotintomadagascar.com/english/bioImpacts.asp (accessed 19 January 2012).

[35] Rio Tinto Madagascar, 'The DINA', online: Rio Tinto Madagascar, www.riotintomadagascar.com/english/sustainSocioDINA.asp (accessed 19 January 2012).

[36] For a discussion of the challenges that have emerged, see C. Rarivoson, 'The Mandena Dina, a Potential Tool at the Local Level for Sustainable Management of Renewable Natural Resources', in J. U. Ganzhorn, S. M. Goodman and M. Vincelette (eds.), *Biodiversity, Ecology, and Conservation of Littoral Ecosystems in Southeastern Madagascar, Tolagnaro* (Washington, DC: Smithsonian Institution, 2007), 309.

processes for rehabilitation and restoration and provide opportunities for the partner conservation organisations to contribute to Rio Tinto's Biodiversity Action Plan.[37]

I only mention here a few of the contracts applicable to environmental regulation of this mine to highlight the importance of contracts as a source of project-specific regulation. This survey of contracts does not attempt to answer the question: will these measures robustly protect the biodiversity in the affected areas?[38] Contracts can be extremely responsive to project-specific contexts and unforeseen issues. But as the concern around the use of stabilisation clauses highlights, contracts can also lead to a gutting or undermining of otherwise applicable environmental regulation. A further concern that contracts raise is the ability to dislodge contractual forms of environmental regulation by exiting the contract. Chad demonstrated this in the context of the Chad–Cameroon pipeline project where it evaded World Bank conditions in a loan agreement by prepaying the loan. Governance through contracts allows parties to contract out of domestic law and apply ambiguous international standards as the only governing law.[39] This concern can be better understood through a richer understanding of the multiple interacting arms of project-specific regulation, and the multiple levels of contractual regulation. The challenge then is to provide for fine-grained analysis of individual contracts but to situate this analysis within the evolving transnational architecture of environmental principles, recommendations, codes and international standards emerging to regulate the environmental dimensions of foreign investment.[40]

[37] The Biodiversity Action Plan was formulated in partnership with Fauna & Flora International. QIT Madagascar Minerals (QMM) was one of the four trial sites. Rio Tinto, *Rio Tinto and Biodiversity: Achieving Results on the Ground* (2008), online: Rio Tinto, www.riotinto.com/documents/ReportsPublications/RTBidoversitystrategyfinal.pdf (accessed 19 January 2012).

[38] This continues to be a subject of heated debate. See e.g. S. Burgin, 'An Environmental Scientist's View of the Role of Biodiversity Banking Offsets in Conservation' (2008) 17 *Biodiversity Conservation* 807; Conservation International, *Review of an Ilmenite Project in Southeastern Madagascar* (2001); Worldwide Fund for Nature (WWF), *An Update on the QMM Mining Project in the Anosy Region* (2005).

[39] For a survey of oil and gas sector practices with respect to this issue, see K. Tienhaara, 'Foreign Investment Clauses in the Oil and Gas Sector: A Survey of Environmentally Relevant Clauses' (2011) 11 *Sustainable Development Law and Policy* 16.

[40] Priscilla Schwartz' work on the Koidu Kimberlite Mining Project in Sierra Leone provides a rich example of such nuanced, project-specific research. See P. Schwartz, 'Corporate Activities and Justice in Sierra Leone Mining', in J. Ebbesson and P. Okawa (eds.), *Environmental Law and Justice in Context* (Cambridge University Press, 2009), 429. For a discussion of the wider transnational environmental architecture relevant to

13.2.2 Transnational conservation contracts

While extractive projects may provide a setting for examining contracts for biodiversity protection where such protection is viewed as a necessary offset or cost of doing business, transnational conservation contracts represent foreign investments where biodiversity protection is the investment. Transnational conservation contracts are agreements which address the protection of discrete areas of land or water to achieve conservation objectives, including the protection of valued, endangered or critical habitat, and involve actors in more than one country. The word 'conservation' is notably contested.[41] It is used intentionally in this definition to emphasise an approach of ecosystem or species preservation which these agreements advance. Many examples of economic instruments that operate through conservation contracts are the subject of other, more detailed, contributions to this volume.[42] The aim of this section is thus to provide an overview of these instruments and their operation as a form of environmental governance, and to argue for a methodological approach that takes seriously a study of contracts as legal texts.

The agreements that fall within the category of 'transnational conservation agreements' admittedly adopt diverse labels: covenants, agreements, contracts, negotiated agreements, voluntary agreements. They have a variety of potential legal consequences. Some are legally binding; others are not. Further, the various parties may have very different assumptions about the legality of the agreement. Framing these agreements as 'contracts' invites a closer look at the text of these agreements and their legality. The term contract also signifies the relevance of private law to these agreements.

13.2.2.1 Conservation concession agreements

Conservation concessions involve lease agreements. National authorities or local resource users may lease public lands or resources to conservation groups who commit to use the lands for conservation

individual projects, see E. Morgera, *Corporate Accountability in International Environmental Law* (Oxford University Press, 2009).

41 Janis Alcorn defines conservation as a 'social and political process by which natural resources … are managed to maintain biodiversity'. J. Alcorn, 'Big Conservation and Little Conservation: Collaboration in Managing Global and Local Heritage' (1995) 98 *Yale School of Forestry and Environmental Studies Bulletin* 15.

42 See Chapters 6, 7 and 8 of this volume.

purposes.[43] The simplest forms of conservation concessions are modelled after extractive industry concession agreements, such as timber or mining concessions. Rather than mine or log the concession area, the conservation investor pays the government for the right not to develop the land. The conservation group commits to protect the lands for conservation purposes. Payments are calculated in a way that intends to compensate the landowner for forgoing extractive use of the land. The contract also typically includes norms and guidelines for monitoring and enforcing the protection of the site.

Legal developments to facilitate the use of concession agreements are being introduced in a number of countries. For example, in 2002, the Peruvian Government included a new provision in its Forestry Law that allows conservation concessions to be adopted as a legal form of land use. The adoption of this law followed discussions between the Peruvian Government and US conservation groups, who helped draft the legislation.[44] International conservation groups have since signed concession agreements with the Peruvian Government, including a forty-year concession agreement in 2006 between the Wildlife Conservation Society and the Government of Peru to protect habitat for the endangered red uakari monkey.[45] This example of Peru is instructive of the deeper legal significance of conservation contracts. In this case, legislative reform was necessary to accommodate this novel form of contract.

13.2.2.2 Conservation performance payments agreements

Conservation performance payments involve a similar approach to that of concession agreements but they do not centre around lease arrangements. Rather, performance payments involve the purchase of a well-defined environmental service (or land use likely to secure that service) with payments that are conditional on the performance of a biodiversity-related outcome such as habitat protection or species preservation.[46] These payments are often made by foreign donors or conservation

[43] Environmental Law Institute, *Legal Tools for Private Lands Conservation in Latin America* (Washington, DC: Environmental Law Institute, 2003), 25.

[44] K. Ellison, 'Renting Biodiversity: The Concessions Approach' (2003) 4 *Conservation Magazine* 20.

[45] See Lago Preto Conservation Concession, www.mbowler.mistral.co.uk/lagopreto/ (accessed 19 January 2012).

[46] This definition is adapted from Sven Wunder's definition of payments for environmental services. S. Wunder, 'The Efficiency of Payments for Environmental Services in Tropical Conservation' (2007) 21 *Conservation Biology* 50.

organisations to local communities or governments in low-income countries to secure the conservation of endangered ecosystems. The motivating idea is to steer economic development away from the most environmentally destructive forms (such as mining or oil and gas development) and to encourage individuals and communities to invest in activities that do not lead to habitat or biodiversity loss (such as ecotourism). An international habitat reserve programme (IHRP) provides one manifestation of this practice. Contracts pursuant to an IHRP require the outside agent (often an international conservation organisation) to make periodic performance payments in exchange for local actors ensuring that target ecosystems remain protected. Compliance monitoring ensures that target levels of species continue to be found in the ecosystem and payments are dependent on these targets being reached.[47]

13.2.2.3 Forest carbon agreements

Forest carbon agreements are a type of performance payment agreement. They reflect an approach of using markets to address the critical role of forests in helping to mitigate the growing threat from anthropogenic climate change. Forest carbon offset agreements are largely transacted between greenhouse gas emitters in industrialised countries and sellers in developing countries. Forest carbon agreements are a growth area for transnational environmental law. But these agreements pose challenges for lawyers. Forest carbon is a new form of property. Voluntary markets have yet to conclude clear rules of property rights for forest carbon. States are still developing legal regimes to allocate property rights in forest carbon.[48] Further, the nature of existing forest carbon markets is such that carbon buyers and sellers are unlikely to be on unequal footing in terms of their commercial experience and legal representation.[49] Some USA-based NGOs have sought to 'level the playing field' between buyers and sellers by drafting prototype agreements for forest carbon emissions reduction purchases, modelled on US contract law.[50] These agreements seek to redress the one-sided legal drafting done by carbon purchasers.

[47] P. J. Ferraro, 'Global Habitat Protection: Limitations of Development Interventions and a Role for Conservation Performance Payments' (2001) 15 *Conservation Biology* 994.

[48] See The Norton Rose Group, *Forest Carbon Rights in REDD+ Countries: A Snapshot of Africa* (London: Norton Rose LLP, 2010); D. Takacs, *Forest Carbon: Law and Property Rights* (Arlington, Va.: Conservation International, 2009), 28–57.

[49] *Contracting for Forest Carbon: Elements of a Model Forest Carbon Purchase Agreement* (Forest Trends and the Katoomba Group, 2010), 1.

[50] See the 'Model Agreement', *ibid.*, 3.

Forest carbon agreements highlight legal issues relevant to many of the other contracts discussed in this article. In many cases, contracting takes place against a backdrop of unclear land tenure, including uncertainties arising from disputes between indigenous peoples and state governments. A legal context that emphasises freedom of contract may be foreign to landowners signing these agreements. Critiques of forest carbon agreements further charge that these agreements allow 'the wealthy to sequester further wealth far out of proportion to the carbon sequestered',[51] that they are based on inadequate scientific knowledge of tropical forests,[52] that they are subject to leakage (that is to say that preserving forests in one location will lead to logging elsewhere) and that they are inadequately geared to protect biodiversity.[53]

A significantly increased role for forest carbon agreements is contemplated through REDD+, a proposed performance-based mechanism under negotiation through the United Nations Framework Convention on Climate Change, as markets for carbon become legally entrenched. These developments are leading to inter-state agreements on forest conservation. For example, a memorandum of understanding was signed between Norway and Guyana in 2009.[54] This agreement provides for payments by Norway of up to US$250 million during a five-year period ending in 2015 in return for Guyana's commitment to limit forest-based greenhouse gas emissions and to protect its rainforest as an asset for the world. A careful reading of this memorandum of understanding reveals the extent to which the agreement is embedded within other forms of transnational law. Guyana is required under the Agreement to show evidence of entering a formal dialogue with the European Union with the intent of joining its forest law enforcement, governance and trade processes towards a voluntary partnership

[51] D. Takacs, 'Carbon into Gold: Forest Carbon Offsets, Climate Change Adaptation, and International Law' (2009) 15 *Hastings West-Northwest Journal of Environmental Law and Policy* 42.

[52] A. Grainger, 'Uncertainty in the Construction of Global Knowledge of Tropical Forests' (2010) 34 *Progress in Physical Geography* 811–12.

[53] O. Venter et al., 'Harnessing Carbon Payments to Protect Biodiversity' (2009) 326 *Science* 1368.

[54] Memorandum of Understanding between the Government of the Cooperative Republic of Guyana and the Government of the Kingdom of Norway regarding Cooperation on Issues Related to the Fight against Climate Change, the Protection of Biodiversity and the Enhancement of Sustainable Development (2009), online: www.regjeringen.no/upload/MD/Vedlegg/Internasjonalt/miljosamarbeid_utviklingsland/mou__norway_guyana.pdf (accessed 19 January 2012).

agreement. Guyana also has to show evidence of its decision to enter a formal dialogue with the Extractive Industries Transparency Initiative (EITI) or an alternative mechanism that the two countries agree will advance similar aims to the EITI.

13.2.2.4 Private protected areas and company reserves

Company protected areas and privately managed reserves involve private forms of land ownership and management and can be distinguished from conservation concessions and performance payments, where ownership resides with the government or community landowners. The extent of privately conserved land is unknown as these reserves do not fall within international efforts to map protected areas such as the World Database of Protected Areas.[55] The existence of privately protected areas is confirmed by the annual reports of both private companies and conservation organisations that document their ownership and use of private lands for conservation purposes.

Countries have developed different legal mechanisms for recognising private protected areas or reserves. Purchase agreements and conservation easements are examples of these legal mechanisms. In Latin America, for example, many countries have legally recognised the private reserve as a device to protect private lands and a number of conservation organisations are experimenting with the use of easements to provide for private land protection.[56]

The creation and funding of private protected areas have long been strategies of internationally minded conservation organisations intent on long-term protection of lands of conservation importance.[57] In Costa Rica, land purchases became a critical aspect of 'save the rainforest' campaigns and led to the creation of globally recognised protected areas such as the Monteverde Rainforest.[58] Companies are also participants in private land conservation, although the extent of 'company reserves' remains unknown. Corporate contributions to land conservation take diverse forms including the sale of land for conservation purposes, ownership and management of land for biodiversity

[55] S. Stolton and N. Dudley, *Company Reserves: Integrating Biological Reserves Owned and Managed by Commercial Companies into the Global Protected Areas Network – A Review of Options*, WWF International White Paper (August 2007), 5.

[56] For examples, see ELI, *Legal Tools*, 16, 21. [57] *Ibid.*, 15.

[58] L. A. Vivanco, *Green Encounters: Shaping and Contesting Environmentalism in Rural Costa Rica* (New York: Berghahn Books, 2006), 60–78.

conservation and the management of land for conservation purposes in cases where the company is not the direct owner.[59] One example of a company owning and managing land for conservation purposes is the Bushmanland Conservation Initiative in Namibia where an agreement provides for private land protection by mining company Anglo Base Metals.[60]

Private and company reserves are particularly significant for forest management and protection. Although much forest land remains owned by governments, it is often leased to international forest companies under long-term leases. Accordingly, conservation management may fall to these companies during their leasehold periods. For example, in January 2006, the Senepis-Buluhala Tiger Conservation Area in Indonesia was approved by the Indonesian Minister of Forestry. The peat swamp forest conservation area is habitat for the Sumatran tiger, but forest companies have been granted concessions to manage the land. These companies will maintain ownership of the land under their concession licences, but, according to a Ministerial letter agreement, the companies are responsible for supporting the mission and activities of the Senepis conservation area in the future.[61]

Distinct from funding and establishing private conservation areas is the practice of international conservation organisations contracting with national governments to establish national forests. Conservation International, for example, signed a 'biodiversity agreement' with the Government of Equatorial Guinea to establish a national forest. Under the agreement, the government commits to establishing a national forest and a national conservation trust fund permanently to support the country's biodiversity conservation.[62]

13.2.2.5 Access and benefit-sharing agreements

Access and benefit-sharing agreements are one of the rare forms of transnational conservation contracts to have already captured the

[59] Stolton and Dudley, *Company Reserves*, 16–20.

[60] *Ibid.* The legal form of this agreement involved a 2006 memorandum of agreement between the Botanical Society of South Africa, Anglo Base Metals and the Department of Tourism, Environment & Conservation, Government of Namibia.

[61] *Ibid.*, 19.

[62] Conservation International, press release, 'Conservation International and Equatorial Guinea Sign Agreement to Collaborate on Conservation' (April 2006), online: Conservation International, www.conservation.org/newsroom/pressreleases/Pages/042506_ci_equatorial_guinea_agreement.aspx (accessed 19 January 2012).

attention of international environmental law.[63] This may be due to the close links between these contracts and the 1992 Convention on Biological Diversity, or it may be a result of the emotive and charged debates over charges of 'biopiracy' and 'biodiversity prospecting'.

A number of different sectors, including the pharmaceutical, biotechnology, seed, cosmetic and food and beverage industries, research and develop commercial products from genetic resources. These industries increasingly enter into agreements with providers of genetic resources. The contractual forms favoured, the terms on which access is ensured, and the legal remedies that companies use for compliance and enforcement, all vary between industries and even between companies.[64] The existing legal regime governing access and benefit-sharing regimes was bolstered by the negotiation of the Nagoya Protocol as part of the tenth Conference of the Parties to the Convention on Biological Diversity in October 2010.[65]

The Nagoya Protocol provides an example of an international instrument which supports and advances the use of contractual approaches to biodiversity governance. It reflects the fact that international treaties and conservation contracts do not stand in competition as governance mechanisms, but rather that contractual approaches often emerge from treaty instruments and aim to implement treaty norms.

13.2.2.6 Debt-for-nature swaps

Debt-for-nature swaps emerged in the 1980s as a mechanism for creating protected areas in developing countries.[66] In return for commitments to

[63] For a detailed discussion of the emergence of benefit-sharing agreements in Southern Africa to develop anti-obesity products from the Hoodia, see R. Wynberg, Doris Schroeder and R. Chennells (eds.), *Indigenous Peoples, Consent and Benefit-Sharing* (Dordrecht: Springer, 2009). On biodiversity prospecting generally, see W. V. Reid et al., *Biodiversity Prospecting: Using Genetic Resources for Sustainable Development* (Washington, DC: World Resources Institute, 1993).

[64] S. Laird and R. Wynberg, 'Study on Access and Benefit-sharing Arrangements – An Overview', *Access and Benefit Sharing in Practice: Trends in Partnerships across Sectors* (Montreal: Secretariat of the Convention on Biological Diversity, 2008), 9–11.

[65] Nagoya Protocol on Access to Genetic Resources and the Fair and Equitable Sharing of Benefits Arising from this Utilisation (Nagoya Protocol). The Protocol opened for signature on 1 February 2011 and will come into force ninety days after the fiftieth ratification. For the Nagoya Protocol text, see online: Convention on Biological Diversity, www.cbd.int/abs/text/ (accessed 19 January 2012).

[66] See S. L. Kokenes, 'Debt for Nature Swaps: Conservancy or Cemetery', doctoral dissertation, College of Business and Public Management, University of La Verne, California, 2007, 111–12 for a partial list of completed swaps.

set aside land as nature reserves or to adopt sustainable management practices, foreign debt is purchased, donated or released. For example, in 1987, Conservation International and the Government of Bolivia entered into an agreement to establish conservation and sustainable use areas in exchange for debt cancellation. The funds were provided to Conservation International from a private US foundation.[67] Between 1987 and 1988, Costa Rica was able to capitalise on donations of over $10 million to convert $69 million of foreign debt into $33 million in local currency bonds within a period of two years.[68] The proceeds from the issuance of bonds were used by the government to support parks and reforest thousands of acres of land.

Three 'generations' of debt-for-nature swaps have now been documented. The first generation of swaps involved large international conservation organisations (the World Wildlife Fund, The Nature Conservancy and Conservation International) and the purchase of commercial debt. These organisations purchased debt through secondary markets and swapped the debt for environmental protection commitments by developing countries. The second generation of swaps saw western governments negotiate agreements to reduce the hard-currency international debt obligations of developing countries in exchange for their agreement to spend the funds on environmental protection. The current, third generation is marked by efforts to combine the best of the earlier approaches, involving public and private actors, with local debt denominated in hard currency and a focus on the performance of funds earmarked for environmental protection. While it is unclear whether these swaps have made a significant impact on the issues of deforestation and biodiversity loss, they are significant in revealing the extent to which private conservation organisations can foster institutional innovations.[69]

[67] In 1987, Conservation International obtained a grant of $100,000 from the Frank Weeden Foundation, which it used to purchase a debt of $650,000 owed to a Swiss Bank by the government of Bolivia. In exchange for cancellation of the debt, the Bolivian government agreed to establish four conservation and sustainable use areas covering over 4 million acres. See S. U. Amin and E. L. Karen, 'A Possible Solution to Tropical Troubles?: Debt-for-Nature Swaps' (1992) 24 *Futures* 658 and 659.

[68] All amounts are in US dollars. These donations were administered through the World Wildlife Fund. See *ibid.*, 659–61.

[69] C. Jakobeit, 'Non-state Actors Leading the Way: Debt-for-Nature Swaps', in R. Keohane and M. Levy (eds.), *Institutions for Environmental Aid* (Cambridge, Mass.: MIT Press, 1996), 127.

The above overview of some key forms of transnational conservation contracts points to the need for further, more detailed and systematic, research on the prevalence of contractual agreements and their wider significance. This effort to delineate and describe six categories of transnational conservation contracts is intended as a preliminary effort to highlight the diversity of contracts that are being negotiated, and how little we know about these contractual arrangements. At the same time as it is critical to emphasise the highly varied form and substance of conservation contracts, common concerns surrounding the significance of governance by contract justify a collective examination of these agreements.

13.2.3 Governance by contract

The legal and cultural significance of contractual forms of governance transcends questions of the legality of individual agreements. This is evidenced by the fact that legal regimes often need to be altered to allow for specific contracts. The example of the Peruvian conservation concession discussed earlier reveals that legislative reforms may be necessary to pave the way for specific conservation agreements. Contractual forms of governance often rely heavily on precedent. The use of standard form contracts and model contracts in natural resource project negotiations can entrench environmental provisions as standard clauses. In the case of transnational conservation contracts, the negotiation of forest carbon agreements or conservation concession agreements often involve repeat players who embed what become standard contractual terms in very diverse settings.

As a form of transnational environmental governance, contracts (and particularly the use of model or standard form contracts) can erase rather than affirm the legal culture of certain negotiating parties. While contracts provide the opportunity for a detailed and highly contextualised agreement, the repeat use of certain contractual forms and language can work against the contextualised potential of contracts. Contracts embed an approach of market liberalism and freedom of contract that may be entirely foreign to certain parties. Contracts are framed as voluntary instruments, while parties may feel compelled to sign agreements or to agree to certain contractual terms. The conceptualisation of contracts as private law instruments may also depoliticise these agreements, obscuring their core political nature. Contracts are not a neutral form of environmental governance. In the context of transnational environmental governance, particular concerns about the use of contracts arise. These include issues around agenda-setting and the uneven patterns of contractual negotiations that may emerge from placing large conservation NGOs ('big NGOs' or BINGOs) in the driver's seat. Contracts can be perceived as part of a paradigmatic shift 'in which economic growth and big business increasingly are presented as essential to successful biodiversity conservation'.[70] Such a neo-liberal view of biodiversity conservation emerges particularly in the context of extractive projects where biodiversity mitigation and offsetting are seen as mechanisms that facilitate the advance of extractive activity in sensitive ecosystems.

13.3 Project-specific research: of materials and methods

There are many reasons to avoid the study of individual contracts. Contracts that deal with biodiversity protection, both extractive industry contracts and transnational conservation contracts, are often private. Considerable efforts may be expended to gain access to these agreements, with no guarantee that they can be publicly disclosed. As few contractual clauses are the subject of dispute resolution, there is a disconnect between the tools available to scholars (arbitration reports) and the subject of study. Contracts are also subject to frequent renegotiation. They may not be implemented and may create an erroneous picture of contractual relations 'on the ground'.

But ignoring contracts results in an impoverished account of not only the role of the private sector in environmental protection in the twenty-first century: it leads to an undeveloped account of law. The need for descriptively thick accounts of individual contractual regimes derives from the unevenness of contracts.[71] Different contractual regimes are adopted in different countries, but also between projects in the same country.[72] Studies that focus solely on national law can thus present an incomplete picture of the legal disparities between regions and between specific project settings.

[70] J. Igoe, S. Sullivan and D. Brockington, 'Problematizing Neoliberal Biodiversity Conservation: Displaced and Disobedient Knowledge' (2009) 3 *Current Conservation* 4.

[71] This is revealed in Lorenzo Cotula's study of land deals in Africa. One contract he cites from Mali brings local farmers into the partnership and applies international social and environmental standards. Other contracts undermine environmental protection goals. They are negotiated in some legal contexts where safeguards for local interests are weak and where environmental issues are not addressed. See L. Cotula, *Land Deals in Africa: What is in the Contracts?* (London: IIED, 2011), 2.

[72] *Ibid.*, 3.

I have already argued for an approach to contracts that resists 'the pull of the policy audience'.[73] A myopic focus on contracts as 'successful tools' looks to replication rather than the project of a deeper illumination of legal architecture. The study of contracts can make room for scholarship that takes 'the social and cultural processes in which legality is embedded and in which legality operates' as a point of departure.[74]

Transcending a view of law as tools comes about by acknowledging complexity, by paying attention to those examples of what has not worked as well as the success stories that are eagerly packaged for transplantation elsewhere. Many of the environmental contracts that have attracted scholarly attention are strong examples of contractual approaches to environmental governance.[75] They are not representative examples. Indeed, they evidence the unevenness of corporate and NGO interest in foreign investment projects. These 'strong cases' thus suggest the need to look at 'less-good cases': what we can learn about environmental regulation from those projects where few useful contracts emerged.

I do not underestimate the difficulties of undertaking fine-grained studies of individual contracts. But the rewards will be seen in a fuller picture of law. To date, legal scholars have readily adopted interdisciplinary approaches to the study of environmental instruments. What is missing in the study of contractual approaches to biodiversity protection is the *intra*disciplinary contribution that builds on insights from private law and private practice. The need to gain access to contracts and better to understand the tensions surrounding their emergence present opportunities for collaborative work between scholars and the practitioners who are drafting these agreements.

CONCLUSION: 'REASONABLE EXPECTATIONS'

I have argued in this chapter that legal scholars can productively enrich our understanding of environmental protection in foreign investment contexts by paying greater attention to individual contracts. My intention

[73] A. D. Sarat and S. Silbey, 'The Pull of the Policy Audience' (1988) 10 *Law and Policy* 97.

[74] A. D. Sarat, 'Redirecting Legal Scholarship in Law Schools' (2000) 12 *Yale Journal of Law and Humanities* 149.

[75] See e.g. Affolder, 'Rethinking Environmental Contracting' (discussing the Ekati Environmental Agreement); D. S. Kenney, *Evaluating the Use of Good Neighbor Agreements for Environmental and Community Protection* (Boulder, Colo.: Natural Resource Law Center, University of Colorado School of Law, 2004) (discussing the Stillwater Good Neighbour Agreement).

is not to discourage scholars from engaging in the valuable studies of dispute resolution processes and investment treaty provisions that are already taking place. My aim is, rather, to complement (and complicate) existing approaches to environmental governance by accounting for project-specific contracts. The larger task upon which this chapter embarks involves resisting a conception of environmental law as tools and a framing of environmental agreements as safeguards.

In concluding, I return to the world of foreign investment law as it is traditionally described. I do so to highlight the rift between the expectations of environmental law that are emerging in these forums (expectations of certainty, stability and the honouring of legitimate expectations) and the messy empirical world of foreign investment projects and environmental law that is the subject of this chapter. Existing accounts of environmental regulation already create a picture of environmental law as one of the most unpredictable regulatory factors facing potential investors.[76] If foreign investment law is to take account of the complex environmental law and policy mix that governs investment projects, contracts need to find a place in legal scholarship.

One scholar suggests that to avoid the conflicts between international investment law's demands for stability and predictability and environmental law's iterative and unpredictable nature, a mechanism for taming environmental law needs to be introduced:

> Because the problem for the foreign investor is not the higher environmental standard as such, but rather the unexpected change towards a higher standard, many of the problems can be addressed if developing and transition economies would engage in more *environmental planning*, combined with *publicity* and *transparency* measures and receive support to that end from developed countries.[77]

Such prescriptions emerge from a focus on what international investment law demands from environmental regulation. Environmental law does not fit into such neat packages. More work needs to be done to reveal, rather than to resist, environmental law's complexity.

I argue in this chapter for a closer study of contractual approaches. This is not to be confused with advocacy for the use of contractual approaches. Contracts are deeply embedded in neo-liberal frameworks.

[76] T. W. Wälde and G. Ndi, 'Stabilizing International Investment Commitments: International Law Versus Contract Interpretation' (1996) 31 *Texas International Law Journal* 230.

[77] Verhoosel, 'Foreign Direct Investment', 478.

The choice to use contracts as a tool of governance is a choice of deep significance. This can be played down if the legal nature of contracts is obscured. It is further played down as the one-off aspect of environmental deal-making is emphasised. Studying contracts is an important task for legal scholars. But it is not a simple exercise of applause or critique: it is about understanding and elucidating how environmental law works.

Select bibliography

Affolder, N., 'Rethinking Environmental Contracting' (2010) 21 *Journal of Environmental Law and Policy* 155.

'Why Study Large Projects? Environmental Regulation's Neglected Frontier' (2011) 44(3) *UBC Law Review* 521–54.

Alcorn, J., 'Big Conservation and Little Conservation: Collaboration in Managing Global and Local Heritage' (1995) 98 *Yale School of Forestry and Environmental Studies Bulletin* 13.

Bowles, I. A., and G. T. Prickett, *Footprints in the Jungle: Natural Resource Industries, Infrastructure and Biodiversity Conservation* (Oxford University Press, 2001).

Collins, H., *Regulating Contracts* (Oxford University Press, 1999).

Cotula, L., *Investment Contracts and Sustainable Development: How to Make Contracts for Fairer and More Sustainable Natural Resource Investments* (London: IIED, 2010).

Land Deals in Africa: What is in the Contracts? (London: IIED, 2011).

Ebbesson, J., and P. Okawa (eds.), *Environmental Law and Justice in Context* (Cambridge University Press, 2009).

Glasbergen, P., F. Biermann and A. P. J. Mol (eds.), *Partnerships, Governance and Sustainable Development: Reflections on Theory and Practice* (Cheltenham: Edward Elgar, 2007).

Head, J. W., 'Environmental Conditionality in the Operations of International Development Finance Institutions' (1991) 1 *Kansas Journal of Law and Public Policy* 15.

O'Faircheallaigh, C., *Environmental Agreements in Canada: Aboriginal Participation, EIA Follow-up and Environmental Management of Major Projects* (Calgary: Canadian Institute of Resources Law, 2006).

O'Faircheallaigh, C., and T. Corbett, 'Indigenous Participation in Environmental Management of Mining Projects: The Role of Negotiated Agreements' (2005) 14 *Environmental Politics* 629.

Orts, E. W., and K. Deketelaere (eds.), *Environmental Contracts: Comparative Approaches to Regulatory Innovation in the United States and Europe* (The Hague: Kluwer, 2001).

Perez, O., 'Using Private–Public Linkages to Regulate Environmental Conflicts: The Case of International Construction Contracts' (2002) 29 *Journal of Law and Society* 77.

Schwartz, P., 'Corporate Activities and Environmental Justice: Perspectives on Sierra Leone's Mining', in J. Ebbesson and P. Okawa (eds.), *Environmental Law and Justice in Context* (Cambridge University Press, 2009), pp. 429–46.

Scott, C., F. Caffagi and L. Senden, 'The Conceptual and Constitutional Challenge of Transnational Private Regulation' (2011) 38 *Journal of Law and Society* 1.

Shihata, I. F. I., 'The World Bank and the Environment: A Legal Perspective' (1992) 16 *Maryland Journal of International Law and Trade* 1.

Stalley, P., 'A Double-edged Sword: Foreign Firms and Environmental Governance in China', PhD dissertation, George Washington University, 2006.

Stewart, R. B., 'A New Generation of Environmental Regulation' (2001) 29 *Capital University Law Review* 21.

Tienhaara, K., 'Mineral Investment and the Regulation of the Environment in Developing Countries: Lessons from Ghana' (2006) 6 *International Environmental Agreement: Politics, Law and Economics* 371.

'Foreign Investment Contracts in the Oil and Gas Sector: A Survey of Environmentally Relevant Clauses' (2011) 11 *Sustainable Development Law and Policy* 15.

14

Socially responsible investing through voluntary codes

BENJAMIN J. RICHARDSON

INTRODUCTION

Can socially conscious investors help abate climate change and other environmental problems and thereby steer the economy towards a more ecologically sustainable future? This chapter examines the role of voluntary codes in promoting and governing sustainable and responsible investment or socially responsible investing (SRI). In examining the design, goals and implementation of voluntary codes, it focuses on the identity of the responsible parties; this is a crucial determinant for a code's quality as a mechanism of governance of the financial market. The chapter concludes with some remarks about the role of such codes in the future governance of financial markets and promotion of SRI.

The financial sector, comprising banks, institutional investors such as pension funds and insurance firms, and retail investors who buy into mutual funds, has come to rival the productive economy in significance. Its role in mobilising capital resources for development, brokering financial transactions and managing investment risks seems to have made it critical for economic growth.[1] Yet, while some commentators such as Niall Ferguson salute finance capitalism as 'an indispensable factor in man's advance from wretched subsistence to the giddy heights of material prosperity that so many people know today',[2] it has been disparaged by others for its evident irrational exuberance[3] and precipitation of

[1] See generally R. G. Hubbard, *Money, the Financial System and the Economy* (Boston, Mass.: Addison-Wesley, 1994); A. T. Rose and M. Marquis, *Money and Capital Markets* (Boston, Mass.: McGraw-Hill/Irwin, 1994).

[2] N. Ferguson, *The Ascent of Money: A Financial History of the World* (New York: Penguin Press, 2008), 3.

[3] R. Shiller, *Irrational Exuberance* (Princeton, NJ: Princeton University Press, 2000).

economic crises.[4] The turmoil in international financial markets since 2008 is the most dramatic example.[5]

The environmental impacts of the finance economy are also increasingly debated. Investors may intensify development pressures on the environment by allowing capital to be transferred readily to those companies able to profit best from exploitation of nature. Being often distant from the environmental consequences of their portfolio companies, especially in a global market, financiers may be unaware or oblivious to the ecological harm they abet. And because corporate financing has traditionally been viewed by the investment community as largely a passive relationship in which financial institutions sit at arm's length to business operations, further disincentives to sustainable finance arise. The only significant exception is where investors' own financial interests are perceived to be jeopardised, such as if a borrower sinks into insolvency because of pollution liability or if a company's share price declines for similar reasons.[6] Otherwise, few financiers would seem willing to act altruistically towards the environment.

The longstanding movement for SRI, which seeks to harness the resources and power of the financial sector as a catalyst to change corporate behaviour, has become increasingly attentive to environmental issues. SRI not only targets individual companies through divestment and shareholder activism but also seeks to promote more systemic change through codes of conduct for investors. Several of these codes specifically address major environmental problems associated with foreign investment. The following section examines the history, aspirations and methods of SRI, before evaluating the codes of conduct as a mechanism of governance of the financial economy.

14.1 The evolution of socially responsible investing

Although dating from at least the 1700s, SRI has gained recognition in mainstream financial markets only since the 1990s.[7] No longer confined

[4] R. Glick, R. Moreno and M. Spiegel (eds.), *Financial Crisis in Emerging Markets* (Cambridge University Press, 2001).

[5] On the emergence of the crisis, see G. Soros, *The New Paradigm for Financial Markets: The Credit Crisis of 2008 and What it Means* (New York: Public Affairs, 2008).

[6] See J. Lipton, 'Project Financing and the Environment: Lender Liability for Environmental Damage in Australia' (1996) 11 *Journal of International Banking Law* 7.

[7] R. Sparkes, *Socially Responsible Investment: A Global Revolution* (Chichester: Wiley, 2002); S. Meeker-Lowry, *Economics as if the Earth Really Mattered: A Catalyst Guide to Socially Conscious Investing* (Philadelphia, Pa.: New Society Publishers, 1988); S. Bruyn, *The Field of Social Investment* (Cambridge University Press, 1987).

to religious and mission-based investors, who once dominated the movement, SRI is now embraced by a variety of actors, including pension plans seeking sustainable, long-term returns, mutual funds selling ethical investments to the general public and banks requiring their borrowers to consider environmental risks.[8] SRI surged to international notoriety in the 1970s during the human rights campaign to divest from South Africa, which was then under the apartheid regime. After a lull during the 1990s, SRI took off again during the past decade as some mainstream financiers began to see opportunities for themselves.

The size of the SRI market is not easily determinable, owing to different survey methodologies and the lack of any widely agreed, authoritative definition of 'socially responsible' finance. In the USA, the Social Investment Forum (SIF) reported in 2010 that approximately US$3 trillion or 'nearly one out of every eight dollars under professional management … is involved in some strategy of socially responsible investing'.[9] The European Social Investment Forum (Eurosif) found in its most recent survey of the European market that at the end of 2009, the SRI sector was worth some €5 trillion, comprising €1.2 trillion of 'core' SRI (i.e., investors using SRI portfolio screens) and €3.8 trillion of 'broad' SRI (incorporating the value of shareholder activism and engagement on SRI issues).[10] By market share, these figures equate to about 10 per cent and 32 per cent respectively of the asset management industry in the European countries surveyed.[11] However, there are substantial variations from country to country; the region's largest economy, Germany, has a tiny SRI sector amounting to slightly less than 1 per cent of its financial market.[12] SRI surveys have also been undertaken in several other countries, including Australia and Canada, revealing trends similar to that observed in Europe overall and the US.[13]

[8] See generally M. Jeucken, *Sustainable Finance and Banking: The Financial Sector and the Future of the Planet* (London: Earthscan, 2001).

[9] Social Investment Forum, *2010 Report on Socially Responsible Investing Trends in the United States* (Social Investment Forum, 2010), 8.

[10] Eurosif, *2010 European SRI Survey* (Eurosif, 2010), 7–11.

[11] *Ibid.*, 13. Eurosif's survey covered nineteen countries: Austria, Belgium, Cyprus, Denmark, Estonia, Finland, France, Germany, Greece, Italy, Latvia, Lithuania, The Netherlands, Norway, Poland, Spain, Sweden, Switzerland and the United Kingdom.

[12] F. J. Preu and B. J. Richardson, 'German Socially Responsible Investment: Barriers and Opportunities' (2011) 12 *German Law Journal* 827.

[13] Corporate Monitor, *Responsible Investment: A Benchmark Report on Australia and New Zealand by the Responsible Investment Association Australasia* (Corporate Monitor,

The principal reason why SRI is attracting more adherents is that many increasingly see a financial advantage for themselves. The movement is no longer dominated by religious-based, limited-issue activism, which began in the 1700s with the Quakers' opposition to the international slave trade. Today, SRI spans a broad constellation of financial actors interested in a diverse set of social and environmental issues such as animal welfare, human rights and climate change.[14] These concerns are no longer addressed by investors as a matter of ethical compulsion but rather because of financial advantage. Take climate change, for instance. Some investors perceive it as a financial risk or opportunity; it might hurt companies exposed to tightening regulations on greenhouse gas (GHG) emissions,[15] or it might yield lucrative opportunities through the burgeoning renewable energies and efficient technologies markets.[16]

Evidence of the changing compulsion for SRI is found not only in popular literature marketed to investors[17] but also in the communications of authoritative bodies. One example is the United Nations Environment Programme Finance Initiative (UNEP-FI), a UN partnership with investors to promote SRI. In its report, *Show Me the Money*, UNEP-FI explains: 'The first – and arguably for investors the most important – reason to integrate [SRI] issues is, simply, to make more money'.[18] Another UNEP-FI publication cajoles financial analysts to 'Communicate on issue-specific, proven, quantifiable, material links to business value … [and to] avoid moral arguments'.[19] The ethos of modern SRI thus often scrutinises social, environmental and corporate governance issues primarily not because they are deemed as ethically significant but because of their perceived financial salience for investors.

2010); Social Investment Organization, *The Canadian Socially Responsible Investment Review 2010* (Social Investment Organization, 2011).

14 R. Sparkes, 'A Historical Perspective on the Growth of Socially Responsible Investment', in R. Sullivan and C. Mackenzie (eds.), *Responsible Investment* (Sheffield: Greenleaf Publishing, 2006), 39.

15 J. Leggett, 'Climate Change and the Banking Industry: A Question of Both Risk and Opportunity' (1996) 179 *Bankers Magazine* 25.

16 S. Labatt and R. White, *Carbon Finance: The Financial Implications of Climate Change* (Chichester: Wiley, 2007).

17 See e.g. R. Lowry, *Good Money: A Guide to Profitable Social Investing in the 90s* (New York: W.W. Norton, 1991); A. Domini, *Socially Responsible Investment: Making a Difference and Making Money* (Chicago, Ill.: Kaplan Press, 2000).

18 UNEP-FI, *Show Me the Money: Linking Environmental, Social and Governance Issues to Company Value* (UNEP-FI, 2006), 4.

19 UNEP-FI, *Generation Lost: Young Financial Analysts and Environmental, Social and Governance Issues: Executive Summary* (UNEP-FI, 2004), 5.

The shifting rationale for SRI has been accompanied by changes to its methods. The exclusionary screening and belligerent shareholder activism redolent of earlier forms of SRI have generally ceded to more polite and inclusive methods of responsible investing. Thus, rather than excluding entire economic sectors judged to be problematic, social investors tend to select firms in any sector that are viewed as 'best-in-class'.[20] This inclusive approach follows from the assumption that corporate environmental and social behaviour should be judged relative to an industry sector's average performance because only firms operating in the same sector face comparable challenges. Investors holding long-term positions in the market also sometimes prefer to influence corporate behaviour from 'within', through exercise of shareholder rights and dialogue with corporate management.[21]

While these changes to SRI's methods and motivations might seem a pragmatic solution to its historical marginalisation, appealing to investors' self-interest carries some significant drawbacks. First, unless investors perceive social and environmental issues to be financially material, they might ignore them. The importance of such issues is not always financially quantifiable.[22] Secondly, a countervailing business case for externalising environmental harm can arise, especially given the ineffectiveness of much conventional environmental regulation. Thirdly, while the SRI community increasingly argues that there is a 'long-term' business case for investing responsibly with regard to issues such as climate change, market pressures to act for the short term can readily prevail. The incentive system for fund managers greatly hinders their willingness to move their focus beyond short-term performance and market valuations.[23]

14.2 Codes of conduct for SRI

Social investors not only target individual companies and projects through screens or engagement, they have designed codes to help coordinate,

[20] A. O'Rourke, 'The Message and Methods of Ethical Investment' (2003) 11 *Journal of Cleaner Production* 683.

[21] R. Sullivan and C. Mackenzie, 'Shareholder Activism on Social, Ethical and Environmental Issues: An Introduction', in Sullivan and Mackenzie, *Responsible Investment*, 150.

[22] S. McGeachie, M. Kiernan and E. Kirzner, *Finance and the Environment in North America* (Ottawa: Public Works and Services Canada, 2005), 57.

[23] C. Juravle and A. Lewis, 'Identifying Impediments to SRI in Europe: A Review of the Practitioner and Academic Literature' (2008) 17 *Business Ethics: A European Review* 290.

standardise and disseminate best practices. The first SRI-related code was the Sullivan Principles, drafted in 1977 by Reverend Leon Sullivan, a pastor and human rights activist who wished to promote non-discriminatory labour standards for US companies operating in South Africa.[24] The subsequent proliferation of SRI codes, which generally have a voluntary character insofar as financiers may subscribe on a take-it-or-leave-it basis, has been influenced not only by investor groups but also by civil society and public sector bodies. The current array of codes is detailed in Table 14.1. These codes are in addition to the plethora of voluntary standards for corporate social responsibility that do not explicitly target the financial sector. While these codes might be interpreted as filling a valuable governance niche, given the limited official regulation at national or international levels to promote SRI they might be viewed less charitably as attempts to pre-empt any unwelcome intensification of governmental regulation in this area.

In addition to these SRI codes, many codes to promote corporate social responsibility (CSR) have been drafted, and some corporations use SRI-related codes such as the Ceres Principles.[25] While financial institutions are not commonly signatories to these CSR codes, they may assist social investors by providing information about best practice standards in a particular industry sector, as well as insights into the behaviour of individual companies. Some codes deal generally with CSR in any business context, while others focus exclusively on a specific economic sector: the former type includes the UN Global Compact and OECD Guidelines for Multinational Enterprises, while the latter includes Responsible Care (designed for the chemical industry) and the Extractive Industries Transparency Initiative.

In theory, all the codes listed in Table 14.1 can improve coordination among social investors, facilitate exchange of information and best practices and build a network of peer pressure to minimise unscrupulous practices. Such effects might seem attainable given the popularity of some codes; for instance, the UN Principles for Responsible Investment as of January 2012 boasted 979 signatories, many of which are major international investment funds.[26]

[24] H. Richardson, 'Leon Sullivan's Principles, Race and International Law' (2001) 15 *Temple International and Comparative Law Journal* 55.

[25] W. Cragg (ed.), *Ethics Codes, Corporations and the Challenge of Globalization* (Cheltenham: Edward Elgar, 2005).

[26] UNPRI, 'Signatories to the Principles for Responsible Investment', www.unpri.org/signatories (accessed 7 March 2012).

Table 14.1 Socially responsible investment-related codes and standards

Code of Conduct	Principal Sponsor
Carbon Disclosure Project (CDP) (2002)	Rockefeller Philanthropy Advisors
Carbon Principles (2008)	Consortium of US banks
Climate Principles (2008)	Climate Group
Coalition for Environmentally Responsible Economies (Ceres) Principles (1989)	Coalition for Environmentally Responsible Economies
Collevecchio Declaration on Financial Institutions (2003)	Coalition of non-governmental organisations
Equator Principles (2003)	Consortium of multinational banks and the World Bank's International Finance Corporation
European Social Investment Forum (Eurosif) Guidelines (2004)	European Social Investment Forum
Global Sullivan Principles (1977)	Revd Leon Sullivan
Investor Network on Climate Risk Action Plan (2003)	Coalition for Environmentally Responsible Economies
London Principles of Sustainable Finance (2002)	UK Department of Environment and Corporation of London
UK Stewardship Code (2010)	UK Financial Reporting Council
UN Principles for Responsible Investment (UNPRI) (2005)	United Nations
UNEP Statement by Financial Institutions on the Environment and Sustainable Development (1997)	United Nations Environment Programme Finance Initiative (UNEP-FI)

Source: B. J. Richardson, 'Financing Sustainability: The New Transnational Governance of Socially Responsible Investment' (2007) 17 *Yearbook of International Environmental Law* 73.

Yet, as for influencing corporate behaviour – ultimately the most relevant indicator of success – evidence is less verifiable. The clearest demonstrated effect has been greater disclosure by companies of their social and environmental performance, such as pursuant to the Carbon Disclosure Project. Improved disclosure enables social investors better to discriminate between corporate leaders and laggards and to apply pressure accordingly. Transparency standards may also foster greater reflection and learning among participants about their practices and impacts, which in turn may stimulate positive behavioural changes.[27]

As voluntary mechanisms, these codes invite scepticism regarding their potential to govern financial markets credibly.[28] Considerable literature has scrutinised the motivations and impact of corporate self-environmental regulation, and although it does not need to be explained here it should be noted that its conclusions are relevant to analysis of SRI codes.[29] That literature emphasises the risks of relying on codes that are rather ambiguous and open-ended in their expectations, and in particular lacking substantive performance standards on social justice or ecological integrity to hold signatories measurably accountable. Voluntary mechanisms tend to lack credible sanctions, with compliance depending on uncertain peer pressure, the discipline of the market or scrutiny from non-governmental organisation (NGO) watchdogs. The corporate hostility to the relatively stringent proposed UN Norms on the Responsibilities of Transnational Corporations perhaps illustrates how many business actors view credible regulation of their social and environmental activities.[30] The most exacting standards for financiers are contained in the Collevecchio Declaration on Financial Institutions, which was drafted by NGOs and has been largely shunned by mainstream investors in favour of discretionary and procedural standards found in other SRI codes.

Apart from their voluntary nature, the most distinctive characteristic of the growing number of SRI codes is their global reach. Most are intended as universal standards for an international market. Their broad scope contrasts with the presently rudimentary intergovernmental regulation of financial markets. Globalisation of financial markets, spurred by technological advances and market deregulation, has greatly accelerated

[27] A. Kolk, D. Levy and J. Pinkse, 'Corporate Responses in an Emerging Climate Regime: The Institutionalization and Commensuration of Carbon Disclosure' (2008) 17 *European Accounting Review* 719.

[28] See I. Maitland, 'The Limits of Business Self-regulation' (1995) 27 *California Management Review* 132.

[29] See e.g. J. Moon, 'The Firm as Citizen? Social Responsibility of Business in Australia' (1995) 30 *Australian Journal of Political Science* 1; R. Gibson (ed.), *Voluntary Initiatives: The New Politics of Corporate Greening* (University of Toronto Press, 1999).

[30] UN Economic and Social Council (ECOSOC), Sub-Commission on Promotion and Protection of Human Rights, *Norms on the Responsibilities of Transnational Corporations and other Business Enterprises with Regard to Human Rights* (ECOSOC, 2003).

the mobility of financial capital across national borders.[31] Globalisation can distance financiers from the social and environmental impacts of the companies they fund, hinder nuanced consideration of such impacts on a case-by-case basis and widen the sources of capital for companies to thereby enable polluters to find alternatives to socially conscious financiers who shun them.[32] These trends have concomitantly diminished the capacity of states to govern financial markets[33] and have possibly created competitive 'race-to-the-bottom' pressures to lessen the regulatory burden.

Global-level regulation of financial markets remains limited and deeply fragmented, serving primarily to facilitate cooperation among national regulators and to promote movement of capital.[34] This governance includes the constitution and working procedures of intergovernmental financial institutions, general rules concerning the behaviour of private institutions, such as data-disclosure principles and capital adequacy rules, and transactional rules that govern aspects of international financial transactions, such as lending and investment criteria.

Within international trade governance, the General Agreement on Trade in Services (GATS)[35] extends to financial services the World Trade Organisation's (WTO) free trade principles.[36] The 1997 GATS Annex on Financial Services[37] aims to eliminate discriminatory and market access-impairing measures so that insurers, banks and other institutions have

[31] C. Williams, 'Corporate Social Responsibility in an Era of Economic Globalization' (2002) 35 *University of California Davis Law Review* 731.

[32] Chinese banks, for instance, have been accused of predatory lending: 'EIB Warns Africa May Suffer as Chinese Banks Move In', *Environmental Finance*, March 2007, at www.environmental-finance.com/2007/0703mar/news.htm#on2 (accessed 7 March 2012).

[33] K. Alexander, R. Dhumale and J. Eatwell, *Global Governance of Financial Systems* (Oxford University Press, 2006), 3.

[34] M. Carlberg, *International Economic Policy Coordination* (Berlin: Springer, 2005).

[35] The General Agreement on Trade in Services (GATS) and Annexes, WTO Agreement, ILM 33 (1994) 1167.

[36] Y. Wang, 'Most-Favoured Nation Treatment under the General Agreement on Trade in Services and its Application in Financial Services' (1996) 30 *Journal of World Trade* 91.

[37] V. Presti, 'Barings Bar None: The Financial Service Agreement of the GATS and its Potential Impact on Derivatives Trading' (1997) 21 *Maryland Journal of International Law and Trade* 145. The legal text of the GATS, including the Annex on Financial Services and the Understanding on Commitments in Financial Services are part of the Final Act Embodying the Results of the Uruguay Round of Multilateral Trade Negotiations. See www.wto.org/english/docs_e/legal_e/final_e.htm (accessed 12 March 2012).

access to financial service markets of all member countries.[38] The GATS does not provide any organisational machinery to supervise financial markets, a function left, if at all, to an assortment of institutions such as the Bank for International Settlements and the International Organization of Securities Commissions. Such bodies hardly address issues of concern to social investors.[39]

At a regional level, the most advanced regulatory framework for financial markets is in the European Union (EU),[40] but the numerous regulations to build a single market for financial services in this region have generally ignored the social and environmental dimensions of financial markets, despite the EU Treaty's expectation that environmental standards be *integrated* across all EU policy sectors.[41]

14.3 Typology of SRI codes

14.3.1 Differentiating voluntary codes

Whether designed solely for SRI or for addressing the business sector more generally, voluntary codes come in many guises. A code may be classified in various ways, including by the identity of the parties who drafted it, its legal consequences, the degree to which it is process- versus performance-oriented, the code's regulatory function and its geographic scope.[42]

One of the more useful ways to understand SRI codes is to locate them on a continuum from process-oriented to performance-based standards,[43]

[38] The agreement was brought into force on 1 March 1999. See further A. Mattoo, *Financial Services and the WTO: Liberalization in the Developing and Transition Economies* (World Trade Organization, 1998).

[39] See M. Giovanoli, 'A New Architecture for the Global Financial Market: An Outline of Legal Issues', in M. Giovanoli (ed.), *International Monetary Law: Issues for the New Millennium* (Oxford University Press, 2000), 3.

[40] By way of introduction, see European Commission, *Institutional Arrangements for the Regulation and Supervision of the Financial Sector* (EC Internal Market Directorate-General, 2000).

[41] Art. 11, Consolidated Version of the Treaty on the Functioning of the European Union, OJ C 83/47 (30 March 2010); see also Art. 6, Consolidated Version of the Treaty Establishing the European Community, OJ C 325/33 (2002).

[42] This discussion draws upon S. Wood, 'Voluntary Environmental Codes and Sustainability', in B. Richardson and S. Wood (eds.), *Environmental Law for Sustainability* (Oxford: Hart Publishing, 2006), 229.

[43] E. Meidenger, '"Private" Environmental Regulation, Human Rights, and Community' (1999) 7 *Buffalo Environmental Law Journal* 123.

although sometimes a single code combines both approaches. Performance-based standards set substantive principles to improve participants' environmental and social behaviour. The content of such standards may vary considerably; some leave considerable room for interpretation, while others are quite prescriptive in directing certain actions or restrictive in discouraging or prohibiting activities. Thus, some codes contain generic performance targets (e.g., to prevent pollution or to minimise adverse environmental impacts), while others are specific (e.g., to reduce GHG emissions by a specific quantity and within a specific timeframe). A good example of the more prescriptive approach is the Collevecchio Declaration, while the UNPRI reflects the more discretionary, general approach.

In contrast, process standards concern the procedures by which institutions manage their interactions with the environment and society, without prescribing specific targets for performance. Such standards commonly address procedures for the assessment, verification and communication of performance. Some examples, notably the Equator Principles, address decision-making procedures to ensure that environmental impacts are considered by banks when financing projects. Other codes prescribe detailed environmental management systems (EMSs) to enable participants to manage their organisational systems to minimise environmental and social impacts. For example, a management system could create a process for a bank to reduce its energy consumption. Of the two main examples of EMSs – the European Community's Eco-Management and Audit Scheme (EMAS)[44] and the International Organization for Standardization (ISO) 14001[45] standard – only the EMAS addresses the financial services sector.[46]

SRI codes can be differentiated along several other dimensions as well. The extent to which their terms are legally binding is one such dimension. Simply because participation in a code is voluntary does not mean that the code, once accepted, is without legal consequences for its participants. An SRI code may be legally binding by virtue of contracts among participating institutions; a bank, for example, may include in

44 European Commission, 'EMAS': http://ec.europa.eu/environment/emas/index_en.htm (accessed 7 March 2012).

45 ISO, 'ISO 1400 essentials', www.iso.org/iso/iso_14000_essentials (accessed 7 March 2012).

46 B. J. Richardson, 'Implications of Recent Changes to the EMAS and Eco-label Regulations for the Financial Services Sector' (2002) 14 *Environmental Law and Management* 131.

its contractual agreement with a borrower that the parties adhere to the Equator Principles' provisions regarding environmental assessment. Also, codes differ greatly in their degree of specificity. Some contain brief aspirational declarations, as in the London Principles of Sustainable Finance, while others posit highly specific operational rules and performance indicators, such as the EMAS. The significance of such differences is that the less specific codes may not be self-executing without additional work to define clearer operational requirements. Another variable is the regulatory function performed by codes. A variety of such functions may be fulfilled by SRI codes, such as agenda-setting, rule-making – including setting targets – administration (such as facilitating exchange of information and verification of compliance) and dispute settlement.[47] Typically, most codes straddle several of these regulatory functions rather than performing merely one.

In reviewing the SRI codes in further detail, this chapter differentiates them according to the identity of the principal protagonists, especially with regard to who designed the code. These parties may be financial or business organisations, government agencies or third parties such as environmental NGOs.[48] Six general types of codes are identified: (i) unilateral commitments by financial institutions; (ii) jointly established codes between financiers and public authorities; (iii) codes developed by public authorities; (iv) third-party codes; (v) joint financier–third-party codes; and (vi) multi-party codes, often involving the establishment of institutional regimes for ongoing collaboration.

Sometimes there is no absolute distinction between these types of codes as classified, as in practice some codes fall clearly within one type, while others blend elements found in several types of codes. For example, with regard to the first type, the Carbon Principles clearly reflect a unilateral commitment by financial institutions, but the Eurosif Transparency Guidelines (which are also classified in this way) contain some minor involvement of other stakeholders, although not to the extent to justify labelling it a multi-party code or other type.

[47] See M. Priest, 'Five Models of Self-regulation' (1997–8) 29 *Ottawa Law Review* 239.

[48] This taxonomy is used by a variety of researchers, such as: Organisation for Economic Co-operation and Development (OECD), *Voluntary Approaches for Environmental Policy* (OECD, 1999); A. Baranzini and P. Thalmann (eds.), *Voluntary Approaches in Climate Policy* (Cheltenham: Edward Elgar, 2004); Wood, 'Voluntary Environmental Codes and Sustainability', 229.

The identity of the parties is arguably the most significant criterion in determining the robustness of a code and the quality of implementation. In general, SRI codes that are designed and controlled by the financial sector attract high levels of support – but often by setting the bar too low and thus risking perpetuation of 'business-as-usual'. On the other hand, codes designed by the public sector or environmental groups are more likely to raise the bar of expected environmental performance; yet such higher expectations may deter potential participants and result in too few adherents. SRI codes that provide for multi-stakeholder involvement may therefore be the most successful in attracting sufficient support, while setting reasonably credible standards.

14.3.2 Financiers' codes

Financiers' codes, involving unilateral commitments, are self-regulatory codes developed by financiers, organisations representing financiers or related actors with commercial interest in the financial economy without direct participation by either governmental authorities or third parties such as NGOs. They range from brief and general statements of principles to more detailed and prescriptive standards.

The main example is the Equator Principles, which were formulated by a group of private-sector banks in order to address environmental impacts in project financing in emerging economies. Development of the Equator Principles was triggered to fend off criticisms that some banks were funding environmentally harmful projects, as well as to avoid the potential loss of business to less scrupulous lenders if some sought to raise standards. In developing the Principles, the banks consulted closely with the World Bank's private-sector lending arm, the International Finance Corporation (IFC), whose performance standards are used to inform the assessment process mandated by the Equator Principles. Although pressure from environmental NGOs spurred creation of the Equator Principles, 'the fast-track process of drafting the Equator Principles prevented [their] meaningful input'.[49]

The Equator Principles are not a static code but rather have been updated considerably since their introduction in 2003.[50] The Principles incorporate the IFC's Safeguard Policies for social and environmental

[49] N. Affolder, 'Cachet Not Cash: Another Sort of World Bank Group Borrowing' (2006) 14 *Michigan State Journal of International Law* 156.

[50] See www.equator-principles.com (accessed 7 March 2012).

impact assessment, forestry, dam safety, indigenous peoples and other issues, and thus the Equator Principles were revised in July 2006 to incorporate revisions to the baseline IFC standards.[51] In July 2010, a set of governance rules were formally adopted, introducing integrity measures to improve implementation of the Equator Principles and establishing the Equator Principles Association, which is comprised of representatives of member signatories.[52]

All Equator Principles signatories pledge to provide loans only to borrowers who conform to the Principles. They apply to projects worth at least US$10 million and require lenders to rate projects based on the magnitude of potential impacts and risks in accordance with the IFC's screening criteria.[53] Project financing banks must also prepare action plans based on the conclusions of the environmental and social assessment.[54] Lenders to category A and B projects, deemed the most significant ones, must ensure that borrowers have consulted affected local communities 'in a structured and culturally appropriate manner'.[55] This requirement falls short of the 'prior informed consent' standard that is demanded by indigenous peoples and other vulnerable communities and is beginning to be recognised in some international instruments.[56] The Equator Principles also require a borrower to establish a 'grievance mechanism' to address any concerns about a project's impacts.[57]

Given that the banking sector designed the Equator Principles, its embrace of the Principles is unsurprising. As of April 2012, at least seventy banks and related financial institutions, accounting for about 95 per cent of the global project financing market, had endorsed the Equator Principles. Most signatories are North American or western European lenders, especially large banks with international operations.[58] A study by the UK law firm Freshfields Bruckhaus Deringer concluded that the Principles' 'impact on the financial market generally and their success in redefining banking considerations has

[51] See E. Morgera, 'Significant Trends in Corporate Environmental Accountability: The New Performance Standard of the International Finance Corporation' (2007) 18 *Colorado Journal of International Environmental Law and Policy* 151.

[52] Equator Principles Association, *Governance Rules* (July 2010).

[53] Principle 1.

[54] Principle 4.

[55] Principle 5.

[56] C. Charters, 'Indigenous Peoples and International Law and Policy' (2007) 18 *Public Law Review* 22.

[57] Principle 6.

[58] P. Kulkarni, 'Pushing Lenders to Over-comply with Environmental Regulations: A Developing Country Perspective' (2010) 22 *Journal of International Development* 470.

been far greater than anyone could have predicted'.[59] The Equator Principles have appealed to banks for several reasons: in order to counter stakeholder and NGO activism, to protect market share, to maintain a level field, to incorporate voluntary standards and to minimise financial risks.[60] While the Principles lack credible sanctions and leave signatories with considerable discretion, each Equator bank must 'at least annually' disclose publicly its 'implementation processes and experience, taking into account appropriate confidentiality considerations'.[61]

While the Equator Principles may enable banks to play an important role as quasi-environmental regulators, especially when some developing countries lack robust environmental laws,[62] perfunctory or negligent implementation of the Principles has drawn criticism.[63] One of several major infrastructure projects funded by Equator banks to have tested their credibility is the Baku–Tbilisi–Ceyhan pipeline bringing Caspian Sea oil to global markets, which poses adverse social and environmental consequences for the affected region.[64] Another is the Sakhalin II oil and gas project in eastern Russia, which risks oil spills that could destroy rich salmon fisheries and endanger rare cetaceans.[65] The financing of Uruguayan pulp mills near the River Uruguay also led to concerns about the adequacy of the environmental assessment process and triggered a dispute between Uruguay and Argentina that was litigated in the International Court of Justice.[66] The Equator Principles' integrity can be also undermined when signatories maintain other types of financial relationships with companies, apart from project financing, which can enable circumvention of the

[59] Freshfields Bruckhaus Deringer (FBD), *Banking on Responsibility* (Freshfields Bruckhaus Deringer, 2005), 1.

[60] *Ibid.*, 50. [61] Principle 10.

[62] See J. Conley and C. Williams, 'Global Banks as Global Sustainability Regulators: The Equator Principles' (2011) 33 *Law and Policy* 542; D. Schepers, 'The Equator Principles: A Promise in Progress?' (2011) 11 *Corporate Governance* 90.

[63] See, in particular, BankTrack: *An Overview of BankTrack–EPFI Engagement on the Equator Principles, 2003–2010* (BankTrack, 2010); N. O'Sullivan and B. O'Dwyer, 'Stakeholder Perspectives on a Financial Sector Legitimation Process: The Case of NGOs and the Equator Principles' (2010) 22 *Accounting, Auditing and Accountability Journal* 553.

[64] 'BTC Project is the First Major Test of the Equator Principles', 27 February 2004, www.equator-principles.com/btc.shtml (accessed 7 March 2012).

[65] M. Bradshaw, 'The "Greening" of Global Project Financing: The Case of the Sakhalin-II Offshore Oil and Gas Project' (2007) 51 *Canadian Geographer* 255.

[66] *Case Concerning Pulp Mills on the River Uruguay (Argentina* v. *Uruguay)*, ICJ, 20 April 2010.

Equator Principles' standards.[67] Nonetheless, some commentators doubt that non-Equator banks are engaged in predatory lending for projects that Equator Principles signatories have avoided.[68]

Another example of a code developed by banks that targets a specific environmental issue is the Carbon Principles. They were developed in early 2008 by three US banks (JPMorgan Chase, Morgan Stanley and Citibank), later joined by three more US lenders. The Principles aim 'to provide a consistent approach for banks and their US power clients to evaluate and address carbon risks in the financing of electric power projects'.[69] The Carbon Principles were prepared in consultation with several US environmental organisations and power utilities. Yet, perhaps because the banks were ultimately responsible for both the drafting of the Principles and their subsequent implementation, they provide latitude for business as usual.

Each signatory to the Principles is expected to incorporate an enhanced due diligence process for assessing potential investments in power generation in the USA and to encourage their clients to switch to low-carbon alternatives such as renewable energy and improved energy efficiency. The due diligence process applies to financing sought by both public and private-sector entities for construction of fossil fuel generation facilities of at least 200 megawatts capacity.[70] The Carbon Principles further provide that if a borrower is unwilling to cooperate, 'the financial institution will not proceed with the financing'.[71] But the Carbon Principles do not mandate adoption of any specific climate mitigation technologies or measures.

While we might thus praise these American banks for taking the lead in climate action over US public authorities, which under the Bush Administration doubted the very existence of climate change, it should not be forgotten that many US business groups, including financiers, have sought to thwart credible regulatory action on GHG

[67] BankTrack, 'Dodgy Deals: Lafayette Mine, Rapu Rapu Island', www.banktrack.org/?show=dodgy&id=26 (accessed 7 March 2012).

[68] P. Q. Watchman, A. Delfino and J. Addison, 'EP2: The Revised Equator Principles. Why Hard-nosed Bankers are Embracing Soft Law Principles' (2007) 1 *Law and Financial Markets Review* 85.

[69] Carbon Principles, http://carbonprinciples.org/ (accessed 7 March 2012).

[70] *The Carbon Principles: Fossil Fuel Generation Financing Enhanced Environmental Diligence Process*, www.morganstanley.com/global/carbon_principles_diligence.pdf (accessed 7 March 2012).

[71] *Ibid.*

emissions.[72] The Carbon Principles themselves do not appear to have reduced financing of fossil fuel projects. A report by the Rainforest Action Network in 2011 found no evidence to distinguish signatory banks from non-signatory banks with regard to financing new carbon-intensive power plants,[73] and no evidence that the Principles 'have stopped, or even slowed financing to carbon-intensive projects'.[74]

The Eurosif Transparency Guidelines, issued in 2004 by the European Social Investment Forum (Eurosif), is another example of a code that can be regarded as developed by financial institutions. Headquartered in Paris, Eurosif is a pan-European association of institutions interested in the SRI market and its governance.[75] While its so-called 'member affiliates' include a few academic institutes and NGOs, and Eurosif is legally a non-profit association, the organisation primarily represents commercial actors in the financial markets such as pension plans, fund managers and retail funds. The Eurosif Transparency Guidelines were designed for use by the retail SRI fund sector to enhance disclosure and increase accountability to investors.[76] Eurosif admits that the Guidelines were introduced partly 'to pre-empt potential regulation that could be enacted without the involvement of the greater SRI community'.[77] The Guidelines expect SRI funds to provide detailed information about their research processes and investment criteria, their methods for voting shareholder proxies and their strategies for engaging corporations to improve CSR. Signatories to the Guidelines must make publicly available disclosures at least once annually. On the other hand, the Eurosif Guidelines do not direct how institutions should invest, nor do they explicitly refer to any ethical motivations that should drive SRI.

14.3.3 Joint financier–public authority codes

This type of code is developed collaboratively by financiers and public authorities. The interests of those affected by investors are therefore not directly represented in the negotiation of such codes. Yet, depending on the extent of involvement of the public sector, as well

[72] C. Jones and D. Levy, 'North American Business Strategies Towards Climate Change' (2007) 25 *European Management Journal* 428.

[73] Rainforest Action Network, *The Principle Matter: Banks, Climate and the Carbon Principles* (Rainforest Action Network, 2010).

[74] *Ibid.*, 13. [75] See www.eurosif.org (accessed 7 March 2012).

[76] Eurosif, *The Eurosif SRI Retail Fund Transparency Guidelines* (Eurosif, 2004).

[77] *Ibid.*, 1.

as the degree of transparency and public consultation, such codes may offer more credible SRI standards than those drafted solely by business interests. The main example is the UN Principles for Responsible Investment (UNPRI), which is treated as a jointly designed code because of the presence of the UN in facilitating and coordinating its development. But the financial sector was and remains very much the senior partner.

Designed primarily for institutional investors, the Principles were developed by the investment community under the auspices of the United Nations through its UNEP-FI and UN Global Compact initiatives. The UNPRI, however, cannot be defined as an intergovernmental initiative in the same manner as many UN initiatives, such as its sponsorship of international environmental treaties, declarations and programmes. While a multi-stakeholder working group with representatives from environmental NGOs, academia and other non-commercial stakeholders were involved in the preparation of the Principles, the financial sector was the most influential voice in the design of the UNPRI. This is reflected in the way the Principles are often labelled just the 'PRI' rather than 'UNPRI'. The present governance of the UNPRI includes an elected Advisory Council of eleven representatives from investor signatory organisations and two representatives from the UN. Day-to-day operations are managed by the UNPRI Secretariat, which is financed by fees paid by signatories to the Principles. They have been well received by the finance sector, with nearly 1,000 signatories as of January 2012.[78]

The UNPRI combine process and performance standards in its six brief principles and supplementary guidance on 'possible actions'. The expectations are broadly defined and do not provide yardsticks to which investors could easily be held measurably accountable. To illustrate, Principle 1 vaguely declares: 'We will incorporate environmental, social and corporate governance (ESG) issues into investment analysis and decision-making processes'.[79] More helpful as an educative tool is the supplementary guidance; for example, concerning the second principle on active shareholding, the suggested actions include to 'exercise voting rights', 'develop an engagement capability' and 'file shareholder resolutions consistent with long-term ESG considerations'.[80] Through such actions, the UNPRI Secretariat sees several benefits:

[78] See the list at www.unpri.org/signatories (accessed 7 March 2012).

[79] UNPRI, www.unpri.org/principles (accessed 7 March 2012). [80] *Ibid.*

> Implementing the Principles will lead to a more complete understanding of a range of material issues, and this should ultimately result in increased returns and lower risk. There is increasing evidence that ESG issues can be material to performance of portfolios, particularly over the long term.
>
> PRI signatories are also part of a network, with opportunities to pool resources and influence, lowering the costs and increasing the effectiveness of research and active ownership practices. The Initiative also supports investors in working together to address systemic problems that, if remedied, may then lead to more stable, accountable and profitable market conditions overall.[81]

Apart from the narrowness of this financial rationale for SRI, the UNPRI have various limitations. Among the list of possible actions for the first principle, there is no stated expectation that investors will actually incorporate social or environmental factors into their ultimate portfolio choices; the principle focuses on 'investment analysis' and 'decision-making processes', not on ensuring that final decisions achieve specific targets, such as to avoid financing carbon-intensive developments. The principles thus do not require a signatory to demonstrate any particular performance standards with regard to human rights or environmental protection. The second principle on active ownership focuses on participation in investee companies but ignores the need to democratise decision-making within financial institutions. Nor do the UNPRI insist on any independent audit or verification mechanism to assess the quality of signatories' implementation. While the one mandatory requirement for signatories that own or manage investments is to complete a reporting and assessment survey annually, the UNPRI secretariat reassures investors that 'There are no legal or regulatory sanctions associated with the Principles. They are designed to be voluntary and aspirational … a direction to head in rather than a prescriptive checklist with which to comply'.[82]

14.3.4 *Public authority codes*

Some SRI codes are initiated by public authorities, whose imprimatur in theory should afford such codes more legitimacy and thus potentially more influence than those that financiers devise for themselves. Nonetheless, the existing examples have not always had this effect.

[81] UNPRI, 'Frequently Asked Questions', www.unpri.org/faqs (accessed 7 March 2012).
[82] *Ibid.*

One unsuccessful example is the London Principles of Sustainable Finance. They were developed in 2002 by the UK Department for Environment Forum for the Future and the Corporation of London. The initiative was designed to address the role of the financial sector in the World Summit on Sustainable Development that year. The London Principles advocate measures to improve financiers' attention to sustainable development when making loans and investments.[83] The Principles, which apply to all activities of finance markets, comprise seven quite brief statements. They include the expectation that signatories, 'where relevant to the product and geographical scope of their business', will 'reflect the cost of environmental and social risks in the pricing of financial and risk management products'. Further, signatories should 'provide access to market finance and risk management products to businesses in disadvantaged communities and developing economies'.

For several reasons, the London Principles have largely failed. First, the finance sector had negligible input into the drafting of the Principles, thus weakening their enthusiasm, even though the Principles are not particularly stringent. Second, the release of the London Principles was timed to give the UK government something concrete to announce at the World Summit on Sustainable Development in Johannesburg; thus, they were not prepared to respond to specific issues that were particularly relevant to the financial sector at that time. Third, the UK government did not provide sufficient resources to facilitate implementation, promotion and monitoring of the Principles. Finally, the close association of the *London* Principles in name and sponsorship to the UK most likely diminished the Principles' standing as a universal code. The implication that 'London knows best' may have been problematic for some foreign investors.

It is thus not surprising that a 2005 review of implementation of the Principles showed a 'mixed picture', concluding that the 'Principles have not maximised the potential to produce change towards sustainability in the manner originally intended'.[84] The review found this gap 'particularly evident in financing environmental technologies and expanding private finance in the developing world, especially for more marginalised and

[83] Corporation of London and the Department for Environment, Food and Rural Affairs (DEFRA), *Financing the Future. The London Principles: The Role of UK Financial Services in Sustainable Development* (DEFRA, 2002), 7.

[84] S. Mills et al., *The London Principles: Three Years on From Johannesburg* (Corporation of London and Forum for the Future, 2005), 5, 13.

underserved groups'.[85] Unlike some SRI codes, the London Principles lack performance benchmarks and rigorous monitoring and are largely just an agenda-setting mechanism to shape debate and stimulate awareness among financiers. At the time of the 2005 review, only eighteen institutions had signed up.

The UK government is also responsible for a second example of a public sector code related to SRI, known as the Stewardship Code.[86] It was released in 2010 by the Financial Reporting Council, the UK's independent regulator responsible for improving corporate governance and reporting to foster investment.[87] The Stewardship Code contains principles and accompanying guidance to encourage institutional investors and fund managers who hold shares in British companies to be active owners and engage in corporate governance in the interests of their beneficiaries. The code expects investors to 'establish clear guidelines on when and how they will escalate their activities as a method of protecting and enhancing shareholder value' and to disclose their own level of compliance with its principles.[88] Among the extensive accompanying guidance, corporate environmental performance is recognised as material to shareholder value: 'Instances when institutional investors may want to intervene include when they have concerns about the company's strategy and performance, its governance or its approach to the risks arising from social and environmental matters'.[89] While the Stewardship Code is not per se enforceable, it relies on a 'comply or explain' approach whereby if fund managers and institutional investors do not comply with any of the principles, they must explain why on their websites, as well as inform the Financial Reporting Council.[90]

In other countries, public authorities rarely issue voluntary SRI codes. South Africa is one exception. The target of the most truculent SRI campaign in modern history, the South African government in the post-apartheid period has sought to improve social responsibility in the financial sector through quasi-regulatory tools such as the Financial

85 *Ibid.*, 5.

86 Financial Reporting Council (FRC), *The UK Stewardship Code* (Financial Reporting Council, July 2010), www.frc.org.uk/images/uploaded/documents/UK%20Stewardship%20Code%20July%2020103.pdf (accessed 7 March 2012).

87 Financial Reporting Council, www.frc.org.uk (accessed 7 March 2012).

88 Financial Reporting Council, *The UK Stewardship Code*, 4.

89 *Ibid.*, 7.

90 The legal compulsion to, at the very least, explain non-compliance with the Stewardship Code stems from the Financial Services and Markets Act 2000, s. 2(4).

Sector Charter.[91] In July 2011, South African authorities adopted a Code for Responsible Investing in South Africa (CRISA). A committee with diverse membership chaired by a representative of South Africa's Government Employees' Pension Fund drafted the code. Modelled on the UNPRI, it contains five main principles, each with supplementary guidance.[92] The first two principles encourage policies that aim to guide institutions towards being responsible shareholders. The other principles require institutional investors to ensure that the principles are implemented and disclosed. Like the UNPRI, the code seeks to ground SRI in fiduciary responsibility; thus, Principle 1 states that 'An institutional investor should incorporate sustainability considerations, including environment, social and governance, into its investment analysis and activities as part of the delivery of superior risk-adjusted returns to the ultimate beneficiaries'. As with South Africa's King Report on Corporate Governance (King III)[93] and the UK's Stewardship Code, the proposed code relies on 'apply or explain' principles to encourage compliance.

14.3.5 Third-party codes

Third-party codes have been developed to promote SRI, to which financiers are invited to subscribe on a take-it-or-leave-it basis. Some codes elaborate detailed requirements, while others espouse broad philosophies for sustainable finance. They have been developed by civil society actors such as environmental and human rights groups, churches and eminent individuals, and they often set demanding performance criteria that only a minority of financiers wish to meet.

The best example of such a code is the Collevecchio Declaration on Financial Institutions,[94] drafted in 2003 by a coalition of NGOs critical of facile, business-friendly codes of conduct such as the Equator Principles. It expects financiers to commit to principles of sustainability, 'no harm',

[91] B. J. Richardson, 'Africa: From Object to Agent of Socially Responsible Investment', in F. Botchway (ed.), *Natural Resource Investment and African Development* (Cheltenham: Edward Elgar, 2011), 247, 268.

[92] Association for Savings and Investment SA, www.asisa.co.za/index.php/info-centre/responsible-investment.html (accessed 7 March 2012).

[93] King Committee on Governance, *Code of Governance Principles for South Africa* (King Committee, 2009).

[94] BankTrack, 'Collevecchio Declaration: The Role and Responsibility of Financial Institutions' (undated), www.banktrack.org/download/collevecchio_declaration_2/0_030401_-collevecchio_declaration.pdf (accessed 7 March 2012).

responsibility, accountability, transparency and sustainable markets and governance. The accompanying Implementation Document outlines immediate steps that financial institutions should take, such as the adoption of internationally recognised industry standards for credit, investing and underwriting transactions. The Declaration differs from other performance standards in its rigorous and detailed requirements. The ambitious 'commitment to sustainability' principle obliges investors to, inter alia, 'fully integrate the consideration of ecological limits, social equity and economic justice into corporate strategies and core business areas (including credit, investing, underwriting, advising), to put sustainability objectives on an equal footing to shareholder maximisation and client satisfaction'. The Declaration's 'do no harm' principle offers a stringent performance benchmark, in contrast to the latitude of many other SRI codes such as the bankers' Carbon Principles.

On the other hand, such uncompromising standards, coupled with the lack of involvement of investors in their design, have led to the Declaration receiving negligible support from investors. Currently, it has about 200 endorsements, mostly from NGOs.[95] The only significant listed endorsement from the financial sector is the pension fund CalPERS (California Public Employees for a Responsible Retirement). The Collevecchio Declaration also lacks the administrative and financial resources enjoyed by some codes, such as the UNPRI, to facilitate its promotion.

A much more successful example of a third-party initiative is the Carbon Disclosure Project (CDP), which maintains on behalf of investors and other interested bodies an international database of corporations' climate-change-related information.[96] It was established in 2000 by the Rockefeller Philanthropy Advisors, a not-for-profit organisation that advises on and manages philanthropic funds. While the CDP is not per se a code of conduct, as an informational instrument that solicits crucial data, it has the capacity to facilitate climate-conscious investing. Transparency can be a governance tool to promote scrutiny and evaluation, and even if financiers make conservative uses of the information, other stakeholders such as NGOs may use it for monitoring and challenging corporations. Reflexive law theorists contend that environmental auditing and reporting processes may help reform the organisational culture of businesses from within by encouraging greater reflection, learning and

[95] See www.foe.org/camps/intl/endorsements.html (accessed 7 March 2012).

[96] Carbon Disclosure Project (CDP), www.cdproject.net/en-US/Pages/HomePage.aspx (accessed 7 March 2012).

behavioural changes.[97] The paucity of well-established legal obligations to report GHG emissions and other climate-related information make the CDP a pioneering tool for SRI.[98]

Essentially, the CDP allows investors collectively to endorse a single global request for disclosure of information regarding companies' GHG emissions, vulnerability to climate change impacts, carbon emission trading activities and their policies on climate change. These requests are made annually to an ever-larger pool of major companies. By 2012, slightly over 3,000 corporations were reporting to the CDP annually, on behalf of approximately 550 investment institutions.[99] The CDP has thus become the largest registry of corporate GHG emissions data in the world. While reporting to the CDP is a voluntary process, some participating companies are probably motivated by the desire to avoid unwelcome pressure and adverse publicity from investors and other groups if they decline to cooperate, while other respondents are likely attracted by the opportunity to gain publicity for their positive efforts.

14.3.6 Joint financier–third-party codes

An SRI code might also be the product of cooperation between investors and third parties, without direct involvement of governmental authorities. As with financier–public authority codes, those designed by financiers and third parties are unlikely to be simple negotiated agreements but rather typically arise from complex multi-stakeholder institutions in which business, environmental and other interests cooperate to develop rules and undertake other initiatives. This model may avoid the pitfalls of the financier-designed codes, which may lack public credibility, and the NGO-driven standards, which can be too abrasive or naive for the business community.

In an SRI context, the leading example is the Ceres Principles.[100] Ceres, standing for the Coalition for Environmentally Responsible

[97] K.-H. Ladeur, 'Coping with Uncertainty: Ecological Risks and the Proceduralization of Environmental Law', in G. Teubner, L. Farmer and D. Murphy (eds.), *Environmental Law and Ecological Responsibility: The Concept and Practice of Ecological Self-Organization* (Chichester: Wiley, 1994), 322–3.

[98] PricewaterhouseCoopers and International Emissions Trading Association, *Uncertainty in Accounting for the EU Emissions Trading Scheme and Certified Emission Reductions* (PricewaterhouseCoopers, 2007), 15–16.

[99] See www.cdproject.net/faqs.asp (accessed 7 March 2012).

[100] V. Zondorak, 'A New Face in Corporate Environmental Responsibility: The Valdez Principles' (1991) 18 *Boston College Environmental Affairs Law Review* 457.

Economies, is a partnership of investors, foundations, trade unions and environmental, religious and other civil society groups. The Ceres Principles are merely one of numerous initiatives of the partnership to promote sustainable finance and corporate social responsibility. Originally known as the Valdez Principles (in the wake of the Exxon Valdez oil spill in 1989), the Ceres Principles combine performance and process standards that focus on environmental rather than social issues. The Principles' ten points commit signatories to protect the biosphere, use natural resources sustainably, reduce waste production, conserve energy, make safe products, provide safe services and report to stakeholders on issues that affect them.[101] Their integrity is enhanced by the rule that a company or financial organisation cannot unilaterally endorse the Ceres Principles. Instead, a prospective signatory must first demonstrate to the Ceres Board of Directors how it would implement the Principles. The Ceres Principles have evidently influenced some SRI practices; for instance, the American Federation of Labor and Congress of Industrial Organizations' (AFL-CIO) Proxy Voting Guidelines refer to them.[102]

Ceres has sponsored a number of initiatives, including the Global Reporting Initiative (GRI), a highly regarded voluntary code for sustainability reporting that is used by some financial institutions for evaluating the environmental impacts of companies and for disclosing their own environmental performance.[103] One advantage of the GRI is its economic-sector-specific supplements, one of which is designed for reporting by providers of financial services and products.[104] Another SRI-related output of Ceres is the Investor Network on Climate Risk (INCR). Launched in 2003, the network aims to support nearly 100 participating investment institutions in identifying the financial risks and opportunities in climate change and in addressing policy and governance issues that impede the development of sustainable capital markets.[105]

[101] Coalition for Environmentally Responsible Economies, at www.ceres.org/coalitionand-companies/principles.phat (accessed 7 March 2012).

[102] American Federation of Labor and Congress of Industrial Organizations (AFL–CIO), 'Proxy Voting Guidelines 2003', www.aflcio.org/corporatewatch/capital/upload/proxy_voting_guidelines.pdf (accessed 7 March 2012).

[103] GRI, at www.globalreporting.org (accessed 7 March 2012).

[104] GRI, at www.globalreporting.org/ReportingFramework/SectorSupplements/Financial-Services/#FS2 (accessed 7 March 2012).

[105] Investor Network on Climate Risk, www.incr.com/Page.aspx?pid=198 (accessed 7 March 2012).

One of its achievements is the INCR Action Plan, which posits nine actions that investors can take to evaluate and reduce the impact of their investments on climate change. The Action Plan covers methods to measure climate change risk in their portfolios, strategies for engaging with portfolio companies on disclosure and mitigation efforts related to climate change risks and opportunities, and ways to support public policy regarding corporate disclosure on climate risks and opportunities.

14.3.7 Multi-party codes and integrated rule-making

Another approach to setting SRI standards is integrated rule-making whereby investors, public authorities and third parties cooperate to create joint rule-making institutions and develop codes. Such approaches have similarities to the so-called 'corporatist' modes of interest group intermediation found in some Western states in the 1970s and 1980s, as a supplement to the traditional polyarchal mechanisms of political decision-making.[106] It is sometimes difficult to distinguish multi-party codes from financier codes because the investors who implement them can exert substantial influence. On the other hand, tripartite negotiated codes are helpfully displacing the closed-door industry–government bargaining that characterised many of the early negotiated environmental codes and agreements.

The best known example is the United Nations Environment Programme's Finance Initiative (UNEP-FI).[107] Established in 1991, UNEP-FI is a global partnership of investor, civil society and government representatives to promote governance standards, education and research on SRI,[108] although in practice financial institutions are its dominant stakeholders. In 1992, UNEP-FI released its first code, the Statement by Banks on Environment and Sustainable Development, to help lenders manage their environmental risks.[109] In 1995, UNEP-FI sponsored a similar statement for the insurance industry.[110] In 1997,

[106] L. Panitch, 'The Development of Corporatism in Liberal Democracies', (1977) 10 *Comparative Political Studies* 61.

[107] UNEP-FI, www.unepfi.org (accessed 7 March 2012).

[108] See e.g. UNEP-FI, 'Managing Environmental Risks in Project Finance', Fact Sheet No.1 (UNEP-FI, 1999).

[109] UNEP, Advisory Committee on Banking and the Environment, *Statement by Banks on Environment and Sustainable Development* (UNEP, 1992).

[110] See www.unepfi.org/signatories/statements/ii/index.html (accessed 7 March 2012). See C. Joly, 'UNEP Insurance Industry Initiative on the Environment: Developments in 1996' (1997) 3 *International Journal of Insurance Law* 171.

UNEP-FI issued a more general code for all financiers, known as the Statement by Financial Institutions on the Environment and Sustainable Development, which as of January 2012 had just over 200 signatories.[111] In an effort to boost financiers' attention to climate change, in 2007, UNEP-FI issued a Declaration on Climate Change by the Financial Services Sector, which calls on financial institutions to take greater action and to integrate climate change considerations (including the reduction of their direct carbon footprints) into their decision-making.[112] Paralleling the growth of SRI over the past decade, UNEP-FI has greatly expanded its own activities, which include workshops, taskforce meetings, global and regional roundtables, and education and training events.[113]

UNEP-FI's 1997 Statement, its main achievement, focuses on financiers' environmental performance with regard to internal operations (e.g., energy and resource use), environmental risk assessment and promotion of financial products and services to enhance environmental protection. Appropriately, the Statement also targets financiers' relationships with their borrowers and clients, and ambitiously expects signatories to 'regard sustainable development as a fundamental aspect of sound business management', 'support the precautionary approach to environmental management' and 'foster openness and dialogue relating to environmental matters with relevant audiences'.[114] However, UNEP-FI does not systematically monitor signatories' implementation of such standards, let alone exert sanctions for non-compliance. A 2007 survey by BankTrack of forty-five international banks, including thirty UNEP-FI signatories, found widespread grounds for concern and concluded that 'voluntary standards and initiatives are no substitute for stringent policies developed by banks themselves'.[115]

Concern about climate change has also triggered the formation of new coalitions dedicated specifically to promoting standards for climate

[111] See www.unepfi.org/signatories/statements/fi/index.html (accessed 7 March 2012). These UNEP-FI signatories represent about 15% of global capital assets under management: N. Purcell, Group General Manager, Westpac (UNEP-FI Global Roundtable, Melbourne, 24–5 October 2007).

[112] Available at www.unepfi.org/fileadmin/documents/cc_statement_jun2007.pdf (accessed 7 March 2012).

[113] See e.g. UNEP-FI, *2009 Overview* (UNEP-FI, 2010).

[114] See www.unepfi.org/signatories/statements/fi/index.html (accessed 7 March 2012).

[115] BankTrack, *Mind the Gap: Benchmarking Credit Policies of International Banks* (BankTrack, 2007), p. xi.

finance. The Climate Principles, subtitled 'A Framework for the Financial Sector', were adopted in 2008 to provide a 'common global standard of best practice not only to assist the finance sector in managing its own climate impact but also to assist the sector in supporting its clients and stakeholders in managing their own impacts'.[116] The Principles were devised by the Climate Group, a coalition of NGOs, businesses and public sector members, in dialogue with some twenty financial institutions. Unlike most SRI codes, the Climate Principles are tailored to specific areas of the finance industry. The insurance sector, for example, is expected to advise clients on climate risks and GHG mitigation technologies, while investment banks should facilitate financing of low-carbon technologies and GHG reduction projects, as well as assess the climate consequences of their investments. For financiers of projects that involve emissions of at least 100,000 tons of CO_2 equivalent annually, the Climate Principles expect them to request that their clients 'quantify and disclose' GHG emissions associated with the project, to 'monitor and report GHG emissions annually in accordance with internationally recognised methodologies' and to 'evaluate technically and financially feasible options to reduce or offset project-related GHG emissions'.[117] The Climate Principles thus provide more concrete performance standards than most SRI codes, and the Climate Group monitors compliance and publishes performance reviews.[118] Yet, like many other examples, individual signatories are not obliged to report their progress, and any detected failure to make meaningful progress does not in itself incur sanctions.

CONCLUSION: THE FUTURE OF SRI GOVERNANCE

The range of voluntary codes to promote SRI is clearly extraordinary, as is their recent and rapid proliferation. While most initiatives have arisen since 2000, it is unlikely that the next decade will see this trend continue. Instead, the focus will most likely shift towards consolidation and coordination of the disparate array of codes, as well as towards improved monitoring and increased compliance. It is debateable, however, whether

[116] Climate Group, www.theclimategroup.org/_assets/files/The-Climate-Principle-English.pdf (accessed 7 March 2012).
[117] Article 2.7.
[118] Climate Group, *Climate Principles: Progress Review* (January 2011).

governance of SRI will be able to continue to rely so heavily on voluntary mechanisms.[119] Some codes suffer from perfunctory implementation or lack robust standards to move the market beyond business-as-usual. The SRI market is also hindered by the continuing presence of legal rules and obligations, especially fiduciary duties, which can constrain financial institutions from investing ethically without a concomitant business case.[120]

SRI will most likely become more widespread and influential only with complementary changes to official regulation to address such legal barriers while offering greater sticks and carrots to stimulate the market for responsible financing. At an international level there remains limited governance of financial markets and no regulatory measures to promote SRI. But some legal reforms to promote SRI have been introduced at a national level in the past decade, especially in the UK, Australia and some Scandinavian countries.[121] As with voluntary codes, these reforms mainly involve market-based and informational tools that alter the procedures and processes of investment decision-making rather than prescribe performance standards. For instance, Australia and several Western European states have enacted legislation to oblige occupational pension funds to disclose their SRI policies (but not *oblige* SRI itself).[122] Another reform, adopted in Canada and the USA, requires mutual funds to disclose their shareholding proxy voting policies and voting records.[123]

Economic incentives for SRI in the form of tax concessions have been offered in a few jurisdictions; the leading example is the Netherlands' Green Project Directive,[124] which studies suggest boosted the Dutch SRI

[119] See the chapter by E. Morgera in this book.

[120] B. J. Richardson, 'From Fiduciary *Duties* to Fiduciary *Relationships* for SRI: Responding to the Will of Beneficiaries' (2011) 1 *Journal of Sustainable Finance and Investment* 1; B. J. Richardson, 'Do the Fiduciary Duties of Pension Funds Hinder Socially Responsible Investment?' (2007) 22 *Banking and Finance Law Review* 145.

[121] B. J. Richardson, *Socially Responsible Investment Law: Regulating the Unseen Polluters* (Oxford University Press, 2008).

[122] See e.g. UK's Occupational Pension Schemes (Investment) Regulations, 2005, cl. 2(3); Australia's Corporations Act, 2001 (Cth), s. 1013D(1)(l).

[123] Securities Exchange Commission, *Disclosure of Proxy Voting Policies and Proxy Voting Records by Registered Management Investment Companies* (31 January 2003); Canadian Securities Administrators, *National Instrument 81-106 Investment Fund Continuous Disclosure and Companion Policy 81-106CP* (2005).

[124] The scheme was revamped and extended in 2002 and 2005: *Regeling groenprojecten buitenland, Staatscourant* 1 (2 January 2002), 31; *Regeling groenprojecten, Staatscourant* 131 (11 July 2005), 13.

market considerably.[125] Substantive duties to invest socially have only been prescribed for sovereign wealth funds and national pension plans, notably in France, New Zealand, Norway and Sweden. New Zealand's Superannuation and Retirement Income Act of 2001 requires the guardians of the national superannuation fund to invest in ways to avoid 'prejudice to New Zealand's reputation as a responsible member of the world community'.[126] However, the open-ended, discretionary nature of this standard appears to have contributed to its perfunctory implementation.[127] The Swedish and Norwegian pension funds, on the other hand, are each guided by an ethics council, which use internationally recognised standards on human rights and sustainable development as benchmarks to fulfil their statutory obligations to invest ethically.[128]

The political obstacles to extending such precedents to private investors are such that it is unlikely for the foreseeable future that governmental regulation will play a decisive role in stimulating SRI. At most, further refinements of existing legal approaches that emphasise greater transparency and financial incentives for SRI will occur. Therefore, voluntary codes for SRI will probably continue to dominate the governance landscape for this market for some time.

This chapter's survey of the types of SRI codes has not provided an opportunity to scrutinise in detail the quality of their implementation. However, it appears that those enjoying the most endorsements and public legitimacy while offering reasonably robust standards are codes resulting from joint- or multi-stakeholder processes that created institutional regimes for ongoing dialogue, rule-making and monitoring. Examples include Ceres and UNEP-FI. While some codes are more ambitious, such as the Collevecchio Declaration on Financial Institutions, they lack support from investors. Conversely, the most popular codes with investors, such as the UNPRI and Equator Principles, do not

125 Vereniging van Beleggers voor Duurzame Ontwikkeling, *Socially Responsible Savings and Investments in the Netherlands: Developments in Volume and Growth of Socially-responsible Savings and Investments in Retail Funds* (Vereniging van Beleggers voor Duurzame Ontwikkeling, 2005), 11; KPMG, *Sustainable Profit: An Overview of the Environmental Benefits Generated by the Green Funds Scheme* (KPMG, 2002), 6.

126 Section 58(2)(c).

127 R. Norman, *Betting the Bank on the Bomb* (Green Party of New Zealand, 2007).

128 UNEP-FI and UK Social Investment Forum, *Responsible Investment in Focus: How Leading Public Pension Funds are Meeting the Challenge* (UNEP-FI, 2007), 7; B. J. Richardson, 'Sovereign Wealth Funds and the Quest for Sustainability: Insights from Norway and New Zealand' (2011) Fall(2) *Nordic Journal of Commercial Law* 1.

offer sufficiently rigorous standards or multi-stakeholder involvement and thus might not dramatically change investors' behaviour.

While the investor community increasingly recognises that it is in their financial self-interest to address climate change and other environmental issues because of the financial risks or opportunities, SRI codes remain essential because this 'business case' approach does not provide a sufficiently comprehensive framework for financing sustainable development. Some financiers may judge that an environmental issue is too remote to affect a company's bottom line, or that there are seemingly more pressing issues affecting investment values. Another hindrance is the general uncertainty that financiers face in determining the tangible implications of climate change or loss of biodiversity, given continuing scientific uncertainties about the magnitude of these environmental problems. Codes of conduct are crucial to help educate investors and provide additional reasons to act sustainably and with precaution when financial cues are lacking. But, ultimately, harder regulation must also have a complementary role. In a capitalist economic system premised on infinite economic growth, competitive advantage and profitability, it is hard to see the financial economy voluntarily accepting the stringent restraints that a low-carbon, sustainable economy demands.

Select bibliography

Baranzini, A., and P. Thalmann (eds.), *Voluntary Approaches in Climate Policy* (Cheltenham: Edward Elgar, 2004).

Bruyn, S., *The Field of Social Investment* (Cambridge University Press, 1987).

Cragg, W. (ed.), *Ethics Codes, Corporations and the Challenge of Globalization* (Cheltenham: Edward Elgar, 2005).

Gibson, R. (ed.), *Voluntary Initiatives: The New Politics of Corporate Greening* (University of Toronto Press, 1999).

Freshfields Bruckhaus Deringer, *A Legal Framework for the Integration of Environmental, Social and Governance Issues into Institutional Investment* (UNEP-FI, 2005).

Jeucken, M., *Sustainable Finance and Banking: The Financial Sector and the Future of the Planet* (London: Earthscan, 2001).

Kulkarni, P., 'Pushing Lenders to Over-comply with Environmental Regulations: A Developing Country Perspective' (2010) 22 *Journal of International Development* 470.

Labatt, S., and R. White, *Carbon Finance: The Financial Implications of Climate Change* (Chichester: Wiley, 2007).

McGeachie, S., M. Kiernan and E. Kirzner, *Finance and the Environment in North America* (Ottawa: Public Works and Services Canada, 2005).

Meidenger, E., '"Private" Environmental Regulation, Human Rights, and Community' (1999) 7 *Buffalo Environmental Law Journal* 123.

O'Rourke, A., 'The Message and Methods of Ethical Investment' (2003) 11 *Journal of Cleaner Production* 683.

O'Sullivan, N., and B. O'Dwyer, 'Stakeholder Perspectives on a Financial Sector Legitimation Process: The Case of NGOs and the Equator Principles' (2010) 22 *Accounting, Auditing and Accountability Journal* 553.

Priest, M., 'Five Models of Self-regulation' (1997–8) 29 *Ottawa Law Review* 233.

Ransome, W., and C. Sampford, *Ethics and Socially Responsible Investment: A Philosophical Approach* (Aldershot: Ashgate Publishing, 2011).

Richardson, B. J., 'Financing Sustainability: The New Transnational Governance of Socially Responsible Investment' (2007) 17 *Yearbook of International Environmental Law* 73.

Socially Responsible Investment Law: Regulating the Unseen Polluters (Oxford University Press, 2008).

'From Fiduciary *Duties* to Fiduciary *Relationships* for SRI: Responding to the Will of Beneficiaries' (2011) 1 *Journal of Sustainable Finance and Investment* 1.

'Are Social Investors Influential?' (2012) 9 *European Company Law* 133.

Schepers, D., 'The Equator Principles: A Promise in Progress?' (2011) 11 *Corporate Governance* 90.

Sparkes, R., *Socially Responsible Investment: A Global Revolution* (Chichester: Wiley, 2002).

Sullivan, R., and C. Mackenzie (eds.), *Responsible Investment* (Sheffield: Greenleaf Publishing, 2006).

Sun, W., C. Louche and R. Pérez (eds.), *Finance and Sustainability: Towards a New Paradigm? A Post-Crisis Agenda* (Bingley: Emerald Books, 2011).

Thornton, R., 'Ethical Investments: A Case of Disjointed Thinking' (2008) 67 *Cambridge Law Journal* 396.

White, M. A., 'Environmental Finance: Value and Risk in an Age of Ecology' (1996) 5 *Business Strategy and the Environment* 198.

Wood, S., 'Voluntary Environmental Codes and Sustainability', in B. Richardson and S. Wood (eds.), *Environmental Law for Sustainability* (Oxford: Hart Publishing, 2006), pp. 1–18.

15

The enforcement of environmental norms in investment treaty arbitration

ZACHARY DOUGLAS

INTRODUCTION

The dense network of more than three thousand treaties[1] for the protection of foreign investments, the majority of which confer rights directly upon non-state actors, is without an analogue in any other branch of international law. The most potent feature of the common investment treaty is the creation of a mechanism for the compulsory adjudication of investment disputes between a national of one of the contracting state parties and the contracting state party that is host to that national's investment. The mechanism is international arbitration: an ad hoc tribunal is created to resolve the dispute and render an award in accordance with an existing set of arbitration rules and that award can be enforced in most countries of the world under a multilateral treaty regime for the recognition and enforcement of arbitral awards.[2] The jurisprudence of these ad hoc tribunals is now vast and is supplemented by new awards on almost a weekly basis. The stakes are high in these cases not just in terms of the quantum of the compensation claimed by the protagonists – which often runs into billions of US dollars – but also in terms of the public interest. Decisions taken at the highest level of all three branches of constitutional power are frequently reviewed and sometimes condemned by the ad hoc tribunals established to hear these cases.[3]

1 UNCTAD, *UNCTAD World Investment Report 2011: Non-Equity Modes of International Production and Development* (2011), 100, available at www.unctad-docs.org/files/UNCTAD-WIR2011-Full-en.pdf (accessed 20 November 2012).

2 The most important of which are the New York Convention on the Recognition and Enforcement of Foreign Arbitral Awards (1958) and the Washington Convention on the Settlement of Investment Disputes between States and Nationals of other States (1965).

3 A brief overview of the investment treaty system is provided in Z. Douglas, *The International Law of Investment Claims* (Cambridge University Press, 2009), 1–6.

The incentive for commercial actors that is created by this network of treaties is to characterise their disputes with public authorities as 'investment disputes' within the criteria designated by an investment treaty that is binding upon the state in question. This may entail, for instance, placing emphasis on certain rights in property as being central to the dispute (so as to discharge the requirement of having a covered investment under the treaty) or selecting an entity within a corporate group as the nominal investor (so as to ensure that the claimant meets the nationality requirements under the treaty). There is nothing inherently wrong with such a litigational strategy: the network of investment treaties has created the incentive and commercial actors cannot be criticised for being incentivised. Indeed the privileged position of investors within the global institutional framework for the settlement of disputes has been made possible only by the international community of states giving priority to investment and trade over and above other matters of international concern such as the environment.

What this does mean, however, is that the ad hoc tribunals established pursuant to investment treaties are adjudicating upon 'investment disputes' that involve questions of environmental protection with increasing frequency. In *Methanex Corporation* v. *United States of America*,[4] for instance, an international tribunal considered the legality of the domestic ban on the commercialisation of a fuel additive in accordance with the investment protection standards set out in Chapter XI of NAFTA. In other cases the host state's measure is said to be mandated by its obligations in international environmental law. In *S.D. Myers* v. *Canada*,[5] Canada justified a ban on the importation of waste materials by reference to the Basel Convention on Hazardous Waste[6] and that justification was rejected by the tribunal. The ongoing dispute in *Chevron* v. *Ecuador* is perhaps the most complex example.[7] A group of indigenous Ecuadorians living in an area of the Amazonian rain forest alleged to have been devastated by the oil extraction activities conducted by a subsidiary of Texaco (which Chevron later acquired) brought a claim before a court in New York. That claim was eventually dismissed on *forum non conveniens*

[4] *Methanex Corporation* v. *United States of America*, UNCITRAL, Award (3 August 2005).

[5] *S.D. Myers Inc.* v. *Canada*, UNCITRAL, Partial Award (13 November 2000).

[6] Basel Convention on the Control of Transboundary Movements of Hazardous Wastes and their Disposal, 22 March 1989, 1673 UNTS 57.

[7] *Chevron Corporation and Texaco Petroleum Company* v. *Republic of Ecuador*, UNCITRAL, PCA Case No. 2009–23 (pending).

grounds but the plaintiffs subsequently refiled their claim against Chevron before their local court in Lago Agrio (Ecuador). While that case was pending, Chevron commenced an investment treaty arbitration against Ecuador. The tribunal upheld its jurisdiction on the theory that investment protection continues until the investment is finally disposed of, such that the contingent liability represented by the court proceedings in Lago Agrio meant that Chevron's investment in Ecuador persisted even though commercial operations had ceased some twenty years earlier, in 1993.[8] The essence of Chevron's claim in the arbitration is that it has suffered a denial of justice before the Lago Agrio court. This case is notable for making domestic accountability regimes for environmental damage subject to the supervisory jurisdiction of an investment treaty tribunal.

Environmental issues are thus often at the core of investment disputes submitted to compulsory third-party adjudication through the mechanism of investor/state arbitration. Given this reality, it is important to enquire as to whether the architecture of the typical investment treaty also allows the vindication of environmental norms under the same roof. In the absence of a comparable network of treaties creating compulsory international adjudicative mechanisms for environmental disputes, the effectiveness of international environmental law is to some extent contingent upon its ability to set up lodgings in the institutions created for other branches of international law.

The focus of this chapter is on the *enforcement* of environmental norms through an action in damages within the context of an investor/state arbitration. It will be immediately obvious that this possibility is at the most challenging end of the spectrum of techniques for reconciling the investment protection and environmental protection regimes. Other techniques at first blush seem far more promising. For instance, the 'greening' of investment protection norms such as the fair and equitable standard of treatment is within the judicial power of every ad hoc international tribunal established to decide an investment dispute.[9] Whether by reference to Article 31(3)(c) of the Vienna Convention of

[8] Third Interim Award on Jurisdiction and Admissibility (27 February 2012), para. 4.13.

[9] See the chapter by J. E. Viñuales in this book. Examples in the jurisprudence are: *Southern Pacific Properties (Middle East) Limited (SPP)* v. *Arab Republic of Egypt*, ICSID Case No. ARB/84/3, Award (20 May 1992) (reference to the UNESCO World Heritage Convention); *Parkerings-Compagniet AS* v. *Republic of Lithuania*, ICSID Case No. ARB/05/08, Award (11 September 2007) (as above); *Chemtura Corporation* v. *Government of Canada*, UNCITRAL, Award (2 August 2010) (reference to the Aarhus Protocol to the Convention on Long-Range Transboundary Air Pollution).

the Law on Treaties or otherwise, there is no obstacle preventing a tribunal from interpreting the fair and equitable standard of treatment in a manner that is sensitive to the legitimate regulatory objectives of the host state as defined by international environmental law. In other words, there is no inevitable conflict between investment protection and environmental norms that is latent in the interstices of the text of the investment treaty. Any clash of such norms in a particular case depends upon a subsequent human failure on the part of a specific tribunal – a failure to utilise the interpretative tools for norm reconciliation that are available to all international tribunals.[10]

In this chapter, I defend an interpretation of the juridical foundations of the investor's claim and the host state's counterclaim that facilitates the operationalisation of international norms extraneous to the investment treaty, including environmental norms. I also provide a brief sketch of how environmental norms might serve as a basis for an action for damages at the suit of the investor and the host state. It is not my intention to survey the field of environmental law for suitable norms as this is the focus of other chapters in this volume.[11]

15.1 The investor's right to claim damages under an investment treaty

15.1.1 *The proper conceptual basis for the investor's rights*

In earlier writings I have identified three possible rationalisations for the investor's rights under an investment treaty.[12] The first is that the

[10] See e.g. the statement of principle in *CDSE* v. *Costa Rica*, ICSID Case No. ARB/96/1, Award (17 February 2000), 5 ICSID Rep 157, 171 ('While an expropriation or taking for environmental reasons may be classified as a taking for a public purpose, and thus may be legitimate, the fact that the Property was taken for this reason does not affect either the nature or the measure of compensation to be paid for the taking … Expropriatory measures – no matter how laudable and beneficial to society as a whole – are, in this respect, similar to any other expropriatory measures that a state may take in order to implement its policies'). Does international law really treat an expropriation of land for the preservation of a wildlife reserve in accordance with international environmental norms in the same way as the expropriation of land to build a golf course for the presidential family? The Tribunal awarded CDSE US$16 million in damages (comprising the principal amount and compound interest). CDSE had purchased the land for US$395,000. This statement of principle was then applied in subsequent cases against Costa Rica: *Marion Unglaube* v. *Republic of Costa Rica*, ICSID Case No. ARB/08/1 and *Reinhard Hans Unglaube* v. *Republic of Costa Rica*, ICSID Case No. ARB/09/20; see www.iareporter.com/articles/20120522_3 (accessed 20 November 2012).

[11] See the chapters by S. Maljean Dubois and V. Richard and E. Morgera in this book.

[12] Douglas, *The International Law of Investment Claims*, 11–38.

investment protection obligations exist purely on an inter-state level and the procedural mechanism allowing the investor to enforce them is a privilege granted by the national state of the investor in derogation of its right of diplomatic protection. In other words, the investor is permitted for convenience to step into the shoes of its national state to assert what is in essence a diplomatic protection claim (and thus the procedural right of the national state). I have set out the arguments against this 'derivative' model elsewhere.[13] It finds support most notably in *Loewen* v. *USA*,[14] but was rejected after a lengthy analysis by the English Court of Appeal in *Occidental* v. *Ecuador*,[15] and since then has not attracted many adherents.

The second and third rationalisations rest upon the (correct) premise that the procedural right to assert claims against the host state in arbitration is vested directly in the investor. The question is then whether the substantive investment protection obligations are owed directly to investors that qualify as such under the investment treaty. An affirmative answer was preferred by the Court of Appeal in *Occidental* v. *Ecuador*[16] and is supported by dicta in some investment awards.[17] This can be labelled the second rationalisation.

There is a third possibility that I have articulated in the following terms:

> Upon the claimant's filing of a notice of arbitration, the claimant investor perfects the host state's unilateral offer to arbitrate, and the two parties thus enter into a direct legal relationship in the form of an arbitration agreement. At the same time, the claimant becomes a counterparty to the host state's obligation to submit to international arbitration for an assessment of its conduct towards the claimant's investment on the basis of the norms of investment protection set out in the treaty. This obligation encompasses the duty of the host state to pay compensation if the international tribunal adjudges its conduct to be violative of these norms. The minimum standards of investment protection could thus be

[13] *Ibid.*, 11–32.

[14] *Loewen Group Inc. and Raymond L. Loewen* v. *United States of America*, ICSID Case No. ARB(AF)/98/3, Award (26 June 2003), para. 233.

[15] *Occidental Exploration and Production Company* v. *Republic of Ecuador* [2005] EWCA Civ 1116 [2006] QB 432.

[16] *Ibid.* para. 18.

[17] See e.g. *CMS Gas Transmission Company* v. *Republic of Argentina*, ICSID Case No. ARB/01/8, Decision on Objections to Jurisdiction (17 July 2003), para. 45; *American Manufacturing and Trading, Inc.* v. *Republic of Zaire*, ICSID Case No. ARB/93/1, Award (21 February 1997), para. 6.06.

> characterised as the applicable adjudicative standards for the claimant's cause of action rather than binding obligations owed directly to the investor.[18]

It is submitted that this third rationalisation is superior to the direct model of the investor's rights represented by the second rationalisation for the reasons that now follow.

15.1.2 The contractual analogy

It is often stated that the triangular arrangement created by an investment treaty as between the investor, the host state and the national state of the investor has an analogy in domestic law in the instances where third parties are permitted to enforce a stipulated benefit under a contract as an exception to the doctrine of privity.[19] But those legal institutions in domestic law either rely upon the fiction that the third party becomes a party to the contract or they grant the third party the same remedies to enforce its rights as if it were a party to that contract. Neither approach can be sustained in the investment treaty context: the investor does not have the capacity to be a party to a treaty in international law and it is not granted the same remedies in international law as its own national state in respect of a breach of the treaty (e.g., the adoption of countermeasures is not available to the investor).

International law, perhaps regrettably, has opted for a division between the law of the instrument and the law of obligations set out in that instrument.[20] An investor does not acquire rights under the law governing the instrument creating the obligation as opposed to the law applicable to the breach of that obligation. By way of example, the general power of the state parties to exercise their rights under the Vienna Convention on the Law of Treaties to amend the investment treaty or

[18] Douglas, *The International Law of Investment Claims*, 35.

[19] This possibility was not permitted in classical Roman law: 'alteri stipulari nemo potest'. A contract for the benefit of a third party is recognised in the principal continental legal systems: in Germany, §§329–31 BGB; in France, Article 1165 Code civil, 'stipulation au profit d'un tiers'. It has been accepted in the USA at least since *Lawrence* v. *Fox* 20 NY 268 (1859). In England the doctrine of privity excluded the recognition of a contract for the benefit of third parties as a legal institution of general application until Parliament intervened with the Contracts (Rights of Third Parties) Act 1999. See generally K. Zweigert and H. Kötz, *An Introduction to Comparative Law* (Oxford University Press, 1998), 456–69.

[20] See generally S. Rosenne, *Breach of Treaty* (Cambridge: Grotius Publications, 1984).

to terminate it in accordance with its terms is unaffected by the existence of a class of third parties with protected interests under that investment treaty (i.e., qualified investors).[21] This may be contrasted with situations in domestic contract law where third parties acquire rights under a contract: the right of the contracting parties to rescind or vary the contract without the consent of a third-party beneficiary is generally limited.[22]

The paradigm of a contract for the benefit of a third party in domestic law does not sit comfortably alongside the mechanism for enforcing investment protection obligations in investment treaties. Investment protection obligations are not defined with sufficient precision so as to constitute a benefit that is capable of being enforced by third parties in the sense permitted under domestic laws (e.g., where A promises B to pay C upon the occurrence of a particular event such as under a life assurance policy).[23] Investment protection obligations are rather formulated as abstract standards of conduct that a host state must adhere to even where the particular investor is not reasonably within its contemplation. Investment treaties in this sense are more accurately described as *traités-loi* than *traités-contrat* and certainly do not exhibit the features of synallagmatic contracts in domestic law.

15.1.3 The tort analogy

A more fruitful analogy can be found in the domestic law of tort for the breach of a statutory duty. The legislature frequently imposes statutory duties upon public authorities (as well as private entities) to comply with minimum standards of conduct. In many countries there is a distinct form of delictual liability for a breach of statutory duty where someone is harmed by conduct falling below the requisite standard fixed by the statute.[24] This form of liability typically plays a prominent role in the area of industrial safety.

[21] It may be otherwise if there is an express provision in the treaty limiting the exercise of this general power.

[22] See e.g. Contracts (Rights of Third Parties) Act 1999 (UK), s. 2.

[23] For this reason investment protection obligations may also be contrasted with the types of treaty provisions that have been characterised as conferring direct rights upon non-state actors in the past by international tribunals outside the field of human rights. See Douglas, *The International Law of Investment Claims*, 34.

[24] In Germany, §823, para. 2 BGB (liability arises when a 'statute designed to protect another' is culpably breached); in England, see e.g. *X* v. *Bedfordshire County Council* [1995] 2 AC 633. On the modern position in England, see K. M. Stanton, 'New Forms of the Tort of Breach of Statutory Duty' (2004) 120 *Law Quarterly Review* 324.

The elements of this cause of action, at least in England, are as follows: (i) the claimant is within the class of persons protected by the statute; (ii) the defendant has breached the statutory provision enshrining the minimum standard of conduct; (iii) the defendant has thereby caused damage to the claimant; and (iv) that damage is of the type contemplated by the statute.

Whether or not the regulatory provisions of a statute are actionable in tort is a question of statutory interpretation that must often be resolved in the absence of any express language in the statute. Nonetheless, an example of an express stipulation can be found in the Financial Services and Markets Act 2000 (UK), s. 150(1):

> A contravention by an authorised person of a rule is actionable at the suit of a private person who suffers loss as a result of the contravention, subject to the defences and other incidents applying to actions for breach of statutory duty.

This model of delictual liability can be readily transposed to the investment treaty context: the state parties confer a right upon investors to assert a claim for damages as a means of obtaining reparation for the breach of one or more of the minimum standards of treatment set out in the investment treaty.

The language of some investment treaties would appear to give direct support for this model for conceptualising the investor's rights. For instance, Article 1116 of NAFTA reads:

> An investor of a Party may submit to arbitration under this Section a claim that another Party has breached an obligation under [Chapter 11 of NAFTA] and that the investor has incurred loss or damage by reason of, or arising out of, that breach.

It is not difficult to extract from this formulation the vesting of a right to pursue a remedy to vindicate a breach of an investment protection obligation.

The important insight from this analogy to the tort for a breach of a statutory duty is that the source for the cause of action is distinct from the source of the norm regulating the conduct in question. The law in Germany provides a clear illustration. The source of the cause of action in tort is §823 para. 2 BGB, which states that liability arises when a 'statute designed to protect another' is culpably breached. The civil code thus provides the cause of action to the claimant, whereas the particular statute that is designed to protect the claimant supplies the standard to adjudge the conduct. The distinction is even more pronounced in the context of delictual liability for a breach of a statutory duty in European Community law. Here the source of the norm regulating the conduct actually comes from a distinct legal order. Thus, where a private entity suffered harm as a result of an abuse of a dominant position in the common market by a trade association in breach of Article 82 of the EEC Treaty,[25] the House of Lords ruled that the English law of torts provided a cause of action for damages for breach of a statutory duty.[26] Another example is provided by the Alien Tort Statute (ATS) in the USA, which reads: 'The district courts shall have original jurisdiction of any civil action by an alien for a tort only, committed in violation of the law of nations or a treaty of the United States'.[27] The ATS vests the district courts with jurisdiction over a cause of action supplied by the federal common law whereas the norms regulating the standards of conduct for the cause of action are to be found in international law.[28]

The situation in investment treaty arbitration can be deconstructed in the following way. The investor/state mechanism for the prosecution of claims against the host state by international arbitration is the source of the procedural right to arbitrate and supplies the cause of action for reparation for a breach of the investment protection obligations. The investment protection obligations are the norms regulating the standards of conduct. The investor is not privy to the substantive investment protection obligations or directly vested with a corresponding right in respect of each. There is no right/duty correlation at this level. In the same way it would be incoherent to describe a general statute regulating the conduct of a public authority in domestic law as creating a web of bilateral relationships between rights-holders and the duty-bearing public authority. Like a statutory regime of this nature, the class of protected persons or entities under an investment treaty is unlikely even to be ascertainable at any given time.

The substantive obligations in investment treaties are better conceived as a set of codified standards for the treatment of foreign investments. Like the tort for breach of a statutory duty, the question is simply whether the person or entity complaining of a breach of those standards falls within the class of protected persons or entities under the treaty. Membership of that protected class allows recourse to the cause of action

[25] Now Article 102 of the Consolidated Version of the Treaty on the Functioning of the European Union, *Official Journal of the European Union*, C83/47, 30.3.2010.

[26] *Garden Cottage Foods* v. *Milk Marketing Board* [1984] AC 130.

[27] 28 USC §1350.

[28] *Sosa* v. *Alvarez-Machain*, 542 US 692 (2004).

created by the treaty to seek reparation for damage caused by a breach of the investment protection standards.

This seems to be a far more promising rationalisation of the investor's cause of action than the contractual model suggested by the theory that investment treaty obligations are owed to investors directly. The investor is not enforcing a promise by the host state to accord fair and equitable treatment to the investor as a third-party beneficiary to the treaty instrument. Rather, the investor is claiming reparation for the failure on the part of the host state to adhere to the standard of fair and equitable treatment in respect of its investment. The investor is not by this analysis invoking the international responsibility of the host state on the international plane. In no sense is the investor stepping into the shoes of its own national state and claiming the performance of secondary obligations that would arise between the host state and the national state of the investor. The investor is making the host state liable in damages but not responsible in international law.

15.1.4 The enforcement of international environmental norms by the investor

The disaggregation of the investor's cause of action from the substantive investment protection obligations in the investment treaty unlocks certain possibilities for the enforcement of environmental norms against the host state. So long as the host state's consent to investor/state arbitration is expressed in broad terms, such as 'all disputes relating to an investment', there is no restriction upon the source of obligations that form the basis of the investor's claim.[29] The investor can, therefore, claim damages for the host state's failure to comply with an environmental obligation in domestic law[30] or international customary or conventional law so long as

[29] See Douglas, *The International Law of Investment Claims*, 234–40.

[30] J. E. Viñuales has unearthed such a claim by a Canadian investor, Peter A. Allard, against Barbados for the failure to enforce domestic environmental law (adopted to implement the international environmental law obligations of Barbados) and it is described in his 'Foreign Investment and the Environment in International Law: An Ambiguous Relationship' (2009) 80 *British Yearbook of International Law* 244, 250: 'the investor, who acquired 34.25 acres of natural wetlands and subsequently developed it into an ecotourism facility, claims that, through its acts and omissions, Barbados has *inter alia* failed (a) to prevent the repeated discharge of raw sewage into wetlands, (b) to investigate or prosecute sources of runoff of grease, oil, pesticides and herbicides from neighbouring areas, and poachers that have threatened the wildlife within the ecosystem'. Apparently

such failure has caused damage to its covered investment. This direct method for enforcing environmental norms against the host state is expressly or at least tacitly permitted by the common applicable law provisions found in investment treaties, which serve merely to confirm that the tribunal is competent to apply the stipulated sources of law, rather than prescribe the connecting factors necessary to determine the applicable laws in any given case.[31] For instance, Article 8(6) of The Netherlands/Czech Republic bilateral investment treaty (BIT) reads:

> The arbitral tribunal shall decide on the basis of the law, taking into account in particular though not exclusively:
>
> the law in force of the Contracting Party concerned;
> the provisions of this Agreement, and other relevant Agreements between the Contracting Parties;
> the provisions of special agreements relating to the investment;
> general principles of international law.[32]

these failures damaged the natural ecosystem adjacent to the investor's ecotourism facility thereby resulting in a fall in tourism revenues.

[31] See e.g. China Model BIT, Art. 9(7), *UNCTAD Compendium*, vol. 3 (1996), 155–6: 'the tribunal shall adjudicate in accordance with the law of the Contracting Party to the dispute accepting the investment including its rules of conflict of laws, the provisions of this Agreement, as well as the generally recognized principles of international law accepted by both Contracting Parties'; Egypt Model BIT, Art. 8(3), *ibid.*, vol. 5 (2000), 296: 'the arbitration tribunal shall decide in accordance with the provisions of this Agreement; the national law of the Contracting Party in whose territory the investment was made; and Principles of International Law'; Sri Lanka Model BIT, Art. 8(3), *ibid.*, 343; OPEC Model BIT, Art. 10.01, *ibid.*, vol. 6, p. 490; Belgo–Luxembourg Economic Union Model BIT, Art. 10(5), *ibid.*, 276; South Africa Model BIT, Art. 7(4), *ibid.*, vol. 8, p. 277; Greece Model BIT, Art. 10(4), *ibid.*, 291–2; Benin Model BIT, Art. 9(4), *ibid.*, vol. 9, p. 284; Burundi Model BIT, Art. 8(5), *ibid.*, 292; Burkina Faso Model BIT, Art. 9(4), *ibid.*, 292; Kenya Model BIT, Art. 12, *ibid.*, vol. 12, p. 310: 'Except as otherwise provided in this Agreement, all investments shall be governed by the laws in force in the territory of the Contracting Party in which such investment are made including such laws enacted for the protection of its essential security interests or in circumstances of extreme emergency provided however that such laws are reasonably applied on a non-discriminatory basis'; Uganda Model BIT, Art. 7(5), *ibid.*, vol. 12, p. 318; Canada Model BIT, Art. 40(1), *ibid.*, vol. 14, p. 247: 'A Tribunal established under this Section shall decide the issues in disputes in accordance with this Agreement and applicable rules of international law'; USA Model BIT (2004), Art. 30; China Model BIT (2003), Art. 9(3): 'the arbitration award shall be based on the law of the Contracting Party to the dispute including its rules on the conflict of laws, the provision of this Agreement as well as the universally accepted principles of international law'; Energy Charter Treaty, Art. 26(6): 'a tribunal established under paragraph (4) shall decide the issues in dispute in accordance with this Treaty and applicable rules and principles of international law'; North American Free Trade Agreement, 17 December 1992, 32 ILM 296, Art. 1131.

[32] Douglas, *The International Law of Investment Claims*, 43.

Such a provision would allow the tribunal to have recourse to treaties between the Contracting Parties in the sphere of environmental law and also to rely upon environmental norms that have passed into custom. But there is little doubt that the tribunal would have such a power in the absence of an express provision.

There is an alternative indirect approach available to the investor, which is to formulate a claim for breach of an environmental norm by reference to one of the investment protection obligations in the treaty, such as the fair and equitable standard of treatment. The essence of the claim would be that a failure on the part of the host state to comply with its international engagements with respect to the environment is indicative of unfair and inequitable treatment in the circumstances of the case, especially if it is accompanied by bad faith or discrimination. There are numerous examples in practice of claims for a breach of the fair and equitable standard that rely upon extraneous international obligations of the host state to supply a threshold for liability that is attuned to the particular subject-matter of the dispute.[33]

In respect of some investment treaties – including NAFTA, the Energy Charter Treaty and treaties concluded on the basis of the USA Model BITs – only the indirect method of enforcing environmental norms is available to investors. The reason is that the consent to investor/state arbitration in these treaties is stipulated on a narrower basis. For instance, Article 24(1) of the USA Model BIT (2012) reads in relevant part:

> [T]he claimant, on its own behalf, may submit to arbitration under this Section a claim … that the respondent has breached (A) an obligation under Articles 3 through 10, (B) an investment authorization, or (C) an investment agreement; and … that the claimant has incurred loss or damage by reason of, or arising out of, that breach.[34]

Unless the host state's international engagements relating to the environment were also encapsulated in the investment authorisation or investment agreement with the investor, then the only course open to the

[33] For instance, in *Saluka* v. *Czech Republic*, the claimant (which owned one of the four leading banks in the Czech Republic) relied upon the EU rules on state aid to demonstrate that the quantum of aid granted by the Czech Government to the claimant's competitors to the exclusion of the claimant violated the fair and equitable standard of treatment as a result of the resultant distortions in the market for banking services. *Saluka Investments BV* v. *Czech Republic*, UNCITRAL, Partial Award (17 March 2006).

[34] USA Model BIT (2012), available at www.ustr.gov.

investor would be to claim damages for a breach of such engagements through the medium of one of the investment protection obligations in the treaty.

15.2 The host state's right to counterclaim under an investment treaty

15.2.1 The source of the host state's right to counterclaim

Whilst investment treaties are silent on the possibility of counterclaims by the respondent host state, numerous international tribunals have uniformly recognised their jurisdiction to hear counterclaims in circumstances where their constitutive instruments do not confer an express power to do so. Thus, for instance, the Permanent Court of Justice,[35] the International Court of Justice[36] and the International Law of the Sea Tribunal[37] have adopted procedural rules for the adjudication of counterclaims, despite the silence of their constitutive instruments on this possibility. The same approach has been taken by several mixed claims commissions[38] and the Iran–US Claims Tribunal in relation to counterclaims by one of the state parties.[39] If a general principle can be discerned from this practice, it is that the jurisdiction *ratione materiae* of an international tribunal extends to counterclaims unless expressly excluded by the constitutive instrument.[40]

35 Statute of the Permanent Court of International Justice (13 December 1920) PCIJ (Ser. D) No. 1; Article 40 of the 1922 Rules of Court, Art. 40; 1936 Rules of Court, Art. 63.

36 Statute of the International Court of Justice (26 June 1945) Acts and Documents concerning the Organization of the Court, No. 5; 1946 Rules of Court, Art. 63; 1972 Rules of Court, Art. 68; 1978 Rules of Court, Art. 80; 2000 Rules of Court, Art. 80.

37 Statute of the International Tribunal for the Law of the Sea, Annex VI of the United Nations Convention on the Law of the Sea, 10 December 1982, 1833 UNTS 3; Rules of the Tribunal, Art. 98.

38 England–Austria, Arts 26–8; England–Bulgaria, Arts 26–8; England–Hungary, Arts 26–8; Italy–Germany, Art. 34; Italy–Austria, Art. 34; Italy–Bulgaria, Art. 34; Italy–Hungary, Art. 34; France–Germany, Art. 14(e); France–Bulgaria, Art. 14(e); France–Austria, Art. 14 (e); France–Hungary, Art. 14(e); Greece–Germany, Art. 14(e); Greece–Bulgaria, Art. 14 (e); Greece–Austria, Art. 14(e); Greece–Hungary, Art. 14(e); Romania–Germany, Art. 13(e); Romania–Hungary, Art. 13(e); Siam–Germany, Art. 14(e); Czechoslovakia–Germany, Art. 24. See *Recueil des Décisions des Tribunaux Arbitraux Mixtes institués par les traités de paix* (vols 1–5 (1922)).

39 *Iran* v. *United States of America* (Case ITL 83-B1-FT, 9 September 2004) (Counterclaims).

40 *Installations Maritimes de Bruges* v. *Hambourg Amerika Linie* 1 RIAA 877 (1921): 'Att. que les deux requêtes introductives sont basées sur un seul et même fait, qui est la

Several investment treaty tribunals have acknowledged the host state's right to counterclaim either explicitly or implicitly.[41] In private international law this would be considered to be a question of procedure[42] and thus it is significant that the most common arbitration rules do recognise the right to counterclaim expressly.

15.2.2 *The scope of permissible counterclaims*

The most common procedural rule governing investor/state arbitrations is Article 47 of the ICSID Convention:

collision survenue le 25 octobre 1911 entre le vapeur Parthia et Duc d'Albe et un mur du port de Zeebruge, et que la seconde requête eût pu prendre la forme d'une simple demande reconventionnelle si l'article 29 du Règlement de procédure ne l'interdisait absolument'. The tribunal in *Saluka* v. *Czech Republic* decided that, as a matter of principle, where the consent to arbitration is expressed in wide terms in an investment treaty, the tribunal is conferred jurisdiction *ratione materiae* over counterclaims by the respondent host state. In that case, Article 8 of The Netherlands/Czech Republic BIT conferred jurisdiction over 'all disputes between a Contracting Party and an investor of the other Contracting Party concerning an investment of the latter'. *Saluka Investments B.V.* v. *The Czech Republic,* UNCITRAL, Decision on Jurisdiction over the Czech Republic's Counterclaim (7 May 2004) (*Saluka* v. *Czech Republic*), para. 39.

41 *Saluka* v. *Czech Republic*; *Alex Genin, Eastern Credit Ltd Inc. and AS Baltoil* v. *Estonia,* ICSID Case No. ARB/99/2, Award (25 June 2001), paras. 201, 376–8 (counterclaim dismissed on the merits without consideration of jurisdiction); *SGS Société Générale de Surveillance SA* v. *Islamic Republic of Pakistan,* ICSID Case No. ARB/01/13, Procedural Order No. 2 (16 October 2002) 8 ICSID Rep 388; Decision on Objections to Jurisdiction (6 August 2003) 8 ICSID Rep 406, 426–7; *SGS Société Générale de Surveillance SA* v. *Republic of the Philippines,* ICSID Case No. ARB/02/6, Decision on Objections to Jurisdiction (29 January 2004) 8 ICSID Rep 518, 528 (host state's right to counterclaim conceded by claimant); *RSM Production Company and others* v. *Grenada,* ICSID Case No. ARB/10/6, Award (13 March 2009), para. 226 (jurisdiction over respondent's counterclaim upheld); *Gustav F W Hamester GmbH & Co KG* v. *Republic of Ghana,* ICSID Case No. ARB/07/24, Award (18 June 2010), paras 353–5 (jurisdiction over respondent's counterclaim upheld); *Paushok and others* v. *Mongolia,* UNCITRAL, Award on Jurisdiction and Liability (28 April 2011), paras 693–9 (jurisdiction over counterclaims rejected but existence of right to counterclaim not disputed); *Spyridon Roussalis* v. *Romania,* ICSID Case No. ARB/06/1, Award (7 December 2011), paras 821–5, 866–76 (jurisdiction over counterclaims rejected but existence of right to counterclaim not disputed; dissenting opinion on this point by Professor Michael Reisman). It has been reported that counterclaims have been made by Ecuador in investment treaty cases brought by Burlington Resources Inc. and Perenco Energy: *Burlington Resources Inc. and others* v. *Republic of Ecuador and Empresa Estatal Petróleos del Ecuador* (*PetroEcuador*), ICSID Case No. ARB/08/5.

42 In England *South African Republic* v. *Compagnie Franco-Belge du Chemin de Fer du Nord* [1897] 2 Ch 487 (CA).

> Except as the parties otherwise agree, the Tribunal shall, if requested by a party, determine any incidental or additional claims or counterclaims arising directly out of the subject-matter of the dispute provided that they are within the scope of the consent of the parties and are otherwise within the jurisdiction of the Centre.

The 'scope of the consent of the parties' in an investment treaty arbitration is defined to some extent by the arbitration agreement that is perfected upon the filing of a notice of arbitration. Some commentators argue that if the investor, upon the filing of its notice of arbitration, 'accepts the offer only in respect of its specific claim, consent will be restricted by the terms of the acceptance' such that the possibility of the host state's assertion of a counterclaim would in essence be eliminated.[43] This interpretation of the investor's acceptance is much too restrictive. When a claimant investor consents to investment treaty arbitration it must be taken to consent to the adjudication of the underlying dispute in accordance with the applicable arbitration rules. If consent were limited to the lowest common denominator represented by the precise formulation of a 'specific claim' by the investor, then the arbitral tribunal's power to order provisional measures would also have to be excluded by this logic. The investor would, moreover, be precluded from amending or supplementing its claims during the course of the arbitration as this would be a derogation from the meeting of the minds of the parties upon the perfection of the arbitration agreement. Such a restrictive interpretation is also at odds with other provisions of the ICSID Convention. Article 25 talks of the submission of a 'dispute' to the Centre and not of an individual 'claim', and Article 26 provides that if the parties have consented to ICSID arbitration then resort to any other remedy is excluded. The latter would be patently unreasonable if the tribunal's jurisdiction were limited to the consideration of the investor's particular claim and nothing more.

Whilst the majority of investment treaties refer simply to 'investment disputes' or 'disputes arising out of an investment' in their provisions on investor/state arbitration,[44] some treaties do use the more restrictive language of 'claims' rather than 'disputes' in describing what is being submitted to investor/state arbitration.[45] But in all cases the content of

[43] C. Schreuer, L. Malintoppi, A. Reinisch and A. Sinclair, *The ICSID Convention: A Commentary* (Cambridge University Press, 2009), 756.

[44] See Douglas, *The International Law of Investment Claims*, 234–5.

[45] See e.g. USA Model BIT (2012).

the arbitration agreement is best defined as the acceptance of an offer to arbitrate the dispute relating to a covered investment in accordance with the rules set out in the investment treaty and the applicable arbitration rules.

Unlike Article 47 of the ICSID Convention, most procedural rules say nothing at all about the scope of permissible counterclaims. Article 21 of the UNCITRAL Arbitration Rules (2010) simply regulates the timing and formal requirements for the respondent to exercise its right to make a counterclaim. The previous Article 19(3) of the 1976 version of the UNCITRAL Rules had limited the scope of counterclaims to those 'arising out of the same contract' and it was noted during the working group sessions for the revision of the rules that this was inappropriate for investment treaty arbitration.[46]

In all cases, the scope of the tribunal's jurisdiction to determine counterclaims by the host state ultimately depends upon a factual nexus between the dispute submitted by the claimant and the counterclaim.[47] That nexus is required by virtue of the consensual basis for the tribunal's jurisdiction. The claimant investor is in the driver's seat to the extent that the outer boundaries of the dispute are fixed by the tribunal's appraisal of the claimant's notice of arbitration. But no symmetry is required in the legal foundations of the claim and counterclaim. The articulation and application of the factual nexus in any given case is a function entrusted to the arbitral tribunal by virtue of its general power to regulate the procedure, which is ubiquitous in all modern arbitration rules.[48]

The subject-matter of the dispute is defined, in turn, by the rights comprising the investment and the disagreement between the investor and host state on questions of law and fact relating to those rights.[49] This is the meaning of the reference to the 'subject-matter of the dispute' in Article 47 of the ICSID Convention. It is, moreover, consistent with other

[46] Douglas, *The International Law of Investment Claims*, 258–60.

[47] *Saluka* v. *Czech Republic*, above, n. 40, para. 61: 'a legitimate counterclaim must have a close connexion with the primary claim to which it is a response'. See also *Amco Asia Corporationa and others* v. *Republic of Indonesia*, ICSID Case No. ARB/81/1, Decision on Jurisdiction (10 May 1988) 1 ICSID Rep 543, 565 (*Amco* v. *Indonesia II*); *Klöckner Industrie-Anlagen GmbH and others* v. *United Republic of Cameroon and Société Camerounaise des Engrais*, ICSID Case No. ARB/81/2, Award (21 October 1983) 2 ICSID Rep 9, 17, 65.

[48] ICSID Convention, Art. 44; UNCITRAL Rules of Arbitration (2010), Art. 17.1; ICC Rules of Arbitration (2012), Art. 19; LCIA Rules of Arbitration (1988), Art. 14.2.

[49] See Douglas, *The International Law of Investment Claims*, 337.

instances where an international or transnational instrument has defined the nexus between claim and counterclaim, such as the EU Regulation on Jurisdiction and the Recognition and Enforcement of Judgments in Civil and Commercial Matters, which provides that a person domiciled in a member state can be sued 'on a counter-claim arising from the same contract or *facts on which the original claim was based*, in the court in which the original claim is pending'.[50]

Contrary to the ruling in *Saluka* v. *Czech Republic*, the test cannot be the identity of the source of the norms underlying the claim and counterclaim. In that case, the tribunal insisted upon the 'interdependence and essential unity of the instruments on which the original claim and counterclaim [are] based'[51] such that if the counterclaims were based upon the general law of the host state they must be resolved exclusively through the appropriate procedures of the host state's law.[52] Such an approach would exclude the tribunal's jurisdiction over counterclaims whenever the investor's claim is based upon a treaty obligation because the host state's counterclaim cannot be based upon the same instrument in this case.

The *Saluka* tribunal cited precedents where the primary claim was based on a contractual relationship with the host state, whereas the counterclaim by the respondent host state was founded upon an obligation in general law such as tax legislation.[53] In *Amco* v. *Indonesia II*,[54]

[50] Council Regulation (EC) No. 44/2001 of 22 December 2000 on jurisdiction and the recognition and enforcement of judgments in civil and commercial matters, Art. 6(3). Emphasis added.

[51] *Saluka* v. *Czech Republic*, above, n. 40, paras 78 and 79.

[52] *Ibid*. The Tribunal in *Hamester* v. *Ghana*, above, n. 41, followed the same approach as in *Saluka*: 'the Counterclaims arise out of Mongolian public law and exclusively raise issues of non-compliance with Mongolian public law, including the tax laws of Mongolia. All these issues squarely fall within the scope of the exclusive jurisdiction of Mongolian courts, are matters governed by Mongolian public law, and cannot be considered as constituting an indivisible part of the Claimants' claims based on the BIT and international law or as creating a reasonable nexus between the Claimants' claims and the Counterclaims justifying their joint consideration by an arbitral tribunal exclusively vested with jurisdiction under the BIT' (para. 694).

[53] *Amco* v. *Indonesia II*, above, n. 47; *Harris International Telecommunications* v. *Iran* (Case 323–409–1, 2 November 1987), 17 Iran–US CTR 31, 57–61 (*Harris* v. *Iran*). See also: *Blount Brothers Corp* v. *Ministry of Housing and Urban Development* (Case 74–62–3, 2 September 1983), 3 Iran–US CTR 225, 226; *Behring International, Inc* v. *Islamic Republic Iranian Air Force* (Case ITM/ITL 52–382–3, 21 June 1985), 8 Iran–US CTR 238, 265; *International Technical Products Corporation* v. *Iran* (Case 196–302–3, 28 October 1985), 9 Iran–US CTR 206, 226–7.

[54] *Amco* v. *Indonesia* II, above, n. 47.

Indonesia raised a counterclaim for 'tax fraud' on the part of the claimants in the second arbitration proceedings and sought the restitution of sums representing the tax allegedly evaded by claimants throughout the relevant period of the investment. The tribunal found that such a claim was outside the tribunal's jurisdiction *ratione materiae*. The tribunal noted that there was no a priori rule or principle that might serve to remove tax claims from the jurisdiction of an ICSID tribunal. The question was simply the nexus between the tax claim and the investment. For the purposes of Article 25(1) of the ICSID Convention, the test was whether the tax claim was a 'legal dispute directly arising out of the investment'. The tribunal identified the relevant principle in the following terms:

> [I]t is correct to distinguish between rights and obligations that are applicable to legal or natural persons who are within the reach of a host State's jurisdiction, as a matter of general law; and rights and obligations that are applicable to an investor as a consequence of an investment agreement entered into with that host State. Legal disputes relating to the latter will fall under Article 25(1) of the Convention. Legal disputes concerning the former in principle fall to be decided by the appropriate procedures in the relevant jurisdiction unless the general law generates an investment dispute under the Convention. The obligation not to engage in tax fraud is clearly a general obligation of law in Indonesia. It was not specially contracted for in the investment agreement and does not arise directly out of the investment.[55]

The *Saluka* tribunal appears to have relied heavily on this passage in excluding from its jurisdiction counterclaims based upon 'rights and obligations which are applicable, as a matter of the general law of the Czech Republic, to persons subject to the Czech Republic's jurisdiction'.[56] But this does not accurately reflect the *Amco* tribunal's finding, which did not rest solely upon the general law nature of the legal obligation forming the basis of the counterclaim. A caveat was added: 'unless the general law generates an investment dispute under the Convention' so that it 'arises directly out of an investment'.[57]

In *Roussalis* v. *Romania*, an ICSID tribunal ruled out the possibility of a counterclaim by Romania for the investor's alleged breach of an investment agreement and misappropriation of funds[58] on account of the text

[55] *Ibid.*, 565. [56] *Saluka* v. *Czech* Republic, above, n. 40, para. 79.
[57] A similar caveat was made in *Harris* v. *Iran*, above, n. 53, pp. 57–61.
[58] *Roussalis* v. *Romania*, above, n. 41, paras 792–6.

of the consent to investor/state arbitration in the Greece/Romania BIT (1997), which defines the scope of disputes that can be submitted by the investor as those 'concerning an obligation of the [host state] under the [BIT], in relation to an investment [of the investor]'.[59] The majority of the tribunal considered that in view of the tribunal's limited jurisdiction over *claims*, it followed that 'the BIT does not provide for counterclaims to be introduced by the host state in relation to obligations of the investor' because the 'meaning of "dispute" is the issuance of compliance by the State with the BIT'.[60] This reasoning should not be endorsed.[61] A limitation upon the scope of the host state's consent to arbitration in respect of the investor's *claims* does not necessarily apply to the host state's *counterclaims*; indeed, there are compelling reasons militating against such a conclusion in the ICSID context, especially given that once a notice of arbitration is filed it must be the exclusive forum for resolving the dispute as noted earlier. The host state's consent to ICSID arbitration requires the full application of Article 47 insofar as it vests the tribunal with the power to adjudicate counterclaims with the required factual nexus to the dispute.[62] Professor Reisman's dissent on this point is to be preferred:

> In rejecting ICSID jurisdiction over counterclaims, a neutral tribunal – which was, in fact, selected by the claimant – perforce directs the respondent State to pursue its claims in its own courts where the very investor who had sought a forum outside the State apparatus is now constrained to become the defendant ... Aside from duplication and inefficiency, the sort of transactions costs which counter-claim and set-off procedures work to avoid, it is an ironic, if not absurd, outcome, at odds, in my view, with the objectives of international investment law.[63]

It follows from this discussion that the legal basis of the claim is not dispositive for determining the scope of the tribunal's jurisdiction over counterclaims. So long as the factual matrix for the counterclaim directly relates to the dispute between the parties concerning the investment in question, the legal basis for the host state's counterclaim could be a contractual obligation, a domestic regulatory obligation and so on.

[59] *Ibid.*, para. 868. [60] *Ibid.*, para. 869.

[61] I have previously expressed a tentative preference for the majority's approach: Douglas, *The International Law of Investment Claims*, 257. I was wrong to do so.

[62] Indeed, by entering into an arbitration agreement in accordance with the BIT provisions, the investor and the host state cannot be taken to have opted out of Article 47, which would require an express agreement to that effect in accordance with its terms.

[63] *Roussalis* v. *Romania* (Dissenting Opinion of Professor Michael Reisman).

15.2.3 *The scope for enforcing international environmental norms through counterclaims by the host state*

International environmental norms may be operationalised within the host state's domestic legal order by the enactment of legislation. To the extent that such legislation grants third parties (whether the host state's government specifically or third parties generally) the right to claim damages against an entity that has violated the environmental norms reflected in that legislation then there is no a priori impediment to such a right being asserted by way of counterclaim by the host state in investment treaty arbitration. In the majority of cases, however, the legislation in question will designate the courts of the host state as having exclusive jurisdiction. For instance, in the USA, the 1980 Comprehensive Environmental Response, Compensation and Liability Act (CERCLA), known as the 'Superfund' Act, provides that the 'owner and operator of a vessel or a facility ... shall be liable for ... all costs of removal or remedial action incurred by the United States Government',[64] but stipulates that the 'United States district court shall have exclusive original jurisdiction'.[65] Those familiar with the jurisprudence of investment treaty arbitration may sense some irony in this conclusion given how frequently tribunals manage to dilute the effectiveness of an exclusive jurisdiction clause in investment agreement when adjudicating upon the investor's claims. Nonetheless, if the host state has established a domestic regime for environmental liability that is self-contained in the sense of conferring exclusive jurisdiction to its own national courts then this must be respected at the transnational level of an investment treaty tribunal.

Another possibility is that international environmental norms are incorporated by reference into a contract between the investor and the host state. By way of example, the Concession Agreement between the Republic of Liberia and Firestone Liberia, Inc., contains an applicable law clause that obliges the investor to act consistently with Liberia's international obligations to the extent that they are recognised in domestic law:

> Applicability of Liberian Law – Except as explicitly provided in this Agreement, Firestone Liberia shall be subject to Law as in effect from time to time, including with respect to labor, environmental, health and safety, customs and tax matters, and shall conduct itself in a manner

[64] 42 USC §9607(a). [65] 42 USC §9613(b).

> consistent with Liberia's obligations under international treaties and agreements insofar as those have the effect of Law in Liberia.[66]

In another concession agreement between the Republic of Liberia and ADA Commercial Inc., the investor is obliged to comply with international standards regardless of their status within domestic law:

> ENVIRONMENTAL MEASURES – Investor's obligations with respect to the environmental shall be as prescribed by Law including the Environmental Protection and Management Law of Liberia and international standards, including the Equator Principles.[67]

An arbitral tribunal apprised of an investment dispute under an investment treaty would be able to adjudicate upon a counterclaim for breach of the investor's contractual undertaking to comply with environmental standards by the host state so long as the dispute submitted by the investor was related to the investment memorialised by the same contract.

15.3 Can a host state enforce international environmental norms by way of counterclaim without a foothold in an investment contract or in domestic law?

The question that must now be addressed is whether the host state can counterclaim for the investor's failure to comply with international environmental norms in the absence of a contractual stipulation of this nature or in circumstances where the host state has failed to give proper effect to international environmental norms within its domestic legal system.

15.3.1 An analogy with the Alien Tort Statute

The disaggregation of the various norms at play in a claim under the ATS is instructive in this context. As already noted, this legislation vests the federal district courts in the USA with jurisdiction over a tort claim for the violation of the law of nations. A cause of action in tort is not created

66 Amended and Restated Concession Agreement between the Republic of Liberia and Firestone Liberia, Inc., Art. 30.1 (on file with author). My thanks to Mikella Hurley for bringing this example to my attention.

67 Concession Agreement between the Republic of Liberia and ADA Commercial Inc., s. 13 (on file with author).

by the ATS; instead the cause of action is a creature of the federal common law and thus developed by federal court judges. The cause of action in tort has the ultimate purpose of enforcing standards reflected in international norms that, in the words of the Supreme Court in *Sosa* v. *Alvarez-Machain*, are 'accepted by the civilized world and defined with a specificity comparable to the features of the 18th-century paradigms'[68] of assaults against ambassadors, violations of safe conducts and piracy.

Unlike the ATS, the investor's cause of action is created by the same instrument that confers adjudicative power to an international arbitral tribunal – the investment treaty. The cause of action allows a non-state entity to enforce, inter alia, the minimum standards reflected in inter-state obligations such as the obligation to accord fair and equitable treatment. The investor is not suing upon an inter-state obligation as such as if it were a contractual entitlement; instead, the normative standard reflected in that obligation becomes the actionable standard for liability sounding in damages. So, just as customary international law supplies the standard of conduct for a claim under the ATS, the investment protection obligation supplies the actionable standard for an investment treaty claim.

The crux of the matter is that the right to assert a claim under an investment treaty is not somehow parasitical upon the substantive investment protection obligations in the treaty: the cause of action and the applicable standards are disaggregated in the same way as a claim under the ATS. Indeed, at least since *SGS* v. *Philippines*,[69] it is generally accepted that an investment treaty with a broad grant of jurisdiction (e.g., 'any disputes relating to an investment') is neutral as to the source of norms that might supply the basis for a claim.

The host state's right to counterclaim is also juridically detached from the investment protection obligations in the treaty. It is simply the procedural counterpart of the claimant's cause of action to recover damages for prejudice to its investment on whatever legal basis the

[68] *Sosa* v. *Alvarez-Machain*, above, n. 28, 724–5. The Supreme Court relied upon *Blackstone's Commentaries on the Laws of England* as to the norms that were actionable at the suit of individuals in the eighteenth century. According to Blackstone, these three paradigms: 'are the principal cases in which the statute law of England interposes to aid and enforce the law of nations as a part of the common law, by inflicting an adequate punishment upon offences against that universal law committed by private persons'. *Blackstone*, book 4, chap. 5, p. 73.

[69] *Société Générale de Surveillance SA* v. *Republic of the Philippines*, ICSID Case No. ARB/02/6, Decision on Jurisdiction (29 January 2004) 8 ICSID Rep 518.

claimant seeks to invoke. If there is an impediment to the host state's ability to invoke international norms in a counterclaim against the investor, then it is not a jurisdictional one (assuming the factual nexus is satisfied) but instead must be found in the structure of the norms themselves.

Once again this leads us back to a discussion of the ATS. In the landmark case of *Filártiga* v. *Peña-Irala*,[70] the US Court of Appeals of the Second Circuit transposed the prohibition of torture as a peremptory norm of international law into an actionable basis of tort liability under the federal common law. In other words, a normative standard of international law was operationalised by recognising a legal right vested in a foreign national to claim damages against a state official who has violated that normative standard.

It is important to recognise that no such legal right could be discerned from international law. As stated by Judge Edwards in *Tel-Oren* v. *Libyan Arab Republic*: 'The Second Circuit [in *Filártiga*] did not require plaintiffs to point to a specific right to sue under the law of nations in order to establish jurisdiction under section 1350; rather, the Second Circuit required only a showing that the defendant's actions violated the substantive law of nations'.[71] It is also the case that no corresponding duty attaching to individual state officials had been recognised by international law either. At the time of *Filártiga* there was no instance of an international tribunal imposing civil or criminal liability upon an individual for acts of torture. The reason that neither the right nor the duty had to be grounded in international law is that international law only supplies the relevant standard of conduct; it is the ATS and the federal common law that determines who can sue, who may be found liable and all the other elements of the cause of action. The current debate before the Supreme Court in *Kiobel* v. *Royal Dutch Petroleum*[72] as to whether corporations are liable for violations of international law *as a matter of international law* starts from a false premise. It is the ATS and the federal common law, and not international law, that govern the question of whether a norm of international law should be actionable by means of a tort action and then whether such a tort action lies against a particular class of defendants.

[70] *Filártiga* v. *Peña-Irala*, 630 F 2d 876 (2nd Cir., 1980).

[71] *Tel-Oren* v. *Libyan Arab Republic*, 726 F 2d 774, 777 (DC Cir., 1984).

[72] No. 10-1491 (pending).

Not all international norms are capable of being transposed into actionable standards for tort liability under the ATS. The Supreme Court in *Sosa*, as already noted, introduced a threshold of determinacy for candidate norms: they must be 'defined with a specificity comparable to the features of the 18th century paradigms we have recognised'.[73] It is implicit from the Supreme Court's reference to these 'paradigms' that the candidate norms must also be suitable for application to the conduct of non-state actors. By suitable I mean that the best interpretation of the norm in question dictates that it is capable of being applied to a spectrum of actors and not just to states. For instance, the rule that states can claim a territorial sea of up to twelve nautical miles from baselines drawn along their coastline certainly satisfies the threshold of determinacy. But it is difficult to imagine how such a norm could be interpreted to apply to non-state actors as a necessary condition for the objectives it serves. The candidate norms in the ATS context are likely to be found primarily among those which create individual responsibility in international law (e.g., various offences under international criminal law), those which oblige states to exercise prescriptive jurisdiction over persons in respect of the proscribed conduct (e.g., the grave breaches regime established by the Geneva Conventions and the Additional Protocol of 1977) and peremptory norms of international law (e.g., the prohibition of torture).

15.3.2 The power of an investment tribunal to operationalise international environmental norms

Reverting to investment treaty arbitration, does an arbitral tribunal have the power to operationalise international norms by transposing them as actionable standards for a counterclaim for damages by the host state? Taking into account the insights from the ATS, the answer cannot be simply that the international norms in question do not bind non-state actors as a matter of international law.

The investor/state arbitration regime establishes a mechanism for the investor to claim damages for prejudice caused to a covered investment and permits counterclaims by host states in relation to activities with a close nexus to that investment. It functions as an autonomous transnational civil liability regime. The proper scope of the tribunal's judicial powers within this regime must be ascertained through the interpretation

[73] *Sosa* v. *Alvarez-Machain*, above, n. 28, p. 725.

of the principles underlying the investment treaty and the consent of the parties to the arbitration of an investment dispute. The state parties conferred a right upon investors to assert a claim for damages as a means of obtaining reparation for the breach of one or more of the minimum standards of treatment set out in the investment treaty. In essence, the state parties created a transnational tort for the benefit of the investor. The question is whether a corresponding right can be inferred for the benefit of host states within the jurisdictional limits of a counterclaim. The relevant standards would not be the minimum standards of treatment in the treaty – those standards are addressed to the contracting states exclusively – but rather those standards reflected in international norms that address the conduct of both states and non-state actors.

A definitive answer to this question cannot be provided within the scope of this chapter. But the roadmap provided up to this point may yet prove to be a guide to a futile journey in the context of international environmental law if it transpires that there is a paucity of suitable norms to supply the relevant standard of conduct for the host state's counterclaim.

Consider the following hypothetical problem, which is designed to illustrate a paradigm case for the utility for such a counterclaim. Suppose a host state adopts a measure to shut down a mining company's operations because it has caused serious environmental damage to the surrounding area over the decades of its operation and that such damage is now posing a health risk to the local population. The foreign owner of the company asserts an expropriation claim in investment treaty arbitration and the host state counterclaims to recover some of the costs of remediation. At the time when the most significant damage was caused to the environment, the mining company enjoyed a privileged relationship with the host state's government such that no environmental regulations were enacted in respect of the company's operations. The mining company is insolvent as a result of the cessation of its activities and the foreign owner is not otherwise subject to the jurisdiction of the host state's courts.

Which norm of international environmental law, which can claim widespread acceptance within the international community, could be transposed to provide an actionable standard for the host state's transnational tort claim against the investor? The potential injustice presented by the hypothetical problem is that the entity responsible for the pollution will not contribute to the costs of cleaning it up in the absence of an enforcement mechanism under the national legal system. The obvious contender to address this injustice is the polluter pays principle. It is described in the 1992 Rio Declaration on Environment and Development in the following terms:

> National authorities should endeavour to promote the internalization of environmental costs and the use of economic instruments, taking into account the approach that the polluter should, in principle, bear the cost of pollution with due regard to the public interest and without distorting international trade and investment.[74]

The principle is stated to be a principle of international law in the preambles of several treaties.[75] Without entering the debate as to whether this designation can be sustained,[76] it is difficult to characterise the polluter pays principle as encapsulating a legal right. It would appear at best to be a guiding policy for the elaboration of legislative texts dealing with environmental protection, whether international or domestic. As one commentator has surmised: 'The true substantive content of the [polluter pays principle] cannot be completely captured without the procedural and institutional framework within which the law and policies operate'.[77] It does not have the same normative value, for instance, as the prohibition of torture, which does encapsulate a legal right in the sense that it is enforceable on demand in adjudicative institutions.

The bulk of international environmental law is found in international treaties rather than in customary law. Those treaties that regulate the

[74] Declaration on Environment and Development, 13 June 1992, UN Doc. A/CONF.151/26, Principle 16.

[75] Kiev Protocol on Liability for Pollution of Transboundary Waters and Lakes (2003); London Protocol on Preparedness, Response, and Co-operation to Pollution Incidents by Hazardous and Noxious Substances (2000); UNECE Convention on the Transboundary Effects of Industrial Accidents (1992); Oil Pollution Preparedness and Response Convention (1990).

[76] Compare P. Birnie, A. E. Boyle and C. Regdwell, *International Law and the Environment*, 3rd edn (Oxford University Press, 2009), 322 (Principle 16 simply lacks the normative character of a rule of law); U. Beyerlin, 'Policies, Principles and Rules', in D. Bodansky, J. Brunnée and E. Hey (eds.), *The Oxford Handbook of International Environmental Law* (Oxford University Press, 2007), 441: 'it is a "(potential legal) rule" that is not part of customary international law but is a "recognized legal rule in the European Community, the Organization of Economic Co-operation and Developments, and the UNECE context"'. See also *Rhine Chlorides Convention Arbitral Award* (France/Netherlands) PCA (2004) para. 103: 'Le Tribunal observe que ce principe figure dans certains instruments internationaux, tant bilatéraux que multilatéraux, et se situe à des niveaux d'effectivité variables. Sans nier son importance en droit conventionnel, le Tribunal ne pense pas que ce principe fasse partie du droit international général'.

[77] P. Schwartz, 'The Polluter-Pays Principle', in M. Fitzmaurice (ed.), *Research Handbook on International Environmental Law* (Cheltenham: Edward Elgar, 2010), 249.

activities of non-state actors generally presuppose the establishment of a domestic institutional framework for their operationalisation. For instance, the Basel Convention on the Control of Transboundary Movements of Hazardous Wastes and Their Disposal obliges the contracting state parties to enact legislation to establish a domestic regulatory regime and it is difficult to read the provisions of this treaty as encapsulating legal rights capable of enforcement against non-state actors. The Protocol on Liability and Compensation for Damage Resulting from Transboundary Movements of Hazardous Wastes and Their Disposal, although not yet in force,[78] may be different. Article 5 states that 'any person shall be liable for damage caused or contributed to by his lack of compliance with the provisions implementing the [Basel] Convention or by his wrongful, intentional, reckless or negligent acts or omissions'. Within the transnational regime for civil liability established by investment treaties, this provision would not appear to require further legislative elaboration to be asserted as a legal right in adjudication so that if the Protocol is in force for the host state and the host state suffers damage caused by the investor in accordance with Article 5 then compensation might be recovered through the mechanism of a counterclaim in investment treaty arbitration. The only obstacle might be Article 17 of the Protocol, within the chapter entitled 'Procedures', which provides that 'Claims for compensation under the Protocol *may* be brought in the courts of a Contracting Party',[79] and then sets out three different territorial links that would establish the necessary basis for the exercise of jurisdiction by the national courts. This provision does not appear to vest the national courts of state parties with exclusive jurisdiction, although it is fair to assume that the possibility of claiming damages before international courts and tribunals was not an immediate concern of the drafters.

The possible utility of a counterclaim based upon the Protocol can be illustrated by a modification of the facts in *S.D. Myers* v. *Canada*. Suppose the USA and Canada are parties to both the Basel Convention and the Protocol. Suppose further that an incident occurs during the loading of polychlorinated biphenyls (PCBs) onto freight trucks by the investor in Canada, causing damage to public lands.[80] Canada subsequently resolves

[78] As of June 2012, there are thirteen signatories and ten parties. Pursuant to Article 29 of the Protocol, there must be twenty ratifications before it comes into force. See www.basel.int (accessed 15 June 2012).

[79] Emphasis added.

[80] And thus within the scope of application of the Protocol pursuant to Article 3.

to ban the export of PCBs to the USA and the investor commences a claim under NAFTA for the resultant losses caused to its investment activities in Canada. The tribunal finds that the export ban can be justified by reference to the Basel Convention and rules that there is no breach of Canada's obligations under Chapter XI of NAFTA. Canada counterclaims on the basis of the Protocol to recover its remediation costs incurred after the incident, which it asserts was caused by the investor's negligence.

CONCLUSION

In this chapter I have defended a particular rationalisation of the investor's claim and the host state's counterclaim in investment treaty arbitration. The consent to investor/state arbitration vests a class of persons with a cause of action and procedural standing to seek reparation for a failure by the host state to adhere to the relevant standard of investment protection in the treaty in circumstances. The investment protection obligations are not directly 'owed' to the investor as a non-party to the treaty in a contractual sense. Instead they supply the conduct regulating norms that are actionable at the suit of the investor by virtue of the cause of action created by the consent to investor/state arbitration. The more appropriate analogy is to the tort for a breach of a statutory duty in domestic law. Likewise, the host state's counterclaim is vested by the same consent to investor/state arbitration and is disaggregated from the source of norms that might supply the actionable standard of liability in respect of the investor's conduct.

This rationalisation may permit both the investor and host state to enforce international environmental norms, albeit in different ways. Depending on the scope of the consent to investor/state arbitration, the investor can assert a claim for the host state's failure to comply with its conventional or customary environmental obligations if damage has been caused by such failure to its investment. It can also rely upon such obligations indirectly as giving content to the investment protection standards in the treaty such as the fair and equitable standard of treatment. The host state can enforce environmental norms entrenched in its own legal system or incorporated in an investment agreement with the investor if it has suffered damage by reason of the investor's conduct so long as the requisite nexus exists between the counterclaim and the facts underlying the dispute submitted by the investor to investor/state arbitration. Whether or not the tribunal can operationalise international environmental norms by transposing them as actionable standards for the host state's counterclaim is more controversial, but an analogy with relevant practice under the ATS suggests that this is a serious possibility in the future.

Select bibliography

Aldrich, G. H., *The Jurisprudence of the Iran–United States Claims Tribunal* (Oxford: Clarendon Press, 1996).

Bellia, A. J., and B. R. Clark, 'The Alien Tort Statute and the Law of Nations' (2011) 78 *University of Chicago Law Review* 445.

Birnie, P., Boyle, A. E. and C. Redgwell, *International Law and the Environment*, 3rd edn (Oxford University Press, 2009).

Bodansky, D., J. Brunnée and E. Hey (eds.), *The Oxford Handbook of International Environmental Law* (Oxford University Press, 2007).

Bradley, C. A., 'The Alien Tort Statute and Article III' (2002) 42 *Virginia Journal of International Law* 587.

Douglas, Z., 'The Hybrid Foundations of Investment Treaty Arbitration' (2003) 74 *British Yearbook of International Law* 151.

The International Law of Investment Claims (Cambridge University Press, 2009).

International Law Association, Reports on Transnational Enforcement of Environmental Law (1997–2006); www.ila-hq.org.

Jaeger, K., 'Environmental Claims under the Alien Tort Statute' (2010) 28 *Berkeley Journal of International Law* 519.

Laborde, G., 'The Case for Host State Claims in Investment Arbitration' (2010) 1 *Journal of International Dispute Resolution* 97.

Lalive, P., and L. Halonen, 'On the Availability of Counterclaims in Investment Treaty Arbitration' (2011) 2 *Czech Yearbook of International Law* 141.

Morgera, E., *Corporate Accountability in International Environmental Law* (Oxford University Press, 2009).

Nollkaemper, A., 'Responsibility of Transnational Corporations in International Environmental Law: Three Perspectives', in G. Winter (ed.), *Multilevel Governance of Global Environmental Change: Perspectives from Science, Sociology and the Law* (Cambridge University Press, 2006), pp. 179–99.

Ong, D., 'The Impact of Environmental Law on Corporate Governance: International and Comparative Perspectives' (2001) 12 *European Journal of International Law* 685.

Richardson, B. J., 'The Equator Principles: The Voluntary Approach to Environmentally Sustainable Finance' (2005) 14 *European Environmental Law Review* 280.

Ratner, S., 'Corporations and Human Rights: A Theory of Liability' (2001) 111 *Yale Law Journal* 443.

'Business', in D. Bodansky, J. Brunnée and E. Hey (eds.), *The Oxford Handbook of International Environmental Law* (Oxford University Press, 2007), pp. 807–28.

Schreuer, C., L. Malintoppi, A. Reinisch and A. Sinclair, *The ICSID Convention: A Commentary* (Cambridge University Press, 2009).

Schwartz P., 'The Polluter-Pays Principle', in M. Fitzmaurice (ed.), *Research Handbook on International Environmental Law* (Cheltenham: Edward Elgar, 2010).

Viñuales, J. E., 'Foreign Investment and the Environment in International Law: An Ambiguous Relationship' (2009) 80 *British Yearbook of International Law* 244.

Foreign Investment and the Environment in International Law (Cambridge University Press, 2012).

Zerk, J. *Multinationals and Corporate Social Responsibility* (Cambridge University Press, 2006).

Concluding observations

PIERRE-MARIE DUPUY AND JORGE E. VIÑUALES

Foreign investment and environmental protection should not be seen as antagonistic terms. As the chapters in this volume suggest, carefully calibrated institutions could achieve significant synergies between these two terms. These synergies must be seen as a combination of incentive mechanisms and appropriate safeguards. The close connection between these two aspects of a properly designed mechanism can be illustrated by several examples reviewed in this book. In these concluding observations, we would like to identify four ways in which incentives and safeguards can be combined.

The first illustration is provided by the variety of codes of conduct relating to sustainable and responsible investment (SRI) discussed most notably in the chapters by M. J. Langer and B. J. Richardson. In this case, the SRI codes may perform both a function of incentivising responsible investment (particularly when, as noted by Richardson and in the chapter by T. Swanson and S. Larcom, complementary regulatory changes, including tax advantages, are granted to foster this form of investment) and a quasi-regulatory one, to the extent that financial intermediaries may exert some pressure on how the operations of multinational corporations are conducted. Yet, the fact that this approach is mostly based on a set of 'standards' or 'primary norms', which are not necessarily consistent with one another, has significant consequences when it comes to actual implementation.

A second type of combination is illustrated by the accountability mechanisms analysed in the chapter by E. Morgera. Unlike the SRI codes discussed by Langer and Richardson, the corporate social responsibility (CSR) initiatives discussed by Morgera (e.g., the Global Compact and the OECD Guidelines, but also the IFC Standards) are more sophisticated in terms of both content and enforcement. Regarding content, as noted by Morgera, the fragmentation of the sources should not hide the increasing convergence of the standards of conduct laid out by the different initiatives. As to their implementation, the application of some of these standards is monitored in a variety of ways ranging from mere reporting (e.g., the Global Compact integrity measures) to quasi-adjudicatory enforcement (e.g., the specific instances procedure before OECD national contact points or the individual complaints before the IFC Ombudsman office). The 'incentives' dimension of these mechanisms, which is a function of corporate image and/or of the need to secure financing, is less pronounced than their 'safeguards' dimension. However, the fact that these accountability mechanisms cover an increasingly converging set of environmental standards suggests that they could be used as a complement to other more incentive-focus instruments, such as SRI codes. An example of this 'assemblage' of perspectives is provided by the IFC Standards (which in many ways can be seen as a SRI code) and their sophisticated accountability mechanism (IFC Ombudsman mechanism).

A third type of combination is the development of an array of contracts governing the access and use of certain natural resources. The highest level of institutionalisation can be found in access and benefit-sharing (ABS) agreements, as discussed in the chapter by R. Pavoni. Under the framework of the Convention on Biological Diversity (CBD) and its ABS Protocol, certain resources (genetic resources or traditional knowledge) can only be accessed on the condition that, among other benefits, the benefits arising from the use of such resources are properly distributed. In addition, several other contractual arrangements have been developed in practice with a thinner institutional basis, at least at the level of international law. These arrangements provide a clearer illustration of how incentives and safeguards can be combined. The payment for environmental or ecosystem services (PES) agreements discussed by R. Pavoni are perhaps the main example of such combination. In this case, the very purpose of the agreement is an investment in environmental protection. The financial transfers aim indeed at maintaining the provision of a variety of ecosystem services (water, purification of air and water, nutrient cycling or simply aesthetic beauty). There are, however, other contractual arrangements where the investment side and the regulatory side of the project are concomitant but distinct. As discussed by N. Affolder, mining projects are often structured in such a way that the operations of the investor have to comply with a layer of social and environmental standards established by contract in order to secure both the legal and the 'social' licence to operate. Here, the investment is not in environmental protection but rather on the extraction of a natural resource. Yet, in order for the investment to be carried out, the investor must enter into a web of contractual arrangements aimed at setting certain environmental safeguards. This category of contractual arrangements, which N. Affolder calls 'transnational environmental contracts', are quite diverse in nature depending on their scope and function. Some may indeed be very similar to PES agreements. A PES agreement may, in fact, be a form of compensatory remedy required for the undertaking of mining operations. But what is most noteworthy in the context of these concluding remarks is the extent to which the international, domestic and contractual levels of regulation are interwoven in this combination of incentives and safeguards.

A fourth possible combination is illustrated by the chapters of S. Maljean-Dubois and V. Richard, J. E. Viñuales and Z. Douglas. The 'incentives' dimension is provided here by the mechanisms for the protection of foreign investors, particularly investment contracts, bilateral investment treaties and investment arbitration. As noted by S. Maljean-Dubois and V. Richard, these mechanisms are rather advantageous for foreign investors who (except in the case of investment contracts) are granted rights – including an important right of action before an investment arbitral tribunal – without correlative obligations. Yet, these correlative obligations could play a role at the enforcement level – investment proceedings – in a variety of ways. Direct application of international environmental standards is possible when such standards have undergone a sort of transformation becoming domestic law or contractual obligations or, at least, CSR commitments. This transformation would allow such standards to be used as a basis for an environmental counterclaim in an investment proceeding, as noted by Z. Douglas. Even when no transformation has taken place, international environmental law can be (and has been) taken into account in interpreting the scope of investment disciplines, as noted by J. Viñuales. In addition, these norms could also be enforced through parallel proceedings, particularly before an array of oversight and compliance bodies established by multilateral environmental agreements, as noted by S. Maljean-Dubois and V. Richard. Again, although the combination of incentives and safeguards in this case is rather complex, it can only be captured analytically if, instead of focusing on one treaty or one mechanism, one looks at 'combinations' of mechanisms.

The four combinations identified above are of course not the only possible ones. Other analytical cuts of the material covered in this book would reveal additional or alternative combinations of incentives and safeguards. But, for current purposes, these four illustrative combinations provide sufficient background to make a basic point, which lies at the origins of this volume: synergies between foreign investment and environmental protection are indeed possible. Even when the existing mechanisms are not sufficiently developed in some respects, the solution to the problems they pose may lie less in the development of new structures than in the combination of existing ones. The challenge of implementation requires innovation not only on how to (re)structure global environmental governance but also, and as importantly, on how better to use what we already have.

INDEX